LSAT®
LOGIC
GAMES

STRATEGIES AND TACTICS

SECOND EDITION

100% OFFICIAL LSAT PrepTest® Questions

GLEN STOHR, JD

Published by Kaplan Publishing, a division of Kaplan, Inc.
395 Hudson Street
New York, NY 10014

Printed in the United States of America

10 9 8 7 6 5 4 3 2 1

ISBN: 978-1-60978-683-0

Kaplan Publishing books are available at special quantity discounts to use for sales promotions, employee premiums, or educational purposes. For more information or to purchase books, please call the Simon & Schuster special sales department at 866-506-1949.

Contents

About the Author

GLEN STOHR, JD, is a 15-year veteran LSAT instructor who has helped thousands of students improve their LSAT scores and present winning applications to their law schools of choice. Glen's students have gone on to matriculate at Yale, Duke, UC Berkeley, Georgetown, and many other top schools. Others have parlayed their LSAT score improvements into full-ride scholarships that made their law school goals a reality. Glen's direct, no-nonsense approach to the LSAT as a test that rewards specific, relevant, and coachable skills has made him one of Kaplan's most sought-after instructors by students at all skill levels. His students' dramatic score improvements and positive feedback made him Kaplan's national Teacher of the Year in 2005. In addition to teaching and tutoring more than 1,500 test takers, Glen's work on Kaplan's courses and curriculum has touched tens of thousands of others. Glen's strategic innovations are found throughout Kaplan's LSAT courses and when Kaplan launched its LSAT Advanced course for top scorers, it turned to Glen to head the curriculum development team. A 95th percentile LSAT scorer, Glen is a *cum laude* graduate of the Sandra Day O'Connor School of Law at Arizona State University, where a background in anthropology led him to specialize in Federal Indian Law. Glen draws on his academic background and his experience in both private and public interest law practice to make his LSAT instruction relevant, engaging, and inspirational.

Introduction to the LSAT

The Law School Admissions Test (LSAT) is probably unlike any other test you've taken in your academic career. Most tests you've encountered in high school and college have been content based—that is, they have required you to recall facts, formulas, theorems, or other acquired knowledge.

The LSAT, however, is a skills-based test. It doesn't ask you to repeat memorized facts or to apply learned formulas to specific problems. In fact, all you'll be asked to do on the LSAT is think—thoroughly, quickly, and strategically. There's no required content to study.

But the lack of specific content to memorize is one of the things that makes preparing for the LSAT so challenging. Before you get the idea that you can skate into the most important test of your life without preparing, remember that learning skills and improving performance take practice. You can't cram for the test.

ABOUT THE LSAT

The LSAT is a standardized test written by the Law School Admissions Council (LSAC) and administered four times each year. The test is a required component of your application to all American Bar Association–approved law schools as well as some others.

The LSAT is designed to measure the skills necessary (according to the governing bodies of law schools) for success in your first year of law school, such as strategic reading, analyzing arguments, understanding formal logic, and making deductions. Because these skills will serve you well throughout law school and your professional life, consider your LSAT preparation an investment in your career.

You may already possess some level of proficiency with LSAT-tested skills. However, you probably haven't yet mastered how to use those skills to your advantage in the context of a standardized, skills-based test that requires careful time management.

The LSAT is also a test of endurance—five 35-minute blocks of multiple-choice testing plus a 35-minute writing sample. Add in the administrative tasks at both ends of the test and a 10- to 15-minute break midway through, and you can count on being in the test room for at least four and a half hours. It's a grueling experience, but it's not as bad if you are familiar with the test and ready to handle every section. You want to approach the test with confidence so that you can maintain your focus, limit your stress, and get your highest score on test day. That's why it's so important to take control of the test, just as you will take control of the rest of the application process.

Our material is as up-to-date as possible at the time of this printing, but test specifications may change at any time. Please visit our website at http://kaptest.com/LSAT for the latest news and updates.

How Do I Register for the LSAT?

The LSAT is administered by the Law School Admissions Council (LSAC). Be sure to register as soon as possible, as your preferred test site can fill up quickly. You can register for the LSAT in three ways:

- Online: Sign up at http://lsac.org.
- Telephone: Call LSAC at (215) 968-1001.
- Email: Contact LSAC for a registration packet at lsacinfo@lsac.org.

If you have additional questions about registration, contact the LSAC by phone or by email.

The LSAT Sections

The LSAT consists of five multiple-choice sections: two Logical Reasoning sections, one Logic Games section, one Reading Comprehension section, and one unscored "experimental" section that looks exactly like one of the other multiple-choice sections. At the end of the test, there is a Writing Sample section during which you'll write a short essay. Here's how the sections break down:

Section	Number of Questions	Minutes
Logical Reasoning	24–26	35
Logical Reasoning	24–26	35
Logic Games	22–24	35
Reading Comprehension	26–28	35
"Experimental"	22–28	35
Writing Sample	n/a	35

The five multiple-choice sections can appear in any order, but the Writing Sample is always last. You will also get a 10- or 15-minute break between the third and fourth sections of the test.

You'll be answering roughly 125 multiple-choice questions (101 of which are scored) over the course of three intense hours. Taking control of the LSAT means increasing your test speed only to the extent that you can do so without sacrificing accuracy.

First, just familiarize yourself with the sections and the kinds of questions asked in each one.

Logical Reasoning

WHAT IT IS: The two Logical Reasoning sections each consist of 24–26 questions that reward your ability to analyze a "stimulus" (a paragraph or a dialogue between two speakers) and make judgments accordingly. You will evaluate the logic and structure of arguments and make inferences from the statements as well as find underlying assumptions, strengthen and weaken arguments, determine logical flaws, and identify parallel argument structures.

WHY IT'S ON THE TEST: Law schools want to see whether you can understand, analyze, evaluate, and manipulate arguments, and draw reliable conclusions—as every law student and attorney must. This question type makes up half of your LSAT score, which means this is a valuable skill to master.

Logic Games

WHAT IT IS: In the Logic Games (a.k.a. Analytical Reasoning) section, you'll find four games (critical-thinking puzzles) with five to seven questions each for a total of 22–24 questions. They reward your ability to make valid deductions from a set of rules or restrictions in order to determine what can, must, or cannot be true in various circumstances.

WHY IT'S ON THE TEST: In law school, your professors will have you read dozens of cases, extract their rules, and apply them to or distinguish them from hypothetical cases. The Logic Games section rewards the same skill set: attention to detail, rigorous deductive reasoning, an understanding of how rules limit and order behavior (the very definition of law), and the ability to discern the conditions under which those rules do and do not apply.

Reading Comprehension

WHAT IT IS: The Reading Comprehension section consists of three passages, each 450–550 words, and a set of two short passages that total 450–550 words. Each passage is followed by five to eight questions. The topics may range from areas of social science, humanities, natural science, and law. Because content isn't tested, you won't need any outside knowledge.

WHY IT'S ON THE TEST: The Reading Comprehension section tests your ability to quickly understand the gist and structure of long, difficult prose—just as you'll have to do in law school and throughout your career.

The Writing Sample

WHAT IT IS: During the Writing Sample section, you will read a paragraph that presents a problem and lists two possible solutions. Each solution will have strengths and weaknesses; you must argue in favor of one based on the given criteria. There is no right or wrong answer, and the writing sample is unscored. However, law schools will receive a copy of your essay along with your LSAT score.

WHY IT'S ON THE TEST: The Writing Sample shows law schools your ability to argue for a position while attacking an opposing argument under timed conditions. In addition, it may be used to verify that your writing style is similar to that in your personal statement.

How the LSAT Is Scored

You'll receive one score for the LSAT ranging between 120 and 180 (no separate scores for Logical Reasoning, Logic Games, and Reading Comprehension). There are roughly 101 scored multiple-choice questions on each exam:

- About 52 from the two Logical Reasoning sections
- About 22 from the Logic Games section
- About 27 from the Reading Comprehension section

Your **raw score,** the number of questions that you answer correctly, will be multiplied by a complicated scoring formula (different for each test, to accommodate differences in difficulty level) to yield the **scaled score**—the one that will fall somewhere in that 120–180 range—which is reported to the schools.

Because the test is graded on a largely preset curve, the scaled score will always correspond to a certain percentile, also indicated on your score report. A score of 160, for instance, corresponds roughly to the 80th percentile, meaning that 80 percent of test takers scored at or below your level. The percentile figure is important because it allows law schools to see where you fall in the pool of applicants.

All scored questions are worth the same amount—one raw point—and there's no penalty for guessing. That means that you should always fill in an answer for every question, whether you get to that question or not.

What's a "Good" LSAT Score?

What you consider a "good" LSAT score depends on your own expectations and goals, but here are a few interesting statistics.

If you got about half of all of the scored questions right (a raw score of roughly 50), you would earn a scaled score of roughly 147, putting you in about the 30th percentile—not a great performance. But on the LSAT, a little improvement goes a long way. In fact, getting only one additional question right every 10 minutes would give you a raw score of about 64, pushing you into the 60th percentile—a huge improvement.

Sample Percentiles Approx. Scaled Score		
Percentile	**(Range 120–180)**	**Approx. Raw Score**
99th percentile	174	~94 correct out of 101
95th percentile	168	~88 correct out of 101
90th percentile	164	~82 correct out of 101
80th percentile	160	~76 correct out of 101
75th percentile	157	~71 correct out of 101
50th percentile	152	~61 correct out of 101

Note: Exact percentile-to-scaled-score relationships vary from test to test.

As you can see, you don't have to be perfect to do well. On most LSATs, you can get as many as 28 questions wrong and still remain in the 80th percentile or as many as 20 wrong and still be in the 90th percentile. Most students who score 180 get a handful of questions wrong.

Although many factors play a role in admissions decisions, the LSAT score is usually one of the most important. And—generally speaking—being average won't cut it. The median LSAT score is somewhere around 152. If you're aiming for the top, you've got to do even better.

By using the strategies in this book, you'll learn how to approach—and master—the test in a general way. As you'll see, knowing specific strategies for each type of question is only part of your task. To do your best, you have to approach the entire test with the proactive, take-control kind of thinking it inspires—the LSAT mindset.

For more information on the LSAT experience, see Part IV of this book.

PART I

HOW LOGIC
GAMES WORK

CHAPTER 1

EVERY QUESTION HAS AN ANSWER

If you've tried an LSAT logic game, you know that it can seem like a bizarre, abstract exercise. For many test takers, the first reaction to the Logic Games section is "I'm not even sure what they're asking for," or "How am I supposed to do all of this in 35 minutes?" If that sounds like you, don't be alarmed. But resolve from this point forward to remember (and follow) one simple principle: Every logic games question on the LSAT has one correct answer. The test always gives you enough information to determine the correct answer (and the four wrong ones). Logic games are unusual, unlike any academic task you've likely faced before, but they're fair and they're designed to reward skills that will be essential to your success as a law student. By adopting the approach laid out in this book, you'll learn how logic games are put together and how you can take them apart efficiently, effectively, and routinely. If you practice the methods and strategies introduced here, your logic games performance, and your LSAT score, will improve.

A SAMPLE LOGIC GAMES QUESTION

Here's a logic games question. See whether you can answer it in 30 seconds.

If the storm passes over Oceana at some time before it passes over Lofton, then which one of the following must be true?

(A) The third town the storm passes over receives only rain.

(B) The fourth town the storm passes over receives only rain.

(C) The fourth town the storm passes over receives hail and rain.

(D) The fifth town the storm passes over receives only rain.

(E) The fifth town the storm passes over receives hail and rain.[1]

I hope your immediate reaction was, "That's not fair. I can't answer this; I don't even know the setup or the rules." And that's the point. The test makers will always supply the preliminary information you need to determine the right answer. They want to reward your critical thinking and your ability to make deductions from the relevant restrictions they provide. In this case, all of the information you need in order to answer this question is in the following paragraph, the game's setup. After reading the setup, try again to answer the question in 30 seconds.

One afternoon, a single thunderstorm passes over exactly five towns—Jackson, Lofton, Nordique, Oceana, and Plattesville—dropping some form of precipitation on each. The storm is the only source of precipitation in the towns that afternoon. On some towns, it drops both hail and rain; on the remaining towns, it drops only rain. It passes over each town exactly once and does not pass over any two towns at the same time. The following must obtain:

   The third town the storm passes over is Plattesville.

   The storm drops hail and rain over the second town it passes over.

   The storm drops only rain on both Lofton and Oceana.

   The storm passes over Jackson at some time after it passes over Lofton and at some time after it passes over Nordique.[2]

If the storm passes over Oceana at some time before it passes over Lofton, then which one of the following must be true?

(A) The third town the storm passes over receives only rain.

(B) The fourth town the storm passes over receives only rain.

(C) The fourth town the storm passes over receives rain and hail.

(D) The fifth town the storm passes over receives only rain.

(E) The fifth town the storm passes over receives rain and hail.[3]

---

[1] PrepTest 46, Sec. 4, Q 16

[2] PrepTest 46, Sec. 4, Game 3

[3] PrepTest 46, Sec. 4, Q 16

If you're thinking, "Well great, how am I supposed to deal with all of that?" or "I'm sure all of the information is there, but it will take me forever to comb through all of that," don't panic. Logic games are designed to feel overwhelming. So is the first year of law school. By the end of this book, you'll see this game as a standard variation, amenable to the Kaplan Method and its strategies. In fact, when you approach the question above, you'll organize the rules and restrictions into a sketch that looks something like this:

If the storm passes over Oceana at some time before it passes over Lofton, then which one of the following must be true?

(A) The third town the storm passes over receives only rain.

(B) The fourth town the storm passes over receives only rain.

(C) The fourth town the storm passes over receives rain and hail.

(D) The fifth town the storm passes over receives only rain.

(E) The fifth town the storm passes over receives rain and hail.[4]

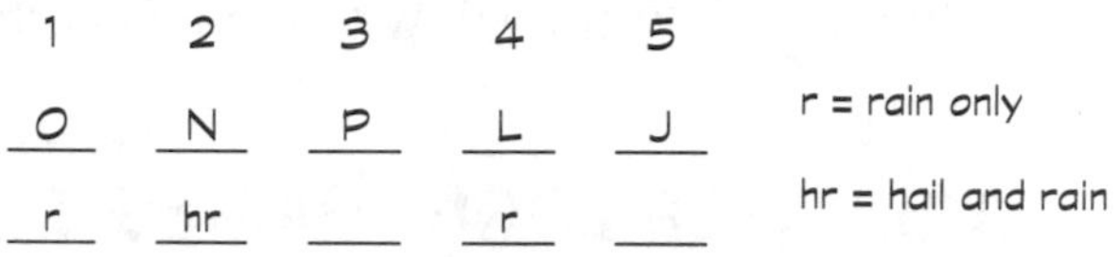

```
      1     2     3     4     5
      O     N     P     L     J        r = rain only
      r     hr    ___   r     ___      hr = hail and rain
```

Figure 1.1

If you try the question now, you'll likely spot the one correct answer in far less than 30 seconds.

The right answer, the one that increases your LSAT score, is (B). A glance at Figure 1.1 confirms that the fourth town receives only rain. Just as importantly, that same glance reveals why each of the wrong answers is wrong. Choice (C) contradicts the sketch. And choices (A), (D), and (E) all deal with spaces that the sketch leaves undetermined, so they don't have to be as true as the question stem calls for.

The Road Ahead

Unfortunately, logic games don't come with pre-drawn sketches like that one. It's the test makers' job to challenge you to demonstrate the reasoning skills you'll need for law school. That's where this book comes in. In the following pages and chapters, you'll learn everything you need to make every logic game, every question, and every correct answer as clear and direct as the one above. You'll discover how to interpret the game's task, turn it into a simple, useful sketch, apply the rules and restrictions, and draw the additional deductions that make the correct answers unequivocal. In short, you'll learn the Kaplan Method for Logic Games.

What you learn about logic games counts for nothing if it doesn't turn into correct answers, quickly and consistently, on test day. A lot of LSAT books and courses set out to show you how much their authors and teachers know about logic games. They sometimes have elaborate, impressive systems for categorizing game types or even fancy names for the rules you'll see. Guess what? You don't get any points on the LSAT for giving a game the right name. You have

---

[4] PrepTest 46, Sec. 4, Q 16

no opportunity to show off your mastery of a new nomenclature. You have four games, 22 to 24 questions, and only 35 minutes to get them all right. Recognizing certain patterns that recur in logic games can be very helpful (and Part II of this book will break down the various game types in detail). Beginning from an understanding of the skills that all logic games are designed to reward, you'll find that a simple, concrete method will earn you more points on logic games time and again, whether the game you're tackling seems as familiar as an old T-shirt or as unexpected as an avant-garde film. So keep your focus on getting the right answers, and the rest of what you need to know will follow.

Job one is to clarify what you're being asked for. Using the Thunderstorm game and a couple of others, I'll illustrate how to identify each task the test makers set out for you.

A SAMPLE LOGIC GAMES TASK
"But What Kind of Game Is This?"

Over the years, I've heard countless students ask this question about a countless number of games. What they're really saying is, "I don't know how to begin unless I recognize the game as one of the predetermined game types, one that I've memorized a sketch for." My answer is always the same: Read the opening paragraph and see what your task is. Imagine you went to work for a lawyer who came in one day and said, "I'm meeting our client in a half hour. Would you please whip up a quick chart showing the order that the defense witnesses are likely to appear in and what each is going to testify about?" I trust that you wouldn't say, "I don't know how to begin that unless you provide me with the defense witness testimony template." You'd simply get the case file, pull the relevant information, and put it into a simple chart or document that would be easy for your boss to read and share with the client. Don't let logic games stymie you. They all involve relatively simple tasks, and you don't get bonus style points for having the "right" diagram.

Take another look at the setup for the game you've already seen:

> One afternoon, a single thunderstorm passes over exactly five towns—Jackson, Lofton, Nordique, Oceana, and Plattesville—dropping some form of precipitation on each. The storm is the only source of precipitation in the towns that afternoon. On some towns, it drops both hail and rain; on the remaining towns, it drops only rain. It passes over each town exactly once and does not pass over any two towns at the same time. The following must obtain:
>> The third town the storm passes over is Plattesville.
>> The storm drops hail and rain over the second town it passes over.

The storm drops only rain on both Lofton and
Oceana.
The storm passes over Jackson at some time after it
passes over Lofton and at some time after it passes
over Nordique.[5]

Your starting point for understanding any logic game on the LSAT is the real-world scenario, or Situation (as you'll come to call it), described in the opening paragraph. Use the Situation to visualize the task; then use that image to begin a simple sketch or chart that will help you organize all of the information in the game's rules and restrictions. In the Thunderstorm game, there are two things you'll need to account for: the order of the towns the storm passes over and the type of precipitation it drops on them.

There are many ways you could logically organize these tasks. The one that will work best is the one that fits the information as it's presented in the game's setup. The key question to ask is "What here is concrete and what's still up in the air?" If the test supplied you with some kind of map or told you the directions among the towns, you might come up with something like this:

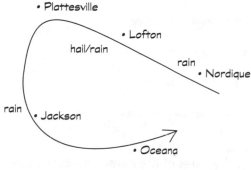

Figure 1.2

That's great for the storm tracker on the news channel, but it's not going to be of any use to you. The towns' locations are completely up in the air. What is certain is that the storm travels in one direction; it passes over each town only once, one at a time. So get ready to organize the information about the order of the towns like this:

J	L	N	O	P
1	2	3	4	5

___ ___ ___ ___ ___

Figure 1.3

That chart will allow you to handle the first task—the order in which the storm passes over the towns—just fine. But there was a second task to deal with, too: determining the type of precipitation dropped on each town. For a lot of test takers, the instinctual response is to create a separate chart for this information, something like this:

---

[5] PrepTest 46, Sec. 4, Game 3

Figure 1.4

That's okay, but it's not as useful as it could be. When the test makers present you with two tasks in a logic game (and they usually do so once or twice per test), they'll ask questions that combine the tasks. In fact, you already saw this in the question examined earlier. It asked you about the type of precipitation dropped on the third, or fourth, or fifth town the storm passed over.

> If the storm passes over Oceana at some time before it passes over Lofton, then which one of the following must be true?
>
> (A) The third town the storm passes over receives only rain.
> (B) The fourth town the storm passes over receives only rain.
> (C) The fourth town the storm passes over receives rain and hail.
> (D) The fifth town the storm passes over receives only rain.
> (E) The fifth town the storm passes over receives rain and hail.[6]

Just as important, notice how the rules of the game combine information about the two tasks. The three highlighted rules illustrate this point: the first tells you about the order of towns the storm passes over, the second about the order of the precipitation dropped, and the third about the type of precipitation dropped on certain towns.

> One afternoon, a single thunderstorm passes over exactly five towns—Jackson, Lofton, Nordique, Oceana, and Plattesville—dropping some form of precipitation on each. The storm is the only source of precipitation in the towns that afternoon. On some towns, it drops both hail and rain; on the remaining towns, it drops only rain. It passes over each town exactly once and does not pass over any two towns at the same time. The following must obtain:
> The third town the storm passes over is Plattesville.
> The storm drops hail and rain over the second town it passes over.
> The storm drops only rain on both Lofton and Oceana.
> The storm passes over Jackson at some time after it passes over Lofton and at some time after it passes over Nordique.[7]

---

[6] PrepTest 46, Sec. 4, Q 16

[7] PrepTest 46, Sec. 4, Game 3

With practice, you'll spot connections like this almost automatically. For now, take to heart that with a good strategic reading of the setup, you can always build a useful sketch for any logic game. Just as it's unlikely that you'd hand your boss, the lawyer, two separate charts—one for the order in which the witnesses appear and another for their likely testimony—it's not really intuitive to separate out the game's tasks either.

For the Thunderstorm game, your sketch or framework should look like this:

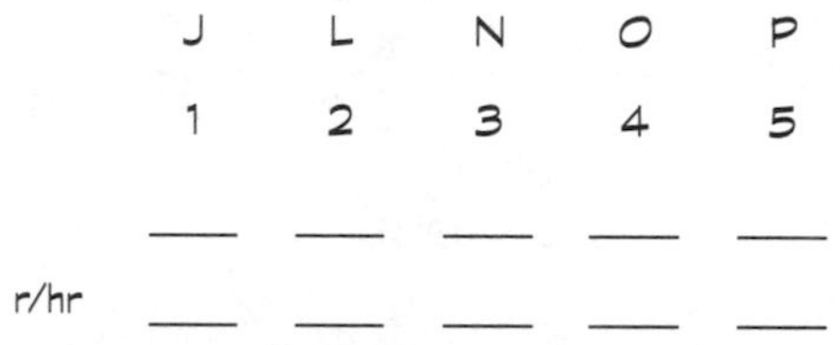

$$J \quad L \quad N \quad O \quad P$$
$$1 \quad 2 \quad 3 \quad 4 \quad 5$$

r/hr   ___ ___ ___ ___ ___

Figure 1.5

In later chapters, you'll come to recognize this as a typical Sequencing-Matching Hybrid game. You'll see other sketches that look a lot like this one because they fit the task so well. But, and this underlines a point I made earlier, you didn't need to know the game's name or have a particular sketch in mind in order to draw an entirely effective diagram. To tell you the truth, I've seen an over-reliance on memorizing game types backfire on many, many test takers. These include students who learn a couple of standard diagrams, get really excited about how well they worked in some games, and then try to fit any and every logic game into one of them, even when the task doesn't fit the sketch. They also include those students who freeze the moment that a game's task doesn't obviously fit something they've previously learned to manage. That's why it's important for you to realize that you can handle any game by carefully reading the Situation, visualizing your task, and creating a sketch that fits the information.

Before moving on to some other typical game tasks, let me make two more points. First, everyone's sketches look a little bit different. That's fine. It's no problem if you saw the Thunderstorm game fitting into a grid, or with the numbers ordering the towns at the bottom, or even arranged vertically instead of horizontally. These variations might look different, but each would organize the game's key information in exactly the same way as the master example, and all would get you the LSAT points you need on test day (which is what matters, right?).

1 2 3 4 5
JLNOP
r/hr
J L N O P
r/hr
1 2 3 4 5
JLNOP
1
2
3
4
5
r/hr

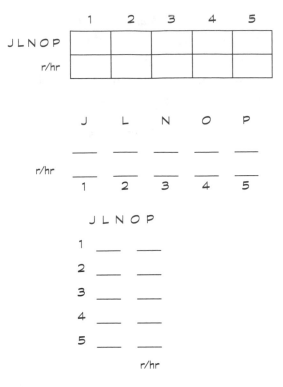

Figure 1.6

You should find the way that's easiest for you to draw accurate, repeatable sketches in the small space that you have in the test booklet. Adopt the best principles for sketching and diagramming given here, and pay attention to the essential notations (I'll always tell you when something is non-negotiable), but don't worry if your sketches aren't carbon copies of what's in this book.

The second point, before I have you look at some other games with different tasks, relates to the rules and deductions that you'll need to add into the diagrams and frameworks you create. Remember the sketch that helped you answer the LSAT question?

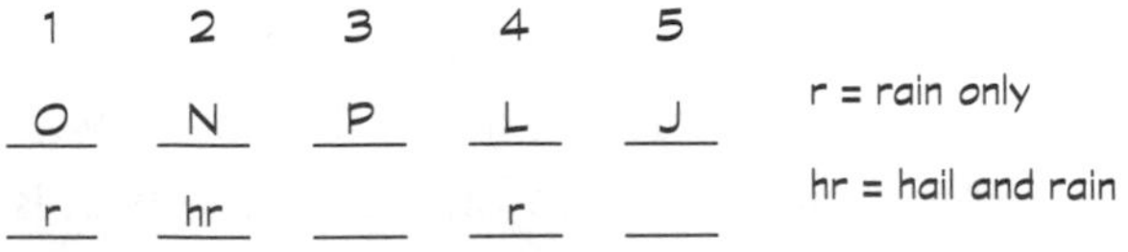

1 2 3 4 5
O N P L J
r hr r
r = rain only
hr = hail and rain

Figure 1.7

This sketch was created specifically for that question. It took all of the rules and deductions from the game setup and added in the restriction from the question's "if" clause.

> If the storm passes over Oceana at some time before it passes over Lofton, then which one of the following must be true?[8]

---

[8] PrepTest 46, Sec. 4, Q 16

You'll learn to build the rules and deductions into your Master Sketch in the remainder of this chapter and perfect your technique over the course of the next three chapters. In the chapter dealing with question types, you'll see how valuable it is to draw new "mini-sketches" for questions containing hypothetical "if" clauses. For now, I just want you to note that it's imperative that you keep your sketches clear, accurate, and simple so they can be just as useful as the mini-sketch for the earlier question was.

DEFINE THE TASK

Although your sketch simplified the tasks in the Thunderstorm game and made them quite manageable, that game—because it contains two actions—is actually among the more complex games found on the LSAT. I hope that's comforting. Before challenging you to identify and begin setting up games on your own, I'll walk you through a few more games' Situations to give you a feel for the variety of tasks you're likely to see on test day.

"Abel, You're Third in Line. Baker, up Front. Space 1."

Here's an example of the task most commonly used on the LSAT. Take a few seconds and look it over. Then go ahead and try to draw the initial framework for this game.

> Exactly six guideposts, numbered 1 through 6, mark a mountain trail. Each guidepost pictures a different one of six animals—fox, grizzly, hare, lynx, moose, or porcupine. The following conditions must apply:
>
> The grizzly is pictured on either guidepost 3 or guidepost 4.
>
> The moose guidepost is numbered lower than the hare guidepost.
>
> The lynx guidepost is numbered lower than the moose guidepost but higher than the fox guidepost.[9]

There are many things you could be asked to do with guideposts. You could be asked to assign each of them a different color. Or you could be asked to determine which of two different artists creates the image for each guidepost. Neither of those tasks would be unusual on the LSAT, but neither of them is your task here. The key phrase in the setup is "numbered 1 through 6." The test makers will ask you questions related to the order of the guideposts. A quick check of the rules confirms this. Each one either restricts a particular guidepost's possible positions or tells you something about certain guideposts' order relative to each other. Your sketch should look like this:

---

[9] PrepTest 46, Sec. 4, Game 1

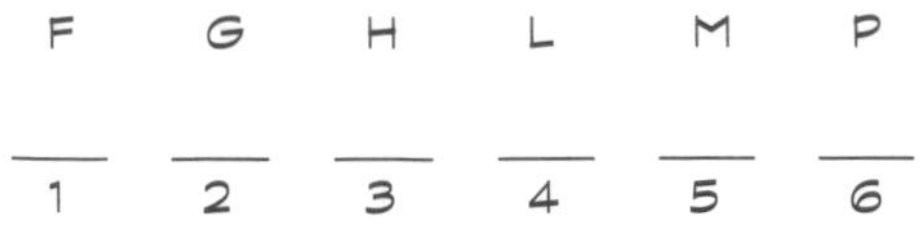

```
F    G    H    L    M    P

___  ___  ___  ___  ___  ___
 1    2    3    4    5    6
```

Figure 1.8

Notice that this game, although it has six signs instead of five towns, tasks you with just the Sequencing half of the Thunderstorm game's setup. That's why I said that the Thunderstorm game is more complex. Complex games aren't necessarily harder or easier than their simpler counterparts (as you'll see in the next chapter, game difficulty is, more than anything, a function of how concrete the rules and restrictions are), but it is essential that you grasp the task or tasks that the questions ask about.

That last point provides the opportunity for an important digression. A lot of test takers go astray by focusing on a game's subject matter. When asked for the game's Situation, they'll say "a thunderstorm" or "trail markers." That tells you nothing. Remember, the test makers could ask you what color each sign is, or which artist painted which signs, or any number of other possible tasks. In logic games, subject matter is irrelevant. Instead, you should look for a clear and descriptive presentation of the Situation that helps you see how the game works. Saying "the Situation is the order of six trail markers" is better. But what I really want you to shoot for is a mental picture of the task. There's a trail in front of you. Under one arm, you have the six signs. In the other hand, you have a mallet to pound them into place. If you put the Grizzly sign in the third space, it's no longer in your hand and no other sign is going in the third space. Now, you can abstract that task into a simple, helpful diagram *and* you can anticipate the kinds of rules, restrictions, and even questions you're going to see. Try that on the next setup.

"Abel, After Charlie. Baker, After Abel."

Take about 30 seconds, compose a picture of the task in your mind, and decide how you'd begin to set this one up. It's similar to the Trail Markers game, but it has a couple of important differences that I'll point out in a moment.

> A courier delivers exactly eight parcels—G, H, J, K, L, M, N, and O. No two parcels are delivered at the same time, nor is any parcel delivered more than once. The following conditions must apply:
> L is delivered later than H.
> K is delivered earlier than O.
> H is delivered earlier than M.
> O is delivered later than G.
> M is delivered earlier than G.
> Both N and J are delivered earlier than M.[10]

---

[10] PrepTest 51, Sec. 4, Game 4

Sure enough, your task is to determine the order of the deliveries. You may have seen that when you read "No two parcels are delivered at the same time, nor is any parcel delivered more than once" in the short opening paragraph. But your mental picture is really fleshed out by the indented rules that follow. Notice that they all restrict the parcels relative to one another. There are no rules here similar to the previous game's restriction of the Grizzly guidepost to spaces 3 or 4. Note, too, that several of the parcels are each mentioned in more than one of the rules. For example, consider the appearance of parcel G in both the fourth and fifth rules:

> A courier delivers exactly eight parcels—G, H, J, K, L, M, N, and O. No two parcels are delivered at the same time, nor is any parcel delivered more than once. The following conditions must apply:
> L is delivered later than H.
> K is delivered earlier than O.
> H is delivered earlier than M.
> O is delivered later than G.
> M is delivered earlier than G.
> Both N and J are delivered earlier than M.[11]

When you have a game like this one—in which all of the rules are relative—you need not create a framework with specific spaces at all. Decide which direction is earlier and which is later, and simply use lines to connect the entities (parcels, in this game) as described by the rules. Without trying to set up the complete game (you'll be doing that soon), here's what the fourth and fifth rules would look like:

Figure 1.9

In this case, earlier deliveries are at the top of the diagram and later ones at the bottom.

Perhaps you pictured yourself as the delivery person arranging the parcels in the back of your truck before you set out on your route. You can't determine the order entirely (there'd be no game if you could), but from the hints in the rules, you can see that some of the packages are going to be dropped off before certain other ones. If this were your real-life job and your route took you to Maple Street before Oak Avenue, you would want to load the Maple deliveries closer to the door of your truck so you wouldn't have to climb over the Oak deliveries to get them.

---

[11] PrepTest 51, Sec. 4, Game 4

By the way, there's a side benefit to doing a quick assessment of the Situation and game tasks: it will reduce your anxiety. With a mental picture of the task, you can arrange your entities logically. You're on your way to law school, so of course you can handle arranging some parcels in a delivery van.

"Abel, You're on Team X. Baker, You're on Team Y."

This next game is quite different from those you've seen thus far, but I'll still challenge you to assess the Situation and task before I explain them in any detail. Take a minute to visualize the Situation, and try to start setting up this game.

> On a field trip to the Museum of Natural History, each of six children—Juana, Kyle, Lucita, Salim, Thanh, and Veronica—is accompanied by one of three adults—Ms. Margoles, Mr. O'Connell, and Ms. Podorski. Each adult accompanies exactly two of the children, consistent with the following conditions:
> > If Ms. Margoles accompanies Juana, then Ms. Podorski accompanies Lucita.
> > If Kyle is not accompanied by Ms. Margoles, then Veronica is accompanied by Mr. O'Connell.
> > Either Ms. Margoles or Mr. O'Connell accompanies Thanh.
> > Juana is not accompanied by the same adult as Kyle; nor is Lucita accompanied by the same adult as Salim; nor is Thanh accompanied by the same adult as Veronica.[12]

The task here is entirely unrelated to the order in which the children go to the museum. But if you picture the Situation, everything becomes clear. There's a classroom, and six kids are standing in alphabetical order. You introduce the three adult chaperones at the front of the room and explain that each grown-up will be responsible for two of the children. Now, just turn that Situation into a simple diagram.

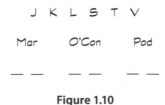

Figure 1.10

It's really beside the point whether you use dashes or boxes or circles to represent each chaperone's assignments, but it's absolutely non-negotiable that you account for exactly two children with each adult. Any of these diagrams would give you what you need:

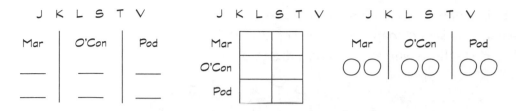

Figure 1.11

You'll come to call this game's action Distribution, dividing a set of entities up into teams. The important thing to notice with this type of game is how clearly the numbers are defined. In the end, it's unimportant that the entities are students and chaperones. What will make this game manageable is that you're splitting six entities into three teams of exactly two players each.

"Abel, You're in This Scene. Baker, You're Not."

Here's one more scenario for you to examine. The sketch will turn out to be remarkably simple (although this game turns out to be pretty challenging for reasons you'll come to appreciate in the chapter on formal logic). Take a few seconds to figure out what you're being asked to do here.

> An album contains photographs picturing seven friends: Raimundo, Selma, Ty, Umiko, Wendy, Yakira, Zack. The friends appear either alone or in groups with one another, in accordance with the following:
>> Wendy appears in every photograph that Selma appears in.
>> Selma appears in every photograph that Umiko appears in.
>> Raimundo appears in every photograph that Yakira does not appear in.
>> Neither Ty nor Raimundo appears in any photograph that Wendy appears in.[13]

This is another game that involves making groups. But this time, there are no chaperones (or coaches, or teams, or whatever) with which the seven friends are being paired. Instead, you're a photographer. You've got the camera set up and you're telling people, "Selma, I want you in this one. Wendy, you too." You could create two lists for any given photo—an "in" group and an "out" group—like so:

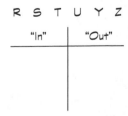

Figure 1.12

---

13 PrepTest 45, Sec. 3, Game 3

An even simpler way to diagram this, and one that would use less of the blank space available on the page (no scratch paper is allowed on test day), is to jot down a list of all seven friends and then circle those who are "in" and strike through those who are "out."

R S T U W Y Z

Figure 1.13

Thus, if you find out that S is in a picture, you know from the rules that W is as well. Since W's appearance knocks out T and R, you'd have a sketch that looks like this:

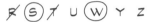

Figure 1.14

This, I'll refer to as a Selection game. This task is almost always straightforward—choose her, reject him. The challenge, as I hinted at above, comes in understanding all of the conditional restrictions the test makers apply to these Situations—"If you include *x*, you have to include *y* but reject *z*," and so on. Fortunately, there are standard ways to interpret and diagram all of the formal logic you'll encounter on the LSAT. But one thing at a time.

Right now, I want you to try your hand at a short drill to test your ability to assess Situations and tasks.

DRILL: DEFINING GAME TASKS

Here are five logic game setups. Take less than one minute with each. Assess the Situation, visualize your task, and use the space next to each one to draw the initial framework or diagram. Don't worry about sketching all of the rules or trying to make additional deductions at this point. You'll be doing all of that soon. Explanations of the game tasks follow the Drill.

1.

In the course of one month Garibaldi has exactly seven different meetings. Each of her meetings is with exactly one of five foreign dignitaries: Fuentes, Matsuba, Rhee, Soleimani, or Tbahi. The following constraints govern Garibaldi's meetings:

> She has exactly three meetings with Fuentes, and exactly one with each of the other dignitaries.
> She does not have any meetings in a row with Fuentes.
> Her meeting with Soleimani is the very next one after her meeting with Tbahi.
> Neither the first nor last of her meetings is with Matsuba.[14]

2.

The three highest-placing teams in a high school debate tournament are the teams from Fairview, Gillom, and Hilltop high schools. Each team has exactly two members. The individuals on these three teams are Mei, Navarro, O'Rourke, Pavlovich, Sethna, and Tsudama. The following is the case:

> Sethna is on the team from Gillom High.
> Tsudama is on the second-place team.
> Mei and Pavlovich are not on the same team.
> Pavlovich's team places higher than Navarro's team.
> The team from Gillom High places higher than the team from Hilltop High.[15]

3.

Three folk groups—Glenside, Hilltopper, Levon—and three rock groups—Peasant, Query, Tinhead—each perform on one of two stages, north or south. Each stage has three two-hour performances: north at 6, 8, and 10; south at 8, 10, and 12. Each group performs individually and exactly once, consistent with the following conditions:

> Peasant performs at 6 or 12.
> Glenside performs at some time before Hilltopper.
> If any rock group performs at 10, no folk group does.
> Levon and Tinhead perform on different stages.
> Query performs immediately after a folk group, though not necessarily on the same stage.[16]

4.

Workers at a water treatment plant open eight valves—G, H, I, K, L, N, O, and P—to flush out a system of pipes that needs emergency repairs. To maximize safety and efficiency, each valve is opened exactly once, and no two valves are opened at the same time. The valves are opened in accordance with the following conditions:

> Both K and P are opened before H.
> O is opened before L but after H.
> L is opened after G.
> N is opened before H.
> I is opened after K.[17]

5.

In a repair facility there are exactly six technicians: Stacy, Urma, Wim, Xena, Yolanda, and Zane. Each technician repairs machines of at least one of the following three types— radios, televisions, and VCRs—and no other types. The following conditions apply:

> Xena and exactly three other technicians repair radios.
> Yolanda repairs both televisions and VCRs.
> Stacy does not repair any type of machine that Yolanda repairs.
> Zane repairs more types of machines than Yolanda repairs.
> Wim does not repair any type of machine that Stacy repairs.
> Urma repairs exactly two types of machines.[18]

Explanations

Now, compare your work to the suggested visualizations and sketches below.

1.
In the course of one month Garibaldi has exactly seven different meetings. Each of her meetings is with exactly one of five foreign dignitaries: Fuentes, Matsuba, Rhee, Soleimani, or Tbahi. The following constraints govern Garibaldi's meetings:

> She has exactly three meetings with Fuentes, and exactly one with each of the other dignitaries.
> She does not have any meetings in a row with Fuentes.
> Her meeting with Soleimani is the very next one after her meeting with Tbahi.
> Neither the first nor last of her meetings is with Matsuba.[19]

F	F	F	M	R	S	T
1	2	3	4	5	6	7

Figure 1.15

Your task is only hinted at in the opening paragraph by the phrases "in the course of one month" and "each of her meetings is with exactly one of five foreign dignitaries." You may already have a mental picture of an appointment calendar in mind. A quick scan of the rules confirms your suspicion: The test makers want you to determine the order of the seven meetings, and you can set up a sketch much like the one you used for the Trail Markers game. There is one unusual feature that I hope you caught. Garibaldi has seven meetings with just five people, but each meeting is with only one dignitary. Rule 1 clears it all up. She'll meet with Fuentes three times. As a result, it's very helpful to list F three times in your roster of the entities: "F F F M R S T." Along the way, a question may give you enough information to determine the position of one or two of the meetings with F, so you could cross those off your roster. This way, you'll still have a visual reminder of all meetings that remain undetermined.

2.
The three highest-placing teams in a high school debate tournament are the teams from Fairview, Gillom, and Hilltop high schools. Each team has exactly two members. The individuals on these three teams are Mei, Navarro, O'Rourke, Pavlovich, Sethna, and Tsudama. The following is the case:

> Sethna is on the team from Gillom High.
> Tsudama is on the second-place team.
> Mei and Pavlovich are not on the same team.
> Pavlovich's team places higher than Navarro's team.
> The team from Gillom High places higher than the team from Hilltop High.[20]

Figure 1.16

Here's another complex game. Your tasks are thoroughly intertwined. You'll need to determine the final ranking of the top three teams and figure out which two debaters competed for each school. Your mental picture may be something like the awards stands at the Olympics, with the

---

[19] PrepTest 44, Sec. 3, Game 1

[20] PrepTest 53, Sec. 2, Game 4

gold, silver, and bronze medalists facing the crowd. When you have two different categories of entities, it's a good idea to abbreviate them in visually distinct ways. In the sample sketch, three-letter abbreviations were used for the schools, one-letter abbreviations for the debaters. Kudos if you noticed a similarity between this game and the Thunderstorm game that kicked off this chapter. In each, your task is to determine an order and make some assignments to each position within the order. There are two key differences, though. In the Thunderstorm game, you could assign "rain" or "hail and rain" multiple times, but once a debater competes for a team in this game, he or she can't be re-used. Of course, in the Thunderstorm game, you matched only one feature—the type of precipitation—with each town or numbered space. Here, you must match two debaters to each school or position. Still, the similarities outweigh the differences, and the rules in this game should seem quite familiar already. One final note: While the order in the Thunderstorm game was arranged horizontally, the rank of the schools here is vertical. That's a matter of taste and not at all crucial to the diagram. For many, the idea of arranging rank vertically from top to bottom will just seem intuitive. Go with it if that's the case.

3.

Three folk groups—Glenside, Hilltopper, Levon—and three rock groups—Peasant, Query, Tinhead—each perform on one of two stages, north or south. Each stage has three two-hour performances: north at 6, 8, and 10; south at 8, 10, and 12. Each group performs individually and exactly once, consistent with the following conditions:

    Peasant performs at 6 or 12.
    Glenside performs at some time before Hilltopper.
    If any rock group performs at 10, no folk group does.
    Levon and Tinhead perform on different stages.
    Query performs immediately after a folk group, though
     not necessarily on the same stage.[21]

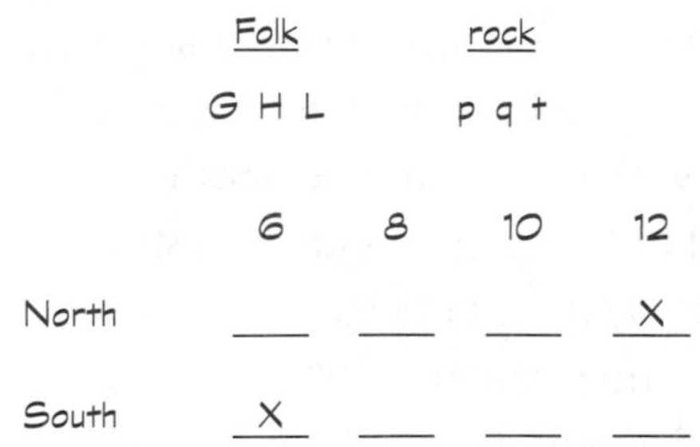

	Folk			rock		
	G H L			p q t		
		6	8	10	12	
North		___	___	___	X	
South		X	___	___	___	

Figure 1.17

Have you ever been to a music festival? It's not hard to picture the two stages or a handbill that announces who'll be on which stage at what time. It's a little subtler than in the Debate Teams game, but you have two tasks here, too. You're going to be asked about the order in which the bands appear *and* about which stage each one's on. That makes it very helpful to

---

[21] PrepTest 48, Sec. 2, Game 4

integrate the sketch so that you can see both the time of the performance and the stage In the same glance. I'm sure you've seen schedules for events that are laid out like this:

North Stage

6 pm	Peasant — rock
8 pm	Tinhead — rock
10 pm	Hilltopper — folk

South Stage

8 pm	Glenside — folk
10 pm	Levon — folk
midnight	Query — rock

Figure 1.18

That makes it a lot harder to manage the information. Note, too, that the sample sketch abbreviates the folk bands in capital letters and the rock bands in lowercase. A clear visual distinction like that is much easier to use on test day than having a separate label next to each entity every time you have draw it into the sketch.

4.
Workers at a water treatment plant open eight valves—G, H, I, K, L, N, O, and P—to flush out a system of pipes that needs emergency repairs. To maximize safety and efficiency, each valve is opened exactly once, and no two valves are opened at the same time. The valves are opened in accordance with the following conditions:

 Both K and P are opened before H.
 O is opened before L but after H.
 L is opened after G.
 N is opened before H.
 I is opened after K.[22]

["Loose Sequencing": No framework needed.]

Figure 1.19

Here's another of those so-called "Loose Sequencing" games (like the Parcel Delivery example). These games task you with determining the order of a set of actions, but they give you rules that restrict the entities only with respect to one another. No framework is required or even very helpful. You'll just link all of the entities with lines showing their relationships. If you see a game like this and automatically draw out eight slots (and, trust me, a lot of us LSAT experts have done that over the years), no problem. You'll just wind up ignoring them. In anticipation of the chapters on rules and deductions, your final sketch here will look like this:

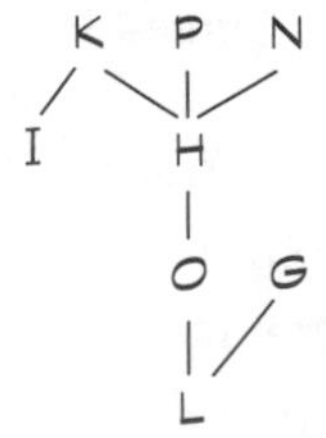

```
        K   P   N
       /  \ | /
      I     H
            |
            O   G
            | /
            L
```

Figure 1.20

Don't worry if you don't see how all of that came together yet. In no time, you'll be making full Master Sketches and attacking the questions with ease.

5.
In a repair facility there are exactly six technicians: Stacy, Urma, Wim, Xena, Yolanda, and Zane. Each technician repairs machines of at least one of the following three types—radios, televisions, and VCRs—and no other types. The following conditions apply:

    Xena and exactly three other technicians repair radios.
    Yolanda repairs both televisions and VCRs.
    Stacy does not repair any type of machine that Yolanda repairs.
    Zane repairs more types of machines than Yolanda repairs.
    Wim does not repair any type of machine that Stacy repairs.
    Urma repairs exactly two types of machines.[23]

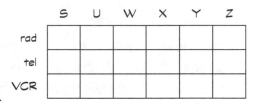

Figure 1.21

Games like this one can give students fits. "How do I know whether to assign the technicians to the gadgets or vice versa?" has been the cry of many a frustrated test taker. Fortunately, the answer is that it doesn't really matter. Probably the most instinctive mental picture is to see the six technicians at a line of work stations and then imagine that some of them are working on only one type of machine while others have two or three different kinds. If you make a chart showing the types of machines and listing who works on each, all you're really doing is flipping the orientation of the same picture.

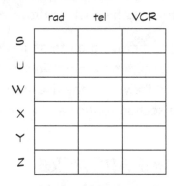

Figure 1.22

Another matter of preference is whether to use a grid (like those shown above) or simply to list the gadgets under each of the technicians. Make your decision based on which is easiest for you to construct and to copy as you handle the various questions. Here's an example of the list approach with the first four rules included:

---

[23] PrepTest 48, Sec. 2, Game 3

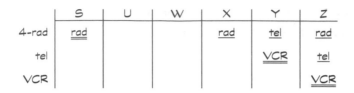

Figure 1.23

The double lines indicate that the technician's assignments have been completely determined. They "close off" the column, so to speak. When we encounter Matching games like this one later in the book, I'll illustrate both approaches to sketching. Practice them and see which variation works best for you. Remember, you don't get style points. Use what works (provided that you capture all of the information accurately).

By the way, if you're getting the impression that a lot of these games are quite similar, that's because they are. The games selected in this chapter and throughout the book are designed to be representative of what you're most likely to see on test day. While there are trends (see chapter 14 for a breakdown of what's appeared on the most recent exams), the core game actions are remarkably consistent. Test-prep books that are more interested in showing off the author's exhaustive store of LSAT logic games esoterica than in helping your prepare for the test often make rare, outdated games seem just as important as those that recent tests have featured most often. By the time you're in Part II of this book, you'll have internalized this knowledge and you'll be handling many logic games without having to stop and think. By test day, they'll be second nature. Nothing will improve your efficiency more than that.

Before wrapping up this chapter and moving on to an in-depth look at logic games rules, I want to respond to a couple of other common complaints that I've heard from hundreds of test takers over the years. I'll also introduce you to the five-step Kaplan Method for Logic Games, which will make your work in this section routine and effective.

RIGHT THINKING, WRONG ANSWERS
"I Think I Just Got The Question Backward."

Almost as common as students saying, "I didn't know how to set this game up," is the comment, "I had everything set up right, but I still got this question wrong. How did that happen?" My answer is always the same. I begin by asking the test taker to read the question back to me and explain what it's asking for. This nearly always reveals that the student misinterpreted the question stem and wound up picking the right answer *for the wrong question*.

In chapter 5, I'll break down all of the question types that the LSAT test makers use in the Logic Games section, and I'll show you how to handle each one correctly. For now, take a look at a handful of questions that illustrate the most common ways in which students waste time and choose the wrong answer even when they've correctly interpreted the game's task, setup, and rules.

Sometimes (more often than students care to admit, actually), it's just a matter of sloppy reading. Here's a question from the Parcel Delivery game:

> If K is the seventh parcel delivered, then each of the
> following could be true EXCEPT:
>
> (A) G is the fifth parcel delivered.
> (B) M is the fifth parcel delivered.
> (C) H is the fourth parcel delivered.
> (D) L is the fourth parcel delivered.
> (E) J is the third parcel delivered.[24]

Four of the answers—the wrong ones—*could be true.* I can't tell you the number of students who I've seen read choice (A) in a question like this one and say, "Yeah, that works." They bubble the answer into their answer grid and move on to the next question. You can see the problem already. Our minds are wired to look for what's okay, what works, what *could be true.* The test makers know this, and they design questions to punish those who aren't reading strategically. In this question, the correct answer is choice (C). It's the only one that *must be false,* which is the characteristic you're actually looking for in the correct choice.

In chapter 5, I'll take you through guided practice and a Drill on characterizing answer choices. For now, just remember that every LSAT question has one correct, credited answer and four unequivocally, demonstrably incorrect ones. There's never a "better" answer, only a right one. It is always worth a few seconds to carefully read each question stem and characterize what the correct answer must contain. Any time you spend producing a wrong answer is wasted time.

Another way in which students who do good work setting up a game wind up choosing a wrong answer is by confusing "must" and "could." Take this example, from the Folk/Rock Festival game.

> Which of the following groups must perform earlier than 10?
>
> (A) Glenside
> (B) Hilltopper
> (C) Levon
> (D) Peasant
> (E) Tinhead[25]

---

24 PrepTest 51, Sec. 4, Q 21
25 PrepTest 48, Sec. 2, Q 19

Remember this question when we revisit this game in later chapters. You'll find that each of the five bands listed in the answer choices could perform earlier than 10. A test taker who makes one sketch that *could* work and sees Hilltopper performing at 8, let's say, might choose (B) and move on. That test taker might not make any mistakes interpreting the game's action or applying its rules, but would nevertheless choose a wrong answer because the question isn't asking which band *could* perform before 10. It's asking which band *must* perform before 10. A more strategic approach to this type of question would be to look for sketches in which bands could perform at 10 or 12 and eliminate the answer choices that include those bands. The correct answer—which happens to be choice (A), by the way—names the only band that can *never* perform at 10 or 12.

As you proceed through this book, look for opportunities to practice *thinking on both sides* of statements and questions like these. The test makers are very fond of checking whether you can interpret both the affirmative and negative ways of saying the same thing. When a rule tells you that one entity *must* be placed on a different team than another, it means that they *cannot* be placed together. If a correct answer *must be false*, all four wrong answers *could be true*. You never know whether the LSAT will use affirmative or negative language in its rules, question stems, and answer choices. You will be rewarded, however, for being able to discern whether statements are equivalent in meaning despite being phrased in different ways.

THE KAPLAN METHOD
"I could have gotten them all right if I'd just had more time."

Of all the gripes students have with the LSAT, this is the most common and the one most likely to lead to poor test-taking decisions. Fortunately, it's also the most preventable. The key is to avoid confusing speed with efficiency. By trying to speed up and going too fast, students get sloppy. They misunderstand game tasks, construct poor sketches, miss deductions, and make the kinds of mistakes with the questions that you just saw. All of that might take less time than would a more patient approach, but it winds up being wasted time because it produces wrong answers (or produces a few right answers only after the student realizes how badly things are going and slows down to redo the game from the start).

Efficiency is found in the optimal mix of speed and correct answers. More than anything else, it's your efficiency that will improve as you follow the principles and strategies laid out in this book. At the top of the list is the 5 Step Kaplan Method for Logic Games. Use this method on every logic game, from the simplest to the most challenging. Use it until it becomes automatic. This method will underlie everything you do in this book from here on out, and it provides the basis for the organization of the rest of Part I.

THE KAPLAN METHOD FOR LOGIC GAMES

STEP 1 Overview
Assess the game's Situation and determine your task(s).

STEP 2 Sketch
Draw a simple, useful framework to organize the game's information and restrictions.

STEP 3 Rules
Add the Rules into the Sketch in clear notation.

STEP 4 Deductions
Combine the Rules and restrictions to determine what must be true and false.

STEP 5 Questions
Answer the questions efficiently using the information from your Master Sketch.

It often surprises students that, for any given game, Steps 1 through 4 may take as long as or longer than Step 5. Given that you have 35 minutes to tackle four games, you should plan on averaging around eight to eight and a half minutes per game. That's eight minutes to read the game, set it up, make your deductions, and answer five to seven questions. Test takers who rush through the earlier parts of a game are those who most often run out of time. That's because they're treating each question as a novel task. If you take a minute or two to answer each question, you'll soon be over the eight minutes allotted for a game.

Following the Kaplan Method, you'll find that spending three, four, or sometimes even five minutes creating a complete and accurate Master Sketch increases your efficiency. Because a complete Master Sketch depicts all of the rules and deductions in a user-friendly chart or diagram, you can often answer most, if not all, of the questions in a matter of seconds each. Think of times when you struggled to understand some complex scientific or historical details in a lecture until the professor put up that one slide that made it all so clear. You could *see* it. That's what the first four steps of the Kaplan Method help you accomplish with logic games. It will take some more explanation (and a lot of practice), but commit now to learning this proven method. It has helped literally hundreds of thousands of test takers improve their logic games performance. It will do the same for you.

The Kaplan Method in Action

To show you how the Kaplan Method works, I'll apply it to the Thunderstorm game. This time, I'll take on the whole thing, from start to finish. Keep in mind that this is just one game, and you'll be seeing all the restrictions, rules, deductions, and questions addressed in subsequent chapters. Here's the Thunderstorm game as it appeared in the June 2005 LSAT:

Questions 12–16

One afternoon a single thunderstorm passes over exactly five towns—Jackson, Lofton, Nordique, Oceana, and Plattesville—dropping some form of precipitation on each. The storm is the only source of precipitation in the towns that afternoon. On some towns, it drops both hail and rain; on the remaining towns, it drops only rain. It passes over each town exactly once and does not pass over any two towns at the same time. The following must obtain:

   The third town the storm passes over is Plattesville.
   The storm drops hail and rain on the second town it passes over.
   The storm drops only rain on both Lofton and Oceana.
   The storm passes over Jackson at some time after it passes over Lofton and at some time after it passes over Nordique.

12. Which one of the following could be the order, from first to fifth, in which the storm passes over the towns?

   (A) Lofton, Nordique, Plattesville, Oceana, Jackson
   (B) Lofton, Oceana, Plattesville, Nordique, Jackson
   (C) Nordique, Jackson, Plattesville, Oceana, Lofton
   (D) Nordique, Lofton, Plattesville, Jackson, Oceana
   (E) Nordique, Plattesville, Lofton, Oceana, Jackson

13. If the storm passes over Oceana at some time before it passes over Jackson, then each of the following could be true EXCEPT:

   (A) The first town the storm passes over is Oceana.
   (B) The fourth town the storm passes over is Lofton.
   (C) The fourth town the storm passes over receives hail and rain.
   (D) The fifth town the storm passes over is Jackson.
   (E) The fifth town the storm passes over receives only rain.

14. If the storm drops only rain on each town it passes over after passing over Lofton, then which one of the following could be false?

   (A) The first town the storm passes over is Oceana.
   (B) The fourth town the storm passes over receives only rain.
   (C) The fifth town the storm passes over is Jackson.
   (D) Jackson receives only rain.
   (E) Plattesville receives only rain.

15. If the storm passes over Jackson at some time before it passes over Oceana, then which one of the following could be false?

   (A) The storm passes over Lofton at some time before it passes over Jackson.
   (B) The storm passes over Lofton at some time before it passes over Oceana.
   (C) The storm passes over Nordique at some time before it passes over Oceana.
   (D) The fourth town the storm passes over receives only rain.
   (E) The fifth town the storm passes over receives only rain.

16. If the storm passes over Oceana at some time before it passes over Lofton, then which one of the following must be true?

   (A) The third town the storm passes over receives only rain.
   (B) The fourth town the storm passes over receives only rain.
   (C) The fourth town the storm passes over receives hail and rain.
   (D) The fifth town the storm passes over receives only rain.
   (E) The fifth town the storm passes over receives hail and rain.[26]

---

[26] PrepTest 46, Sec. 4, Game 3, Qs 12–16

STEPS 1 AND 2: Overview and Sketch

Believe it or not, you've already got a great head start on Steps 1 and 2 of the Kaplan Method from the work you did determining game tasks earlier in this chapter. There, I encouraged you to look at the game's Situation, the real-life scenario described in the setup. As I said, it's not enough to simply say, "It's about a thunderstorm." The test could involve any of many tasks related to thunderstorms. To get better at conducting the Overview, you can actually divide your assessment of the setup into four questions (a lot of Kaplan teachers call them the SEAL questions, creating an acronym out of their keywords):

> *What is the **S**ituation?*
>
> *Who or what are the **E**ntities?*
>
> *What's the **A**ction?*
>
> *What are the **L**imitations?*

Answering these four questions will yield a thorough understanding of the scenario that allows you to create a mental picture of your task. Take a few seconds now to refresh your memory of this game's setup. Ask the SEAL questions and develop a mental picture of what the game entails.

One afternoon, a single thunderstorm passes over exactly five towns—Jackson, Lofton, Nordique, Oceana, and Plattesville—dropping some form of precipitation on each. The storm is the only source of precipitation in the towns that afternoon. On some towns, it drops both hail and rain; on the remaining towns, it drops only rain. It passes over each town exactly once and does not pass over any two towns at the same time. The following must obtain:
   The third town the storm passes over is Plattesville.
   The storm drops hail and rain over the second town it passes over.
   The storm drops only rain on both Lofton and Oceana.
   The storm passes over Jackson at some time after it passes over Lofton and at some time after it passes over Nordique.[27]

The *situation* involves a storm passing over five towns, of course. The towns are the first set of *entities* described in the setup. The *limitations*—the storm passes over each town only once, one town at a time—reveal that the *action* involves Sequencing. You're also told that the storm will drop one of two kinds of precipitation—this is your second set of entities—on each town. So Matching either hail and rain or just rain to each town or position is the second *action* you're asked to perform. Seeing all of that (in your mind, at least) leads to starting a sketch like this one:

---

[27] PrepTest 46, Sec. 4, Game 3

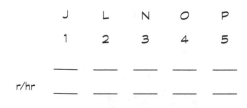

Figure 1.24

Go ahead and copy that down on the page displaying the complete game. This particular game left a lot of space at the bottom of the page (remember, you don't get any scratch paper for the LSAT), so I'd encourage you to write it in small, neat writing an inch or so below question 13.

STEP 3: Rules

Now, you're ready to add the rules into the sketch. Notice that I said *into*. Whenever possible, you'll want to leverage the full power of your visual description of the game. Just reading the rules or jotting them down off to the side isn't nearly as powerful as using them to show the restrictions that are occurring within the game's framework. The rules are your greatest allies in handling games. They restrict the possible arrangements that will work. At the outset of this game, there are 3,840 possible arrangements of the towns and the types of precipitation. By the time you're done with the rules and deductions, there will be only 10. That's powerful. Here's how it works.

Rule 1 deals with the order of the towns.

> The third town that the storm passes over is Plattesville.[28]

	J	L	N	O	P̸
	1	2	3	4	5
	—	—	P	—	—
r/hr	—	—	—	—	—

Figure 1.25

That goes directly into the sketch in an obvious way. It makes P what you'll come to call an Established Entity.

Rule 2 does the same thing on the line representing precipitation.

---

[28] PrepTest 46, Sec. 4, Game 3

The storm drops hail and rain on the second town it passes over.[29]

Figure 1.26

Rule 3 determines the type of precipitation that two of the towns receive. Since you don't yet know which position those towns will take in the storm's path, show the connection within your roster of entities.

The storm drops only rain on both Lofton and Oceana.[30]

Figure 1.27

Rule 4 gives the relationship between Jackson and Lofton and between Jackson and Nordique. (Don't make more of a rule than what's actually there. This rule doesn't tell you anything about the relationship between Lofton and Nordique.)

The storm passes over Jackson at some point after it passes over Lofton and at some point after it passes over Nordique.[31]

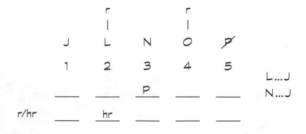

Figure 1.28

---

29 PrepTest 46, Sec. 4, Game 3

30 PrepTest 46, Sec. 4, Game 3

31 PrepTest 46, Sec. 4, Game 3

This is a rule that you have to jot down in shorthand beneath or beside the framework. There's just no way, at this point, to build it into the framework. When you get this kind of rule, don't be haphazard. Depict the rule in the same "visual vocabulary" that you've used for the Sketch. Make the letters depicting the entities about the same size as the spaces you've created for them, and make sure the orientation is the same as what you've used in the framework diagram.

If you haven't done so already, add these illustrations of the rules to the Master Sketch you constructed in Step 2. You're just about ready to make deductions. That's where the magic will happen.

STEP 4: Deductions

The sketch as you currently have it, with the rules represented as simple graphics, is about as far as the average LSAT test taker is likely to go. It's not far enough to maximize your efficiency when it comes to the questions. You could muddle through the questions (try it if you want to), but you'd soon find that the more complex questions are costing you an inordinate amount of time. After you complete the Deductions step, you'll find that you're able to answer any of the questions here in 30 seconds or less.

Deductions are valid inferences (facts that *must be true* or *must be false*) that you can make by combining the game's individual rules and restrictions. As you identify them, build them right into the Master Sketch so that you have them visually represented. In chapter 4, you'll learn that there are five types of rules that combine to create logic games deductions. For now, follow this principle: Start with the most concrete information and work your way down until you've exhausted all that you can know with certainty. This principle is extremely important, and following it will make your logic games experience much more pleasant. But more on that later. Back to the game at hand.

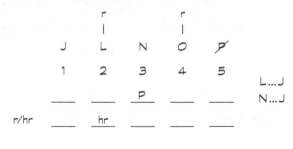

Figure 1.29

Look first at the line representing the order of towns that the storm passes over. Established Entity P sits in space 3. Which other rule restricts the order of towns? It's Rule 4, the one that says L and N must both come before J. Consider what must be true when you combine that rule with the one placing P in space 3.

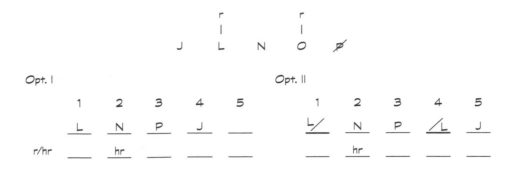

Figure 1.30

J comes after at least two towns—L and N—and P already occupies space 3. That means J has to be in either space 4 or space 5. Throughout the book, we'll refer to deductions like this one, in which every acceptable arrangement conforms to one of two patterns, as Limited Options. Whenever you find Limited Options, draw both acceptable arrangements in your Master Sketch.

By the way, do you see why town N must take space 2 in either option? You know from the second rule that the second town receives hail and rain. That was already in your Master Sketch from Rule 2. You also knew that L and O (the only remaining towns) receive only rain. That's Rule 3. In fact, go ahead and add that to your deductions.

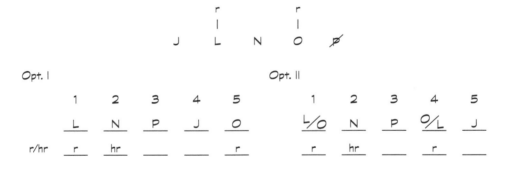

Figure 1.31

In Option I, O has to take space 5. In Option II, you don't know which of L and O takes space 1 and which takes space 4, but you know either way that spaces 1 and 4 will receive only rain.

Put the completed Master Sketch (with both options) at the bottom of the page with the full game on it. With this Sketch, you're ready to tackle the questions. This game doesn't include all of the question types you'll see on test day (it's very rare that any one game does), but it provides a great example of the power of the Kaplan Method, the rules, and the deductions.

STEP 5: Questions

I'll answer the questions for this game in the order in which they appear. At times, it's advantageous to tackle the questions out of order (you'll see this discussed in Part III of the book, when I talk about managing the games and sections), but going straight through is the most efficient approach in this case. If you'd like to try any of the questions on your own now that you have the Master Sketch, feel free. But pay very close attention to the explanations below, because the takeaway message at this point in the book is to see how to tackle the questions with maximum effectiveness.

12. **(A)**

Which one of the following could be the order, from first to fifth, in which the storm passes over the towns?

(A)   Lofton, Nordique, Plattesville, Oceana, Jackson
(B)   Lofton, Oceana, Plattesville, Nordique, Jackson
(C)   Nordique, Jackson, Plattesville, Oceana, Lofton
(D)   Nordique, Lofton, Plattesville, Jackson, Oceana
(E)   Nordique, Plattesville, Lofton, Oceana, Jackson[32]

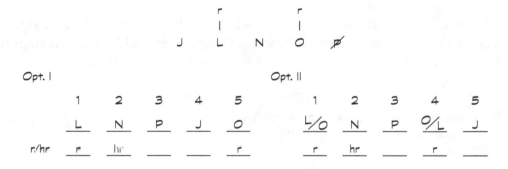

Figure 1.32

This is called an Acceptability question. The correct answer is simply the one that works, that violates no rules. Use the rules (or in this case, your Master Sketch) to eliminate answers that violate the rules. You can see that in either Option, the only acceptable town for space 1 is L or O. That gets rid of choices (C), (D), and (E). Cross out those answers completely; you have no reason to look at them again.

---

[32] PrepTest 46, Sec. 4, Q 12

Which one of the following could be the order, from first to fifth, in which the storm passes over the towns?

(A) Lofton, Nordique, Plattesville, Oceana, Jackson
(B) Lofton, Oceana, Plattesville, Nordique, Jackson
(C) ~~Nordique, Jackson, Plattesville, Oceana, Lofton~~
(D) ~~Nordique, Lofton, Plattesville, Jackson, Oceana~~
(E) ~~Nordique, Plattesville, Lofton, Oceana, Jackson~~[33]

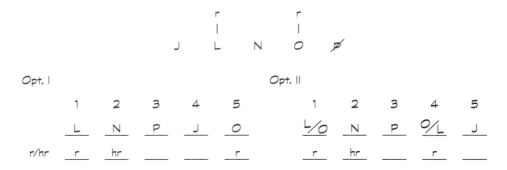

Figure 1.33

Now check space 2. N is acceptable. O is not. Choice (A) is correct. That would take you all of 10 seconds on test day. Your investment in the initial Sketch, Rules, and Deductions steps pays dividends immediately.

13. **(C)**

If the storm passes over Oceana at some time before it passes over Jackson, then each of the following could be true EXCEPT:

(A) The first town the storm passes over is Oceana.
(B) The fourth town the storm passes over is Lofton.
(C) The fourth town the storm passes over receives hail and rain.
(D) The fifth town the storm passes over is Jackson.
(E) The fifth town the storm passes over receives only rain.[34]

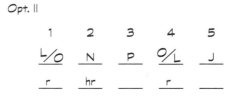

Figure 1.34

All of the remaining questions are "If" questions. That is, they begin with an additional, hypothetical restriction. Such restrictions apply only to the individual question in which they appear. They don't carry over to restrict other questions that follow. In this game, the "if" questions demonstrate the power of your Limited Options deduction. Here, for example, the "if" says that O precedes J. That can only happen in Option II. So you know which part of your Master Sketch to refer to.

---

[33] PrepTest 46, Sec. 4, Q 12

[34] PrepTest 46, Sec. 4, Q 13

Now, characterize the answer choices. The four wrong answers *could be true*. They're all things that *could* happen in Option II. But the "EXCEPT" tells you that the correct answer *must be false*. The answer you're looking for will violate Option II. Go through the choices one at a time:

Choice (A) says that O is the first town. That's okay in Option II. Cross out the answer completely and move on.

Choice (B) puts L in space 4. That's acceptable in Option II. Cross it out.

Choice (C) has town 4 getting hail and rain. That's impossible in Option II. This is the correct answer. Circle it. You're done.

You may wonder whether you need to check answer choices (D) and (E). The answer is "no." But it's "no" because you had a complete Master Sketch with all of the deductions, because you used the "if" to narrow your search to Option II, *and* because you characterized the answer choices before evaluating them. Without those essential steps in the Kaplan Method, you'd still be floundering around with this question.

14. **(E)**

If the storm drops only rain on each town it passes over after passing over Lofton, then which one of the following could be false?

(A) The first town the storm passes over is Oceana.
(B) The fourth town the storm passes over receives
      only rain.
(C) The fifth town the storm passes over is
      Jackson.
(D) Jackson receives only rain
(E) Plattesville receives only rain.[35]

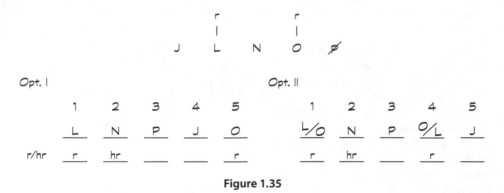

Figure 1.35

This is another "If" question. This time, the "if" restricts all towns after L to receiving only rain. Checking the options, that clearly cannot happen in Option I, where the very next town after L receives hail and rain. In Option II, it can only happen when L is the fourth town the storm passes over. And if every town after L receives only rain, you know that's what J receives. If it's helpful, you can draw this as a mini-sketch next to the question.

	1	2	3	4	5
	O	N	P	L	J
	r	hr	__	r	r

Figure 1.36

If you're already looking at the answer choices, wait. Did you characterize what you're looking for? The correct answer here *could be false*. It's something that doesn't have to be true in the mini-sketch from Option II. That means that all four wrong answers *must be true*. When you see an answer that *must be true* in the mini-sketch, cross it out.

Choice (A) must be true. O is right there in space 1. Cross this one out.

Choice (B) must also be true. In Option II, town 4 always gets only rain. Cross it out.

Choice (C) must be true. J is last in Option II. Gone.

Choice (D) must be true in this case. The "if" restricts towns following L to receiving only rain. J follows L. Ergo, cross it out.

That means choice (E) is the winner. The only town for which you cannot determine the type of precipitation is P, in space 3. Since you can't determine its precipitation, it *could be false* that it receives only rain.

Learning when to draw a new mini-sketch to help you with an individual question takes some experience and practice. I'll always point out when and where a new sketch is beneficial.

15. **(D)**

If the storm passes over Jackson at some time before it passes over Oceana, then which one of the following could be false?

(A) The storm passes over Lofton at some time before it passes over Jackson.

(B) The storm passes over Lofton at some time before it passes over Oceana.

(C) The storm passes over Nordique at some time before it passes over Oceana.

(D) The fourth town the storm passes over receives only rain.

(E) The fifth town the storm passes over receives only rain.[36]

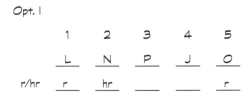

Opt. I

	1	2	3	4	5
	L	N	P	J	O
r/hr	r	hr	__	__	r

Figure 1.37

Same singer, different tune. In this question, the "if" puts J earlier than O in the storm's path. How can that happen? Only in Option I. Again, the question asks what *could be false*. That means that the wrong answers *must be true*. Be bold. Check each answer against Option I and eliminate those that have to be true there.

Choice (A) actually must be true in every instance. Rule 4 told you that L comes earlier than J. Eliminate.

Choice (B) is definitely true in Option I. Get rid of it, too.

Choice (C) must be true in Option I. N is in space 2. O is in space 5. Strike through this one.

Choice (D) could be false in Option I. The type of precipitation that falls on J in space 4 is undetermined here. Circle choice (D) and move on.

The more you work with the Kaplan Method, the more confident you will be in tackling all types of questions. Early in this book (and early in your practice), don't be afraid to slow down and learn to master all of the strategies and techniques. Your speed (and more importantly, your efficiency) will increase naturally as you get more and more comfortable thinking along with the test.

16. **(B)**

If the storm passes over Oceana at some time before it passes over Lofton, then which one of the following must be true?

(A) The third town the storm passes over receives only rain.
(B) The fourth town the storm passes over receives only rain.
(C) The fourth town the storm passes over receives hail and rain.
(D) The fifth town the storm passes over receives only rain.
(E) The fifth town the storm passes over receives hail and rain.[37]

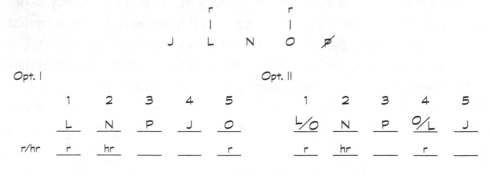

Figure 1.38

You already know the answer to this one from the opening of the chapter, but I'll review it in the context of the Kaplan Method in order to close the loop. I hope you'll see how far you've already come in understanding what makes logic games tick.

---

[37] PrepTest 46, Sec. 4, Q 16

The "if" in this question—O positioned earlier than L—puts you squarely in Option II and, in fact, limits you to the following mini-sketch (the one you saw earlier, though you didn't know how it was derived at that point).

1	2	3	4	5
O	N	P	L	J
r	hr	___	r	___

Figure 1.39

You're asked for the answer that *must be true*. Each of the wrong answers, therefore, *could be false*. Evaluate them one at a time, just for practice.

Choice (A) could be false. The mini-sketch shows that the type of precipitation in space 3 is undetermined. So it need not be true that it's only rain. Cross out choice (A).

Choice (B) must be true. Indeed, the town in space 4 always gets only rain in Option II. Circle choice (B). You've gotten all the points from this game.

That's the Kaplan Method in a nutshell. In the following chapters, I'll elaborate on Steps 3, 4, and 5 in detail. By the time you've worked through those chapters, you'll have seen the variety of rules and restrictions used by the test makers, the types of deductions you're consistently rewarded for making, and every type of question that appears in the logic games section of the LSAT. You're well on your way to logic games mastery. I'll make just one more comment about efficiency before closing the chapter.

Don't Let Perfect Be the Enemy of Good (and Vice Versa)

On one hand, the desire to be perfect can be frustrating. You'll have a tendency to get hung up on one difficult game, or even one tough question, and have the sinking feeling that you'll never get this stuff. (That's compounded by the fact that it's much easier to see later, in hindsight, how each logic games question should have been done.) The test can use that tendency against you, if you let it, by placing difficult games and questions at exactly the points where you'll grind to a halt. If you take the bait, you can wind up spending five precious minutes to get one point, only to miss out on five or six eminently "gettable" points because you ran out of time.

On the other hand, the desire to see quick gains leads some students to compromise when they don't need to. I've had hundreds of students over the years who, after a little practice, find themselves still struggling to finish a section. They come to me with questions like "Should I just try to do three games as well as I can and give up on the last one?" That question is almost always premature. Students want to see more points *now*. But as with anything that rewards skill, there are growing pains during your LSAT practice. Don't give up on what you know to be the best approach because it's difficult at first. By the time test day rolls around, you want to get as many points as possible from all of the games. Don't abandon the methods and strategies that will get you there in order to make practice feel easier or more immediately gratifying.

The only real solution to this dilemma is patience, both with yourself and with the test. Spend the time now to thoroughly understand and internalize all of the information in Part I of this book. As the right approach—the strategic one—becomes second nature, you'll see the gains in efficiency (and, therefore, LSAT points) that are the reason you bought this book in the first place. Mastering the LSAT isn't easy; it's not supposed to be. You're going to law school, after all. But it's going to be worth it.

CHAPTER 2

RULES AND SKETCHES

LEARN TO "THINK WITH RULES"

As a future law student, you probably have a good intuitive understanding of rules, and you're probably quite comfortable in a world where the rule of law helps keep things running smoothly and helps ensure a level playing field. So there's no reason to have an adverse reaction to the rules in logic games. In fact, there's every reason to embrace the rules as your greatest allies. In this chapter, you'll see how the rules can turn directly into points. You'll also see how the set of rules always allows you to answer one particular question type—Acceptability questions—quickly and accurately. Finally, I'll show you how to assess the power of rules, a skill that allows you to take control of the entire game by spotting its most restricted entities.

Rules Reduce Uncertainty

It's the rules and limitations that reduce the task from an unmanageable riot of possible arrangements down to fewer than a couple dozen. Recall that the rules (and their concomitant deductions) allowed you to take the Thunderstorm game from 3,840 possible arrangements down to just 10. Take a closer look at how the rules enable you to take control of all logic games.

To appreciate how much help rules are giving you, first take a look at just how many arrangements a typical game task permits. In every LSAT course I teach, I ask my students a math question. I'll ask you the same thing. (Now, there's no math on the LSAT and this certainly isn't something you'll need to do on test day, but indulge me for a moment.) Imagine a straightforward Sequencing game; let's say seven students are to be assigned to seven different desks, with one student per desk. How many possible acceptable arrangements does that task permit? It's not unusual for students to answer, "Umm . . . 49?" Some guess a little higher. Some have no idea at all. The correct answer is that there are 7-factorial possible arrangements. That's $7 \times 6 \times 5 \times 4 \times 3 \times 2 \times 1$, or 5,040 acceptable arrangements. No wonder logic games are challenging.

But now consider what happens when I add just one rule. Let's call the students A, B, C, D, E, F, and G and number the desks 1 through 7. If I tell you "D always sits in desk 3," the number of possible arrangements falls from 7-factorial to 6-factorial.

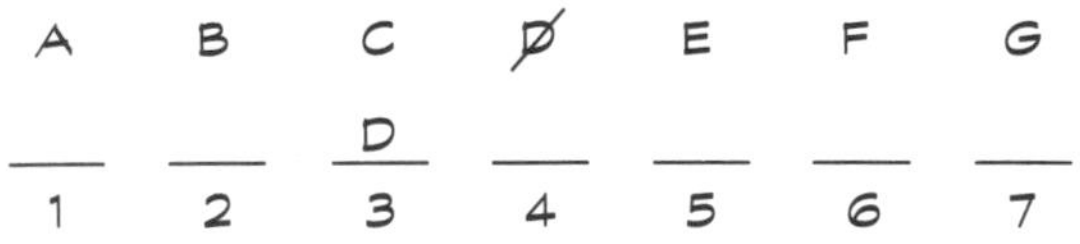

A	B	C	D̸	E	F	G
		D				
1	2	3	4	5	6	7

Figure 2.1

You're down to 720 acceptable arrangements. If I add another rule—"C sits in a lower-numbered desk than B"—then you're down to 330 acceptable permutations.

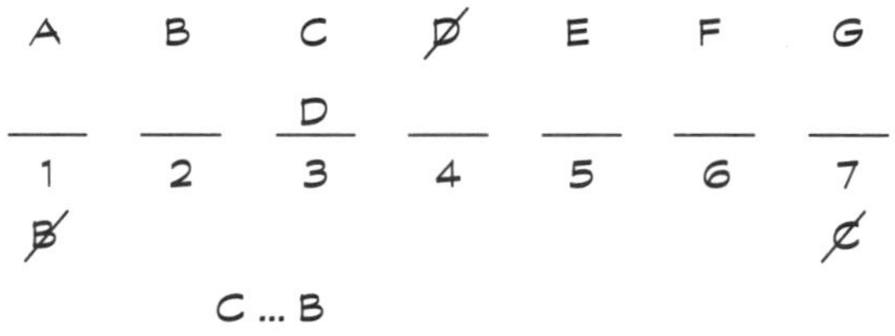

A	B	C	D̸	E	F	G
		D				
1	2	3	4	5	6	7
B̸						C̸

C … B

Figure 2.2

That rule restricts two entities, but it's nowhere near as concrete as the first rule, which established D's position exactly. Keeping D in seat 3, but making the second rule stronger by telling you that "C sits in a desk numbered exactly one number lower than the desk B sits in" reduces the number of acceptable arrangements to just 56.

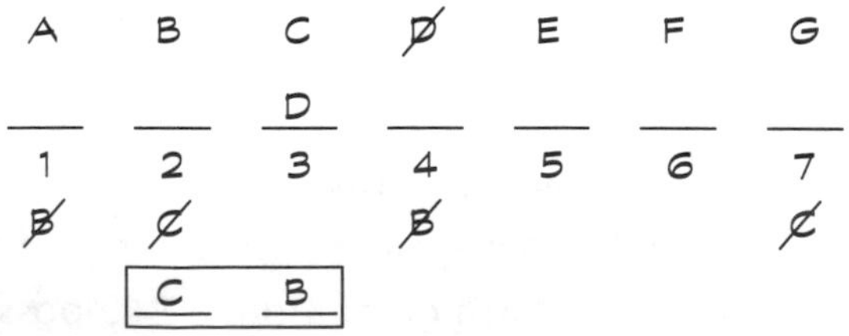

A	B	C	D̸	E	F	G
		D				
1	2	3	4	5	6	7
B̸	C̸		B̸			C̸

C	B

Figure 2.3

Given that most logic games on the LSAT have between three and six rules, it's no surprise that they typically wind up with fewer than a couple dozen acceptable arrangements, sometimes far fewer. I'll bring you back to this example and show you how the rules have the same helpful impact on some released games later in this chapter, but first I want to show you how you can sometimes turn the rules directly into LSAT points.

RULES TURN (DIRECTLY) INTO POINTS

It's rare that a legal case (at least one that goes to trial) turns on just one rule. On the LSAT, though, it does happen that a single rule can get you a right answer. Learning to *think with rules*, to see what they forbid and what they allow, is a first, small step in your legal education, but a giant leap on the test. Recall the game from PrepTest 52 with the students and their chaperones going on a field trip to the natural history museum.

On a field trip to the Museum of Natural History, each of six children—Juana, Kyle, Lucita, Salim, Thanh, and Veronica—is accompanied by one of three adults—Ms. Margoles, Mr. O'Connell, and Ms. Podorski. Each adult accompanies exactly two of the children, consistent with the following conditions:

> If Ms. Margoles accompanies Juana, then Ms. Podorski accompanies Lucita.
> If Kyle is not accompanied by Ms. Margoles, then Veronica is accompanied by Mr. O'Connell.
> Either Ms. Margoles or Mr. O'Connell accompanies Thanh.
> Juana is not accompanied by the same adult as Kyle; nor is Lucita accompanied by the same adult as Salim; nor is Thanh accompanied by the same adult as Veronica.[1]

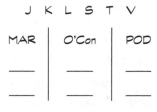

Figure 2.4

Now, take a look at two of the five questions that accompanied that game. Take less than one minute to consider each and try to zero in on the rule(s) that would allow you to answer it.

11. Ms. Podorski CANNOT accompany which one of the following pairs of children?

   (A) Juana and Lucita
   (B) Juana and Salim
   (C) Kyle and Salim
   (D) Salim and Thanh
   (E) Salim and Veronica[2]

12. Mr. O'Connell CANNOT accompany which one of the following pairs of children?

   (A) Juana and Lucita
   (B) Juana and Veronica
   (C) Kyle and Thanh
   (D) Lucita and Thanh
   (E) Salim and Veronica[3]

How did you do? Did you see that the questions could be answered with reference to just one rule each?

---

[1] PrepTest 52, Sec. 2, Game 2
[2] PrepTest 52, Sec. 2, Q 11
[3] PrepTest 52, Sec. 2, Q 12

The correct answer to question 11 came from Rule 3. Since T has to go with either Ms. Margoles or Mr. O'Connell, Ms. Podorski cannot accompany T regardless of who the other student is. That makes choice (D) correct.

Question 12 needed only Rule 2, which makes clear that when K is not with Ms. Margoles, V must be with Mr. O'Connell. Thus, choice (C) is a pair that cannot go together with Mr. O'Connell. It takes K away from Ms. Margoles without placing V with Mr. O'Connell.

More often, of course, the test rewards you for synthesizing multiple rules. That's why the Deductions step in the Kaplan Method for Logic Games is so important. You'll see its full payoff in chapter 4. Still, it's worth noting that even without a fully rendered sketch or the comprehensive deductions you'll soon learn to make, you need not be daunted by the prospect of combining rules to get a correct answer.

In fact, the most common way to get points using nothing but the rules comes from Acceptability questions. You can always get these points in a matter of seconds using nothing but the rules. The next section will show you how.

ACCEPTABILITY QUESTIONS
Each Wrong Answer Breaks a Rule

Most LSAT Logic Games sections feature three or four Acceptability questions; most often, there's one per game (though, of course, there are exceptions). When they include Acceptability questions, the test makers usually make them the first question after the game's setup and rules. Here are a couple of representative question stems. You may recognize the games from which these questions were pulled; you saw them in chapter 1.

> Which one of the following could be an accurate list of the animals pictured on the guideposts, listed in order from guidepost 1 to guidepost 6?[4]
> Which one of the following could be the order of deliveries from first to last?[5]

Occasionally, the test makers will even use the phrase "acceptable arrangement."

Regardless of how they word the question stem, the correct answer to an Acceptability question is simply the one that violates no rules. Each and every one of the four wrong answers breaks one or more of the rules in the game. This simple fact allows you to answer Acceptability questions accurately in a matter of seconds.

Consider again the Museum Field Trip game. Take a look at the setup, rules, and first question—the Acceptability question—from that game.

---

[4] PrepTest 46, Sec. 4, Q 1

[5] PrepTest 51, Sec. 4, Q 16

On a field trip to the Museum of Natural History, each of six children—Juana, Kyle, Lucita, Salim, Thanh, and Veronica— is accompanied by one of three adults—Ms. Margoles, Mr. O'Connell, and Ms. Podorski. Each adult accompanies exactly two of the children, consistent with the following conditions:

If Ms. Margoles accompanies Juana, then Ms. Podorski accompanies Lucita.

If Kyle is not accompanied by Ms. Margoles, then Veronica is accompanied by Mr. O'Connell.

Either Ms. Margoles or Mr. O'Connell accompanies Thanh.

Juana is not accompanied by the same adult as Kyle; nor is Lucita accompanied by the same adult as Salim; nor is Thanh accompanied by the same adult as Veronica.[6]

8. Which one of the following could be an accurate matching of the adults to the children they accompany?

(A)   Ms. Margoles: Juana, Thanh; Mr. O'Connell: Lucita, Veronica; Ms. Podorski: Kyle, Salim

(B)   Ms. Margoles: Kyle, Thanh; Mr. O'Connell: Juana, Salim; Ms. Podorski: Lucita, Veronica

(C)   Ms. Margoles: Lucita, Thanh; Mr. O'Connell: Juana, Salim; Ms. Podorski: Kyle, Veronica

(D)   Ms. Margoles: Kyle, Veronica; Mr. O'Connell: Juana, Thanh; Ms. Podorski: Lucita, Salim

(E)   Ms. Margoles: Salim, Veronica; Mr. O'Connell: Kyle, Lucita; Ms. Podorski: Juana, Thanh[7]

The mistake that most test takers make is searching through the answer choices to find one that works. That can take an inordinate amount of time because you have no idea which (if any) rule a given answer choice violates. I suggest a far more efficient approach. Simply take the rules, one at a time, and eliminate any answer choice that breaks the rule. Do that along with me here.

Look for one or more answers that break Rule 1. That is, find every answer in which J is with Ms. Margoles, but L isn't with Ms. Podorski.

That eliminates choice (A). Strike it through and look for a choice that violates Rule 2.

---

[6] PrepTest 52, Sec. 2, Game 2

[7] PrepTest 52, Sec. 2, Q 8

8. Which one of the following could be an accurate matching of the adults to the children they accompany?

(A) ~~Ms. Margoles: Juana, Thanh; Mr. O'Connell: Lucita, Veronica; Ms. Podorski: Kyle, Salim~~
(B) Ms. Margoles: Kyle, Thanh; Mr. O'Connell: Juana, Salim; Ms. Podorski: Lucita, Veronica
(C) Ms. Margoles: Lucita, Thanh; Mr. O'Connell: Juana, Salim; Ms. Podorski: Kyle, Veronica
(D) Ms. Margoles: Kyle, Veronica; Mr. O'Connell: Juana, Thanh; Ms. Podorski: Lucita, Salim
(E) Ms. Margoles: Salim, Veronica; Mr. O'Connell: Kyle, Lucita; Ms. Podorski: Juana, Thanh[8]

To violate Rule 2, an answer must place K with either Mr. O'Connell or Ms. Podorski (in other words, "not accompanied by Ms. Margoles") *and* place V with an adult other than Mr. O'Connell (in other words, with Ms. Margoles or Ms. Podorski). Do you see any such answers?

Choice (C) has both K and V with Ms. Podorski, and choice (E) has K with Mr. O'Connell and V with Ms. Margoles. Get rid of both.

8. Which one of the following could be an accurate matching of the adults to the children they accompany?

(A) ~~Ms. Margoles: Juana, Thanh; Mr. O'Connell: Lucita, Veronica; Ms. Podorski: Kyle, Salim~~
(B) Ms. Margoles: Kyle, Thanh; Mr. O'Connell: Juana, Salim; Ms. Podorski: Lucita, Veronica
(C) ~~Ms. Margoles: Lucita, Thanh; Mr. O'Connell: Juana, Salim; Ms. Podorski: Kyle, Veronica~~
(D) Ms. Margoles: Kyle, Veronica; Mr. O'Connell: Juana, Thanh; Ms. Podorski: Lucita, Salim
(E) ~~Ms. Margoles: Salim, Veronica; Mr. O'Connell: Kyle, Lucita; Ms. Podorski: Juana, Thanh~~[9]

Rule 3 is easy to look for. It's unacceptable to find T with Ms. Podorski. Do any of the remaining choices have that problem?

No. Neither choice (B) nor choice (D) has T with Ms. Podorski. Move on to the fourth rule. You know exactly what to do. Either choice (B) or choice (D) must include one of the forbidden pairs listed in Rule 4: J and K, L and S, or T and V. Find the violator.

It's choice (D), which has L and S both accompanied by Ms. Podorski. So choice (B) is the correct answer.

8. Which one of the following could be an accurate matching of the adults to the children they accompany?

(A) ~~Ms. Margoles: Juana, Thanh; Mr. O'Connell:~~
~~Lucita, Veronica; Ms. Podorski: Kyle, Salim~~

(B) Ms. Margoles: Kyle, Thanh; Mr. O'Connell:
Juana, Salim; Ms. Podorski: Lucita, Veronica

(C) ~~Ms. Margoles: Lucita, Thanh; Mr. O'Connell:~~
~~Juana, Salim; Ms. Podorski: Kyle, Veronica~~

(D) ~~Ms. Margoles: Kyle, Veronica; Mr. O'Connell:~~
~~Juana, Thanh; Ms. Podorski: Lucita, Salim~~

(E) ~~Ms. Margoles: Salim, Veronica; Mr. O'Connell:~~
~~Kyle, Lucita; Ms. Podorski: Juana, Thanh~~[10]

That's it. Once you're comfortable with this approach, you'll never need more than 15 to 30 seconds to answer an Acceptability question.

Before I have you look at another example, let me be explicit about a couple of things you saw in the previous question. First, once you found that an answer violated one of the rules, I had you cross it out completely. That's a practice you should adopt because it prevents you from wasting time figuring out whether the answer violated any other rules. Once you determine that an answer is wrong, don't look at it again. Second, this question happened to have two answer choices that violated one rule. That won't always happen. In fact, it's more common to find that a single rule is violated by only one wrong answer. Check for any and all violators of the rule you're evaluating, but don't expect to find multiple wrong answers from a given rule.

Try another example. Here are the setup and rules from the Water Treatment Plant game you saw in chapter 1. This time, it's accompanied by its Acceptability question. (As usual, the Acceptability question was the first one in the question set.)

Workers at a water treatment plant open eight valves—G, H, I, K, L, N, O, and P—to flush out a system of pipes that needs emergency repairs. To maximize safety and efficiency, each valve is opened exactly once, and no two valves are opened at the same time. The valves are opened in accordance with the following conditions:

Both K and P are opened before H.
O is opened before L but after H.
L is opened after G.
N is opened before H.
I is opened after K.[11]

---

[10] PrepTest 52, Sec. 2, Q 8

[11] PrepTest 52, Sec. 2, Game 1

1. Which one of the following could be the order, from first
    to last, in which the valves are opened?

    (A)   P, I, K, G, N, H, O, L
    (B)   P, G, K, N, L, H, O, I
    (C)   G, K, I, P, H, O, N, L
    (D)   N, K, P, H, O, I, L, G
    (E)   K, I, N, G, P, H, O, L[12]

Use the same approach. The challenge in this Loose Sequencing example will be to keep straight whether you're looking for a given letter before or after another. If L is required to be after G, an answer that has L before G will be the violator.

Assess Rule 1. The violator will be a choice in which either K or P comes after H in the list.

It turns out that none of the answer choices violates this rule. Don't despair. The same approach will work. The test makers just didn't happen to use this rule to distinguish a wrong answer.

Approach Rule 2 carefully. It has O before L but after H. In other words, it requires this sequence: H-O-L. If an answer violates any aspect of the order, eliminate it.

That rule gets rid of choice (B), where L precedes both H and O.

Which one of the following could be the order, from
first to last, in which the valves are opened?

    (A)   P, I, K, G, N, H, O, L
    (B)   ~~P, G, K, N, L, H, O, I~~
    (C)   G, K, I, P, H, O, N, L
    (D)   N, K, P, H, O, I, L, G
    (E)   K, I, N, G, P, H, O, L[13]

On to Rule 3: L must come after G. Look for an answer or answers in which L comes before G.

Choice (D) should jump out, not least because G is in last place and you know from Rule 3 that L must come after it in an acceptable sequence.

1. Which one of the following could be the order, from first
    to last, in which the valves are opened?

    (A)   P, I, K, G, N, H, O, L
    (B)   ~~P, G, K, N, L, H, O, I~~
    (C)   G, K, I, P, H, O, N, L
    (D)   ~~N, K, P, H, O, I, L, G~~
    (E)   K, I, N, G, P, H, O, L[14]

---

[12] PrepTest 52, Sec. 2, Q 1

[13] PrepTest 52, Sec. 2, Q 1

[14] PrepTest 52, Sec. 2, Q 1

You've got two answers left to eliminate and two rules left to check. You can see just what's going to happen. Check Rule 4 next. Any answer choice that places N after H violates this one.

That gets rid of choice (C).

> Which one of the following could be the order, from first
> to last, in which the valves are opened?
>
> (A)   P, I, K, G, N, H, O, L
> (B)   ~~P, G, K, N, L, H, O, I~~
> (C)   ~~G, K, I, P, H, O, N, L~~
> (D)   ~~N, K, P, H, O, I, L, G~~
> (E)   K, I, N, G, P, H, O, L[15]

And so, either choice (A) or choice (E) is going to place I before K, breaking Rule 5.

Choice (A) incorrectly orders I and K. Eliminate it. Choice (E) is the correct answer.

> Which one of the following could be the order, from first
> to last, in which the valves are opened?
>
> (A)   ~~P, I, K, G, N, H, O, L~~
> (B)   ~~P, G, K, N, L, H, O, I~~
> (C)   ~~G, K, I, P, H, O, N, L~~
> (D)   ~~N, K, P, H, O, I, L, G~~
> (E)   K, I, N, G, P, H, O, L[16]

Now try your hand at a few more Acceptability questions on your own.

---

[15] PrepTest 52, Sec. 2, Q 1
[16] PrepTest 52, Sec. 2, Q 1

DRILL: ANSWERING ACCEPTABILITY QUESTIONS

Each game setup is followed by that game's Acceptability question. Take about a minute to acquaint (or reacquaint) yourself with the game. Then use the Kaplan Method to answer each Acceptability question in no more than 30 seconds by systematically assessing each rule and eliminating any answer choices that violate it. The correct answers and explanations follow the Drill.

1.
In the course of one month Garibaldi has exactly seven different meetings. Each of her meetings is with exactly one of five foreign dignitaries: Fuentes, Matsuba, Rhee, Soleimani, or Tbahi. The following constraints govern Garibaldi's meetings:

   She has exactly three meetings with Fuentes, and exactly one with each of the other dignitaries.
   She does not have any meetings in a row with Fuentes.
   Her meeting with Soleimani is the very next one after her meeting with Tbahi.
   Neither the first nor last of her meetings is with Matsuba.

Which one of the following could be the sequence of the meetings Garibaldi has with the dignitaries?
   (A)   Fuentes, Rhee, Tbahi, Soleimani, Fuentes, Matsuba, Rhee
   (B)   Fuentes, Tbahi, Soleimani, Matsuba, Fuentes, Fuentes, Rhee
   (C)   Fuentes, Rhee, Fuentes, Matsuba, Fuentes, Tbahi, Soleimani
   (D)   Fuentes, Tbahi, Matsuba, Fuentes, Soleimani, Rhee, Fuentes
   (E)   Fuentes, Tbahi, Soleimani, Fuentes, Rhee, Fuentes, Matsuba[17]

2.
Three short seminars—Goals, Objections, and Persuasion—and three long seminars—Humor, Negotiating, and Telemarketing—will be scheduled for a three-day sales training conference. On each day, two of the seminars will be given consecutively. Each seminar will be given exactly once. The schedule must conform to the following conditions:

   Exactly one short seminar and exactly one long seminar will be given each day.
   Telemarketing will not be given until both Goals and Objections have been given.
   Negotiating will not be given until Persuasion has been given.

Which one of the following could be an accurate schedule for the sales training conference?
   (A)   first day: Persuasion followed by Negotiating
         second day: Objections followed by Telemarketing
         third day: Goals followed by Humor
   (B)   first day: Objections followed by Humor
         second day: Goals followed by Telemarketing
         third day: Persuasion followed by Negotiating
   (C)   first day: Objections followed by Negotiating
         second day: Persuasion followed by Humor
         third day: Goals followed by Telemarketing
   (D)   first day: Objections followed by Goals
         second day: Telemarketing followed by Persuasion
         third day: Negotiating followed by Humor
   (E)   first day: Goals followed by Humor
         second day: Persuasion followed by Telemarketing
         third day: Objections followed by Negotiating[18]

---

[17] PrepTest 44, Sec. 3, Game 1, Q 1   [18] PrepTest 52, Sec. 2, Game 3, Q 13

3.

A summer program offers at least one of the following seven courses: geography, history, literature, mathematics, psychology, sociology, zoology. The following restrictions on the programs must apply:

> If mathematics is offered, then either literature or sociology (but not both) is offered.
>
> If literature is offered, then geography is also offered but psychology is not.
>
> If sociology is offered, then psychology is also offered but zoology is not.
>
> If geography is offered, then both history and zoology are also offered.

Which one of the following could be a complete and accurate list of the courses offered by the summer program?

- (A) history, psychology
- (B) geography, history, literature
- (C) history, mathematics, psychology
- (D) literature, mathematics, psychology
- (E) history, literature, mathematics, sociology[19]

---

[19] PrepTest 49, Sec. 1, Game 3, Q 13

Explanations

1. (C)

In the course of one month, Garibaldi has exactly seven different meetings. Each of her meetings is with exactly one of five foreign dignitaries: Fuentes, Matsuba, Rhee, Soleimani, or Tbahi. The following constraints govern Garibaldi's meetings:

> She has exactly three meetings with Fuentes and exactly one with each of the other dignitaries.
> She does not have any meetings in a row with Fuentes.
> Her meeting with Soleimani is the very next one after her meeting with Tbahi.
> Neither the first nor last of her meetings is with Matsuba.

Which one of the following could be the sequence of the meetings Garibaldi has with the dignitaries?

    (A) ~~Fuentes, Rhee, Tbahi, Soleimani, Fuentes, Matsuba, Rhee~~   Rule 1

    (B) ~~Fuentes, Tbahi, Soleimani, Matsuba, Fuentes, Fuentes, Rhee~~   Rule 2

    (C) Fuentes, Rhee, Fuentes, Matsuba, Fuentes, Tbahi, Soleimani

    (D) ~~Fuentes, Tbahi, Matsuba, Fuentes, Soleimani, Rhee, Fuentes~~   Rule 3

    (E) ~~Fuentes, Tbahi, Soleimani, Fuentes, Rhee, Fuentes, Matsuba~~[20]   Rule 4

You're familiar with this Sequencing game from the first chapter. Here, each of the rules eliminated one wrong answer. Rule 1 requires three meetings with F. That eliminates choice (A), in which she has only two. Rule 2 forbids consecutive meetings with F. That gets rid of choice (B). Rule 3 places the meeting with S immediately after the one with T. Choice (D) violates this rule. Finally, Rule 4 proscribes the M meeting from being first or last. The M meeting is last in choice (E), making that answer incorrect. You're left with choice (C), the correct response.

2. (B)

Three short seminars—Goals, Objections, and Persuasion— and three long seminars—Humor, Negotiating, and Telemarketing—will be scheduled for a three-day sales training conference. On each day, two of the seminars will be given consecutively. Each seminar will be given exactly once. The schedule must conform to the following conditions:

> Exactly one short seminar and exactly one long seminar will be given each day.
> Telemarketing will not be given until both Goals and Objections have been given.
> Negotiating will not be given until Persuasion has been given.

---

[20] PrepTest 44, Sec. 3, Game 1, Q 1

Which one of the following could be an accurate
schedule for the sales training conference?

(A) ~~first day: Persuasion followed by Negotiating~~
 ~~second day: Objections followed by~~
  ~~Telemarketing~~ Rule 2
 ~~third day: Goals followed by Humor~~

(B) first day: Objections followed by Humor
 second day: Goals followed by Telemarketing
 third day: Persuasion followed by Negotiating

(C) ~~first day: Objections followed by Negotiating~~
 ~~second day: Persuasion followed by Humor~~ Rule 3
 ~~third day: Goals followed by Telemarketing~~

(D) ~~first day: Objections followed by Goals~~
 ~~second day: Telemarketing followed by~~
  ~~Persuasion~~ Rule 1
 ~~third day: Negotiating followed by Humor~~

(E) ~~first day: Goals followed by Humor~~
 ~~second day: Persuasion followed by~~
  ~~Telemarketing~~ Rule 2
 ~~third day: Objections followed by Negotiating~~[21]

In this Sequencing-Matching Hybrid game, you're tasked with deciding the order and the pairing of six seminars over three days. The answer choices in the Acceptability question actually give you a great idea of the sketch you'll use for the complete game. You may have noticed that this game is quite similar to the one from PrepTest 53 that asked you to pair the debaters and rank their schools' teams. The biggest difference is that, in this game, the order of presentation within each pairing also matters.

Here, you were given only three rules, so you know that at least one of them eliminates two or more answer choices. Rule 1 restricts each day to a pair with one long (H, N, or T) and one short (g, o, or p) seminar. (Remember to make a visual distinction, such as upper- and lowercase letters, between different categories of entities.) Any answer that includes a day with two long or two short seminars would be a violator. Answer choice (D) breaks this rule on both the first day and the third day. Rule 2 requires T to come after both g and o. Choice (A) has T on the second day and g on the third. Choice (E) has T on the second day and o on the third. Eliminate choices (A) and (E). So one of the two remaining choices must violate the third rule. Rule 3 dictates that N come after p. The rule-breaker is choice (C), where N is on the first day and p is on the second. That leaves correct answer choice (B) as the only acceptable arrangement.

---

[21] PrepTest 52, Sec. 2, Game 3, Q 13

3. (A)

A summer program offers at least one of the following seven courses: geography, history, literature, mathematics, psychology, sociology, zoology. The following restrictions on the programs must apply:

> If mathematics is offered, then either literature or sociology (but not both) is offered.
>
> If literature is offered, then geography is also offered but psychology is not.
>
> If sociology is offered, then psychology is also offered but zoology is not.
>
> If geography is offered, then both history and zoology are also offered.

Which one of the following could be a complete and accurate list of the courses offered by the summer program?

> (A)   history, psychology
> (B)   ~~geography, history, literature~~   Rule 4
> (C)   ~~history, mathematics, psychology~~   Rule 1
> (D)   ~~literature, mathematics, psychology~~   Rule 2
> (E)   ~~history, literature, mathematics, sociology~~[22]   Rule 1

Here's a game in which the rules are all conditional ("if/then") formal logic, but that shouldn't affect your approach to the Acceptability question. You can still eliminate violators one by one. The first rule is the most complicated. It states that anytime M is offered, you have to have just one of L or S. So an answer with M and neither L nor S, or one with M and both L and S, will be a violator. Choice (C) makes the first mistake, having M but neither L nor S. Choice (E) violates the second provision, having M with both L and S. Eliminate both choices. To test Rule 2, look for L in the remaining choices. If an answer has L but doesn't have G *or* has L and has P, it violates Rule 2. Choice (D) makes both mistakes. Neither of the remaining choices—(A) and (B)—has S, so there's no way either could violate Rule 3. Move on to Rule 4, which requires that both H and Z accompany G. Choice (B) is the rule-breaker this time. It has G and H but lacks Z. Only choice (A) remains, and you've got another LSAT point.

---

[22] PrepTest 49, Sec. 1, Game 3, Q 13

THE POWER OF RULES AND LIMITATIONS

Now, think back to the discussion of the power of rules—of how they allow you to take control of games—that opened this chapter. In this section, you'll see how being able to think with rules and to assess the restrictions they place on games allows you to identify easier games and to get all of their points.

You can take control of logic games. In fact, the test makers provide you with exactly what you need to do so. You don't need an in-depth mathematical analysis of the games on your test to see a couple of important takeaways here: First, games with fewer possible arrangements are easier; second, games with more concrete restrictions are the ones with fewer possible arrangements. With a little practice, you can get a feel for spotting easier games. The easiest of all have only a few entities, a strict task, and concrete restrictions. In fact, concreteness and simplicity are more important factors in assessing a game's difficulty than is the game type.

Not All Rules Are Created Equal

On LSAT logic games, all rules are helpful, but some are more helpful than others. The most helpful, of course, are those that contribute the greatest restriction. It takes practice to spot, at a glance, the strongest rules, but three guidelines will go a long way toward making you better at this.

THE STRONGEST RULES . . .

1. **Create Established Entities**
   Established Entities wind up affecting all others because they take up one slot, match, or position, keeping others out.

2. **Control More Than One Entity**
   A rule restricting three entities is generally stronger than a rule restricting two; a rule restricting two entities is generally stronger than a rule restricting just one.

3. **Contain Concrete Language**
   Look for words such as "exactly," "cannot," or "must"; relative or conditional rules provide less certainty.

To see these guidelines in action, recall our hypothetical game with the seven students—A, B, C, D, E, F, and G—and seven desks, numbered 1 through 7. Allow for the typical one-student-per-desk limitation to apply (as it likely would in any similar game on the test). As I noted earlier, this setup allows for 5,040 acceptable arrangements. There isn't space to show all of those possibilities here, but seeing how to get that number will be helpful in understanding the impact of the possible rules. Take desk 1. There are seven possibilities for who could sit there.

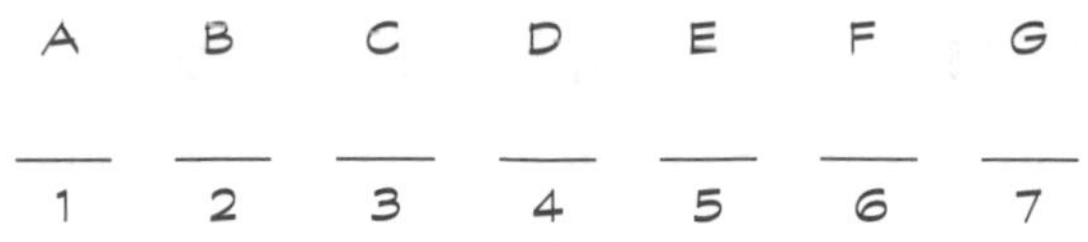

```
A     B     C     D     E     F     G
___   ___   ___   ___   ___   ___   ___
 1     2     3     4     5     6     7
```

Figure 2.7

Once you determine who is in that desk, there are six possibilities left for desk 2.

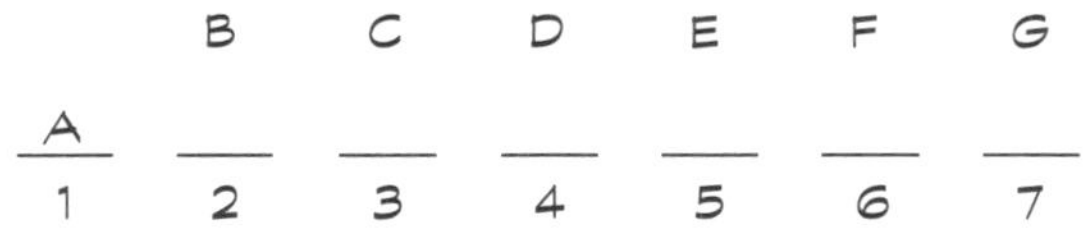

```
      B     C     D     E     F     G
 A    ___   ___   ___   ___   ___   ___
___
 1     2     3     4     5     6     7
```

Figure 2.8

Determining who is in desk 2 leaves five potential occupants for desk 3. And so on.

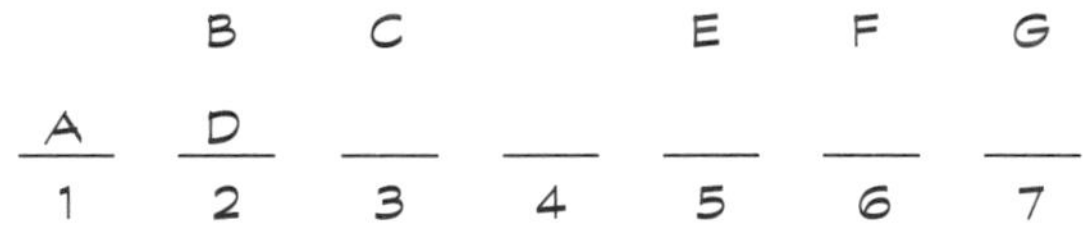

```
      B     C           E     F     G
 A    D     ___   ___   ___   ___   ___
___  ___
 1     2     3     4     5     6     7
```

Figure 2.9

Remember, you have all of those possible permutations when A is in desk 1, when B is in desk 1, when C is in desk 1, and on and on. But the good news is that every time you determine or restrict a possible placement, you dramatically reduce the overall number of possible assignments.

Consider the following rules as they apply to the students and desks. Using the "strong rule" guidelines, see which ones provide more restriction (and, thus, most help you to solve the game). Don't worry about combining the rules at this point; that's for the chapter on deductions. (All of the following rules are identical in meaning to rules that have appeared on actual released LSATs, just not all at the same time.)

Seven students—A, B, C, D, E, F, and G—are assigned to seven desks, numbered 1 through 7. Each student occupies exactly one desk. The following restrictions apply:

D occupies desk 4.

G sits in a lower-numbered desk than the desk C sits in.

At least one desk separates the desks in which E and F sit.

B sits in a desk numbered exactly one higher than the desk C sits in.

G sits in either desk 1 or desk 7.

There are exactly two desks between the desks in which A and B sit.

A's desk is numbered lower than E's desk but higher than C's.

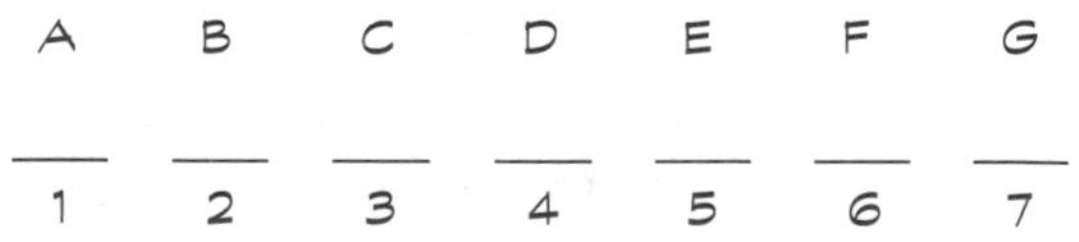

```
A     B     C     D     E     F     G
___   ___   ___   ___   ___   ___   ___
 1     2     3     4     5     6     7
```

Figure 2.10

As I have you review each of the rules, I'll go over your considerations for how to depict the rule visually. Making rules concrete—being able to literally *see* them in action—is vital to your ability to use them when answering questions. Pay attention to the suggested sketches and depictions of the rules throughout Part I of this book. When drawing rules, follow this plan:

TO ADD RULES TO A SKETCH

1 Consider what the rule does (and does not) tell you.

2 Whenever possible, draw the rule directly into the framework.

3 Failing that, add the rule beneath or beside your framework using the same visual vocabulary.

By "visual vocabulary," I mean: Make the rule look just like the framework you've used in the sketch. For example, if your sequencing spaces are dashes on which you picture the entities sitting, use dashes with the entities sitting on them in your depiction of the rules as well. Have the dashes and letters you use for the entities be the same size as those in your framework. That way, you can mentally picture where the entities in the rule will and won't fit within the framework. Keeping everything visually consistent will help you enormously when it comes to using the rules to answer the questions.

Here are the rules in action:

D occupies desk 4.

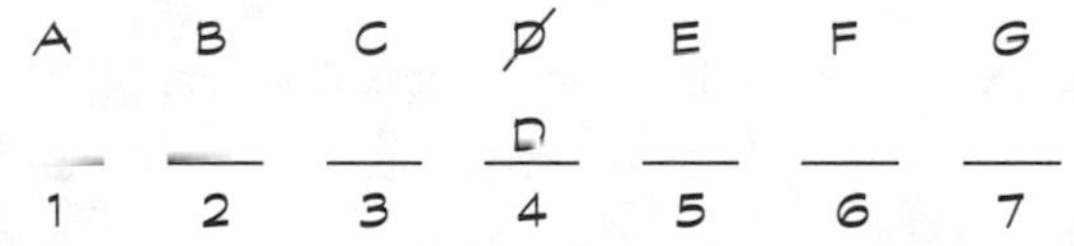

Figure 2.11

This rule is quite powerful. It makes D an Established Entity and, as such, you can draw the rule directly into the framework of your sketch. D will never take another position, and no other student will ever occupy desk 4. By itself, this rule reduces the number of possible arrangements from 5,040 to just 720. D is locked in place, while the other six entities can move wherever they like (besides desk 4, of course).

G sits in a lower-numbered desk than the desk C sits in.

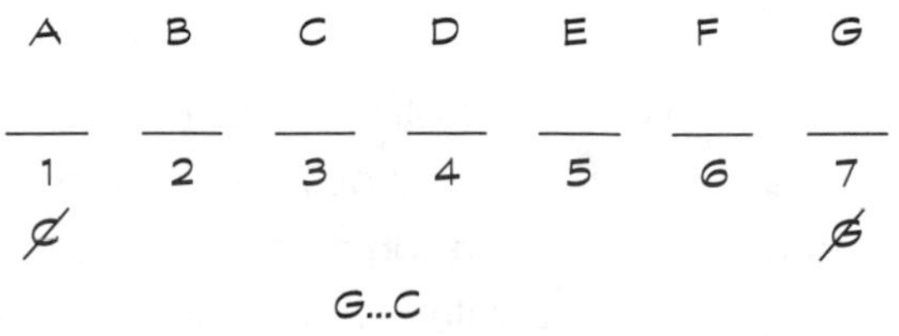

Figure 2.12

This rule affects two entities, but it gives only their relative positions. Thus, the sample scratch work uses an ellipsis to indicate that the order of the entities is known, but the number of spaces between them isn't. You can, however, enter two concrete, negative pieces of information into your sketch. C can never sit in desk 1 and G can never sit in desk 7. This rule by itself reduces the number of acceptable arrangements from 5,040 to 2,520. It leaves 21 acceptable arrangements for G and C (six when G is in desk 1, five when G is in desk 2, 4 when G is in desk 3, etc.), while the other five entities move wherever they like.

At least one desk separates the desks in which E and F sit.

Figure 2.13

Be very careful with a rule like this one. It tells you something about the relative distance between E and F, but nothing about their order. Notice that there is a blank slot *and* an ellipsis between the two occupied positions in the drawing of the rule. The entities could be farther apart, but no closer, since the rule states that "[a]t least one desk" separates them. This rule by itself is less powerful than the previous one, allowing for 3,600 acceptable arrangements. The reason that it's less restrictive is that either E or F could be the entity taking the lower-numbered seat.

B sits in a desk numbered exactly one higher than the desk C sits in.

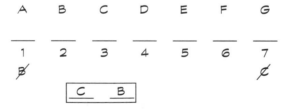

Figure 2.14

While it's impossible to place this block exactly within the framework, the certainty of the relationship between B and C makes this a very powerful rule. Make sure your drawing indicates that no spaces separate the two entities and that they are consecutive. You can also indicate that B will never appear in the first slot and that C will never appear in the final slot. Since it limits the C-B block to just six possible placements (1 and 2, 2 and 3, 3 and 4, 4 and 5, 5 and 6, or 6 and 7), this rule allows for only 720 possible arrangements. The word "exactly" always indicates strong, helpful restrictions in logic games. Not to get too far ahead, but if you combined the C-B block with the first rule establishing D in desk 4, you'd have only 96 possible arrangements. In the chapter devoted to deductions, you'll learn to always look for the interaction of Established Entities and blocks of entities in Sequencing games.

G sits in either desk 1 or desk 7.

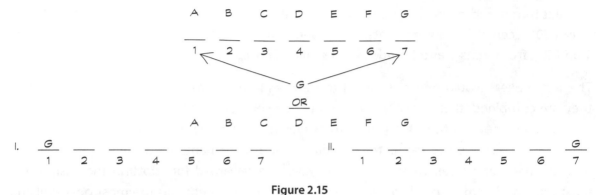

Figure 2.15

While not making G an Established Entity, this rule is still quite strong. You may choose to depict this rule with arrows indicating the two possible positions for G. But if G is duplicated in any other rules or if its placement affects other entities directly, it creates Limited Options (the scenario—like that in the Thunderstorm game—in which only two arrangements are possible), and you should make two separate frameworks, one for each possible position for G. Then you would fill in the other rules as acceptable in each option. The rule by itself limits the game to 1,440 possible arrangements (720 for each possible placement of G).

There are exactly two desks between the desks in which A and B sit.

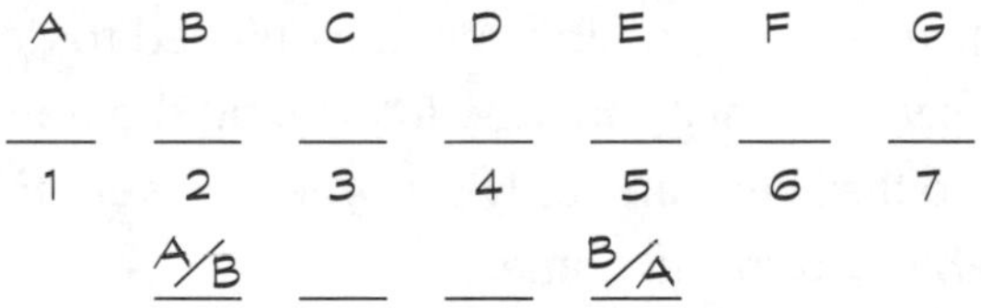

Figure 2.16

Here's another rule that defines the distance between two entities without telling you their order. Make sure to depict the slots separating A and B concretely. There are only eight ways to arrange A and B without violating the rules. You must place one entity each in either seats 1 and 4, 2 and 5, 3 and 6, or 4 and 7, remembering that either one could be placed earlier or later. With the other five entities still able to move around at will, this rule on its own leaves 960 acceptable arrangements.

A's desk is numbered lower than E's desk but higher than C's.

C ... A ... E

Figure 2.17

This rule's strength derives from its restriction of three entities relative to one another. Despite the fact that it doesn't determine the exact number of spaces between the entities, it leaves only 850 acceptable arrangements. Moreover, you can confidently eliminate A from seats 1 and 7, E from seats 1 and 2, and C from seats 6 and 7.

The test makers would never use all of these rules in the same game because, by the time they are combined, there are only two acceptable solutions left for the entire sequence. But as examples, they illustrate the power that rules have to make games manageable. On test day, you'll never need to calculate the number of arrangements that would be acceptable after applying any given rule. You will, however, be rewarded for spotting the easiest and most restricted games and doing them first, as well as for identifying the most powerful and concrete rules and using those as the basis for making deductions and answering questions.

Now, put those skills to work on a couple of real LSAT games.

Rules Determine What You Know and What You Don't: Practice

Here, again, is the setup for the Trail Markers game, which you saw in chapter 1. Start by thinking through the setup and reconstructing the framework of your sketch. This time, I want you to assess the rules, too. Try to add each to your sketch. Remember the strategy for depicting rules: Think clearly about what the rules tell you and what they don't. Add the rules directly into the sketch framework whenever possible. When you need to depict the rule beneath the sketch, use the same visual vocabulary you used in drawing the framework. Make your sketch and rules look consistent so that you can easily see where the entities restricted by the rule(s) will and won't be acceptable within the game.

As you try that here, consider which rules provide the most restriction. Hint: There's one entity that escapes restriction altogether. After you finish your scratch work, review the setup and rules. Then I'll have you try the questions from this game. And, as a word to the wise, don't worry about being fast just yet. Efficiency comes with practice. Right now, just get your feet wet and see how your newfound appreciation for the rules can turn into points.

Exactly six guideposts, numbered 1 through 6, mark a mountain trail. Each guidepost pictures a different one of six animals—fox, grizzly, hare, lynx, moose, or porcupine. The following conditions must apply:

The grizzly is pictured on either guidepost 3 or guidepost 4.

The moose guidepost is numbered lower than the hare guidepost.

The lynx guidepost is numbered lower than the moose guidepost but higher than the fox guidepost.[23]

I'll review the setup and sketch by taking you through the steps in the Kaplan Method.

---

[23] PrepTest 46, Sec. 4, Game 1

STEPS 1 AND 2: **Overview and Sketch**

By now, you're getting used to seeing Sequencing tasks, so whether you remembered the sketch from chapter 1 or not, I imagine you came up with something much like this:

$$F \quad G \quad H \quad L \quad M \quad P$$
$$\underline{} \quad \underline{} \quad \underline{} \quad \underline{} \quad \underline{} \quad \underline{}$$
$$1 \quad 2 \quad 3 \quad 4 \quad 5 \quad 6$$

Figure 2.18

The setup states that "[e]ach guidepost pictures a different one of six animals," so you know that you'll be sequencing the entities one per slot. In case you're interested, this setup—six pictures on six signs, one per sign—allows for 720 possible arrangements (before the rules, that is).

STEP 3: **Rules**

There were just three rules here, but two of them—the first and the third—were very restrictive. Before reviewing the questions, check your sketch and see whether you interpreted each of the rules correctly. Compare your diagrams to those that follow.

The grizzly is pictured on either guidepost 3 or guidepost 4.[24]

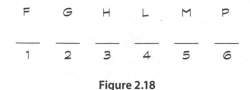

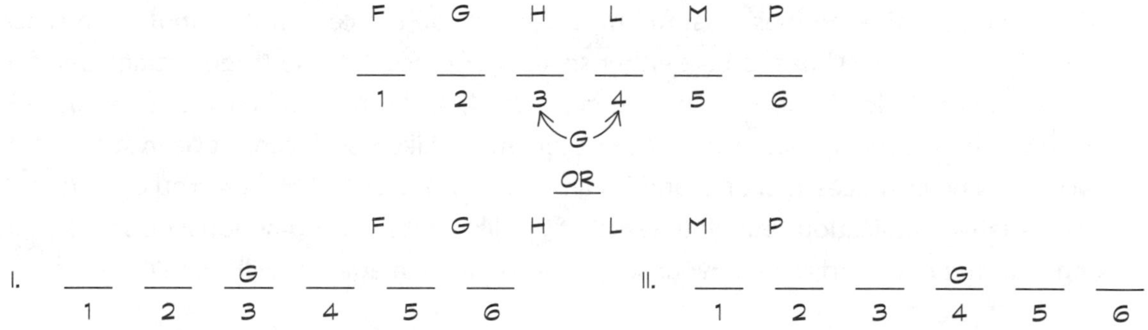

Figure 2.19

Either of these depictions of this rule about G would work. G is not quite an Established Entity, but its wiggle room has been reduced to just one of two spots. This rule reduces the number of acceptable arrangements to just 240. Well over half of your work disappeared with just one rule.

The moose guidepost is numbered lower than the hare guidepost.[25]

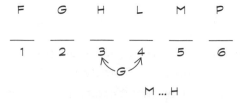

Figure 2.20

24 PrepTest 46, Sec. 4, Game 1
25 PrepTest 46, Sec. 4, Game 1

On its own, this rule is pretty loose. It establishes the order, but not the relative distance of M and H. Note, however, that you can absolutely rule out M in space 6 and H in space 1. Adding this rule to the sketch along with Rule 1 reduces the number of acceptable arrangements to 120.

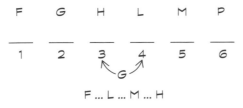

Figure 2.21

This rule, which restricts three entities, really locks things down. Make sure that you depicted it accurately in your scratch work. The best way to approach it is to realize that you already have "M . . . H" diagrammed. So when the first part of Rule 3 says L is on a lower-numbered guidepost than M, you can just supplement the picture you made for Rule 2: "L . . . M . . . H." Then the second half of Rule 3 connects F to this string, restricting it to a space before L's: "F . . . L . . . M . . . H." This scratch work allows you to see that F can never appear in spaces 4, 5, or 6, since three other entities must follow it. But did you notice that it cannot be in space 3, either? That's because G has to take either space 3 or space 4. If the three entities that follow F as a result of Rules 2 and 3 are placed in spaces 4, 5, and 6, G will have to take space 3. (There's a question coming that rewards this observation.) Likewise, L cannot be in spaces 1, 5, or 6; M cannot be in spaces 1, 2, or 6; and H cannot be in spaces 1, 2, 3, or 4. You can draw all of those negative implications into your sketch if you like, but by test day, you'll be so adept at thinking with the rules and reading your scratch work that I imagine it will seem unnecessary.

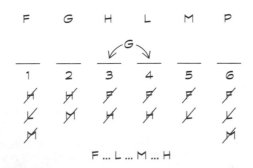

Figure 2.22   Optional sketch with negative implications included

Before moving on, there's just one more thing you should do: Figure out what you *don't* know. Remember my hint? One entity is entirely unrestricted. It's P. Put a little star or asterisk above P in the list of entities to remind yourself that it can be placed anywhere within the sequence. One question rewards you directly for making that observation.

---

[26] PrepTest 46, Sec. 4, Game 1

STEP 4: **Deductions**

There really aren't any deductions to add to this game. Rules 2 and 3 combined via the shared entity M, but you were able to accommodate that as you drew out the two rules. Games like this, with no (or very few) deductions, will pop up from time to time. When they do, rest assured that you have all you need to answer the questions. Here, then, is your completed Master Sketch:

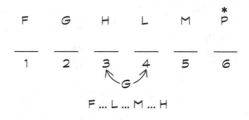

Figure 2.23

STEP 5: **Questions**

Compare your scratch work to what's here. On the next page, you'll see the game laid out in its entirety, questions and all, just as it was in PrepTest 46. Copy your sketch and rules onto that page, then try the questions. You'll find that you can answer some directly from your depiction of the rules. Others may require a new mini-sketch that incorporates the "if" clause from the question stem. Again, don't worry at this point about speed. Just practice implementing what you've learned so far. If you get stuck on a question, don't let it stress you. Just take your best shot and, after you finish, review the explanations for each question to see whether you applied the rules accurately.

Questions 1–6

Exactly six guideposts, numbered 1 through 6, mark a mountain trail. Each guidepost pictures a different one of six animals—fox, grizzly, hare, lynx, moose, or porcupine. The following conditions must apply:

The grizzly is pictured on either guidepost 3 or guidepost 4.

The moose guidepost is numbered lower than the hare guidepost.

The lynx guidepost is numbered lower than the moose guidepost but higher than the fox guidepost.

1. Which one of the following could be an accurate list of the animals pictured on the guideposts, listed in order from guidepost 1 through guidepost 6?

   (A) fox, lynx, grizzly, porcupine, moose, hare
   (B) fox, lynx, moose, hare, grizzly, porcupine
   (C) fox, moose, grizzly, lynx, hare, porcupine
   (D) lynx, fox, moose, grizzly, hare, porcupine
   (E) porcupine, fox, hare, grizzly, lynx, moose

2. Which one of the following animals CANNOT be the one pictured on guidepost 3?

   (A) fox
   (B) grizzly
   (C) lynx
   (D) moose
   (E) porcupine

3. If the moose is pictured on guidepost 3, then which one of the following is the lowest numbered guidepost that could picture the porcupine?

   (A) guidepost 1
   (B) guidepost 2
   (C) guidepost 4
   (D) guidepost 5
   (E) guidepost 6

4. If guidepost 5 does not picture the moose, then which one of the following must be true?

   (A) The lynx is pictured on guidepost 2.
   (B) The moose is pictured on guidepost 3.
   (C) The grizzly is pictured on guidepost 4.
   (D) The porcupine is pictured on guidepost 5.
   (E) The hare is pictured on guidepost 6.

5. Which one of the following animals could be pictured on any one of the six guideposts?

   (A) fox
   (B) hare
   (C) lynx
   (D) moose
   (E) porcupine

6. If the moose guidepost is numbered exactly one higher than the lynx guidepost, then which one of the following could be true?

   (A) Guidepost 5 pictures the hare.
   (B) Guidepost 4 pictures the moose.
   (C) Guidepost 4 pictures the porcupine.
   (D) Guidepost 3 pictures the lynx.
   (E) Guidepost 3 pictures the porcupine.[27]

---

[27] PrepTest 46, Sec. 4, Game 1, Qs 1–6

Answer Explanations follow on the next page.

Explanations

Review your work to see how the rules revealed each of the correct answers unequivocally.

1. (A)

> Which one of the following could be an accurate list
> of the animals pictured on the guideposts, listed in
> order from guidepost 1 through guidepost 6?
>
> (A) fox, lynx, grizzly, porcupine, moose, hare
> (B) fox, lynx, moose, hare, grizzly, porcupine
> (C) fox, moose, grizzly, lynx, hare, porcupine
> (D) lynx, fox, moose, grizzly, hare, porcupine
> (E) porcupine, fox, hare, grizzly, lynx, moose[28]

This is a run-of-the-mill Acceptability question. Did you use the rules to eliminate violators? Here's the best way to handle this question.

Rule 1 said that G must be in either space 3 or space 4. That eliminated answer (B), where G is found in space 5.

> Which one of the following could be an accurate list
> of the animals pictured on the guideposts, listed in
> order from guidepost 1 through guidepost 6?
>
> (A) fox, lynx, grizzly, porcupine, moose, hare
> (B) ~~fox, lynx, moose, hare, grizzly, porcupine~~
> (C) fox, moose, grizzly, lynx, hare, porcupine
> (D) lynx, fox, moose, grizzly, hare, porcupine
> (E) porcupine, fox, hare, grizzly, lynx, moose[29]

Rule 2 had you check to make sure that M always preceded H. Choice (E) broke this rule.

> Which one of the following could be an accurate list
> of the animals pictured on the guideposts, listed in
> order from guidepost 1 through guidepost 6?
>
> (A) fox, lynx, grizzly, porcupine, moose, hare
> (B) ~~fox, lynx, moose, hare, grizzly, porcupine~~
> (C) fox, moose, grizzly, lynx, hare, porcupine
> (D) lynx, fox, moose, grizzly, hare, porcupine
> (E) ~~porcupine, fox, hare, grizzly, lynx, moose~~[30]

Finally, Rule 3 gave you the "F . . . L . . . M" lineup. Choice (C), where the order went F-M-L, and choice (D), where it went L-F-M, both violated this one. Choice (A) is the correct answer.

---

[28] PrepTest 46, Sec. 4, Game 1, Q 1

[29] PrepTest 46, Sec. 4, Game 1, Q 1

[30] PrepTest 46, Sec. 4, Game 1, Q 1

Which one of the following could be an accurate list of the animals pictured on the guideposts, listed in order from guidepost 1 through guidepost 6?

(A)   fox, lynx, grizzly, porcupine, moose, hare
(B)   ~~fox, lynx, moose, hare, grizzly, porcupine~~
(C)   ~~fox, moose, grizzly, lynx, hare, porcupine~~
(D)   ~~lynx, fox, moose, grizzly, hare, porcupine~~
(E)   ~~porcupine, fox, hare, grizzly, lynx, moose~~[31]

2. (A)

Which one of the following animals CANNOT be the one pictured on guidepost 3?

(A)   fox
(B)   grizzly
(C)   lynx
(D)   moose
(E)   porcupine[32]

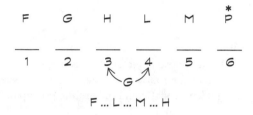

Figure 2.24

This question rewarded you for seeing something that the rules made impossible. I went over why F can never appear in spaces 3, 4, 5, or 6 in the review of the rules. According to Rules 2 and 3, L, M, and H must all follow F. Even if you squeezed those three into spaces 4, 5, and 6, Rule 1 told you that G needed to take one of spaces 3 and 4. So F is never going to get into space 3, making choice (A) the correct answer. As for the wrong answers, there are five acceptable arrangements with G in space 3. Any one of them allows you to eliminate choice (B).

P	F	G	L	M	H
1	2	3	4	5	6

F	P	G	L	M	H
1	2	3	4	5	6

F	L	G	P	M	H
1	2	3	4	5	6

F	L	G	M	P	H
1	2	3	4	5	6

F	L	G	M	H	P
1	2	3	4	5	6

Figure 2.25

For each of the remaining answers, G would take space 4. Here are the acceptable arrangements illustrating how choices (C), (D), and (E) are all possible.

---

[31] PrepTest 46, Sec. 4, Game 1, Q 1
[32] PrepTest 46, Sec. 4, Game 1, Q 2

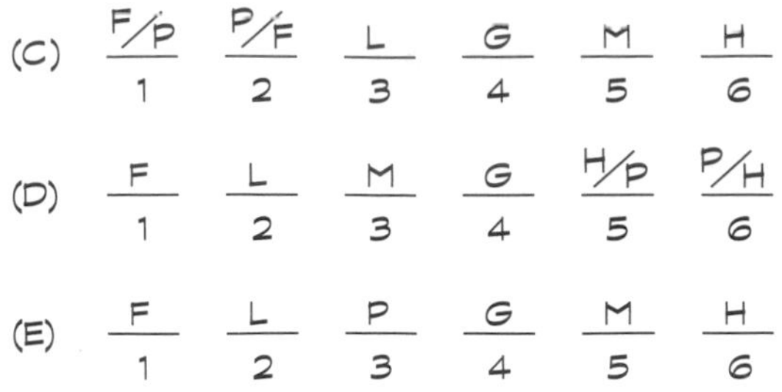

$$\text{(C)} \quad \frac{F/P}{1} \quad \frac{P/F}{2} \quad \frac{L}{3} \quad \frac{G}{4} \quad \frac{M}{5} \quad \frac{H}{6}$$

$$\text{(D)} \quad \frac{F}{1} \quad \frac{L}{2} \quad \frac{M}{3} \quad \frac{G}{4} \quad \frac{H/P}{5} \quad \frac{P/H}{6}$$

$$\text{(E)} \quad \frac{F}{1} \quad \frac{L}{2} \quad \frac{P}{3} \quad \frac{G}{4} \quad \frac{M}{5} \quad \frac{H}{6}$$

Figure 2.26

3. **(D)**

If the moose is pictured on guidepost 3, then which one of the following is the lowest numbered guidepost that could picture the porcupine?

(A) guidepost 1
(B) guidepost 2
(C) guidepost 4
(D) guidepost 5
(E) guidepost 6[33]

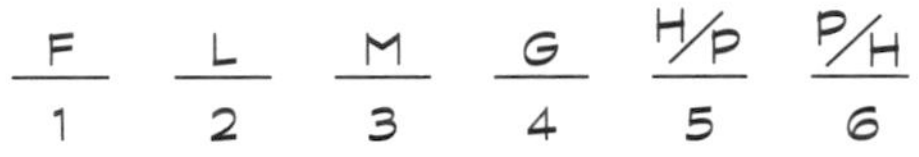

$$\frac{F}{1} \quad \frac{L}{2} \quad \frac{M}{3} \quad \frac{G}{4} \quad \frac{H/P}{5} \quad \frac{P/H}{6}$$

Figure 2.27

This question—with its "if" clause—is one that benefitted from a mini-sketch based on the new restriction in the question stem. It's pictured above. Here's how you should have created it. Start with the "if" clause. Place M in space 3.

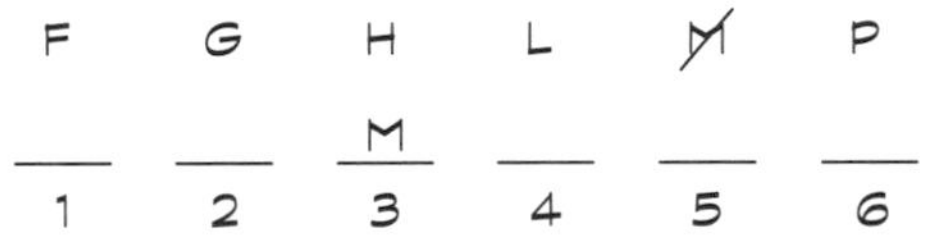

$$\begin{array}{cccccc} F & G & H & L & \cancel{M} & P \\ \underline{} & \underline{} & \underline{M} & \underline{} & \underline{} & \underline{} \\ 1 & 2 & 3 & 4 & 5 & 6 \end{array}$$

Figure 2.27A

With M taking space 3, Rule 1 requires G to take space 4.

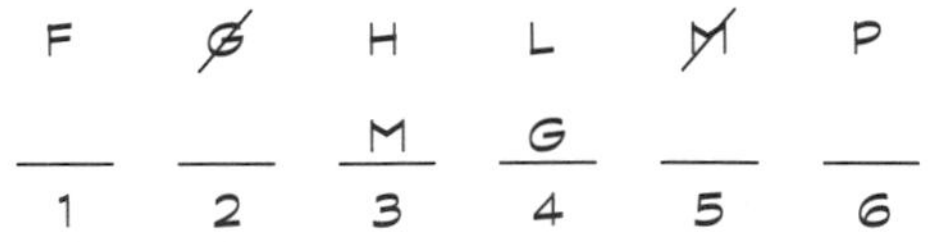

$$\begin{array}{cccccc} F & \cancel{G} & H & L & \cancel{M} & P \\ \underline{} & \underline{} & \underline{M} & \underline{G} & \underline{} & \underline{} \\ 1 & 2 & 3 & 4 & 5 & 6 \end{array}$$

Figure 2.28

Likewise, Rules 2 and 3 require F and L to take spaces numbered lower than M's. In this case, those are spaces 1 and 2, respectively.

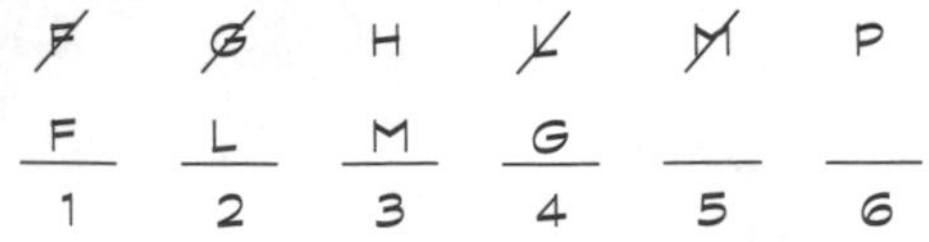

$$\begin{array}{cccccc} \cancel{F} & \cancel{G} & H & \cancel{L} & \cancel{M} & P \\ \underline{F} & \underline{L} & \underline{M} & \underline{G} & \underline{} & \underline{} \\ 1 & 2 & 3 & 4 & 5 & 6 \end{array}$$

Figure 2.29

---

[33] PrepTest 46, Sec. 4, Game 1, Q 3

The only two remaining entities are H, which just has to take a spot following M's, and P, which can go anywhere.

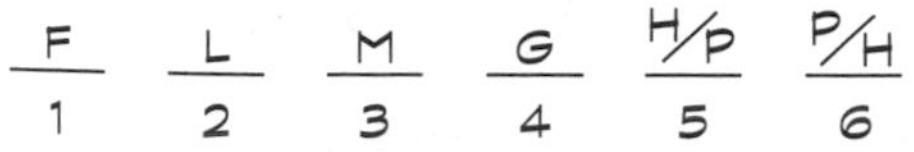

$$\underset{1}{\underline{F}} \quad \underset{2}{\underline{L}} \quad \underset{3}{\underline{M}} \quad \underset{4}{\underline{G}} \quad \underset{5}{\underline{^H\!/_P}} \quad \underset{6}{\underline{^P\!/_H}}$$

Figure 2.30

In this case, P can take space 5 or space 6, so the correct answer to the question—which is "the lowest numbered" spot P can take—is choice (D).

Students often hesitate to create new mini-sketches for "If" questions, fearing that it will take them too long to draw the new scratch work. But with your framework and rules in order as you have them, the new sketch takes a matter of seconds. Moreover, just look at how quickly and clearly the correct answer shows itself. Do the same thing with the "if" in the next question.

4. (A)

If guidepost 5 does not picture the moose, then which one of the following must be true?

(A)   The lynx is pictured on guidepost 2.
(B)   The moose is pictured on guidepost 3.
(C)   The grizzly is pictured on guidepost 4.
(D)   The porcupine is pictured on guidepost 5.
(E)   The hare is pictured on guidepost 6.[34]

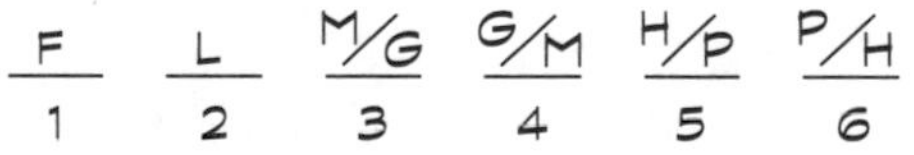

$$\underset{1}{\underline{F}} \quad \underset{2}{\underline{L}} \quad \underset{3}{\underline{^M\!/_G}} \quad \underset{4}{\underline{^G\!/_M}} \quad \underset{5}{\underline{^H\!/_P}} \quad \underset{6}{\underline{^P\!/_H}}$$

Figure 2.31

Another "if" clause means another mini-sketch. Here's how you get to this one.

Start with the question stem. If M isn't in space 5, where could it be? Check your original Master Sketch. M can't be in space 6, since H must follow it. It also can't be in spaces 1 or 2, since both F and L must precede it. That leaves only spaces 3 and 4. Whichever one M doesn't take will be taken by G.

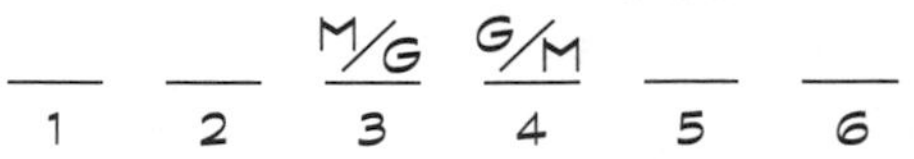

$$\underset{1}{\underline{}} \quad \underset{2}{\underline{}} \quad \underset{3}{\underline{^M\!/_G}} \quad \underset{4}{\underline{^G\!/_M}} \quad \underset{5}{\underline{}} \quad \underset{6}{\underline{}}$$

Figure 2.32

The scratch work for Rules 2 and 3 makes it clear that F and L must take spaces 1 and 2, respectively.

---

[34] PrepTest 46, Sec. 4, Game 1, Q 4

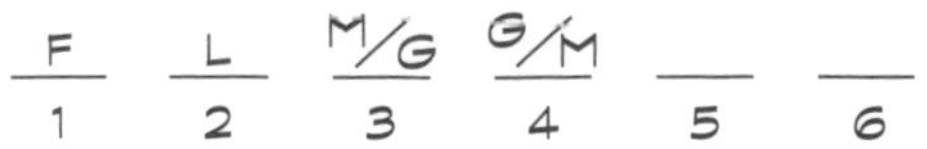

$$\frac{F}{1} \quad \frac{L}{2} \quad \frac{^M/_G}{3} \quad \frac{^G/_M}{4} \quad \frac{}{5} \quad \frac{}{6}$$

Figure 2.33

The remaining entities are H and P. Spaces 5 and 6 are open to them, and nothing restricts either H or P from taking either of those positions.

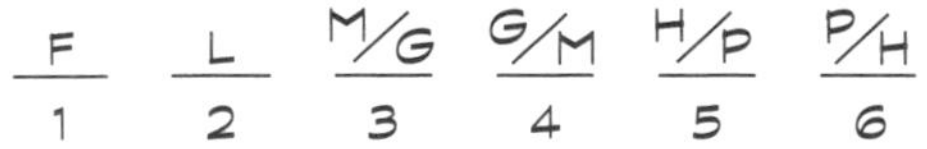

$$\frac{F}{1} \quad \frac{L}{2} \quad \frac{^M/_G}{3} \quad \frac{^G/_M}{4} \quad \frac{^H/_P}{5} \quad \frac{^P/_H}{6}$$

Figure 2.34

Now that you've got your ticket to a quick, definite answer, get on the train. The question stem asks for what *must be true*. Notice that your mini-sketch established the positions of two of the entities absolutely: F in space 1 and L in space 2. One of those has to be the correct answer, since those are the two things that must be true in this case. Choice (A) turns out to have L in space 2 and is the correct answer. Notice that all of the wrong answers deal with entities that still have wiggle room—M, G, P, and H. Because of that wiggle room, none of these could be the correct answer to a *must be true* question.

5. **(E)**

Which one of the following animals could be pictured on any one of the six guideposts?

(A) fox
(B) hare
(C) lynx
(D) moose
(E) porcupine[35]

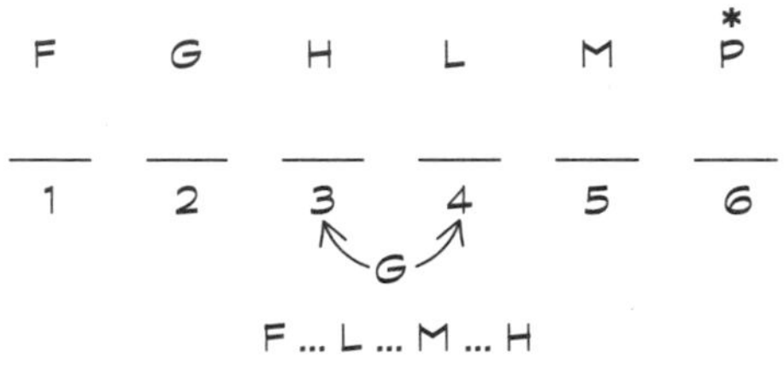

$$\overset{F}{\underline{}} \quad \overset{G}{\underline{}} \quad \overset{H}{\underline{}} \quad \overset{L}{\underline{}} \quad \overset{M}{\underline{}} \quad \overset{*}{\overset{P}{\underline{}}}$$
$$1 \qquad 2 \qquad 3 \qquad 4 \qquad 5 \qquad 6$$

F ... L ... M ... H

Figure 2.35

As a savvy test taker—one trained by Kaplan, that is—you can get this point in five seconds. Look at your Master Sketch. Who had the asterisk? P, the entity unrestricted by any rule. Of course, that's the one that can take any position. Choose (E) and you're done, just that fast.

6. **(A)**

If the moose guidepost is numbered exactly one higher than the lynx guidepost, then which one of the following could be true?

(A) Guidepost 5 pictures the hare.
(B) Guidepost 4 pictures the moose.
(C) Guidepost 4 pictures the porcupine.
(D) Guidepost 3 pictures the lynx.
(E) Guidepost 3 pictures the porcupine.[36]

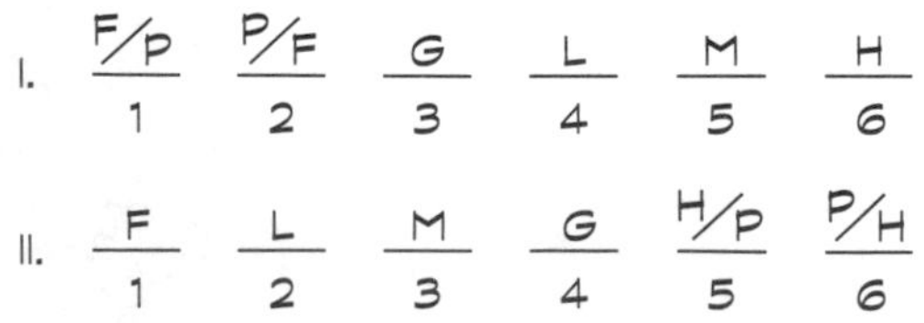

I.
$$\frac{^F/_P}{1} \quad \frac{^P/_F}{2} \quad \frac{G}{3} \quad \frac{L}{4} \quad \frac{M}{5} \quad \frac{H}{6}$$

II.
$$\frac{F}{1} \quad \frac{L}{2} \quad \frac{M}{3} \quad \frac{G}{4} \quad \frac{^H/_P}{5} \quad \frac{^P/_H}{6}$$

Figure 2.36

---

[35] PrepTest 46, Sec. 4, Game 1, Q 5

[36] PrepTest 46, Sec. 4, Game 1, Q 6

This was the toughest question in the set, the toughest even to draw a mini-sketch for. The "if" clause told you to make L and M a solid block; they must be consecutive entities. That part is easily depicted as a variation on your picture of Rules 2 and 3.

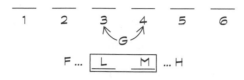

Figure 2.37

What's tougher is seeing how that relates to Rule 1. To take control of the question, simply make two frameworks. Put G in space 3 in one of them, space 4 in the other.

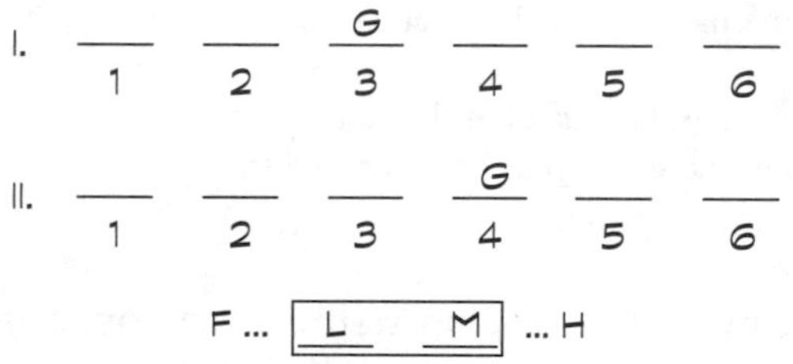

I.
—	—	G	—	—	—
1	2	3	4	5	6

II.
—	—	—	G	—	—
1	2	3	4	5	6

F ... [L   M] ... H

Figure 2.38

Now consider how the revised Rule 2/3 block of entities could fit in. The solid L-M block must follow G when G is in space 3. It must precede G when G is in space 4. There's not enough room to accommodate the block any other way.

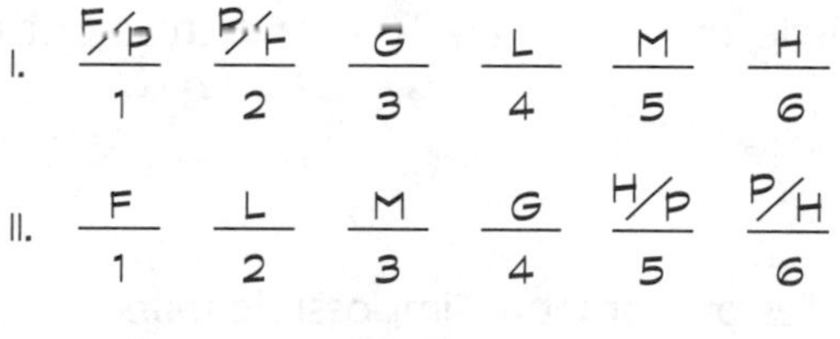

I.
F̸/P	P̸/F̸	G	L	M	H
1	2	3	4	5	6

II.
F	L	M	G	H/P	P/H
1	2	3	4	5	6

Figure 2.39

Now that you have a perfect pair of mini-sketches, make sure you've understood the question. The correct answer will be the only one that's acceptable in one of these mini-sketches. The wrong answers will all be impossible in both. Choice (A) does the trick. H could appear in space 5 in the second option, the one with G in space 4. Check them if you want to, but all of the remaining choices have to violate both mini-sketches.

Rules Create Key Entities

Another way in which the rules allow you to take control of a game is by creating key entities, players that restrict several of the other entities or limit much of the action. In the preceding game, G was limited to just one of two spaces, and P was important because it was completely unrestricted. Still, the real heavy lifting in that game was done by the string of four entities that kept pushing each other to the front or the back.

In this next game, the opposite is true. It's a game you haven't seen before, so take some time and review the setup and rules. Try your hand at sketching them out and then use the review to see how you did. Above all, see if your assessment of the rules helps you find two key entities, those that will be involved in every question.

> Henri has exactly five electrical appliances in his dormitory
> room: a hairdryer, a microwave oven, a razor, a television,
> and a vacuum. As a consequence of fire department
> regulations, Henri can use these appliances only in accordance
> with the following conditions:
>> Henri cannot use both the hairdryer and the razor
>> simultaneously.
>> Henri cannot use both the hairdryer and the television
>> simultaneously.
>> When Henri uses the vacuum, he cannot at the same time
>> use any of the following: the hairdryer, the razor, and the
>> television.[37]

How'd you do? I'll take you through the Kaplan Method as it applies to this game. As you see the setup, sketch, and rules come together, take note of the two entities that will drive the action.

STEPS 1 AND 2: **Overview and Sketch**

Your job here is to determine which appliances Henri can use simultaneously and which ones he needs to keep turned off to avoid blowing a fuse. That makes this a Selection game. Each entity is either "off" or "on" at any given time. You needn't draw a framework or chart. Just list the entities. You can circle those that are "on" and cross out those that are "off" as the questions require it.

STEP 3: **Rules**

Each of the three rules creates one or more "impossible pairs."

> Henri cannot use both the hairdryer and the razor
> simultaneously.[38]

Figure 2.40

[37] PrepTest 48, Sec. 2, Game 1

[38] PrepTest 48, Sec. 2, Game 1

You might choose to depict this rule in any of the ways pictured. I'll stick with the first one as I proceed, though some test takers find that striking through impossible pairs makes it harder to read their scratch work. Choose the way that works best for you, but be consistent within any particular game to avoid confusion about what the rules mean.

Henri cannot use both the hairdryer and the television simultaneously.[39]

Figure 2.41

There's the hairdryer again. That thing must really use a lot of juice. At any rate, it's starting to look pretty important to account for the hairdryer in any given scenario, isn't it?

When Henri uses the vacuum, he cannot at the same time use any of the following: the hairdryer, the razor, and the television.[40]

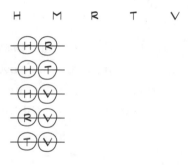

Figure 2.42

This rule introduces three more impossible pairs. All of them involve the vacuum. It, too, has become a key entity in this game. Notice that this rule also creates a third impossible pair for the hairdryer. In fact, if Henri wants to use another appliance along with either the hairdryer or the vacuum, his only option is the microwave. The television and razor, on the other hand, have only two exclusions each. Those two exclusions are, of course, the hairdryer and the vacuum.

Did you also account for what you don't know? Like P in the previous game, the microwave here is a "floater," an entity completely unrestricted by any of the rules. It's the one entity that can accompany any of the others. Put a star or asterisk above it. Here's your final sketch:

---

[39] PrepTest 48, Sec. 2, Game 1
[40] PrepTest 48, Sec. 2, Game 1

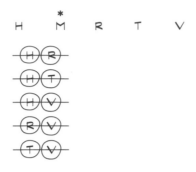

Figure 2.43

STEP 4: Deductions

This is another game with very little to do in the Deductions step. The one thing to consider is what you've uncovered about the maximum number of appliances Henri could use at the same time. To do so, Henri will need to avoid using the hairdryer or the vacuum, each of which knock out three other entities. So the maximum that he can use together is three: the razor, the television, and the unrestricted entity, the microwave.

STEP 5: Questions

With your rules sketched out and considered, you should be able to nail down the questions associated with this game. Copy your diagrams of the rules over onto the page with the questions. Then take your time with the questions. Be systematic as you apply the rules, and jot out a list of your entities when there is a new "if" clause at the beginning of a question stem.

Questions 1–3

Henri has exactly five electrical appliances in his dormitory room: a hairdryer, a microwave oven, a razor, a television, and a vacuum. As a consequence of fire department regulations, Henri can use these appliances only in accordance with the following conditions:

Henri cannot use both the hairdryer and the razor simultaneously.

Henri cannot use both the hairdryer and the television simultaneously.

When Henri uses the vacuum, he cannot at the same time use any of the following: the hairdryer, the razor, and the television.

1. Which one of the following is a pair of appliances Henri could be using simultaneously?

    (A)   the hairdryer and the razor
    (B)   the hairdryer and the television
    (C)   the razor and the television
    (D)   the razor and the vacuum
    (E)   the television and the vacuum

2. Assume that Henri is using exactly two appliances and is not using the microwave oven. Which one of the following is a list of all the appliances, other than the microwave oven, that Henri CANNOT be using?

    (A)   hairdryer
    (B)   razor
    (C)   vacuum
    (D)   hairdryer, razor
    (E)   hairdryer, vacuum

3. Which one of the following CANNOT be true?

    (A)   Henri uses the hairdryer while using the microwave oven.
    (B)   Henri uses the microwave oven while using the razor.
    (C)   Henri uses the microwave oven while using two other appliances.
    (D)   Henri uses the television while using two other appliances.
    (E)   Henri uses the vacuum while using two other appliances.[41]

---

[41] PrepTest 48, Sec. 2, Game 1, Qs 1-3

Explanations

Only question 2 had new "if" clauses (although it used the word "assume" instead of "if"). All of the other questions could be answered with nothing more than your expertly sketched set of the rules. Take a look.

1. (C)

Which one of the following is a pair of appliances Henri could be using simultaneously?

(A)   the hairdryer and the razor
(B)   the hairdryer and the television
(C)   the razor and the television
(D)   the razor and the vacuum
(E)   the television and the vacuum[42]

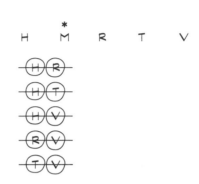

Figure 2.44

Your scratch work made short work of this one. The wrong answers all list forbidden pairs. In fact, they list the first two and the last two from your sketch. The correct answer, choice (C), is the only one that lists a pair not forbidden by the rules.

2. (E)

Assume that Henri is using exactly two appliances and is not using the microwave oven. Which one of the following is a list of all the appliances, other than the microwave oven, that Henri CANNOT be using?

(A)   hairdryer
(B)   razor
(C)   vacuum
(D)   hairdryer, razor
(E)   hairdryer, vacuum[43]

Figure 2.45

For this question, it was efficient to create a new mini-sketch based on the "if" clause in the question stem. Don't let the word change—"assume" instead of "if"—throw you. The hypothetical situation introduced at the beginning of the question is just the same here as it is in any other new "if" question.

The condition you need to account for states that Henri is using two appliances, neither of which is the microwave. Start your mini-sketch like this:

2 "on"   H   M̸   R   T   V

Figure 2.46

---

[42] PrepTest 48, Sec. 2, Q 1
[43] PrepTest 48, Sec. 2, Q 2

Now, consider the rules. With the microwave (remember, it's the only appliance with no restrictions) out of the picture, the only pair that is not forbidden is the razor and television. The rules had already identified the hairdryer and vacuum as the most difficult appliances to find matches for. So cross the hairdryer and the vacuum off of the list in your mini-sketch, too.

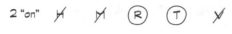

Figure 2.47

The question stem is long, but your mini-sketch helps you interpret it. The correct answer is simply the one that includes everything you crossed off your list besides the microwave. That's choice (E).

3. **(E)**

Which one of the following CANNOT be true?

(A)   Henri uses the hairdryer while using the microwave oven.

(B)   Henri uses the microwave oven while using the razor.

(C)   Henri uses the microwave oven while using two other appliances.

(D)   Henri uses the television while using two other appliances.

(E)   Henri uses the vacuum while using two other appliances.[44]

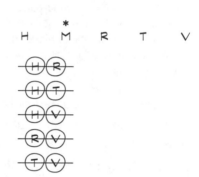

Figure 2.48

The correct answer here is the one that is impossible given the rules. That means that all four wrong answers are acceptable. If you approached this question by eliminating wrong answers, you should have noticed that both choices (A) and (B) mention exactly two appliances including the microwave, the unrestricted entity. It can be used with anything, so both (A) and (B) give possible scenarios and are therefore wrong answers. Choices (C) and (D) both assign Henri three appliances. You knew, from considering the rules, that Henri could use the razor, television, and microwave simultaneously. So both (C) and (D) give acceptable selections. By process of elimination, you know that choice (E) is the correct answer. It has Henri using the vacuum with two other appliances. Impossible. The vacuum can only be used with the microwave.

It's exciting to see how much you can accomplish with a strategic understanding of the rules. Not all games can be handled as easily as the previous two were with just the rules. That's why there's a chapter on Deductions in this book. Still, it should boost your confidence to realize that even when there aren't a lot of additional inferences to pull from the rules, the game will always give you enough information to answer every question. That's true no matter how complicated the action is.

---

[44] PrepTest 48, Sec. 2, Q 3

Rules Remove Complications

Of course, the test makers won't announce the difficulty of each game in the section on test day. Sometimes students see what appears to be a complicated task and assume that they've encountered a difficult game. But if the rules are sufficiently concrete, your task will ultimately be quite manageable. As a case in point, revisit the Debate Teams game you saw in the Game Tasks Drill in chapter 1.

> The three highest-placing teams in a high school debate tournament are the teams from Fairview, Gillom, and Hilltop high schools. Each team has exactly two members. The individuals on these three teams are Mei, Navarro, O'Rourke, Pavlovich, Sethna, and Tsudama. The following is the case:
>> Sethna is on the team from Gillom High.
>> Tsudama is on the second-place team.
>> Mei and Pavlovich are not on the same team.
>> Pavlovich's team places higher than Navarro's team.
>> The team from Gillom High places higher than the team from Hilltop High.[45]

For a test taker who is trained only to see the "game type," this is a dreaded Hybrid game: You have to Sequence the order of the schools, Distribute the students into teams of two, and Match the student pairs to the schools. Described that way, the game sounds daunting. But now consider this game from the perspective of its restrictions. It's going to seem much easier in a moment. First, there are just six possible ways to Sequence the schools:

1	Frv	Frv	Gil	Gil	Hil	Hil
2	Gil	Hil	Frv	Hil	Frv	Gil
3	Hil	Gil	Hil	Frv	Gil	Frv

Figure 2.49

One of the three high schools is in first place, and then there are just two ways to arrange the remaining schools. (Remember, the math is just here to help you see the restrictions more clearly; by test day, you'll be able to assess game difficulties by feel and experience.)

There are actually only 90 ways to combine and match the students. (Feel free to roll your eyes at the idea of "only 90," but remember that the "simple" seven students, seven desks game had 5,040 permutations.) The simplicity comes from the fact that once you have one combination, say M and N, there are only four debaters remaining, so they can combine in only three ways: OP, ST; OS, PT; or OT, PS. So once you assign any given pair to a rank—first, second, or third place—there are only six ways to complete the picture. Here are the possibilities when you rank the MN pair first:

---

[45] PrepTest 53, Sec. 2, Game 4

Figure 2.50

Since there are 15 possible first-place pairings, there are 90 possible ways to pair and match the debaters. With six ways to sequence the teams and 90 ways to combine and match the students, this game has 540 acceptable arrangements, already much simpler than our hypothetical seven students, seven desks game.

But you haven't considered the impact of the rules yet, and it's a big impact. Take a moment and think about how each of the rules limits the acceptable "solutions" to this game. Start sketching the rules. It will help.

> The three highest-placing teams in a high school debate tournament are the teams from Fairview, Gillom, and Hilltop high schools. Each team has exactly two members. The individuals on these three teams are Mei, Navarro, O'Rourke, Pavlovich, Sethna, and Tsudama. The following is the case:
> Sethna is on the team from Gillom High.
> Tsudama is on the second-place team.
> Mei and Pavlovich are not on the same team.
> Pavlovich's team places higher than Navarro's team.
> The team from Gillom High places higher than the team from Hilltop High.[46]

The most restrictive of the rules is actually the fifth. It cuts the number of solutions in half. By eliminating any sequence in which Hilltop finishes higher than Gillom, there are only three ways to rank the teams:

Figure 2.51

46 PrepTest 53, Sec. 2, Game 4

You can use this as the framework for your Master Sketch. You're limited to just three options.

The remaining rules all eliminate a number of the possible pairings and matches. Since Rule 5 means that Gillom High will place first or second, Rule 1 gets rid of all cases in which S could be matched to the third-place team. You've just eliminated 30 more possible solutions.

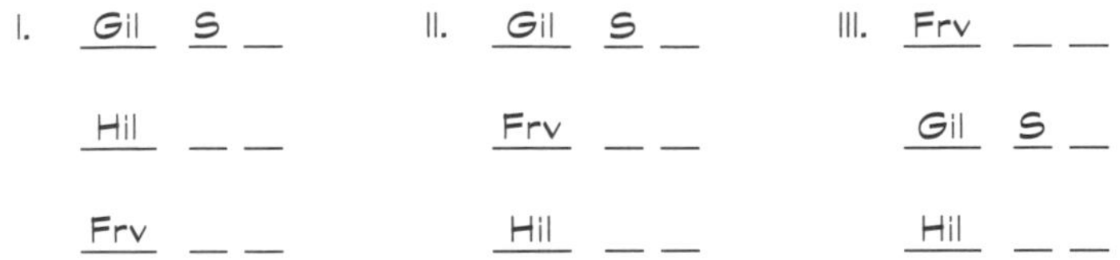

I. Gil S __   II. Gil S __   III. Frv __ __

    Hil __ __   Frv __ __   Gil S __

    Frv __ __   Hil __ __   Hil __ __

Figure 2.52

The second rule is stronger, since it gets rid of all arrangements in which T could be on the first-place or third-place teams. So it removes 60 possible solutions.

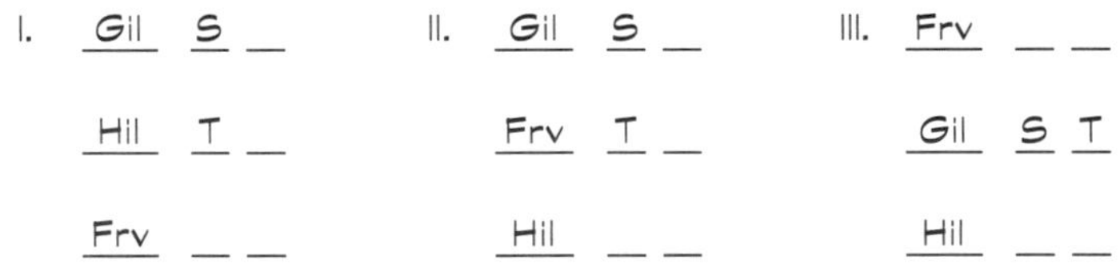

I. Gil S __   II. Gil S __   III. Frv __ __

    Hil T __   Frv T __   Gil S T

    Frv __ __   Hil __ __   Hil __ __

Figure 2.53

Rules 3 and 4 ensure that the MP and NP pairs are never permitted. Moreover, Rule 4 tells you that you'll never find P on the third-place team and you'll never find N on the first-place team.

I. Gil S __   II. Gil S __   III. Frv __ __

    Hil T __   Frv T __   Gil S T

    Frv __ __   Hil __ __   Hil __ __

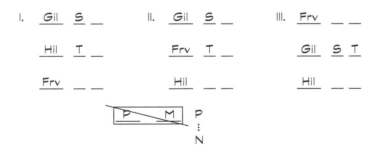

Figure 2.54

To find out just how limited the possible solutions are, consider the three ranking options in light of the rules restricting potential pairs and matches.

There are five ways to complete the picture in Option I. P must be on a higher-ranking team than N. That can happen in three ways:

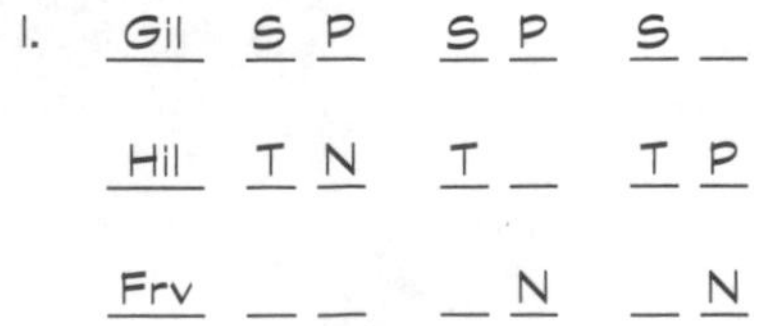

I. Gil S P   S P   S __

    Hil T N   T __   T P

    Frv __ __   N   __ N

Figure 2.55

Those arrangements make it easy to see where M and O could fit in:

I.

Gil	S	P	S	P	S	O/M
Hil	T	N	T	O/M	T	P
Frv	M	O	M/O	N	M/O	N

Figure 2.56

Since M and O could swap places in the second and third of these possible solutions, there are five ways to finish Option I.

Option II, where Fairview finishes second and Hilltop third, has the same five possible pairings and matches:

II.

Gil	S	P	S	P	S	O/M
Frv	T	N	T	O/M	T	P
Hil	M	O	M/O	N	M/O	N

Figure 2.57

In Option III, where the TS pair is assigned to second-place Gillom High, there's only one way to complete the sketch. P must go in first place and N in third place. Since the MP pair is forbidden, this is the only solution:

III.

Frv	P	O
Gil	T	S
Hil	N	M

Figure 2.58

Those in the business of trying to scare you about the LSAT rather than to help you master it would characterize this as a daunting, complex triple-hybrid. But with the rules and restrictions fully considered, this game in fact has only 11 possible solutions. Period. Of course, I would never encourage a student to sketch out all 11 possible solutions. The Master Sketch I'd recommend would stop here:

The three highest-placing teams in a high school debate
tournament are the teams from Fairview, Gillom, and Hilltop
high schools. Each team has exactly two members. The
individuals on these three teams are Mei, Navarro, O'Rourke,
Pavlovich, Sethna, and Tsudama. The following is the case:
    Sethna is on the team from Gillom High.
    Tsudama is on the second-place team.
    Mei and Pavlovich are not on the same team.
    Pavlovich's team places higher than Navarro's team.
    The team from Gillom High places higher than the team
     from Hilltop High.[47]

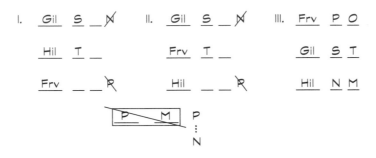

Figure 2.59

But this exercise has given you a much greater appreciation of just how many possible arrangements are taken off the table because of the rules that forbid the MP pair and place P on a higher-ranked team than N. Not surprisingly, one of the questions associated with this game directly rewards students for being able to count acceptable arrangements. Take a look (and get the right answer while you're at it).

21. If Pavlovich and Tsudama are teammates, then for how many of the individuals can it
    be exactly determined where his or her team placed?

    (A)   two
    (B)   three
    (C)   four
    (D)   five
    (E)   six[48]

The "if" clause here means that you can only be in Options I or II. Once you place P on the second-place team with T, you know that N has to be on the third-place team. That leaves only M and O to swap places.

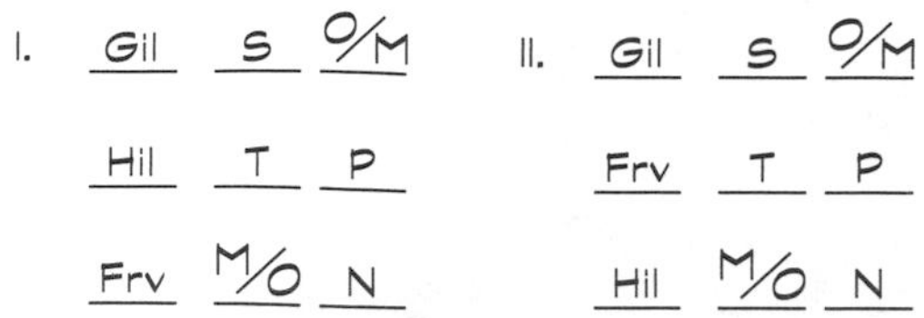

I. $\underline{\text{Gil}}$ $\underline{\text{ S }}$ $\underline{\text{ O/M }}$ II. $\underline{\text{Gil}}$ $\underline{\text{ S }}$ $\underline{\text{ O/M }}$

 $\underline{\text{Hil}}$ $\underline{\text{ T }}$ $\underline{\text{ P }}$ $\underline{\text{Frv}}$ $\underline{\text{ T }}$ $\underline{\text{ P }}$

 $\underline{\text{Frv}}$ $\underline{\text{ M/O }}$ $\underline{\text{ N }}$ $\underline{\text{Hil}}$ $\underline{\text{ M/O }}$ $\underline{\text{ N }}$

Figure 2.60

Four of the students' rankings are determined for sure, making choice (C) the correct answer.

Rules Help You Score Points

In games of any complexity level, rules are your best friends. They reduce a galaxy of options down to just a few acceptable arrangements. In the next chapter, you'll see how to combine the rules and restrictions to makes games even more definite. It's something that untrained test takers are rarely able to do accurately or efficiently (if at all), and it will provide you with the greatest possible advantage over your competition.

In Part II of this book, by the way, you'll find lists and descriptions of all the rules most commonly associated with each game type. For now, keep your attention on the Kaplan Method and the steps you need to take in all games. Doing so will make Part II's exhaustive discussion of game types and variations even more valuable.

CHAPTER 3

FORMAL LOGIC

USING FORMAL LOGIC ON THE LSAT

Over the years, I've found that one type of logic games rule seems to intimidate students more than all the others: formal logic. Formal logic in the Logic Games section consists of the conditional, or "if-then" rules that dictate what must follow from a certain situation and what's necessary for that situation to occur. I understand why students get anxious about formal logic. Philosophers and other academics refer to it with daunting terms like "first-order predicate calculus," "predicate logic," and "quantification theory." Look it up on the Internet and you'll encounter a dizzying array of terms and symbol systems. But take a deep breath. You don't get any LSAT points for knowing *about* formal logic, just for being able to use it to answer LSAT questions. If you follow what's laid out for you in this book, there's no need for you to take a formal logic class unless you have a personal interest in it. A philosophy- or math-department logic course provides excellent thinking practice, but it won't do much to change your LSAT score.

How to Use Formal Logic on the LSAT

My main goal for this chapter is to help you overcome your trepidation about formal logic and learn to *use* it. To do that, you'll need to be able to do four things. I'll outline them here and then elaborate on each in its own subsection.

1. Recognize formal logic statements.

Look at this rule:

> If literature is offered, then geography is also offered
> but psychology is not.[1]

Its "if-then" grammar is a dead giveaway that it is standard, conditional formal logic. Once you've practiced the techniques in this section, you'll be able to handle the rule flawlessly and rake in the associated LSAT points. But what if the test makers had written it like this?

> Literature is offered only if geography is also offered
> and only if psychology is not offered.

The two rules are actually identical in meaning and have precisely the same impact on the logic game. But if you fail to recognize that the second version represents the same conditional rule, if you fail to see that it dictates a "sufficient-necessary" relationship among its terms, then you won't be able to use it to score points on the LSAT.

2. Translate formal logic statements.

This skill has two elements. The first is directly related to recognizing formal logic. You must be able to turn any English sentence that expresses a conditional rule into its "if-then" equivalent. For example, the sentence "Bobby won't go to the dance unless Jane goes to the dance" has the same meaning as "If Bobby goes to the dance, then so does Jane." I'll have you spend some time learning to assess the implications of these sentences, however they're written, so that you can use them effectively as logic games rules.

The second element involves translating the "if-then" proposition into simple, consistent symbols. The rule about Bobby and Jane can thus be written as:

$$\text{If } B_d \rightarrow J_d$$

Figure 3.1

Don't try to run before you walk, though. Translating formal logic rules into symbolic notation doesn't get you any LSAT points unless you understand what the symbols, and the rules they depict, actually mean. Symbolism is a great way to organize information once you've understood it.

3. Determine the statement's contrapositive.

Here's one of those fancy-sounding terms that sometimes confuses students. A statement's "contrapositive" is simply another way of saying the same thing. It's the logical equivalent of

---

[1] PrepTest 49, Sec. 1, Game 3

the original statement, constructed using negated terms. For the rule that says "If Bobby goes to the dance, then so does Jane," the contrapositive is "If Jane does not go to the dance, then neither will Bobby." In symbols, it looks like this:

$$\text{If } J_{\not{}} \rightarrow B_{\not{}}$$

Figure 3.2

The reason why finding the contrapositive is so valuable to you in logic games is that it essentially doubles the restrictions on the game's action (or at least doubles your ability to spot them). As you saw in chapter 2, restrictions are what make games easier and more manageable. Additionally, the test makers often relate the questions directly to the contrapositive expression of a rule. In the case of Bobby and Jane, the question might ask, "If Jane does not go to the dance, which one of the following must be true?" Because you've already considered the contrapositive, it's easy to see at least one fact that must follow from the seemingly new "if" clause: Bobby will not go to the dance.

4. Combine formal logic rules.

When the test makers include formal logic rules, they most often provide additional rules with which you can combine them. For example, in the imaginary game with Bobby and Jane, they might give you a rule that says, "If Bobby does not go to the dance, then Martha will not go to the football game." Translating this, you get:

$$\text{If } B_{\not{}} \rightarrow M_{\not{}}$$

Figure 3.3

Notice that this allows for a deduction. By combining the contrapositive of the rule about Bobby and Jane with the rule about Bobby and Martha, you can see the connection between Jane and Martha.

$$\text{If } J_{\not{}} \rightarrow B_{\not{}}$$
$$\text{If } B_{\not{}} \rightarrow M_{\not{}}$$
$$\text{Thus, if } J_{\not{}} \rightarrow M_{\not{}}$$

Figure 3.4

If Jane avoids the dance, then so does Bobby. And when Bobby avoids the dance, Martha avoids the football game. Thus, if Jane doesn't go to the dance, Martha won't go to the football game. As your skill with contrapositives grows, you'll see that the statement "If Martha goes to the football game, then Jane goes to the dance" also follows from this combination of rules. (A great number of LSAT Logical Reasoning questions reward the same skill, by the way. The practice you're doing here will help you on other sections of the test.)

The test makers consistently reward your ability to spot these types of connections. In games with multiple formal logic rules, every question may turn on your ability to make the correct combinations.

"But I don't get the whole 'if-then' thing."

I've lost count of the hours that I've spent thinking about how best to present formal logic material to future test takers. I know that dozens (if not hundreds) of other Kaplan teachers have pondered this, too. In this chapter, you'll reap the fruits of that thinking: the discussion of necessity and sufficiency, suggested symbols, "translations," and a foolproof system for determining statements' contrapositives. These tools will allow you to manage the formal logic that you encounter in the logic games section. But those students who've made greatest breakthroughs with formal logic are the ones who have put it in perspective. They've seen that formal logic is itself a tool, one that helps them get correct answers. For them, formal logic transformed from obstacle to opportunity. I'll help you learn from their experiences.

To help reduce your anxiety, here are a few reasons why you should learn to love formal logic on the LSAT:

You use formal logic every day.

Formal logic, or at least the small part of it that appears on the LSAT, is actually something that you use consistently without even realizing it. Every time you make a statement such as "The TV has to be plugged in if you want it to work" or "You can't travel to China without a visa," you're using exactly the same conditional logic that is used on the test. You can draw on that nearly intuitive understanding of conditional rules as you learn to master the test.

Formal logic is a small part of logic games.

Understanding formal logic is one of the Core 4 LSAT Skills. That being said, it's actually a bigger part of Logical Reasoning than it is of Logic Games on most administrations of the exam. On some recent exams (PrepTests 50, 52, and 53, for example, from which many of the games in this book are drawn), you won't find more than one or two formal logic statements in the Logic Games section. Arguably, there are tests (such as PrepTest 46) where you find none at all. Every once in a while, of course, you'll find a game that turns entirely on formal logic rules. You'll deal with a couple of those at the end of this chapter. By then, you'll have everything you need to master such games (and to do so much more easily than your competition).

Formal logic brings certainty.

Some test takers love learning how to diagram formal logic statements and their contrapositives. There's a feeling of mathlike precision that can be very comforting. Others find the algebraic approach overwhelming and deal with the statements as regular sentences providing rules for the game. Use the approach that fits your learning style. Regardless, learn to appreciate the fact that formal logic rules lead you to absolute certainty about the right answer. When formal logic is involved, you can determine without doubt what must, cannot, or could be true or false in a given case.

Formal logic is often just a complicated way to say simple things.

Consider the following rule:

> Neither Ty nor Raimundo appears in any photograph that
> Wendy appears in.[2]

You could diagram it, in all its formal logic glory, like this:

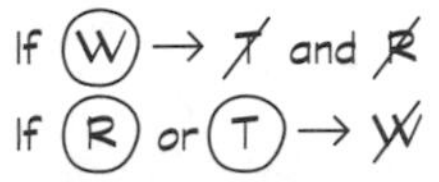

Figure 3.5

As you'll see shortly, that's an accurate depiction of the rule. But think about what the rule means, the restrictions that it places on the game. It's just telling you to keep Wendy apart from Ty and from Raimundo. So if it's clearer to you, just jot the rule like this:

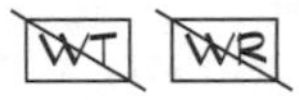

Figure 3.6

Keep formal logic rules simple and represent them in helpful ways. In logic games, your goals should always be to seek clarity and to avoid confusion. You'll find that when you think through what formal logic rules mean to the game, they're often quite easy to visualize, and thus to represent symbolically without a lot of fancy (and unnecessary) gibberish.

IDENTIFY FORMAL LOGIC: DISTINGUISH BETWEEN *SUFFICIENT* AND *NECESSARY*

The Sufficient-Necessary Relationship

At the heart of all formal logic statements on the LSAT are the twin concepts of sufficiency and necessity. Don't let the terms intimidate you; just use their ordinary meanings. "Sufficient" means "enough by itself" and "Necessary" means "required." Don't confuse the two. Plenty of things are necessary for a given result without being sufficient for it, or vice versa. If your car has an internal combustion engine, gasoline is necessary for it to run, but gasoline by itself isn't enough. The car might have plenty of gas, but if it doesn't have spark plugs, or if the battery is dead, it's not going to work. Having gasoline is necessary, but not sufficient, for your car to run. On the flip side, winning the lottery is sufficient to make you rich, but it's not necessary.

---

[2] PrepTest 45, Sec. 3, Game 3

You could also get rich by working hard, investing well, discovering a sunken treasure, or inheriting a large sum of money. The takeaway message is that you already understand these concepts, almost intuitively.

To make sure you get the idea, consider the following example. Say there's a watch you'd like to buy. It costs $100. Each of the following statements tells you something that is *sufficient but not necessary*, *necessary but not sufficient*, or *both sufficient and necessary* in order for you to purchase the watch. Consider each statement and label it accordingly.

You have at least $50. _____

You have exactly $100. _____

You have $400. _____

You have at least $100. _____

Here are the answers:

You have at least $50: *Necessary, but not sufficient*. If you don't have at least $50, there's no way you can have the $100 you would need to buy the watch. But, $50 is not enough, by itself, for you to buy the watch. So, it's not sufficient.

You have exactly $100: *Sufficient, but not necessary*. With $100, you can definitely buy the watch. But, it's not necessary for you to have exactly $100. You could buy the watch if you had $101 or $105 or $5,000. Always pay attention to the wording of LSAT rules, questions, and answer choices. The test makers' word choice is always intentional.

You have $400: *Sufficient, but not necessary*. You could buy the watch and plenty more. So, it's sufficient (and nice) for you to have $400, but it's not necessary that you have so much in order to get the watch.

You have at least $100: *Both sufficient and necessary*. Knowing that you have at least $100 guarantees that you can buy the watch. It's also necessary. If you don't have at least $100, you can't buy the watch.

You can write conditional statements in the same language the test makers use for formal logic rules on the LSAT. Think back to the first example, the one identifying gasoline as necessary (but not sufficient) for your car to run.

If the car runs, then it has gasoline.

If the car does not have gasoline, then it will not run.

The car runs only if it has gasoline.

Only when the car has gasoline will it run.

The car will not run unless it has gasoline.

All of those statements mean exactly the same thing. Moreover, switching the places of the key terms—the car's running and its having gas—would create nonsense. Make sure you see why.

If the car has gasoline, then it will run: Not necessarily; it might have a dead battery or lack spark plugs.

The car has gasoline only if it runs: Same problem; you could have a full tank in a nonfunctioning car.

The car does not have gasoline unless it runs: yet another variation on the same faulty logic.

Why don't any of the latter three statements work? Because they've mistaken the sufficient term for the necessary one. The test makers test your understanding of necessity and sufficiency throughout the test, and they design wrong answers to catch those who mistake one for the other.

Interpreting a Formal Logic Rule

In chapter 2, I said that logic games rules are like laws. Nowhere is this truer than in formal logic rules. To see this, and to see how important it will be to use formal logic in logic games, consider this legal rule:

> To legally vote in Country X, you must be at least 18 years of age and you must be properly registered.

First, determine the sufficient-necessary relationship. Which of the terms is enough, by itself, to establish the truth of other term(s)? Which are needed in order to have another condition? If you're confused, try fitting the terms—there are three this time: "vote legally," "at least 18," and "properly registered"—into the following sentences:

If _____, then _____.

You cannot _____ unless you are _____.

If not _____, then not _____.

You can _____ only if you are _____.

The sufficient term is "vote legally." Someone who has voted legally in Country X must be both 18 or older *and* properly registered. The necessary terms are "at least 18" and "properly registered." You cannot legally vote in Country X unless you are both at least 18 *and* properly registered. So a potential voter who fails to satisfy either of the necessary conditions cannot vote legally. Thus, if you are not at least 18 *or* are not properly registered, then you cannot vote legally. Remember that "only" and "only if" signify necessity. Here's how each sentence might be properly completed:

If *legally voting*, then *at least 18* and *properly registered*.
You *cannot legally vote* unless you are at least 18 and properly registered.
If *not at least 18* or *not properly registered*, then *not voting legally*.
You can *vote legally* only if you are *at least 18* and *properly registered*.

The LSAT is always interested in what must, cannot, or could be true given a particular set of circumstances or rules, especially in the Logic Games section. That is, the test wants to know what you can validly infer. Imagine a citizen of Country X named John. Try to complete the following conditional sentences based on the voting rule above. Here's a hint: The correct inference may be something that must be true, something that must be false, or it may be "I don't know; there's not enough information to draw a conclusion from the rule."

If John is 15 years old, then _____.

If John is 35 years old, but not registered to vote, then _____.

If John is 20 years old and he is properly registered to vote, then _____.

If John can vote legally in Country X, then _____.

Check and see how you did.

The first sentence should read: "If John is 15 years old, then *he cannot legally vote in Country X.*" It doesn't matter whether he's registered. When you lack either of two necessary conditions, whatever is in the sufficient term cannot be true.

The second sentence should read: "If John is 35 years old, but not registered to vote, then *he cannot legally vote in Country X.*" Again, failure to meet either of the necessary terms is enough to know that John cannot cast his ballot legally.

The third sentence is the trickiest (and one that the test makers love to use). It should read: "If John is 20 years old and he is properly registered to vote, then *I don't know whether John can vote legally in Country X or not.*" Being above the minimum age and being properly registered to vote are requirements for legal voting, but they are not assurances of it. That is, they are necessary but not sufficient. Perhaps a past criminal conviction makes him ineligible to vote. Maybe he's been found mentally unfit to vote. Maybe in order to vote in Country X, you have to be registered with the military draft board and John isn't. Remember, there could be necessary conditions that haven't been stated in the rule. The test makers include many wrong answers that catch test takers who confuse necessity and sufficiency. The best you can do with the third sentence is to say that John fulfills two of the requirements for legal voting in Country X. He may be able to vote legally, but he also may not.

The fourth sentence should read: "If John can vote legally in Country X, then *he is at least 18 years old* and *he is legally registered to vote.*" This sentence begins by affirming the sufficient condition. Given that, you know unequivocally that both the necessary conditions must be true.

Now, try your hand at recognizing the sufficient and necessary terms in some actual LSAT rules.

DRILL: IDENTIFYING SUFFICIENT AND NECESSARY TERMS

For each of the following rules, determine which of the terms is sufficient and which necessary. Then complete the sentences that follow by jotting down what must be true or must be false, or by saying, "I don't know." (NOTE: All of these rules are taken from official, recently released LSAT exams. However, you should *not* combine rules in this exercise. Even if you notice that some of the rules come from the same game as each other, contain your analysis to one rule at a time.)

1.

If the keeshond is placed on Monday, the greyhound is placed on Tuesday.[3]

Sufficient: _____

Necessary: _____

    (a) If the greyhound is placed on Tuesday, then _____.

    (b) If the greyhound is placed on Wednesday, then

    _____

    (c) If the keeshond is placed on Tuesday, then

    _____.

    (d) If the keeshond is placed on Monday, then

    _____.

2.

Selma appears in every photograph that Umiko appears in.[4]

Sufficient: _____

Necessary: _____

    (a) If Umiko appears in the photograph, then

    _____

    (b) If Selma appears in the photograph, then

    _____.

    (c) If Umiko does not appear in the photograph, then _____.

    (d) If Selma does not appear in the photograph, then _____.

3.

Raimundo appears in every photograph that Yakira does not appear in.[5]

Sufficient: _____

Necessary: _____

    (a) If Raimundo does not appear in the photograph, then _____.

    (b) If Yakira appears in the photograph, then _____.

    (c) If Raimundo appears in the photograph, then

    _____.

    (d) If Yakira does not appear in the photograph, then _____.

4.

If Figueroa's delivery is earlier than Malpighi's, then Leacock's delivery is earlier than Harris's.[6]

Sufficient: _____

Necessary: _____

    (a) If Figueroa's delivery is earlier than Malpighi's, then _____.

    (b) If Figueroa's delivery is later than Malpighi's, then _____.

    (c) If Leacock's delivery is earlier than Harris's, then _____.

    (d) If Leacock's delivery is later than Harris's, then _____.

5.

If sociology is offered, then psychology is also offered but zoology is not.[7]

Sufficient: _____

Necessary: _____

    (a) If psychology is not offered, then _____.

    (b) If psychology is offered and zoology is offered, then

    _____.

    (c) If sociology is not offered, then _____.

    (d) If psychology is offered and zoology is not offered, then

    _____.

6.

A film in Greek is not shown unless a film in Italian is going to be shown the next day.[8]

Sufficient: _____

Necessary: _____

    (a) If a film in Greek is shown on day two, then _____.

    (b) If a film in Italian is shown on day three, then _____.

    (c) If a film in Italian is not shown on day five, then _____.

    (d) If a film in Greek is not shown on day two, then _____.

---

[3] PrepTest 44, Sec. 3, Game 2

[4] PrepTest 45, Sec. 3, Game 3

[5] PrepTest 45, Sec. 3, Game 3

---

[6] PrepTest 52, Sec. 2, Game 4

[7] PrepTest 49, Sec. 1, Game 3

[8] PrepTest 49, Sec. 1, Game 1

7.
If G is more expensive than H, then neither K nor L
is more expensive than J.[9]
[For this rule, assume that no entities are the same price.]
Sufficient: _____
Necessary: _____

    (a) If K is more expensive than J and L is less expensive than
        K, then _____.

    (b) If G is less expensive than H, then _____.

    (c) If both K and L are more expensive than J, then _____.

    (d) If H is less expensive than G, then _____.

8.
If Nation Y exports rice, then Nations X and Z both export tea.[10]
Sufficient: _____
Necessary: _____

    (a) If Nation X exports tea and Nation Z does not export tea,
        then _____.

    (b) If Nation Y does not export rice, then _____.

    (c) If Nation Y exports oranges, then _____.

    (d) If Nation X and Nation Y both export tea, then _____.

---

[9] PrepTest 51, Sec. 4, Game 2
[10] PrepTest 45, Sec. 3, Game 4

Explanations

1.

If the keeshond is placed on Monday, the greyhound is
placed on Tuesday.[11]
Sufficient: *The keeshond is placed on Monday.*
Necessary: *The greyhound is placed on Tuesday.*

(a) If the greyhound is placed on Tuesday, then *I don't know*.

The greyhound being placed on Tuesday is necessary, but not sufficient, for the keeshond to be placed on Monday. The best you can say here is that the keeshond *could* go on Monday, but you don't know that it will.

(b) If the greyhound is placed on Wednesday, then *the keeshond cannot be placed on Monday*.

The greyhound being placed on Tuesday is necessary for the keeshond to be placed on Monday. Once you know that the greyhound goes anywhere other than Tuesday, you can conclude that the keeshond goes on a day other than Monday.

(c) If the keeshond is placed on Tuesday, then *I don't know*.

When the keeshond is placed on Monday, you know that the greyhound is placed on Tuesday. When the keeshond goes on any other day, you cannot make any determination about the greyhound. The greyhound could be placed on any day, as far as this rule is concerned.

(d) If the keeshond is placed on Monday, then *the greyhound must be placed on Tuesday*.

This is just a restatement of the rule. The keeshond's being placed on Monday is sufficient to conclude that the greyhound is placed on Tuesday. The greyhound cannot be placed on any other day.

2.

Selma appears in every photograph that Umiko appears in.[12]
Sufficient: *Umiko appears in the photograph.*
Necessary: *Selma is in the photograph.*

(a) If Umiko appears in the photograph, then *Selma appears in the photograph*.

This rule wasn't written in "if-then" form, but the sufficient-necessary relationship is the same. Selma is required (necessary) to be in any photograph that Umiko appears in. In this sentence, Umiko is in the picture, so Selma must be, too.

(b) If Selma appears in the photograph, then *I don't know*.

The rule requires Selma to be included whenever Umiko is, but it doesn't preclude her from appearing solo. Knowing that Selma is in the photo tells you nothing about whether Umiko is in it. The best you can say is that Umiko *might* be in the photo, but she also might not.

(c) If Umiko does not appear in the photograph, then *I don't know*.

The rule requires Selma's appearance when Umiko *appears* in a photo. When Umiko *does not appear*, you can't make any deductions about Selma. The best you can say here is that Selma *might* appear in the photo.

(d) If Selma is not in the photograph, then *Umiko does not appear in the photograph*.

Since the rule requires Selma's appearance in any photo featuring Umiko, you know that Umiko cannot appear without Selma. Take away what's necessary, and you can't have the sufficient condition occur.

---

[11] PrepTest 44, Sec. 3, Game 2

[12] PrepTest 45, Sec. 3, Game 3

3.

Raimundo appears in every photograph that Yakira does
not appear in.[13]

Sufficient: *Either Yakira or Raimundo not appearing in the photograph*

Necessary: *The other person appearing in the photograph*

At first glance, it may seem that only Yakira's not appearing is a sufficient term, but think about it for a moment. If Raimundo is in *every* photo in which Yakira doesn't appear, it must be true that Yakira is in *every* photo in which Raimundo does not appear. If she weren't there, he'd have to be. You can simplify this rule like so: "At least one of Yakira and Raimundo appears in every photograph."

(a) If Raimundo does not appear in the photograph, then *Yakira appears in the photograph*.

Since the rule tells you that Raimundo is always included when Yakira is not, it's impossible for both of them to be missing from the same photo. Since this sentence begins by excluding Raimundo from the photo, you can conclude that Yakira is included.

(b) If Yakira appears in a photograph, then *I don't know*.

The rule tells you that Raimundo must be included when Yakira *does not* appear, but it says nothing about what happens when Yakira *does* appear. A rule like this one tells you that *at least one* of the two is in every picture; it does not preclude any photo from featuring both of them.

(c) If Raimundo appears in a photograph, then *I don't know*.

Just as you saw in the previous sentence, *including* one of the two friends tells you nothing about the other. If Raimundo were left out of the picture, you'd know that Yakira must be in. Since this sentence begins by including Raimundo, you can only say that Yakira may or may not be in the picture.

(d) If Yakira does not appear in a photograph, then *Raimundo appears in the photograph*.

This is really just a restatement of the original rule. Since Raimundo appears whenever Yakira doesn't, and this sentence begins by telling you that Yakira is left out of the photo, you can conclude that Raimundo is in the photo.

4.

If Figueroa's delivery is earlier than Malpighi's, then
Leacock's delivery is earlier than Harris's.[14]

Sufficient: *Figueroa's delivery is before Malpighi's* (or *Malpighi's delivery is after Figueroa's*).

Necessary: *Leacock's delivery is before Harris's* (or *Harris's delivery is after Leacock's*).

(a) If Figueroa's delivery is earlier than Malpighi's, then *Leacock's delivery is earlier than Harris's*.

This is just a restatement of the rule. Knowing that Figueroa gets a delivery before Malpighi is sufficient to ensure that Leacock gets a delivery before Harris.

(b) If Figueroa's delivery is later than Malpighi's, then *I don't know*.

According to the rule, you know what happens when Figueroa receives a delivery before Malpighi, but not what happens when Malpighi gets a delivery earlier than Figueroa. In this case, Leacock's delivery might still come before Harris's, but Harris's might come before Leacock's. That wouldn't violate the rule, since the rule is only triggered when Figueroa gets a delivery earlier than Malpighi.

(c) If Leacock's delivery is earlier than Harris's, then *I don't know*.

Leacock getting a delivery before Harris is necessary for Figueroa to get one before Malpighi, but it is not sufficient to know that Figueroa gets a delivery before Malpighi. All you can safely say here is that Figueroa *might* get a delivery before Malpighi. Whether that happens or not, the rule is satisfied.

(d) If Leacock's delivery is later than Harris's, then *Malpighi's delivery is earlier than Figueroa's*.

According to the rule, *whenever* Figueroa gets delivery before Malpighi, Leacock gets one before Harris. Since this sentence begins by telling you that Harris gets a delivery prior to Leacock, you know that this cannot be a case in which Figueroa gets a delivery before Malpighi. Malpighi must, in this case, get a delivery prior to Figueroa and not the other way around.

---

[13] PrepTest 45, Sec. 3, Game 3

[14] PrepTest 52, Sec. 2, Game 4

5.

If sociology is offered, then psychology is also offered
but zoology is not.[15]

Sufficient: *Sociology is offered.*

Necessary: *Psychology is offered and zoology is not offered.*

    (a) If psychology is not offered, then *sociology is not offered.*

       According to the rule, two things are necessary in order for sociology to be offered: Psychology must be offered and zoology must not be. Since this sentence begins by taking away one of the things that's necessary in order for sociology to be offered, you can be certain that sociology is off of the schedule. This sentence doesn't allow you to draw any conclusions at all about zoology. It may or may not be offered in this case.

    (b) If psychology is offered and zoology is offered, then *sociology is not offered.*

       Be careful with statements like this one. One of the requirements for sociology to be offered—that psychology is offered—has been met. But the other requirement (the other necessary term)—that zoology is off of the schedule—has been negated. Since zoology is being offered, you can conclude that sociology is not, regardless of what's true about psychology.

    (c) If sociology is not offered, then *I don't know.*

       "Sociology is offered" is the sufficient term. Negating it doesn't tell you anything about psychology or zoology. Psychology "in" and zoology "out" are required when sociology is offered, but this sentence begins by telling you that sociology is not offered. Thus, you have no way of making any valid deductions about whether psychology or zoology are offered or not.

    (d) If psychology is offered and zoology is not offered, then *I don't know.*

       The two terms that begin this sentence—offering psychology and not offering zoology—are necessary, but not sufficient, for sociology to be offered. So knowing that they are both true means that sociology could be offered but not that it must be.

6.

A film in Greek is not shown unless a film in Italian
is going to be shown the next day.[16]

Sufficient: *A film in Greek is shown on day X.*

Necessary: *A film in Italian is shown on day X + 1.*

    (a) If a film in Greek is shown on day two, then *a film in Italian is shown on day three.*

       A film in Greek being shown is the sufficient term. It's all you need in order to be certain that a film in Italian is being shown the next day.

    (b) If a film in Italian is shown on day three, then *I don't know.*

       Showing an Italian film is necessary for the Greek film to be shown a day earlier. But showing the Italian film is not sufficient to establish anything about when the Greek film is shown. The best you can do with this sentence is to say, "A film in Greek may be shown on day two, but a film from another country might be shown instead."

    (c) If a film in Italian is not shown on day five, then *a film in Greek is not shown on day four.*

       Remember, an Italian film the next day is necessary for a Greek film to be shown. So knowing that Italian is ruled out on day five ensures that Greek is ruled out on day four.

    (d) If a film in Greek is not shown on day two, then *I don't know.*

       Showing a Greek film is sufficient to determine what's shown the following day. However, saying that a Greek film is not shown doesn't tell you anything about whether an Italian film is shown the next day. The rule doesn't limit Italian films to following only Greek films, after all.

---

[15] PrepTest 49, Sec. 1, Game 3

[16] PrepTest 49, Sec. 1, Game 1

7.

If G is more expensive than H, then neither K nor L
is more expensive than J.[17]
[For this rule, assume that no entities are the same price.]

Sufficient: *G is more expensive than H (or H is less expensive than G).*
Necessary: *J is more expensive than both K and L (or Both K and L are less expensive than J).*

    (a) If K is more expensive than J and L is less expensive than J, then *G is less expensive than H.*
        In order for G to be more expensive than H, both K and L must be priced less than J. Since this sentence has K priced higher than J, it must be the case that G is less expensive than H. Remember, when two things are necessary, losing either one or both of them means that the sufficient term cannot be true.

    (b) If G is less expensive than H, then *I don't know.*
        The part of the rule relating K and L to J is triggered when G is more expensive than H. Since, in this case, it's less expensive, you cannot draw any valid inferences about the relationship among K, L, and J. Negating the sufficient term tells you nothing about the necessary one(s).

    (c) If both K and L are more expensive than J, then *G is less expensive than H.*
        In order for G to be more expensive than H, the rule requires that K and L both be less expensive than J. Here, the necessary terms are negated, so the sufficient term must be, too.

    (d) If H is less expensive than G, then *both K and L must be less expensive than J.*
        Be careful with simple changes in wording that leave the meaning of a rule intact. The rule is triggered by the sufficient term—G is more expensive than H. This sentence posits that H is less expensive than G. That's just another way of saying the sufficient term in the original rule. Thus, both necessary terms—K is less expensive than J and L is less expensive than J—must be true.

8.

If Nation Y exports rice, then Nations X and Z both
export tea.[18]

Sufficient: *Nation Y exports rice.*
Necessary: *Nations X and Z both export tea.*

    (a) If Nation X exports tea and Nation Z does not export tea, then *Nation Y does not export rice.*
        Here, the necessary condition is violated, so the sufficient term cannot be true. In order for Nation Y to export tea, both Nations X and Z must export tea. This sentence, however, has Nation Z not exporting rice. You can, therefore, conclude that Nation Y does not export rice in this case.

    (b) If Nation Y does not export rice, then *I don't know.*
        When Nation Y exports rice, you can validly infer that Nations X and Z export tea. When Nation Y doesn't export rice, you know nothing about the other two countries. Negating the sufficient term always leaves the necessary terms up in the air.

    (c) If Nation Y exports oranges, then *I don't know.*
        This sentence introduces a term that isn't even included in the original rule. Indeed, knowing that Nation Y exports oranges tells you nothing about whether it exports rice, so you cannot determine whether the necessary term has or has not been negated. If you assumed that a nation could only export one crop, check yourself. You would need another rule or restriction to make that determination. As it turns out, this game actually has nations exporting two crops apiece.

    (d) If Nation X and Nation Y both export tea, then *I don't know.*
        This sentence fulfills half of the necessary condition. So it may be that Nation Y exports rice, but there's no way to say for sure from the information here. Having Nation Y export tea is completely outside the scope of the rule, so it adds nothing helpful.

---

[17] PrepTest 51, Sec. 4, Game 2
[18] PrepTest 45, Sec. 3, Game 4

Sufficient and Necessary Terms Help Unlock Formal Logic

You can see from that drill that the test makers present conditional "if-then" rules in a variety of ways. Learning to recognize the sufficient-necessary relationship whenever it appears and however it's worded is actually the heavy-lifting part of dealing with formal logic. What follows will help you organize and keep track of these rules on the pages of your test booklet. It provides a very useful shorthand notation system and shows you how to spot all of the additional deductions that come from combining formal logic rules. But remember, this work will be for naught if you've mistaken the sufficient and necessary terms or failed to appreciate what they tell you must, can, and cannot be true within the logic game.

TRANSLATE FORMAL LOGIC: SYMBOLIZE AND ABBREVIATE

As you've seen already, formal logic statements can be wordy. That's why translating them into a simple "if-then" shorthand is so helpful on test day. This is one place in which the test makers are quite helpful. Since they always create lists of entities that can be shortened into one- or two-letter abbreviations, your symbolic representations of formal logic rules can be clear and compact.

Common Examples

The most straightforward examples occur when the rule is written in "if-then" terms from the start.

> If the stand carries kiwis, then it does not carry pears.[19]

You don't need to "translate" the language of this rule in order to identify the sufficient-necessary relationship. The sufficient term—"carries kiwis"—is in the "if" clause, and the necessary term—"not carry pears"—follows "then." To write this in symbols, simply jot it down like this:

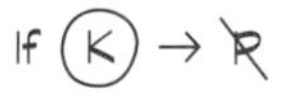

$$\text{If } \textcircled{K} \rightarrow \cancel{R}$$

Figure 3.7

The arrow stands in place of "then," indicating that what precedes it is sufficient and what follows it is necessary. The strike-through indicates negation; the stand does *not* carry pears. As always, I'll encourage you to use the symbols that are clearest and easiest for you. So if you prefer to use a tilde (~) or the word "NOT" to indicate negation, feel free.

---

[19] PrepTest 36, Sec. 4, Game 1

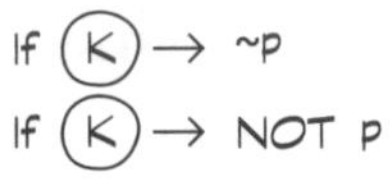

$$\text{If } (K) \rightarrow \text{~p}$$
$$\text{If } (K) \rightarrow \text{NOT } p$$

Figure 3.8

Just make sure that by test day you've settled on a single, consistent symbol set that makes every rule crystal clear for you.

Students sometimes hesitate to symbolize formal logic rules as they become more complex or when they move away from the standard "if-then" grammar. Don't fall into that trap. When the test makers choose to phrase formal logic differently, simply apply what you've already learned in this section. Once you've identified the statement as formal logic, distinguish the sufficient term(s) from the necessary term(s). Then symbolize the logic as you would with a straightforward "if-then." Take this rule from the Friends' Photographs game, for instance:

> Selma appears in every photograph that Umiko appears in.[20]

Since Selma is required (necessary) in every photo that has Umiko, Selma's appearance is the necessary term and Umiko's the sufficient term. The rule is thus symbolized as:

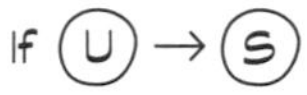

$$\text{If } (U) \rightarrow (S)$$

Figure 3.9

Twists on Common Examples

Here are a few more common twists that you should learn to symbolize.

When the rule involves both an entity and a particular location or characteristic, use a subscript for the secondary characteristic. For example, you can depict this rule

> If the keeshond is placed on Monday, the greyhound is
> placed on Tuesday.[21]

neatly like this:

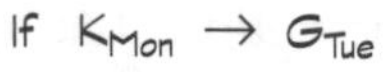

$$\text{If } K_{Mon} \rightarrow G_{Tue}$$

Figure 3.10

The subscript Mon and Tue are clear. If you want to reflect the layout of your framework, something along these lines works just as well:

---

[20] PrepTest 45, Sec. 3, Game 3
[21] PrepTest 44, Sec. 3, Game 2

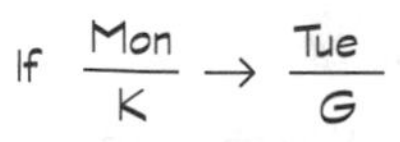

$$\text{If} \quad \frac{\text{Mon}}{K} \rightarrow \frac{\text{Tue}}{G}$$

Figure 3.11

When a formal logic rule contains two terms in either the sufficient clause or the necessary clause, determine whether the rule is requiring both terms (X *and* Y) or at least one of the terms (X *or* Y) and use the appropriate conjunction—"and" or "or"—between the two terms in your symbolism of the rule. Look at this rule:

> If sociology is offered, then psychology is also offered
> but zoology is not.[22]

The inclusion of sociology requires both the inclusion of psychology and the exclusion of zoology. Thus, your scratch work would look like this:

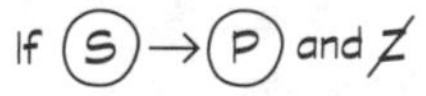

$$\text{If} \quad \textcircled{S} \rightarrow \textcircled{P} \text{ and } \cancel{Z}$$

Figure 3.12

Occasionally, a rule will call on you to translate the language and to use creative symbolism. This is especially true in Sequencing games where you need to represent the entities' relative positions. Consider this rule:

> A film in Greek is not shown unless a film in Italian
> is going to be shown the next day.[23]

Now, identify the sufficient and necessary terms, and use your Sequencing scratch work to illustrate the relevant restriction within the game.

$$\text{If} \quad G \rightarrow \boxed{\begin{array}{c|c} G & I \end{array}}$$

Figure 3.13

There are no right or wrong ways for formal logic symbolism to *look*, although there are, of course, right and wrong arrangements for the sufficient and necessary terms. And there are helpful and unhelpful depictions of all rules on the test. Use the following Drill to jump-start your practice with symbolizing formal logic. Use the explanations that follow to check your work. If you misplace or make mistakes with any of the sufficient or necessary terms, go back and review the rule to avoid making similar mistakes in the future.

---

[22] PrepTest 49, Sec. 1, Game 3
[23] PrepTest 49, Sec. 1, Game 1

DRILL: SYMBOLIZING RULES

For each of the following rules, first identify the sufficient and necessary terms. Then, symbolize the rule using the previously outlined principles.

1.
If Traugott signs with Star Agency, West also signs with
Star Agency.[24]
Sufficient: _____
Necessary: _____
Symbolism: _____

2.
None of the nations exports both wheat and oranges.[25]
Sufficient: _____
Necessary: _____
Symbolism: _____

3.
If the stand carries watermelons, then it carries figs or
tangerines or both.[26]
Sufficient: _____
Necessary: _____
Symbolism: _____

4.
If geography is offered, then both history and
zoology are also offered.[27]
Sufficient: _____
Necessary: _____
Symbolism: _____

5.
If a site dates from the eighth century, it was discovered
by Oliphant.[28]
Sufficient: _____
Necessary: _____
Symbolism: _____

---

[24] PrepTest 53, Sec. 2, Game 1

[25] PrepTest 45, Sec. 3, Game 4

[26] PrepTest 36, Sec. 4, Game 1

[27] PrepTest 49, Sec. 1, Game 3

[28] PrepTest 44, Sec. 3, Game 3

Answer Explanations follow on the next page.

Explanations

1.

If Traugott signs with Star Agency, West also signs with
Star Agency.[29]
    Sufficient: *Traugott signs with Star.*
    Necessary: *West signs with Star.*
    Symbolism:

$$\text{If}\quad T_S \rightarrow W_S$$

Figure 3.14

The rule is in standard "if-then" format. Use subscript to designate the specific agency (Star) that triggers this rule. Make sure not to misinterpret this rule; it does not mean that Traugott and West must always sign with the same agency as each other.

2.

None of the nations exports both wheat and oranges.[30]
    Sufficient: *A nation exporting either wheat or oranges*
    Necessary: *The nation not exporting the other crop*
    Symbolism:

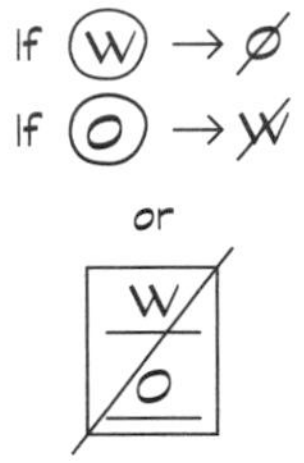

Figure 3.15

It doesn't matter which of the crops you use as your trigger. In fact, in the next section you'll learn that the two "if-then" statements are one another's contrapositives. Of course, the simplest visual depiction of the rule is just to strike through or negate the WO pair.

3.

If the stand carries watermelons, then it carries figs or
tangerines or both.[31]
    Sufficient: *Carries watermelons*
    Necessary: *Carries figs or tangerines*
    Symbolism:

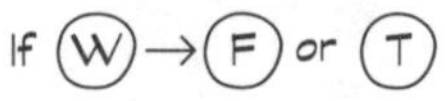

Figure 3.16

---

[29] PrepTest 53, Sec. 2, Game 1

[30] PrepTest 45, Sec. 3, Game 4

[31] PrepTest 36, Sec. 4, Game 1

There are two terms in the necessary statement this time. The rule requires only one of them to happen, however. You need to use the word "or" between the terms in the "then" clause. It's worth noting that the "or both" on the end is superfluous. In order to carry watermelons, the stand must carry either figs or tangerines. If it has both, then it has clearly met the requirement. So there's no need to add that to your symbolism.

4.

If geography is offered, then both history and
zoology are also offered.[32]
   Sufficient: *Geography is offered.*
   Necessary: *History is offered* and *zoology is offered.*
   Symbolism:

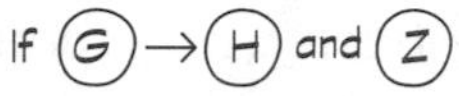

$$\text{If } \textcircled{G} \rightarrow \textcircled{H} \text{ and } \textcircled{Z}$$

Figure 3.17

This time, both of the terms in the "then" clause are necessary for the sufficient condition. Therefore, use "and" to link H and Z in your symbolism. Knowing that geography is offered is sufficient to show that both history and zoology are also on the schedule.

5.

If a site dates from the eighth century, it was discovered
by Oliphant.[33]
   Sufficient: *The site dates from the eighth century.*
   Necessary: *The site was discovered by Oliphant.*
   Symbolism:

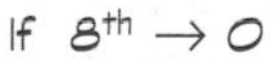

$$\text{If } 8^{th} \rightarrow O$$

Figure 3.18

This rule is in the standard "if-then" formal logic format. The only thing that might have given you pause is that it restricts a match rather than a selection or sequence. Don't let that concern you. The sufficient-necessary relationship is still the same. If you've organized the Matching action in your sketch with slots for the age of the site and its discoverer, you could also symbolize the rule like so:

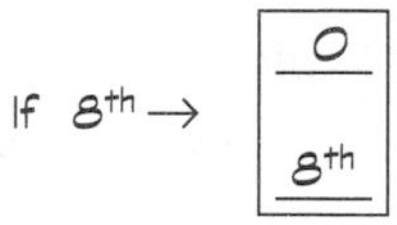

$$\text{If } 8^{th} \rightarrow \boxed{\begin{array}{c} O \\ \hline 8^{th} \end{array}}$$

Figure 3.19

---

[32] PrepTest 49, Sec. 1, Game 3
[33] PrepTest 44, Sec. 3, Game 3

Translate and Symbolize for Success on Test Day

Once you've mastered these first two techniques—identifying sufficiency and necessity and translating formal logic rules into symbols—you'll be ready to use any formal logic rule that you encounter on the test. Next, you'll see how to double your advantage by determining the contrapositives of formal logic rules and adding them to your scratch work.

DETERMINE THE CONTRAPOSITIVE: REVERSE AND NEGATE
Simple "If-Thens"

The contrapositive is one of those confusing-sounding aspects of formal logic that's actually quite straightforward. In fact, you've been using contrapositives already in this section. A contrapositive is the logical equivalent of any conditional formal logic statement, with the key (sufficient and necessary) terms reversed and negated. Here's how it works.

Say you want to go to a club to see a concert. At the door of the concert hall, a bouncer greets you with a rule in formal logic: "You cannot enter the club unless I see your ID." Since you're an LSAT test taker, you identify the statement as formal logic and distinguish the sufficient condition—"enter the club"—from the necessary one—"show ID." Knowing that the necessary condition follows the arrow, you translate the statement into symbols.

If   enter club   →   Show ID

Figure 3.20

Maybe the bouncer grows impatient with you as you're working this out and says, "Do you know what happens if you don't show me your ID?" Of course you do. Failure to show your ID negates the necessity clause of the rule, which means that you cannot have the sufficient condition. You answer, "If I do not show my ID, I cannot enter the club," and show the bouncer your new scratch work.

If   NOT show ID   →   NOT enter club

Figure 3.21

That's the contrapositive of the original rule. Actually, it is better to say that the two statements are contrapositives of one another. It doesn't matter whether you start with the terms expressed affirmatively or negatively. For any formal logic statement, reversing and negating the key terms forms the contrapositive. Both ways of expressing the rule are valid restrictions within the logic game.

Try it with another example from earlier in the chapter. Identify the sufficient and necessary terms in the following statement. Translate it into symbols. Then reverse and negate the terms to form the contrapositive.

The car will run only if it has gasoline.
Sufficient: _____
Necessary: _____
Translation: _____
Contrapositive: _____

What did you come up with? Check your work against the following:
The car will run only if it has gasoline.
Sufficient: *Car runs*
Necessary: *Car has gasoline*
Translation:

$$\text{If} \quad C_{runs} \quad \rightarrow \quad C_{gas}$$

Figure 3.22

Contrapositive:

$$\text{If} \quad \cancel{C_{gas}} \quad \rightarrow \quad \cancel{C_{runs}}$$

Figure 3.22A

If you translated the rule into negative terms first and then wrote the contrapositive in the affirmative, no problem. Remember, both expressions are just different ways of writing the same rule.

Before I go on, here's an important warning: Never ever reverse without negating or negate without reversing. Doing so confuses the sufficient and necessary terms in the rule and will lead straight to wrong answers. Showing your ID may not be enough to get you into the concert. A car can have gasoline and still not run. The logic is just as flawed when you make these mistakes with logic game's rules. Try it out with this one. Translate it and then reverse and negate to form the contrapositive.

If Traugott signs with Star Agency, West also signs with
Star Agency.[34]
Translation: _____
Contrapositive: _____
Translation:

$$\text{If} \quad T_S \quad \rightarrow \quad W_S$$

Figure 3.23

Contrapositive:

$$\text{If} \quad \cancel{W_S} \quad \rightarrow \quad \cancel{T_S}$$

Figure 3.24

Notice what the rule, expressed in contrapositives, tells you and what it doesn't. Whenever Traugott signs with Star, West must also sign with Star. When West does not sign with Star,

---

[34] PrepTest 53, Sec. 2, Game 1

neither does Traugott. But be careful. Knowing that Traugott signs with an agency other than Star tells you nothing about West. Likewise, learning that West signs with Star doesn't allow for any valid inferences about Traugott. The first of these incorrect translations negates without reversing. The second reverses without negating. Rest assured that the test makers will design wrong answers to catch students who cannot correctly interpret and contrapose the rule.

Complex "If-Thens": Change "And" to "Or"

When either of the clauses in a formal logic rule has more than one term linked with either "and" or "or," you must complete one more step in making the contrapositive. To see how it works, consider the following example.

> If a painting is by Monet, then it is by a famous artist *and* it is by a French artist.

If you like, you can symbolize that statement this way:

$$\text{If} \quad \text{Monet} \quad \rightarrow \quad A_{famous} \text{ and } A_{French}$$

Figure 3.25

Now, imagine that your friend shows you a painting. You ask, "Who painted it?" Your friend answers, "I don't know the artist's name, but I know that he was relatively unknown." What can you infer? Right. The painting isn't by Monet.

$$\text{If} \quad \cancel{A}_{famous} \quad \rightarrow \quad \cancel{Monet}$$

Figure 3.26

Rewind. This time, when you ask your friend who painted the picture, she says, "I don't know the artist's name, but I know he was Italian." Again, you can safely conclude that you're not looking at a Monet.

$$\text{If} \quad \cancel{A}_{French} \quad \rightarrow \quad \cancel{Monet}$$

Figure 3.27

Now, put those two inferences together and compare them to the original statement.

$$\text{If} \quad \cancel{A}_{famous} \text{ or } \cancel{A}_{French} \quad \rightarrow \quad \cancel{Monet}$$

Figure 3.28

Here, the contrapositives are formed by reversing and negating the terms and by changing "and" to "or." It works just as well the other way around. Here's a rule in which the sufficient clause has two terms:

If you're male and you have children, then you are a father.
Take a moment to write the rule and its contrapositive in formal logic symbols.
    Translations: _____
    Contrapositive: _____
Here's how it should look:

If   male and children   →   ~~father~~

If   ~~father~~   →   m~~a~~le or chil~~d~~ren

Figure 3.29

Notice that the "and" must change to "or" in order to make the contrapositive valid. You could have children, but if you're female, you're not a father. Likewise, you may be male, but if you have no children, you're not a father. In short, if you're not a father, at least one of the terms in the sufficient clause of the original rule must be negated.

Now, apply this procedure to a rule from an LSAT logic game. Translate the rule into symbols and form its contrapositive.

If geography is offered, then both history and
zoology are also offered.[35]
    Translations: _____
    Contrapositive: _____

How did you do? Compare your work to the correct contrapositives.

If (G) → (H) and (Z)

If ~~H~~ or ~~Z~~ → ~~G~~

Figure 3.30

Having the "or" in a contrapositive is important because a question might read, "If zoology is not offered, which one of the following must be true?" The "or" tells you that excluding zoology is enough, by itself, to infer that you must exclude geography.

Form the Contrapositive in Two Steps

That's the sum total of what you need to know to form the correct contrapositives of any formal logic rule you will encounter on the LSAT.

TO FORM THE CONTRAPOSITIVE . . .

1. Reverse and negate the sufficient and necessary terms.

2. If needed, change "and" to "or," or vice versa.

---

[35] PrepTest 49, Sec. 1, Game 3

Contrapositives in Sequencing Rules

Most formal logic rules in Selection, Distribution, and Matching games are pretty straightforward once you get the hang of translating and forming contrapositives. Even the complex rules in these games use all of the familiar terms.

> If the stand carries oranges, then it carries both pears and watermelons.[36]

Your symbolization of the translation and contrapositive follows exactly the steps you've just seen.

If (O) → (P) and (W)

If P̶ or W̶ → O̶

Figure 3.31

Everything in these statements is *by the numbers*: reverse, negate, change "and" to "or."

Formal logic Sequencing rules can throw students for a loop at first because they often have multiple terms but lack the standard "and/or" conjunctions. Instead, the sufficient and necessary terms show the relative order of two entities. Here's an example:

> If Figueroa's delivery is earlier than Malpighi's, then Leacock's delivery is earlier than Harris's.[37]

(For the purposes of this rule, assume that none of the deliveries occur at the same time.)

You should symbolize the rule this way:

$$\text{If } \begin{matrix} F \\ | \\ M \end{matrix} \rightarrow \begin{matrix} L \\ | \\ H \end{matrix} \quad \text{or} \quad \text{If } F...M \rightarrow L...H$$

Figure 3.32

To form the contrapositive, do what you would with any formal logic statement: reverse and negate the terms. Here, since no two deliveries occur simultaneously, the negation of "Leacock's delivery is earlier than Harris's" is "Harris's delivery is earlier than Leacock's." Likewise, the negation of "Figueroa's delivery is earlier than Malpighi's" is "Malpighi's delivery is earlier than Figueroa's." Thus, you can symbolize the contrapositive like this:

$$\text{If } \begin{matrix} H \\ | \\ L \end{matrix} \rightarrow \begin{matrix} M \\ | \\ F \end{matrix} \quad \text{or} \quad \text{If } H...L \rightarrow M...F$$

Figure 3.33

---

[36] PrepTest 36, Sec. 4, Game 1
[37] PrepTest 52, Sec. 2, Game 4

When you depict the game's action or framework within your scratch work for the rule, use it in forming the contrapositive as well. As always, the most important thing is for your symbols to be clear and helpful to you. No one else will see your test-day scratch work; they'll only see how many correct answers you produce.

"If, but Only If": A Special Case

One variant that has appeared very rarely on the LSAT is the so-called "bi-conditional" statement, in which two terms are linked by "if, and only if" or "if, but only if." Here's a recent example:

> Nation X exports soybeans if, but only if, Nation Y does also.[38]

This rule contains not just one, but two conditional, formal logic statements. The phrase "if, but only if" designates Nation Y's exporting soybeans as both sufficient ("if") and necessary ("only if") for Nation X to export them. There are two ways you can add this rule into your scratch work. You could write out the two formal logic rules and their contrapositives:

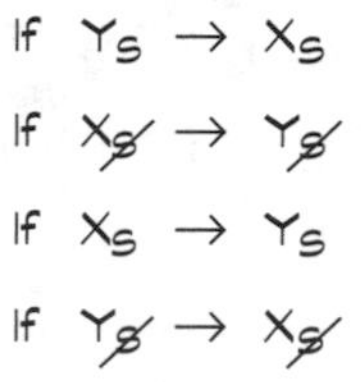

$$\text{If } Y_S \rightarrow X_S$$
$$\text{If } X_{\cancel{S}} \rightarrow Y_{\cancel{S}}$$
$$\text{If } X_S \rightarrow Y_S$$
$$\text{If } Y_{\cancel{S}} \rightarrow X_{\cancel{S}}$$

Figure 3.34

Or you could summarize the impact of the rule:

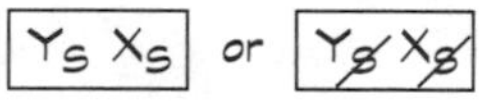

$$\boxed{Y_S\ X_S}\ \ or\ \ \boxed{Y_{\cancel{S}}\ X_{\cancel{S}}}$$

Figure 3.35

In every acceptable arrangement in this game, either both X and Y will export soybeans or neither of them will. In the unlikely event that you encounter a biconditional statement on test day, keep in mind that "if" signals sufficiency while "only if" signals necessity, and you'll interpret the rule correctly. Regardless of the context, the rule you see will function exactly as the one you've just seen.

Continue your practice with translating formal logic and forming the contrapositives of each of the rules in the following Drill.

---

[38] PrepTest 45, Sec. 3, Game 4

DRILL: WRITING CONTRAPOSITIVES

First, translate each of the following rules into formal logic symbols. Then, determine and write the rule's contrapositive.

1.
If the stand carries kiwis, then it does not carry pears.[39]
　　Translation: _____
　　Contrapositive: _____

2.
Onawa is at Souderton if Juarez is at Randsborough.[40]
　　Translation: _____
　　Contrapositive: _____

3.
A film in Italian is not shown unless a film in
Norwegian is going to be shown the next day.[41]
　　Translation: _____
　　Contrapositive: _____

4.
If the schnauzer is placed on Wednesday, the husky is
placed on Tuesday.[42]
　　Translation: _____
　　Contrapositive: _____

5.
If Nation Y exports rice, then Nations X and Z both
export tea.[43]
　　Translation: _____
　　Contrapositive: _____

---

[39] PrepTest 36, Sec. 4, Game 1

[40] PrepTest 34, Sec. 4, Game 4

[41] PrepTest 49, Sec. 1, Game 1

[42] PrepTest 44, Sec. 3, Game 2

[43] PrepTest 45, Sec. 3, Game 4

Answer Explanations follow on the next page.

Explanations

As you review these explanations, don't worry if your "translation" matches the given contrapositive, and vice versa. As long as the two statements you've written match the two suggested symbolizations, you've done the right work. Remember, the two statements are simply contrapositives of one another.

1.

If the stand carries kiwis, then it does not carry pears.[44]
  Translation:

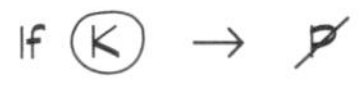

If (K) → P̸

Figure 3.36

Contrapositive:

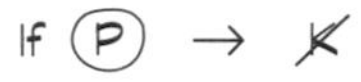

If (P) → K̸

Figure 3.37

This is a common rule to see in Selection, Distribution, and Matching games. Essentially, it just tells you that the two entities must be kept apart. While it's important to understand the translation and its contrapositive, on test day, you'll likely want to symbolize this rule more simply:

Figure 3.38

2.

Onawa is at Souderton if Juarez is at Randsborough.[45]
  Translation:

If J_R → O_S

Figure 3.39

Contrapositive:

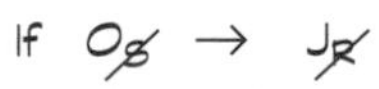

If $O_S̸$ → $J_R̸$

Figure 3.40

This is another fairly straightforward "if-then." One thing to be careful of here is the fact that the "if" clause (the sufficient condition) follows the "then" (necessary) clause in the sentence. Also note that if there are only two groups into which you can place the entities (in this game, everyone has to be assigned to only one clinic, either Souderton or Randsborough), you can also symbolize the rule this way:

---

[44] PrepTest 36, Sec. 4, Game 1
[45] PrepTest 34, Sec. 4, Game 4

$$\text{If } O_R \rightarrow J_S$$

Figure 3.41

This is possible because, with only two possible placements, *not* being placed in Souderton is the same thing as being placed at Randsborough, and vice versa. Use discretion, though, because this would not work in a case where more than two placements are possible or where not every entity had to be used.

3.

A film in Italian is not shown unless a film in
Norwegian is going to be shown the next day.[46]
    Translation:

Figure 3.42

Contrapositive:

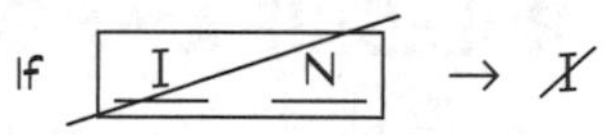

$$\text{If } \boxed{\cancel{\text{I} \quad \text{N}}} \rightarrow \cancel{I}$$

Figure 3.43

This rule provides a golden opportunity to exploit the framework of your sketch. The more that your scratch work allows you to "see" which arrangements follow the rules and which ones break them, the faster you'll be able to eliminate wrong answers and zero in on the correct choice.

4.

If the schnauzer is placed on Wednesday, the husky is
placed on Tuesday.[47]
    Translation:

$$\text{If } S_{Wed} \rightarrow H_{Tue}$$

Figure 3.44

Contrapositive:

$$\text{If } H_{\cancel{Tue}} \rightarrow S_{\cancel{Wed}}$$

Figure 3.45

This is a rule that requires you to account not only for the entity, but also for the day. In this game, by the way, there were more than two days on which each dog could be placed, so the alternative symbolism suggested for the previous rule would not work here.

---

[46] PrepTest 49, Sec. 1, Game 1
[47] PrepTest 44, Sec. 3, Game 2

5.

If Nation Y exports rice, then Nations X and Z both export tea.[48]

Translation:

$$\text{If } \quad Y_r \quad \rightarrow \quad X_t \text{ and } Z_t$$

Figure 3.46

Contrapositive:

$$\text{If } \quad X_{\cancel{t}} \text{ or } Z_{\cancel{t}} \quad \rightarrow \quad Y_{\cancel{r}}$$

Figure 3.47

This is your run-of-the-mill, complex "if-then," meaning simply that it restricts three entities. Provided that you correctly swap the "and" in the necessary clause for an "or" in the sufficient clause of the contrapositive, this one should pose no special problems.

COMBINE FORMAL LOGIC RULES: IF A ➜ B + IF B ➜ C = IF A ➜ C

There's just one more thing that you need to learn to do with formal logic to have complete mastery of the topic on test day. In this section, I'll teach you how to combine formal logic rules in order to achieve even greater certainty about the acceptable arrangements or selections. This will be your first foray into the Deductions step of the Kaplan Method, and it makes a perfect springboard for the next chapter. As you'll soon see, for some LSAT logic games, combinations of the formal logic rules are the only deductions you need to make in order to get all of the questions right.

Create Strings of Logic

Somewhere along the line, you've probably seen someone reason by means of a syllogism. They used two (or more) premises that shared a common term to reach a valid deduction. Here are a couple of examples:

> Socrates is human.
> All humans are mortal.
> Therefore, Socrates is mortal.

> All dogs are mammals.
> All mammals are warm-blooded.
> Therefore, dogs are warm-blooded.

---

[48] PrepTest 45, Sec. 3, Game 4

Those logical deductions probably sound familiar (at least in the form they take). What you may not have realized is that they're created by linking two conditional "if-then" formal logic statements in order to draw a valid inference. Look at the two syllogisms again, this time symbolized as formal logic.

$$\text{If } S \rightarrow h$$
$$\text{If } h \rightarrow M$$
$$\text{Thus, If } S \rightarrow M$$

$$\text{If } d \rightarrow M$$
$$\text{If } M \rightarrow Wb$$
$$\text{Thus, If } d \rightarrow Wb$$

Figure 3.48

Notice that, in each case, the two premises can be combined because the necessary ("then") clause of the first contains precisely the same term as the sufficient ("if") clause of the second.

This is another reason why your ability to correctly form the contrapositive of formal logic rules is so valuable. Imagine that you have two rules for assigning students to various Physical Education activities:

1. If Dave plays soccer, then Carl must play soccer.
2. If Evelyn plays basketball, then Carl cannot play soccer.

Carl is duplicated in both rules, but it may not be immediately apparent how the rules can be combined. One of them has a condition sufficient to demonstrate that Carl plays soccer, while the other has a condition sufficient to prevent his playing soccer. But take a moment to translate the rules and form their contrapositives, and it will become clear.

$$1. \text{ If } D_s \rightarrow C_s$$
$$\text{If } C_{\not{s}} \rightarrow D_{\not{s}}$$
$$2. \text{If } E_b \rightarrow C_{\not{s}}$$
$$\text{If } C_s \rightarrow E_{\not{b}}$$

Figure 3.49

The translation of Rule 1 combines perfectly with the contrapositive of Rule 2. By combining the two, you can infer that whenever Dave plays soccer, Evelyn does not play basketball. Moreover, the translation of Rule 2 combines with the contrapositive of Rule 1. When Evelyn plays basketball, Carl cannot play soccer. And when Carl doesn't play soccer, Dave can't either. Thus, you have an additional, valid restriction available to limit the acceptable assignments of students to teams: Whenever Evelyn plays basketball, Dave cannot play soccer.

Students often ask whether they should take the time to write out all of the combinations and connections they spot among formal logic rules before they tackle the questions on test day. I'd recommend against it, provided that you make a clear, easy-to-reference list of the formal logic rules and their contrapositives as I have done. With a list like that one, you can quickly spot any "then" results that trigger other "if" clauses. From there, you'll be able to assemble the strings of logic: "When A is chosen, so is B. And if B is chosen, D is ruled out. If no D, then no F," and so on.

Look for "Thens" that Trigger "Ifs"

Now, take a look at how the LSAT test makers design logic games to reward you for recognizing these strings of logic.

Below, I've reproduced the setup and rules from a Selection game. You've seen a couple of the rules already in your translation and contrapositive practice. As you see the setup in its entirety, notice that every one of the rules is a conditional, formal logic "if-then." Take a couple of minutes to symbolize each of the rules and form their contrapositives. Try to follow the suggestion above and line them up neatly, so that you'll be able spot the connections among the rules. When you're done, check your scratch work for each of the individual rules against the sample symbolizations I've provided. Then I'll quiz you on your ability to spot the connections and combine the rules to make additional deductions.

A fruit stand carries one of the following kinds of fruit: figs, kiwis, oranges, pears, tangerines, and watermelons. The stand does not carry any other kind of fruit. The selection of fruits the stand carries is consistent with the following conditions:

If the stand carries kiwis, then it does not carry pears.
If the stand does not carry tangerines, then it carries kiwis.
If the stand carries oranges, then it carries both pears and watermelons.
If the stand carries watermelons, then it carries figs or tangerines or both.[49]

---

[49] PrepTest 36, Sec. 4, Game 1

Explanations

How did you do?

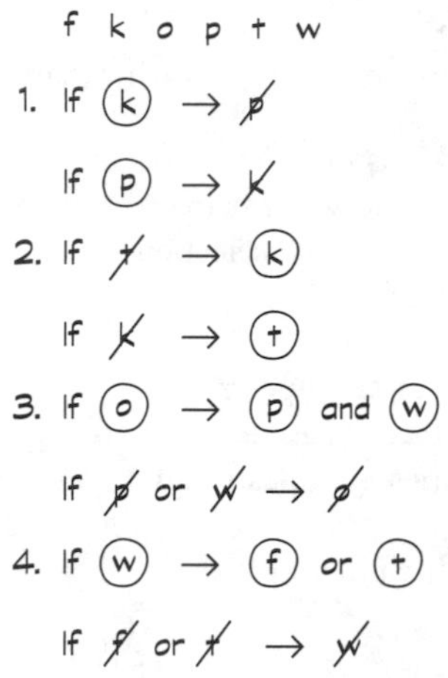

Figure 3.50

If your scratch work matches what's here, you've absorbed the earlier portions of this chapter expertly already. If you missed (or messed up) any of the translations or contrapositives, make sure you review the rule to see where you went off course. For now, you can consult the sample scratch work provided in order to see how the rules combine to yield additional deductions. I've numbered the rules here to make this discussion easier to follow. You won't need to number them on test day.

Here's an example of what I'll be asking you to do.

If the stand carries kiwis, what else can you determine? _____

The correct answer here would be: "The stand does not carry pears and does not carry oranges."

Make sure you see how you get to that answer. The sufficient condition in the question is that the stand carries kiwis. "If k" appears in Rule 1. It's sufficient to rule out pears. That result (no pears) appears in the "if" clause of Rule 3's contrapositive: If pears *or* watermelons are out, then so are oranges. You know nothing about watermelons in this case, but since you've ruled out pears, you can rule out oranges as well. Scan down the list of "ifs." "No oranges" doesn't appear in any of them. So you know that you've exhausted the available deductions.

Try another one.

If the stand carries figs, what else can you determine? _____

The correct answer this time is: "Nothing."

Scan down the list of statements. Choosing figs never appears as the sufficient ("if") condition in any of the rules or contrapositives. Only *not* carrying figs has additional implications (as seen in the contrapositive of Rule 4).

DRILL: COMBINING FORMAL LOGIC RULES

Use the same game setup and scratch work to answer the questions below. For each, push the "string of logic" deductions as far as they can go with certainty, but no farther. Remember, some of the questions may produce no further deductions. In such cases, answer "Nothing."

A fruit stand carries one of the following kinds of fruit: figs, kiwis, oranges, pears, tangerines, and watermelons. The stand does not carry any other kind of fruit. The selection of fruits the stand carries is consistent with the following conditions:

    If the stand carries kiwis, then it does not carry pears.
    If the stand does not carry tangerines, then it carries kiwis.
    If the stand carries oranges, then it carries both pears and watermelons.
    If the stand carries watermelons, then it carries figs or tangerines or both.[50]

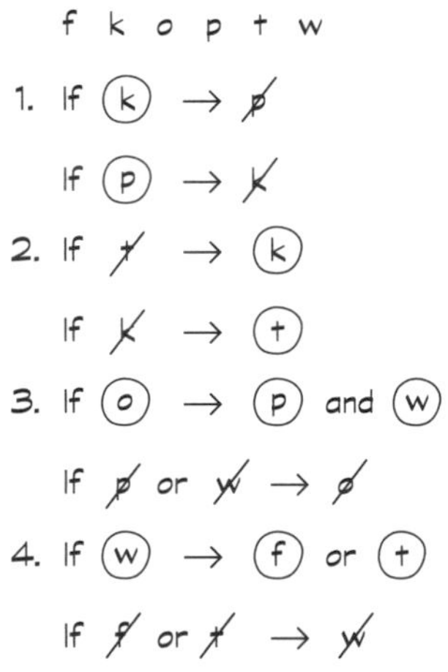

Figure 3.51

1. If the stand does not carry figs, what else can you determine?

_____

2. If the stand does not carry kiwis, what else can you determine?

_____

3. If the stand carries oranges, what else can you determine?

_____

4. If the stand does not carry oranges, what else can you determine?

_____

5. If the stand carries pears, what else can you determine?

_____

[50]PrepTest 36, Sec. 4, Game 1

Answer Explanations follow on the next page.

Explanations

1. If the stand does not carry figs, what else can you determine?

Nothing. "No figs *and* no tangerines" is a trigger in the contrapositive of Rule 4. So if you also knew that tangerines were forbidden, learning that figs are out would allow you to make additional deductions. But knowing only that figs are out doesn't trigger any of the rules' "if" clauses.

2. If the stand does not carry kiwis, what else can you determine?

The stand carries tangerines. "No kiwis" is the sufficient condition in the contrapositive of Rule 2, resulting in "carries tangerines." The stand carrying tangerines doesn't trigger any other rules, so no additional deductions are available.

3. If the stand carries oranges, what else can you determine?

The stand carries pears, watermelons, and tangerines; the stand does not carry kiwis. This one has huge implications for the game. "Carries oranges" is the sufficient trigger in Rule 3, resulting in "carries pears *and* carries watermelons." Pursue each of those results separately. "Carries pears" is the sufficient condition in the contrapositive of Rule 1, resulting in "no kiwis." "No kiwis" is the sufficient condition in the contrapositive of Rule 2, resulting in "carries tangerines." That exhausts one string of logic, but you still need to find out what's triggered by "carries watermelons." That's the trigger in Rule 4, resulting in "carries at least one of figs or tangerines." Since tangerines are already definitely in, the best you can say is that the stand *could* carry figs. It's not certain that the stand will carry figs, however.

4. If the stand does not carry oranges, what else can you determine?

Nothing. "No oranges" isn't found in any "if" clause. So knowing that it's true doesn't lead to any additional combinations or deductions.

5. If the stand carries pears, what else can you determine?

The stand does not carry kiwis; the stand carries tangerines. "Carries pears" is the trigger in the contrapositive of Rule 1. It results in "no kiwis." "No kiwis" is then the trigger in the contrapositive of Rule 2, resulting in "carries tangerines." That result is not found in the "if" clause of any further rules, so your string of logic runs out here.

Notice how some of the hypothetical situations posed in the questions led to long strings of deductions, while others yielded nothing at all. That's the way it will always be in games that feature formal logic. Don't feel that you've failed when you find out that some rules or conditions don't lead to additional deductions. In fact, you've succeeded anytime you can say, with certainty, "Nothing else can be determined here." Remember, the test makers ask for what must, cannot, and could be true. Sometimes you can infer, "The stand will not carry oranges in this case." Other times, you wind up saying, "The stand might carry oranges, but it doesn't have to." Depending on the question, either of those could be the right answer.

Speaking of question and answers, it's time to apply all that you've learned about formal logic to some complete logic games. In the section that follows, I'll have you translate all of the rules, form their contrapositives, and look for the strings of logic that are likely to be most limiting and helpful. Finally, I'll show that you can answer all of the questions associated with the games using nothing more than what you've learned in this chapter.

COMPLETE GAME PRACTICE

From time to time, the test makers will present you with games that turn entirely on formal logic rules. You may or may not get a game like this one on your official LSAT, but if you do, think back to this chapter and put all of the skills and techniques discussed here into practice. You've already seen the following game setup, but now you can look at it knowing that you've been exposed to everything you'll need in order to handle it flawlessly.

Start by taking around four minutes to set it up. Sketch it out. List out all of the rules and their contrapositives, and look for rules that can be combined for additional deductions. Then I'll review the correct step-by-step application of the Kaplan Method.

> An album contains photographs picturing seven friends:
> Raimundo, Selma, Ty, Umiko, Wendy, Yakira, Zack. The
> friends appear either alone or in groups with one another, in
> accordance with the following:
>> Wendy appears in every photograph that Selma appears in.
>> Selma appears in every photograph that Umiko appears in.
>> Raimundo appears in every photograph that Yakira does
>>   not appear in.
>> Neither Ty nor Raimundo appears in any photograph that
>>   Wendy appears in.[51]

STEPS 1 AND 2: Overview and Sketch

It's not hard to get a picture (pun intended) of your task here. You're a photographer, and you have to ensure that the correct groups are together in the shots. Sometimes that will mean calling for someone else to get in the shot; sometimes you'll have to ask someone to step out of the frame. "Choose her; reject him"—this is a Selection game. As such, there's no need for you to create any framework within your sketch. Just maintain a list of the entities. You'll circle those who are included and strike through those who are excluded in any given question.

---

[51] PrepTest 45, Sec. 3, Game 3

STEP 3: Rules

All of the rules are formal logic, albeit in language that requires some careful translation to be sure that you've correctly identified the sufficient and necessary terms. Compare your list of translations and contrapositives with the scratch work below. Again, I've numbered the rules for convenience in referencing them in the discussion and explanations.

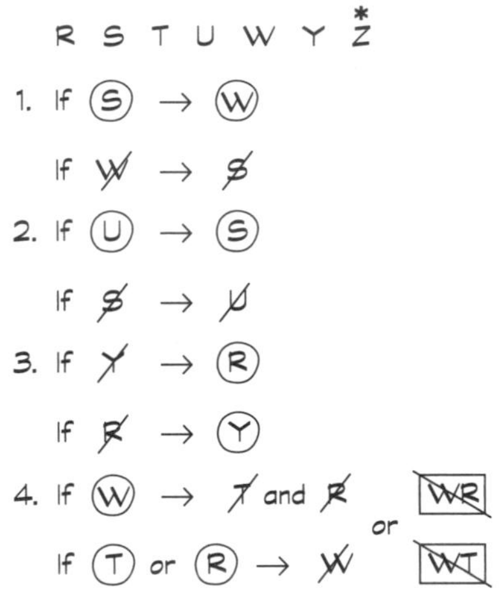

Figure 3.52

Here are a few key questions to ask as you're reviewing your setup work:

- Did you get the correct terms in the "if" and "then" positions in Rules 1 and 2?
- Did you remember that Rule 3 means "At least one of Y or R is included every time"?
- Did you recognize that Rule 3 allows Y and R to be together in a photograph?
- Did you translate the "Neither . . . nor . . ." construction in Rule 4 correctly?
- Did you remember to swap the "and" for "or" in the contrapositive of Rule 4?
- Did you indicate that Z is the floater, unrestricted by any of the rules?

If you got the rules and contrapositives sketched correctly, you're ready for the Deductions step..

STEP 4: Deductions

While the next chapter will cover all of the various types of deductions you'll be rewarded for making on test day, you have learned enough about formal logic in this chapter to cover all the deductions in this game. If you haven't done so already, take a moment to note which rules can be combined.

Here's the list:

- Rules 1 and 2 combine because they share Selma. Together, they allow you to deduce that whenever Umiko is chosen, Wendy will be, too. Combining their contrapositives, you can see that whenever Wendy is not in the photo, Umiko will not be, either.

- Rules 1 and 4 combine because they share Wendy. Together, they allow you to deduce that whenever Selma appears in the photo, Ty and Raimundo must stay out of the picture. Likewise, the contrapositives of the two rules tell you that if either Ty or Raimundo is included in the picture, Selma must stay out.
- Finally, Rules 3 and 4 combine because they share Raimundo. Thus, whenever Yakira does not appear, Wendy must not appear. Conversely—link the two contrapositives—when Wendy is in the picture, Raimundo is out, so Yakira must be in.

Because of all these shared entities, the combinations can actually allow you to link all four rules into one long string of logic, depending on your starting point. For example, if Umiko appears, Rule 2 tells you that Selma must also appear. Rule 1 is triggered, and Wendy must also get into the photo. That puts Rule 4 into play; both Ty and Raimundo are excluded. Raimundo's exclusion triggers Rule 3, and Yakira must step into the shot. Only floater Zack remains untouched in this string of valid inferences.

On test day, I encourage you *not* to try to determine (or write out) all of the various possible linkages. Rather, make your list of rules and contrapositives clear and easy to consult. You can note the "likely suspects," but the various "if" questions will trigger your strings of logic, which will lead you straight to the right answers.

STEP 5: Questions
Go ahead and try the question set now. You've seen a couple of these questions before, but doing them again with a complete sketch will be good practice.

An album contains photographs picturing seven friends: Raimundo, Selma, Ty, Umiko, Wendy, Yakira, Zack. The friends appear either alone or in groups with one another, in accordance with the following:

Wendy appears in every photograph that Selma appears in.
Selma appears in every photograph that Umiko appears in.
Raimundo appears in every photograph that Yakira does not appear in.
Neither Ty nor Raimundo appears in any photograph that Wendy appears in.

13. Which one of the following could be a complete and accurate list of the friends who appear together in a photograph?

    (A)   Raimundo, Selma, Ty, Wendy
    (B)   Raimundo, Ty, Yakira, Zack
    (C)   Raimundo, Wendy, Yakira, Zack
    (D)   Selma, Ty, Umiko, Yakira
    (E)   Selma, Ty, Umiko, Zack

14. If Ty and Zack appear together in a photograph, then which one of the following must be true?

    (A)   Selma also appears in the photograph.
    (B)   Yakira also appears in the photograph.
    (C)   Wendy also appears in the photograph.
    (D)   Raimundo does not appear in the photograph.
    (E)   Umiko does not appear in the photograph.

15. What is the maximum number of friends who could appear in a photograph that Yakira does not appear in?

    (A)   six
    (B)   five
    (C)   four
    (D)   three
    (E)   two

16. If Umiko and Zack appear together in a photograph, then exactly how many of the other friends must also appear in that photograph?

    (A)   four
    (B)   three
    (C)   two
    (D)   one
    (E)   zero

17. If exactly three friends appear together in a photograph, then each of the following could be true EXCEPT:

    (A)   Selma and Zack both appear in the photograph.
    (B)   Ty and Yakira both appear in the photograph.
    (C)   Wendy and Selma both appear in the photograph.
    (D)   Yakira and Zack both appear in the photograph.
    (E)   Zack and Raimundo both appear in the photograph.[52]

---

[52] PrepTest 45, Sec. 3, Game 3, Qs 13–17

Answer Explanations follow on the next page.

Explanations

13. **(B)**

Which one of the following could be a complete and
accurate list of the friends who appear together in a photograph?

(A)   Raimundo, Selma, Ty, Wendy
(B)   Raimundo, Ty, Yakira, Zack
(C)   Raimundo, Wendy, Yakira, Zack
(D)   Selma, Ty, Umiko, Yakira
(E)   Selma, Ty, Umiko, Zack[53]

You've seen this Acceptability question in chapter 2. Did you remember to eliminate answers
rule-by-rule as you spotted violations? Rule 1 got rid of choices (D) and (E), both of which have
Selma but not Wendy. Rule 4 eliminated choices (A) and (C), both of which have Wendy and
Raimundo appearing together in the photograph. That left (B) as the correct answer, the only
one to violate none of the rules.

14. **(E)**

If Ty and Zack appear together in a photograph, then
which one of the following must be true?

(A)   Selma also appears in the photograph.
(B)   Yakira also appears in the photograph.
(C)   Wendy also appears in the photograph.
(D)   Raimundo does not appear in the photograph.
(E)   Umiko does not appear in the photograph.[54]

Here's the first question that put your formal logic deductions to the test. The "if" clause at
the beginning of the question prompts you to create a mini-sketch consisting of your list of
entities. Circle T and Z as prescribed by the question stem.

R S (T) U W Y (Z)

Figure 3.53

Zack is the floater, so his inclusion won't trigger any additional deductions. But the inclusion
of Ty in the photo calls for the contrapositive of Rule 4. Since T is in, cross W off the list.

R S (T) U W̸ Y (Z)

Figure 3.54

"No Wendy" triggers the contrapositive of Rule 1. Thus, cross S off the list, too.

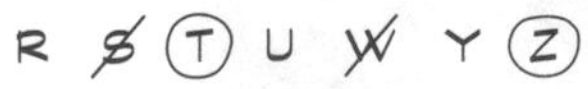

R S̸ (T) U W̸ Y (Z)

Figure 3.55

[53] PrepTest 45, Sec. 3, Q 13
[54] PrepTest 45, Sec. 3, Q 14

"No Selma" puts the contrapositive of Rule 2 into play. Exclude U from the photo.

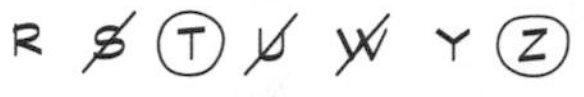

$$R \not{S} \; \textcircled{T} \; \not{U} \; \not{W} \; Y \; \textcircled{Z}$$

Figure 3.56

You can't make any further deductions, so you're ready for the answer choices. The only one that must be true according to your mini-sketch is choice (E). Choices (A) and (C) must be false, while choices (B) and (D) could be either true or false in this case.

15. **(D)**

What is the maximum number of friends who could appear in a photograph that Yakira does not appear in?

(A) six
(B) five
(C) four
(D) three
(E) two[55]

This question stem doesn't begin with an "if" clause, but it still presents you with a hypothetical condition: "a photograph that Yakira does not appear in." Begin your work with a list of the entities with Y struck out.

$$R \; S \; T \; U \; W \; \not{Y} \; Z$$

Figure 3.57

Y's exclusion triggers Rule 3, of course, and that means that Raimundo must be in the photograph. Circle R in your list.

$$\textcircled{R} \; S \; T \; U \; W \; \not{Y} \; Z$$

Figure 3.58

Including R in the photo means excluding W, according to Rule 4's contrapositive. So cross out W.

$$\textcircled{R} \; S \; T \; U \; \not{W} \; \not{Y} \; Z$$

Figure 3.59

"No Wendy" triggers the contrapositive of Rule 1. That means that you must cross S off the list.

$$\textcircled{R} \; \not{S} \; T \; U \; \not{W} \; \not{Y} \; Z$$

Figure 3.60

---

[55] PrepTest 45, Sec. 3, Q 15

Finally, eliminating S is the sufficient condition in the contrapositive of Rule 2. Eliminate U from your mini-sketch list.

$$\text{\textcircled{R}} \; \cancel{S} \; \text{T} \; \cancel{U} \; \cancel{W} \; \cancel{Y} \; \text{Z}$$

Figure 3.60A

You've exhausted all four rules here, so evaluate the answer choices. According to your list Raimundo is definitely in the picture, while Ty and floater Zack could be. The maximum number of friends who could appear is three, making (D) the correct answer.

16. **(B)**

> If Umiko and Zack appear together in a photograph, then exactly how many of the other friends must also appear in that photograph?

(A) four
(B) three
(C) two
(D) one
(E) zero[56]

Here's yet another question that calls for a mini-sketch and a string of logic. This will be no surprise to you by test day. Begin your work this time with a list of entities with U and Z circled as per the question stem.

$$\text{R} \; \text{S} \; \text{T} \; \text{\textcircled{U}} \; \text{W} \; \text{Y} \; \text{\textcircled{Z}}$$

Figure 3.61

Floater Zack doesn't impact any other entities, so the deductions will come as a result of including Umiko. Do you remember the long string of inferences that her appearance triggers? Here it is again.

Rule 2: Including Umiko means including Selma.

$$\text{R} \; \text{\textcircled{S}} \; \text{T} \; \text{\textcircled{U}} \; \text{W} \; \text{Y} \; \text{\textcircled{Z}}$$

Figure 3.62

Rule 1: Including Selma means including Wendy.

$$\text{R} \; \text{\textcircled{S}} \; \text{T} \; \text{\textcircled{U}} \; \text{\textcircled{W}} \; \text{Y} \; \text{\textcircled{Z}}$$

Figure 3.63

---

[56] PrepTest 45, Sec. 3, Q 16

Rule 4: Including Wendy means excluding Ty and Raimundo.

$$\cancel{R}\ \textcircled{S}\ \cancel{T}\ \textcircled{U}\ \textcircled{W}\ Y\ \textcircled{Z}$$

Figure 3.64

Finally, Rule 3's contrapositive: Excluding Raimundo means including Yakira.

$$\cancel{R}\ \textcircled{S}\ \cancel{T}\ \textcircled{U}\ \textcircled{W}\ \textcircled{Y}\ \textcircled{Z}$$

Figure 3.65

Your entire list is determined. Everyone is either in or out. There are a total of five friends in the picture, which means that there are three in addition to Umiko and Zack. Choice (B) is the correct answer.

17. **(A)**

> If exactly three friends appear together in a photograph, then each of the following could be true EXCEPT:
>
> (A) Selma and Zack both appear in the photograph.
> (B) Ty and Yakira both appear in the photograph.
> (C) Wendy and Selma both appear in the photograph.
> (D) Yakira and Zack both appear in the photograph.
> (E) Zack and Raimundo both appear in the photograph.[57]

This question doesn't provide a hypothetical "if" that you can easily write out as a mini-sketch. Rather, it provides a number-based restriction: Exactly three friends are in the photograph. Moreover, the correct answer will be the one that *cannot* have exactly three friends in it. Still, you can apply what you've learned from this chapter and get the correct answer straightaway. Simply turn each answer into a mini-sketch and make the deductions that follow. One, and only one, of the answers will not allow you to have exactly three friends in the picture.

Starting with choice (A), write out the list of entities and circle S and Z.

$$R\ \textcircled{S}\ T\ U\ W\ Y\ \textcircled{Z}$$

Figure 3.66

According to Rule 1, including Selma means including Wendy.

$$R\ \textcircled{S}\ T\ U\ \textcircled{W}\ Y\ \textcircled{Z}$$

Figure 3.67

---

[57] PrepTest 45, Sec. 3, Q 17

Wendy's appearance triggers Rule 4, meaning that you can cross off R and T.

$$\cancel{R} \; \textcircled{S} \; \cancel{T} \; \cup \; \textcircled{W} \; Y \; \textcircled{Z}$$

Figure 3.68

Removing Raimundo from the photograph triggers the contrapositive of Rule 3 and requires Yakira to get into the picture.

$$\cancel{R} \; \textcircled{S} \; \cancel{T} \; \cup \; \textcircled{W} \; \textcircled{Y} \; \textcircled{Z}$$

Figure 3.69

Voilà! Choice (A) requires at least four friends to be in the photograph. That means it cannot be true under the conditions of the question. You've got the right answer.

All four of the other choices would allow you to stop with exactly three friends in the photo. Try sketching them out for practice. But on test day, stop right here. You have the right answer and you can move on to the next game.

COMPLETE GAME PRACTICE

Speaking of the next game, there's one more formal logic-intensive game that I'd like you to try before moving on to the next chapter. Again, it's a Selection game and again, all of the rules are conditional, formal logic statements. The challenge in the Friends' Photograph game was in translating the rules. In the game that follows, all of the rules are presented in the standard "if-then" format. But be careful. They are quite complex. Take your time and make sure you've gotten your symbolism for the rules and contrapositives clear and correct. If you want to double-check your setup work before tackling the questions, turn to the Explanations and review Steps 1 through 4 of the Kaplan Method. Then come back and try the questions. I'm confident that with the rules and their contrapositives sketched correctly, you can get all of the points available here.

Complete this game and all of its questions. Do not time yourself. Your goal, at this point, should be to interpret each of the rules correctly, determine their contrapositives, and make all of the deductions as called for by the questions. Your speed and efficiency will improve with additional practice.

Questions 13–17

A summer program offers at least one of the following seven courses: geography, history, literature, mathematics, psychology, sociology, zoology. The following restrictions on the program must apply:

> If mathematics is offered, then either literature or sociology (but not both) is offered.
>
> If literature is offered, then geography is also offered but psychology is not.
>
> If sociology is offered, then psychology is also offered but zoology is not.
>
> If geography is offered, then both history and zoology are also offered.

13. Which one of the following could be a complete and accurate list of the courses offered by the summer program?

    (A) history, psychology
    (B) geography, history, literature
    (C) history, mathematics, psychology
    (D) literature, mathematics, psychology
    (E) history, literature, mathematics, sociology

14. If the summer program offers literature, then which one of the following could be true?

    (A) Sociology is offered.
    (B) History is not offered.
    (C) Mathematics is not offered.
    (D) A total of two courses are offered.
    (E) Zoology is not offered.

15. If history is not offered by the summer program, then which one of the following is another course that CANNOT be offered?

    (A) literature
    (B) mathematics
    (C) psychology
    (D) sociology
    (E) zoology

16. If the summer program offers mathematics, then which one of the following must be true?

    (A) Literature is offered.
    (B) Psychology is offered.
    (C) Sociology is offered.
    (D) At least three courses are offered.
    (E) At most four courses are offered.

17. Which one of the following must be false of the summer program?

    (A) Both geography and psychology are offered.
    (B) Both geography and mathematics are offered.
    (C) Both psychology and mathematics are offered.
    (D) Both history and mathematics are offered.
    (E) Both geography and sociology are offered.[58]

---

[58] PrepTest 49, Sec. 1, Game 3, Qs 13–17

Explanations

A summer program offers at least one of the following
seven courses: geography, history, literature, mathematics,
psychology, sociology, zoology. The following restrictions
on the program must apply:

> If mathematics is offered, then either literature or
> sociology (but not both) is offered.
>
> If literature is offered, then geography is also offered
> but psychology is not.
>
> If sociology is offered, then psychology is also offered
> but zoology is not.
>
> If geography is offered, then both history and
> zoology are also offered.[59]

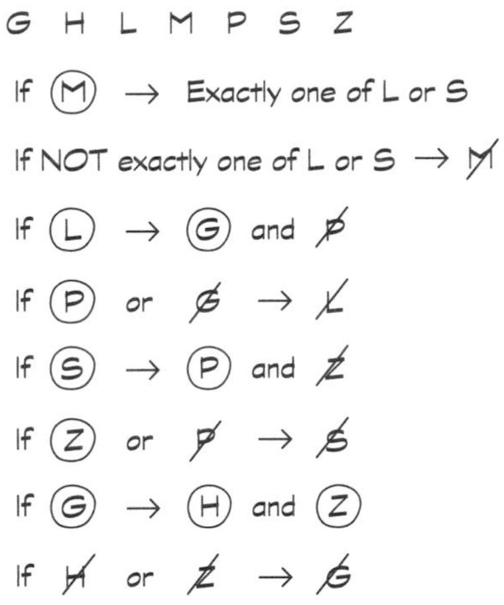

Figure 3.70

STEPS 1 AND 2: Overview and Sketch

The opening paragraph of this setup is brief and to the point. You're working in some sort of academic administration office, and your task is to create a list of the courses that will and will not be offered in the summer program. "Choose this one, reject that one"—it's another Selection game, and you need only jot down a list of the entities in order to have a starting point for your Sketch. Circle those courses that are offered and strike through those that are not.

STEP 3: Rules

All four rules in this game are conditional formal logic statements. What's more, they're written in straightforward "If-Then" format. The challenge comes from the fact that all four of the rules restrict three entities each. Compare your scratch work with the correct translations and contrapositives above. If there are any you missed, make sure to go back and correct the mistakes in your Master Sketch while going over the rules to make sure you won't fall into the same trap again.

---

[59] PrepTest 49, Sec. 1, Game 3

The first rule is the toughest of the bunch. There's probably no better way to write it out than to simply say "exactly one of L or S." The alternative would be to split the contrapositive into two separate statements, like so:

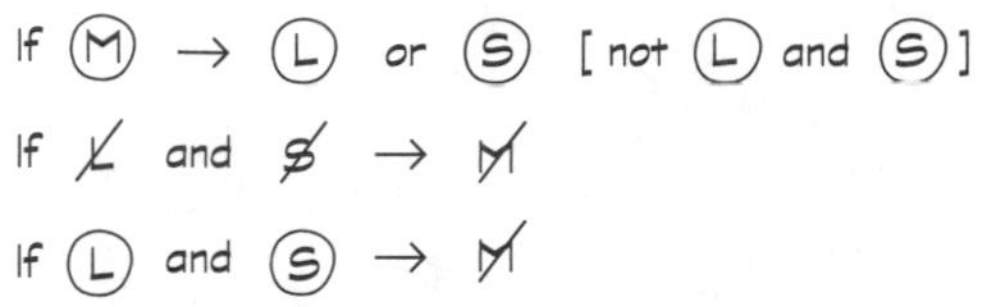

$$\text{If } \textcircled{M} \rightarrow \textcircled{L} \text{ or } \textcircled{S} \quad [\text{ not } \textcircled{L} \text{ and } \textcircled{S}]$$

$$\text{If } \cancel{\textcircled{L}} \text{ and } \cancel{\textcircled{S}} \rightarrow \cancel{\textcircled{M}}$$

$$\text{If } \textcircled{L} \text{ and } \textcircled{S} \rightarrow \cancel{\textcircled{M}}$$

Figure 3.71

Take your choice. So long as the rule and its implications are clear to you, you'll be able to leverage it to your advantage on test day.

The remaining rules are more direct. Provided that you kept the negations clear and always swapped "and" for "or," you should be fine.

STEP 4: Deductions

Several of these rules share entities and can be combined. Don't fall into the trap of trying to sort out all of the possible combinations up front. Just make sure that your list of rules and contrapositives is easy for you to interpret, and have confidence that you'll be able to make all of the Deductions you need when the questions call for them.

You may have noted some of the combinations as you were sketching out the rules. Take Rule 2, for example. Offering literature means offering geography and nixing psychology. Each of those results triggers a string of logic. Offering geography, according to Rule 4, means offering zoology. Offering zoology, in turn, triggers the contrapositive of Rule 3 and results in ruling out sociology. You derive the same conclusion from the exclusion of psychology. It, too, triggers the contrapositive of Rule 3.

Trying to track down or write out all of the possible connections here would be a waste of your time on test day. Make a clear, accurate list of the rules and contrapositives and use it to whip through the question set.

STEP 5: Questions

13. **(A)**

Which one of the following could be a complete and accurate list of the courses offered by the summer program?

(A) history, psychology
(B) geography, history, literature
(C) history, mathematics, psychology
(D) literature, mathematics, psychology
(E) history, literature, mathematics, sociology[60]

This is the game's Acceptability question, a type you're eminently prepared to handle at this point. Going rule-by-rule and eliminating the choices that break them, you should have had this point in a matter of seconds. Rule 1 got rid of choice (C), which offers M without either L or S, and choice (E), which offers M with both L and S. Rule 2 took out choice (D), where L is offered without G. Finally, Rule 4 eliminated (B), which has G offered without Z. Choice (A) is the correct answer.

14. **(C)**

If the summer program offers literature, then which one of the following could be true?

(A) Sociology is offered.
(B) History is not offered.
(C) Mathematics is not offered.
(D) A total of two courses are offered.
(E) Zoology is not offered.[61]

Here's one that gives you the chance to show off your newfound deductive capacity. Begin with a list of the entities and circle L in accordance with the question stem.

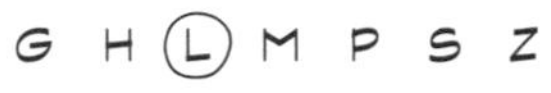

$$G \quad H \quad Ⓛ \quad M \quad P \quad S \quad Z$$

Figure 3.72

Offering literature is the sufficient condition in Rule 2. It tells you to circle G and strike through P in your roster of entities.

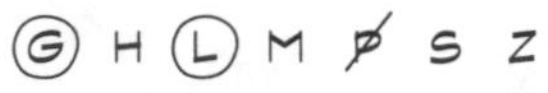

$$Ⓖ \quad H \quad Ⓛ \quad M \quad \cancel{P} \quad S \quad Z$$

Figure 3.73

Circling G draws your eye to Rule 4. Offering geography means offering history and zoology as well. Circle H and Z in the list.

Ⓖ Ⓗ Ⓛ M P̸ S Ⓩ

Figure 3.74

The inclusion of zoology (and the exclusion of psychology, for that matter) means the exclusion of sociology according to the contrapositive of Rule 3. Cross S off of your list.

Ⓖ Ⓗ Ⓛ M P̸ S̸ Ⓩ

Figure 3.75

The only entity that remains undetermined is M. Mathematics requires the inclusion of either literature or sociology, but not both. That condition is met here, so mathematics could be offered, though it doesn't have to be. That makes choice (C) the correct answer. All of the other answers must be false as you can see by checking them against the mini-sketch you made.

15. **(A)**

> If history is not offered by the summer program,
> then which one of the following is another course
> that CANNOT be offered?

(A) literature
(B) mathematics
(C) psychology
(D) sociology
(E) zoology[62]

This time, the question stem presents you with a hypothetical that eliminates an entity—H— from consideration. Start your work with a list of the entities, and cross out H right off the bat.

G H̸ L M P S Z

Figure 3.76

The exclusion of history triggers the contrapositive of Rule 4. Getting rid of H means getting rid of G.

G̸ H̸ L M P S Z

Figure 3.77

---

[62] PrepTest 49, Sec. 1, Game 3, Q15

Eliminating geography activates the contrapositive of Rule 2. That forces you to cross L off of your list, too.

$$\cancel{G} \;\; \cancel{H} \;\; \cancel{L} \;\; M \;\; P \;\; S \;\; Z$$

Figure 3.78

Excluding literature from the offerings doesn't trigger any additional deductions, so you're ready for the answer choices. The correct one will be a course that's been crossed off of your list. Choice (A)—literature—is the only one that fits the bill. It's not for nothing that there are four entities that could be included in your list and that they are represented in the four wrong answers to this question.

16. **(D)**

> If the summer program offers mathematics, then which one of the following must be true?

(A)   Literature is offered.
(B)   Psychology is offered.
(C)   Sociology is offered.
(D)   At least three courses are offered.
(E)   At most four courses are offered.[63]

Before I explain how to answer this question, I want you to notice the stem and the answer choices. The correct answer is the one that must be true. The first three choices suggest particular, individual courses will be offered, while the last two deal with minimum-maximum number requirements. Keep that in mind as you review the scratch work. The question stem tells you to list the entities and circle M.

$$G \;\; H \;\; L \;\; \boxed{M} \;\; P \;\; S \;\; Z$$

Figure 3.79

The inclusion of mathematics raises the specter of the complicated Rule 1. All you can know is that either literature or sociology will be offered along with mathematics. You can't even circle one or the other for sure. But since the correct answer *must be true*, you can eliminate choices (A) and (C). Either *could be true*, but neither *must be true*.

Now, look at Rules 2 and 3. They spell out the implications of offering either literature or sociology. Both options are on the table, but only one of them (offering sociology) would trigger the inclusion of psychology. Eliminate choice (B). It's another statement that *could* but doesn't have to be true.

---

[63] PrepTest 49, Sec. 1, Game 3, Q16

What must be true, then, is that whichever way you proceed—offering literature or offering sociology—you'll have to add at least one more course. No matter which way you turn, at least three courses will be offered. Choice (D) is the correct answer.

17. **(E)**

> Which one of the following must be false of the summer program?
>
> (A)   Both geography and psychology are offered.
> (B)   Both geography and mathematics are offered.
> (C)   Both psychology and mathematics are offered.
> (D)   Both history and mathematics are offered.
> (E)   Both geography and sociology are offered.[64]

This question calls for an answer that must be false. Given that each of the answers suggests a pair of courses, the correct answer will be the one in which the rules make the pairing incompatible. Rules 3 and 4 combine to make choice (E) the correct answer. According to Rule 4, offering geography means offering zoology. According to the contrapositive of Rule 3, offering zoology rules out offering sociology.

If you approached this question by eliminating the wrong answers—those that could be true—you may have noticed that you got some help from your scratch work in question 14. There, mathematics was compatible with geography and history, proof that choices (B) and (D) could be true. Rules 1 and 3 combine to show that choice (C) is possible. Choice (A), meanwhile, doesn't contradict any of the rules. If you needed to demonstrate that it could be true, create a list of the entities and circle G and P. Push the deductions from each of those conditions as far as possible, and you'll wind up with an acceptable selection.

(Don't Fear) Formal Logic

If you were a test taker who came to this book intimidated by formal logic with its jargon and symbols, I hope this chapter has given you some confidence. There's no way to know whether formal logic will feature prominently in the logic games section on your LSAT, but by learning (and, more importantly, by practicing) the principles and techniques presented here, you'll be able to turn any formal logic you encounter into certain LSAT points.

The strings of logic you can create by combining formal logic statements are just one type of deduction that will put you in control of logic games. In the next chapter, I'll outline the others, five types of deductions that will make it possible for you to answer any logic games question that the test makers can devise.

---

[64] PrepTest 49, Sec. 1, Game 3, Q17

CHAPTER 4

DEDUCTIONS

WHY YOU MAKE DEDUCTIONS

You're standing on the edge of logic games mastery. Step 4 of the Kaplan Method—Deductions—is so important that I want to pause for a moment to put it in context. Remember back to chapter 1, where I gave you an example of a real-world task that you might have working in a law office. Your boss, the attorney, asks you for a document showing the order of witnesses for an upcoming trial and what each witness will testify about. In chapter 1, you were just concerned with understanding your task and with picturing how you'd lay out such a document so that it would be easy to use in a meeting with the client. As you get ready for the meeting, you're going to consult the case files and start pulling the information together. It will have notes that resemble logic games rules: Jones cannot testify about payroll; we don't want Martin to be the first witness; if we have Norris testify about investments, we'll have O'Brien cover payroll; etc.

You don't want to head into the meeting with the client with a bunch of scattered papers and sticky notes. So you start entering what you know into your document. And you anticipate what your boss and the client will ask. They'll want to know what's determined and what still needs to be decided. You'll go in ready to say, "Jones has to be the first witness," or, "Either Norris or Paulino will testify about the investments." That same work, figuring out from your notes what must, can't, or could be the case, is what you're doing when you make deductions in logic games. At work, it will impress your boss that you're so organized and ready for the meeting. On the LSAT, it will get you the right answers and add points to your score.

Start with What's Most Certain

Learning to make deductions quickly and accurately takes some time. Almost all test takers realize the need to make games visual, even when they aren't yet very adept at doing so. They realize the need to account for the game's rules, even when they haven't learned to analyze them or add them into the sketch. But it is only the best test takers who develop the patience and rigor that it takes to make deductions.

The shortest path from the scramble of rules and restrictions to the clarity of deductions is to move from the most concrete restrictions in a game to the least. Fortunately, you've got a great head start on that from the work you did analyzing rules in chapter 2. To see how helpful deductions can be and to see what I mean by moving from the most to the least concrete restrictions, take a look at a fairly challenging game from PrepTest 53. Apply Steps 1 through 3 of the Kaplan Method—that is, conduct your overview to get a handle on the task, draw out your initial sketch, and analyze the rules. Afterward, I'll review the rules and show you how making the available deductions will allow you to answer the questions flawlessly in a matter of a few seconds each.

Questions 12–17

Detectives investigating a citywide increase in burglaries questioned exactly seven suspects—S, T, V, W, X, Y, and Z—each on a different one of seven consecutive days. Each suspect was questioned exactly once. Any suspect who confessed did so while being questioned. The investigation conformed to the following:

T was questioned on day three.
The suspect questioned on day four did not confess.
S was questioned after W was questioned.
Both X and V were questioned after Z was questioned.
No suspects confessed after W was questioned.
Exactly two suspects confessed after T was questioned.

12. Which one of the following could be true?

    (A)   X was questioned on day one.
    (B)   V was questioned on day two.
    (C)   Z was questioned on day four.
    (D)   W was questioned on day five.
    (E)   S was questioned on day six.

13. If Z was the second suspect to confess, then each of the following statements could be true EXCEPT:

    (A)   T confessed.
    (B)   T did not confess.
    (C)   V did not confess.
    (D)   X confessed.
    (E)   Y did not confess.

14. If Y was questioned after V but before X, then which one of the following could be true?

    (A)   V did not confess.
    (B)   Y confessed.
    (C)   X did not confess.
    (D)   X was questioned on day four.
    (E)   Z was questioned on day two.

15. Which one of the following suspects must have been questioned before T was questioned?

    (A)   V
    (B)   W
    (C)   X
    (D)   Y
    (E)   Z

16. If X and Y both confessed, then each of the following could be true EXCEPT:

    (A)   V confessed.
    (B)   X was questioned on day five.
    (C)   Y was questioned on day one.
    (D)   Z was questioned on day one.
    (E)   Z did not confess.

17. If neither X nor V confessed, then which one of the following must be true?

    (A)   T confessed.
    (B)   V was questioned on day two.
    (C)   X was questioned on day four.
    (D)   Y confessed.
    (E)   Z did not confess.[1]

---

[1] PrepTest 53, Sec. 2, Game 3, Qs 12–17

Hopefully, you were able to apply Steps 1 through 3 of the Kaplan Method on this game without too much trouble.

STEPS 1 AND 2: Overview and Sketch

Your task is to set out a schedule of seven interrogations that happen, one per day, over the course of seven days. Along with the schedule, you'll need to keep track of who did and did not confess during questioning. Just like the Thunderstorm game from chapter 1, this is a hybrid of Sequencing and Matching. It's a little harder on the Sequencing side than the Thunderstorm game was (seven suspects versus five towns), but the sketch should look almost identical.

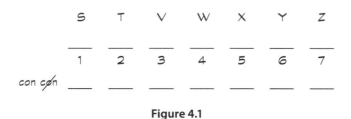

Figure 4.1

STEP 3: Rules

Seeing six rules should be a comfort; there simply has to be a great deal of restriction on the action. Make sure you jotted them down accurately.

Rule 1 was easy. T goes right into the sketch.

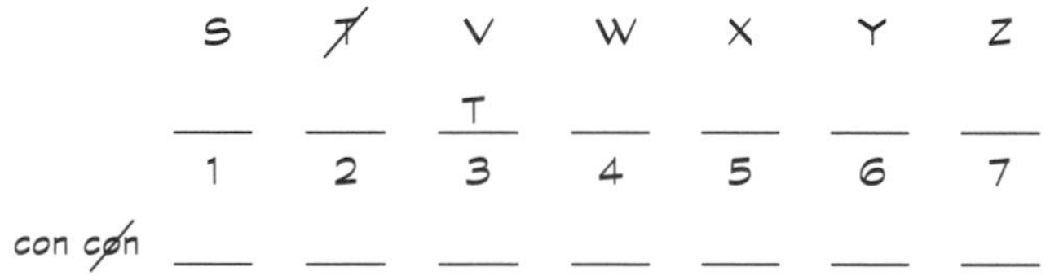

$$\begin{array}{ccccccc} S & \not{T} & V & W & X & Y & Z \\ \rule{1em}{0.5pt} & \rule{1em}{0.5pt} & T & \rule{1em}{0.5pt} & \rule{1em}{0.5pt} & \rule{1em}{0.5pt} & \rule{1em}{0.5pt} \\ 1 & 2 & 3 & 4 & 5 & 6 & 7 \end{array}$$

Figure 4.2

Rule 2 goes right in, too.

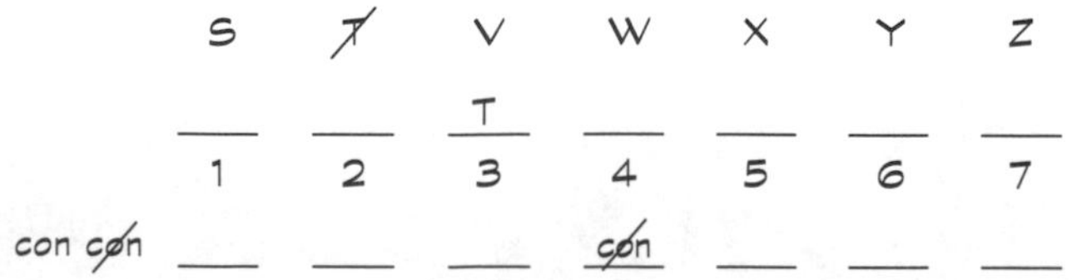

$$\begin{array}{ccccccc} S & \not{T} & V & W & X & Y & Z \\ \rule{1em}{0.5pt} & \rule{1em}{0.5pt} & T & \rule{1em}{0.5pt} & \rule{1em}{0.5pt} & \rule{1em}{0.5pt} & \rule{1em}{0.5pt} \\ 1 & 2 & 3 & 4 & 5 & 6 & 7 \end{array}$$

Figure 4.3

Rules 3 and 4 both restrict entities relative to each other. Make sure you recognize that Rule 4 does not give you any information about V and X relative to one another, only relative to Z.

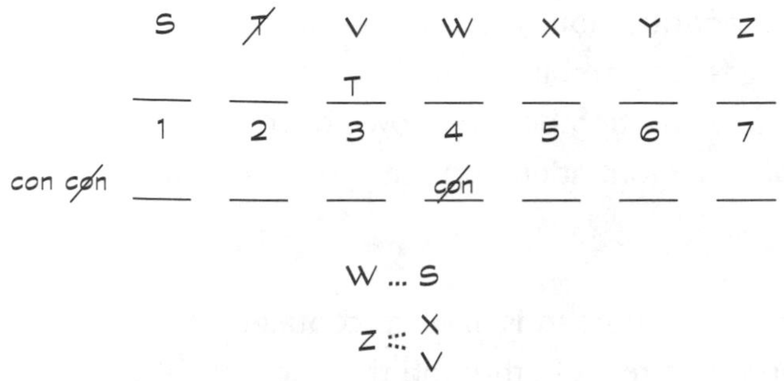

S T̸ V W X Y Z
___
T
___ ___ ___ ___ ___ ___ ___
1 2 3 4 5 6 7
con cøn ___ ___ ___ cøn ___ ___ ___

W ... S

Z ::: X over V

Figure 4.4

Rule 5 tells you that no one confessed after W's questioning, although it doesn't tell you whether W confessed.

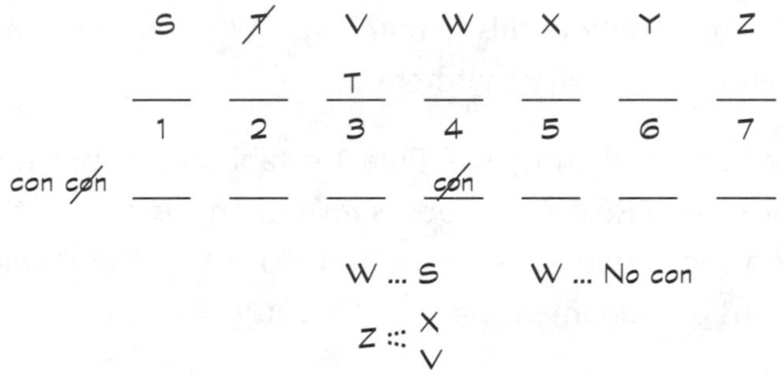

S T̸ V W X Y Z
___
T
___ ___ ___ ___ ___ ___ ___
1 2 3 4 5 6 7
con cøn ___ ___ ___ cøn ___ ___ ___

W ... S   W ... No con

Z ::: X over V

Figure 4.5

Finally, Rule 6 restricts three positions. There will be two cons on the bottom row after T's space on the top row.

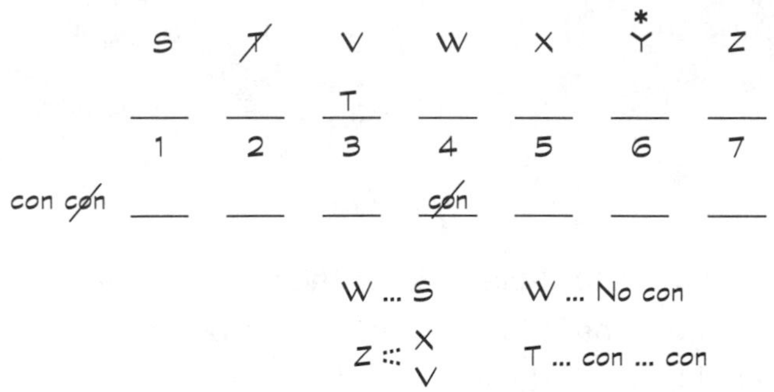

S T̸ V W X Ẏ* Z
___
T
___ ___ ___ ___ ___ ___ ___
1 2 3 4 5 6 7
con cøn ___ ___ ___ cøn ___ ___ ___

W ... S   W ... No con

Z ::: X over V   T ... con ... con

Figure 4.6

Notice, too, that Y is starred in that last sketch. It's the floater, unaffected by any rule.

This is about as far as most students ever learn to go. While it's always a good thing to get more rules in logic games, without deductions all of those rules can feel like the jumble of sticky notes in the case file. That's not how you wanted to go into the client meeting, and it's not how you want to go into the LSAT question set, either. If you have to deal with all six rules individually for every question, you can feel overwhelmed, make sloppy mistakes, and run out of time. If you're feeling ambitious, go back and try the questions. But don't spend too long. If you feel that you're getting bogged down or confused, I'll show you how making the deductions sorts all of this information and puts you in control of the questions.

STEP 4: Deductions

All of the information that you need is, in fact, contained in the setup and the rules, but it will still take you a long time to work through the questions if you don't pause to synthesize that information. The solution is Step 4 of the Kaplan Method: Deductions. There, you'll take a couple of minutes to organize the rules within your sketch. Before tackling the question set, you'll know precisely what is and isn't determined within the game.

The key to effective deductions is to work from what's concrete to what's less defined. Ask, "Who is the most restricted entity in this game?" and "Who presents the greatest restriction for the other entities and spaces?" Try that here.

In this game, the most restricted entity is T. Rule 1 establishes its position once and for all in space 3. Moreover, because of Rule 6, T imposes restrictions on two of the four positions that follow it. By combining those two rules, you can deduce that there will be two confessions and two non-confessions among interrogations 4 through 7.

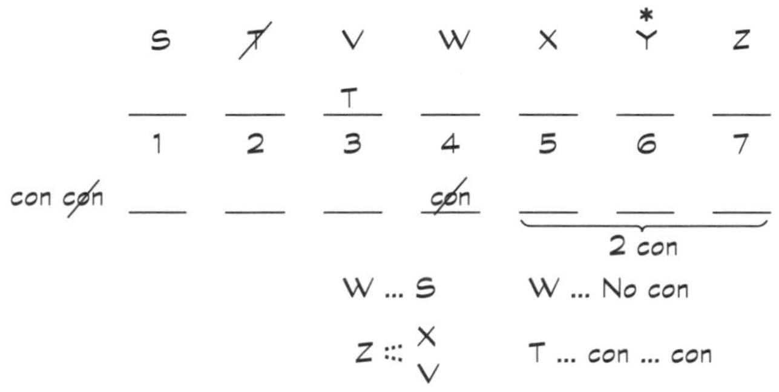

Figure 4.7

That deduction, in turn, implicates Rule 2. Since the fourth interrogation does not produce a confession, the two confessions following T must be from interrogations 5 and 6, 5 and 7, or 6 and 7. Who's affected by that? The answer is W, the other entity that shows up in two of the rules.

From Rules 3 and 5, you can conclude that S does not confess. Now that you've made the deductions regarding T and the interrogations that must produce confessions, you can add W and S right into the sketch. Since two people confess after T and no one confesses after W, W has to follow T. And according to Rule 3, S follows W.

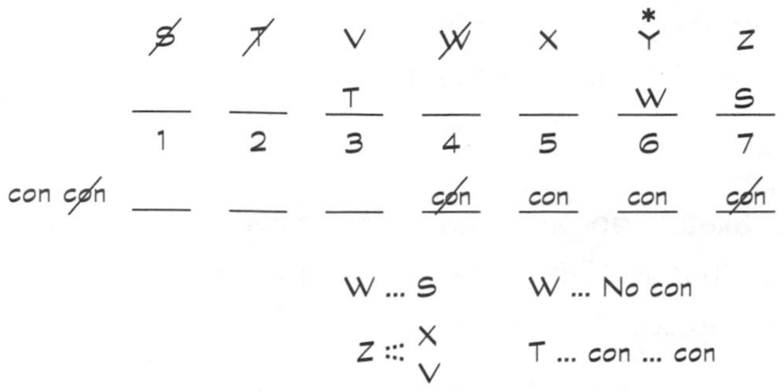

Figure 4.8

Since S must follow W (Rule 3), W cannot be the seventh suspect questioned. Since no one can confess after W is questioned (Rule 5), W must be the sixth suspect interrogated. That makes S seventh, and it locks down interrogations 5 and 6 as the two that produce confessions following T's questioning.

Now you can see that Z, X, and V, all of whom are restricted in Rule 4, and floater Y, are the only entities left for interrogations 1, 2, 4, and 5. Of those entities, Z, which we know must precede both X and V is the most restricted. Z will wind up in either space 1 or space 2. You can write out the implications of those two Options:

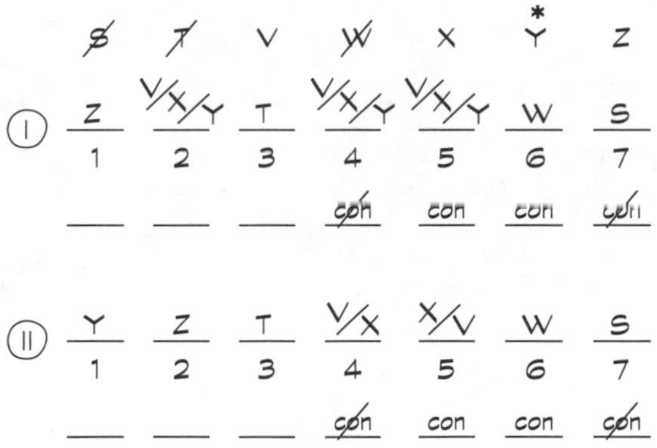

Figure 4.9

When Z is first, V, X, and Y can be arranged in any order among spaces 2, 4, and 5. When Z is second, Y will be the first suspect interrogated and V and X will take positions 4 and 5 in either order. At this point, the only thing you have no idea about is whether spaces 1 through 3 will produce any confessions.

You were able to add an enormous amount of additional certainty to this game. Reflect on how you did it. You started from the most restricted entity—T—and asked, "Which entities or spaces does its placement limit?" Adding your answer to that question into the sketch, you asked, "And what does *that* restrict?" and so on. Throughout this chapter, you'll get better at taking those steps, but that's essentially what making deductions always entails. When you get to the point at which you're just speculating—"I guess space 1 could confess, but it doesn't have to," for example—you're ready for the questions. You know all that can be known.

STEP 5: Questions

Using the final Master Sketch, go back and try to answer the question set. With a complete Master Sketch, I predict that you'll be able to answer all of the questions far more accurately (and much faster) than you could have before.

Explanations

I've reproduced the setup and Master Sketch here, for your reference. But, really, the sketch is all that you'll need. Take a look.

Detectives investigating a citywide increase in burglaries questioned exactly seven suspects—S, T, V, W, X, Y, and Z—each on a different one of seven consecutive days. Each suspect was questioned exactly once. Any suspect who confessed did so while being questioned. The investigation conformed to the following:

T was questioned on day three.
The suspect questioned on day four did not confess.
S was questioned after W was questioned.
Both X and V were questioned after Z was questioned.
No suspects confessed after W was questioned.
Exactly two suspects confessed after T was questioned.[2]

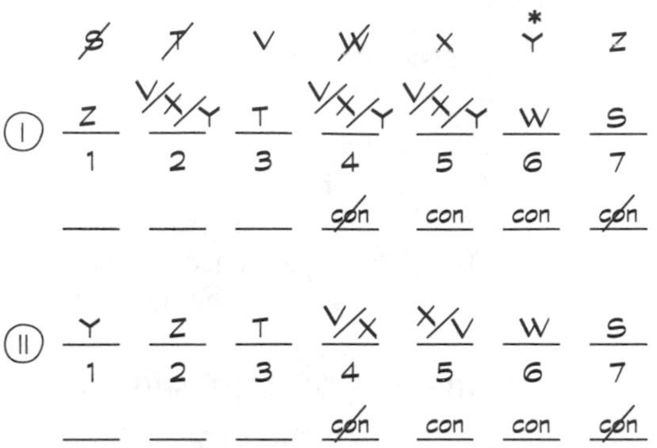

Figure 4.10

12. **(B)**

Which one of the following could be true?

(A)   X was questioned on day one.
(B)   V was questioned on day two.
(C)   Z was questioned on day four.
(D)   W was questioned on day five.
(E)   S was questioned on day six.[3]

This question can be answered with nothing but a glance at your Master Sketch. Only choice (B) is possible (see Option I).

13. **(C)**

If Z was the second suspect to confess, then each of the following statements could be true EXCEPT:

(A)   T confessed.
(B)   T did not confess.
(C)   V did not confess.
(D)   X confessed.
(E)   Y did not confess.[4]

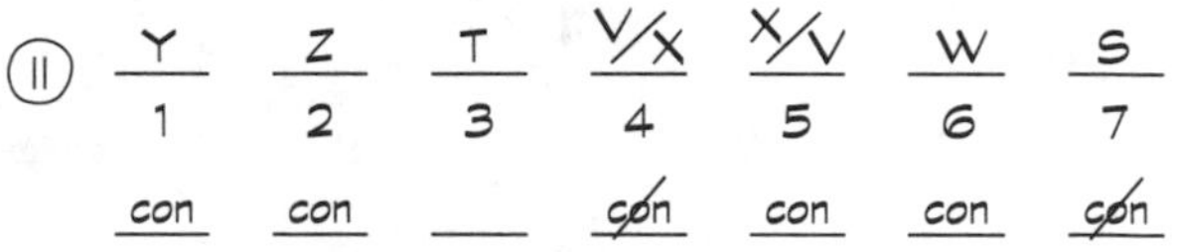

Figure 4.11

This question begins with a new "if" clause. If Z produces the second confession, you must consult Option II (after all, Z is in space 1 in Option I, so that won't work). Moreover, you now know that the first two interrogations produced confessions. That gives you the mini-sketch to use as you evaluate the answers for this question.

---

[2] PrepTest 53, Sec. 2, Game 3
[3] PrepTest 53, Sec. 2, Q 12
[4] PrepTest 53, Sec. 2, Q 13

The correct answer is the one that *must be false*, because the question stem says that the four wrong answers *could be true*. Only choice (E) *must be false*. Y must confess in this scenario, since it takes space 1 and Z produces the second confession in space 2.

14. (A)

If Y was questioned after V but before X, then which one of the following could be true?

(A) V did not confess.
(B) Y confessed.
(C) X did not confess.
(D) X was questioned on day four.
(E) Z was questioned on day two.[5]

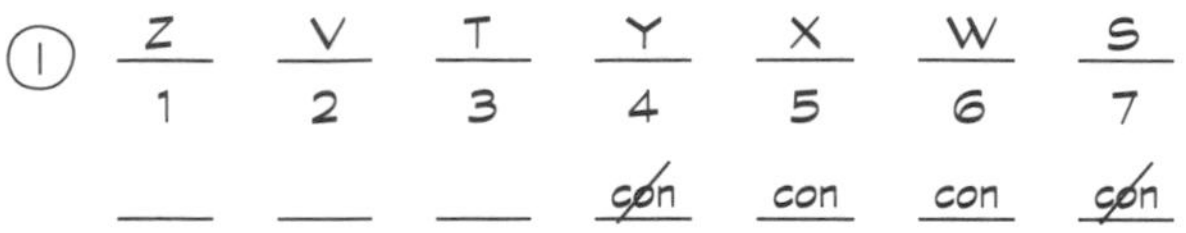

Figure 4.12

Here, the new "if" results in a completely determined sequence of interrogations. The only way to produce the order "V . . . Y . . . X" called for in the question stem is to use Option I. (In Option II, Y has to be in space 1.) Complete your mini-sketch with V in space 2, Y in space 4, and X in space 5. The only wiggle room left is whether spaces 1 through 3 did or didn't produce confessions.

The correct answer *could be true*. Choice (A) gives you such a statement. Since V is in space 2 and you don't know whether the second interrogation produced a confession, it might be the case that V didn't confess. Consult your mini-sketch to see that all four wrong answers *must be false*. Y is in space 4 and did not confess. Choice (B) is out. X is in space 5 and did confess. That knocks out choices (C) and (D). In this scenario, Z must be the first interrogation. Choice (E) is impossible, too.

15. (E)

Which one of the following suspects must have been questioned before T was questioned?

(A) V
(B) W
(C) X
(D) Y
(E) Z[6]

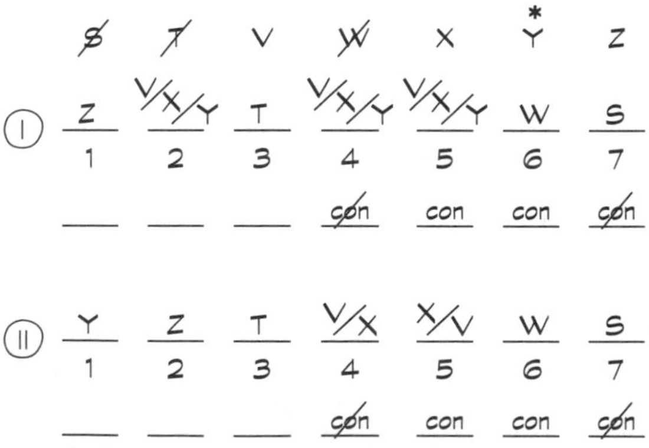

Figure 4.13

There's no new "if" restriction here, so as you did with question 12, answer this one directly from your Master Sketch. Which of the five entities in the answer choices comes prior to T in either Option? It's Z, of course, which must take either space 1 or space 2. That's choice (E), and you're done.

---

[5] PrepTest 53, Sec. 2, Q 14
[6] PrepTest 53, Sec. 2, Q 15

This question is a perfect illustration of the value of Step 4. If you try to forgo the time and effort of making a complete Master Sketch that includes your deductions, getting this answer could take you minutes as you work through the permutations of the six rules to be sure that V, W, X, and Y can each be acceptably placed after T. With the Deductions step behind you, this question takes all of five to ten seconds to answer correctly.

16. **(A)**

If X and Y both confessed, then each of the following could be true EXCEPT:

(A)   V confessed.
(B)   X was questioned on day five.
(C)   Y was questioned on day one.
(D)   Z was questioned on day one.
(E)   Z did not confess.[7]

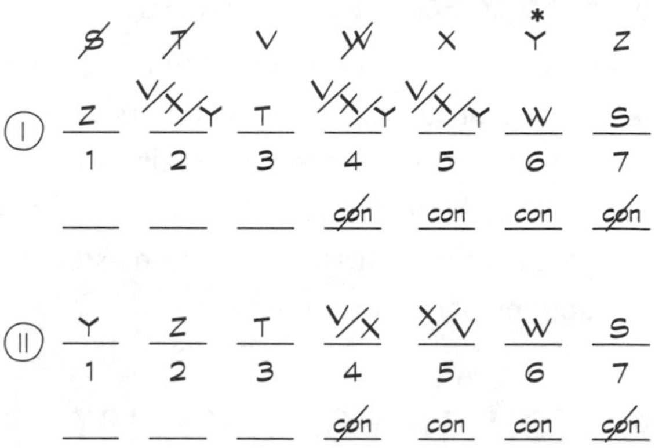

Figure 4.14

The "if" in this question can be accommodated in either Option I or Option II. What's important is to keep both X and Y out of space 4, where you know that the suspect does *not* confess.

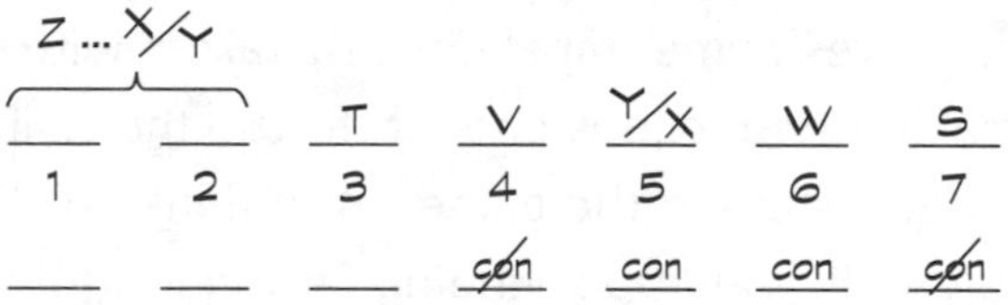

Figure 4.15

In either option, this forces V into the fourth slot. Thus, it cannot be true that V confessed. Choice (A) is the correct answer.

17. **(D)**

If neither X nor V confessed, then which one of the following must be true?

(A)   T confessed.
(B)   V was questioned on day two.
(C)   X was questioned on day four.
(D)   Y confessed.
(E)   Z did not confess.[8]

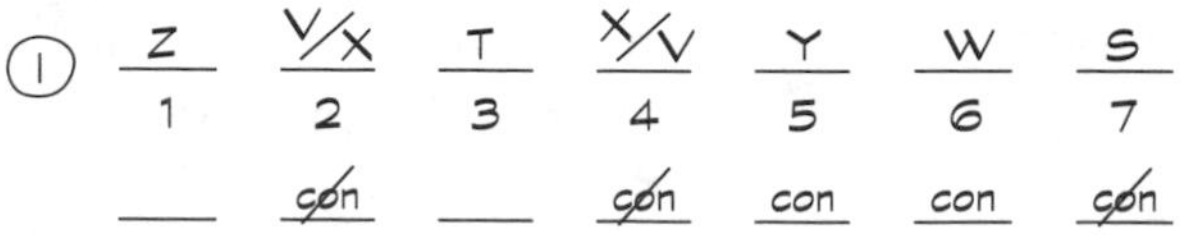

Figure 4.16

---

[7] PrepTest 53, Sec. 2, Q 16
[8] PrepTest 53, Sec. 2, Q 17

This time, the "if" can occur only in Option I. (In Option II, one of V or X must take the fifth slot and confess.) To keep V and X from confessing in Option I, you have to put them in spaces 2 and 4, forcing Y into the fifth spot (see the mini-sketch). The fifth suspect questioned always confesses, so choice (D) *must be true*. That's the correct answer.

Step Four Scores You Points

Step 4 of the Kaplan Method is what separates logic games amateurs from logic games masters. I've heard hundreds of students proclaim how easy the questions are once they have a "complete sketch." Those who really took their own words to heart and learned to make the available deductions every time are the ones who transformed their logic games performance. Take a closer look at the Deductions step as I outline the five types of rules that will lead to deductions game after game.

A DEDUCTIONS CHECKLIST
"How do I know if I've made all the deductions?"

When you're first practicing Step 4, the hardest thing to get a feel for is when you've made all of the available deductions. This is a double-edged sword. On the one hand, you may miss a crucial deduction and head into the questions without much more than what you got from the rules. That experience leaves some impatient test takers with a "why bother" attitude, and they don't practice making deductions enough to use the skill effectively. On the other hand, perfectionists will sit and stare at the game setup thinking, "There must be more that I can figure out." As a result, they wind up spending far too long before they move on to the questions and concluding that they just can't afford the time that the Deductions step takes.

Fortunately, there is a way to avoid both aspects of that dilemma, a checklist of the kinds of rules that lead to deductions. Learning it will ensure that you quickly find all available deductions *and* that you know when you've found them all so that you can move on to the questions with confidence.

RULES AND LIMITATIONS THAT LEAD TO DEDUCTIONS

Blocks of Entities
> Rules that join two or more entities such that when one is placed, the other must follow or move in response; e.g., "A and B occupy consecutive seats," "D and E play on the same team."

Limited Options
> Rules or restrictions that force all acceptable arrangements to follow one of two patterns; e.g., "F is either in position 1 or position 6," "Either three or four of the seven bills are paid on Wednesday and the rest on Thursday."

> **Established Entities**
>
> Rules that place an entity in one position or within one group once and for all; e.g., "T is assigned to boat 3," "Y is the fourth client interviewed."
>
> **Number Restrictions**
>
> Rules or restrictions that limit the numerical dimensions of the game; e.g., "Each committee has three members," "No more than two clients are interviewed per day."
>
> **Duplications**
>
> Two or more rules that restrict a common entity or space; e.g., "M is assigned to boat 1" and "M and N are assigned to different boats;" "If T is chosen, then U is not chosen" and "If S is chosen, then U is chosen."

Not all LSAT logic games have all five of these types of rules and restrictions. As you've seen, games featuring formal logic may include nothing but a string of duplications. Sequencing actions are likely to have blocks of entities—"K and L are separated by exactly one space"—but rarely allow for numerical deductions, since they usually provide for one entity per space. As you're setting up a game and analyzing the rules, simply catalogue the potential deductions and look for the points of greatest restriction (i.e., the most restrictive or restricted entities).

The first letters of these five types of rules create the acronym BLEND. That's helpful for remembering what to look for while you're learning how to make deductions, but don't confuse it for an ordered series of steps. You don't look for blocks of entities first, Limited Options second, and so on. Remember, work from what's most concrete down to what's least concrete. In order to give you a better handle on the BLEND rule types, I'll point them out next in a handful of games, some of which you've seen in earlier chapters.

GUIDED PRACTICE: BLEND IN ACTION
Duplications and Number Restrictions

Here's another game with a lot of rules. That's good, of course, because it will provide a lot of restriction to where the entities can be placed. But it puts a high premium on your ability to make deductions. Go through Steps 1 through 3 of the Kaplan Method on your own. I'll review the setup and analysis of the rules before moving on to Step 4.

In a repair facility there are exactly six technicians: Stacy, Urma, Wim, Xena, Yolanda, and Zane. Each technician repairs machines of at least one of the following three types—radios, televisions, and VCRs—and no other types. The following conditions apply:

>   Xena and exactly three other technicians repair radios.
>   Yolanda repairs both televisions and VCRs.
>   Stacy does not repair any type of machine that Yolanda repairs.
>   Zane repairs more types of machines than Yolanda repairs.
>   Wim does not repair any type of machine that Stacy repairs.
>   Urma repairs exactly two types of machines.[9]

STEPS 1 AND 2: Overview and Sketch

You might remember this game from the discussion of game tasks. Likely, you pictured the six technicians at their work stations. Walking by, you could see that so-and-so has only radios at her station or that what's-his-name has televisions and VCRs. So your initial framework sketch looks like this:

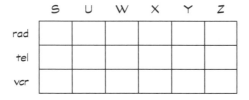

Figure 4.17

You can put a check mark to indicate a match and an X when you've ruled out a match. When you're unsure whether a given technician repairs a given machine, just leave the box blank.

STEP 3: Rules

As always, your goal should have been to build the rule inside the framework if possible. You can do that with the first rule. Put a check mark in Xena's radio box. Don't forget to also account for the number restriction given by this rule: You'll need a total of four of the radio boxes checked.

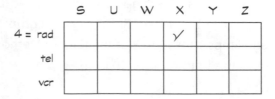

Figure 4.18

---

[9] PrepTest 48, Sec. 2, Game 3

Rule 2 can also go into the sketch. Don't make more of the rule than is there, though. You don't know whether Yolanda repairs radios.

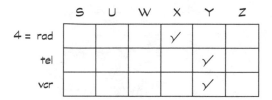

Figure 4.19

You can jot down the third rule in shorthand underneath the sketch. Because Rules 2 and 3 share Yolanda, you've now got duplications. You'll be coming back to them to make an important deduction.

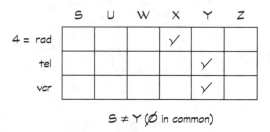

S ≠ Y (∅ in common)

Figure 4.20

Rule 4 goes beneath the sketch as well.

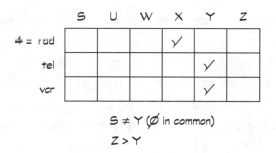

S ≠ Y (∅ in common)

Z > Y

Figure 4.21

Rule 5 is just like Rule 3. Notice that Stacy is mentioned in both. She's on her way to becoming very important in the Deductions step.

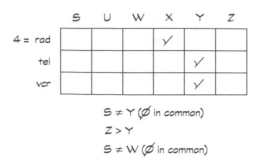

Figure 4.22

Finally, you can note Rule 6 above or below Urma's column within the framework.

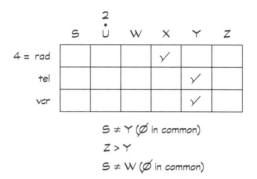

Figure 4.23

This is, at a minimum, what you should have on the page at the end of Step 3.

You may have noticed one or more deductions already. Students sometimes ask, "If I see some deductions while I'm diagramming the rules, should I put them in the sketch right then or should I wait until after I've written out all of the rules?" The answer is that, as you first begin to practice, you should probably wait until you have all of the rules down. That way, you'll learn to be more systematic and thorough. The truth of the matter, however, is that as you get more and more adept at this Step, you'll likely start making some deductions as you go. There's nothing wrong with that, as long as you've learned to catch all available deductions and you don't allow yourself to be sloppy.

STEP 4: Deductions

Here's what you're looking at as you begin Step 4:

In a repair facility there are exactly six technicians: Stacy, Urma, Wim, Xena, Yolanda, and Zane. Each technician repairs machines of at least one of the following three types—radios, televisions, and VCRs—and no other types. The following conditions apply:

Xena and exactly three other technicians repair radios.
Yolanda repairs both televisions and VCRs.
Stacy does not repair any type of machine that Yolanda repairs.
Zane repairs more types of machines than Yolanda repairs.
Wim does not repair any type of machine that Stacy repairs.
Urma repairs exactly two types of machines.[10]

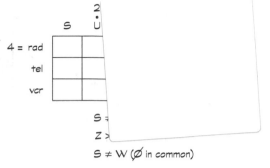

Figure 4.24

To get yourself started, determine the most restricted (or restrict*ive*) entity. No technician's column is completely established, but Xena and Yolanda each have at least some of their cells checked. Of the two, notice that Yolanda is a "duplicator"—she's present in two more rules. Without a doubt, Yolanda is your starting point for deductions.

Start with Rule 4, which shares Yolanda with Rule 2 and adds a number restriction. Since Yolanda already repairs two types of machines, Zane must repair all three types in order to obey the rule. Moreover, you now know that Yolanda does not repair radios. (If she did, Zane couldn't repair more types of machines than she does.)

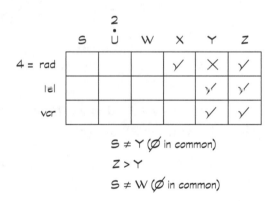

Figure 4.25

Just like that, two columns—Y's and Z's—are completely established.

Now, consider Yolanda's role in Rule 3, the other rule in which she is a duplicator. Since Yolanda and Stacy can have nothing in common, you now know that Stacy repairs only radios. A third column is locked down.

---

[10] PrepTest 48, Sec. 2, Game 3

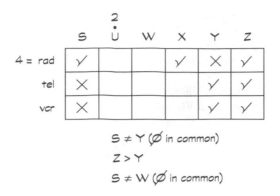

Figure 4.26

Stacy, whose column you just determined, is also a duplicator, present in Rules 3 and 5. Since you now know that she will repair radios, you know that Wim won't repair them.

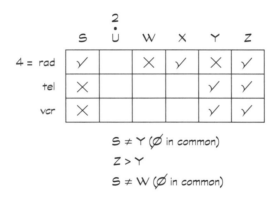

Figure 4.27

Don't push this further than what you can validly deduce, though. You cannot determine, at this point, whether Wim repairs televisions, VCRs, or both.

You've wrung everything you can from Rules 2, 3, 4, and 5. But there's still more that you can determine. Remember that Rule 1 contained a number restriction: Four of the technicians will repair radios. You noted that next to the "radio" row. What you've now added to your sketch allows you to see that Urma must also repair radios. And one of your rows is now completely determined, too.

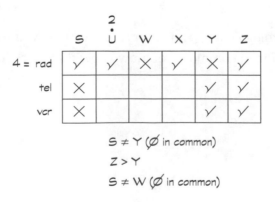

Figure 4.28

Urma is the subject of Rule 6. You can't make any concrete deductions from this rule, but you can now see that she'll repair either radios and televisions *or* radios and VCRs.

You were able to add a lot of certainty to this game. Consider how you did it. The bulk of the restrictions—and this is typical of Matching games—came from duplications and number restrictions. You started with the most restricted and restrictive entity, Yolanda, who appeared in three rules. She allowed you to determine Zane's column and set off a string of deductions that ran through Stacy, Wim, and Urma. By the end of the Deductions step, you are able to see precisely which cells are determined and which are still in play. I'll have you come back to this game in the next chapter, where you'll focus on the questions. For now, take a look at a game in which the most important deductions come from different elements in the BLEND checklist.

Established Entities and Blocks of Entities

Here's a game that you haven't seen before, but I'm sure that its action and arrangement will seem familiar once you conduct your overview and visualize the task. Take a couple of minutes and complete Steps 1 through 3 of the Kaplan Method. Once you're done, review your analysis of the rules. Then, I'll take you through this game's all-important Deductions step.

> In a single day, exactly seven trucks—S, T, U, W, X, Y, and Z—are the only arrivals at a warehouse. No truck arrives at the same time as any other truck, and no truck arrives more than once that day. Each truck is either green or red (but not both). The following conditions apply:
>> No two consecutive arrivals are red.
>> Y arrives at some time before both T and W.
>> Exactly two of the trucks that arrive before Y are red.
>> S is the sixth arrival.
>> Z arrives at some time before U.[11]

STEPS 1 AND 2: Overview and Sketch

It's not hard to imagine the scene. You'll need to lay out a series of seven numbered slots in which you'll keep track of the trucks' arrival order. Beneath each numbered slot (or beside it, if you arrange your sketch vertically), you'll put another slot to account for the color of each truck, either red or green.

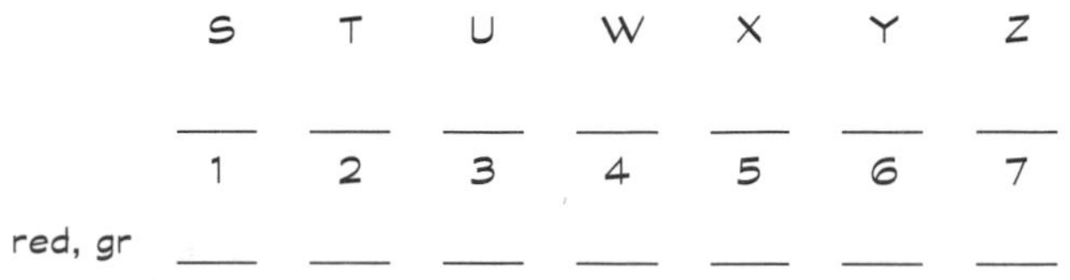

Figure 4.29

---

[11] PrepTest 37, Sec. 3, Game 2

STEP 3: **Rules**

The rules that accompany this game are succinct and, at first, may appear to restrict the entities loosely. Only one of them can be placed immediately within the framework.

Rule 1 creates an "anti-block." It tells you that you can never see red trucks next to each other.

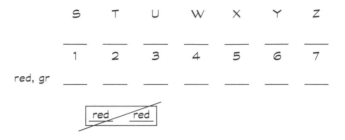

Figure 4.30

Notice that the rule is phrased negatively: Red trucks *cannot* arrive consecutively. Think about its affirmative implications, though. It tells you that any red truck must have a green truck in the space right before or right after it. Don't confuse this with a rule that says that red and green must alternate throughout the order, though; green trucks *can* arrive consecutively.

Rule 2 creates a loose block, but it restricts three entities. Y precedes both T and W. Remember, this rule doesn't tell you anything about the relationship between T and W.

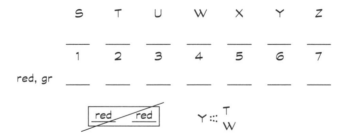

Figure 4.31

Rule 3 creates another loose block, and again, three spaces are restricted. Rule 2 restricts truck Y with regard to two other named trucks. This time, Y is restricted with regard to the number of red trucks that precede its arrival.

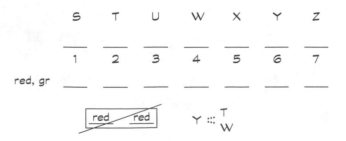

Figure 4.31A

Finally, Rule 4 gives you something concrete. S can go right into the framework.

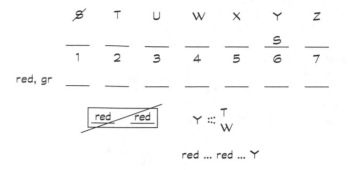

Figure 4.32

Rule 5 creates another loose block, giving the relative order of two trucks that hadn't been mentioned before. You'll just have to write this down below the framework, too.

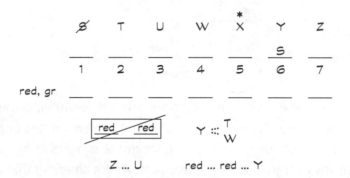

Figure 4.32A

Finally, notice that truck X is the floater, the unrestricted entity, as shown with the asterisk.

So far, so good. Your current understanding of the rules would allow you to trudge through the questions. But as you'll see, making the available deductions puts you in a far better position to breeze through the question set.

STEP 4: **Deductions**

Here's the state of the game at the outset of Step 4:

In a single day, exactly seven trucks—S, T, U, W, X, Y, and Z—are the only arrivals at a warehouse. No truck arrives at the same time as any other truck, and no truck arrives more than once that day. Each truck is either green or red (but not both). The following conditions apply:

No two consecutive arrivals are red.

Y arrives at some time before both T and W.

Exactly two of the trucks that arrive before Y are red.

S is the sixth arrival.

Z arrives at some time before U.[12]

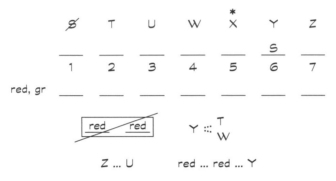

Figure 4.33

This game presents a great example of the importance of identifying the greatest point of restriction within a game. There's no doubt that S is the most restric*ted* entity. It's established in space 6, after all. But beyond occupying a space in the order, S is not at all restric*tive*—it doesn't appear explicitly in any other rule. There is, however, an entity that restricts (and, thus, is restricted by) a great number of other entities and/or spaces. Do you spot which one it is?

Truck Y is the entity that will initiate your deductions here. It's a duplicator, appearing in both Rule 2 and Rule 3, each of which makes Y part of a block of entities. Consider the effect of these two blocks as they work in concert to establish Y's position in the game. The latest Y can appear is in space 4. Both T and W must follow Y in the order of arrival. Because space 6 is already occupied by Established Entity S, a minimum of three other entities must follow Y in the sequence. So you can push Y no farther toward the back of the list than space 4.

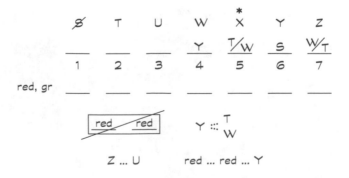

Figure 4.34

[12] PrepTest 37, Sec. 3, Game 2

In fact, you can't push Y any closer to the front of the list than space 4, either. Because of Rule 3, Y must be preceded by two red trucks. And because of Rule 1, those red trucks must be separated by at least one green truck. Thus, the combination of the two loose blocks (along with the presence of the established entity in space 6) locks Y firmly in space 4.

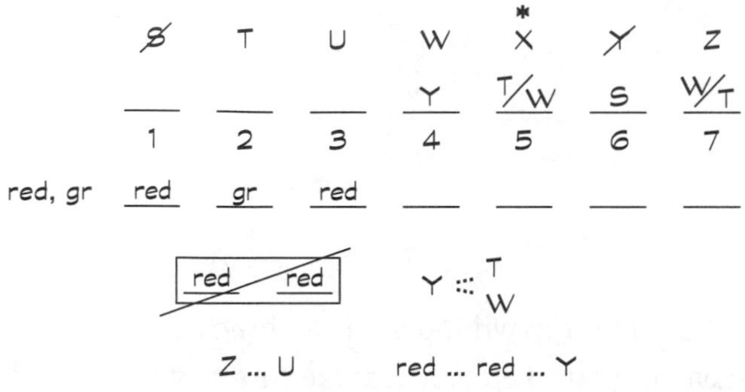

Figure 4.35

Note that with Y in space 4, you know that one of T and W will take space 5 and the other will take space 7. Likewise, you now know that the first and third trucks are red (they're the two red trucks that must precede Y's arrival) and that the second truck is green.

In fact, there's another truck whose color you can determine: You know with certainty that the fourth truck—truck Y—is green. Were it red, Rule 1 would be violated.

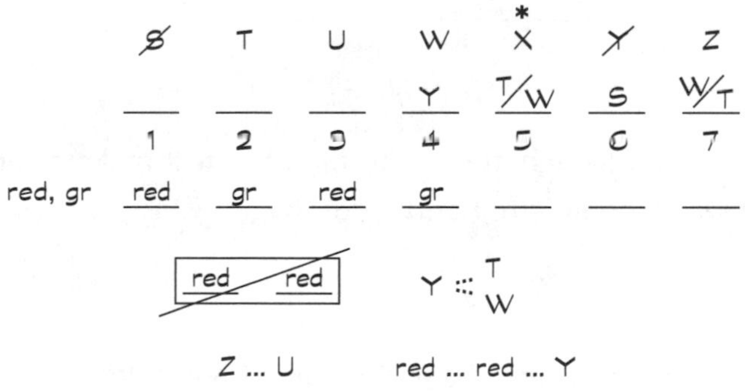

Figure 4.36

The remaining trucks are Z and U (in that order, according to Rule 5) and floater X. They'll take the only open spaces—spaces 1 through 3—in one of the following orders:

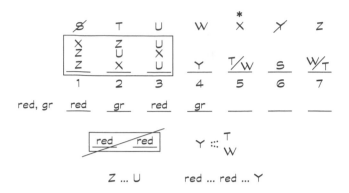

Figure 4.37

On test day, you may choose to forgo writing in those three possibilities for X, Z, and U, depending on the space you have for your sketch. Just make sure that you've seen how restricted even these loosely related entities and the floater are by the time you've completed your deductions.

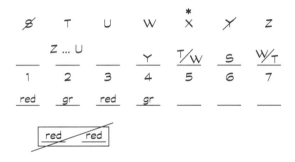

Figure 4.38

With this as your final Master Sketch, there's nothing the test makers can throw at you in the question set that you won't be able to handle quickly.

Limited Options

Limited Options, the scenario in which the entire game breaks down into one of two possibilities, is often the most helpful type of deduction you can make. Think of Limited Options as the test maker's way of saying "either . . . or . . ." Indeed, at times the rules giving rise to Limited Options are that literal. When a game offers you Limited Options, make two complementary sketches, one for each option. Once you've created the dual sketches and filled in the additional deductions that arise within each, you're usually left with only a handful of acceptable arrangements. You'll be close to being able to see all of the ways that the game can be completed.

Limited Options stem from one of three conditions. It's worth remembering what they are.

LIMITED OPTIONS COME FROM . . .

1. A "Key Player"
When a particular entity can take exactly two positions or placements, either of which give rise to additional restrictions among the remaining entities

2. Number Restrictions
When exactly two numerical arrangements are acceptable; for example, Committee A has three members and Committee B has four, or vice versa

3. Blocks of Entities
When a block can occupy exactly two different positions or be placed on exactly two different teams, either of which gives rise to additional restrictions among the remaining entities

You've seen Limited Options games already in this book, and you'll see several more. They're often the subtlest of all deductions to spot, and it will take practice before you're an expert. But whenever they're available, they're invaluable. Keep a keen eye out for the possibility of Limited Options in Parts II and III of this book, where I'll discuss game types and have you do full section practice. Here are a couple of tips: Occasionally, Limited Options will be announced by a single rule. This is especially true of key players—"G is either in seat 1 or else in seat 6." More often, you'll need to combine rules to derive the Limited Options. In fact, the very first game I had you look at in chapter 1—the Thunderstorm game—is a great example. In that game, the rules combined to limit the town Jackson to the two spaces at the end of the sequence. Review that game after this discussion and see how you'd now be able to deduce the Limited Options scenario yourself.

First, take a look at a game that you haven't seen before. Start by performing Steps 1 through 3 of the Kaplan Method: Conduct an overview, create the basic sketch, and fill in the rules. When you've finished those Steps, pause for a moment and see if you can spot the rule or rules that lead to a valuable Limited Options deduction.

Exactly six people—Lulu, Nam, Ofelia, Pachai, Santiago, and Tyrone—are the only contestants in a chess tournament. The tournament consists of four games, played one after the other. Exactly two people play in each game, and each person plays in at least one game. The following conditions must apply:

Tyrone does not play in the first or third game.

Lulu plays in the last game.

Nam plays in only one game and it is not against Pachai.

Santiago plays in exactly two games, one just before and one just after the only game that Ofelia plays in.[13]

STEPS 1 AND 2: Overview and Sketch

In this game, you're being asked to set up a schedule of four games in a chess tournament. The order of the games is important; you're told that they're "played one after the other." Naturally, you'll need to match the two contestants in each game as well. You could arrange this game horizontally or vertically. Either way, you'll have four numbered positions with spaces for two players each.

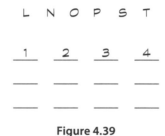

Figure 4.39

It's worth noting that you have six players for eight game positions. Since "each person plays in at least one game," either one player will have to participate in three games or two of them will have to participate in two games each. The others will play only once each.

STEP 3: Rules

You can depict Rule 1 within the framework of the sketch, but only negatively.

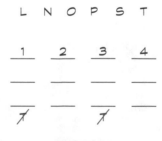

Figure 4.40

Without knowing whether Tyrone plays in one game or two, you can't place him affirmatively in game 2, game 4, or both.

---

[13] PrepTest 45, Sec. 3, Game 2

Rule 2 is also amenable to placement within the framework.

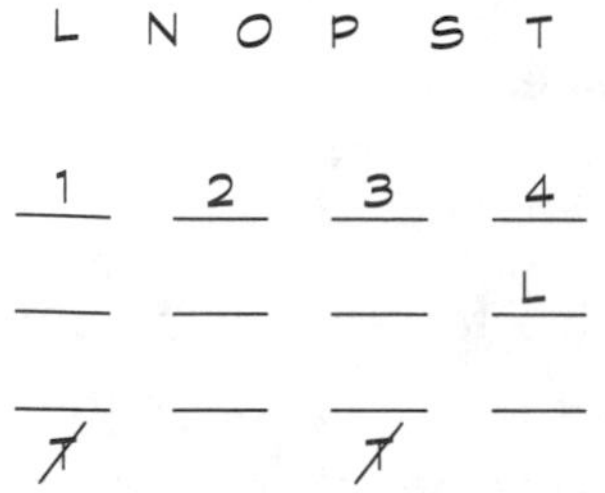

Figure 4.41

Here again, exercise restraint. You don't know that game 4 is Lulu's only appearance in the tournament.

Rule 3 has two elements, but you can't draw either of them in the sketch at this point. Make a note above N in the roster of entities to indicate that Nam makes only one appearance in the tournament. Beside your framework, diagram the "anti-block" that prevents N and P from being opponents.

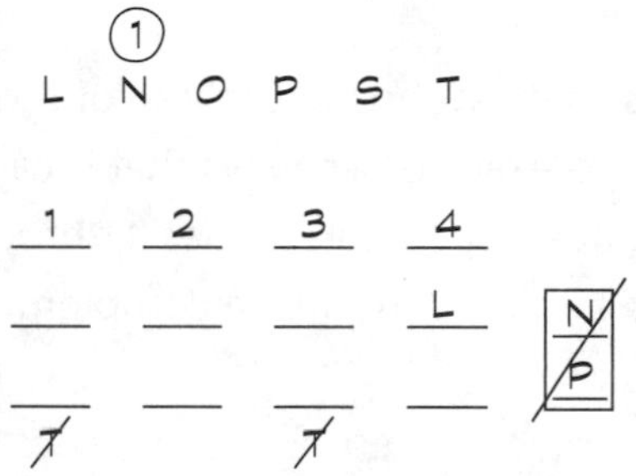

Figure 4.42

The final rule is huge. It restricts two entities and determines a block of three consecutive spaces. Make note of what you learn about the numbers: O appears only once, and S appears exactly twice. More importantly, draw out this order of game assignments in a way that reflects your framework.

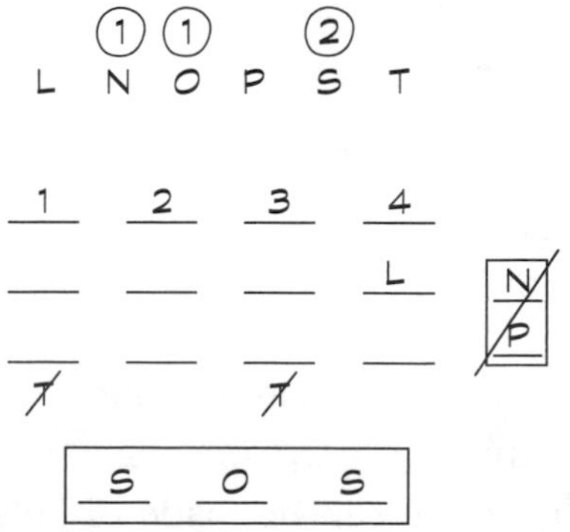

Figure 4.43

If you tried the questions from this game with nothing more than what you have here, you'd be in for a fairly tiring slog. But with just a little more effort, this game's acceptable arrangements begin to take fairly clear shape.

STEP 4: Deductions

Looking at the game as you have it after diagramming the rules, can you see an "either/or" scenario that will allow you to determine a chunk of the possible arrangements here? Think about which of the rules creates the greatest restriction within the game.

Exactly six people—Lulu, Nam, Ofelia, Pachai, Santiago, and Tyrone—are the only contestants in a chess tournament. The tournament consists of four games, played one after the other. Exactly two people play in each game, and each person plays in at least one game. The following conditions must apply:

Tyrone does not play in the first or third game.
Lulu plays in the last game.
Nam plays in only one game and it is not against Pachai.
Santiago plays in exactly two games, one just before and one just after the only game that Ofelia plays in.[14]

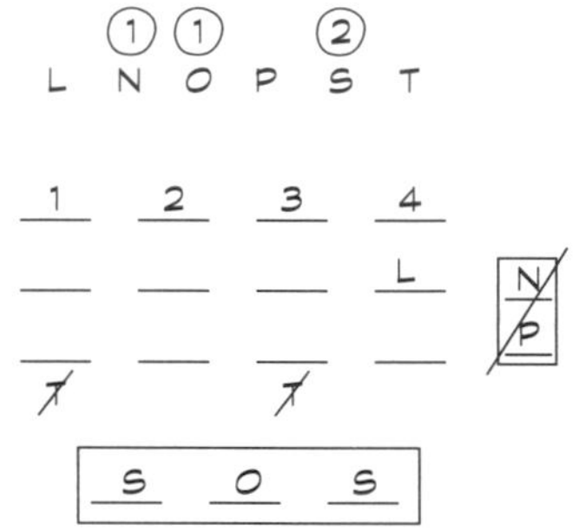

Figure 4.44

Rule 4 creates a block of entities that extends over three of the four games played in the tournament. That means that there are exactly two ways that it can be placed into the framework of the game: *Either* the S-O-S block appears in games 1 through 3, *or* it appears in games 2 through 4. Represent those two Limited Options in complementary sketches.

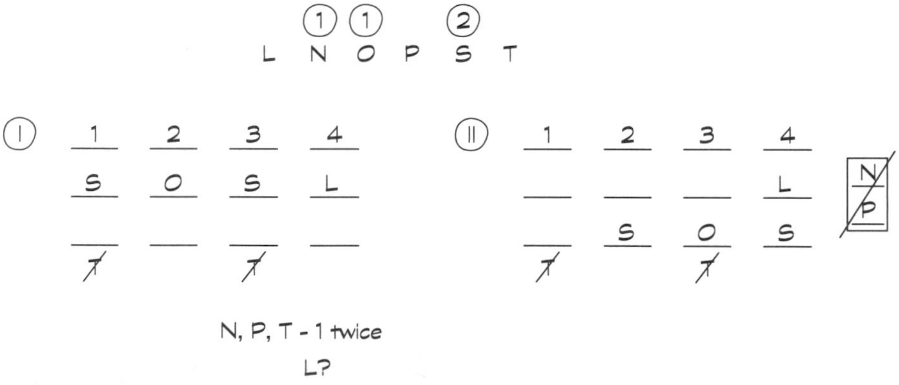

Figure 4.45

Drawing out the two options gives the game much more coherence. Consider what else you're able to deduce in each option.

In Option I, you still need to place N, P, and T. In the fourth open spot, you'll place L, P, or T a second time. Make note of that beneath the Option I diagram. There's no risk of N and P being opponents in this scenario, so no more can be made of Rule 3. Nor does Rule 1 apply any

---

[14] PrepTest 45, Sec. 3, Game 2

additional restriction. It's possible for T to appear in game 2, game 4, or both. You've learned as much as possible from Option I.

Option II is another story. There's only one position open to Tyrone, so you can safely place T in game 2, competing against S.

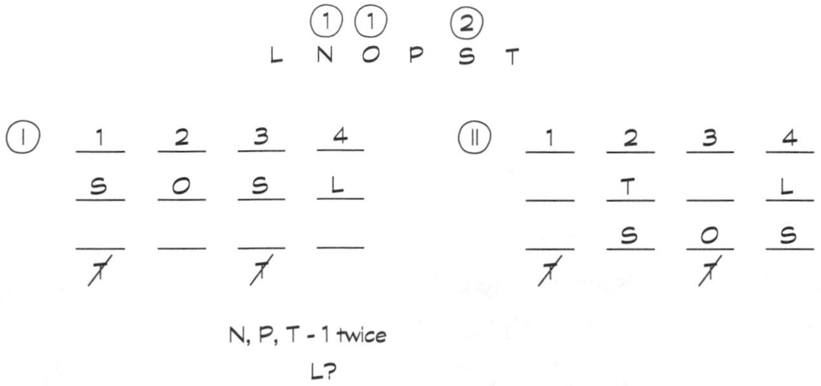

Figure 4.46

Rule 3 prevents N and P from being opponents. One must be assigned to game 1 and the other to game 3. Represent those alternatives as follows:

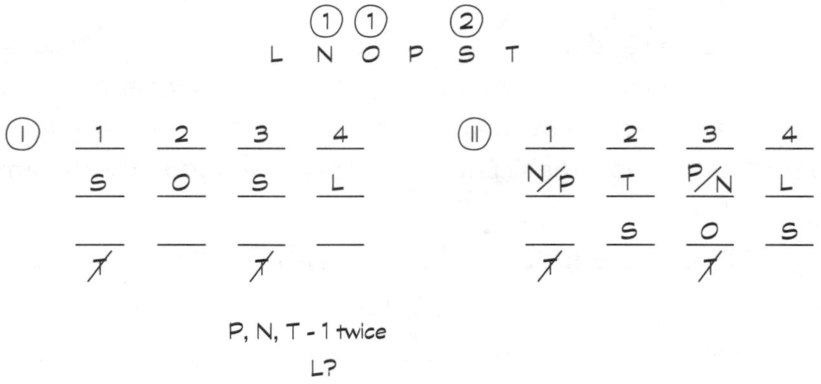

Figure 4.47

There's only one entity that can take the final open space in game 1. Since either N or P is playing in the game already, Rule 3 prevents the other one from taking the open seat. O and S are already placed within the game (and Rule 4, remember, dictates that S plays exactly twice and O exactly once). T can never play in the first game by virtue of Rule 1. So in Option II, L will play twice, once in game 4 and once in game 1.

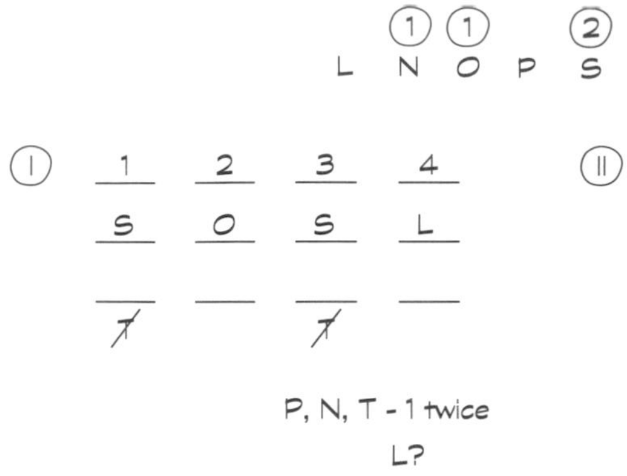

Figure 4.48

Your Master Sketch, and this is always the case with Limited Options, consists of both options, presented side by side or one under the other.

It's quite common in Limited Options games to have one option that is almost completely determined while the other has much more wiggle room. In the Chess Tournament game, Option II was the more determined. Savvy test takers will anticipate a couple of questions that call attention to one of the options, a couple more that require considering the other option, and a couple that take both into account.

As profoundly helpful as the Deductions step can be, most Logic Games sections also include a game with few, if any, deductions beyond the original rules. It's very important to know when you've made all of the available deductions and be confident that it's time to move on to the question set. Take a look at how the BLEND checklist can help you in such games.

Don't Struggle to Find Deductions That Aren't There

Here's a game you haven't seen before. Its task should seem quite familiar by now. Take a few minutes to assess what you're being asked to do. Try to design the framework for the sketch and add the rules as best you can. Then I'll show you how the Deductions step will work on a game like this one.

> There are exactly six groups in this year's Civic Parade: firefighters, gymnasts, jugglers, musicians, puppeteers, and veterans. Each group marches as a unit; the groups are ordered from first, at the front of the parade, to sixth, at the back. The following conditions apply:
> At least two groups march behind the puppeteers but ahead of the musicians.
> Exactly one group marches behind the firefighters but ahead of the veterans.
> The gymnasts are the first, third, or fifth group.[15]

---

[15] PrepTest 43, Sec. 4, Game 1

STEPS 1 AND 2: Overview and Sketch

The setup of this game provides a pretty clear mental picture. You can see the six groups marching one at a time. This is a typical Sequencing action. What's more, the inclusion in the rules of specific numbers of spaces between groups tells you to draw this with a Strict Sequencing framework. At this point, your sketch looks something like this:

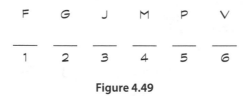

Figure 4.49

STEP 3: Rules

The rules in this game provide fairly strong restrictions, but they require you to read carefully and analyze their impact before writing them down. A sloppy mistake with one of the rules in this game could wind up costing you four or five points, so make sure you pay close attention.

The first rule is the most complicated. It tells you the relative order and distance between the puppeteers and the musicians. The puppeteers are earlier in the parade order, and *at least* two groups march between them and the musicians' group. Diagram the rule with something along these lines:

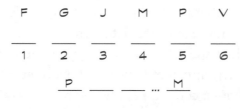

Figure 4.50

Note that despite the specificity of this rule, you can't place the groups precisely within the framework. The puppeteers will be limited to spaces 1 through 3 and the musicians to spaces 4 through 6. Beyond that, it's impossible to nail down their positions.

Rule 2 presents a similar restriction on the firefighters and the veterans, but this rule's distance restriction is more precise: *Exactly* one space intervenes here. Here's the rule added to the sketch:

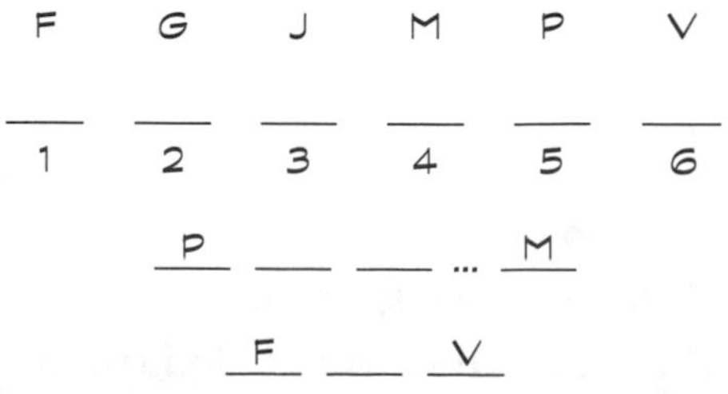

F   G   J   M   P   V
___ ___ ___ ___ ___ ___
 1   2   3   4   5   6
          P   ___ ___ ... M
               F   ___   V

Figure 4.51

Again, there's no way to place the block of entities precisely within the framework. It might take spaces 1 and 3, 2 and 4, 3 and 5, or 4 and 6.

The final rule controls just one of the entities, the gymnasts. It restricts them to one of the odd-numbered spaces within the parade order. Enter that rule into your diagram like this, at least initially:

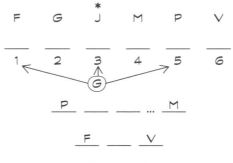

Figure 4.52

Note, too, that the jugglers are unrestricted. Entity J is your floater, acceptable in any open space. That's where you are at the end of the Rules step. Your job in the Deductions step is to see how the restrictions interact to reveal further limitations on the game.

STEP 4: Deductions

Right away, you get a big clue that there will be few, if any, deductions: It's difficult to spot a particular entity that qualifies as the most restricted. The puppeteers, musicians, and gymnasts are restricted to three possible spaces each and the firefighters and veterans to four each. Even worse, it's not immediately apparent how any of the rules interact, though they must at some level. None of them share a common entity and none mentions a common position or slot in the order.

For many test takers, especially those who are very diligent about finding all possible restrictions, the temptation is to forgo making deductions and give in to random speculation. Going about things this way will leave you breathless: "If the gymnasts are third, then the puppeteers could be first and the musicians could be last. Of course, the puppeteers could also be second and the musicians fifth. Then the firefighters and veterans could take spaces four and six. That means…" If you get caught up in trying to reason through every possible permutation, you'll have no time left to actually answer the questions and get the LSAT points.

Instead, turn to the BLEND checklist and reason through Step 4 like so:

Blocks of Entities: There are two blocks here, one each from Rules 1 and 2. Do they allow for any further certainty? In this game, they don't. Your initial diagram for each rule allows the blocks to shift up and down the order. There are no deductions here.

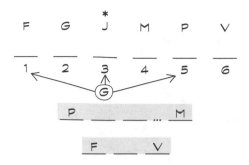

Figure 4.53

Limited Options: Arguably, Rule 3 provides a three-way Limited Options set for the gymnasts. LSAT experts can argue pretty heatedly about whether it's beneficial to draw out three alternate sketches for Limited Options (although we all agree that two-sketch Limited Options are of enormous value). The real takeaway from Rule 3 in this game is that, even if you did draw out three framework lines in order to show where G could be placed, you wouldn't give the game any further clarity.

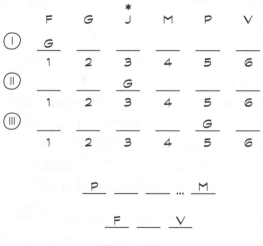

Figure 4.54

The gymnasts don't restrict any other entities directly, and both blocks still have wiggle room within any of the three potential options.

Established Entities: There are none here.

Number Restrictions: The entities are limited to one space each—the setup said, "Each group marches as a unit"—but that distribution is as simple as possible already. Numbers won't give you any additional deductions here.

Duplications: No rules share common entities or restrict common spaces.

In this game, there just aren't any deductions to make beyond understanding the restrictions that the rules provide. That will happen in some games. In situations like this, rather than doubt yourself, just run down the BLEND checklist. If none of the elements lead to additional certainties, you're ready for the questions. You could, I suppose, write out the negative implications of the two sequence rules like so:

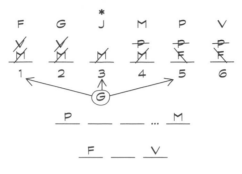

Figure 4.55

Some LSAT prep books make a big deal out these negative inferences. But really, those crossed-out letters are implied by the rules as you originally wrote them. Jot them down if doing so is helpful to you, but realize that they fall short of true deductions in the sense of combining rules to reveal additional restrictions.

STEP 5: Questions

Don't allow a lack of earth-shattering deductions to shake your confidence. When there are no additional restrictions to build into your sketch, simply turn directly to the questions. One thing you'll likely notice is that games with few up-front deductions usually have a high number of "If" questions. Each of these "ifs" supplies an additional restriction that will lead to additional deductions within that question. Start by drawing a mini-sketch containing the new "if," and work out from there. In a sense, it's as if these questions defer the Deductions step until you're already in the question set. The upside is that they always provide a starting point for your work.

Here's the Civic Parade game, complete with its Master Sketch and three questions. Take about four or five minutes to try the questions. You'll see that you can answer them all with nothing more than the information you already have. Make sure to draw a mini-sketch and use it for a "mini-Deductions step" on each of the three "If" questions.

Questions 1–3

There are exactly six groups in this year's Civic Parade: firefighters, gymnasts, jugglers, musicians, puppeteers, and veterans. Each group marches as a unit; the groups are ordered from first, at the front of the parade, to sixth, at the back. The following conditions apply:

At least two groups march behind the puppeteers but ahead of the musicians.

Exactly one group marches behind the firefighters but ahead of the veterans.

The gymnasts are the first, third, or fifth group.

1. Which one of the following could be an accurate list of the groups in the Civic Parade in order from first to last?

   (A) firefighters, puppeteers, veterans, musicians, gymnasts, jugglers

   (B) gymnasts, puppeteers, jugglers, musicians, firefighters, veterans

   (C) veterans, puppeteers, firefighters, gymnasts, jugglers, musicians

   (D) jugglers, puppeteers, gymnasts, firefighters, musicians, veterans

   (E) musicians, veterans, jugglers, firefighters, gymnasts, puppeteers

2. If the gymnasts march immediately ahead of the veterans, then which one of the following could be the fourth group?

   (A) gymnasts
   (B) jugglers
   (C) musicians
   (D) puppeteers
   (E) veterans

3. If the veterans march immediately behind the puppeteers, then which one of the following could be the second group?

   (A) firefighters
   (B) gymnasts
   (C) jugglers
   (D) musicians
   (E) veterans[16]

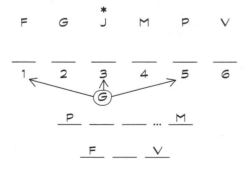

Figure 4.56

[16] PrepTest 43, Sec. 4, Game 1, Qs 1–3

Explanations

1. (D)

> Which one of the following could be an accurate list of
> the groups in the Civic Parade in order from first to last?
>
> (A) firefighters, puppeteers, veterans, musicians,
>   gymnasts, jugglers
> (B) gymnasts, puppeteers, jugglers, musicians,
>   firefighters, veterans
> (C) veterans, puppeteers, firefighters, gymnasts,
>   jugglers, musicians
> (D) jugglers, puppeteers, gymnasts, firefighters,
>   musicians, veterans
> (E) musicians, veterans, jugglers, firefighters,
>   gymnasts, puppeteers[17]

This is a run-of-the-mill Acceptability question. You know how to approach these efficiently: Go rule-by-rule and eliminate the answers that break them.

Rule 1 takes care of choices (A) and (B), each of which has only one space between the puppeteers and the musicians, and choice (E), which has the musicians earlier in the parade than the puppeteers. Rule 2 knocks out the remaining violator, choice (C), where the veterans precede the firefighters. That leaves choice (D), the correct answer.

Acceptability questions rarely reward the Deductions step. They turn on your understanding of what each rule individually allows and prohibits. Your approach to Acceptability questions should not change, regardless of how many deductions you were able to find.

2. (E)

> If the gymnasts march immediately ahead of the
> veterans, then which one of the following could be the fourth group?
>
> (A) gymnasts
> (B) jugglers
> (C) musicians
> (D) puppeteers
> (E) veterans[18]

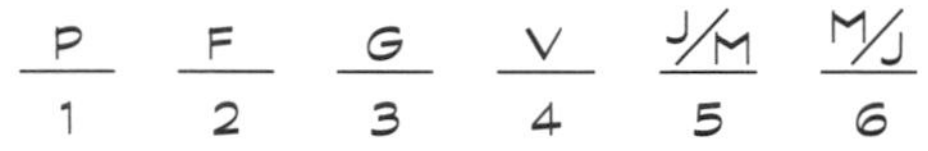

$$\frac{P}{1} \quad \frac{F}{2} \quad \frac{G}{3} \quad \frac{V}{4} \quad \frac{J/M}{5} \quad \frac{M/J}{6}$$

Figure 4.57

Take note how the "if" in this question stem triggers additional deductions. The stem tells you to place the gymnasts right before the veterans. Thus, G goes in the middle of the F-V block.

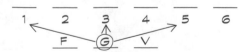

Figure 4.58

---

[17] PrepTest 43, Sec. 4, Q 1
[18] PrepTest 43, Sec. 4, Q 2

Now, the restriction from Rule 3 kicks in. G cannot go in space 1 in this case because there would be no room for F at the beginning of the parade. Likewise, if you tried to put G in space 5, F would occupy space 4 and V space 6, leaving no room for the P-M block in your game. Thus, G must take space 3, with F in 2 and V in 4.

$$\underset{1}{\underline{\quad}} \quad \underset{2}{\underline{F}} \quad \underset{3}{\underline{G}} \quad \underset{4}{\underline{V}} \quad \underset{5}{\underline{\quad}} \quad \underset{6}{\underline{\quad}}$$

Figure 4.59

Now you can see that Rule 1 requires P to take space 1 and M to take either space 5 or space 6. Whichever space isn't occupied by M will go to floater J.

$$\underset{1}{\underline{P}} \quad \underset{2}{\underline{F}} \quad \underset{3}{\underline{G}} \quad \underset{4}{\underline{V}} \quad \underset{5}{\underline{J/M}} \quad \underset{6}{\underline{M/J}}$$

Figure 4.60

With that mini-sketch to consult, choice (E) is clearly correct. In fact, the veterans *must* be the fourth group in the parade under these conditions.

3. **(A)**

If the veterans march immediately behind the puppeteers, then which one of the following could be the second group?

(A) firefighters
(B) gymnasts
(C) jugglers
(D) musicians
(E) veterans[19]

$$\underset{1}{\underline{F}} \quad \underset{2}{\underline{P}} \quad \underset{3}{\underline{V}} \quad \underset{4}{\underline{J}} \quad \underset{5}{\underline{G}} \quad \underset{6}{\underline{M}}$$

$$\underset{1}{\underline{G/J}} \quad \underset{2}{\underline{F}} \quad \underset{3}{\underline{P}} \quad \underset{4}{\underline{V}} \quad \underset{5}{\underline{J/G}} \quad \underset{6}{\underline{M}}$$

Figure 4.61

This time, the new "if" combines Rules 1 and 2. By placing the puppeteers right before the veterans (and thus in the middle of the F-V block), you can see a string of five spaces.

$$\underline{F} \quad \underline{P} \quad \underline{V} \quad \underline{\quad} \quad \dots \quad \underline{M}$$

Figure 4.62

There are only six spaces available in the parade, so the firefighters must march either first or second. In any other position, they'd push M right off the other end of the framework.

$$\underset{1}{\underline{F}} \quad \underset{2}{\underline{P}} \quad \underset{3}{\underline{V}} \quad \underset{4}{\underline{J}} \quad \underset{5}{\underline{G}} \quad \underset{6}{\underline{M}}$$

$$\underset{1}{\underline{G/J}} \quad \underset{2}{\underline{F}} \quad \underset{3}{\underline{P}} \quad \underset{4}{\underline{V}} \quad \underset{5}{\underline{J/G}} \quad \underset{6}{\underline{M}}$$

Figure 4.63

---

[19] PrepTest 43, Sec. 4, Q 3

So there are only two groups who could march second, the firefighters or the puppeteers. Of the two, only one is mentioned in an answer choice, of course. That's the firefighters, in choice (A).

LSAT logic games always reward the Deductions step. Sometimes they shift the burden up front and design questions that can be answered quickly from the deductions you make from the rules. Other times, as you saw here with the Civic Parade game, they offer almost nothing in the way of initial deductions but reward your ability to combine the rules triggered by the new "if" conditions in the question stems. Learn to make all of the deductions that you can in Step 4, but don't be stymied or shell-shocked when they don't appear. Go through the BLEND checklist systematically. When you've gotten all that's available, even when that's nothing, head into the question set with complete confidence that you'll have the information necessary to get all of the points.

The Power of Deductions

When you finish Step 4 of the Kaplan Method, you will be ready to handle the set of questions associated with any logic game. As you've seen in this chapter, Step 4 may involve stringing together several deductions that leave you with near-certainty about the acceptable arrangements of the entities in the game. At other times, you'll find few deductions available from the rules themselves and anticipate "If" questions that will precipitate further deductions within the questions. Either way, use the BLEND checklist to find all of the available deductions. Make them and account for them within your Master Sketch. Being able to conduct this step efficiently and effectively may be the most powerful tool in your LSAT toolkit. With it now available to you, turn to the final step in the Kaplan Method: answering the questions.

CHAPTER 5

THE QUESTIONS (AND WHAT THEY'RE ASKING FOR)

THE ANATOMY OF LOGIC GAMES QUESTIONS

It all comes down to Step 5 of the Kaplan Method, answering the questions. The four preceding steps are for naught if they don't turn into points. As you've seen, creating a complete setup and making all of the available deductions gives you all of the information you need to answer every logic games question. At times, the right answers can seem nearly inevitable once your Master Sketch is in place. Indeed, you've been answering logic games questions since chapter 1. But as I discussed there, the most common mistake that test takers make is to answer the wrong question. They choose an answer that *must be true* when the question calls for what *could be false*, for example.

So if it's just a matter of paying attention to the call of the question stem, why have a separate chapter for the Questions step? Because even here, and even with all of your setup work done perfectly, you have a chance to improve your logic games speed and accuracy. Once you learn how the test makers put together their various question types, you'll be able to approach each in the most strategic way.

"If" or Not "If": That Is the Question Stem

The first thing to notice about any LSAT logic games question is whether it has an "if" clause, a conditional clause that adds a further restriction applicable to that particular question. You've seen questions without the "if" clause in now-familiar Acceptability questions:

> Which one of the following could be an accurate list
> of the animals pictured on the guideposts, listed in
> order from guidepost 1 through guidepost 6?[1]

"Non-If" questions might also ask simply what must, can, or cannot be true within a game:

> Which one of the following must be true?[2]
> Which one of the following must be false?[3]
> Each of the following could be true EXCEPT:[4]

Or "Non-If" questions might ask complex questions specific to the action and restrictions of a particular game:

> Which one of the following is a pair of songs that must
> occupy consecutive tracks on the CD?[5]
> Which one of the following statements, if true,
> guarantees that Henri is using no more than one of the
> following: the hairdryer, the razor, the television?[6]

There are even a couple of rarer "Non-If" question types that I'll address later in this chapter. What all "Non-If" questions have in common is that they can be answered from the information in your completed Master Sketch, or in the case of Acceptability questions, from the rules themselves.

"If" questions, of course, are defined by the additional restrictions they add to the game. They offer, if you like, hypothetical situations within which you apply the game setup and deductions. By definition, those additional constraints mean that "If" questions are testing fewer possible arrangements than their "Non-If" counterparts. But to leverage that advantage, you need to be able to visualize the new restriction. That's why making a new mini-sketch based on the hypothetical is so important.

In the clause that follows the hypothetical, the test makers ask the same range of questions that they do in "Non-If" stems. They may simply follow the "If" with a question about what must, can, or cannot be true:

> If K is the fourth valve opened, then which one of the
> following could be true?[7]
> If there are exactly two colors in the costume, then
> which one of the following must be false?[8]

---

[1] PrepTest 46, Sec. 4, Q 1

[2] PrepTest 48, Sec. 2, Q 14

[3] PrepTest 51, Sec. 4, Q 4

[4] PrepTest 51, Sec. 4, Q 20

[5] PrepTest 51, Sec. 4, Q 12

[6] PrepTest 48, Sec. 2, Q 5

[7] PrepTest 52, Sec. 2, Q 5

[8] PrepTest 51, Sec. 4, Q 2

Or the call of the question—the part of the stem following the "if"—may be more complex and game-specific:

> If Henri were to use exactly three appliances, then what is the total number of different groups of three appliances any one of which could be the group of appliances he is using?[9]
> If two films in French are going to be shown, one on day 3 and one on day 5, which one of the following is a pair of films that could be shown on day 1 and day 6, respectively?[10]

In short, "If" questions can and will mimic all of the same tasks found in "Non-If" questions, just with the added restriction in the stem. You may even see "If" questions that call for an "acceptable arrangement" under the hypothetical situation. In that case, the "If" clause becomes one more rule. You can eliminate any answer choice that violates it.

Characterize the Right Choice and the Wrong Ones

You'll learn to distinguish between "If" and "Non-If" questions and to handle each appropriately, in short order. It's mostly a matter of familiarity and practice. The second aspect of handling logic games questions efficiently requires a bit more discipline.

Before evaluating the answer choices, you need to characterize what the stem is asking for. To do this properly—to be completely prepared to evaluate the answer choices—you need to articulate (to yourself, of course) the characteristics that distinguish the one right answer *and* the four wrong ones. Take this question from the Water Treatment Plant game as an example; I've included the Master Sketch for your reference:

> Workers at a water treatment plant open eight valves—G, H, I, K, L, N, O, and P—to flush out a system of pipes that needs emergency repairs. To maximize safety and efficiency, each valve is opened exactly once, and no two valves are opened at the same time. The valves are opened in accordance with the following conditions:
> > Both K and P are opened before H.
> > O is opened before L but after H.
> > L is opened after G.
> > N is opened before H.
> > I is opened after K.[11]

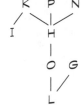

Figure 5.1

2. Each of the following could be the fifth valve opened EXCEPT:

    (A)   H
    (B)   I
    (C)   K
    (D)   N
    (E)   O[12]

---

[9] PrepTest 48, Sec. 2, Q 4

[10] PrepTest 49, Sec. 1, Q 5

[11] PrepTest 52, Sec. 2, Game 1

[12] PrepTest 52, Sec. 2, Q 2

Here, each of the four wrong answers *could* be the fifth valve opened. So the correct answer is the one with the entity that *cannot* be fifth. Now, you're ready for the answer choices. Looking at choice (A), you ask, "Can H ever be fifth?" Consult your Master Sketch or your work from other questions. Your answer will be, "Yes, it can." In this question, that's the characteristic of a *wrong* answer. Cross out choice (A) and move on. When you get to the right answer—it happens to be choice (C) in this case—your answer will be, "No, it can't be opened fifth." Characterizing the answer choices allows you to get to the correct answer efficiently and confidently.

Characterizing the answer choices means mentally preparing the question that you will ask as you read each one. Never read answer choices passively. Be ready to distinguish the *relevant* aspect of the choice. Think of it as knowing the chief characteristic of a "likely suspect." If I showed you a lineup of five people and told you "The culprit was over six feet tall," you'd be wasting time if you studied their eye colors or tattoos.

For *could be true* or *must be false* question stems, the question you'll ask to distinguish the likely suspect is straightforward. "Is choice (A) acceptable?" "How about choice (B)?" And so on. For a handful of questions, though, you'll need to tailor your query to the wording of the question stem. Consider an example that you'll recognize from the preceding chapter:

A locally known guitarist's demo CD contains exactly seven different songs—S, T, V, W, X, Y, and Z. Each song occupies exactly one of the CD's seven tracks. Some of the songs are rock classics; the others are new compositions. The following conditions must hold:
  S occupies the fourth track of the CD.
  Both W and Y precede S on the CD.
  T precedes W on the CD.
  A rock classic occupies the sixth track of the CD.
  Each rock classic is immediately preceded on the CD by a new composition.
  Z is a rock classic.[13]

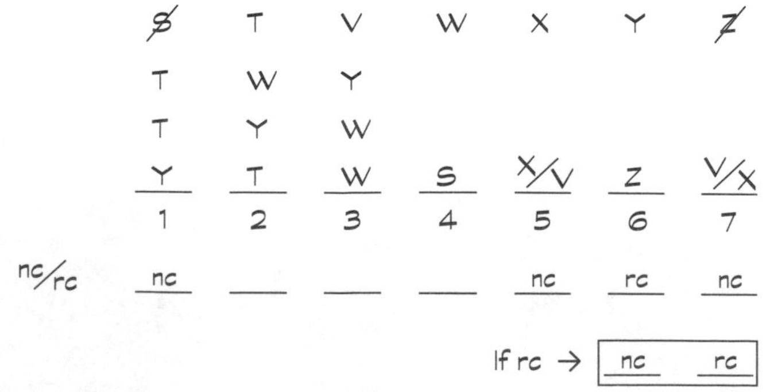

Figure 5.2

13 PrepTest 51, Sec. 4, Game 3

12. Which one of the following is a pair of songs that must occupy consecutive tracks on the CD?

   (A)   S and V
   (B)   S and W
   (C)   T and Z
   (D)   T and Y
   (E)   V and Z[14]

In this case, you can't ask, "Does this choice have to be true?" The right approach here is to ask instead, "Can I separate these two entities?" The answer to this question will be "yes" for every wrong answer and "no" for the correct answer. So you'd approach choice (A) by asking, "Can I separate S and V?" A glance at your Master Sketch shows that S is in space 4 and V can be in either space 5 or space 7. So you answer, "Yes, they can be separated." That's the characteristic of a wrong answer. Cross out choice (A) and ask the same question about the pair of entities in choice (B).

I'll have you practice characterizing right and wrong answers for each of the question types that you'll see on the test. It's something that will soon become second nature and won't cost you any time as you're taking the section. But, it is a non-negotiable part of your overall strategic approach to logic games questions.

Question Sets Are Clues

In a typical Logic Games *section*, about half of the questions will have new "Ifs" and about half will be of the "Non-If" variety. But that won't be the case with individual games. In fact, seeing a concentration of "if" or of "Non-If" questions often reveals the extent to which you can deduce the game's acceptable arrangements before you reach the Questions step.

In the Electronics Technician game, for instance, you were able to establish 12 of the 18 possible matches before attacking the questions. You completely determined Stacy's, Yolanda's, and Zane's columns and knew exactly who did and did not repair radios.

In a repair facility there are exactly six technicians: Stacy, Urma, Wim, Xena, Yolanda, and Zane. Each technician repairs machines of at least one of the following three types—radios, televisions, and VCRs—and no other types. The following conditions apply:

   Xena and exactly three other technicians repair radios.
   Yolanda repairs both televisions and VCRs.
   Stacy does not repair any type of machine that Yolanda repairs.
   Zane repairs more types of machines than Yolanda repairs.
   Wim does not repair any type of machine that Stacy repairs.
   Urma repairs exactly two types of machines.[15]

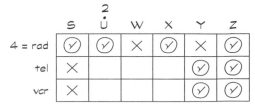

Figure 5.3

14 PrepTest 51, Sec. 4, Q 12

15 PrepTest 48, Sec. 2, Game 3

With two-thirds of the possible matches predetermined, the test makers don't have a lot of room for new "ifs", so they'll design the questions to reward you for front-loading your work. Take a look at the question stems that accompanied this game:

13. For exactly how many of the six technicians is it possible to determine exactly which of the three types of machines each repairs?

14. Which one of the following must be true?

15. Which one of the following must be false?

16. Which one of the following pairs of technicians could repair all and only the same types of machines as each other?

17. Which one of the following must be true?[16]

There's not an "If" question in the bunch. That's not by accident. Each of the questions associated with this game rewards you for making all of the available deductions. When you see this kind of question set, you can rest assured that there is a good deal of certainty involved in the initial setup even before you've completed Steps 1 through 4 of the Kaplan Method.

In contrast, take a look at the following game setup. You first saw it in chapter 1, where you determined that its task involves creating the schedule of Garibaldi's meetings. Take three to four minutes to sketch it, add in the rules, and make any possible deductions.

> In the course of one month, Garibaldi has exactly seven different meetings. Each of her meetings is with exactly one of five foreign dignitaries: Fuentes, Matsuba, Rhee, Soleimani, or Tbahi. The following constraints govern Garibaldi's meetings:
> She has exactly three meetings with Fuentes, and exactly one with each of the other dignitaries.
> She does not have any meetings in a row with Fuentes.
> Her meeting with Soleimani is the very next one after her meeting with Tbahi.
> Neither the first nor last of her meetings is with Matsuba.[17]

Here's what your Master Sketch should look like:

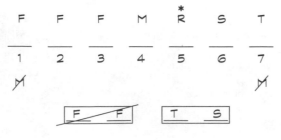

Figure 5.4

---

[16] PrepTest 48, Sec. 2, Qs 13–17

[17] PrepTest 44, Sec. 3, Game 1

The standard Sequencing task is reflected in the seven numbered slots. Rule 1 is shown in the list of entities, which has F repeated three times. Rules 2 and 4 are negative restrictions limiting the acceptable arrangements within the game but not leading to any further deductions immediately. Rule 3 creates a block of entities out of T and S but isn't connected to any other rules or any specific spaces. A run through the BLEND checklist doesn't produce any further deductions. An untrained test taker might be alarmed at the lack of specificity and spend precious minutes fruitlessly speculating about the possible arrangements here. But a look at the question set shows that you should expect little concreteness from this setup.

1. Which one of the following could be the sequence of the meetings Garibaldi has with the dignitaries?

2. If Garibaldi's last meeting is with Rhee, then which one of the following could be true?

3. If Garibaldi's second meeting is with Fuentes, then which one of the following is a complete and accurate list of the dignitaries with any one of whom Garibaldi's fourth meeting could be?

4. If Garibaldi's meeting with Rhee is the very next one after Garibaldi's meeting with Soleimani, then which one of the following must be true?

5. If Garibaldi's first meeting is with Tbahi, then Garibaldi's meeting with Rhee could be the

6. If Garibaldi's meeting with Matsuba is the very next meeting after Garibaldi's meeting with Rhee, then with which one of the following dignitaries must Garibaldi's fourth meeting be?[18]

This question set signals a game in which it's unlikely that you'll be able to make many (if any) big deductions. The first question is a standard Acceptability question, and then it's all "ifs" the rest of the way. Seeing all of those "If" questions tells you that the test makers know that there are many acceptable permutations remaining to be explored. A quick scan of this question set should tell you not to spend extra time trying to chase a phantom "big deduction." You'll get all of the additional restrictions you need to answer the questions once you add each "if" to the rules.

Those two examples are, of course, at the extreme ends of the spectrum. Most games have a mix of "If" questions and their various "Non-If" counterparts. And not surprisingly, most games fall somewhere in between these two in terms of how much can be deduced up front. It's impossible to predict whether you'll see games like these on test day, but it's worth your time to take a quick glance over the question set for each game you face, especially if you're hesitant about whether you've made all of the available deductions.

---

[18] PrepTest 44, Sec. 3, Qs 1–6

Next, turn your attention to the various question types you'll see on the LSAT. For each, I'll point out the language in the question stem that identifies the type, go through a few representative examples, and explain the most strategic approach for you to take.

ACCEPTABILITY QUESTIONS

You're already thoroughly familiar with Acceptability questions. I covered this question type in chapter 2 because of its close association with the rules. Typically, Acceptability question stems ask for the answer that could be an "accurate" or "acceptable" arrangement, list, or order of the entities or groups in the game.

> Which one of the following could be an accurate list of the contestants who play in each of the four games?[19]

> Which one of the following is an acceptable order of the films for the retrospective, listed by their language, from day 1 through day 6?[20]

As I mentioned in chapter 2, the most common pattern is to have one Acceptability question per game and for it to be the first question in the set. Every once in a while, you'll find a game with no Acceptability question and, very rarely, you may find an Acceptability question later in the set. But you won't go wrong to expect the "one-and-first" pattern most of the time.

It's worth commenting briefly here on question stems that ask for a "complete and accurate list" of entities within a game. These are usually, but not always, Acceptability questions. Consider two examples:

> Which one of the following could be a complete and accurate list of the performers who sign with each agency?[21]

> Which one of the following is a complete and accurate list of the days, any one of which is a day on which a film in Italian could be shown?[22]

The first of these stems indicates an Acceptability question. The wording—"list of the performers who sign with each agency"—tells you that the answer choices will cover all of the entities and groups within the game. You should treat this question exactly as you would any other Acceptability question.

---

[19] PrepTest 45, Sec. 3, Q 7

[20] PrepTest 49, Sec. 1, Q 1

[21] PrepTest 53, Sec. 2, Q 1

[22] PrepTest 49, Sec. 1, Q 4

The second stem limits your focus to just one of the entities. It's asking for the answer choice that has *any and all* acceptable placements for Italian films. We'll cover this type shortly under the heading "Complete and Accurate List Questions." You'll deal with it in a different way.

The takeaway from these examples is to always read question stems thoroughly and strategically. It should also come as no surprise that the first of those two stems belonged to the first question in its set (the position in which Acceptability questions are nearly always found), while the second belonged to the fourth question in the set for its game.

Eliminate Answers Rule by Rule

As you'll recall, the best strategy for Acceptability questions is to eliminate wrong answers rule by rule. Trying to evaluate choice by choice is a fool's errand. Take a look at this example:

Workers at a water treatment plant open eight valves—G, H, I, K, L, N, O, and P—to flush out a system of pipes that needs emergency repairs. To maximize safety and efficiency, each valve is opened exactly once, and no two valves are opened at the same time. The valves are opened in accordance with the following conditions:

Both K and P are opened before H.
O is opened before L but after H.
L is opened after G.
N is opened before H.
I is opened after K.

1. Which one of the following could be the order, from first to last, in which the valves are opened?

   (A)   P, I, K, G, N, H, O, L
   (B)   P, G, K, N, L, H, O, I
   (C)   G, K, I, P, H, O, N, L
   (D)   N, K, P, H, O, I, L, G
   (E)   K, I, N, G, P, H, O, L[23]

If you took the approach of saying, "Is choice (A) acceptable? Let me check," you'd wind up checking all five rules before determining that, in fact, choice (A) is a violator. Then you'd start the process all over again for choice (B). That inefficiency is compounded by the fact that the correct answer is the one that won't violate any of the rules. What winds up happening to many test takers is that they find the right answer but still question whether they missed something. They wind up going over the list of rules two or three times before they're confident enough to circle the correct choice and move on.

[23] PrepTest 52, Sec. 2, Q 1

As you know from chapter 2, the efficient approach is to work rule by rule, systematically eliminating the violators. In the example from the Water Treatment Plant, Rule 1 is never broken. Choice (B) breaks Rule 2. Choice (D) breaks Rule 3. Choice (C) breaks Rule 4. Finally, choice (A) breaks Rule 5. Your efficiency is increased by the fact that once you've eliminated a choice, you need not consider it again. Once you've eliminated an answer choice, strike through it completely in your test booklet. It doesn't matter if it breaks any other rules; you've already determined that it's unacceptable.

Using this approach, no Acceptability question should take you more than a few seconds on test day. Moreover, you'll be able to get the Acceptability points even in games that you struggle to set up completely.

Partial Acceptability: A Partial Exception

Partial Acceptability questions are cousins of Acceptability questions, which you will handle *almost* identically. The answer choices in Partial Acceptability questions have the same characteristics as those in Acceptability questions. That is, the four wrong answers each break one or more of the rules, while the correct answer breaks none of them. The difference is that Partial Acceptability answer choices don't contain the entire arrangement of entities in the game. Here's an example:

> Three folk groups—Glenside, Hilltopper, Levon—and three rock groups—Peasant, Query, Tinhead—each perform on one of two stages, north or south. Each stage has three two-hour performances: north at 6, 8, and 10; south at 8, 10, and 12. Each group performs individually and exactly once, consistent with the following conditions:
>> Peasant performs at 6 or 12.
>> Glenside performs at some time before Hilltopper.
>> If any rock group performs at 10, no folk group does.
>> Levon and Tinhead perform on different stages.
>> Query performs immediately after a folk group, though not necessarily on the same stage.

18. Which one of the following could be a complete and accurate ordering of performances on the north stage, from first to last?

   (A)   Glenside, Levon, Query
   (B)   Glenside, Query, Hilltopper
   (C)   Hilltopper, Query, Peasant
   (D)   Peasant, Levon, Tinhead
   (E)   Peasant, Query, Levon[24]

---

[24] PrepTest 48, Sec. 2, Game 4, Q 18

The question is looking for an acceptable arrangement, but the answer choices display the bands on the north stage only. In order for the north-stage arrangement to be acceptable, it will have to allow for an acceptable south-stage program as well. You have to keep that in mind as you assess the choices. It would help to be able to see the south stage, too. That's why it's more important to wait until you have your sketch, rules, and deductions all diagrammed before evaluating the answers. Go through the process here, and you'll see what I mean.

Rule 1 provides that Peasant must perform at 6 or 12, that is, first or last in the program. If you merely glance at the answers, the violator might not jump out at you. But remember that in this game, the north stage has bands only at 6, 8, and 10.

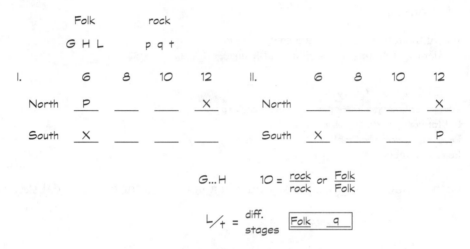

Figure 5.5

So answer (C) violates Rule 1 by having Peasant perform at 10.

18. Which one of the following could be a complete and accurate ordering of performances on the north stage, from first to last?

    (A)   Glenside, Levon, Query
    (B)   Glenside, Query, Hilltopper
    (C)   ~~Hilltopper, Query, Peasant~~
    (D)   Peasant, Levon, Tinhead
    (E)   Peasant, Query, Levon[25]

Rule 2 requires Glenside to perform before Hilltopper. You see Glenside in choices (A) and (B), and they perform first in both cases. So there's no problem there. In choices (D) and (E), Glenside and Hilltopper perform on the south stage (you can't see them). Still, there's nothing to suggest that Glenside couldn't perform earlier than Hilltopper on the south stage, so it doesn't appear that Rule 2 is broken.

---

[25] PrepTest 48, Sec. 2, Q 18

Rule 3 is another one that is impossible to assess with only the north stage visible. Rock bands perform at 10 in choices (A) and (E), but since you can't see who's on the south stage at that time, this doesn't give you any way to spot violations. Press on.

Rule 4 eliminates two wrong answers. See if you can determine which ones are the rule-breakers. Saying that Levon and Tinhead must perform on different stages is just another way of saying you must have exactly one of them on the north stage and exactly one on the south stage. Choice (D) is a clear violator, since you can see both bands on the north stage. But this rule also eliminates choice (B), where you see neither. Thinking with rules in Partial Acceptability questions can involve taking stock of what *doesn't* show up in the answer choices as well as what does.

18. Which one of the following could be a complete and accurate ordering of performances on the north stage, from first to last?

    (A)   Glenside, Levon, Query
    (B)   ~~Glenside, Query, Hilltopper~~   Neither L nor T
    (C)   ~~Hilltopper, Query, Peasant~~
    (D)   ~~Peasant, Levon, Tinhead~~
    (E)   Peasant, Query, Levon[26]

Rule 5 is another that's more easily assessed when you can refer to the initial sketch.

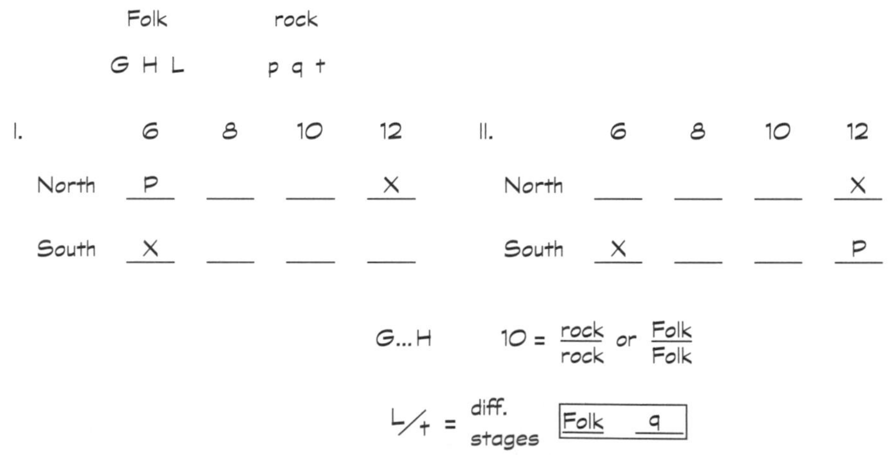

Figure 5.6

Recognizing that there is only one performance at 6 reveals that choice (E) violates Rule 4. In that choice, Query performs at 8 and there is no way a folk group can perform at 6, since Peasant is on the north stage and the south stage is empty at that time.

---

[26] PrepTest 48, Sec. 2, Game 4, Q 18

18. Which one of the following could be a complete and
     accurate ordering of performances on the north stage,
     from first to last?

     (A)   Glenside, Levon, Query
     (B)   ~~Glenside, Query, Hilltopper~~
     (C)   ~~Hilltopper, Query, Peasant~~
     (D)   ~~Peasant, Levon, Tinhead~~
     (E)   ~~Peasant, Query, Levon~~[27]

Thus, choice (A) is the correct answer.

Partial Acceptability questions are not as common as their standard Acceptability cousins.
It's unlikely that you'll see more than one in the entire Logic Games section, and many tests
feature none at all. Unlike standard Acceptability questions, they may appear anywhere in the
question set.

Often, when they appear in the middle or at the end of a question set, Partial Acceptability
questions will contain language that clearly identifies them.

> Which one of the following could be an accurate partial
> list of the architects, each matched with his or her
> design's place in the order in which the designs are
> presented?[28]

That's all you need to know in order to handle Acceptability questions and Partial Acceptability
questions with minimum effort and maximum efficiency. They won't constitute the bulk of your
points, but they're fast and they're certain. Treat them as the starting blocks for the race, and
use the strategic approach outlined here to get a jump on the section and on your competition.

MUST BE/COULD BE TRUE/FALSE QUESTIONS

Recognizing these questions is a no-brainer. Most often, the question stems are simple and
short.

> Which one of the following could be true?[29]
> Which one of the following must be false?[30]

From time to time, you'll see game-specific variants, like this twist on a *must be true* question:

> Which one of the following suspects must have been
> questioned before T was questioned?[31]

---

[27] PrepTest 48, Sec. 2, Game 4, Q 18

[28] PrepTest 53, Sec. 2, Q 11

[29] PrepTest 53, Sec. 2, Q 2

[30] PrepTest 52, Sec. 2, Q 23

[31] PrepTest 53, Sec. 2, Q 15

Or this slightly more complex variation on a *must be false* question stem:

> Sethna's teammate could be any one of the following
> EXCEPT:[32]

Do you see why I categorized that as a *must be false* question? The "EXCEPT" at the end means that the correct answer is an entity who *cannot* be Sethna's teammate. That analysis anticipates the most important step you'll need to take when tackling this question type: how to correctly characterize the answer choices.

Characterize the Answer Choices

You can always derive the correct answer to Must/Could be True/False question types from your Master Sketch. But as I emphasized earlier in this chapter, you have to know what you're looking for. To analyze these questions' answer choices, you need to picture two columns. The first represents the level of certainty, and the second represents the affirmative or negative "charge" of the question stem.

Level of Certainty	"Charge"
Must	True
Could	False

The correct answer combines one of the levels of certainty with one of the charges. The four wrong answers combine the other two terms. Here's a straightforward example:

> Which one of the following must be true?[33]

Since the correct answer clearly combines "must" and "true" in this question, you know beyond a shadow of a doubt that the four wrong answers all *could be false*. I'll put the question in context to show you how that analysis plays out.

> Five performers—Traugott, West, Xavier, Young, and Zinser—are recruited by three talent agencies—Fame Agency, Premier Agency, and Star Agency. Each performer signs with exactly one of the agencies and each agency signs at least one of the performers. The performers' signing with the agencies is in accord with the following:
> Xavier signs with Fame Agency.
> Xavier and Young do not sign with the same agency as each other.
> Zinser signs with the same agency as Young.
> If Traugott signs with Star Agency, West also signs with Star Agency.

---

[32] PrepTest 53, Sec. 2, Q 23
[33] PrepTest 53, Sec. 2, Q 3

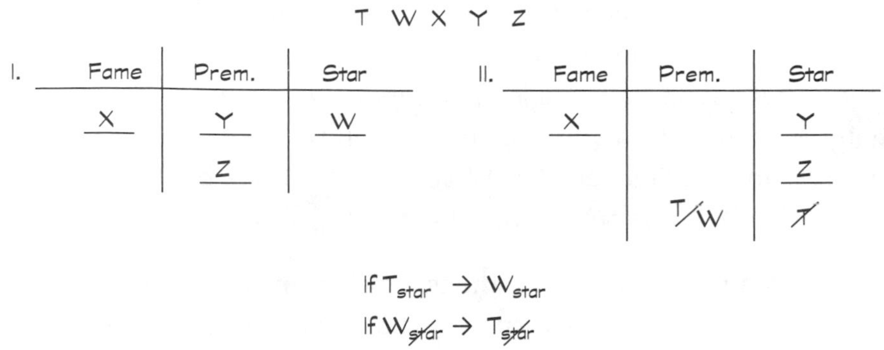

T W X Y Z

I.	Fame	Prem.	Star
	X	Y	W
		Z	

II.	Fame	Prem.	Star
	X		Y
			Z
		T/W	~~T~~

If $T_{star} \rightarrow W_{star}$

If $W_{\cancel{star}} \rightarrow T_{\cancel{star}}$

Figure 5.7

3. Which one of the following must be true?

   (A) West and Zinser do not sign with the same
       agency as each other.
   (B) Fame Agency signs at most two of the
       performers.
   (C) Fame Agency signs the same number of the
       performers as Star Agency.
   (D) Traugott signs with the same agency as West.
   (E) West does not sign with Fame Agency.[34]

This is the Talent Agency game that you set up in the Deductions chapter. You can see the Limited Options Master Sketch next to the game's setup. Knowing that the correct answer *must be true*, you can evaluate the answer choices without hesitation.

Look at answer choice (A). Must West and Zinser sign with different agencies? Not in Option II. There, both West and Zinser could sign with Star, provided that Traugott signs with Premier. So the statement in choice (A) *could be false.*

Turn to choice (B). Must it be true that Fame signs a maximum of two artists? Yes. In Option I, Fame could sign Xavier and Traugott, but everyone else is already assigned. In Option II, either Traugott or West could join Xavier, but the other has to sign with Premier. So it *must be true* that Fame signs at most two of the performers. Choice (B) is the correct answer. On test day, you could stop right here. For practice, evaluate the remaining choices to identify how they *could be false.*

Examine choice (C). Must it be true that Fame and Star sign the same number of performers? No. In Option I, one of the two agencies will sign two performers, while the other signs only one. You may notice that in Option II, it is possible for both Fame and Star to sign two performers, but that's not enough to make this a correct answer to a *must be true* question. Remember, if a statement does not have to be true, it *could be false.*

---

34 PrepTest 53, Sec. 2, Game 1

The statement in choice (D) could be true in either option. Traugott and West could both sign with Star Agency in Option I, and both could sign with Premier in Option II. But the statement *could be false* in either option, too. Nothing prevents Traugott from signing with Fame or Premier, in Option I. In Option II, Traugott could sign with Fame while West signs with Premier, or Traugott could sign with Premier while West signs with Fame or Star. Since the statement could be false, choice (D) is a wrong answer.

Negative language can be confusing, and the test makers most assuredly know it. Make sure you understand what it would mean to say that choice (E) must be true. Evaluate the answer choice by asking, "Must it be true that West does *not* sign with Fame?" If West can sign with Fame, then this choice's statement could be false. West can, of course, sign with Fame in Option II. Choice (E) does not have to be true, so it's a wrong answer.

Take a look at one more question from that game. Characterize the one correct and the four wrong answers, and then use the Master Sketch to identify the correct answer.

2. Which one of the following could be true?

   (A)   West is the only performer who signs with Star Agency.

   (B)   West, Young, and Zinser all sign with Premier Agency.

   (C)   Xavier signs with the same agency as Zinser.

   (D)   Zinser is the only performer who signs with Star Agency.

   (E)   Three of the performers sign with Fame Agency.[35]

Since the correct answer takes "could" as its level of certainty and "true" as its charge, the four wrong answers *must be false*. Were you able to stop as soon as you saw choice (A)? On test day, you'll be able to. You know that the one, correct choice *could be true*. West could be Star Agency's only client in Option I. Choice (A) must be correct.

For the record, all four of the wrong choices offer statements that are impossible within the restrictions of the game. Take choice (B). West, Young, and Zinser can never be together at Premier Agency. They could all join Star Agency in Option II, but that's not what the answer choice states. Move on to choice (C). Xavier joins Fame Agency in both options, while Zinser is a client of either Premier or Star, so choice (C) must be false. Likewise for choice (D): A glance at the Master Sketch reminds you that Young accompanies Zinser (Rule 3) no matter where the latter signs.

Choice (E) deserves a more in-depth look. It *must be false*, of course. In Option I, Fame Agency could sign Xavier and Traugott, but not anyone else. In Option II, either Traugott or West could join Fame, but the other would have to sign with Premier. So there's no way Fame Agency could ever sign three performers. What I want you to notice, though, is the relationship between this wrong answer and the correct answer to question 3 from this game.

---

[35] PrepTest 53, Sec. 2, Q 2

2. Which one of the following could be true?

    …

    (E)   Three of the performers sign with Fame Agency.

3. Which one of the following must be true?

    …

    (B)   Fame Agency signs at most two of the
           performers.[36]

Although the two mean exactly the same thing, choice (E) in question 2 is a wrong answer and choice (B) in question 3 is the correct answer. If it *must be true* that Fame signs at most two performers, it *must be false* that the agency signs three performers.

This illustrates what it means to *evaluate* the answer choices. Understanding what the choice *says* is necessary but not sufficient to know whether it's a right or wrong answer. You must know whether the characteristics of the statement in each answer choice fit those of the correct answer or the incorrect answers in a given question. The test makers are acutely aware of a statement's charge, but they'll flip the language around again and again: If Bob is scheduled before Dave, Bob is not scheduled after Dave; and Dave is scheduled after Bob; and Dave is *not* scheduled before Bob. Characterize the answer choices' meaning, but be ready for the statements in the choices to be phrased in any of those ways.

Now, try characterizing the choices in a slightly more complex question stem.

    Each of the following could be true EXCEPT:[37]

In this case, the correct answer *must be false*. Each of the four wrong answers could be true. Don't let "EXCEPT" confuse you. It's simply telling you that the correct answer takes the two attributes *not* assigned to the wrong answers. Since the wrong answers have "could" as their level of certainty and "true" as their charge, the correct answer will take "must" and "false." Learn to recognize what you do *and* what you don't know for certain about the arrangement within a game. The test makers reward you for being able to pop back and forth between certainty and possibility, or between truth and falsity, in almost every question in the section.

Variations on the Must/Could Theme

Occasionally, the test makers will reward the same analysis that you've been using on the preceding questions but apply it to question stems that are more game-specific. Don't let that rattle you. Identify the level of certainty ("must" or "could") called for in the question stem, and then characterize the correct answer. The four wrong answers will take the opposite attributes and will negate the rest of the stem. Here's an example.

---

[36] PrepTest 53, Sec. 2, Qs 2–3
[37] PrepTest 51, Sec. 4, Q 20

> Which one of the following suspects must have been
> questioned before T was questioned?[38]

Since the correct answer here lists a suspect who *must* have been questioned *before* T, the four wrong answers will contain entities that *could* have been questioned *after* T. This question is simply a variation on questions in which the right answer *must be true* and the wrong answers *could be false*. If you want to see the question in context again, flip back to the beginning of chapter 4, where I explained it in association with the game's deductions.

Here's a question stem from another game that you've already seen. Characterize its right and wrong answers.

> Which one of the following animals could be
> pictured on any one of the guideposts?[39]

This time, you have a variation on the *could be true* question stem. Since the correct choice will contain an animal that *could* go on any of the signposts, the four wrong answers will list animals that *must* avoid certain signposts. Put even more simply, the animal in the correct answer can go anywhere. The animals in the wrong answers can't. This one is worth seeing in its original context. Take a couple of moments to get reacquainted with the game's task, rules, and deductions. Then see whether you can zero in on the correct answer.

> Exactly six guideposts, numbered 1 through 6, mark a mountain trail. Each guidepost pictures a different one of six animals—fox, grizzly, hare, lynx, moose, or porcupine. The following conditions must apply:
>   The grizzly is pictured on either guidepost 3 or guidepost 4.
>   The moose guidepost is numbered lower than the hare guidepost.
>   The lynx guidepost is numbered lower than the moose guidepost but higher than the fox guidepost.

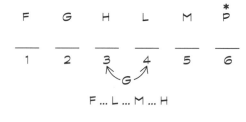

Figure 5.8

5. Which one of the following animals could be pictured on any one of the six guideposts?

(A) fox
(B) hare
(C) lynx
(D) moose
(E) porcupine[40]

Remember, the correct answer lists an animal that *could* be pictured anywhere, without restriction. That's choice (E), the porcupine. Unsurprisingly, a glance at your Master Sketch shows

---

[38] PrepTest 53, Sec. 2, Q 15
[39] PrepTest 46, Sec. 4, Q 5
[40] PrepTest 46, Sec. 4, Q 5

that P is the floater, the entity unrestricted by any rules. The wrong answers each contain an animal that is restricted within the rules, as reflected in the Master Sketch. Fox, hare, lynx, and moose are all part of the big, loose block of entities created by Rules 2 and 3, and thus *cannot* be featured on some of the guideposts; they each have a restriction. Let this question stand as a reminder of just how integrated the Kaplan Method and the Logic Games section really are.

Before I move on, try your hand at characterizing the answer choices for a few more questions. This practice will benefit you with the "If" questions that follow, too, since most of them append similar questions to the hypothetical restrictions in their opening clauses.

DRILL: CHARACTERIZING ANSWER CHOICES

For each of the following question stems, jot down the characteristics of the correct answer and those of four wrong answers. Where appropriate, consider the level of certainty and the charge of both the right and the wrong answers.

Level of Certainty	"Charge"
Must	True
Could	False

1. Which one of the following must be true?[41]

   Correct answer characteristics: _____
   Incorrect answer characteristics: _____

2. Each of the following could be the fifth valve opened EXCEPT:[42]

   Correct answer characteristics: _____
   Incorrect answer characteristics: _____

3. Mr. O'Connell CANNOT accompany which one of the following pairs of children?[43]

   Correct answer characteristics: _____
   Incorrect answer characteristics: _____

4. Which one of the following could be true?[44]

   Correct answer characteristics: _____
   Incorrect answer characteristics: _____

5. Which one of the following is a pair of songs that must occupy consecutive tracks on the CD?[45]

   Correct answer characteristics: _____
   Incorrect answer characteristics: _____

6. Each of the following could be true EXCEPT:[46]

   Correct answer characteristics: _____
   Incorrect answer characteristics: _____

7. Which one of the following must be false of the summer program?[47]

   Correct answer characteristics: _____
   Incorrect answer characteristics: _____

8. Which one of the following CANNOT be true?[48]

   Correct answer characteristics: _____
   Incorrect answer characteristics: _____

9. Which one of the following pairs of technicians could repair all and only the same types of machines as each other?[49]

   Correct answer characteristics: _____
   Incorrect answer characteristics: _____

10. Which one of the following groups could perform at 6?[50]

    Correct answer characteristics: _____
    Incorrect answer characteristics: _____

---

[41] PrepTest 52, Sec. 2, Q 5

[42] PrepTest 52, Sec. 2, Q 2

[43] PrepTest 52, Sec. 2, Q 12

[44] PrepTest 46, Sec. 4, Q 20

[45] PrepTest 51, Sec. 4, Q 12

[46] PrepTest 51, Sec. 4, Q 20

[47] PrepTest 49, Sec. 1, Q 17

[48] PrepTest 48, Sec. 2, Q 3

[49] PrepTest 48, Sec. 2, Q 16

[50] PrepTest 48, Sec. 2, Q 20

Explanations

1. Which one of the following must be true?[51]

   Correct answer characteristics: Must be true.

   Incorrect answer characteristics: Could be false.

This is a straightforward question stem. The correct answer takes "must" as its level of certainty and "true" as its charge. The wrong answers will simply take the counterparts in each column.

2. Each of the following could be the fifth valve opened EXCEPT:[52]

   Correct answer characteristics: Must *not* be the fifth valve opened. Alternately, must be a valve other than the fifth one opened.

   Incorrect answer characteristics: Could be the fifth valve opened.

3. Mr. O'Connell CANNOT accompany which one of the following pairs of children?[53]

   Correct answer characteristics: Must be a pair that cannot go with Mr. O'Connell. Alternately, must be a pair that goes with Ms. Margoles or Ms. Podorski.

   Incorrect answer characteristics: Could be a pair that goes with Mr. O'Connell. Alternately, a pair that is not limited to Ms. Margoles or Ms. Podorski.

4. Which one of the following could be true?[54]

   Correct answer characteristics: Could be true.

   Incorrect answer characteristics: Must be false.

5. Which one of the following is a pair of songs that must occupy consecutive tracks on the CD?[55]

   Correct answer characteristics: Must be a contiguous pair.

   Incorrect answer characteristics: Could be separated by intervening tracks.

6. Each of the following could be true EXCEPT:[56]

   Correct answer characteristics: Must be false.

   Incorrect answer characteristics: Could be true.

7. Which one of the following must be false of the summer program?[57]

   Correct answer characteristics: Must be false.

   Incorrect answer characteristics: Could be true.

---

[51] PrepTest 52, Sec. 2, Q 5
[52] PrepTest 52, Sec. 2, Q 2
[53] PrepTest 52, Sec. 2, Q 12
[54] PrepTest 46, Sec. 4, Q 20
[55] PrepTest 51, Sec. 4, Q 12
[56] PrepTest 51, Sec. 4, Q 20
[57] PrepTest 49, Sec. 1, Q 17

8. Which one of the following CANNOT be true?[58]

   Correct answer characteristics: Must be false.

   Incorrect answer characteristics: Could be true.

Note that examples 6, 7, and 8 are all exactly the same kind of question. Don't lose sight of how much the test makers like to play with positive and negative language while saying the same thing.

9. Which one of the following pairs of technicians could repair all and only the same types of machines as each other?[59]

   Correct answer characteristics: Could have exactly the same matches in their respective columns. Alternately, could repair exactly the same machines as one another.

   Incorrect answer characteristics: Must have some difference between their columns.

Note the phrase "all and only." The wrong answers contain pairs of technicians who must repair different types of machines *or* must repair a different number of machines. The correct answer gives a pair of technicians who could repair *exactly* the same machines as one another.

10. Which one of the following groups could perform at 6?[60]

    Correct answer characteristics: Could perform at 6.

    Incorrect answer characteristics: Must not perform at 6. Alternately, must perform at 8, 10, or 12.

Get Familiar with Must/Could Be True/False Questions

Along with the new "If" questions, which you'll explore next, Must/Could be True/False questions are your bread and butter in the Logic Games section. Their question stems can be either deceptively simple or deceptively hard. The fact of the matter is that, beneath the veneer of "must" and "could" and "EXCEPT," this is just one more way in which the test makers are rewarding you for honing the core LSAT skills of making deductions and understanding formal logic. Indeed, saying that something *must* occur is equivalent to saying that it's necessary. With these questions, rather than having you wrestle with "if-then" statements, the test makers want you to show that you've already determined what must or must not happen in the course of the game.

NEW "IF" QUESTIONS

I'll stay on the theme of understanding formal logic as I lead you through the "If" question type. Recall from chapter 3 that every conditional "if-then" rule defines a sufficient-necessary relationship. Whatever is stated in the "if" clause is sufficient to make what's stated in the

---

[58] PrepTest 48, Sec. 2, Q 3

[59] PrepTest 48, Sec. 2, Q 16

[60] PrepTest 48, Sec. 2, Q 20

"then" clause happen. Whatever's in the "then" clause is necessary for what's in the "if" clause to occur. Here's an example to help refresh your memory:

If Ms. Margoles accompanies Juana, then Ms. Podorski accompanies Lucita.[61]

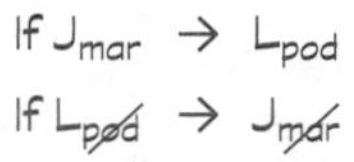

If $J_{mar} \rightarrow L_{pod}$

If $\cancel{L_{pod}} \rightarrow \cancel{J_{mar}}$

Figure 5.9

In this game, any time that Juana's chaperone is Ms. Margoles, Lucita's must be Ms. Podorski. Likewise, if Lucita goes with anyone other than Ms. Podorski—if Ms. Podorski is *not* Lucita's chaperone—Juana must go with someone other than Ms. Margoles. To use the precise terminology, Ms. Margoles accompanying Juana is *sufficient* to establish that Ms. Podorski accompanies Lucita. Ms. Podorski's accompanying Lucita is *necessary* for Ms. Margoles to be able to accompany Juana.

That same relationship is mirrored in "if" questions, except that instead of a complete conditional statement, the test makers are giving you just the "if" clause and then asking you to supply the result, the "then" that follows. In other words, the beginning of the question stem is sufficient to tell you that something must, can't, or could occur. Here's an example from the Water Treatment Plant game. I've included the Master Sketch for your reference.

Workers at a water treatment plant open eight valves—G, H, I, K, L, N, O, and P—to flush out a system of pipes that needs emergency repairs. To maximize safety and efficiency, each valve is opened exactly once, and no two valves are opened at the same time. The valves are opened in accordance with the following conditions:
  Both K and P are opened before H.
  O is opened before L but after H.
  L is opened after G.
  N is opened before H.
  I is opened after K.

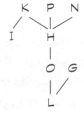

Figure 5.10

4. If L is the seventh valve opened, then each of the following could be the second valve opened EXCEPT:

   (A) G
   (B) I
   (C) K
   (D) N
   (E) P[62]

The new condition imposed here is that L is opened seventh. Checking the Master Sketch, you see that, in order for that to happen, I will have to be opened eighth. I is, in fact, the only valve that can be opened after L. Jot down a new mini-sketch (more on these in a minute) that contains the condition imposed by the "if" clause.

---

[61] PrepTest 52, Sec. 2, Game 2
[62] PrepTest 52, Sec. 2, Q 4

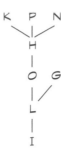

Figure 5.11

Now, consider the question in the "then" clause of the stem and then characterize the right and wrong answers. The wrong answers have entities that *could* be opened second. Thus, the correct answer contains an entity that *must not* be opened second. That's choice (B). The "if" clause, which said that L is opened seventh, is sufficient to establish that I is the eighth valve in the sequence. I can't be opened second, making choice (B) the right answer.

Notice that you didn't consider the question in the stem until after you'd dealt with the deductions triggered by the new "if." That's how you should always approach these questions. Read the "if." Determine its implications, what it's sufficient to establish. Then, and only then, proceed to the question itself. You're not ready for the question until you've played out the results of the "if."

In rare cases, the Master Sketch is so complete that there is no need for a new mini-sketch to deal with the "if" restriction. For the most part, however, train yourself to make a quick, accurate copy of the Master Sketch in which to work out the new deductions that follow from the "if" restriction. This must become a part of your logic games training.

New "Ifs" Call for New Sketches and New Deductions

You've seen this many times already in the first few chapters of this book. A new "If" question imposes a new restriction on the game. In order to see its effect, you need to combine the new "if" information with what's in your Master Sketch and add in the resulting implications. The problem is that you don't want to mess with your actual Master Sketch. The new "If" is applicable only to its one, particular question. If you wrote it and its deductions into the Master Sketch, you'd have to erase them back out before the next question. That costs you time and effort, and it dramatically increases the possibility of introducing an error into your Master Sketch. That last risk is one you can't afford to take.

The solution is the mini-sketch, a small, abbreviated copy of the Master Sketch that you draw right next to the question. There, you can put in the new "if" information and play out all of the available deductions. It should only take you 10 or 15 seconds to create a mini-sketch, but your reward is enormous. It will reveal precisely what can, can't, and must happen in the situation that results from the new "if." You'll be able to see the correct answer directly.

Students who try to save time by skipping the mini-sketch process are chasing a false efficiency. Logic games are simply too complex to keep all of their moving parts straight in your head. Without a concrete diagram, you'll wind up taking longer on the question as well as risking sloppy mistakes. Making mini-sketches and their resulting deductions is essential to your overall efficiency in the section.

Here are a few examples. Sometimes the new "if" produces a single deduction and leads directly to the right answer. Other times, it will produce a string of consequences, all of which you'll need to capture on the page. Don't rush through these examples. Take the time to re-familiarize yourself with the game's task, its rules, and its Master Sketch. Then try each of the questions in turn. Learning the mini-sketch process will make you faster and more accurate in the long run.

In a single day, exactly seven trucks—S, T, U, W, X, Y, and Z—are the only arrivals at a warehouse. No truck arrives at the same time as any other truck, and no truck arrives more than once that day. Each truck is either green or red (but not both). The following conditions apply:

No two consecutive arrivals are red.
Y arrives at some time before both T and W.
Exactly two of the trucks that arrive before Y are red.
S is the sixth arrival.
Z arrives at some time before U.

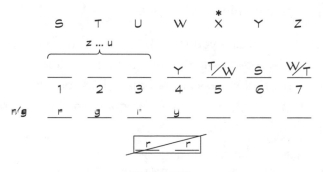

Figure 5.12

9. If exactly three of the trucks are green, then which one of the following trucks must be green?

(A) S
(B) T
(C) U
(D) W
(E) Z[63]

This is a game you'll remember from the chapter on deductions. By combining the two rules involving Y with the established entity S, you were able to lock Y into space four. As a result, you determined the colors of the first four trucks to arrive and learned that T and W were limited to spaces 5 and 7.

---

[63] PrepTest 37, Sec. 3, Q 9

The new "if" in this question draws your attention back to the color line. It tells you that exactly three of the trucks will be green. Combine the "if" with the rule that forbids red trucks from arriving consecutively. Since you already have two green trucks in spaces 2 and 4 in your Master Sketch, you can complete the color line by including the new restriction.

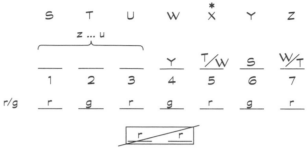

Figure 5.13

The third green truck has to arrive in the sixth spot. That's the only way to avoid consecutive red arrivals. That's just what you need to figure out which truck *must* be green.

Choice (A) is the correct answer. The new "if" allowed you to deduce that the sixth arrival is green, and Rule 4 has had truck S locked into space 6 all along. In this situation, trucks T and W will definitely be red, and there's no way to tell about trucks U and Z. All four of the trucks in the wrong answers most certainly *could* be red.

The next question is going to require you to make a longer string of deductions. The game—Garibaldi's Meetings—was featured earlier in this chapter. You'll recall that its setup and rules allowed for no additional restrictions. Because of that, I had you note that, with the exception of the Acceptability question, each question in the question set began with an "if." The one you'll try here is particularly illustrative.

> In the course of one month Garibaldi has exactly seven different meetings. Each of her meetings is with exactly one of five foreign dignitaries: Fuentes, Matsuba, Rhee, Soleimani, or Tbahi. The following constraints govern Garibaldi's meetings:
>> She has exactly three meetings with Fuentes, and exactly one with each of the other dignitaries.
>> She does not have any meetings in a row with Fuentes.
>> Her meeting with Soleimani is the very next one after her meeting with Tbahi.
>> Neither the first nor last of her meetings is with Matsuba.

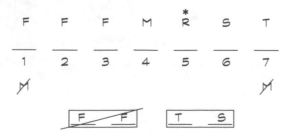

Figure 5.14

5. If Garibaldi's first meeting is with Tbahi, then
   Garibaldi's meeting with Rhee could be the

   (A) second meeting
   (B) third meeting
   (C) fifth meeting
   (D) sixth meeting
   (E) seventh meeting[64]

As soon as you see the "if," you can copy the framework slots from your Master Sketch and plug in the new restriction. Here, that means putting T in space 1:

$$\frac{\text{T}}{1} \quad \frac{\quad}{2} \quad \frac{\quad}{3} \quad \frac{\quad}{4} \quad \frac{\quad}{5} \quad \frac{\quad}{6} \quad \frac{\quad}{7}$$

Figure 5.15

Checking the rules as they're depicted in the Master Sketch, you see that S always follows immediately after T.

$$\frac{\text{T}}{1} \quad \frac{\text{S}}{2} \quad \frac{\quad}{3} \quad \frac{\quad}{4} \quad \frac{\quad}{5} \quad \frac{\quad}{6} \quad \frac{\quad}{7}$$

Figure 5.16

Now, you have five open spaces. Three of them must belong to F and the other two to M and R. Which rule allows you to make some of those spaces concrete? It's Rule 2, the one forbidding consecutive meetings with F. There's only one way to fit in three noncontiguous meetings with F:

$$\frac{\text{T}}{1} \quad \frac{\text{S}}{2} \quad \frac{\text{F}}{3} \quad \frac{\quad}{4} \quad \frac{\text{F}}{5} \quad \frac{\quad}{6} \quad \frac{\text{F}}{7}$$

Figure 5.17

Looking at your Master Sketch, you can see that there's nothing more to determine concretely. R is the floater. His meeting can go anywhere. M is restricted from meetings 1 and 7, but you're at no risk of running afoul of that rule in this case. You can't say for sure which of M or R takes space 4 or space 6, so just write them in as alternatives.

$$\frac{\text{T}}{1} \quad \frac{\text{S}}{2} \quad \frac{\text{F}}{3} \quad \frac{\text{M/R}}{4} \quad \frac{\text{F}}{5} \quad \frac{\text{R/M}}{6} \quad \frac{\text{F}}{7}$$

Figure 5.18

Now, examine the question in the stem. It asks for a space in which R *could* go. You know that the right answer will say either "fourth" or "sixth." Choice (D) is the one that has an acceptable placement for R. Voilà. Choice (D) is the right answer.

---

64 PrepTest 44, Sec. 3, Q 5

That took a little patience, but imagine trying to test the answer choices in your head. You'd still be trying them out, and you'd likely wind up sketching them anyway to see which one worked.

Learn to deal with all "if" questions in the two-phase process I've just described. Combine the "if" information with what's in the Master Sketch, and derive all of the available deductions. Then turn to the question itself and characterize the choices. Most of the time, a mini-sketch will be invaluable to you as you go through those steps.

There is one exception, though. When a game breaks down into Limited Option sketches, new "ifs" often simply point you to the appropriate option. Take a look at how this works.

New "Ifs" in Limited Options Games

You'll recall Limited Options (the L in the BLEND checklist) as the Deductions triggered by "either . . . or" rules and restrictions. Because they limit the acceptable arrangements of games into one of two possible solutions, I taught you to make *twin* sketches in these cases. Those dual sketches are incredibly powerful ways to organize logic games that break down into just two alternative arrangements. The time you spend making the two sketches really pays you back when the game has "if" questions associated with it. Because you've determined so much of what must be true in the game, the new "ifs" here usually don't require a mini-sketch at all. Take a look at the following examples and take note of how the "if" question(s) in each tell you which option to examine in order to derive the correct answer.

Five performers—Traugott, West, Xavier, Young, and Zinser—are recruited by three talent agencies—Fame Agency, Premier Agency, and Star Agency. Each performer signs with exactly one of the agencies and each agency signs at least one of the performers. The performers' signing with the agencies is in accord with the following:

Xavier signs with Fame Agency.

Xavier and Young do not sign with the same agency as each other.

Zinser signs with the same agency as Young.

If Traugott signs with Star Agency, West also signs with Star Agency.

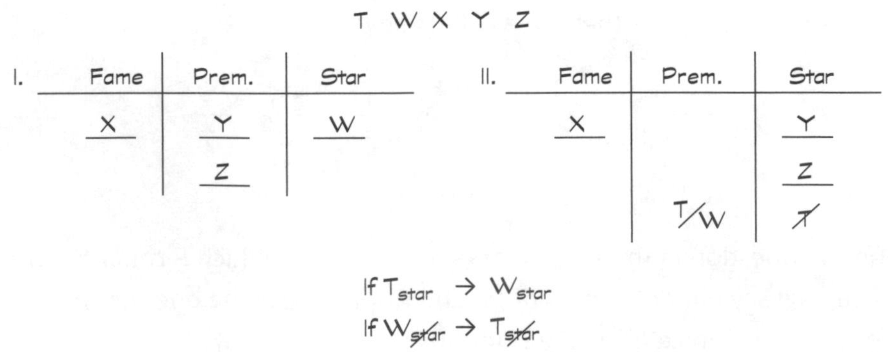

Figure 5.19

5. If Zinser signs with Star Agency, which one of the following must be false?

(A) Premier Agency signs exactly one performer.
(B) Star Agency signs exactly three of the performers.
(C) Traugott signs with Star Agency.
(D) West signs with Star Agency.
(E) None of the other performers signs with the same agency as Xavier.[65]

The basis for the Limited Options sketches in this game is the placement of the Young-Zinser block. You knew from Rules 2 and 3 that Young had to accompany Zinser and avoid Xavier. And from Rule 1, you knew that Xavier was a Fame Agency client. Thus, the Young-Zinser block was signing with either Premier Agency (Option I) or Star Agency (Option II).

The "if" in this question places you solidly in Option II. Check that option, and you can see that Traugott is forbidden from signing with Star.

It's no coincidence that the question asks for what *must be false*. You know that Traugott cannot sign with Star Agency, and that's exactly what choice (C) says. It's your right answer, just that quickly.

In that example, the "if" language echoed the very language you used in setting up the Limited Option scenario. Occasionally, a game's Limited Options are so clear that all of the "ifs" relate directly to criteria you used to create the two sketches. In these games, you may be able to handle the question set in a matter of a minute or two. Try it out in the game about the Clown Costume that you first saw in chapter 4. I've included all three "If" questions from its question set. By test day, you'll be handling all three more quickly than you would have handled just one of them when you first cracked open this book.

A clown will select a costume consisting of two pieces and no others: a jacket and overalls. One piece of the costume will be entirely one color, and the other piece will be plaid. Selection is subject to the following restrictions:

If the jacket is plaid, then there must be exactly three colors in it.
If the overalls are plaid, then there must be exactly two colors in them.
The jacket and overalls must have exactly one color in common.
Green, red, and violet are the only colors that can be in the jacket.
Red, violet, and yellow are the only colors that can be in the overalls.

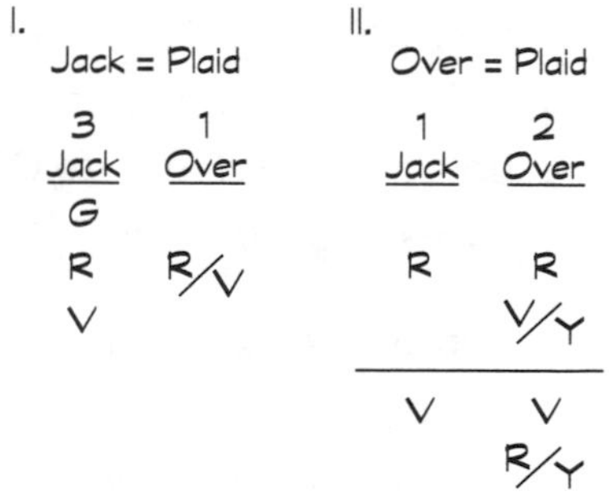

Figure 5.29

---

2. If there are exactly two colors in the costume, then which one of the following must be false?

    (A)   At least part of the jacket is green.
    (B)   At least part of the jacket is red.
    (C)   The overalls are red and violet.
    (D)   The overalls are red and yellow.
    (E)   The overalls are violet and yellow.

3. If at least part of the jacket is green, then which one of the following could be true?

    (A)   The overalls are plaid.
    (B)   No part of the jacket is red.
    (C)   No part of the jacket is violet.
    (D)   At least part of the overalls are yellow.
    (E)   At least part of the overalls are violet.

5. If there are exactly three colors in the costume, the overalls must be

    (A)   entirely red or else red and violet plaid
    (B)   entirely yellow or else violet and yellow plaid
    (C)   entirely violet or else red and violet plaid
    (D)   entirely red or else entirely yellow
    (E)   entirely red or else entirely violet[66]

You'll recall that the Limited Options in this game derived from the fact that either the jacket or the overalls were plaid and the other item plain. When the jacket is the plaid piece (Option I), it has three colors—green, red, and violet—and the plain overalls are either entirely red or entirely violet. When it's the overalls that are plaid (Option II), they have two colors from among red, violet, and yellow. The jacket in that case is one color, either red or violet, matching one of the colors in the overalls.

Now, look back at the three question stems. Question 2 put you in Option II (in Option I, there are three colors in the costume) and asked you what *must be false*. Question 3 put you in Option I (the jacket cannot have green in Option II) and asked you what *could be true*. Finally, question 5 again referred to Option I (that's where the costume has three colors) but, this time, asked what *must be true*.

You'd probably like to know the correct answers. For question 2, the right answer was choice (A). It *must be false* that the jacket has any green in Option II. For question 3, the right choice was (E). The overalls *could* be violet in Option I. For number 5, the correct choice was again (E). In Option I, the overalls *must be* entirely one color, either red or violet. Review the wrong answer choices on your own. Remember that all four must take the characteristics opposite those of the correct answer. In question 2, the four wrong answers could be true; in question 3, they must be false; and in question 5, they could be false.

---

[66] PrepTest 51, Sec. 4, Qs 2, 3, and 5

Those three questions serve as a nice microcosm illustrating what you need to remember about "If" questions in the Limited Options context. Use the "if" to identify which of the options to refer to. Then characterize the right and wrong answers and evaluate the choices. You're coming to the point where you've learned the Kaplan Method from top to bottom. Your ability to pull out these various tools and strategies and use them in harmony to get points quickly and confidently is almost complete.

In the remainder of this chapter, I'll have you look at the handful of other question types you may see on test day. These are much rarer than those you've practiced so far, but each comes with its own little twist.

MINIMUM/MAXIMUM QUESTIONS

Of the remaining logic games question types, those asking for the minimum or maximum number of entities or spaces that can be acceptably selected, grouped, or matched are the most common. Even so, you're unlikely to see more than two or three in a section; depending on the types of games represented in the section, you may see none at all. Minimum/maximum questions are most likely to accompany a Selection task ("What's the greatest/smallest number you can choose?"), but as you'll see, the test makers find subtle ways to ask about numbers in all types of logic games.

> What is the maximum number of friends who could
> appear in a photograph that Yakira does not appear in?[67]
> The tour group could visit at most how many sites that
> were discovered by Ferrara?[68]

The first thing to recognize is that, regardless of the game's task, the test makers cannot ask this kind of question unless the number restrictions within the game are in play. They can't, for example, ask you for the maximum number of candidates you can select if the game setup says, "Exactly four of the seven candidates will be selected." They can't ask you for the minimum number of entities recruited to the red team if the game setup or a rule states, "Each team recruits exactly three players." So you have a good heads-up that a question like this may be coming when, at the end of the Deductions step, you still don't have a definitive answer to some issue involving the game's numbers.

That was the case in the Friends Photograph game I presented as an illustration of the Selection task and of formal logic rules. Refresh your memory of the game's setup and rules. Take note of which rules can be combined into further deductions. Then I'll discuss the Maximum/Minimum question that follows.

---

[67] PrepTest 45, Sec. 3, Q 15
[68] PrepTest 44, Sec. 3, Q 17

An album contains photographs picturing seven friends: Raimundo, Selma, Ty, Umiko, Wendy, Yakira, Zack. The friends appear either alone or in groups with one another, in accordance with the following:

Wendy appears in every photograph that Selma appears in.
Selma appears in every photograph that Umiko appears in.
Raimundo appears in every photograph that Yakira does not appear in.

15. What is the maximum number of friends who could appear in a photograph that Yakira does not appear in?

(A) six
(B) five
(C) four
(D) three
(E) two[69]

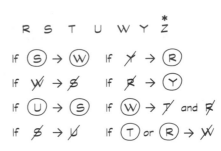

Figure 5.30

In this game, all of the rules involve conditional, formal logic statements. Depending on who appears in the photograph, other friends must be included or excluded. Nothing in the setup or rules gives you a set number of entities that must be in a given photo, so this game is a likely candidate to have a minimum/maximum question. The particular question asks for a maximum number, but it places a condition on the question. It asks for the maximum number of friends who could appear *when Yakira does not appear*. That's like a hidden "if." A question asking for the maximum number who could appear *in any case* would be a different question and have a different answer.

So start with the condition that Yakira is excluded from the list.

R S T U W Y̶ Z̶*

Figure 5.31

Checking the rules, you see that when Yakira is out, Raimundo is in.

Ⓡ S T U W Y̶ Z̶*

Figure 5.32

Raimundo's presence knocks out Wendy, pursuant to Rule 4.

Ⓡ S T U W̶ Y̶ Z̶*

Figure 5.33

69 PrepTest 45, Sec. 3, Q 15

The loss of Wendy triggers Rule 1, which says that without Wendy, you can't have Selma.

Figure 5.34

And finally, that triggers Rule 2, which tells you that if you get rid of Selma, you must also get rid of Umiko.

Figure 5.35

Now, you can see the correct answer unequivocally. The maximum number of friends available for the photograph is three: Raimundo, Ty, and Zack. Don't be surprised when elements of more than one question type appear together. You probably wouldn't have categorized this as an "If" question right off the bat, but once you see that there is a limiting condition in the question stem, you know to deal with it by way of a mini-sketch before evaluating the answer choices.

The next example lacks any conditional, "if"-type language.

A tour group plans to visit exactly five archaeological sites. Each site was discovered by exactly one of the following archaeologists—Ferrara, Gallagher, Oliphant—and each dates from the eighth, ninth, or tenth century (A.D.). The tour must satisfy the following conditions:

The site visited second dates from the ninth century.
Neither the site visited fourth nor the site visited fifth was discovered by Oliphant.
Exactly one of the sites was discovered by Gallagher, and it dates from the tenth century.
If a site dates from the eighth century, it was discovered by Oliphant.
The site visited third dates from a more recent century than does either the site visited first or that visited fourth.

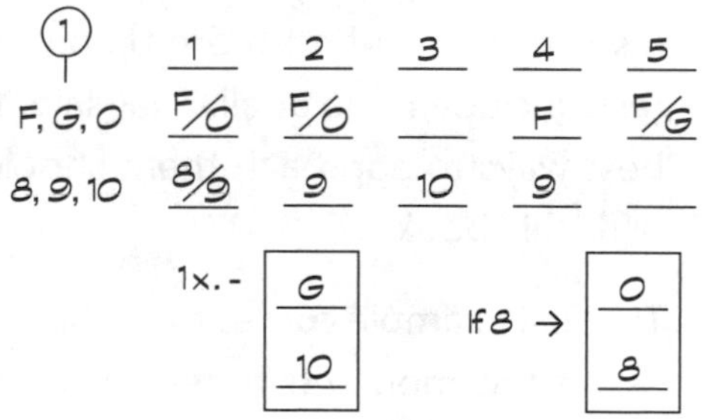

Figure 5.36

17. The tour group could visit at most how many sites that were discovered by Ferrara?

(A) one
(B) two
(C) three
(D) four
(E) five[70]

This time, all you have to do is check the Master Sketch to see how many of the sites could have been discovered by Ferrara. You can see that nothing prevents Ferrara from discovering any given one of the five sites. The third rule, though, tells you that Gallagher must have discovered exactly one site, so Ferrara cannot have discovered *all* of the sites. Oliphant *may* have discovered a site, but you don't know that for sure. The maximum number Ferrara could have found is thus four. With this kind of minimum/maximum question, you can predict the correct answer before evaluating the choice. In this case, it's choice (D).

COMPLETE AND ACCURATE LIST QUESTIONS

Most of the time, when you see "complete and accurate list" in a question stem, it is part of a regular Acceptability question. But as I mentioned in the section on Acceptability questions, you will occasionally see Complete and Accurate List questions that focus on a narrower part of the game, such as a single entity or a specific space.

> Which one of the following could be a complete and accurate list of the lunch trucks, each of which serves all three of the office buildings?[71]

> Which one of the following is a complete and accurate list of the sites each of which CANNOT be the site discovered by Gallagher?[72]

These questions are less common than the other question types covered so far in this chapter. It's very rare to find more than one or two of these in the Logic Games section, and many tests include none at all. That said, take a look at a couple of examples in context to learn the best ways to approach them should you encounter one on test day or later in your practice with this book.

The first example comes from the Archaeological Site Tour game you saw earlier in this chapter. Take a few moments to refresh your memory of the game and review the deductions that led to the Master Sketch.

A tour group plans to visit exactly five archaeological sites. Each site was discovered by exactly one of the following archaeologists—Ferrara, Gallagher, Oliphant—and each dates from the eighth, ninth, or tenth century (A.D.). The tour must satisfy the following conditions:

    The site visited second dates from the ninth century.
    Neither the site visited fourth nor the site visited fifth was discovered by Oliphant.
    Exactly one of the sites was discovered by Gallagher, and it dates from the tenth century.
    If a site dates from the eighth century, it was discovered by Oliphant.
    The site visited third dates from a more recent century than does either the site visited first or that visited fourth.

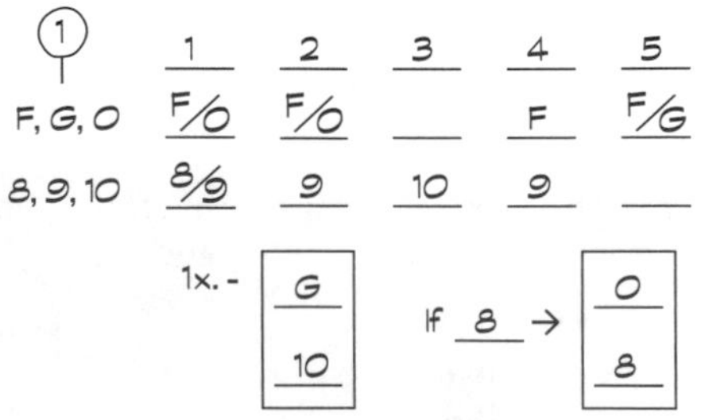

Figure 5.37

---

[71] PrepTest 43, Sec. 4, Q 21

[72] PrepTest 44, Sec. 3, Q 16

16. Which one of the following is a complete and accurate
    list of the sites each of which CANNOT be the site
    discovered by Gallagher?

    (A)   third, fourth, fifth
    (B)   second, third, fourth
    (C)   first, fourth, fifth
    (D)   first, second, fifth
    (E)   first, second, fourth[73]

In a case like this one, you can predict the correct answer with precision before you evaluate
the choices. Looking at the Master Sketch, you see that Gallagher is ruled out of the first, second, and fourth sites and no others. That's your complete and accurate list, and it fits answer
choice (E) exactly.

It's great when your answer is as clear-cut as that one, but it won't always happen. In the next
example, I'll go over a Complete and Accurate List question where you're better off eliminating
the wrong choices than you are trying to figure out the correct response before evaluating
the answer choices.

Exactly six people—Lulu, Nam, Ofelia, Pachai, Santiago, and
Tyrone—are the only contestants in a chess tournament. The
tournament consists of four games, played one after the other.
Exactly two people play in each game, and each person plays
in at least one game. The following conditions must apply:
    Tyrone does not play in the first or third game.
    Lulu plays in the last game.
    Nam plays in only one game and it is not against Pachai.
    Santiago plays in exactly two games, one just before and
    one just after the only game that Ofelia plays in.

Figure 5.38

11. Which one of the following is a complete and accurate
    list of the contestants who CANNOT play against Tyrone in any game?

    (A)   Lulu, Pachai
    (B)   Nam, Ofelia
    (C)   Nam, Pachai
    (D)   Nam, Santiago
    (E)   Ofelia, Pachai[74]

---

[73] PrepTest 44, Sec. 3, Q 16
[74] PrepTest 45, Sec. 3, Q 11

This time, there's no way to simply look at the Master Sketch and say, "Oh, those are the players who can't compete against Tyrone." Instead, you'll need to first examine the options and eliminate answers containing players who *can* be matched against Tyrone in the tournament. Cross out wrong answers completely. Option II is quite clear. There, Tyrone is scheduled to face off against Santiago in Game 2. That eliminates choice (D). In Option I, Tyrone could face Ofelia in Game 2. That gets rid of choices (B) and (E). Tyrone could also face Lulu in Option I, Game 4. So strike out choice (A). That leaves only choice (C), the correct answer.

Whenever you encounter Complete and Accurate List questions, you'll work through them in one of those two ways, either determining the content of the correct answer from the Master Sketch *or* using the restrictions shown in the Master Sketch to eliminate wrong answers. Remember that the correct answer to a Complete and Accurate List question must include *any and all* entities, groups, or spaces that fit the call of the question. That means that an answer can be incorrect not only for being inaccurate (including the wrong entities or spaces) but also for being incomplete (not including all of the right entities or spaces).

Complete and Accurate List questions are never going to make or break your Logic Games section performance. There simply aren't enough of them to have that kind of impact. Just make sure you know how to approach them and keep your focus on the Rules and Deductions steps of the Kaplan Method. If you do, Complete and Accurate List questions should become just one more small element of the Logic Games section that you can handle flawlessly.

COMPLETE SOLUTION QUESTIONS

Very occasionally, the test makers will pose a question that asks you what additional restriction would allow you to completely determine the arrangement of all entities in the game.

> Which one of the following, if known, would allow one to determine the entire lecture schedule and identify for each week the philosopher who is lectured on that week?[75]

> It can be determined in which department each of the seven applicants is hired if which one of the following statements is true?[76]

Questions like these can be associated with any task, but the game must be close enough to completion that the addition of one restriction will lock all of the entities into place. That tells you to look for one of two alternatives as you evaluate the answer choices. Either a floater or loosely restricted entity will be established into position, or an entity that restricts several others will be further limited. Take a look at this example from the Talent Agency game:

---

[75] PrepTest 34, Sec. 4, Q 10

[76] PrepTest 38, Sec. 2, Q 16

Five performers—Traugott, West, Xavier, Young, and
Zinser—are recruited by three talent agencies—Fame Agency,
Premier Agency, and Star Agency. Each performer signs with
exactly one of the agencies and each agency signs at least one
of the performers. The performers' signing with the agencies
is in accord with the following:

> Xavier signs with Fame Agency.
> Xavier and Young do not sign with the same agency as
> each other.
> Zinser signs with the same agency as Young.
> If Traugott signs with Star Agency, West also signs with
> Star Agency.

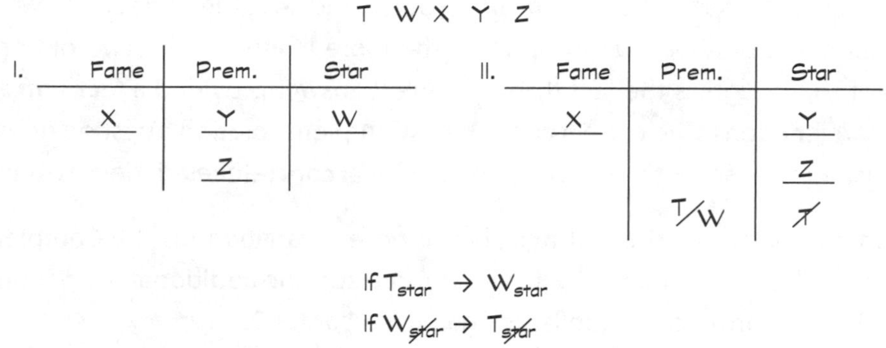

T W X Y Z

I.	Fame	Prem.	Star
	X	Y	W
		Z	

II.	Fame	Prem.	Star
	X		Y
			Z
		T/W	~~T~~

If $T_{star} \rightarrow W_{star}$

If $W_{\not{star}} \rightarrow T_{\not{star}}$

Figure 5.39

4. The agency with which each of the performers signs is
    completely determined if which one of the following is true?

    (A) Traugott signs with Fame Agency.
    (B) Traugott signs with Star Agency.
    (C) West signs with Premier Agency.
    (D) Xavier signs with Fame Agency.
    (E) Zinser signs with Premier Agency.[77]

One of the answers will provide the last puzzle piece, so to speak. Think about each of the
entities mentioned in the choices. Who would it be most helpful to know more about?

Start with choice (D). Xavier is already established in Fame Agency. That much you've known
since you first read Rule 1. And yet there's some ambiguity left in the game. Eliminate choice (D).

Choice (E) focuses on Zinser. Along with Young, Zinser provided the trigger for your Limited
Options deduction. Zinser can sign with either Premier or Star, but in neither case does knowing about Zinser finish the picture. Eliminate choice (E).

The remaining answers focus on West and Traugott, both of whom are restricted by the formal
logic in Rule 4. That makes choices (A), (B), and (C) all more likely than choices (D) and (E) were,
but choice (B) should stand out. The statement in choice (B) exactly matches the "if" clause of
Rule 4. Traugott can be placed in Star's column only in Option I. In fact, Traugott is the only

---

[77] PrepTest 53, Sec. 2, Q 4

entity yet to be placed in Option I. So knowing that Traugott signs with Star Agency is, indeed, enough to determine every performer's placement in the game.

For the record, Traugott could sign with Fame Agency in either option, so choice (A) doesn't determine everyone's placement. And while placing West under the Premier heading definitely puts you in Option II, it doesn't tell you whether Traugott signs with Fame or Premier. So choice (C) doesn't quite get the job done either.

It shouldn't surprise you that this question type accompanied a Limited Options game, where a restricted set of potential arrangements could be predetermined. And, once you see the answer choices in action, it shouldn't surprise you to find that the correct answer involved a statement that could only be true in Option I, the more limited of the two options. Perhaps most telling of all, though, is the fact that the correct answer provided a fact *sufficient* to trigger additional restrictions. The correct answer to a Complete Solution question doesn't have to trigger formal logic per se, but it must lead to additional concrete restrictions within the game.

Every once in a great while, the test makers will pose a variation on the Complete Solution question that asks for a fact that would lead to more specific additional restrictions. You saw one of these in the Dorm Room Appliances game in chapter 2.

5.   Which one of the following statements, if true, guarantees that Henri is using no more than one of the following: the hairdryer, the razor, the television?[78]

These questions are rare indeed. If you should chance upon one on test day or in your further practice, remember to keep your eyes peeled for the answer choice that triggers additional restrictions. You'll know, coming out of Step 4, where ambiguity and wiggle room remain within the setup. The correct answer to one of these Complete Solution questions will focus exactly there. It will hit the target so precisely that only one position is available to each of the entities.

"RULE-CHANGERS"

Nearly as rare as Complete Solution questions (there were, again, two of these among all of the logic games from PrepTest 39 through PrepTest 53), "Rule-Changers" are questions that ask you to replace one of the original rules with a new restriction applicable only to this question.

Suppose the restriction that Miller rows closer to the front than Singh is replaced by the restriction that Singh rows closer to the front than Miller. If the other two restrictions remain in effect, then each of the following could be an accurate matching of athletes to seats EXCEPT:[79]

---

[78] PrepTest 48, Sec.2, Q 5
[79] PrepTest 43, Sec. 4, Q 12

> Assume that the original condition that the linen dress hangs immediately to the right of the silk dress is replaced by the condition that the wool dress hangs immediately to the right of the silk dress. If all the other initial conditions remain in effect, which one of the following must be false?[80]

These question stems are long, but they look more intimidating than they are. In effect, they're super-"Ifs", because they force you to alter your original Master Sketch. But as with a regular "If" question, you can take control of them through a new mini-sketch. Notice, too, that the questions they ask after instructing you to swap positions are exactly the same ones you practiced earlier in this chapter: What must/could be true/false? What is or is not an acceptable arrangement? Moreover, they're always explicit—not only about the rule that is changing, but also that the other original restrictions are not.

"Rule-Changers" Always Appear Last

Something that many test takers fail to realize is that these questions, when they do occur, are always the last of the questions in the set for that game. The test makers bank on "Rule-Changers" being time-consuming, and at least part of the reason for their inclusion is almost certainly to slow down test takers who aren't being strategic with their time. Don't fall into that trap. If you find a "Rule-Changer" too time-consuming, skip it and leave yourself ample time to get all of the remaining points in the Logic Games section. It's far better to sacrifice that one question than to find yourself unable to complete one of the remaining games. I'll talk more about strategic time management in Part III of this book. For now, just remember that your goal must be to get as many right answers as you can overall. Don't overinvest your time in one complex question.

The placement of these questions at the end of the question set has one other consequence. Assuming you've finished all of the other questions, this is the one exceptional circumstance in which I'd tell you that it's okay to mess with your Master Sketch if doing so is easier or more efficient than making a new mini-sketch. Since the question stem is changing or replacing one of the original restrictions, you'll need to see the ripple effect that the rule change has on the other deductions you made in Step 4.

"Rule-Changer" Practice

Here's an example from a game that you've already seen. I've included the game's setup, its original Master Sketch, and the question. Give it a try, and then I'll go over it. Make sure that you take the time to consider which parts of the Master Sketch the "Rule-Changer" does and doesn't alter.

---

[80] PrepTest 41, Sec. 2, Q 7

A fruit stand carries at least one kind of the following kinds of fruit: figs, kiwis, oranges, pears, tangerines, and watermelons. The stand does not carry any other kind of fruit. The selection of fruits the stand carries is consistent with the following conditions:

> If the stand carries kiwis, then it does not carry pears.
> If the stand does not carry tangerines, then it carries kiwis.
> If the stand carries oranges, then it carries both pears and watermelons.
> If the stand carries watermelons, then it carries figs or tangerines or both.

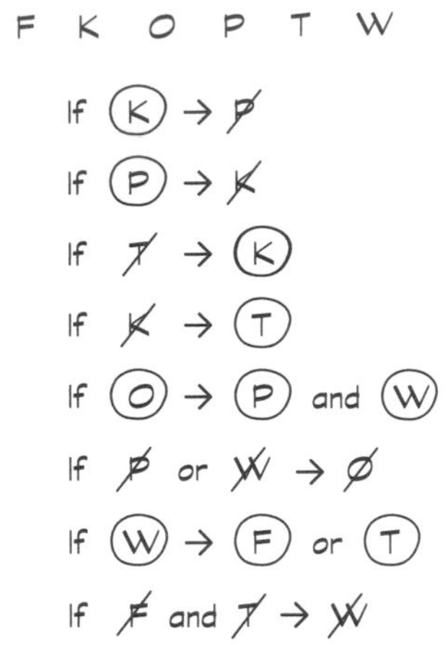

F K O P T W

If (K) → P̷

If (P) → K̷

If T̷ → (K)

If K̷ → (T)

If (O) → (P) and (W)

If P̷ or W̷ → O̷

If (W) → (F) or (T)

If F̷ and T̷ → W̷

Figure 5.40

6. If the condition that if the fruit stand does not carry tangerines then it does carry kiwis is suspended, and all other conditions remain in effect, then which one of the following CANNOT be a complete and accurate list of the kinds of fruit the stand carries?

(A) pears
(B) figs, pears
(C) oranges, pears, watermelons
(D) figs, pears, watermelons
(E) figs, oranges, pears, watermelons[81]

In this example, one of the original rules—Rule 2—is suspended. The presence of Rule 2 in the original Master Sketch told you that you had to have at least one of kiwis or tangerines. Now, that restriction is lifted and an arrangement with neither kiwis nor tangerines is fine, provided that it meets the game's other requirements. You needn't do more than cross Rule 2 off the list and you're ready to evaluate the answer choices.

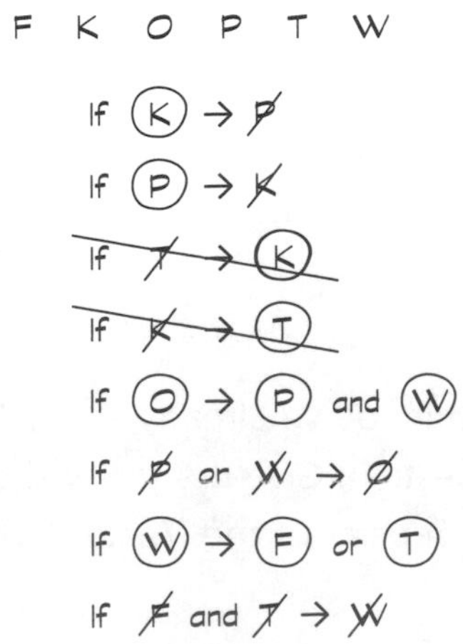

F K O P T W

If (K) → P̷

If (P) → K̷

~~If T̷ → (K)~~

~~If K̷ → (T)~~

If (O) → (P) and (W)

If P̷ or W̷ → O̷

If (W) → (F) or (T)

If F̷ and T̷ → W̷

Figure 5.41

[81] PrepTest 36, Sec. 4, Q 6

The question calls for the one *un*acceptable arrangement. This is the opposite of an Acceptability question stem: The right answer will violate a rule, but the wrong answers will not.

Choice (A) is acceptable. The only thing that including pears triggers is the exclusion of kiwis. Notice that under the original rules, this would have necessitated the inclusion of tangerines. Now that Rule 2 has been suspended, that second requirement is gone. Since choice (A) is acceptable, it's a wrong answer.

Choice (B), too, offers an acceptable arrangement and is, therefore, a wrong answer. Including figs doesn't trigger any additional rules, so figs and pears is a fine combination for the fruit stand's offerings.

Choice (C), though, runs afoul of Rule 4, which is still in effect under this question stem's terms. Including watermelons requires including either figs or tangerines, neither of which is included in the answer choice. As a rule-violator, choice (C) is the correct answer.

Choices (D) and (E) offer acceptable arrangements, of course. There are always one correct and four demonstrably incorrect answer choices. That point really encapsulates the final takeaway message of both this chapter and Part I of this book.

TAKEAWAY: ANSWER THE QUESTION THE TEST IS ASKING

I'll say it one more time: One right, four rotten. Unlike some tests you may have encountered in school, there is no "best" answer on the LSAT. There is always one unequivocally correct choice and four unequivocally wrong ones. And remember the very first point I made in chapter 1: Every question has an answer. The test always provides you with enough information to determine the correct answer.

The LSAT is tough but fair. If you encounter any question that seems to have more than one right answer (or one that seems to have no right answer), you can rest assured that you've made one of two mistakes: Either you missed a rule or deduction in the game's setup, or you misread the question stem. Avoiding the first of those mistakes is a matter of practicing with Steps 1 through 4 of the Kaplan Method, something you've already made great strides with. To avoid the latter mistake—to ensure that you're answering the right question—you must remain diligent. Characterize the choices before you evaluate them. Discipline yourself to do that on every question, because it's tempting to let the easiest questions make you sloppy. Avoid those two pitfalls and you're on the road to a great Logic Games section and a great LSAT score.

In the next chapter, I'll have you work through a few games from top to bottom, putting all five steps of the Kaplan Method into action.

CHAPTER 6

COMPLETE GAME PRACTICE

PUT IT ALL TOGETHER

You're ready to try your hand at some full games, top to bottom, start to finish. I won't be interrupting you with hints or analyses this time. You've learned how to manage any logic game effectively using the Kaplan Method. Now, use it systematically to practice the five steps in order, exactly as you'll use them on test day.

THE 5-STEP KAPLAN METHOD FOR LOGIC GAMES

STEP 1 Overview
Assess the game's Situation and determine your task(s).

STEP 2 Sketch
Draw a simple, useful framework to organize the game's information and restrictions.

STEP 3 Rules
Add the Rules into the Sketch in clear notation.

STEP 4 Deductions
Combine the Rules and restrictions to determine what must be true and false.

STEP 5 Questions
Answer the question efficiently using the information from your Master Sketch.

Take the games one at a time. They're laid out just as they will be on the real exam, so practice using the space on the page to manage your scratch work and mini-sketches. You won't get any scratch paper for your official LSAT, so get used to working in the test booklet now.

After you've completed each one, review it thoroughly using the explanations that follow it. That will help you see where you've mastered the concepts and strategies and where your approach still needs some polishing. More importantly, don't limit yourself to reviewing only the questions you got wrong. Even when you wound up with the correct answer, you need to be sure that you did so as efficiently as possible.

Those are your Dos. Now, for a couple of Don'ts. First, don't try to go too fast. You'll have the chance to practice timing and efficiency in Part III of this book. Use this chapter as a chance to practice being methodical, accurate, and effective; after all, you must be able to do logic games properly before you can do them fast. That's another reason why, at this point in your practice, it's so important to study the explanations to those questions you got right as well as those you got wrong.

Second, don't worry too much about categorizing each game. Part II of this book will outline and teach you to recognize the game types. For now, assess each game as you read it. Try to understand your task and to create a helpful, logical sketch. I want you to be confident that you can handle every game you see on test day, even if you can't give it a special name.

The four games in this chapter constitute a fairly representative sample of the games you're most likely to see on test day. You may recognize bits and pieces of some of them, but you haven't worked through the complete set of rules or deductions for any of them at this point. Challenge yourself to employ the relevant strategies from chapters 1–5. You may be surprised at how routine much of this is beginning to feel.

GAME 1

Questions 1–7

A closet contains exactly six hangers—1, 2, 3, 4, 5, and 6—hanging, in that order, from left to right. It also contains exactly six dresses—one gauze, one linen, one polyester, one rayon, one silk, and one wool—a different dress on each of the hangers, in an order satisfying the following conditions:

> The gauze dress is on a lower-numbered hanger than the polyester dress.
> The rayon dress is on hanger 1 or hanger 6.
> Either the wool dress or the silk dress is on hanger 3.
> The linen dress hangs immediately to the right of the silk dress.

1. Which one of the following could be an accurate matching of the hangers to the fabrics of the dresses that hang on them?

   (A) 1: wool; 2: gauze; 3: silk; 4: linen; 5: polyester; 6: rayon
   (B) 1: rayon; 2: wool; 3: gauze; 4: silk; 5: linen; 6: polyester
   (C) 1: polyester; 2: gauze; 3: wool; 4: silk; 5: linen; 6: rayon
   (D) 1: linen; 2: silk; 3: wool; 4: gauze; 5: polyester; 6: rayon
   (E) 1: gauze; 2: rayon; 3: silk; 4: linen; 5: wool; 6: polyester

2. If both the silk dress and the gauze dress are on odd-numbered hangers, then which one of the following could be true?

   (A) The polyester dress is on hanger 1.
   (B) The wool dress is on hanger 2.
   (C) The polyester dress is on hanger 4.
   (D) The linen dress is on hanger 5.
   (E) The wool dress is on hanger 6.

3. If the silk dress is on an even-numbered hanger, which one of the following could be on the hanger immediately to its left?

   (A) the gauze dress
   (B) the linen dress
   (C) the polyester dress
   (D) the rayon dress
   (E) the wool dress

4. If the polyester dress is on hanger 2, then which one of the following must be true?

   (A) The silk dress is on hanger 1.
   (B) The wool dress is on hanger 3.
   (C) The linen dress is on hanger 4.
   (D) The linen dress is on hanger 5.
   (E) The rayon dress is on hanger 6.

5. Which one of the following CANNOT be true?

   (A) The linen dress hangs immediately next to the gauze dress.
   (B) The polyester dress hangs immediately to the right of the rayon dress.
   (C) The rayon dress hangs immediately to the left of the wool dress.
   (D) The silk dress is on a lower-numbered hanger than the gauze dress.
   (E) The wool dress is on a higher-numbered hanger than the rayon dress.

6. Which one of the following CANNOT hang immediately next to the rayon dress?

   (A) the gauze dress
   (B) the linen dress
   (C) the polyester dress
   (D) the silk dress
   (E) the wool dress

7. Assume that the original condition that the linen dress hangs immediately to the right of the silk dress is replaced by the condition that the wool dress hangs immediately to the right of the silk dress. If all the other initial conditions remain in effect, which one of the following must be false?

   (A) The linen dress is on hanger 1.
   (B) The gauze dress is on hanger 2.
   (C) The wool dress is on hanger 4.
   (D) The silk dress is on hanger 5.
   (E) The polyester dress is on hanger 6.[1]

---

[1] PrepTest 41, Sec. 2, Game 1, Qs 1–7

Explanations—Game 1

STEPS 1 AND 2: Overview and Sketch

This is an easy game to visualize: a closet with six hangers, numbered 1 through 6. That easily turns into a standard Sequencing framework.

1 2 3 4 5 6
G L P R S W
1 2 3 4 5 6

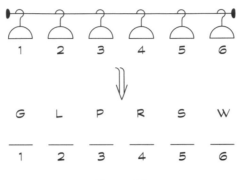

Figure 6.1

Make sure that you notice when games establish a direction for the numbering of slots. Here, the numbers increase as you go from left to right. Just a glance at the rules shows you that some of them pinpoint specific spaces. Anticipate being able to draw some of the restrictions right into the picture.

STEP 3: Rules

Rule 1 is relative, or "loose."

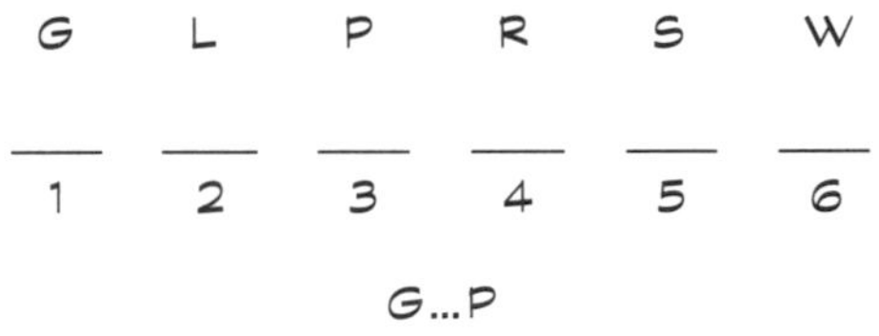

G L P R S W
1 2 3 4 5 6
G...P

Figure 6.2

Rule 2 presents an "either/or" situation, but since the rayon dress isn't implicated in any other rule, it's probably overkill to make dual Limited Options sketches here. Simply depict it like this:

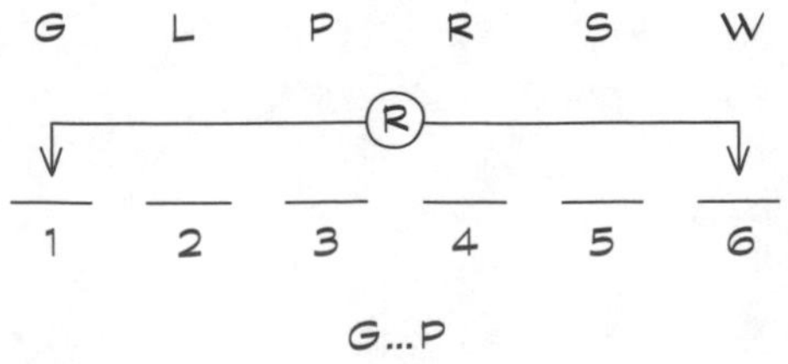

G L P R S W
R
1 2 3 4 5 6
G...P

Figure 6.3

Rule 3 provides for another "either/or," this time involving a space rather than an entity.

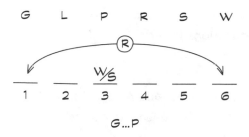

Figure 6.4

Rule 4 makes a strong block of entities S and L. You know both their order and their proximity.

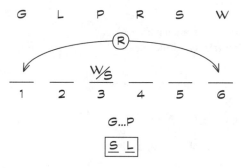

Figure 6.5

Not one of those rules should seem unfamiliar at this point. You haven't seen precisely this combination, but you've seen several examples of how similar rules work together. There are no floaters in this game. Every entity is restricted by at least one rule.

STEP 4: Deductions

You can combine only two of the four rules in this game, Rules 3 and 4. They share entity S, the silk dress. So place the result of that duplicated entity into your framework and you have your Master Sketch.

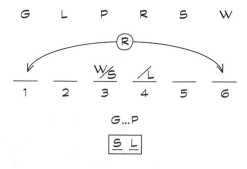

Figure 6.6

One of the key questions to ask yourself is whether you spent time unnecessarily looking for additional deductions that weren't there to find. Did you consult the BLEND checklist? If so, you knew that only the block created by Rule 4 and the duplicated entity S would help you. That meant getting to the questions faster.

STEP 5: Questions

The question set here is fairly balanced: one Acceptability question, three "If" questions, two Must Be False questions, and one "Rule-Changer." The fact that there are seven questions means that this game is especially important to your performance on the section. This one game represented close to 30 percent of the logic games points available on PrepTest 41. If you handled the questions here efficiently, you had the foundation for an outstanding section performance. See how you did.

1. **(A)**

Which one of the following could be an accurate matching of the hangers to the fabrics of the dresses that hang on them?

(A)   1: wool; 2: gauze; 3: silk; 4: linen; 5: polyester; 6: rayon

(B)   1: rayon; 2: wool; 3: gauze; 4: silk; 5: linen; 6: polyester

(C)   1: polyester; 2: gauze; 3: wool; 4: silk; 5: linen; 6: rayon

(D)   1: linen; 2: silk; 3: wool; 4: gauze; 5: polyester; 6: rayon

(E)   1: gauze; 2: rayon; 3: silk; 4: linen; 5: wool; 6: polyester[2]

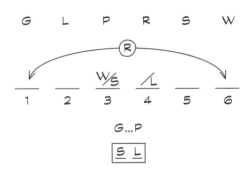

Figure 6.7

Once you recognized this as an Acceptability question, you should have had one point in a matter of seconds. Did you eliminate the violators rule by rule? Rule 1 knocked out choice (C), where P hangs below G. Rule 2 eliminated choice (E), where R is given hanger 2. Rule 3 took care of choice (B), where neither S nor W is on hanger 3. Rule 4 got rid of choice (D), where L hangs to the left of S, not to its right. Four rules, four wrong answers, just like that. The credited response is choice (A), and you have one point in the bag.

---

[2] PrepTest 41, Sec. 2, Q1

2. (B)

If both the silk dress and the gauze dress are on odd-numbered hangers, then which one of the following could be true?

(A) The polyester dress is on hanger 1.
(B) The wool dress is on hanger 2.
(C) The polyester dress is on hanger 4.
(D) The linen dress is on hanger 5.
(E) The wool dress is on hanger 6.[3]

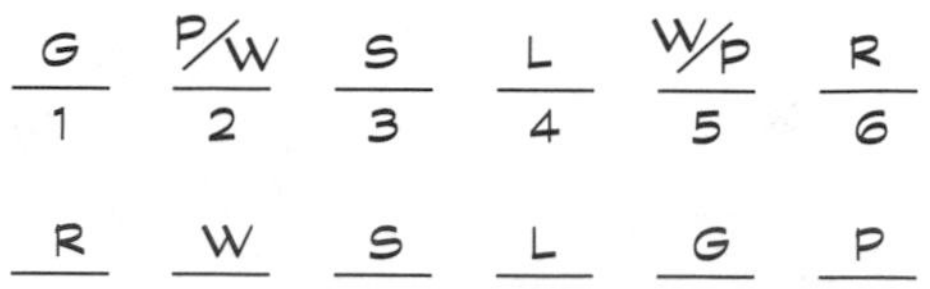

G	P/W	S	L	W/P	R
1	2	3	4	5	6

R	W	S	L	G	P

Figure 6.8

Question 2 kicks off a string of three straight "If" questions. All of them can be managed with mini-sketches. Make sure to check your scratch work. If you tried to handle any of these three questions in your head, you likely weren't as efficient as you could have been, even if you wound up getting the right answers.

The new "If" on question 2 tells you to place both G and S in odd numbered slots. Use what you know about working with the greatest limitations first to determine how that might work. S is more constricted than G because it has to have L immediately to its right. If you tried to put S in space 1, you'd be unable to place G in an odd-numbered space. W would have to take space 3 in that case, and R would take space 6. Although the fifth hanger is open, there'd be no room for P to follow G in such an arrangement.

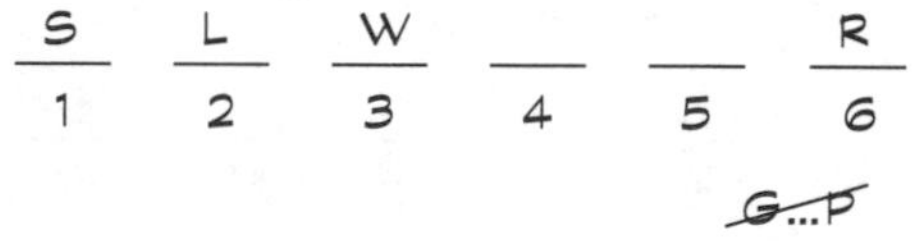

S	L	W	_	_	R
1	2	3	4	5	6

~~G...P~~

Figure 6.9

Similarly, you cannot place S in space 5. In this instance, W would again take space 3, R would take space 1, and you're fresh out of odd-numbered spaces for G.

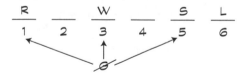

Figure 6.10

So you quickly know that for G and S to both take odd-numbered spaces, S will have to take space 3, leaving either space 1 or space 5 for G. Here's the start of your mini-sketch:

---

[3] PrepTest 41, Sec. 2, Q2

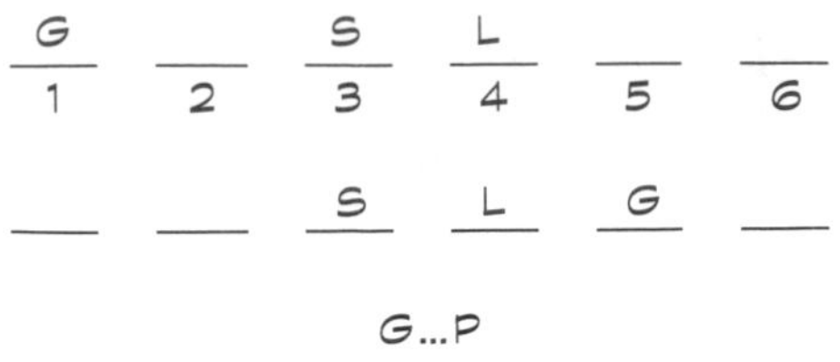

$$\frac{G}{1} \quad \frac{}{2} \quad \frac{S}{3} \quad \frac{L}{4} \quad \frac{}{5} \quad \frac{}{6}$$

$$\frac{}{} \quad \frac{}{} \quad \frac{S}{} \quad \frac{L}{} \quad \frac{G}{} \quad \frac{}{}$$

G...P

Figure 6.11

In either case, L hangs on hanger 4, immediately to the right of S per Rule 4.

The next most restricted entity is R. When G is in space 1, R will take space 6. When G is in space 5, P must follow it in space 6, so R will take space 1.

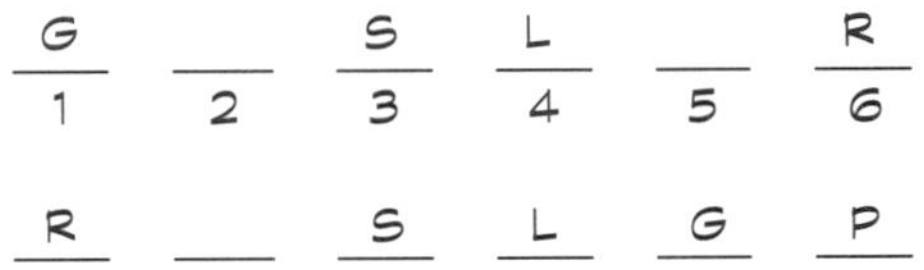

$$\frac{G}{1} \quad \frac{}{2} \quad \frac{S}{3} \quad \frac{L}{4} \quad \frac{}{5} \quad \frac{R}{6}$$

$$\frac{R}{} \quad \frac{}{} \quad \frac{S}{} \quad \frac{L}{} \quad \frac{G}{} \quad \frac{P}{}$$

Figure 6.12

In the first alternative, P and W are able to swap positions in spaces 2 and 5. In the second, W takes the only open slot, hanger 2.

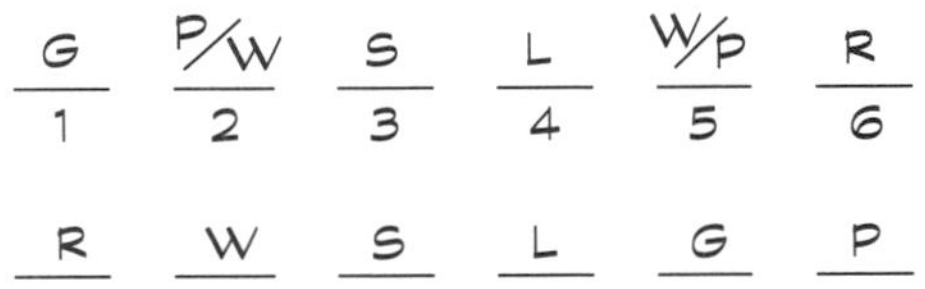

$$\frac{G}{1} \quad \frac{P/W}{2} \quad \frac{S}{3} \quad \frac{L}{4} \quad \frac{W/P}{5} \quad \frac{R}{6}$$

$$\frac{R}{} \quad \frac{W}{} \quad \frac{S}{} \quad \frac{L}{} \quad \frac{G}{} \quad \frac{P}{}$$

Figure 6.13

Your patience in making a solid mini-sketch is rewarded by how easy it now is to evaluate the choice. The correct answer could be true, so the four wrong choices must be false. Choice (B) is the only answer that appears as acceptable in your mini-sketch, so it's correct.

3. **(E)**

If the silk dress is on an even-numbered hanger, which one of the following could be on the hanger immediately to its left?

(A) the gauze dress
(B) the linen dress
(C) the polyester dress
(D) the rayon dress
(E) the wool dress[4]

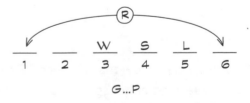

G...P

Figure 6.14

Much like question 2, you can reduce the potential solutions very quickly here by considering the restrictions on entity S. Of the three even-numbered hangers in the closet, S can only acceptably take number 4. If you tried to put S on hanger 2, W and L would be in conflict, as both would be required to take hanger 3. If you tried to put S on hanger 6, there'd simply be no hanger for L. So your mini-sketch must start like this:

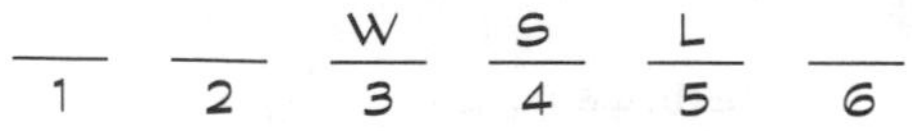

$$\underline{}\ \underline{}\ \underset{3}{\underline{W}}\ \underset{4}{\underline{S}}\ \underset{5}{\underline{L}}\ \underline{}$$
$$\quad 1\quad\ \ 2\quad\ \ 3\quad\ \ 4\quad\ \ 5\quad\ \ 6$$

Figure 6.15

That's enough to answer the question. Without S in space 3, W has to take it per Rule 3. That means that the wool dress is immediately to the left of the silk dress. Choice (E) is correct.

4. (E)

> If the polyester dress is on hanger 2, then which one of the following must be true?
>
> (A)   The silk dress is on hanger 1.
> (B)   The wool dress is on hanger 3.
> (C)   The linen dress is on hanger 4.
> (D)   The linen dress is on hanger 5.
> (E)   The rayon dress is on hanger 6.[5]

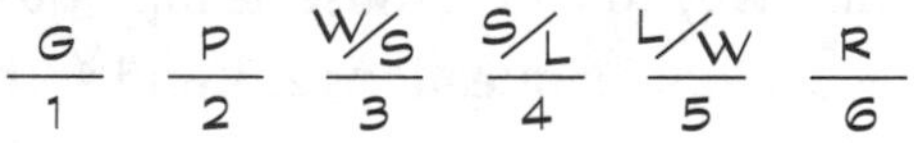

$$\underset{1}{\underline{G}}\ \underset{2}{\underline{P}}\ \underset{3}{\underline{W\!/\!S}}\ \underset{4}{\underline{S\!/\!L}}\ \underset{5}{\underline{L\!/\!W}}\ \underset{6}{\underline{R}}$$

Figure 6.16

Question 4 is the ideal counterpart to question 3. The former locked in entities W, S, and L. This one locks in entities G, P, and R. The "If" tells you to place P in space 2. That means that G must take space 1 to accord with Rule 1.

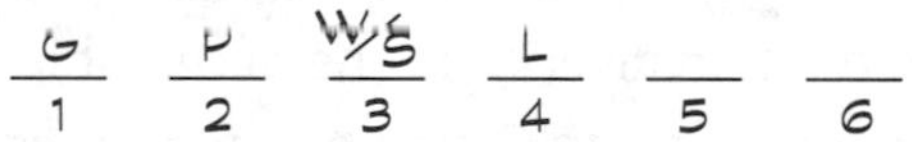

$$\underset{1}{\underline{G}}\ \underset{2}{\underline{P}}\ \underset{3}{\underline{W\!/\!S}}\ \underset{4}{\underline{L}}\ \underline{}\ \underline{}$$
$$\quad 1\quad\ \ 2\quad\ \ 3\quad\ \ 4\quad\ \ 5\quad\ \ 6$$

Figure 6.17

Once space 1 is occupied, Rule 2 dictates that R will take space 6.

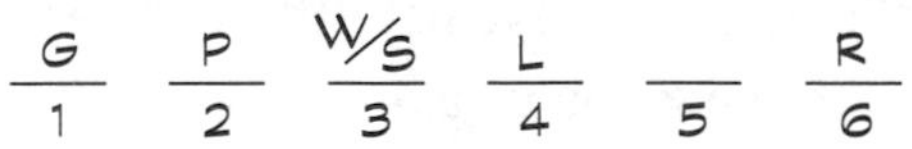

$$\underset{1}{\underline{G}}\ \underset{2}{\underline{P}}\ \underset{3}{\underline{W\!/\!S}}\ \underset{4}{\underline{L}}\ \underline{}\ \underset{6}{\underline{R}}$$

Figure 6.18

That means that choice (E) must be true, which is the characteristic of the right answer here. It's worth noting that all four wrong answers contain one of entities W, S, or L, the three entities whose positions are not determined by the "If." The sketch next to the question shows the two possible positions for each of W, S, and L. That's no coincidence given the question stem.

---

[5] PrepTest 41, Sec. 2, Q4

5. (B)

Which one of the following CANNOT be true?

(A)   The linen dress hangs immediately next to the gauze dress.

(B)   The polyester dress hangs immediately to the right of the rayon dress.

(C)   The rayon dress hangs immediately to the left of the wool dress.

(D)   The silk dress is on a lower-numbered hanger than the gauze dress.

(E)   The wool dress is on a higher-numbered hanger than the rayon dress.[6]

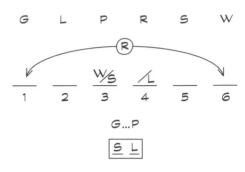

Figure 6.19

There's no new "If" for this question, so all you need to do is to characterize the answer choices before evaluating them. The correct answer here "CANNOT be true." That's just another way of saying it must be false. It also means that the four wrong answers could be true. I'll show you a quick way to tackle must be false questions in a game like this one. You've already done the scratch work for questions 2, 3, and 4. That scratch work shows several acceptable arrangements for the entities in this game. Any answer choice in question 5 that appears as acceptable is a wrong answer because it could be true. Look at the scratch work for question 2:

G	P/W	S	L	W/P	R
1	2	3	4	5	6
R	W	S	L	G	P

Figure 6.20

Specifically, look at the second alternative. That one acceptable arrangement knocks out all four wrong answers here. It shows L next to G, getting rid of choice (A). It shows R immediately left of W in spaces 1 and 2. That eliminates choices (C) and (E). S is on hanger 3 and G is on hanger 5 there. That takes care of choice (D). The correct answer, the one that must be false, is choice (B).

Characterizing the answers allows you to evaluate the choices in whatever way is the most effective. Given all of the scratch work you've already done for this game, it's much easier to look for what could be true and eliminate the wrong answers than it would be to analyze each choice to try to prove that it had to be false. The next question works much the same way.

---

[6] PrepTest 41, Sec. 2, Q5

6. **(D)**

Which one of the following CANNOT hang immediately next to the rayon dress?

(A) the gauze dress
(B) the linen dress
(C) the polyester dress
(D) the silk dress
(E) the wool dress[7]

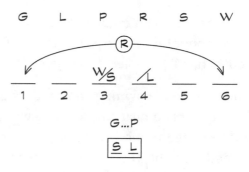

Figure 6.21

Again, put your scratch work to use. Here, the correct choice is a dress that cannot hang next to the rayon dress. So you will eliminate any answer choice containing an entity that can go next to R. The scratch work for question 2 shows that W and P could hang next to R.

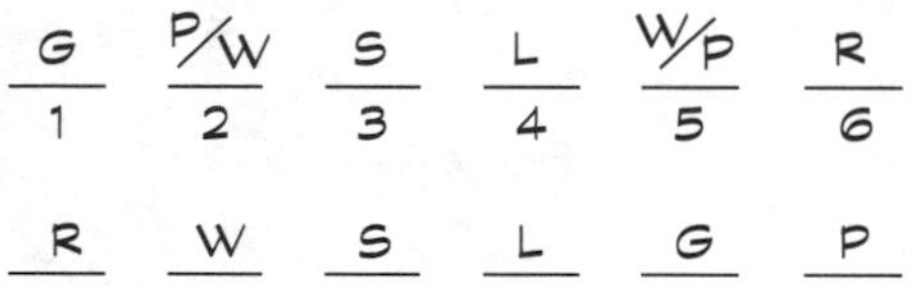

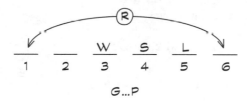

Figure 6.22

That gets rid of choices (C) and (E).

The scratch work for question 3 shows that G could hang next to R, in spaces 1 and 2.

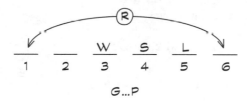

Figure 6.23

That eliminates choice (A).

Finally, the scratch work from question 4 shows that L and R can be in consecutive spots on hangers 5 and 6.

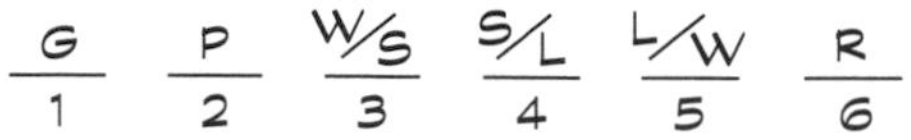

Figure 6.24

---

[7] PrepTest 41, Sec. 2, Q6

That takes out choice (B) and leaves you with the correct answer: choice (D). It's tough to see who cannot be next to R, but it's easy to determine who can, especially with all of the "If"s you've handled earlier in this game.

Now that you know that choice (D) is the correct answer, take a moment to consider why S can never hang next to R. It will give you a clearer picture of how games like this one work. R is restricted to the end points of the closet, hangers 1 or 6. S is restricted by having L to its immediate right. The S-L block prevents S from taking space 5 when R is in space 6.

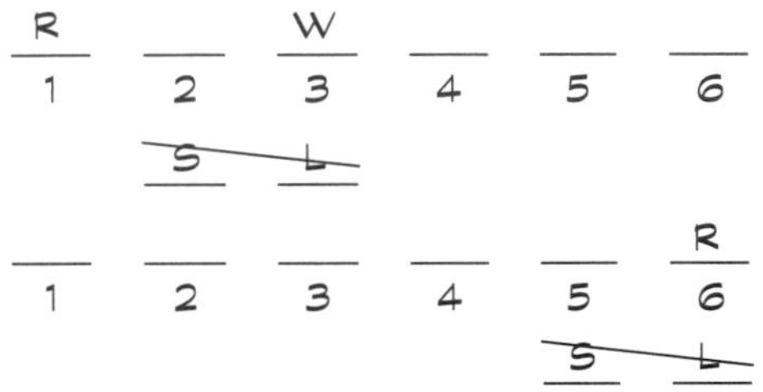

$$
\begin{array}{cccccc}
\underset{1}{\overset{R}{\rule{1.5em}{0.4pt}}} & \underset{2}{\rule{1.5em}{0.4pt}} & \underset{3}{\overset{W}{\rule{1.5em}{0.4pt}}} & \underset{4}{\rule{1.5em}{0.4pt}} & \underset{5}{\rule{1.5em}{0.4pt}} & \underset{6}{\rule{1.5em}{0.4pt}}
\end{array}
$$

Figure 6.25

Rule 3 provides that either S or W take the third hanger. That means that the S-L block also prevents S from taking space 2 when R is in space 1. However you slice it, the silk dress cannot wind up hanging next to the rayon dress.

7. **(D)**

Assume that the original condition that the linen dress hangs immediately to the right of the silk dress is replaced by the condition that the wool dress hangs immediately to the right of the silk dress. If all the other initial conditions remain in effect, which one of the following must be false?

(A) The linen dress is on hanger 1.
(B) The gauze dress is on hanger 2.
(C) The wool dress is on hanger 4.
(D) The silk dress is on hanger 5.
(E) The polyester dress is on hanger 6.[8]

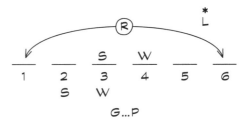

Figure 6.26

And now for a "rule-changer." As soon as you see that one of the original rules will be replaced by a new restriction, you know you're in for a new sketch. The S-L block is replaced by the new S-W block. Rule 3, requiring either S or W to take hanger 3, remains in effect, however. So your new situation looks like this:

---

[8] PrepTest 41, Sec. 2, Q7

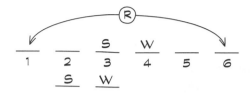

Figure 6.27

R is still constrained to the ends of the closet, and the loose order of G and P stands. L has effectively become a floater.

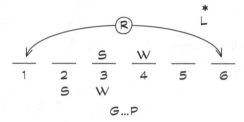

Figure 6.28

Before launching into the choices, characterize the answers. The correct answer must be false; the four wrong ones could be true. You're ready.

Choice (A) could be true, as L has become a floater. Eliminate it.

Choice (B) is also possible. With G in space 2, P would have either space 5 or 6 available. Eliminate this one, too.

You can see that choice (C) is possible just by looking at the new mini-sketch. Cross it out.

Just as easily, you can see from the mini-sketch that S cannot go in space 5. It's now restricted to either the third or fourth hanger. Choice (D) must be false and, therefore, is correct.

For the record, your analysis of choice (B) provided that P could acceptably be placed on hanger 6. So you know already that choice (E) could be true under the altered circumstances of this question stem.

Sequencing games like this one have been the most common games to appear on the LSAT over the past two decades. This example is almost stereotypical. The level of restriction here is standard, neither overly constrained nor overly vague. Even the question set is balanced, with just enough new "If" questions to allow you to work out several acceptable permutations that you can then leverage against the more opened-ended Must Be False questions. Consider this game to be the archetype of Strict Sequencing. That will give proper context to the variations on this game type that you'll see in Part II.

GAME 2

Questions 6–10

Six hotel suites—F, G, H, J, K, L—are ranked from most expensive (first) to least expensive (sixth). There are no ties. The ranking must be consistent with the following conditions:

H is more expensive than L.

If G is more expensive than H, then neither K nor L is more expensive than J.

If H is more expensive than G, then neither J nor L is more expensive than K.

F is more expensive than G, or else F is more expensive than H, but not both.

6. Which one of the following could be the ranking of the suites, from most expensive to least expensive?

(A)   G, F, H, L, J, K
(B)   H, K, F, J, G, L
(C)   J, H, F, K, G, L
(D)   J, K, G, H, L, F
(E)   K, J, L, H, F, G

7. If G is the second most expensive suite, then which one of the following could be true?

(A)   H is more expensive than F.
(B)   H is more expensive than G.
(C)   K is more expensive than F.
(D)   K is more expensive than J.
(E)   L is more expensive than F.

8. Which one of the following CANNOT be the most expensive suite?

(A)   F
(B)   G
(C)   H
(D)   J
(E)   K

9. If L is more expensive than F, then which one of the following could be true?

(A)   F is more expensive than H.
(B)   F is more expensive than K.
(C)   G is more expensive than H.
(D)   G is more expensive than J.
(E)   G is more expensive than L.

10. If H is more expensive than J and less expensive than K, then which one of the following could be true?

(A)   F is more expensive than H.
(B)   G is more expensive than F.
(C)   G is more expensive than H.
(D)   J is more expensive than L.
(E)   L is more expensive than K.[9]

---

[9] PrepTest 51, Sec. 4, Game 2, Qs 6–10

Answer Explanations follow on the next page.

Explanations—Game 2

STEPS 1 AND 2: Overview and Sketch

The notion of ranking should put you on immediate notice that you're dealing with a Sequencing action. It's also likely that your instinctive reaction is to arrange this game vertically. The very words *higher* and *lower* ranked imply this orientation. If you started to scratch out six slots, that's fine. But there's really no need for a framework here at all. All of the rules are "loose"; they give only the relative positions of the entities they restrict.

STEP 3: Rules

Sometimes, Loose Sequencing rules are so integrated that you can simply start with Rule 1 and then add on the remaining rules to the sketch one at a time. Here, however, the formal logic in Rules 2 and 3 makes that direct approach too difficult. So jot down all four rules and then combine them in Step 4: Deductions.

Rule 1 is the only one that's truly straightforward: H is ranked above L.

H
|
L

Figure 6.29

Rules 2 and 3 create two incompatible alternative scenarios. Don't worry if you didn't see that as you sketched Rule 2. Once you saw that the conditional clauses of the two rules are contradictions of one another, you'd know that you have to consider two arrangements.

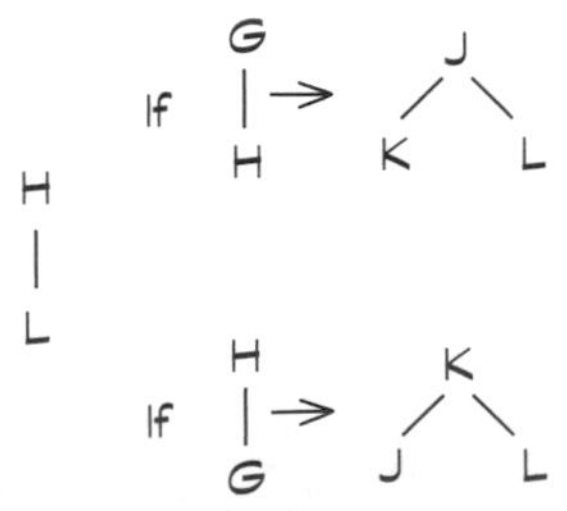

Figure 6.30

Rule 4 also gives you alternative arrangements. It's easy to depict F as either more expensive than G or more expensive than H, but the "but not both" at the end is what gives this rule its true power. When F is more expensive than G, F must be less expensive than H. When F is more expensive than H, F must be less expensive than G.

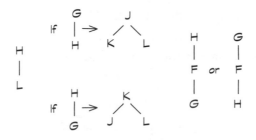

Figure 6.31

Creating a complete picture of Rule 4 is the springboard to the additional deductions that give this game its full concreteness.

STEP 4: Deductions

If you struggled with the questions in this game, it's likely that Step 4 is actually where you went off course. Review this step carefully and make sure you wound up with the recommended Master Sketch.

Your starting point—the point of greatest restriction in this game—is Rule 4. It creates the fundamental Limited Options sketches you'll build off of. Every acceptable ranking contains either the order H–F–G or the order G–F–H among the entities.

Figure 6.32

Next, add Rule 1 to each of the options.

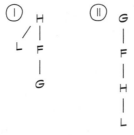

Figure 6.33

In Option I, you don't know anything about the relationship between L and the F-G portion of the string. In Option II, you can see that the order G–F–H–L is required.

Now, consider Rules 2 and 3 in light of the Limited Options. The alternate orderings of G and H relative to F in Rule 4 match the two sufficient clauses of the formal logic rules. Rule 2 is triggered by Option II, while Rule 3 is triggered by Option I. So add J and K into each option accordingly.

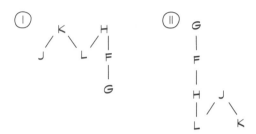

Figure 6.34

This Master Sketch puts you fully in control of the game. You can already anticipate "If" questions that will indicate which of the two options you need to use.

STEP 5: Questions

There are only five questions this time. The key to handling them lies in using the Limited Options sketches effectively. As you review, check not only whether you got the correct answer, but also if you got it as quickly *and confidently* as possible. Review your work.

6. (B)

> Which one of the following could be the ranking of
> the suites, from most expensive to least expensive?

(A) G, F, H, L, J, K
(B) H, K, F, J, G, L
(C) J, H, F, K, G, L
(D) J, K, G, H, L, F
(E) K, J, L, H, F, G[10]

Here's a standard Acceptability question. The conditional nature of the rules makes them a little bit more challenging than usual to check, perhaps, but that shouldn't make you alter your rule-by-rule approach.

Rule 1 eliminates choice (E), where L is more expensive than H. Rule 2 gets rid of choice (A); there, G is more expensive than H, but L is more expensive than J. Rule 3 gets rid of choice (C); H is more expensive than G in this answer, but J is more expensive than K. Finally, Rule 4 eliminates choice (D), where F is less expensive than both G and H. That leaves choice (B), the correct answer.

---

[10] PrepTest 51, Sec. 4, Q6

7. (C)

If G is the second most expensive suite, then which one of the following could be true?

(A) H is more expensive than F.
(B) H is more expensive than G.
(C) K is more expensive than F.
(D) K is more expensive than J.
(E) L is more expensive than F.[11]

Figure 6.35

Recall what you learned in chapter 5 about "If" questions in games with Limited Options sketches. The "If" will nearly always place you into one of the two options. For this question, you need to use Option II, because there is no way for G to be higher than third place in Option I. In Option II, J and K could be ranked higher than G. For G to be second-highest, J must be ranked most expensive and K must be ranked beneath G. That gives you the mini-sketch next to the question. Use it to evaluate the answer choices. The correct answer could be true, so each of the wrong answers must be false.

Both choices (A) and (B) must be false. The G-F-H ranking is the defining feature of Option II. Eliminate both.

Choice (C), on the other hand, is undefined. K could be either more or less expensive than F. That's the very essence of a could be true answer, meaning that choice (C) is correct.

A glance at the mini-sketch shows that both choices (D) and (E) must be false. J has to be the most expensive hotel suite pursuant to the "If" in the question stem, and L is always less expensive than F in Option II.

8. (A)

Which one of the following CANNOT be the most expensive suite?

(A) F
(B) G
(C) H
(D) J
(E) K.[12]

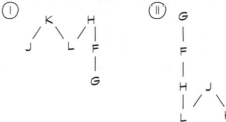

Figure 6.36

Provided that you characterize the answers correctly, this question should take you only a few seconds to answer. Since the correct answer is an entity that cannot be ranked at the top, all four of the wrong answers are entities that can be ranked at the top. You already know, from Rule 4, that F will always be sandwiched between G and H. F can never be the most expensive suite, making choice (A) the correct answer.

---

[11] PrepTest 51, Sec. 4, Q7
[12] PrepTest 51, Sec. 4, Q8

To no one's surprise, it turns out that there are precisely four entities that could be ranked at the top, two in Option I—K and H—and two in Option II—G and J. Those four entities are listed in the wrong answers, choices (B), (C), (D), and (E).

9. **(D)**

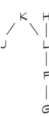

Figure 6.37

> If L is more expensive than F, then which one of the following could be true?
>
> (A) F is more expensive than H.
> (B) F is more expensive than K.
> (C) G is more expensive than H.
> (D) G is more expensive than J.
> (E) G is more expensive than L.[13]

Like question 7, this question has an "If" clause that limits you to considering only one of the two options. Not surprisingly, since question 7 had you checking Option II, question 9 has you working with Option I. The "If" in question 9's stem tells you to place L above F. That would directly contradict Option II, but it works fine in Option I provided that you place L between H and F, as shown in the mini-sketch above. Using that mini-sketch, evaluate the answer choices. You're looking for the one that could be true; all four wrong answers must be false.

Notice that choices (A) and (B) each address suite F. The mini-sketch shows that F must be less expensive than K, H, and L. Thus, both choices (A) and (B) must be false and are wrong answers.

The next three choices all address G. G is highly restricted in Option I, and especially so in this question, where you know that G is also less expensive than K and L. Since being less expensive than L automatically means being less expensive than H, choices (C) and (E) must be eliminated. That makes choice (D) the right answer here since it is the only one that could be true.

10. **(D)**

Figure 6.38

> If H is more expensive than J and less expensive than K, then which one of the following could be true?
>
> (A) F is more expensive than H.
> (B) G is more expensive than F.
> (C) G is more expensive than H.
> (D) J is more expensive than L.
> (E) L is more expensive than K.[14]

[13] PrepTest 51, Sec. 4, Q9

[14] PrepTest 51, Sec. 4, Q10

The "If" in this stem calls for the order K-H-J. That's only possible in Option I. (In Option II, K must follow J.) Jot down the K-H-J order from the stem to begin your mini-sketch:

Figure 6.39

Now add what you know about L, F, and G from Option I.

Figure 6.40

Characterize the answers and use that mini-sketch to make short work of this one. The correct answer here could be true; the wrong answers all must be false.

Choices (A), (B), and (C) all must be false as soon as you know you're in Option I, which is, after all, based on the H-F-G order.

Choice (D) is the correct answer. J and L must both be less expensive than H in this question, but they don't restrict one another in any way. Either could take any position from third through sixth.

For the record, choice (E) must be false. L follows H in Option I, and the "If" from the stem told you that H followed K in this question. This yields the order K-H-L.

This game, like the first game in this chapter, tasked you with determining the entities' order or sequence. The big difference is that, in the Hotel Suites game, all of the rules were relative, or "loose." None of the rules lock an entity into a particular space or dictate a specific distance that separates any of the entities. In the past, Loose Sequencing games were typically very simple, and you were able to link all of the entities within a single "tree" framework. More recently—and I'll go into more detail about this in Part II of the book—the test makers have been more creative, and Loose Sequencing games have become more complex. This example is somewhere in between the simplest and most complex of these games. The inclusion of formal logic rules and the presence of the Limited Options deduction are reminders that what you've learned about Steps 3 and 4 of the Kaplan Method applies to all logic games.

GAME 3

Questions 18–22

Each of exactly six lunch trucks sells a different one of six kinds of food: falafel, hot dogs, ice cream, pitas, salad, or tacos. Each truck serves one or more of exactly three office buildings: X, Y, or Z. The following conditions apply:

The falafel truck, the hot dog truck, and exactly one other truck each serve Y.

The falafel truck serves exactly two of the office buildings.

The ice cream truck serves more of the office buildings than the salad truck.

The taco truck does not serve Y.

The falafel truck does not serve any office building that the pita truck serves.

The taco truck serves two office buildings that are also served by the ice cream truck.

18. Which one of the following could be a complete and accurate list of each of the office buildings that the falafel truck serves?

    (A) X
    (B) X, Z
    (C) X, Y, Z
    (D) Y, Z
    (E) Z

19. For which one of the following pairs of trucks must it be the case that at least one of the office buildings is served by both of the trucks?

    (A) the hot dog truck and the pita truck
    (B) the hot dog truck and the taco truck
    (C) the ice cream truck and the pita truck
    (D) the ice cream truck and the salad truck
    (E) the salad truck and the taco truck

20. If the ice cream truck serves fewer of the office buildings than the hot dog truck, then which one of the following is a pair of lunch trucks that must serve exactly the same buildings as each other?

    (A) the falafel truck and the hot dog truck
    (B) the falafel truck and the salad truck
    (C) the ice cream truck and the pita truck
    (D) the ice cream truck and the salad truck
    (E) the ice cream truck and the taco truck

21. Which one of the following could be a complete and accurate list of the lunch trucks, each of which serves all three of the office buildings?

    (A) the hot dog truck, the ice cream truck
    (B) the hot dog truck, the salad truck
    (C) the ice cream truck, the taco truck
    (D) the hot dog truck, the ice cream truck, the pita truck
    (E) the ice cream truck, the pita truck, the salad truck

22. Which one of the following lunch trucks CANNOT serve both X and Z?

    (A) the hot dog truck
    (B) the ice cream truck
    (C) the pita truck
    (D) the salad truck
    (E) the taco truck[15]

Answer Explanations follow on the next page.

Explanations—Game 3

STEPS 1 AND 2: Overview and Sketch

The most important language in this game's setup text is that "[e]ach truck serves *one or more*" of the office buildings. This game would play out differently (and be much easier) if the trucks were assigned to only one building each. At any rate, you can see your task: Construct a list or chart showing the trucks that serve (and those that don't serve) each of the buildings. The buildings don't move, of course, but the trucks might. So you'll set up your framework in one of these ways:

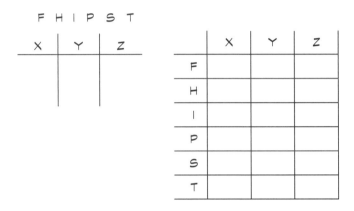

Figure 6.41

It's pretty much a matter of taste whether you want to jot down lists of the trucks under each building's column or make a grid with checks and *X*s. I'll illustrate both here so that you can check your handling of the rules and deductions either way.

STEP 3: Rules

Rule 1 is very restrictive. You can affirmatively indicate F's and H's inclusion in building Y's column. You also need to note that Y's column will have exactly three matches.

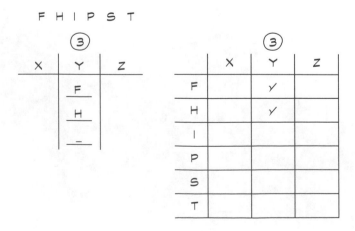

Figure 6.42

Rule 2 gives you the precise number of buildings that F will serve. Since one of F's matches has already been indicated by Rule 1, you can see that further deductions for F are forthcoming.

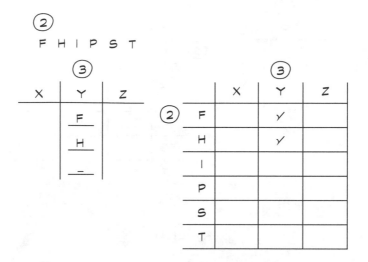

Figure 6.43

Rule 3 cannot be drawn into the framework yet, but as the game becomes clearer, expect all of these numerical restrictions to start acting in concert during the Deduction step.

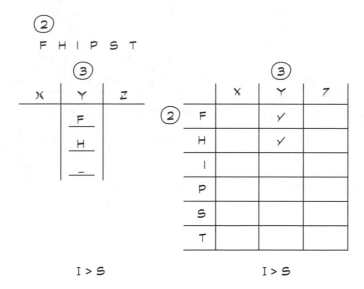

Figure 6.44

Rule 4 is negative but absolute. Diagram it right into the framework, regardless of whether you used a list or a grid.

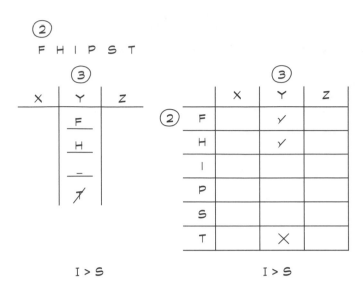

Figure 6.45

Rule 5 is yet another that touches on F. You can anticipate that the relationship between F and P will be central to how the game plays out.

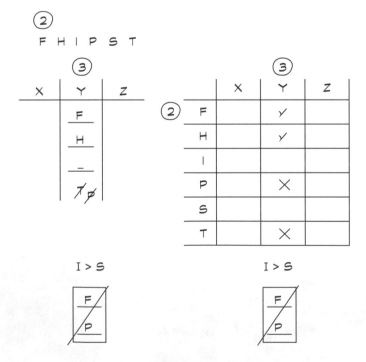

Figure 6.46

Rule 6 might seem tricky to diagram. But since T is excluded from building Y already, you can actually put this rule right into the framework. Make sure you don't read too much into this rule, though. Truck T can't serve building Y, but truck I still might.

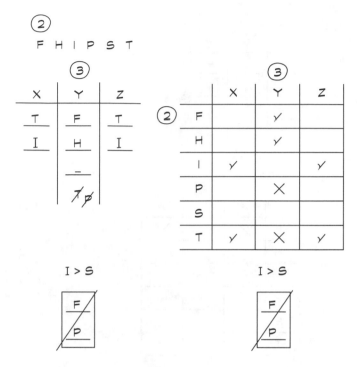

Figure 6.47

There are several rules that duplicate entities in this game and several that impose numerical limitations on the rows and columns. Their interactions should be your focus in the Deduction step.

STEP 4: Deductions

Three entities are each duplicated in two or more rules: F (Rules 1, 2, and 5), I (Rules 3 and 6), and T (Rules 4 and 6). Truck T is the most restricted, but it's so restricted that you've already learned all you can about it. T will serve buildings X and Z and won't serve building Y. T's row is closed.

Truck F will serve exactly two buildings, one of which is building Y. So F yields Limited Options, serving either buildings X and Y or buildings Y and Z. In a grid-type framework, you may choose to depict the two options without two separate sketches. Draw whichever is clearest. It's the information (not the style) that gets you LSAT points.

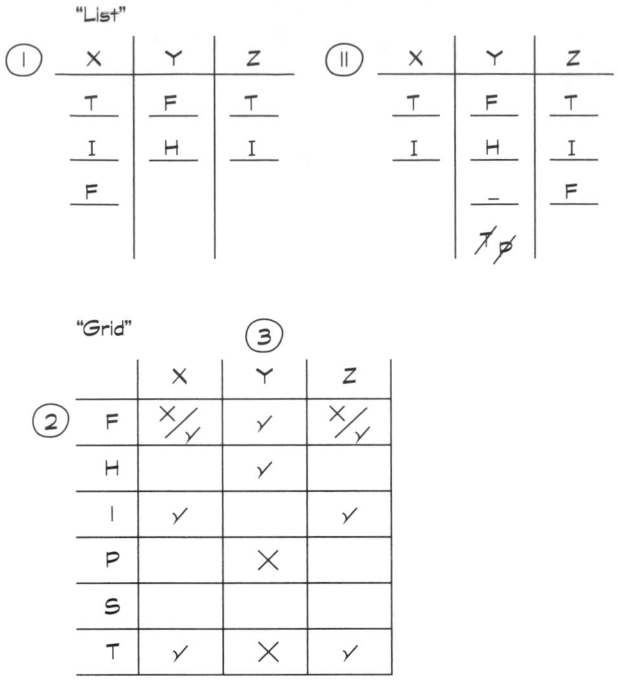

"List"

(I)

X	Y	Z
T	F	T
I	H	I
F		

(II)

X	Y	Z
T	F	T
I	H	I
	_	F
	̸I ø	

"Grid"   (3)

(2)

	X	Y	Z
F	X/✓	✓	X/✓
H		✓	
I	✓		✓
P		X	
S			
T	✓	X	✓

Figure 6.48

When you add in Rule 5, truck P becomes part of the Limited Options as well. It will serve *only* the one building *not* served by F.

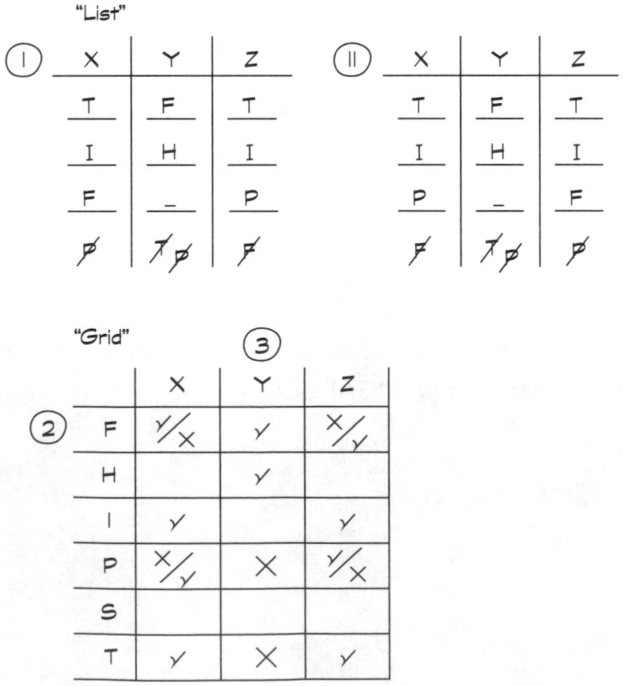

"List"

(I)

X	Y	Z
T	F	T
I	H	I
F	_	P
ø	̸I ø	̸F

(II)

X	Y	Z
T	F	T
I	H	I
P	_	F
̸F	̸I ø	ø

"Grid"   (3)

(2)

	X	Y	Z
F	✓/X	✓	X/✓
H		✓	
I	✓		✓
P	X/✓	X	✓/X
S			
T	✓	X	✓

Figure 6.49

So no matter what, you know the acceptable arrangements for trucks F, P, and T. Now, consider I and S. One of them (but not both) will serve building Y, which must have three trucks serving it (Rule 1). Notice that if S serves building Y, that's the only building it can serve. Rule 3 requires that I serve more buildings than S. If I serves building Y, then S could serve either or both of buildings X and Z. I recommend against drawing out even more options to depict these permutations. Rather, just highlight the numerical restrictions between I and S and keep an eye on how they play out.

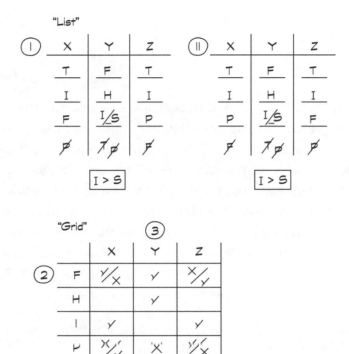

Figure 6.50

That leaves only truck H. You know from Rule 1 that it will serve building Y. Since it's otherwise unrestricted and unrestrictive, it can serve either or both of the other two buildings, but it need not do so. It's the closest thing you have to a floater in this game.

STEP 5: Questions

Of the five questions in this set, only one has a new "if." Seeing that should prompt you to be extra patient in the Rules and Deductions steps, since you'll need to have a big chunk of this game worked out before you answer the questions. Review your answers.

18. **(B)**

Which one of the following could be a complete and accurate list of each of the office buildings that the falafel truck serves?

(A)   X
(B)   X, Z
(C)   X, Y, Z
(D)   Y, Z
(E)   Z[16]

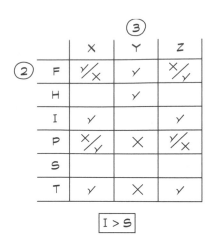

Figure 6.51

Truck F was at the center of the rules and deductions, so it's no surprise to see it featured in a Complete and Accurate List question like this one. Make sure that you read the question stem carefully. The correct answer here will give one of the two pairs of buildings that F could serve. There are a number of ways you can approach the answer choices. You could start by eliminating any answer choice without building Y (the one building truck F always serves) in it. That would eliminate choices (A), (B), and (E). Alternately, you could eliminate any answer that doesn't have exactly two buildings because having truck F serve one or three buildings would violate Rule 2. Going that route would eliminate choices (A), (C), and (E). Finally, you could simply predict the correct answer: It must have pair X, Y or pair Y, Z. Choice (D), which has the second of the two acceptable pairs, is the correct answer.

19. **(C)**

For which one of the following pairs of trucks must it be the case that at least one of the office buildings is served by both of the trucks?

(A)   the hot dog truck and the pita truck
(B)   the hot dog truck and the taco truck
(C)   the ice cream truck and the pita truck
(D)   the ice cream truck and the salad truck
(E)   the salad truck and the taco truck[17]

		X	Y	Z
②	F	Y/X	Y	X/Y
	H		Y	
	I	Y		Y
	P	X/Y	X	Y/X
	S			
	T	Y	X	Y

I > S

Figure 6.52

---

[16] PrepTest 43, Sec. 4, Q18

[17] PrepTest 43, Sec. 4, Q19

Here's another question stem that requires a careful reading. At first, the language of the stem may appear convoluted. In fact, though, it's very precise. The correct answer is a pair of entities that must have some overlap; they have to serve at least one building together. That means that each of the wrong answers contains a pair of entities that could serve completely different buildings than one another. With that characterization, evaluate the answers.

The two trucks in choice (A) need not have any overlap. The one building that H serves for sure—building Y—is never served by P. Eliminate choice (A).

Nothing requires trucks H and T to serve any of the same buildings, either. Truck H might serve only building Y, a building T never serves. Eliminate choice (B) as well.

The two entities in choice (C) must serve at least one building together. Whether truck P serves building X or building Z, truck I is already there. That's the characteristic of the correct answer in this question.

The pairs listed in choices (D) and (E) can be kept apart. In choice (D), truck I might serve only buildings X and Z while truck S serves only building Y. As for choice (E), truck S might serve only building Y, the one building T never serves.

This question stem doesn't fit the standard must be/could be or true/false pattern, but this makes it even more important to characterize the answers properly. You must know what it is that distinguishes correct from incorrect answers before you evaluate the choices.

20. **(E)**

If the ice cream truck serves fewer of the office buildings than the hot dog truck, then which one of the following is a pair of lunch trucks that must serve exactly the same buildings as each other?

(A) the falafel truck and the hot dog truck
(B) the falafel truck and the salad truck
(C) the ice cream truck and the pita truck
(D) the ice cream truck and the salad truck
(E) the ice cream truck and the taco truck[18]

③	X	Y	Z
② F	Y̶/X	Y	X̶/Y
H	Y	Y	Y
I	Y	X	Y
P	X̶/Y	X	Y̶/X
S	X	Y	X
T	Y	X	Y

$$I > S$$

Figure 6.53

[18] PrepTest 43, Sec. 4, Q20

Here, the new "If" rewards your understanding of the implications of Rules 3 and 6. For truck H to serve more buildings than truck I, truck H will have to serve all three buildings.

	X	Y	Z
F	Y/X	Y	X/Y
H	Y	Y	Y
I	Y	X	Y
P	X/Y	X	Y/X
S			
T	Y	X	Y

Figure 6.54

So truck I is limited to buildings X and Z. That means that truck S must be the third truck serving building Y.

③

	X	Y	Z
② F	Y/X	Y	X/Y
H	Y	Y	Y
I	Y	X	Y
P	X/Y	X	Y/X
S	X	Y	X
T	Y	X	Y

I > S

Figure 6.55

Everything is determined here except truck F's second building and which building—X or Z—truck P takes.

Before evaluating the answer choices, characterize them. The correct answer here is a pair of trucks locked into exactly the same buildings as one another. The wrong answers are pairs of trucks that could serve different buildings than one another or trucks that simply aren't locked down at all in this question.

Choices (A), (B), and (C) all include either truck F or truck P. Since the placement of those trucks is not determined by the new "If" in this question stem, there's no way to say that these answers have pairs of trucks that must be assigned to the same buildings as one another.

The two trucks in choice (D)—trucks I and S—are definitely determined in this scenario, but truck I will serve buildings X and Z while truck S serves building Y. So this is another wrong answer.

That leaves choice (E). You know from the process of elimination that it must be the correct choice. Checking it against the mini-sketch, you can see that both truck I and truck T serve buildings X and Z and only buildings X and Z.

21. **(A)**

Which one of the following could be a complete and accurate list of the lunch trucks, each of which serves all three of the office buildings?

(A) the hot dog truck, the ice cream truck
(B) the hot dog truck, the salad truck
(C) the ice cream truck, the taco truck
(D) the hot dog truck, the ice cream truck, the pita truck
(E) the ice cream truck, the pita truck, the salad truck[19]

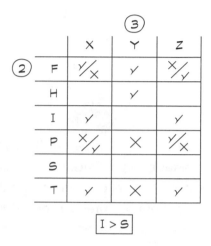

Figure 6.56

The correct answer here includes any and all trucks that could serve all three of the buildings. You can attack the answers by eliminating incomplete or inaccurate choices. You know from your Master Sketch (and from question 20) that truck H can serve all three buildings. So choices (C) and (E)—which lack truck H—are incomplete. The Master Sketch also shows that truck I must be included in the correct answer. That means that choice (B) is out. The only difference between the two remaining choices—choices (A) and (D)—is the inclusion of truck P in choice (D). You know that P can serve only one of the buildings, X or Z, so choice (D) is a clear violator. Choice (A) is the correct answer.

If you approached that question by eliminating choices that contained incorrect trucks (instead of those that were incomplete), you would still have gotten choice (A) in short order. One or more of trucks P, S, and T are present in each of the four wrong answers here.

---

[19] PrepTest 43, Sec. 4, Q21

22. (C)

Which one of the following lunch trucks CANNOT serve both X and Z?

(A) the hot dog truck
(B) the ice cream truck
(C) the pita truck
(D) the salad truck
(E) the taco truck[20]

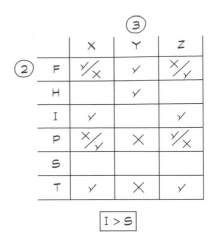

Figure 6.57

With a complete Master Sketch containing all of the available Deductions, this question is straightforward. Since the correct answer names a truck that can't serve both X and Z, all four wrong answers contain entities that can serve both of those buildings. Trucks H and I, as you know from the previous question, are the two trucks that can serve all three buildings. That makes choices (A) and (B) incorrect. A glance at the Master Sketch shows truck T serving both X and Z; that knocks out choice (E). The toughest wrong answer to eliminate is choice (D), but truck S can, in fact, serve both X and Z provided that truck I serves building Y.

That makes choice (C)—truck P—the correct answer. Note that the question stem asks for a truck that cannot serve both X and Z. Again, the wording of the stem is very precise. Truck P can serve either X or Z, but not both.

That is by no means an easy game, but it is a perfect example of how far you've come already. By accomplishing Steps 1–4 of the Kaplan Method, you were able to remove the largest part of the game's ambiguity before diving into the question set.

---

[20] PrepTest 43, Sec. 4, Q22

GAME 4

Questions 19–23

An airline has four flights from New York to Sarasota—flights 1, 2, 3, and 4. On each flight there is exactly one pilot and exactly one co-pilot. The pilots are Fazio, Germond, Kyle, and Lopez; the co-pilots are Reich, Simon, Taylor, and Umlas. Each pilot and co-pilot is assigned to exactly one flight.

   The flights take off in numerical order.

   Fazio's flight takes off before Germond's, and at least one other flight takes off between their flights.

   Kyle is assigned to flight 2.

   Lopez is assigned to the same flight as Umlas.

19. Which one of the following pilot and co-pilot teams could be assigned to flight 1?

   (A)   Fazio and Reich
   (B)   Fazio and Umlas
   (C)   Germond and Reich
   (D)   Germond and Umlas
   (E)   Lopez and Taylor

20. If Reich's flight is later than Umlas's, which one of the following statements cannot be true?

   (A)   Fazio's flight is earlier than Simon's.
   (B)   Kyle's flight is earlier than Reich's.
   (C)   Kyle's flight is earlier than Taylor's.
   (D)   Simon's flight is earlier than Reich's.
   (E)   Taylor's flight is earlier than Kyle's.

21. If Lopez's flight is earlier than Germond's, which one of the following statements could be false?

   (A)   Fazio's flight is earlier than Umlas's.
   (B)   Germond is assigned to flight 4.
   (C)   Either Reich's or Taylor's flight is earlier than Umlas's.
   (D)   Simon's flight is earlier than Umlas's.
   (E)   Umlas is assigned to flight 3.

22. What is the maximum possible number of different pilot and co-pilot teams, any one of which could be assigned to flight 4?

   (A)   2
   (B)   3
   (C)   4
   (D)   5
   (E)   6

23. If Simon's flight is later than Lopez's, then which one of the following statements could be false?

   (A)   Germond's flight is later than Reich's.
   (B)   Germond's flight is later than Taylor's.
   (C)   Lopez's flight is later than Taylor's.
   (D)   Taylor's flight is later than Reich's.
   (E)   Umlas's flight is later than Reich's.[21]

---

[21] PrepTest 36, Sec. 4, Game 4, Qs 19–23

Explanations—Game 4

STEPS 1 AND 2: Overview and Sketch

Your mental picture of this game probably begins with the four numbered airplanes. More specifically, you likely picture the cockpits, with seats for the pilots and co-pilots, respectively. It's not tough to turn that into a useful framework for the game.

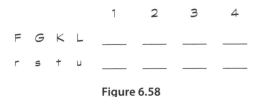

Figure 6.58

The numbers of the game work out simply and evenly: four planes, four pilots, four co-pilots, with one of each type of operator per plane. The number of acceptable arrangements will decrease dramatically with each of the pilots or co-pilots that you place.

STEP 3: Rules

Rule 1 is a little deceptive. You already knew that the flights were numbered 1 through 4, but it's not until this rule that you know that those are more than names. The numbers are connected to the action as well. This doesn't change or add to your sketch, but you can now anticipate other rules and questions that reward you for keeping track of who flies earlier or later than someone else.

Rule 2 delivers immediately on the promise of Rule 1; it defines the relative order and minimum proximity of two pilots' flights.

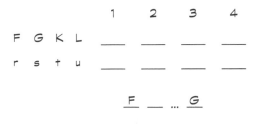

Figure 6.59

Rule 3 establishes the position of yet another pilot.

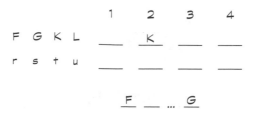

Figure 6.60

Rule 4 gives one of the pairings.

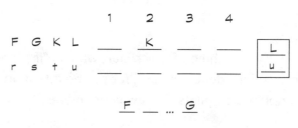

Figure 6.61

By this point, the game should be reminiscent of at least a couple of the games you saw earlier in the book. It shares the same Sequencing-Matching combination of tasks as the Thunderstorm and Suspects' Confessions games. The chief distinction is that, in this game, you have just as many entities to order on the second line as you do on the first. Still, you can anticipate the questions that the test makers will ask: What are the acceptable orders and pairings of pilots and co-pilots? See what additional information you can obtain in the Deductions step.

STEP **4: Deductions**

As always, work with the most concrete restrictions first. Three of the four rules restrict the pilots, while only one deals with a co-pilot. On the pilots' line, you know that K is established in flight 2. Given that restriction, the F-G sequence from Rule 2 creates a Limited Options scenario.

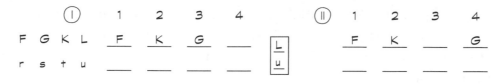

Figure 6.62

Given the requirement that at least one flight takes off after F's and before G's, F can only take flight 1. That leaves either flight 3 or flight 4 for G.

With three of the four pilots placed in each option, fitting in pilot L is a snap. And per Rule 4, U goes wherever L does.

Figure 6.63

The remaining three spaces, all on the co-pilot line, belong to R, S, and T in any order. It's certainly not worth the time to try to draw out the six different arrangements available to those three entities in each of the options. But expect at least one or two of the "If" questions to impose restrictions involving the remaining undefined co-pilots.

STEP 5: Questions

There are five questions in the set, three of which start with an "if." Expect to be rewarded for having made the Limited Options deduction and for paying attention to what can or cannot be true among the yet-unplaced co-pilots. Review your answers.

19. **(A)**

Which one of the following pilot and co-pilot teams could be assigned to flight 1?

(A)   Fazio and Reich
(B)   Fazio and Umlas
(C)   Germond and Reich
(D)   Germond and Umlas
(E)   Lopez and Taylor[22]

Figure 6.64

This is a very limited Partial Acceptability question. It asks only for who could be assigned to flight 1. You know from the Master Sketch that the only pilot who could take the first flight is F. That eliminates choices (C), (D), and (E). Since U has to accompany L in either flight 3 or 4, you can also cross out choice (B). That leaves only the correct answer, choice (A), and you have one point in the bag.

---

[22] PrepTest 36, Sec. 4, Q19

20. **(C)**

If Reich's flight is later than Umlas's, which one of the following statements cannot be true?

(A)   Fazio's flight is earlier than Simon's.
(B)   Kyle's flight is earlier than Reich's.
(C)   Kyle's flight is earlier than Taylor's.
(D)   Simon's flight is earlier than Reich's.
(E)   Taylor's flight is earlier than Kyle's.[23]

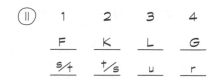

Figure 6.65

The new "If" in this stem not only tells you which option to consult, it allows you to add information by way of a mini-sketch. The new condition tells you that U must take an earlier flight than R. That can only happen in Option II, where U takes flight 3. That allows you to place both U and R with certainty.

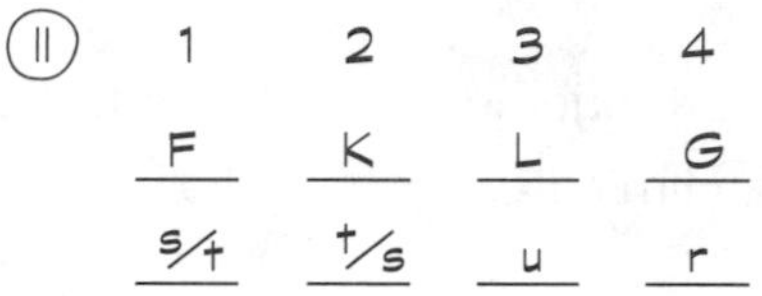

Figure 6.66

With that mini-sketch, you can evaluate the choices. The correct answer must be false. That means that the four wrong answers could be true.

Choice (A) is a wrong answer. You know that F takes flight 1, and it could be true that S takes flight 2 in this question.

Choice (B) is also incorrect. In this case, it must be true that K, who takes flight 2, comes earlier than R, who takes flight 4 under this "If" condition.

Choice (C) is the right answer here. It must be false that K, who takes flight 2, is earlier than T, who takes either flight 1 or flight 2. While the two might be on the same flight, there's no

way that K can be on an earlier flight than T.

You know that the final two answers are incorrect. Choice (D) contains another statement that must be true. Since R is the copilot for flight 4 in this case, S takes an earlier flight for sure.

Finally, choice (E) could be true and is therefore incorrect. K is the pilot for flight 2, and T could be the copilot for flight 1.

[23] PrepTest 36, Sec. 4, Q20

21. **(D)**

If Lopez's flight is earlier than Germond's, which one of the following statements could be false?

(A) Fazio's flight is earlier than Umlas's.
(B) Germond is assigned to flight 4.
(C) Either Reich's or Taylor's flight is earlier than Umlas's.
(D) Simon's flight is earlier than Umlas's.
(E) Umlas is assigned to flight 3.[24]

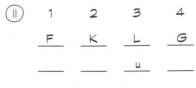

Figure 6.67

In this case, the "If" clause in the question stem simply points you to Option II. That's where L takes an earlier flight than G. There's nothing else you can add or deduce, so there's no need for a mini-sketch this time. Characterize the answers and evaluate them. The correct answer could be false, meaning that the four wrong answers must be true.

Choice (A) must be true in every arrangement possible in this game let alone under the conditions of this particular question. Eliminate.

Choice (B) must be true in Option II, the option called for by the "If" here. Get rid of this one, too.

Choice (C) is worded cleverly, but it must be true that either R or T is on an earlier flight than U. After all, there's only one flight after U's, and there's no way that R and T can both be the copilots on flight 4.

Choice (D) is the correct answer, the one that could be false. S might be the copilot on flight 4.

For the record, choice (E) must be true anytime you're looking at Option II, the one that applies in this question.

22. **(C)**

What is the maximum possible number of different pilot and co-pilot teams, any one of which could be assigned to flight 4?

(A) 2
(B) 3
(C) 4
(D) 5
(E) 6[25]

```
( I )   1     2     3     4            ( II )   1     2     3     4

        F     K     G     L                     F     K     L     G

r  s  t  ___   ___   ___   u      r  s  t  ___   ___   u    ___
```

Figure 6.68

Read this question stem carefully. A little patience is rewarded with an easy point. How many different pairings are acceptable on flight 4? Start with Option I. There's just one pairing that's okay there: L and U. In Option II, on the other hand, there are three acceptable pairings: G

---

[24] PrepTest 36, Sec. 4, Q21
[25] PrepTest 36, Sec. 4, Q22

and R, G and S, G and T. That makes a total of four acceptable pairs overall. Choice (C) is the correct answer.

23. **(D)**

If Simon's flight is later than Lopez's, then which one of the following statements could be false?

(A) Germond's flight is later than Reich's.
(B) Germond's flight is later than Taylor's.
(C) Lopez's flight is later than Taylor's.
(D) Taylor's flight is later than Reich's.
(E) Umlas's flight is later than Reich's.[26]

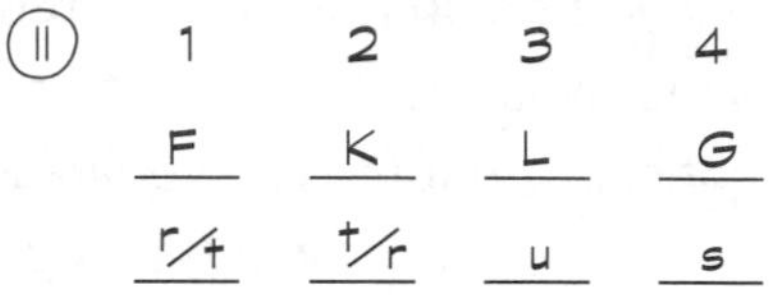

Figure 6.69

The "If" clause in this question is quite similar to its counterpart in question 20. Once again, the "If" puts you in Option II (in Option I, after all, L would pilot the final flight). As you did in question 20, you should make a quick mini-sketch here to depict the restrictions following from the question stem. You know from the "If" that S will copilot flight 4.

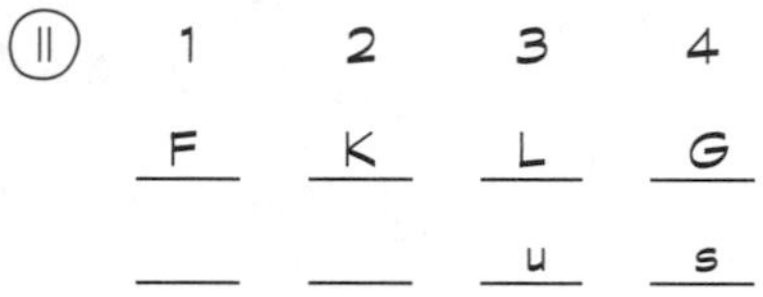

Figure 6.70

That means that R and T will copilot flights 1 and 2 in either order.

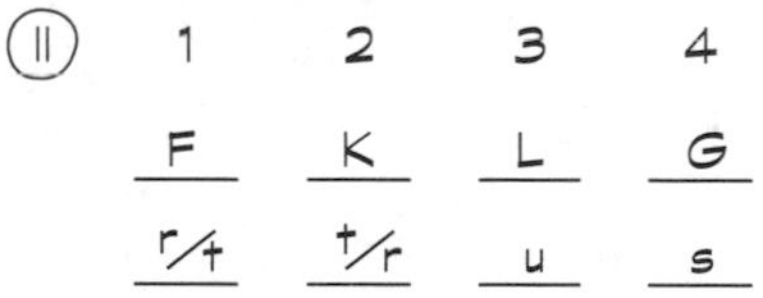

Figure 6.71

Take a moment to characterize the answers. Since the correct answer could be false, all four of the wrong ones must be true.

Given that you're dealing with Option II in this question, G will always be in flight 4. Your minisketch shows that R and T will copilot flights 1 and 2. Thus, choices (A) and (B) must be true. You can eliminate both.

Notice that choices (C) and (E) compare the positions of L and U to those of R and T. L and U man flight 3 in Option II, and R or T is the copilot of either flight 1 or flight 2. So both (C) and (E) must be true and can be eliminated.

---

[26] PrepTest 36, Sec. 4, Q23

Choice (D) is the correct answer. It could be false because it compares R and T, the two copilots who can swap positions between flight 1 and flight 2. There's no way to say for sure which of the two is earlier or later than the other.

What you see in this game is representative of what you've seen throughout this chapter and, indeed, what you'll see on test day. The games you'll encounter from this point on won't be identical to games you've already done, but they'll be similar enough to seem familiar. The actions, the rules, even the deductions will follow patterns that you've seen and worked with. In the next part of this book, I'll show you how to make the most of that familiarity to maximize your efficiency without becoming so pigeonholed that you lose the ability to look at new games holistically. First, I want to break down a few of the ways in which the test makers make game setups and questions harder. As I introduce you to game types and variations, I want you to be able to distinguish games that are simply *different* than usual from those that are truly more *difficult* than usual.

CHAPTER 7

HOW THE LSAT MAKES GAMES HARDER

I hope I've shown you by now that the Kaplan Method will allow you to get through any logic game with maximum efficiency and accuracy. Still, as you've already seen, some games are harder than others. By studying test takers' responses and noting which games consistently produce a lower percentage of correct answers, Kaplan has been able to determine four factors that make games more difficult.

WHAT MAKES LOGIC GAMES HARDER

Easier	Harder
Concrete	Ambiguous
Simple	Complex
Brief	Long
Familiar	Strange

As you can see, some of these factors are purely objective; a complex game, for example, is complex for all test takers, though some test takers will handle that complexity better than others will. On the other hand, a factor like familiarity with the game is at least somewhat subjective; it's within your control to become familiar with as many game patterns and tasks as you can. By studying this book, you're making yourself familiar with games, rules, and strategies that at least some of your competition simply won't know.

In this chapter, I'll show you how to recognize and respond to the higher-difficulty games you encounter. In Part III of the book, I'll come back to these factors when I teach you to "triage" the Logic Games section and prioritize the easiest games to maximize your score in the 35 minutes you're given on test day.

REDUCING AMBIGUITY

As you know from the chapter on rules, restrictions make games easier. They reduce the enormous number of acceptable permutations to a manageable handful. So it stands to reason that games with fewer restrictions—less concreteness, if you will—are harder than games that lock entities into place. Be careful, though: A failure to interpret the rules or make the available deductions in the setup should not be confused with true ambiguity.

Actual versus Perceived Ambiguity

Any logic game can appear ambiguous and incomplete prior to the Deductions step. The game that tasked you with sequencing the red and green trucks' arrivals is a good example of one in which untrained students fail to make all of the available deductions. As a result, they struggle with the questions, either missing them entirely or spending far too long to get what should be a straightforward answer.

> In a single day, exactly seven trucks—S, T, U, W, X, Y, and Z—are the only arrivals at a warehouse. No truck arrives at the same time as any other truck, and no truck arrives more than once that day. Each truck is either green or red (but not both). The following conditions apply:
>
> No two consecutive arrivals are red.
> Y arrives at some time before both T and W.
> Exactly two of the trucks that arrive before Y are red.
> S is the sixth arrival.
> Z arrives at some time before U.[1]

If you record all of the rules correctly, you'd have this to work with:

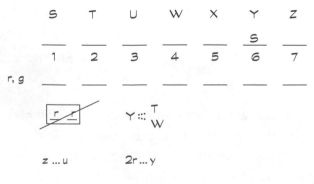

Figure 7.1

---

[1] PrepTest 37, Sec. 3, Game 2

That's a far cry from the Master Sketch you learned to create in chapter 4. As a Kaplan-trained test taker, you're already aware of how much certainty the game's setup and rules signal here. This game's rules use words like "exactly" and "no." None of the rules is conditional; there's not even an "either/or" type of restriction. Using the BLEND checklist and starting with the most restricted entity (you'll recall that it's truck Y), you were able to produce a Master Sketch that determined or severely limited most of the slots in the game.

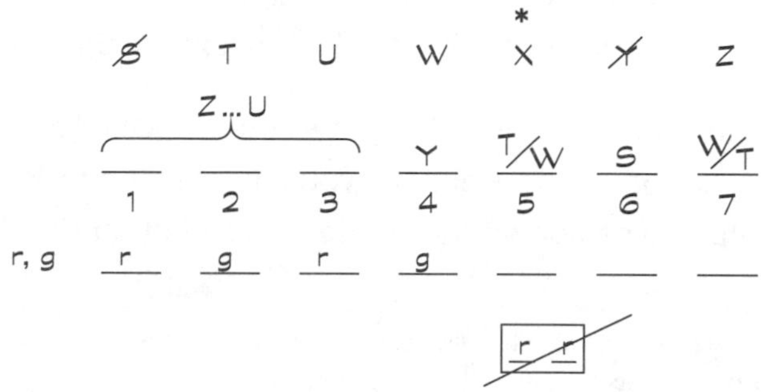

Figure 7.2

The result was a set of questions you could answer in a matter of seconds each.

So your greatest ally in combating ambiguity is Step 4 of the Kaplan Method. That's true even when there aren't many deductions to make. Recall the Civic Parade game in chapter 4? There, you had almost nothing to add to your Master Sketch beyond the original rules. Indeed, the key to your efficiency on that game was to recognize that you had all the information available to handle the question set.

The Kaplan Method is not only for games with lots of deductions and intricate diagrams. Following the method—sketching the rules and using the BLEND checklist to determine how much additional certainty Step 4 can add—puts you in the driver's seat every time. While you'll always prefer concreteness to ambiguity, what's most important is that you create a Master Sketch that shows exactly what can and what cannot be determined. That's what LSAT logic games questions always reward.

Recognizing Ambiguous Setups

What are the signs that a game is less concrete, or more ambiguous, than most? You already know that words like "exactly," "must," and "not" or "never" are good indicators of certainty. On the other hand, seeing a plethora of conditional rules or either/or restrictions stated in the alternative (e.g., "H ranks higher than P or else H ranks lower than L, but not both") is a sign that you'll find less concreteness.

But your assessment of a game's ambiguity actually begins as soon as you identify the task. If asked to schedule appointments, you'd prefer to schedule six appointments over six days, one per day, than, say, to schedule those same six appointments over the course of four days with no more than two appointments per day. The latter scenario means that you might have two days with two appointments each and two days with one each. Or you might have three days with two appointments each and one with zero.

Other tasks contain their own built-in signals of ambiguity. Would you rather be asked to select *exactly* four new hires from a pool of six applicants or to select *at least* one new hire? Emphatically, you'd prefer the former. Indeed, as you've already seen in multiple examples, a little extra complexity in a game's task can easily be offset by extra concreteness in its restrictions.

Review the following game's setup and rules to determine whether you find it concrete or ambiguous and to what extent. Here's a hint: As you consider the task, think about what kind of information would help you nail down the answers and whether that information is present.

> Each of exactly six doctors—Juarez, Kudrow, Longtree, Nance, Onawa, and Palermo—is at exactly one of two clinics: Souderton or Randsborough. The following conditions must be satisfied:
> Kudrow is at Randsborough if Juarez is at Souderton.
> Onawa is at Souderton if Juarez is at Randsborough.
> If Longtree is at Souderton, then both Nance and Palermo are at Randsborough.
> If Nance is at Randsborough, then so is Onawa.
> If Palermo is at Randsborough, then both Kudrow and Onawa are at Souderton.[2]

The task here is straightforward: You need to make a simple chart showing which doctors are assigned to each clinic. That should be easy, but this game turns out to be quite challenging. The reason is its lack of concreteness.

Remember my hint suggesting that you think about what you'd like to know in order to make your job easier? First on your list should have been, "Tell me how many doctors are assigned to each clinic." Numerical restrictions are enormously helpful in a Distribution game like this one. But here, you get none. For all you know, it's possible to have all six doctors at one of the clinics and none at the other, five doctors at one and one at the other, four and two, three and three, two and four, etc. The rules will serve to keep some of the doctors apart, but even there you get little of what you hoped for. You'd prefer rules that create Established Entities ("Doctor so-and-so is at Randsborough") or, at the very least, rules that tell you who had to be placed together or who had to be kept apart. Unfortunately, you get none of that. Every rule here is conditional. Take Rule 1, for instance. When Doctor Juarez is at Souderton, Doctor Kudrow is not. When Juarez is at Randsborough, though, you can't reach any conclusions about Kudrow's location. There's nothing unfamiliar or even very complex about this game, but its lack of concreteness makes it a formidable exercise.

---

2 PrepTest 34, Sec. 4, Game 4

A quick read of this game's setup and rules is enough to tell you that it's not the easiest game you'll encounter in the section; indeed, it may well be the toughest. In fact, I'll have you come back to this game in Part II as an example of a challenging Distribution action. There, you'll see how to manage it as efficiently as possible, though I doubt that it will ever be one of your favorites.

Being able to spot games that lack concreteness is valuable for two reasons. As I'll discuss further in Part III of this book, you'll want to be able to locate the easiest games in the section on test day. Prioritizing the easiest games will help you manage your time effectively to get the greatest number of points. Deferring an ambiguous, and therefore challenging, setup like this one is a good idea. The other benefit is psychological. When you know that the game in front of you is challenging (and even more so when you know *why* it's so challenging), it helps you avoid panic and frustration that could derail your performance throughout the entire section. "Forewarned is forearmed," as they say, and that's certainly true when it comes to recognizing ambiguous logic games.

PEELING BACK THE LAYERS OF COMPLEXITY
"Hybrid" Doesn't Have to Mean "Hard"

The number-one way in which the test makers increase games' complexity is to "hybridize" them, or blend two or more tasks together. This can be especially perplexing for students who become over-reliant on giving each task a specific name: "This is Sequencing" or "This is Matching." The fact is, most LSATs include at least one Hybrid game, made up of a combination of common game actions. It's important not to think that all Hybrid games are "hard" games. Each of the following is a Hybrid game that you've already handled successfully in the earlier chapters of this book. You can see that they cover a range of difficulty levels. Consider what makes each of these games easier or harder and how you were able to take control of each one.

In a single day, exactly seven trucks—S, T, U, W, X, Y, and Z—are the only arrivals at a warehouse. No truck arrives at the same time as any other truck, and no truck arrives more than once that day. Each truck is either green or red (but not both). The following conditions apply:

No two consecutive arrivals are red.
Y arrives at some time before both T and W.
Exactly two of the trucks that arrive before Y are red.
S is the sixth arrival.
Z arrives at some time before U.[3]

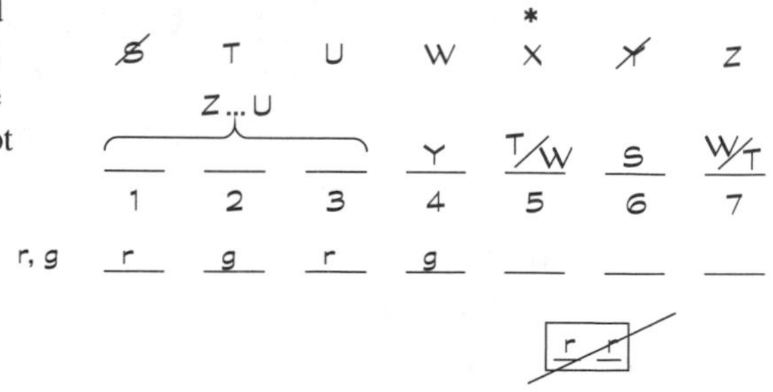

Figure 7.3

This game is a hybrid of Sequencing (determining the order in which the trucks arrive) and Matching (assigning each truck a color). As you'll learn in Part II, Sequencing-Matching is the most common Hybrid variant on the LSAT. The Thunderstorm game, the Pilots and Co-pilots

---

[3] PrepTest 37, Sec. 3, Game 2

game, and the Guitarist's CD game are all examples of this combination of actions. Typically, the Sequencing action dominates the game and serves as the anchor for your sketch. By drawing the sketch in a way that allows you to see the interaction between the two actions—the color assignments limit the possible order and vice versa, for instance—you are able to boil this game down to two lines: one for the trucks and one for their colors. Depicting both actions within the same sketch is the key to handling almost all Hybrid games. And here, the Sketch and Deductions steps make this Hybrid much easier than several of the single-action games you've already encountered.

> Exactly six people—Lulu, Nam, Ofelia, Pachai, Santiago, and Tyrone—are the only contestants in a chess tournament. The tournament consists of four games, played one after the other. Exactly two people play in each game, and each person plays in at least one game. The following conditions must apply:
> Tyrone does not play in the first or third game.
> Lulu plays in the last game.
> Nam plays in only one game and it is not against Pachai.
> Santiago plays in exactly two games, one just before and one just after the only game that Ofelia plays in.[4]

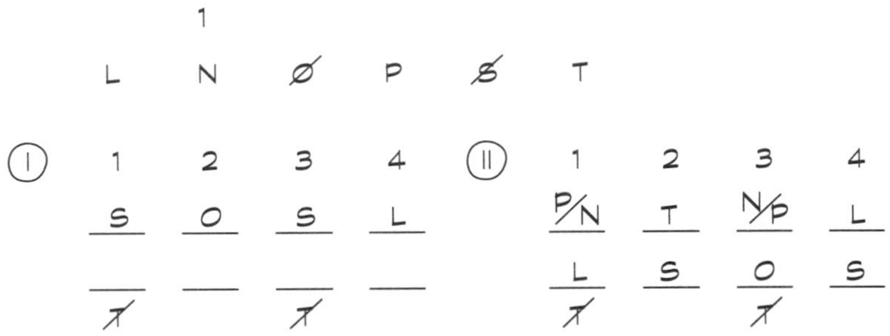

Figure 7.4

This is another game in which the test makers have blended Sequencing and Matching elements. This time, though, the complexity stems from the fact that you must decide how the chess players pair up against one another rather than being asked to assign each player an attribute. The other thing that makes this game intimidating is that you must determine the number of games in which each person plays. As you remember from chapter 4—and as you can see in the sketch above—you were able to turn the tables on the test maker by employing a Limited Options sketch. It's always worth remembering that with additional complexity comes additional restriction. The concreteness of the S-O-S block more than makes up for the complexity of the action.

---

4 PrepTest 45, Sec. 3, Game 2

The three highest-placing teams in a high school debate tournament are the teams from Fairview, Gillom, and Hilltop high schools. Each team has exactly two members. The individuals on these three teams are Mei, Navarro, O'Rourke, Pavlovich, Sethna, and Tsudama. The following is the case:

Sethna is on the team from Gillom High.

Tsudama is on the second-place team.

Mei and Pavlovich are not on the same team.

Pavlovich's team places higher than Navarro's team.

The team from Gillom High places higher than the team from Hilltop High.[5]

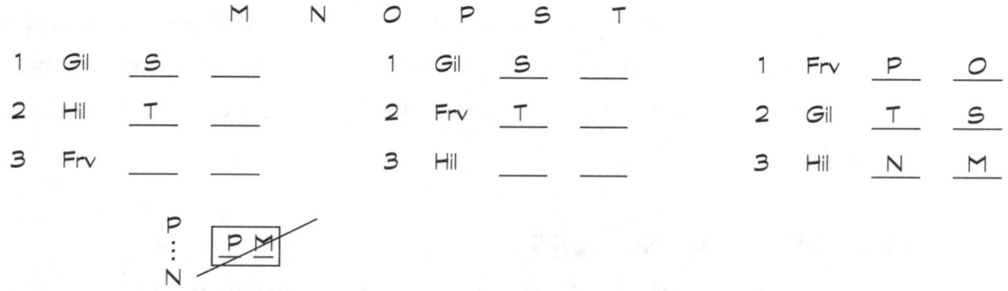

Figure 7.5

This game's task is the most complex you've yet seen in this book. Here, you must sequence the schools by rank, match team members in pairs, and distribute the members among the three schools' teams. That's a Hybrid game combining three tasks. But look again and refresh your memory of the Master Sketch. By the time you've made the available deductions, only three patterns are possible and, in one of them, every entity's place is determined. Let this game stand as a reminder of rules' power to make your job easier. With three schools to rank, there are six acceptable arrangements. But adding just Rule 5—Gillom places higher than Hilltop—cuts that number in half.

This game illustrates a second consideration as well. Whenever the test makers combine tasks, they will also simplify each one. In a typical Sequencing game, you must order six or seven entities; here, only three schools. Likewise, most Distribution games don't specify the exact number of entities in each group. Here, the six students form three teams of two members each, a very concrete and simple pattern. Even the Matching element—one team per school—is too easy to stand on its own as a logic game.

Now, you can conceive of all types of enormous and difficult games. The test makers could come up with something in which you're asked to sequence six entities and then match between one and three attributes to each. To picture this, imagine that the following game asked you to place the technicians at Workstations 1 through 6 as well as to determine which kinds of devices each repairs.

---

[5] PrepTest 53, Sec. 2, Game 4

In a repair facility there are exactly six technicians: Stacy, Urma, Wim, Xena, Yolanda, and Zane. Each technician repairs machines of at least one of the following three types—radios, televisions, and VCRs—and no other types. The following conditions apply:[6]

Nothing makes a game like that impossible *in theory*, but it would simply be too time-consuming to include on the test. Even the very best test takers would be unable to finish such a game and still have time left for the other three games in the section. Remember, the test maker's objective is to make a test that distinguishes levels of ability with the Core 4 LSAT Skills. They'll use complexity to make some games more challenging than others, but they still set out to design a section in which the top scorers can get to every question. Indeed, the section is designed so that a small handful of test takers will even get every question right. I'd like to see you among that select group.

Thinking Exercises: Complex Tasks

There's one more consideration that will help you master complex games: When a game includes multiple tasks, one of the tasks may logically precede or restrict the other(s). Take a look at how recognizing this makes your job easier.

Jewelry Display Case

Imagine you work in a jewelry store that has a display case containing four pedestals, numbered 1 through 4 from left to right. The store's inventory includes seven necklaces, one each of coral, garnet, jade, onyx, pearl, ruby, sapphire, and turquoise. Your manager tells you to put exactly one of those necklaces on each of the four display pedestals. Think about the decisions you must make and the order in which they must be made: Before you can sequence necklaces on pedestals 1 through 4, you must first determine which four of the seven necklaces will be displayed. In a Selection-Sequencing Hybrid, the Selection element logically precedes the Sequencing element.

Now, indeed, in real life, just as in a logic game, your boss could give you restrictions on either the selection of necklaces or on their positions in the display case. Think about their effects on your job. He might say, "Put the onyx necklace just to the right of the sapphire one." In that case, you have some guidance about the sequence. The sapphire and onyx necklaces will go on pedestals 1 and 2, 2 and 3, or 3 and 4, respectively. But more importantly, you know that the onyx and sapphire necklaces will be among those displayed. Two of your four selected entities are now determined. Think about how much more powerful that would be, as a logic game rule, than if your boss had said, "*If* you put the onyx necklace on display, I want it to be just to the right of the sapphire one." Now, your boss's instruction is conditional. Selecting the onyx necklace requires selecting the sapphire and determines their relative order. But if

---

[6] PrepTest 48, Sec. 2, Game 3

you leave the onyx necklace out of the display case, you know nothing. That, in turn, is more powerful than if your boss said, "Should you choose to put both the sapphire and the onyx necklaces on display, I want the sapphire necklace to be just to the right of the onyx one." This rule gives you no guidance about which necklaces to select, only about the sequence of onyx and sapphire *if* you put both on display. The LSAT rewards your ability to identify the most powerful and restrictive rules in all games; in games with complex tasks, rules that impose concrete restrictions on multiple elements of your task will, of necessity, be more powerful.

Basketball Scrimmage

Here's another complex task—far larger and more unwieldy than any you'd see on test day—to get you thinking about how the test makers design Hybrid games and their rules.

Imagine you're a basketball coach. You have a team with 12 players on the roster: Anna, Betty, Carolyn, Danielle, Evelyn, Francis, Gwendolyn, Helen, Iris, Jane, Karla, and Lorraine. At today's practice, you'll have them scrimmage on two teams—the gold team and the purple team—of five players each. Each team will have one center, one power forward, one small forward, one shooting guard, and one point guard. If this were a logic game, which tasks would it include? Which of those tasks logically precedes or follows the other(s)? What types of rules or restrictions would the test makers be likely to include? Which of those would be most helpful to you? Take a few minutes and brainstorm your answers to those questions. Sketch out the framework you'd use to organize the information. Then review your thinking with the discussion that follows. See how complete a picture you had of the tasks and potential rules.

Basketball Scrimmage: Discussion

If the basketball scrimmage scenario were a logic game, you'd identify it as a three-part Hybrid. First, you'd have to choose which 10 of your 12 team members would play in the game. That's Selection. Then, you'd need to divide the 10 selected players into two teams of 5 players each. That's Distribution. Finally, you'd need to assign each player to a position. Consider that a Matching task (or if you number the positions—point guard is 1, shooting guard is 2, etc.—you could think of it as Sequencing). Your framework for such a game would look like this:

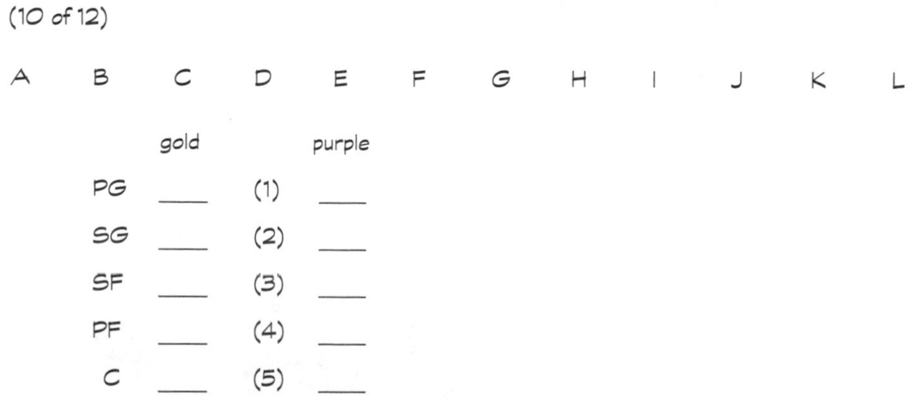

(10 *of* 12)

A   B   C   D   E   F   G   H   I   J   K   L

	gold		purple
PG	____	(1)	____
SG	____	(2)	____
SF	____	(3)	____
PF	____	(4)	____
C	____	(5)	____

Figure 7.6

In making this into a logic game, the test makers could give you rules that covered any of the three tasks. But the farther up the logical chain the rule is, the more restrictive (and helpful) it will be. For example:

"Karla plays power forward for the gold team." This tells you that Karla is selected and gives you the team and position she's assigned to. Karla is a completely established entity in this case.

(10 of 12)
A B C D E F G H I J K L
gold
purple
PG
SG
SF
PF
K
C

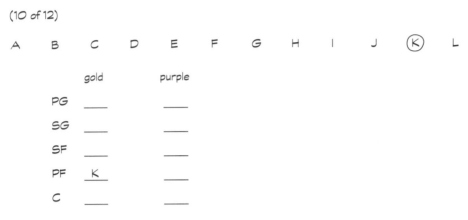

Figure 7.7

"Karla plays for the gold team." This is slightly less helpful. Karla is selected and assigned to a team, but her position is still up in the air.

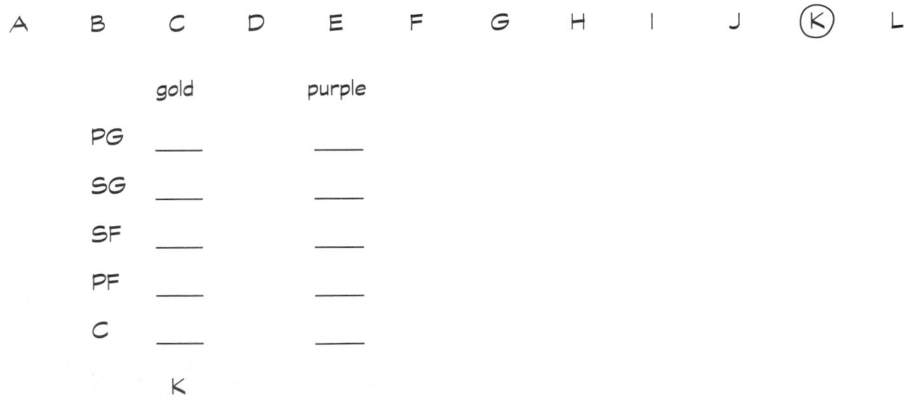

A B C D E F G H I J K L
gold
purple
PG
SG
SF
PF
C
K

Figure 7.8

"If Betty plays in the game, then Danielle plays in the game." This rule affects only the Selection element of the game. Moreover, it's conditional. It restricts the game only if Betty plays or if Danielle doesn't.

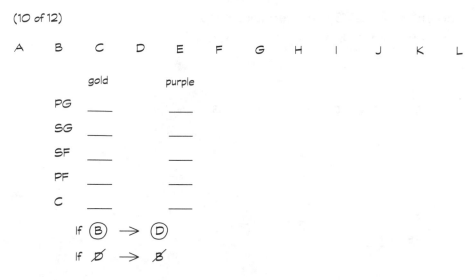

Figure 7.9

"If Betty plays in the game, then Danielle is the point guard on the purple team." This rule is also conditional, but its necessary term—"Danielle plays point guard on the purple team"—is much more specific. If you determine that Betty is selected, you can place Danielle precisely. And if Danielle does not play, does not play on the purple team, or does not play point guard, then Betty won't be selected at all.

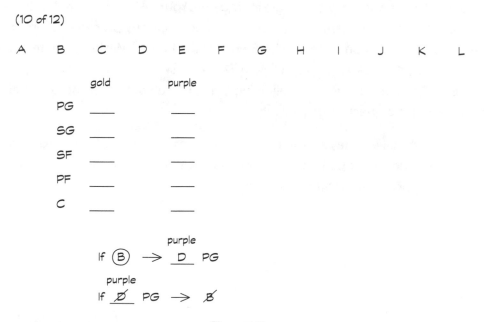

Figure 7.10

"Gwendolyn and Anna cannot play together on a team." Be careful with a rule like this one. If you know that Gwendolyn is playing on the gold team, then either Anna plays on the purple team *or* she doesn't play at all. Since being selected to play in the scrimmage logically precedes assignment to a team, a rule like this presents more than one alternative.

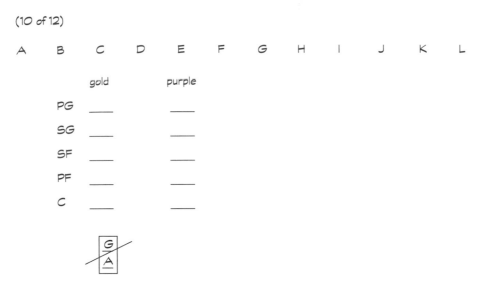

Figure 7.11

You could—and maybe you did—go on and on designing rules for a hypothetical game like this one. It's good mental practice for you, and exercises like this one give you a much clearer understanding of what goes into creating a logic game. Your takeaway here should be that the internal logic of all complex games requires that some decisions precede others. In the end, your mastery of any logic game starts with Step 1 of the Kaplan Method, where you conduct your overview and get a clear picture of your task or tasks. With that, you'll be able to see the restrictions that the rules impose, allowing you to take control of the game all the way through answering the questions.

Very rarely, the test makers may "complexify" a single task. They might, for example, ask you to determine the order of six patients' appointments with each of two health professionals, a dietician and a physician. Something like this:

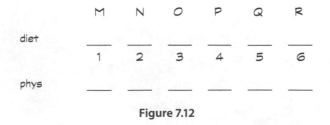

Figure 7.12

I'll go over a few of the recent variations on single-action games in Part II of this book, so it's very unlikely you'll encounter some wholly novel twist on logic games when you take your test.

Remember that no matter how many tasks the test makers put into a game, there will always be a trade-off between complexity and concreteness. By sticking to the Kaplan Method and using the Rules and Deductions steps to their fullest capacities, you will have all of the information you need to answer every question. When the test makers don't give you enough information to determine where an entity *must* be placed, they can ask you where it *could* be placed, but they never leave you hanging.

GETTING TO THE HEART OF LONG GAMES

For the most part, you should be happy when the text of a game's setup is long and detailed. Why? Because the extra text will usually mean additional rules and restrictions, providing more certainty and making your job easier. So don't fear a long setup just because it's long. For sure, there are times when the test makers are unnecessarily descriptive. Remember the Water Treatment Plant game?

> Workers at a water treatment plant open eight valves—G, H, I, K, L, N, O, and P—to flush out a system of pipes that needs emergency repairs. To maximize safety and efficiency, each valve is opened exactly once, and no two valves are opened at the same time. The valves are opened in accordance with the following conditions:[7]

Knowing that there's "a system of pipes that needs emergency repairs" or that the reason for opening the pipes one at a time is to "maximize safety and efficiency" adds nothing to your understanding of the game. You might prefer it if the test makers just cut to the chase like so:

> Workers at a water treatment plant open eight valves—G, H, I, K, L, N, O, and P. Each valve is opened exactly once, and no two valves are opened at the same time. The valves are opened in accordance with the following conditions:

But the extra information doesn't really make the game any harder to understand, either. In minor cases like this, just tune out the redundant or background language and jump right into your task using the Kaplan Method.

The real problem comes when the test makers use unnecessarily convoluted phraseology. This could happen in a rule, a question stem, or even an answer choice. In such cases, untangle the language and find the straightest line of reasoning from the restrictions to the right answer.

---

[7] PrepTest 52, Sec. 2, Game 1

Paraphrase Convoluted Language

Paraphrasing is a skill rewarded throughout the LSAT (and in law school, too). Your ability to transform dense, confusing prose into clear statements is vital to your success in understanding logical reasoning arguments and reading comprehension passages. Many of the correct answers in those sections are simply accurate rewordings of what the author of the passage or argument said. Naturally, on a test as integrated and skills-based as the LSAT, the test makers find a way to reward paraphrasing in the Logic Games section, too.

Take this question stem from the Red and Green Trucks game:

> For exactly how many of the seven trucks can one
> determine exactly how many trucks arrived before it?[8]

Any test taker would prefer it if the test makers simply asked, "How many of the trucks are locked into one certain arrival space?" But since that's what the question means, it's within your power (and it's to your advantage) to paraphrase the question stem for yourself before you evaluate the choices. Knowing exactly how many trucks arrive before a given truck means nothing more than knowing exactly when that truck arrives. Use that certainty to gain the advantage over your competition on test day.

The most important thing to remember is that *LSAT language is never imprecise*. However wordy the test makers get, however much they use double negatives or say, "each of the following could be true EXCEPT," instead of, "which one of the following must be false," they never leave instructions or limitations open to interpretation. You can rest absolutely assured that the rule or question means just what the test makers want it to.

One area in which you've already made great strides at taking control of complex language is in dealing with formal logic rules. If you think about it, you're paraphrasing every time you translate a formal logic rule. The following rule, as an English-language sentence, is pretty unruly:

> F is more expensive than G, or else F is more expensive
> than H, but not both.[9]

But dealing with the following diagram is fairly straightforward.

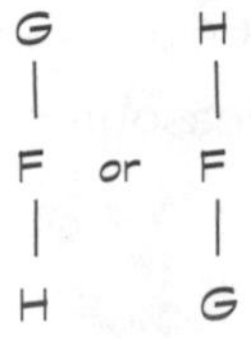

Figure 7.13

---

[8] PrepTest 37, Sec. 3, Q 10

[9] PrepTest 51, Sec. 4, Game 2

The LSAT Always Defines "Special" Terms

There is one other way in which the test makers can use language to make games longer or trickier. It's by using or defining a term in a special way to impose additional restrictions within the game. They don't do this very often, but it can catch the untrained test taker off guard when they do. Here's an example:

> Exactly seven professors—Madison, Nilsson, Orozco, Paton, Robinson, Sarkis, and Togo—were hired in the years 1989 through 1995. Each professor has one or more specialties, and any two professors hired in the same year or in consecutive years do not have a specialty in common. The professors were hired according to the following conditions:
>
> Madison was hired in 1993, Robinson in 1991.
> There is at least one specialty that Madison, Orozco, and Togo have in common.
> Nilsson shares a specialty with Robinson.
> Paton and Sarkis were each hired at least one year before Madison and at least one year after Nilsson.
> Orozco, who shares a specialty with Sarkis, was hired in 1990.[10]

This game's setup is long and dense, but the task is simple: Sequence the professors by hiring year.

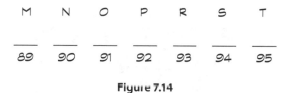

Figure 7.14

The unusual term (or more precisely, the term used in an unusual way) is "specialty." It's clearly important, as it shows up in three of the rules. But what does it mean? And why aren't you told what the specialties are? Don't let a term like this throw you. Simply look for the definition that must be present in the game's setup. The test makers will never introduce a term or use a word in a special way without defining it. The importance of a professor's specialty is given in the setup text: "[A]ny two professors hired in the same year or in consecutive years do not have a specialty in common." (Notice that the test makers could have called a "specialty" anything they wanted to: "Each professor hired has one or more *frim frams*, and any two professors hired in the same year or in consecutive years do not have a *frim fram* in common" would have served the same purpose.) Now, use that definition and create a Master Sketch for this game. Draw out the rules and make all available deductions. You'll be surprised by how much certainty the shared "specialties" add to the game.

---

[10] PrepTest 35, Sec. 3, Game 4

I gave you the basic framework for this game earlier. So consider Steps 1 and 2 complete; you start out with a clear idea of your task. But there's one thing I wonder if you caught. It's actually something that the setup *didn't* say. In this game, there's no requirement that one professor was hired each year. Never take restrictions for granted. When the test is silent on something, it's silent intentionally. To solve this game correctly, in fact, one year must see no professors hired while another sees two hired. If you didn't catch that, take a look at the rules and deductions to see why it must be true.

Rules

The first rule establishes two of the professors' hiring years; Madison and Robinson can go right into the framework.

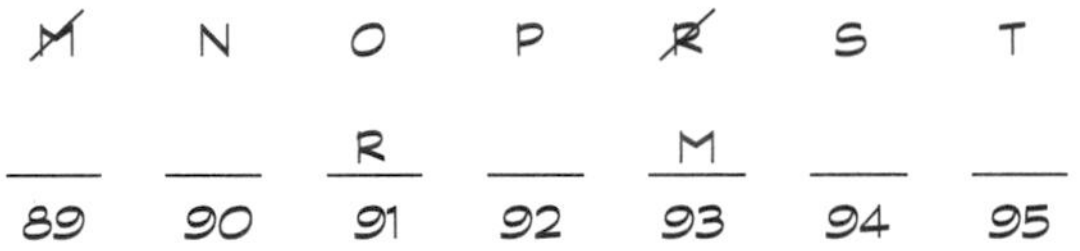

M̶   N   O   P   R̶   S   T

| | | R | M | |
| 89 | 90 | 91 | 92 | 93 | 94 | 95 |

Figure 7.15

Rule 2 tells you that three of the professors share a specialty. Make note of that to the side.

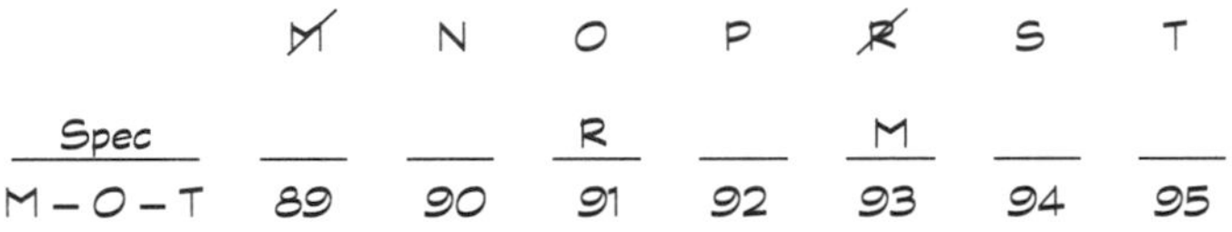

M̶   N   O   P   R̶   S   T

Spec   R   M
M – O – T   89   90   91   92   93   94   95

Figure 7.16

Rule 3 gives you another pair who share a specialty. Add them to the list.

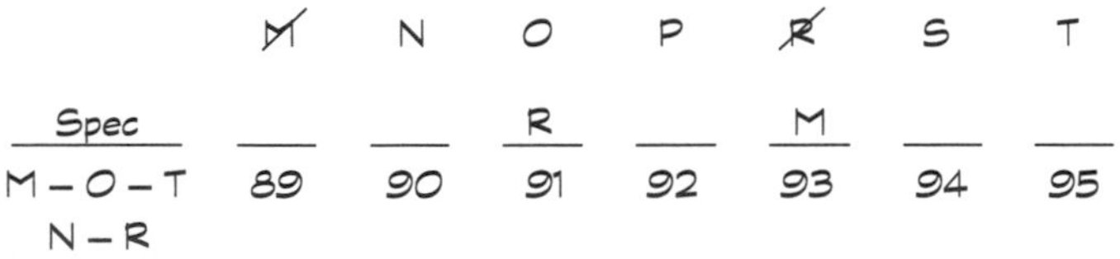

M̶   N   O   P   R̶   S   T

Spec   R   M
M – O – T   89   90   91   92   93   94   95
N – R

Figure 7.17

Rule 4 makes two loose blocks of three professors each. Record that beneath the framework for easy reference.

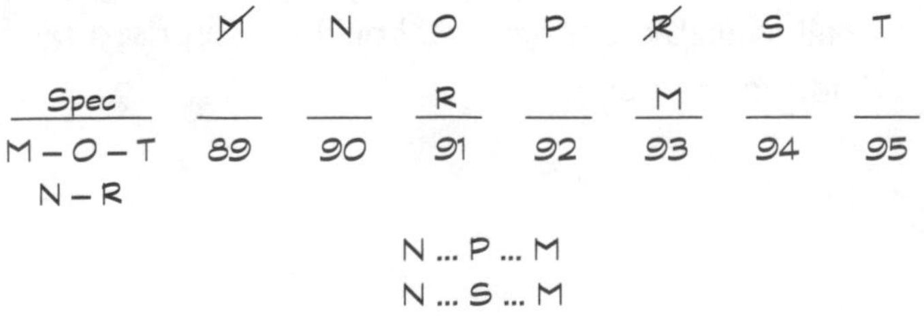

M̶   N   O   P   R̶   S   T

Spec   R   M
M – O – T   89   90   91   92   93   94   95
N – R

N ... P ... M
N ... S ... M

Figure 7.18

Read Rule 5 carefully. It allows you to place Orozco into the framework directly, but it also tells you to add Orozco-Sarkis under the shared-specialty list.

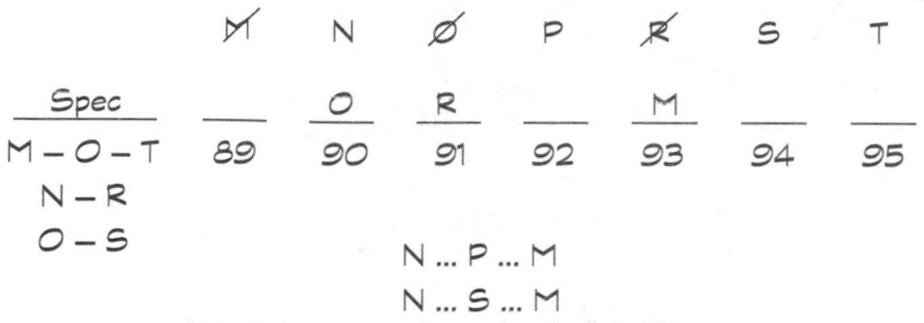

Figure 7.19

With the rules recorded effectively, turn to the Deductions step. All of these rules combine in one way or another to add additional certainty to the game.

Deductions

Start, as always, with what's most clearly established. Rule 1 put Madison in 1993. Think about whom Madison affects. In Rule 2, you are told that Madison, Orozco, and Togo all share a specialty. Orozco's hiring year is already established (by Rule 5) as 1990, but what about Togo? Since professors sharing a specialty can't be hired in the same year or in consecutive years, Rule 2 means that Togo cannot have been hired in '89, '90, or '91 (because of Orozco) or in '92, '93, or '94 (because of Madison). Togo must have been hired in 1995, and you now have four of the seven professors locked into place.

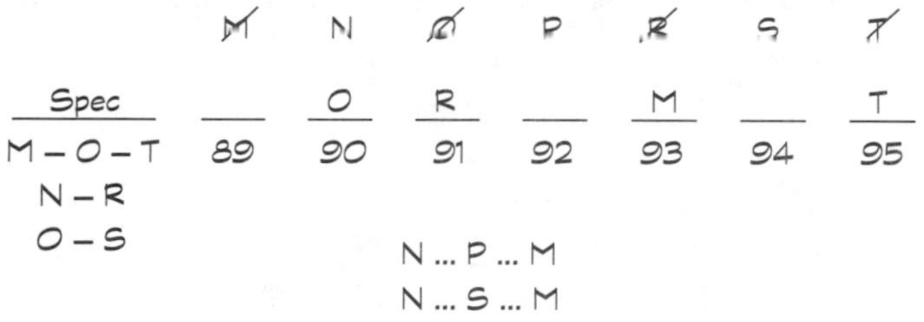

Figure 7.20

Madison's influence isn't exhausted in Rule 2. In Rule 4, you see that Nilsson, Paton, and Sarkis were all hired prior to Madison. Of those three, consider Nilsson first. Since Rule 3 tells you that Nilsson shares a specialty with Robinson, Nilsson's blocked out of '90, '91, and '92. The only way for Nilsson to obey both Rule 4 and Rule 3 is to take 1989. Yet another professor's hiring has been precisely determined.

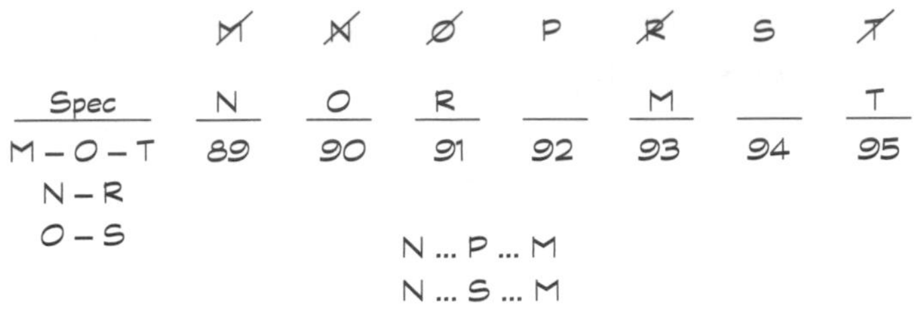

```
        M̸   N̸   O̸   P   R̸   S   T̸
  Spec   N   O   R   _   M   _   T
M-O-T   89  90  91  92  93  94  95
 N-R
 O-S
              N ... P ... M
              N ... S ... M
```

Figure 7.21

Now, go back to Rule 4 for Paton and Sarkis. Sarkis, who shares a specialty with Orozco according to Rule 5, is blocked out of '89, '90, and '91. In order for Sarkis's hiring year to fall between those of Nilsson and Madison, Sarkis must have been hired in 1992. Add that to the sketch.

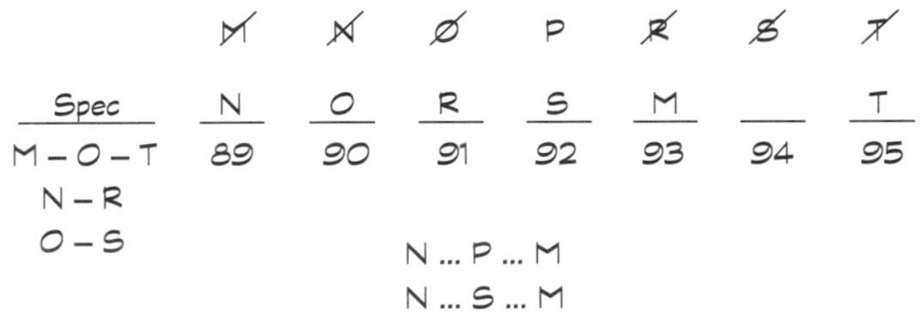

```
        M̸   N̸   O̸   P   R̸   S̸   T̸
  Spec   N   O   R   S   M   _   T
M-O-T   89  90  91  92  93  94  95
 N-R
 O-S
              N ... P ... M
              N ... S ... M
```

Figure 7.22

The only professor you haven't completely locked down is Paton. He must have been hired after Nilsson and before Madison (Rule 4), but otherwise has no restrictions. He shares no specialties with any other professor. So indicate that Paton could have been hired in '90, '91, or '92, and you're done.

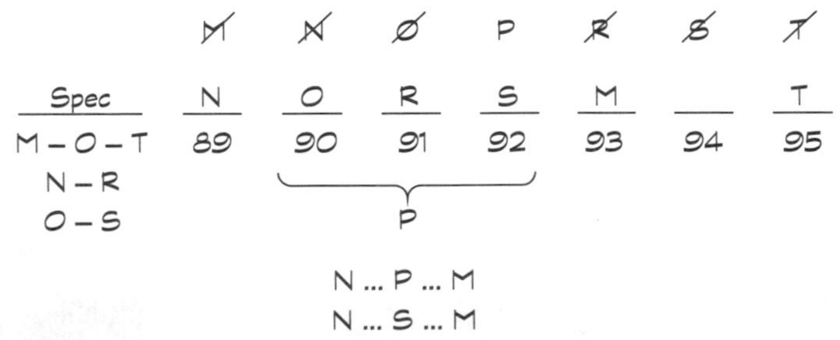

```
        M̸   N̸   O̸   P   R̸   S̸   T̸
  Spec   N   O   R   S   M   _   T
M-O-T   89  90  91  92  93  94  95
 N-R            ⌣‾‾‾‾‾⌣
 O-S               P
              N ... P ... M
              N ... S ... M
```

Figure 7.23

Far from being a problem, the special definition of "specialty" turned out to provide some of the strongest restrictions in the game. I'll have you come back to this game (and try its questions) in Part II when I discuss variations on Sequencing. For now, just appreciate how you turned a tricky term into a powerful restriction.

So in short, don't fear long or convoluted language in LSAT logic games. The guidelines and questions are always precise; a simple, accurate paraphrase just makes them more useful.

CONFRONTING UNFAMILIARITY

I won't say a lot at this point about what to do when you encounter an unfamiliar game. After all, the goal of Part II of this book is to ensure that it simply won't happen to you. It's within your power to encounter all of the game types that the test makers have used. From test to test, the game types change very little, and it's likely that all of the games on your test will seem familiar from this book. You may be flipping switches on an electrical grid instead of opening valves in a water treatment plant, but the task won't be much (if any) different.

I will caution now—and I'll repeat this caution throughout Part II—that you don't become over-reliant on being able to name or categorize a game. The Kaplan Method will allow you to handle anything that the test makers can design. It's done so for hundreds of thousands of test takers over the years. By conducting an overview of the game—defining your task, the entities you're manipulating, and the broad limitations on the action—you'll be able to draw an initial sketch with which to manage all of the rules and deductions that give you the information you need. When you first saw the Debate Teams game, it's nearly certain you'd never encountered a logic game like it before, nor would you have known to call it a Sequencing-Matching-Distribution Hybrid game.

> The three highest-placing teams in a high school debate tournament are the teams from Fairview, Gillom, and Hilltop high schools. Each team has exactly two members. The individuals on these three teams are Mei, Navarro, O'Rourke, Pavlovich, Sethna, and Tsudama. The following is the case:
> Sethna is on the team from Gillom High.
> Tsudama is on the second-place team.
> Mei and Pavlovich are not on the same team.
> Pavlovich's team places higher than Navarro's team.
> The team from Gillom High places higher than the team from Hilltop High.[11]

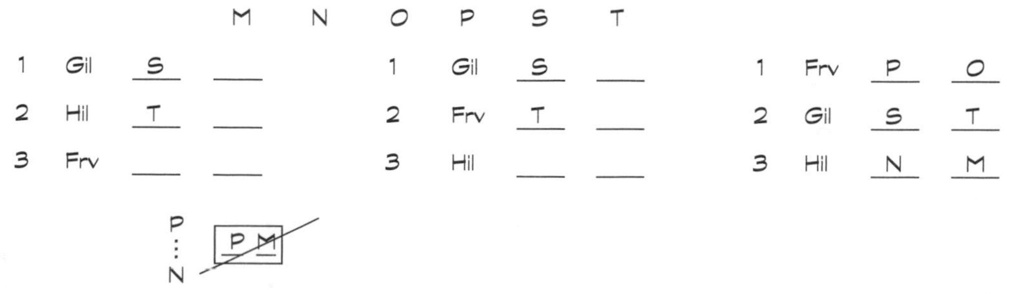

Figure 7.24

[11] PrepTest 53, Sec. 2, Game 4

Nor would it matter if you called it an Ordering-Pairing-Association game, for that matter. By getting a handle on the task and understanding the inherent restrictions within the rules, you're able to turn this into a short, manageable puzzle with a handful of acceptable solutions. Do that on test day, and you'll be rocking the Logic Games section … and your competition.

Given the time you're devoting to practice and the resources available in this book and through all of Kaplan's other materials and services, encountering an unfamiliar game on your test should be way, way down on your list of concerns.

HOW THE LSAT MAKES GAMES HARDER . . . AND WHAT YOU CAN DO ABOUT IT

On any given LSAT, there is almost always one easy game, two of medium difficulty, and one harder one. The criteria in this chapter can help you identify which is which. The easiest game is usually quite concrete, simple, short, and familiar. The medium-difficulty games typically add one or two complicating factors. The hardest game throws in everything. (But remember, your diligent practice deprives the test maker of using unfamiliarity as a way to make games harder for you.)

As I'll discuss at greater length in Part III of this book, it's in your best interest to manage the Logic Games section strategically and tackle the easiest games first. That will allow you to rack up the quickest points and, perhaps, even bank some extra time for the toughest game. When you do dive into the hardest game, remember the strategies from this chapter to help you deal with any lack of concreteness, complex tasks, or difficult language you encounter.

Above all, remember the very first point that I made in chapter 1: Every question has an answer. The test makers set out to create a challenging, but fair, test. They always provide the information you need to distinguish the one correct answer from the four wrong ones. In that sense, you should approach the hardest logic games exactly as you approach the easiest ones. Adhering to the Kaplan Method is the best way to ensure that you glean that information clearly, accurately, and completely in every logic game you do.

PART II

GAME TYPES

CHAPTER 8

THE LOGIC GAMES TASKS

In Part II, I'll take you through each of the standard logic game types you'll see on the LSAT. I'll show you the routine versions of each game type, as well as examples of the variations and twists that have appeared on recent tests. I'll also go through the best ways to set up the sketches for each game type, cover the most common rules associated with them, and even show you how real-world versions of these puzzles can help you manage the process. There's no cognitive task tested by logic games that you haven't managed successfully in your personal, professional, or academic life. But the connections aren't always obvious, to say the least. Taking the mystery out of logic games is a valuable step.

While the test makers will offer variations on the standard game setups, the basic tasks that underlie the game types have remained remarkably consistent. Your chances of seeing familiar games on test day are far greater than those of seeing something novel or surprising. You're better off mastering the most common game types than you would be scouring old tests for variations you're unlikely to see on test day. Use what you learn in this section to make your work more efficient. By recognizing familiar game patterns, you can make better sketches faster and tackle the rules and deductions with greater confidence—and add points to your score.

IDENTIFYING GAME TYPES

If you've completed Part I of this book, you've already seen examples of every common logic games task. There, I deliberately mixed in various game types in order to keep the focus on the steps in the Kaplan Method and to illustrate how you can use them to master all LSAT logic games. In Part II, I'll break the games down by type to show you how recognizing certain patterns can make you even more efficient. Once you see the games arranged by type, you'll notice that the test makers consistently employ the same types of tasks but incorporate different rules, limitations, and number restrictions to make each game unique. Students who learn logic games' underlying similarities and use their common features to create the most useful sketches are those who become the most effective test takers. I'll now give you a brief overview of the common tasks posed by logic games. I'll then elaborate each with its own chapter.

The Standard Tasks

The LSAT test makers reuse the standard games tasks test after test. With maybe a dozen exceptions since 1991 (and *none* since 2003), every logic game that's appeared on the 60-plus released LSATs falls into one of the five main categories listed below. Even those games that fall into the Hybrid category are devised by combining two or three of the tasks listed in the first four main groupings. Logic games aren't identical from test to test, but they have far more commonalities than they do distinctions—a fact you can use to your advantage.

Sequencing Games

Far and away the most common game task (and the one most often combined into Hybrid games), Sequencing games task you with determining schedules, rankings, or numerical orderings of entities. As you already know from Part I, the test may give you a Strict Sequencing task, in which entities are limited to specific days or numbered slots within the order, or in which the exact number of spaces separating entities is given. Alternatively, the test might serve up Loose Sequencing, providing only relative restrictions among the entities, such as "M ranks higher than P" or "L is visited later than both C and D." It's not uncommon for a test to include each type of Sequencing game. Over the years, the test makers have very occasionally used other twists on the task; these include Circular Sequencing, in which entities are ordered around a table, and Double Sequencing, in which the same set of players must be ordered twice. I'll show you recent variations like these, but your main goal should be to master the basics of Sequencing games. Even in the most unusual examples, the fundamental questions—Which entities are before, after, or beside others? And how far are these two entities separated?—will give you the insights you need to answer the questions.

Matching Games

Matching games—the second most popular category, albeit a distant second—are defined by having two sets of entities. One of the entity sets is static, and your job is to assign the attributes or players that make up the second set to particular entities from the first group. In Part I, you saw the Electronics Technicians game, in which various types of machines were assigned to each of six technicians, and the Lunch Trucks game, in which three buildings were served by a fleet of lunch trucks that each sold a different kind of food. It's important to remember that in Matching games you may assign each of the "moveable" entities more than once. Four of the technicians, for example, repaired radios. The ice cream truck served at least two of the buildings. You'll come to see that this provides a huge clue for how to attack these games.

Determining how many matches a given entity can have or how many times a certain attribute can be assigned is always important to the limitations that make Matching games manageable.

Selection Games

Selection games are the type most closely associated with formal logic. Your job is always to take a list of entities and distinguish those that are chosen, or included, from those rejected, or excluded. So rules that designate entities whose inclusion is sufficient or necessary for the inclusion of others are particularly well suited to this action. In some of the Selection examples you saw in Part I—think of the Friends' Photographs game—all of the rules were in the form of conditional formal logic statements. Beyond handling the formal logic tasks, your main concern in Selection games is to determine the numerical possibilities. The test makers are fond of asking Minimum/Maximum questions that reward you for being able to count how many or how few entities could constitute an acceptable selection. Pay close attention to whether the test makers have determined up front the number of entities to be chosen—have they said, "Exactly five of the seven applicants will be hired"?—or whether they've left the numbers open-ended—for example, "The company will hire at least one of the applicants." That distinction provides the basis for the two basic subtypes within the Selection family.

Distribution Games

Cousins of Matching games, Distribution games ask you to divide a group of entities into two, three, or sometimes four groups. The primary distinction between Matching and Distribution is that in the latter, each entity can be placed only one time. Think of choosing sports teams at recess as a good model for Distribution: Once you place Bobby on the red team, you can't place him anywhere else. Numbers are just as important to Distribution games as they are to Selection. Once you recognize a game a presenting a Distribution task, your first question should be, "How many entities go into each group or team?" The more definite that aspect of the game is—for example, "Nine players will be divided among three teams, three players per team"—the easier the game is likely to be. But when the test makers don't specify how many entities go on each team—"Seven doctors will each serve at one of two hospitals, with at least one doctor at each hospital"—your task will be more challenging. Knowing how to quickly assess a game's difficulty is one of the major benefits of learning the game types and their characteristics.

Hybrid Games

I talked a little about Hybrid games in Part I. There's no doubt that combining two or three tasks can make a game more difficult, but in the chapter on Hybrid games that follows, I'll show you how identifying a Hybrid game's constituent tasks allows you to avoid many potential complications. Make sure you recognize the four preceding tasks, and know what makes each one easier or harder before you turn to the chapter on Hybrids. What you'll come to realize is that, while Hybrid games combine two or more of these other tasks, the individual tasks that comprise them are, on their own, quite simple. For example, a game might ask you to divide a group of six entities into two teams and rank each team's members from first through third. Dividing six entities into two teams of exactly three each is about as simple as Distribution tasks get. Similarly, ranking three entities would never stand on its own as a Sequencing task; it simply presents too few permutations to be challenging. As your familiarity with the patterns in Hybrid games increases, their ability to intimidate you will decrease. When you learn how to represent compound tasks with simple sketches, you'll find that Hybrids are susceptible to precisely the same limitations and deductions as are single-action games.

Rare Games

There's no special chapter of the book for the Mapping and Process games, the only game types that have appeared on the LSAT that don't fit easily into one of the above categories. That's because, with the exception of one Mapping game from PrepTest 40 (June 2003), none of the rare games has appeared on a released test since 1997. It's very unlikely that one of these will appear on a new exam.

THE LIMITS OF TAXONOMY
You Don't Get Any Points for Knowing the Game Type

"What kind of game is this one?" I've heard this a thousand times. But the fact is that it means different things depending on the context in which it's asked. Sometimes the student is saying, "I messed up this game somehow, and I don't have the information I need to answer the questions." Knowing the game type *might* set the student on the right track, but what's more important here is trusting in the Overview step of the Kaplan Method to reveal the task and goal of each game so that the rules and deductions have meaning. At other times, the student is really saying, "I was torn about how to sketch this game; show me what you'd do." Certain game types are definitely associated with certain sketch structures, but the sketch should ultimately flow organically from the game's task. No one, including the law school admissions committee, will ever see the scratch work you put in the test booklet. There's no "right" sketch, just one that's best for you in the context of the game. Worst of all is when the student asking the question is saying, "I'm stuck; I need this to be like a game I've already done," implying that there's no way forward unless the game matches something completely familiar.

That's the problem with prioritizing taxonomy and memorization ahead of the principles and fundamentals that allow you to answer the questions to any logic game. You're far better off learning the fundamentals of how to recognize and complete the types of games the test makers use most often. That way, the test won't throw you off by changing one tiny thing and making you think you've never seen a similar game before.

You don't get any points for giving the game the right name. You get points for answering the questions. That's the great advantage of studying and practicing for the test the way you did in Part I of this book. You're prepared to tackle any game of any type using the Kaplan

Method. You're not dependent on recognizing certain buzzwords, and you won't be hamstrung if the test makers decide to throw in an unusual rule or scenario. You're in a position to use a taxonomy of game types in the right way, by engaging your knowledge of the characteristics of the standard game types to help you make good strategic choices about how best to manage all of the games in your section. If you're on an outing in the desert, it's great to have memorized exactly which snakes you might encounter. What's more important, though, is that you know the characteristics of those that are poisonous and those that are harmless and can identify them at a moment's notice. Approaching this portion of the book with a similar goal will help you avoid getting bitten by logic games on test day.

Keeping the Taxonomy Up-to-Date

If you take the time to catalogue the games covered in this book (although, to be honest, I don't know why you would), you'll find that all of them appeared on tests administered within the last decade or so.

Now, there's nothing wrong *per se* with practicing games from earlier PrepTests. Many of those games are just additional examples of the standard game types that continue to appear on the LSAT. But I will caution you against two things. Don't comb those old tests just to find one more variation or oddity and then spend time analyzing that one old twist at the expense of learning the fundamentals of the games that the test makers use most often *now*. That leads to the second caution: Don't set your study priorities according to the frequency of game types found in those older tests. Loose Sequencing games are just one example of games that have appeared more frequently than they used to and have gotten much tougher than they used to be. In the chapter on Recent Trends at the end of Part II, I'll go over what has been on the latest tests released by the LSAC so that you can assess what you're most likely to see on test day.

CHAPTER 9

SEQUENCING GAMES

As I indicated in the previous chapter, Sequencing games are far and away the most common game type found on the LSAT. Many recent exams feature two, or even three, Sequencing games or Hybrid games in which Sequencing is one of the actions. Perhaps as a result of how often they're employed by the test makers, Sequencing tasks also show the broadest range of variations. Some variations—like the Circular Sequencing game covered near the end of this chapter—are so unusual that there's no way you'll miss them. Other variations—such as omitting the requirement that you schedule one entity per space (you saw this in the Professors' Hiring Year game in chapter 7)—are more subtle, and as such, potentially more dangerous. Taking a few minutes to think about the real-world tasks that require you to arrange, sequence, and schedule items in your life and work will help you visualize this range of Sequencing variations more clearly.

REAL-LIFE SEQUENCING

If you think about it, you'll realize that there's probably not a day in your adult life in which you don't sequence something. Every time you alphabetize, schedule, rank, or decide the order of steps in a process, you're sequencing. The most common scenario—the *default*, if you will—is that things in the sequence happen one at a time or that items are ranked without ties, one per space. If I asked you to rank your 10 favorite songs, I doubt you'd ask, "Are 3 songs supposed to be tied at number two?" or "Should I avoid repeating the same song twice in my list?" You might have difficulty ranking your favorites, but you'd *assume* that I intended the list to have 10 songs and 10 slots with one song per slot.

Never assume anything on LSAT logic games. While it's true that most (it's fair to say the *vast* majority of) Sequencing games contain one-at-a-time, one-per-space restrictions, the test makers must be, and will be, explicit about all restrictions that are to apply. Make sure you always pay attention to the overall limitations that affect a game's action and account for them in your sketch.

If your analysis of the setup reveals the expected one-at-a-time, one-per-space format, great. But, don't let variations throw you off or undermine your confidence. After all, you deal with different sequencing scenarios just fine in everyday life. If I asked you to list the order of people you met with at work last week, it might well be the case that you had a single meeting with each of four coworkers but met with another person three times. So your final list of meetings would look something like this:

Mon	Tue	Wed	Thurs	Fri
Tom	Ed	Jane	Tom	
Hiromi	Tom		Paul	

Figure 9.1

Don't let the test makers throw you by saying, "Thomas will schedule seven meetings with five potential investors. He'll have one meeting with each of investors A, B, C, and D and three meetings with investor E."

A class schedule presents another understandable variation. It might be that a law student has some classes only on Tuesdays and Thursdays, others only on Mondays, Wednesdays, and Fridays. For good measure, throw one of those long, once-per-week classes into the mix. You have no problem interpreting this student's schedule at a glance.

	Mon	Tues	Wed	Thurs	Fri
9 – 10 am	Tort		Tort		Tort
10:30 – noon		Civ Pro		Civ Pro	
1 – 2:30 pm		Prop		Prop	
2 – 3 pm	Crim		Crim		Crim
6 – 9 pm		Leg writing			

Figure 9.2

So even if a game asks you to use some entities multiple times or to leave a slot open, it's nothing you haven't done before.

Another trap that the test makers employ is revealed by considering your real-world assumptions. If I ask you to create a sequence of eight departments in a certain company, your default would almost certainly be to start with a sketch like one of these:

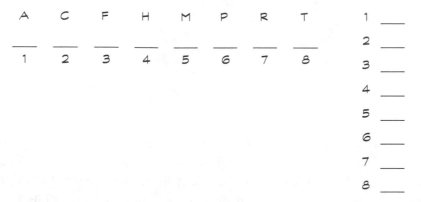

Figure 9.3

Our default orientations are generally top to bottom and left to right. But now imagine if I said that the eight departments occupy one floor each in an eight-story building. If I include a rule like "Human Resources occupies a higher floor than Marketing," your sketch needs to be numbered from the bottom up.

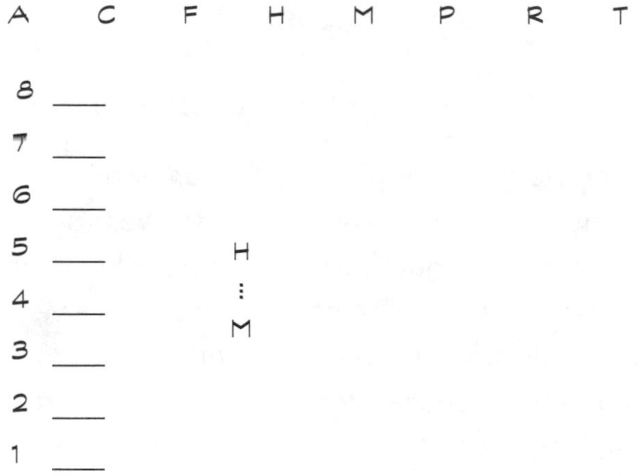

```
          A    C    F    H    M    P    R    T

     8  ___

     7  ___

     6  ___

     5  ___         H

     4  ___         ⋮

     3  ___         M

     2  ___

     1  ___
```

Figure 9.4

The same confusion can be avoided by paying attention to the differences between games in which entities are ranked and those in which they're assigned to numbered positions. Consider two examples: If I tell you that seven salespeople will be ranked on their performance over the past quarter, a rule such as "Baker was ranked lower than Carty" should be depicted like this:

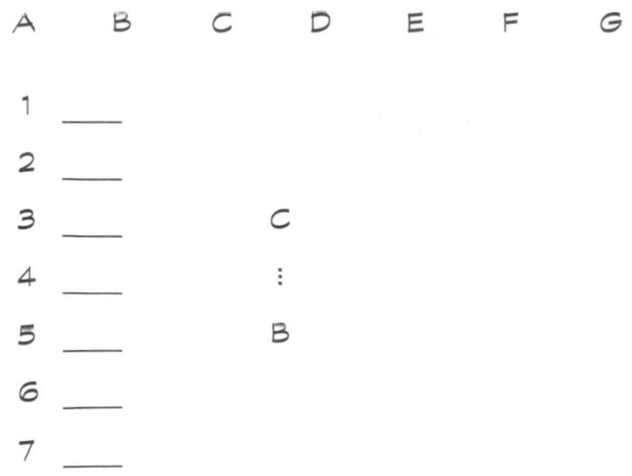

```
        A    B    C    D    E    F    G

    1  ___

    2  ___

    3  ___         C

    4  ___         ⋮

    5  ___         B

    6  ___

    7  ___
```

Figure 9.5

Being ranked lower means taking a position closer to number seven. On the other hand, if the game assigns seven salespeople to seven offices, numbered 1 through 7, the rule "Baker is assigned a lower-numbered office than Carty" should be written like this:

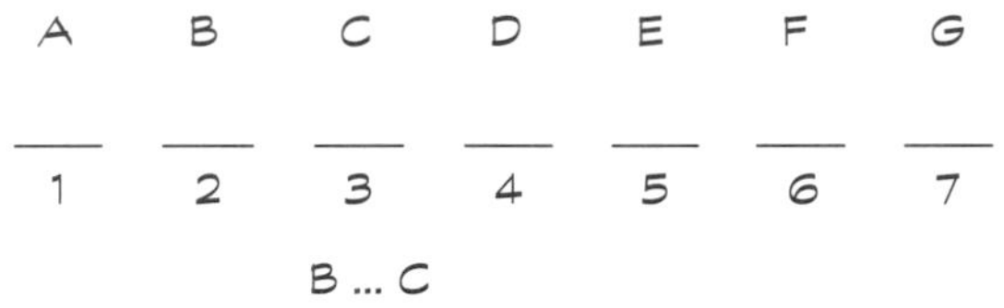

```
        A    B    C    D    E    F    G
       ___  ___  ___  ___  ___  ___  ___
        1    2    3    4    5    6    7
                 B ... C
```

Figure 9.6

Here, having a *lower-numbered* office means taking an office *closer to number 1*.

The test makers can even reward you for paying attention to the criterion on which items are ranked. Imagine a game show host telling you, "Put these five products in order by price" or a gym teacher who says, "Line up by height." You'd make sure to know whether you are supposed to arrange the products from cheapest to most expensive or vice versa, whether the students were supposed to go from tallest to shortest or the other way around. The test makers will always be explicit about the order you're supposed to use. There have been many examples over the years of relatively simple Sequencing games that test takers missed or struggled with because they failed to catch these distinctions. In fact, you'll be given the opportunity to make this very mistake in the Hotel Suites game later in this chapter, so stay alert.

When you're conducting your overview in Step 1 of the Kaplan Method, use the real-world scenario that's described to your advantage. Ask the logical questions about your task and make sure you reflect all of the restrictions or definitions in your sketch framework. It's better to jot down "Cheapest" at the top of your sketch and "Most Expensive" at the bottom than to set up the whole game incorrectly and have to start over from scratch.

STANDARD SEQUENCING GAMES

You've already seen the two basic subcategories of Sequencing games: strict and loose. Strict Sequencing games contain rules and restrictions that associate certain entities with specific slots, or rules that tell you precisely how many spaces separate two or more entities. The framework for such games should always be numbered slots or spaces, and entities should be placed as definitely as possible within them.

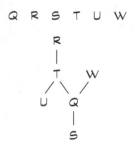

Figure 9.7

Even when you're unable to place many of the entities within the framework initially, the strict framework will enhance your understanding of the rules and acceptable arrangements.

In Loose Sequencing games, on the other hand, all of the rules are "relative." That is, they tell you only the relative order of two or more entities, with no restrictions as to the specific slots that the entities must take or avoid and no information about how close to or far from each other the entities must be placed. In these games, you will use the "tree" model for your framework. Numbered slots do nothing to give you further concreteness in the sketch.

```
         Q  R  S  T  U  W

               R
               |
               T        W
              /| \      /
             U   Q
                 |
                 S
```

Figure 9.8

Strict Sequencing

In the most routine Strict Sequencing games, the number of slots and entities will be the same and the setup will be unequivocal in telling you to arrange the entities one per slot. The Trail Markers game is representative of this pattern.

Exactly six guideposts, numbered 1 through 6, mark a mountain trail. Each guidepost pictures a different one of six animals—fox, grizzly, hare, lynx, moose, or porcupine. The following conditions must apply:

    The grizzly is pictured on either guidepost 3 or guidepost 4.

    The moose guidepost is numbered lower than the hare guidepost.

    The lynx guidepost is numbered lower than the moose guidepost but higher than the fox guidepost.[1]

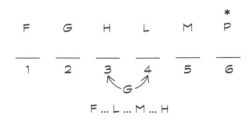

Figure 9.9

In this case, it's Rule 1 that signals the usefulness of the strict framework. You need to be able to *see* the impact of placing G in either space 3 or space 4. Note, too, that the orientation of the sketch is irrelevant. The relative restrictions in Rules 2 and 3 refer to lower- or higher-*numbered* guideposts. Guidepost 1 is the lowest-numbered and guidepost 6 the highest-numbered, no matter how you draw it. So the presumptive left-to-right slot numbering is fine. But top-to-bottom or bottom-to-top would be just as good, so long as it's logical and clear to you.

Here's another standard Strict Sequencing setup. Take a few moments to look it over and determine which rule(s) make it clear that a numbered-slot framework is called for.

Exactly eight computer processor chips—F, G, H, J, K, L, M, and O—are ranked according to their speed from first (fastest) to eighth (slowest). The ranking must be consistent with the following:

    There are no ties.

    Either F or G is ranked first.

    M is not the slowest.

    H is faster than J, with exactly one chip intermediate in speed between them.

    K is faster than L, with exactly two chips intermediate in speed between them.

    O is slower than both J and L.[2]

F	G	H	J	K	L	M	O
F/G	___	___	___	___	___	___	___
1	2	3	4	5	6	7	8
							M̸

    H ___ J
   K ___ ___ L ⋯ O

Figure 9.10

This time, Rule 1 explicitly mentions the first position. Moreover, Rules 3 and 4 both designate the specific number of spaces that separate pairs of entities. Even though you weren't able to put a lot of these entities into the framework at the outset, it would be nearly impossible

[1] PrepTest 46, Sec. 4, Game 1
[2] PrepTest 49, Sec. 1, Game 4

to assess the impact without the accompanying framework. Being able to quickly see that placing K in space 2 means placing L in space 5 is vital, and this sketch allows you to do that.

The two preceding games also stand as good reminders of what leads to most deductions within Strict Sequencing games: Established Entities and Blocks of Entities. In the Trail Markers game, no entity is completely determined, but the G comes very close. Combining G's restriction to either space 3 or 4 with the long F-L-M-H block leaves only 10 acceptable arrangements for the game. Likewise, in the Processor Chip game, no entity is entirely established, but you know for certain that space 1 is occupied by either F or G. That means that the K-L block, which has to be followed by O, can only fit in spaces 2 and 5, 3 and 6, or 4 and 7, severely limiting the number of acceptable solutions. At times, the position taken by an Established Entity leaves a Block of Entities only two acceptable positions. That's relatively rare, but when it happens, you can create a Limited Options sketch. What's more common, and is seen in both of the previous examples, is the presence of Duplications. In the Trail Markers game, the moose allows you to combine Rules 2 and 3. In the Processor Chip game, J appears in Rules 4 and 6 and L in Rules 5 and 6, allowing the three rules to be combined into a long string. The one element of the BLEND checklist that's unlikely to be of help in most Strict Sequencing games is Number Restrictions. That's because the numbers—one entity per space—are as simple as they can be. You can see a couple of exceptions under the "Uneven Numbers" heading below. But for the most part, once you've confirmed that you're working with a standard one-per-space format, you can take the numbers out of consideration. There's just no way to make them any clearer than they are.

Loose Sequencing

For many years, Loose Sequencing games were (rightly) considered easier than their strict counterparts. If you're prepping with outdated materials, you will (wrongly) get the impression that it's still the case. In the easiest of these games (the majority of them prior to PrepTest 33), all of the rules were relatively straightforward—"X ranks lower than Y," and "W ranks higher than Y"—and all of the rules combined. So you wound up with a single "tree" diagram that, while not completely determining the exact lineup, gave the relative position of every entity. A few of the more recent examples preserve that format. The Water Treatment Plant game is a perfect illustration.

Workers at a water treatment plant open eight valves—G, H, I, K, L, N, O, and P—to flush out a system of pipes that needs emergency repairs. To maximize safety and efficiency, each valve is opened exactly once, and no two valves are opened at the same time. The valves are opened in accordance with the following conditions:

Both K and P are opened before H.
O is opened before L but after H.
L is opened after G.
N is opened before H.
I is opened after K.[3]

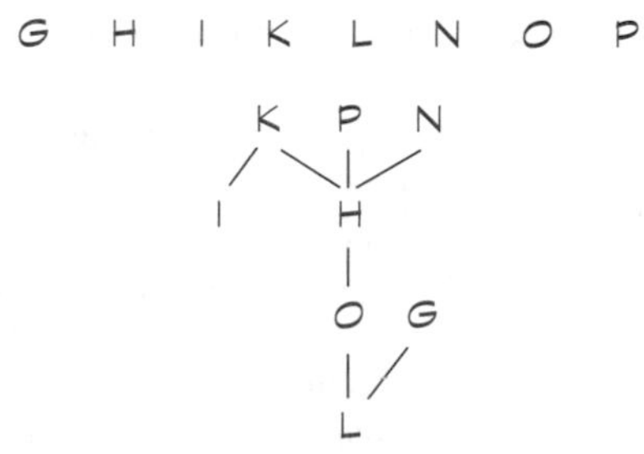

Figure 9.11

---

[3] PrepTest 52, Sec. 2, Game 1

Take note of how you knew to draw this one with a loose sketch. None of the rules mentions a specific slot, and none gives you any idea of how distant two entities are from one another. All of the rules give you the relative positions of two or more entities. There would be nothing to place into slots even if you drew them. But there's a lot to learn by combining the relative restrictions. That puts a huge premium on Duplications, the most important of the BLEND elements in Loose Sequencing deductions. As is typical in Loose Sequencing games, every entity in this game relates to at least one other.

Once you've created your Loose Sequencing sketch, you can figure out the acceptable positions for any of the entities. In the Water Treatment Plant game, for example, H could only be opened fourth, fifth, or sixth. There are eight entities in total, and H must come after K, P, and N and before O and L. H is pretty heavily restricted here. G, on the other hand, has only one restriction: It must be opened before L. So G could be opened in any position first through seventh. Be very careful not to make unwarranted assumptions based on the drawing. In the previous sketch, G may be lower on the page than K, P, N, or H, but it isn't restricted by any entity except L.

Don't misinterpret the name Loose Sequencing to indicate a lack of concreteness. Although there are no Established Entities in the Water Treatment Plant game, notice that all of the rules are direct and restrictive. There are no conditional rules and none that offer restrictions in the alternative (e.g., "Either K is opened before P but after I, or else K is opened after P but before I"). The absence of those types of rules is a good sign that this is one of the easier Loose Sequencing games you'll encounter, and it makes the Water Treatment Plant game reminiscent of the stereotypical older Loose Sequencing games.

PrepTest 52, the test that featured the Water Treatment Plant game, had another Loose Sequencing game as well. In fact, this second game from PrepTest 52 is much more representative of Loose Sequencing as it has appeared recently. Take a couple of minutes and review the setup and rules. Note what makes the Bread Truck game more challenging to set up and how it rewards deductions beyond the string of Duplications that allowed you to stitch together all of the entities in the Water Treatment Plant game.

A bread truck makes exactly one bread delivery to each of six restaurants in succession—Figueroa's, Ginsberg's, Harris's, Kanzaki's, Leacock's, and Malpighi's—though not necessarily in that order. The following conditions must apply:

> Ginsberg's delivery is earlier than Kanzaki's but later than Figueroa's.
> Harris's delivery is earlier than Ginsberg's.
> If Figueroa's delivery is earlier than Malpighi's, then Leacock's delivery is earlier than Harris's.
> Either Malpighi's delivery is earlier than Harris's or it is later than Kanzaki's, but not both.[4]

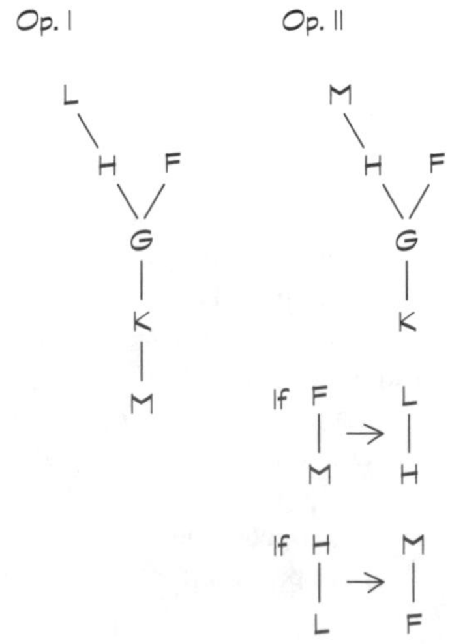

Figure 9.12

4 PrepTest 52, Sec. 2, Game 4

The scenario and the first two rules could come from any Loose Sequencing game. They're direct and, unsurprisingly, they share a duplicated entity, G. Combined, Rules 1 and 2 start a sketch that might appear in any Loose Sequencing game.

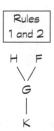

Figure 9.13

It's the third and fourth rules that set this game apart from the Water Treatment Plant and from most of the older Loose Sequencing games. Because they are conditional and present alternative possibilities respectively, Rules 3 and 4 cannot simply be snapped onto the block created by Rules 1 and 2 in order to create a single Master Sketch. A lot of the newer Loose Sequencing games reward a Limited Options approach. Here's how it works in this game.

Rule 4 creates the Limited Options. Either M is earlier than both H and K, or it is later than both H and K.

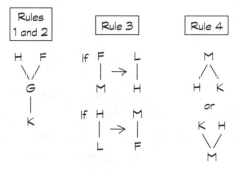

Figure 9.14

Since H and K are included in the block created by Rules 1 and 2, you can simply add M after K to create Option I or before H to create Option II.

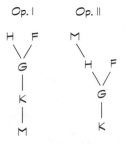

Figure 9.15

Now, consider the applicability of the conditional rule, Rule 3.

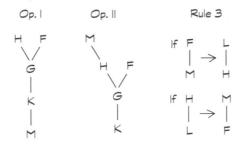

Figure 9.16

In Option I, F must come before M. Therefore, L must come before H. In this option, all six entities are related and you're done.

Figure 9.17

In Option II, however, three possibilities remain. On test day, you probably wouldn't write out all three, provided that you can see how they work. I'll illustrate the three possibilities now, so that you can be sure you've got them straight. (By the way, take another look at the sample Master Sketch above; now you can see why I wrote Rule 3 next to Option II, where its conditions are still applicable.) It could be the case that F comes before M. That's the sufficient trigger in Rule 3's formal logic, meaning that L would have to come before H.

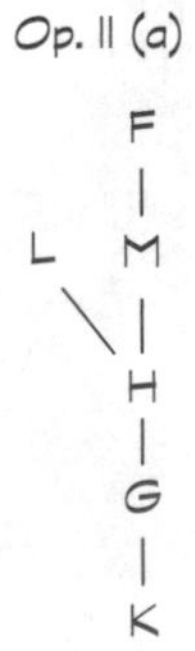

Figure 9.18

Likewise, it could be that H comes before L. That's the sufficient trigger in Rule 3's contrapositive, meaning that F would come after M.

Op. II (b)

Figure 9.19

Finally, it could be that neither of the sufficient triggers in Rule 3 is present. F could come after M and H could come after L.

Op. II (c)

Figure 9.20

That's a lot to keep track of and, indeed, this is one of the toughest Loose Sequencing games you're likely to see. But it's a good reminder not to take Loose Sequencing for granted and to practice using recent materials. A lot of test takers could be caught off guard if they ran into something like the Bread Delivery game. Fortunately, knowing how to deal with alternative possibilities by using a Limited Options sketch means that you'll be far more likely to take control of this game than will someone who hasn't trained with the Kaplan Method. Chances are that if you have a Loose Sequencing game on your test, it will fall somewhere in between the difficulty levels presented by these two examples. I'll have you take another crack at Loose Sequencing with Limited Options shortly. For now, take a look at how the test makers throw some more variety into their favorite game type.

SEQUENCING TWISTS
Uneven Numbers

As I discussed above, when asked to put things in an order—to rank, schedule, or arrange them in a row—your default is to assume that there are no ties. Most of the time, the test makers want you to adhere to one-at-a-time, one-per-space limitations. But when they do, they'll be explicit about it. Taking one-entity-per-space for granted is a good way to go off track on games in which the test makers don't include that restriction.

You saw the setup for this next game in chapter 7. Refresh your memory of the overview, sketch, rules, and deductions, keeping in mind that while there are seven professors hired over seven years, nothing in the setup text says that one professor must be hired each year. If you're fuzzy on how you were able to deduce so much about the arrangement of professors to hiring years, revisit chapter 7, where I took you through Steps 1–4 of the Kaplan Method on this game.

> Exactly seven professors—Madison, Nilsson, Orozco, Paton, Robinson, Sarkis, and Togo—were hired in the years 1989 through 1995. Each professor has one or more specialties, and any two professors hired in the same year or in consecutive years do not have a specialty in common. The professors were hired according to the following conditions:
>
> Madison was hired in 1993, Robinson in 1991.
> There is at least one specialty that Madison, Orozco, and Togo have in common.
> Nilsson shares a specialty with Robinson.
> Paton and Sarkis were each hired at least one year before Madison and at least one year after Nilsson.
> Orozco, who shares a specialty with Sarkis, was hired in 1990.[5]

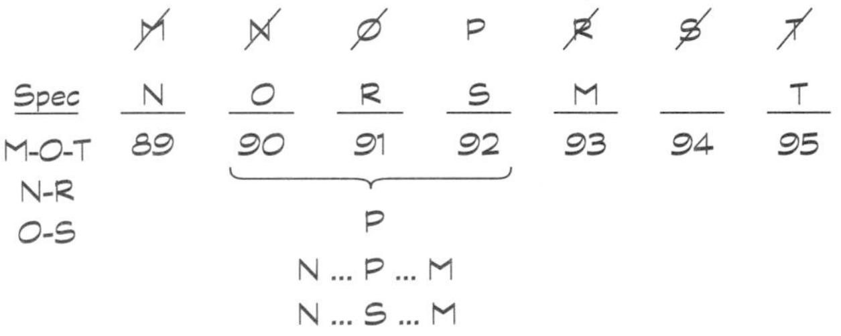

Figure 9.21

There are two big takeaways from this game. First, you must pay attention to the restrictions that are and *are not* included in the setup. Test takers who struggle with this game make unwarranted assumptions and then fail to be patient and methodical enough in the Deductions step to demonstrate that Paton will have to be hired in the same year as one of the other professors. Second, variations don't necessarily make games harder. It's certainly the exception to have a Sequencing game in which you don't place one entity per slot. The test makers count on unfamiliar twists to throw off a certain percentage of test takers. But remember that familiarity is entirely within your control. Your practice with this book and other Kaplan resources immunizes you against the very difficulties the test makers will present to throw off much of your competition. Here, your expert use of the Kaplan Method has allowed you to establish the hiring years of six of the seven professors. Now, tackling the question set has to be pretty

---

[5] PrepTest 35, Sec. 3, Game 4

easy; there's just not much left to account for. Try it out. Give yourself five minutes for the six questions. Pay special attention to Paton, the only professor whose hiring year isn't locked down in the Master Sketch. Remember, too, what it means to "share a specialty." Professors who share a specialty cannot be hired in the same year as each other or in consecutive years.

18. Which one of the following is a complete and accurate list of the professors who could have been hired in the years 1989 through 1991?

    (A)   Nilsson, Orozco, Robinson
    (B)   Orozco, Robinson, Sarkis
    (C)   Nilsson, Orozco, Paton, Robinson
    (D)   Nilsson, Orozco, Paton, Sarkis
    (E)   Orozco, Paton, Robinson, Sarkis

19. If exactly one professor was hired in 1991, then which one of the following could be true?

    (A)   Madison and Paton share a specialty.
    (B)   Robinson and Sarkis share a specialty.
    (C)   Paton was hired exactly one year after Orozco.
    (D)   Exactly one professor was hired in 1994.
    (E)   Exactly two professors were hired in 1993.

20. Which one of the following must be false?

    (A)   Nilsson was hired in 1989.
    (B)   Paton was hired in 1990.
    (C)   Paton was hired in 1991.
    (D)   Sarkis was hired in 1992.
    (E)   Togo was hired in 1994.

21. Which one of the following must be true?

    (A)   Orozco was hired before Paton.
    (B)   Paton was hired before Sarkis.
    (C)   Sarkis was hired before Robinson.
    (D)   Robinson was hired before Sarkis.
    (E)   Madison was hired before Sarkis.

22. If exactly two professors were hired in 1992, then which one of the following could be true?

    (A)   Orozco, Paton, and Togo share a specialty.
    (B)   Madison, Paton, and Togo share a specialty.
    (C)   Exactly two professors were hired in 1991.
    (D)   Exactly two professors were hired in 1993.
    (E)   Paton was hired in 1991.

23. If Paton and Madison have a specialty in common, then which one of the following must be true?

    (A)   Nilsson does not share a specialty with Paton.
    (B)   Exactly one professor was hired in 1990.
    (C)   Exactly one professor was hired in 1991.
    (D)   Exactly two professors were hired in each of two years.
    (E)   Paton was hired at least one year before Sarkis.[6]

---

[6] PrepTest 35, Sec. 3, Qs 18–23

Explanations

In this question set, the question types are equally divided: three of them have a new "if" and three don't. Reviewing them in two groups will point out a valuable pattern. For the "if" questions, Paton (the one professor whose hiring year is not completely determined) will have to be involved. Let's begin with those that lack a new "if"; these are questions you can answer with just a glance at your Master Sketch.

18. **(C)**

Which one of the following is a complete and accurate list of the professors who could have been hired in the years 1989 through 1991?

(A) Nilsson, Orozco, Robinson
(B) Orozco, Robinson, Sarkis
(C) Nilsson, Orozco, Paton, Robinson
(D) Nilsson, Orozco, Paton, Sarkis
(E) Orozco, Paton, Robinson, Sarkis[7]

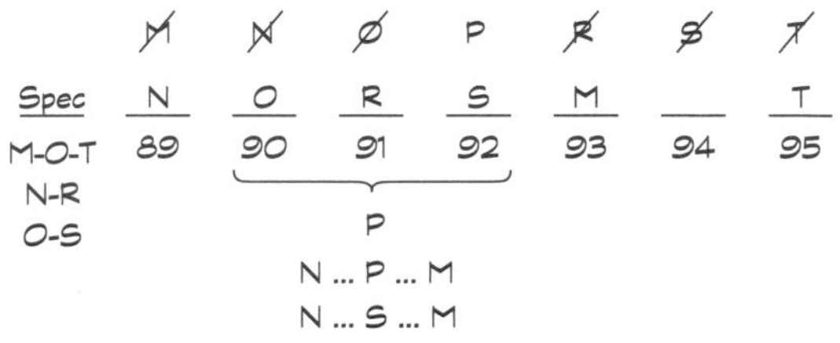

Figure 9.22

This question asks for a "complete and accurate list," in other words *any and all* of the professors who could have been hired between '89 and '91. As the Master Sketch illustrates, the correct answer must include N, O, R, and P and cannot include S, M, or T, who were all hired in '92 or later. That makes choice (C) the correct answer. Choice (A) misses Paton, while choices (B), (D), and (E) all incorrectly include Sarkis and miss one or more of the professors who should be included. Notice the role that Paton, the one entity who can still move, plays here. Paton *could* have been hired within the years in question, and so must be included in the correct answer.

20. **(E)**

Which one of the following must be false?

(A) Nilsson was hired in 1989.
(B) Paton was hired in 1990.
(C) Paton was hired in 1991.
(D) Sarkis was hired in 1992.
(E) Togo was hired in 1994.[8]

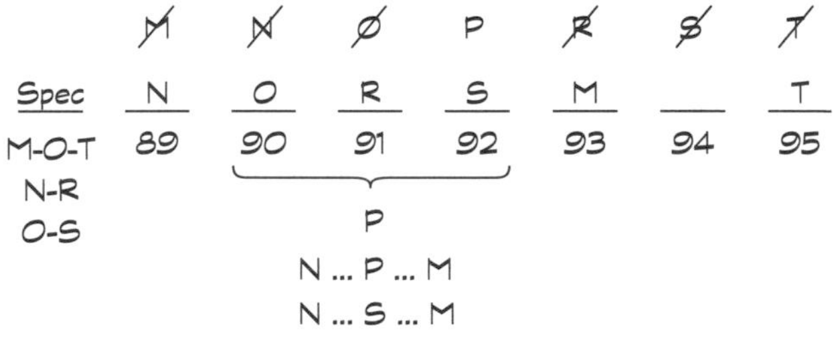

Figure 9.23

Here, the correct answer *must be false*. Togo, you can see from the Master Sketch, must be hired in 1995, making choice (E) the correct answer. Note that here, Paton, who could have been hired in '90, '91, or '92, is included in two of the wrong answers, both of which *could be true*.

---

21. **(D)**

Which one of the following must be true?

(A) Orozco was hired before Paton.
(B) Paton was hired before Sarkis.
(C) Sarkis was hired before Robinson.
(D) Robinson was hired before Sarkis.
(E) Madison was hired before Sarkis.[9]

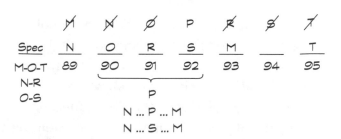

Figure 9.24

This time, the correct answer *must be true*. Since R was hired in '91 and S in '92, choice (D) fits the bill. As with question 20, it's no surprise to find Paton in two of the wrong answers here. P could have been hired before S, but P could also have been hired the same year as S. So choice (B) *could be false*. And P could have been hired the same year as or later than O. Therefore, choice (A) could also be false.

P's status as the one professor that can be hired the same year as another played a role in those "Non-If" questions, but it will become even more central in the "If" questions. As the only entity who can move, Paton must be involved in any conditional statements.

19. **(A)**

If exactly one professor was hired in 1991, then which one of the following could be true?

(A) Madison and Paton share a specialty.
(B) Robinson and Sarkis share a specialty.
(C) Paton was hired exactly one year after Orozco.
(D) Exactly one professor was hired in 1994.
(E) Exactly two professors were hired in 1993.[10]

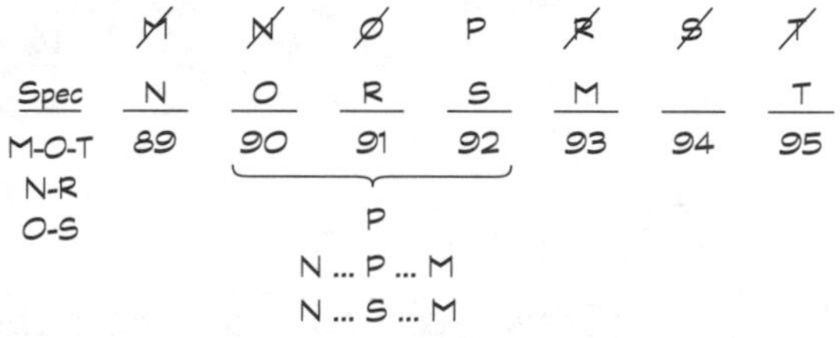

Figure 9.25

Usually, a new "if" calls for a mini-sketch. There's no harm in making one here. If only one professor is hired in '91, you know that P was hired in either '90 or '92.

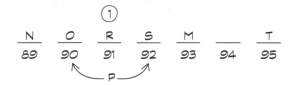

Figure 9.26

---

[9] PrepTest 35, Sec. 3, Q 21
[10] PrepTest 35, Sec. 3, Q 19

With so much certainty in this game, though, you may just have elected to answer this one from your Master Sketch, telling yourself "P can't be in '91." Either way, you can tell that P is the focus of this question. The correct answer is one that *could be true*, after all. If hired in '90, P could share a specialty with M, which would require that they not be hired in the same or consecutive years. Choice (A) is the correct answer. The only other choice involving P is ruled out by the "if" condition in the question stem. Since P can't be hired in '91, choice (C) *must be false*. The other three choices must be false because they contradict the Master Sketch.

22. **(A)**

If exactly two professors were hired in 1992, then which one of the following could be true?

(A) Orozco, Paton, and Togo share a specialty.
(B) Madison, Paton, and Togo share a specialty.
(C) Exactly two professors were hired in 1991.
(D) Exactly two professors were hired in 1993.
(E) Paton was hired in 1991.[11]

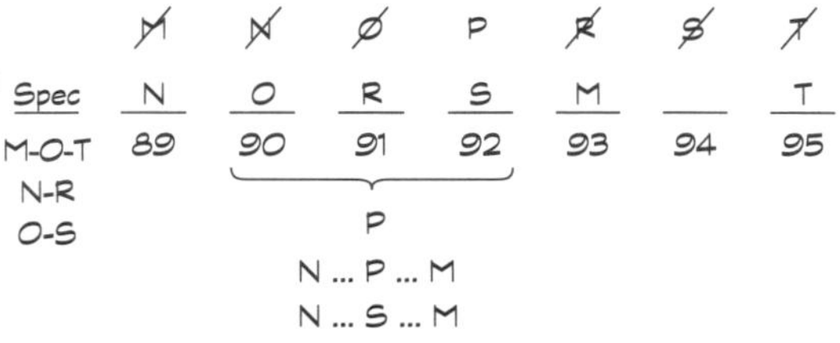

Figure 9.27

Again, with so much certainty, a mini-sketch is optional. The new "if" simply means that P was hired in '92, something you can likely keep clear in your head.

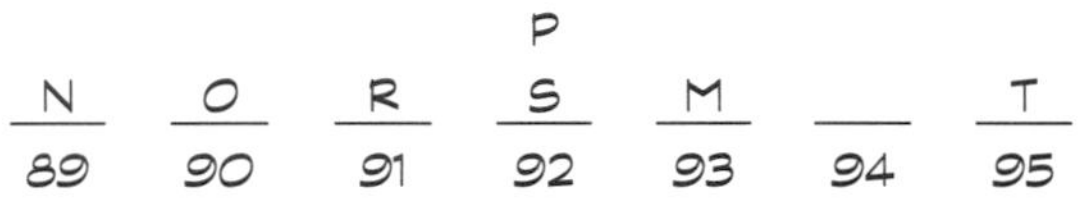

Figure 9.28

The correct answer *could be true*. That's choice (A). With P in '92, O, P, and T are all kept apart by more than a year, meaning that they can share a specialty. The four wrong answers *must be false*. The "if" condition puts P and M in consecutive years, meaning that they cannot share a specialty. That eliminates choice (B). Moreover, with P hired in '92, choices (C), (D), and (E) are all impossible.

---

[11] PrepTest 35, Sec. 3, Q 22

23. (E)

If Paton and Madison have a specialty in common, then which one of the following must be true?

(A) Nilsson does not share a specialty with Paton.
(B) Exactly one professor was hired in 1990.
(C) Exactly one professor was hired in 1991.
(D) Exactly two professors were hired in each of two years.
(E) Paton was hired at least one year before Sarkis.[12]

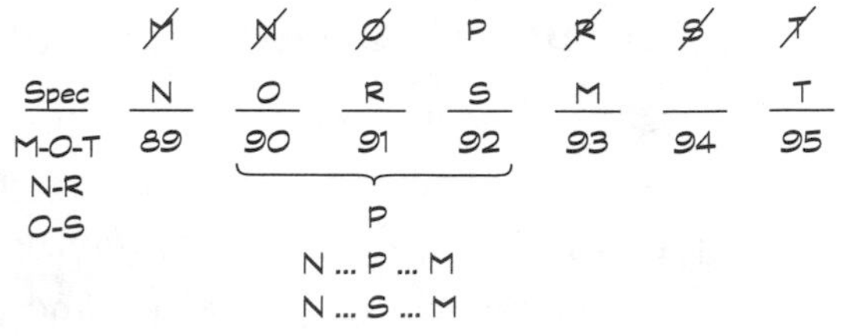

	N̶	M̶	O̶	P	R̶	S̶	T̶
Spec	N	O	R	S	M		T
M-O-T	89	90	91	92	93	94	95
N-R							
O-S			P				

P

N … P … M

N … S … M

Figure 9.29

This is the toughest of the "if" conditions. It requires applying the restriction that comes from having a specialty in common. If P and M share a specialty, they cannot have been hired in the same or consecutive years. That means that, for this question, P was hired in either '90 or '91.

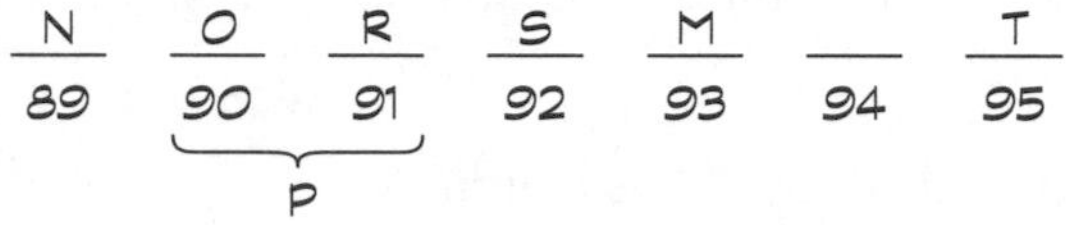

N	O	R	S	M		T
89	90	91	92	93	94	95

P

Figure 9.30

The correct answer *must be true*, leading you to choice (E). If P was hired in '90 or '91, S was hired later. Note that choices (B) and (C) could be false. P could be hired in either '90 or '91. Likewise with choice (A): If hired in '91, P could share a specialty with N, who was hired in '89. Choice (D) makes a statement that is always false in this game, regardless of when P was hired.

That game has derailed many test takers over the years. Students who try to impose a one-entity-per-space requirement where none exists get confused and frustrated and never make the deductions that wind up precisely determining six of the seven entities' positions. By training yourself to recognize when the test makers have departed from their usual modus operandi, you'll be at a double advantage. First, by not insisting on a restriction that doesn't exist, you'll manage the Deductions step effectively. Second, you'll realize that the exceptional situation (here, the fact that P must be the second professor hired during one of the years) must be the focus of at least some of the questions. The test makers have no reason to create unusual situations unless they want to reward the test takers who can notice and correctly analyze them.

Another way the test makers present Sequencing actions with uneven numbers is through Selection-Sequencing Hybrid games. There, they ask you to select some number of entities and then arrange those that you've selected in order. This has a different effect on the game than what you saw in the Professor Hiring scenario. Once you've selected your entities, the test makers will likely have you sequence them in routine one-per-space fashion. Instead of having the possibility of having an empty slot or a slot with multiple entities, you'll have to consider the impact of certain entities being included or excluded in the selection process. I'll take you through an example of such a game in the chapter on Hybrids.

---

[12] PrepTest 35, Sec. 3, Q 23

Strict Sequencing with Conditional Rules

You've already seen how the test can use conditional formal logic rules in Loose Sequencing games (the Bread Truck Deliveries setup featured them). In recent years, formal logic has appeared more often in Loose Sequencing games than it has in their Strict Sequencing counterparts. Still, it's worth taking the time to see how the test makers use conditional rules in Strict Sequencing games. The following game, which first appeared on the June 2003 exam, is a great example.

I'll let you try the game on your own and then review it in its entirety after you're done. Give yourself eight and a half minutes to try the game and all of its questions. If you find that you're struggling, stop and review Steps 1–4 of the Kaplan Method. Once you're sure that you've got a good Master Sketch and an understanding of the how the game works, go back and try the question set again.

> Charlie makes a soup by adding exactly six kinds of foods—
> kale, lentils, mushrooms, onions, tomatoes, and zucchini—to a
> broth, one food at a time. No food is added more than once.
> The order in which Charlie adds the foods to the broth must be
> consistent with the following:
>> If the mushrooms are added third, then the lentils are
>> added last.
>> If the zucchini is added first, then the lentils are added at some
>> time before the onions.
>> Neither the tomatoes nor the kale is added fifth.
>> The mushrooms are added at some time before the
>> tomatoes or the kale, but not before both.

1. Which one of the following could be the order in which the foods are added to the broth?

    (A) kale, mushrooms, onions, lentils, tomatoes, zucchini
    (B) kale, zucchini, mushrooms, tomatoes, lentils, onions
    (C) lentils, mushrooms, zucchini, kale, onions, tomatoes
    (D) zucchini, lentils, kale, mushrooms, onions, tomatoes
    (E) zucchini, tomatoes, onions, mushrooms, lentils, kale

2. Which one of the following foods CANNOT be added first?

    (A) kale
    (B) lentils
    (C) mushrooms
    (D) onions
    (E) tomatoes

3. If the lentils are added last, then which one of the following must be true?

    (A) At least one of the foods is added at some time before the zucchini.
    (B) At least two of the foods are added at some time before the kale.
    (C) The mushrooms are added third.
    (D) The zucchini is added third.
    (E) The tomatoes are added fourth.

4. Which one of the following could be an accurate partial ordering of the foods added to the broth?

    (A) lentils: second; mushrooms: third
    (B) mushrooms: fourth; lentils: last
    (C) onions: second; mushrooms: fifth
    (D) zucchini: first; lentils: last
    (E) zucchini: first; mushrooms: second

5. If the zucchini is added first, then which one of the following CANNOT be true?

    (A) The kale is added second.
    (B) The tomatoes are added second.
    (C) The lentils are added third.
    (D) The lentils are added fourth.
    (E) The onions are added fourth.[13]

---

[13] PrepTest 40, Sec. 2, Game 1, Qs 1–5

Explanations

STEPS 1 AND 2: **Overview and Sketch**

You're able to identify this as a Sequencing game right from the start. The entities—the six kinds of foods—will be added to the broth one at a time, with restrictions on the order in which they're added. It's an easy task to picture. There's a big pot of water on the stove, and six kinds of food are being prepared and arrayed in bowls in front of you. The task is clear: What goes into the pot first, second, third, and so on?

Up to this point, the game could be either Strict or Loose Sequencing. But a quick check of the rules tells you that they definitely implicate specific slots in the order. The first, third, fifth, and last spots are all mentioned explicitly. So a Strict Sequencing framework is in order.

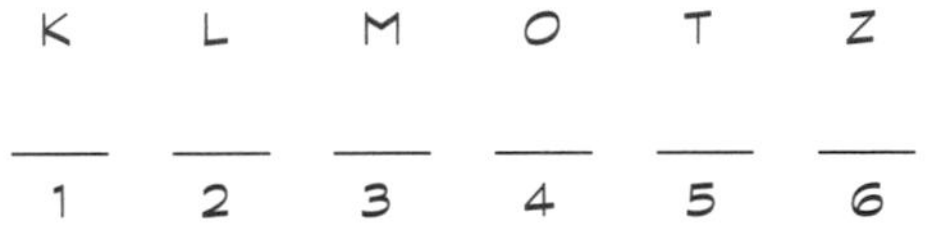

$$\begin{array}{cccccc} K & L & M & O & T & Z \\ \underline{} & \underline{} & \underline{} & \underline{} & \underline{} & \underline{} \\ 1 & 2 & 3 & 4 & 5 & 6 \end{array}$$

Figure 9.31

STEP 3: **Rules**

Here's where things start to seem a little out of the ordinary. The rules themselves aren't strange. It's just that, with the exception of Rule 3, you don't normally associate them with Strict Sequencing.

Rules 1 and 2 are formal logic statements. You know that their conditional nature won't allow you to build them directly into the sketch, so record each, along with its contrapositive, below the framework slots.

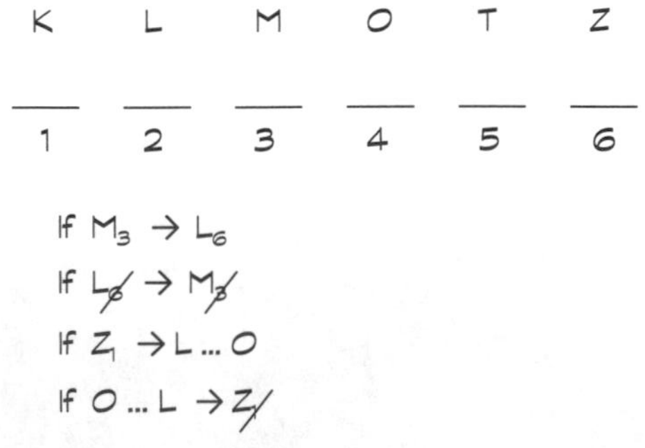

$$\begin{array}{cccccc} K & L & M & O & T & Z \\ \underline{} & \underline{} & \underline{} & \underline{} & \underline{} & \underline{} \\ 1 & 2 & 3 & 4 & 5 & 6 \end{array}$$

If $M_3 \rightarrow L_6$

If $\cancel{L_6} \rightarrow \cancel{M_3}$

If $Z_1 \rightarrow L \ldots O$

If $O \ldots L \rightarrow \cancel{Z_1}$

Figure 9.32

Make sure you got the negation correct for Rule 2. In a game where each item goes into the pot "one food at a time," negating "the lentils are added at some time before the onions" means that the onions would have to be added at some time before the lentils.

Rule 3 is a standard negative restriction. Record it beneath space 5 in the framework.

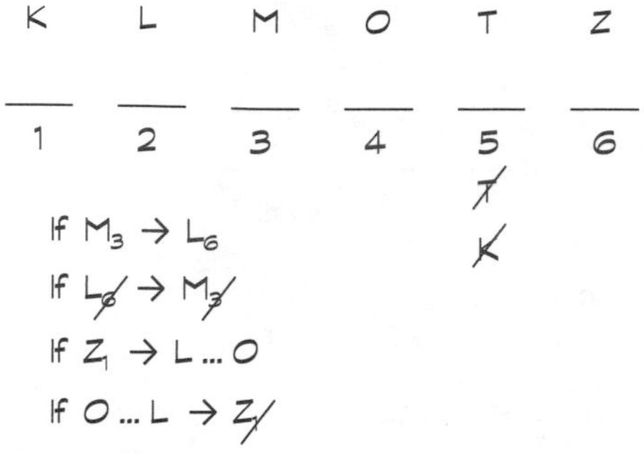

$$K \quad L \quad M \quad O \quad T \quad Z$$

$$\overline{}_1 \quad \overline{}_2 \quad \overline{}_3 \quad \overline{}_4 \quad \overline{}_5 \quad \overline{}_6$$

$$\cancel{T}$$
$$\cancel{K}$$

If $M_3 \rightarrow L_6$
If $\cancel{L_6} \rightarrow \cancel{M_3}$
If $Z_1 \rightarrow L \ldots O$
If $O \ldots L \rightarrow \cancel{Z_1}$

Figure 9.32A

Rule 4 presents two alternatives. The mushrooms must be added either after the tomatoes and before the kale, or after the kale and before the tomatoes. Again, there's no way to put this firmly into the sketch (there are just too many open slots), so record the options beneath the framework. You can add notes below the framework indicating that the mushrooms can never be first or sixth, but you can't determine affirmatively where they will go.

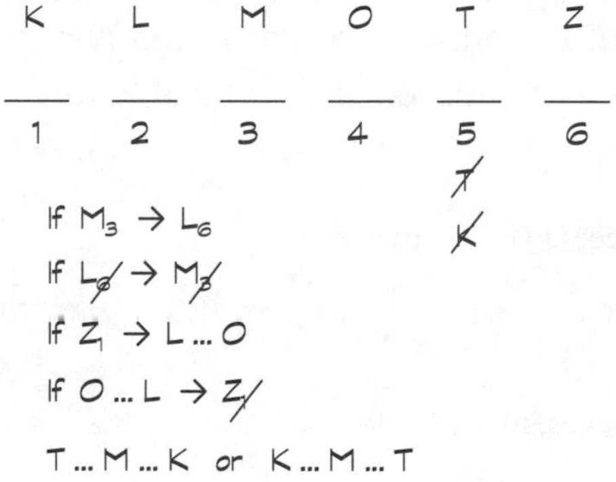

$$K \quad L \quad M \quad O \quad T \quad Z$$

$$\overline{}_1 \quad \overline{}_2 \quad \overline{}_3 \quad \overline{}_4 \quad \overline{}_5 \quad \overline{}_6$$

$$\cancel{T}$$
$$\cancel{K}$$

If $M_3 \rightarrow L_6$
If $\cancel{L_6} \rightarrow \cancel{M_3}$
If $Z_1 \rightarrow L \ldots O$
If $O \ldots L \rightarrow \cancel{Z_1}$

T ... M ... K   or   K ... M ... T

Figure 9.33

You may have been tempted to create dual Limited Options sketches based on Rule 4. But ask yourself what you'd be able to do with such sketches. Rule 4 doesn't trigger any of the other restrictions here (at least until you have more certainty about the mushrooms' placement), so the "or" in the diagram will serve to remind you that one of these two patterns must apply.

STEP 4: Deductions

In Strict Sequencing, the strongest deductions derive from Established Entities and Blocks of Entities. You have no Established Entities in this game, and the only blocks you're given are too loose to allow for any additional headway in the sketch. Sometimes when you have multiple conditional statements, they combine, with the result of one triggering the other. But not here.

Rules 1 and 2 cover entirely different entities. Your Master Sketch is just the framework with the rules diagrammed below.

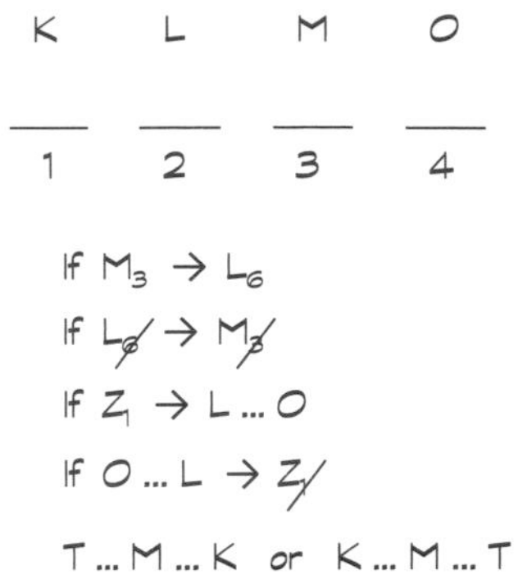

K   L   M   O   T   Z

—   —   —   —   —   —
1   2   3   4   5   6

If M₃ → L₆

If L̸ → M̸

If Z₁ → L … O

If O … L → Z̸

T … M … K or K … M … T

Figure 9.34

STEP 5: Questions

What can you expect from the questions in this game? The question set is a routine collection: an Acceptability question, a Partial Acceptability question, two "If" questions, and one "Non-If" question. But you should expect that the "If" questions will trigger one of the two conditional rules. So will at least some of the answer choices in the Acceptability-based questions. The "Non-"If" question, on the other hand, you should be able to answer using Rules 3 or 4.

1. **(D)**

Which one of the following could be the order in which the foods are added to the broth?

(A)   kale, mushrooms, onions, lentils, tomatoes, zucchini

(B)   kale, zucchini, mushrooms, tomatoes, lentils, onions

(C)   lentils, mushrooms, zucchini, kale, onions, tomatoes

(D)   zucchini, lentils, kale, mushrooms, onions, tomatoes

(E)   zucchini, tomatoes, onions, mushrooms, lentils, kale[14]

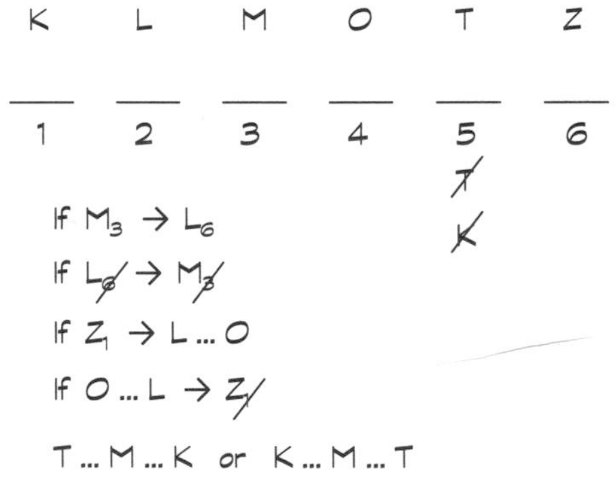

K   L   M   O   T   Z

—   —   —   —   —   —
1   2   3   4   5   6

If M₃ → L₆

If L̸ → M̸

If Z₁ → L … O

If O … L → Z̸

T … M … K or K … M … T

Figure 9.35

Approach this Acceptability question as you would any other, by using the rules to eliminate violators. Given that Rules 1 and 2 will only apply in certain conditions, though, it will be easier to start with Rules 3 and 4. Rule 3 eliminates choice (A), which has tomatoes added fifth. Rule 4 knocks out choice (C), where mushrooms are found before both tomatoes and kale. With those two choices out of the way, it's easier to check the conditional rules. To check Rule 1, look for an answer in which mushrooms are added third. That's only true in choice (B). Since choice (B) doesn't have lentils in the sixth spot, it breaks Rule 1. Get rid of it. Both of choices (D) and (E) have zucchini in the first spot. That implicates Rule 2 and requires that lentils precede onions into the broth. Choice (E) reverses the order of lentils and onion and breaks the rule. Choice (D) complies with the rule and is correct.

When a game offers you a mix of concrete and conditional rules, attack Acceptability questions using the more definite rules first. This makes it easier to spot the choices containing the conditions that trigger the formal logic.

2. **(C)**

Which one of the following foods CANNOT be added first?

(A) kale
(B) lentils
(C) mushrooms
(D) onions
(E) tomatoes[15]

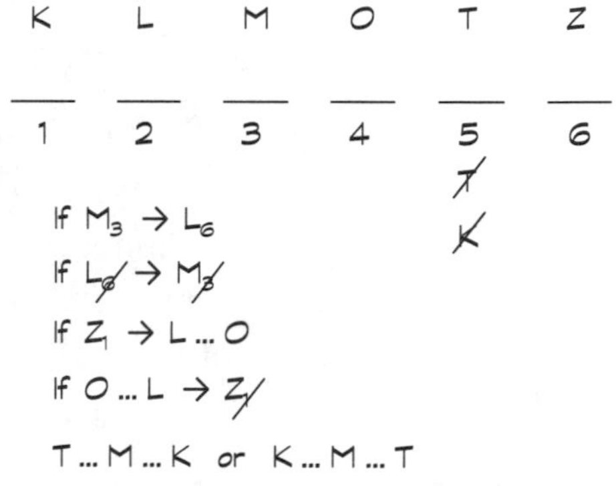

$$K \quad L \quad M \quad O \quad T \quad Z$$

$$\underline{} \quad \underline{} \quad \underline{} \quad \underline{} \quad \underline{} \quad \underline{}$$

$$1 \quad 2 \quad 3 \quad 4 \quad 5 \quad 6$$

If $M_3 \rightarrow L_6$

If $\cancel{L_6} \rightarrow \cancel{M_3}$

If $Z_1 \rightarrow L \ldots O$

If $O \ldots L \rightarrow \cancel{Z}$

$T \ldots M \ldots K$ or $K \ldots M \ldots T$

Figure 9.36

Since this question lacks an "if" condition, it's unlikely to involve either of the conditional rules. Since it involves the first space, there's no way it can involve Rule 3. Go directly to Rule 4 and get your answer. The food that can never be added first is mushrooms, which always follow either tomatoes or kale into the broth. Choice (C) is correct.

3. **(A)**

If the lentils are added last, then which one of the following must be true?

(A) At least one of the foods is added at some time before the zucchini.
(B) At least two of the foods are added at some time before the kale.
(C) The mushrooms are added third.
(D) The zucchini is added third.
(E) The tomatoes are added fourth.[16]

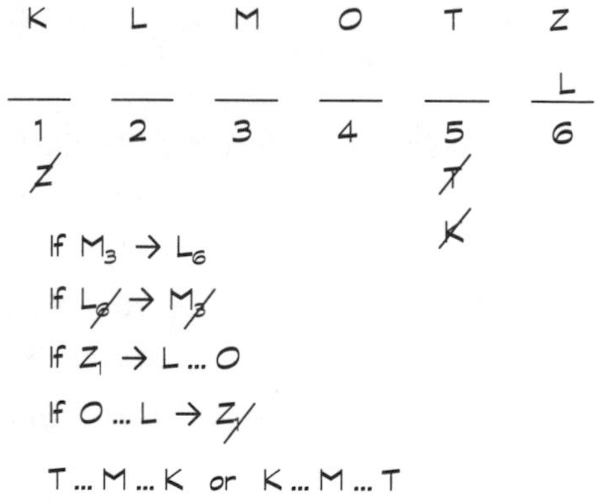

$$K \quad L \quad M \quad O \quad T \quad Z$$

$$\underline{} \quad \underline{} \quad \underline{} \quad \underline{} \quad \underline{} \quad \underline{L}$$

$$1 \quad 2 \quad 3 \quad 4 \quad 5 \quad 6$$

$\cancel{Z}$ ... $\cancel{T}$

$\cancel{K}$

If $M_3 \rightarrow L_6$

If $\cancel{L_6} \rightarrow \cancel{M_3}$

If $Z_1 \rightarrow L \ldots O$

If $O \ldots L \rightarrow \cancel{Z}$

$T \ldots M \ldots K$ or $K \ldots M \ldots T$

Figure 9.37

Seeing the "if" in the question stem, your instinct at this point should be to draw a mini-sketch like the one next to the question. You won't get far, though, before you realize that the "if"

---

[15] PrepTest 40, Sec. 2, Q 2
[16] PrepTest 40, Sec. 2, Q 3

condition here is simply meant to trigger Rule 2. As soon as you make L the final ingredient in the soup, you know that O must precede it. That's the sufficient condition in Rule 2's contrapositive.

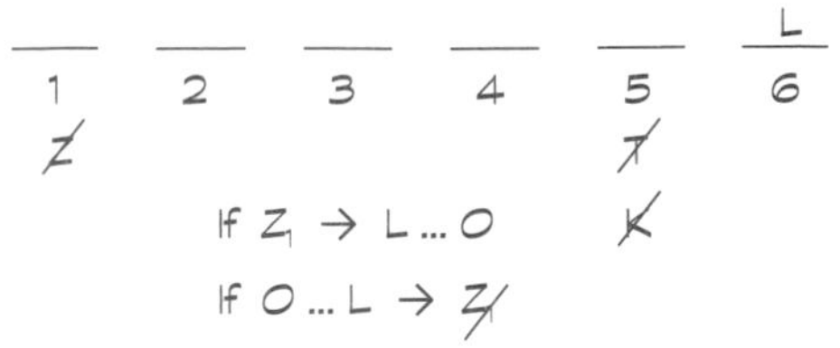

$$\underset{1}{\underline{}} \quad \underset{2}{\underline{}} \quad \underset{3}{\underline{}} \quad \underset{4}{\underline{}} \quad \underset{5}{\underline{}} \quad \underset{6}{\underline{L}}$$

$$\underset{1}{\cancel{Z}} \qquad\qquad\qquad \underset{5}{\cancel{\nearrow}}$$

If $Z_1 \rightarrow$ L ... O $\qquad \cancel{K}$

If O ... L $\rightarrow \cancel{Z}$

Figure 9.38

The result is that zucchini cannot be the first ingredient. That means that choice (A) *must be true*, which makes it the correct answer. Since there's nothing else that you can conclude from the "if" condition, none of the four remaining choices must be true.

4. **(C)**

    Which one of the following could be an accurate partial ordering of the foods added to the broth?

    (A) lentils: second; mushrooms: third
    (B) mushrooms: fourth; lentils: last
    (C) onions: second; mushrooms: fifth
    (D) zucchini: first; lentils: last
    (E) zucchini: first; mushrooms: second[17]

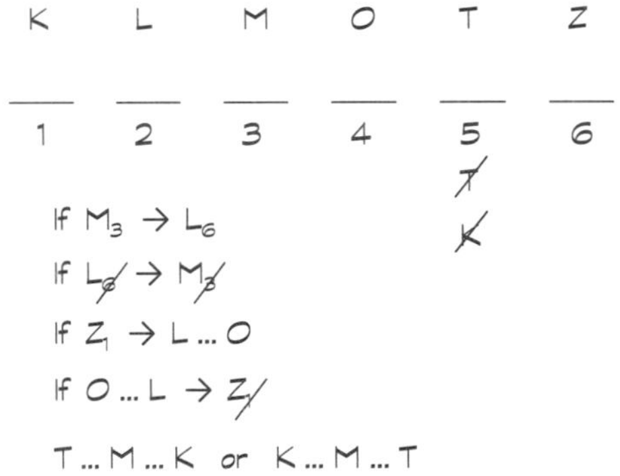

K L M O T Z

$$\underset{1}{\underline{}} \quad \underset{2}{\underline{}} \quad \underset{3}{\underline{}} \quad \underset{4}{\underline{}} \quad \underset{5}{\underline{}} \quad \underset{6}{\underline{}}$$

$$\underset{5}{\cancel{\nearrow}}$$
$$\cancel{K}$$

If $M_3 \rightarrow L_6$

If $\cancel{L_6} \rightarrow \cancel{M_3}$

If $Z_1 \rightarrow$ L ... O

If O ... L $\rightarrow \cancel{Z}$

T ... M ... K or K ... M ... T

Figure 9.39

You can tackle this Partial Acceptability question just as you would a regular Acceptability question, indeed, just as you tackled question 1. Use the rules and eliminate the violators, remembering that you can only see two of the spaces in any of the answer choices this time. Start with the most concrete rule, Rule 3. Only one of the answers—choice (C)—mentions the fifth spot, and it doesn't have kale or tomatoes there. So Rule 3's not a problem for any of the answers. Rule 4 is, though. Choice (E) has mushrooms second. That's okay, provided that either tomatoes or kale is first. But choice (E) has lentils being added first. It violates Rule 4's placement of mushrooms between tomatoes and kale. So does choice (B), albeit in a subtler way. With mushrooms added fourth, either tomatoes or kale must come afterwards. Unfortunately, you know from Rule 3 that tomatoes and kale are excluded from space 5 and choice (B) blocks them out of space 6, too, by placing lentils there. That leaves choices (A), (C), and (D). Two of them must violate the conditional rules. Look no further than choice (A) to find the choice that violates Rule 1; it has mushrooms third and lentils first, instead of sixth. It's choice (D)

---

[17] PrepTest 40, Sec. 2, Q 4

that violates Rule 2; it has zucchini as the first vegetable but places lentils in sixth place, when the rule requires onions to follow lentils. Only choice (C) remains. It's the correct answer.

5.   **(D)**

If the zucchini is added first, then which one of the following CANNOT be true?

(A)   The kale is added second.
(B)   The tomatoes are added second.
(C)   The lentils are added third.
(D)   The lentils are added fourth.
(E)   The onions are added fourth.[18]

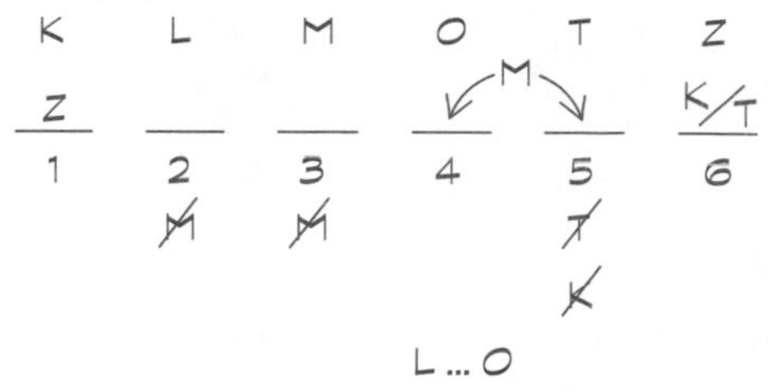

Figure 9.40

At this point, you could have expected it. The final question's "if" condition will, naturally, trigger one of the conditional rules. As soon as you see zucchini being added first, you know you're dealing with Rule 2.

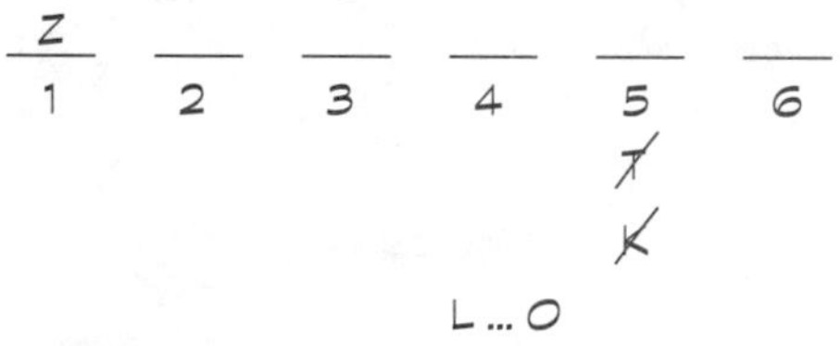

Figure 9.41

Did that make you realize that you were, by extension, dealing with Rule 1, as well? Since lentils must precede onions pursuant to Rule 2, lentils can't be in space 6. That triggers the contrapositive of Rule 1. With lentils not in space 6, mushrooms can't take space 3.

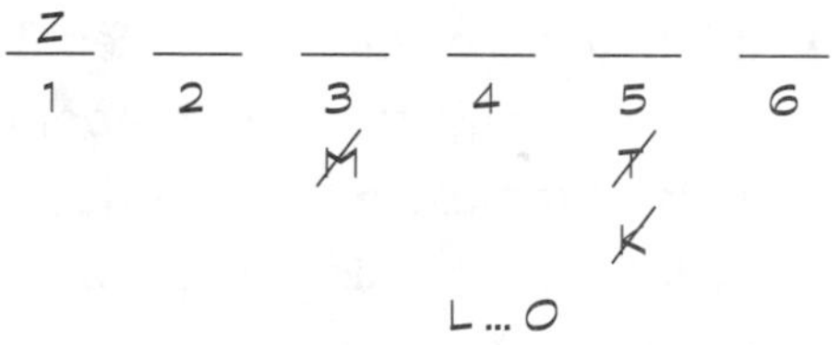

Figure 9.42

Nor can mushrooms take space 2. Rule 4 requires that the mushrooms be added in between the tomatoes and kale. With zucchini in space 1, there's no way to abide by Rule 4 with the mushrooms in space 2.

---

[18] PrepTest 40, Sec. 2, Q 5

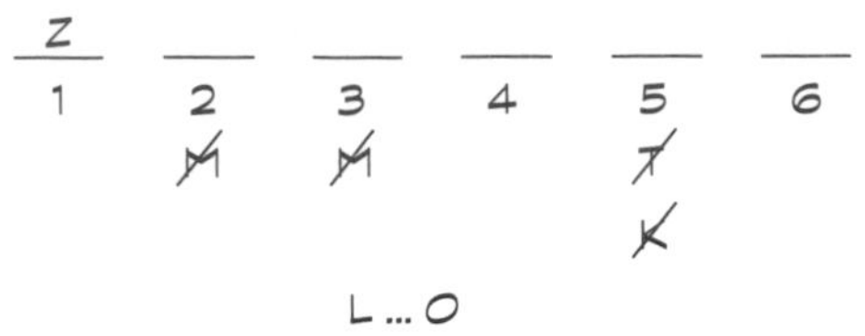

Figure 9.43

So the mushrooms will take either space 4 or space 5, and either tomatoes or kale—one of which must follow the mushrooms—will take space 6. Those two foods are excluded from space 5 by Rule 3.

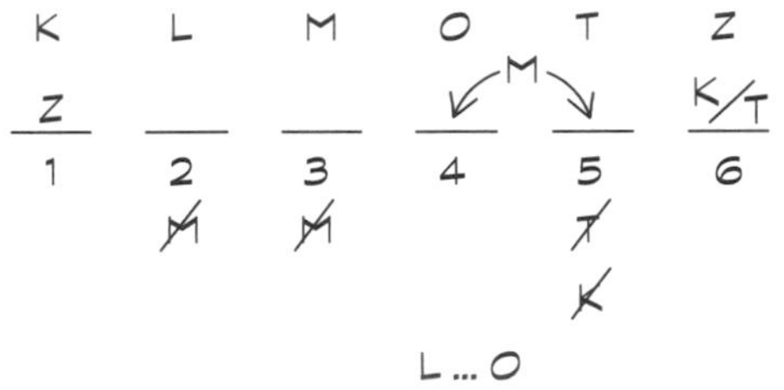

Figure 9.44

There's a little wiggle room left for lentils, onions, and whichever of tomatoes and kale isn't in space 6, but this is enough information to answer the question. Remember: When you've pushed your deductions as far as they'll go, you *always* have enough information to answer the question.

The correct answer *must be false*. Nothing prevents either tomatoes or kale from being added second. So both choice (A) and choice (B) are possible. Eliminate them. In fact, eliminate choice (C) as well, because with either tomatoes or kale added second, lentils would be added third. But slow down on choice (D). In this scenario, adding lentils fourth would mean adding mushrooms fifth. But if tomatoes or kale must follow mushrooms in space 6, then there's no space left for onions to follow lentils, as it must in this question. Choice (D) must be false and is, therefore, the right answer. For the record, onions could be fourth with mushrooms fifth. Nothing is violated by that arrangement, so choice (E) could be true.

That's not a hard game. Indeed, that's the point. Variations aren't difficult just because they're variations. You're less likely to see a Strict Sequencing game that prominently features formal logic rules than to see one without them. If you happen to have one on your test, remember a few takeaways from this game. First, you know how to diagram formal logic and to form the contrapositives of conditional statements. Many of your competitors on test day won't. That's one advantage for you right from the outset. Second, since conditional formal logic rules are only triggered by the presence of their sufficient conditions, use the more concrete, universal rules to eliminate violators first. Then turn to the conditional rules and see which remaining answer choices they apply to. Finally, expect the "If" questions—at least some of them—to trigger the conditional rules. Here, both of them did.

See how it's all coming together? Knowing the standard form that game types take allows you to spot the exceptions. Spotting the exceptions allows you to focus on what the test makers intend to reward or punish by using the unusual rules or limitations. As you progress through the rest of this chapter and the remainder of Part II, keep in mind that you're eliminating any possibility of being thrown off your game by anything out of the ordinary.

I'll show you a couple of extremely rare variations on the Strict Sequencing game type shortly. First, though, I want you to tackle a couple of the hardest Sequencing games out there; one is strict and one loose. They'll show you that if you've taken Part I of this book and the Kaplan Method to heart, you're ready for just about anything.

DIFFICULT SEQUENCING GAMES

On any given administration of the LSAT, the test makers are likely to include one easy game, two of medium difficulty, and one that they intend to be the hardest for all test takers. There's no way to anticipate which types of game they'll use for the various difficulty levels. There have even been tests on which the easiest and hardest games were both Sequencing games. As you try the toughest examples of each game type here and in the remaining chapters of this section, take note of what they all have in common: a lack of concreteness, complexity in the task, and long and tricky wording in either the rules or the questions.

While it's a fact that you're going to see a hard game on test day, your best chance of conquering it will be in recognizing the game type and seeing what makes this particular game more challenging. Including the toughest games in your preparation gives you a psychological edge, too. You'll go in to the test confident that you've seen the worst it can offer and knowing that the same method and strategies allowed you to handle it effectively.

Difficult Strict Sequencing

In chapter 2, you learned to assess the power of rules, distinguishing those that provided a great deal of certainty from those that offered only relative or conditional restrictions. Harder games will nearly always include fewer concrete rules. To compound that inherent difficulty, the test makers can give you more open-ended tasks, leaving more ambiguity in the framework of your sketch. The following game does both, making it a truly challenging Strict Sequencing example. Take your time with this game. I'd rather you spend the time to explore its intricacies than try to rush through it and miss what makes it tough. You'll have the opportunity to do more difficult games under timed conditions in Part III of this book. By the way, this was the third game in the Logic Games section on this test. That's the most common place to find the toughest game, though the test makers have placed the toughest game second or fourth in the section on occasion. Give this one a try. If you are really confused by the setup, check the explanations for Steps 1–4 of the Kaplan Method as they apply here. Then go back and try the questions.

A bakery makes exactly three kinds of cookie—oatmeal, peanut butter, and sugar. Exactly three batches of each kind of cookie are made each week (Monday through Friday) and each batch is made, from start to finish, on a single day. The following conditions apply:

No two batches of the same kind of cookie are made on the same day.

At least one batch of cookies is made on Monday.

The second batch of oatmeal cookies is made on the same day as the first batch of peanut butter cookies.

The second batch of sugar cookies is made on Thursday.

13. Which one of the following could be a complete and accurate list of the days on which the batches of each kind of cookie are made?

   (A)   oatmeal: Monday, Wednesday, Thursday
         peanut butter: Wednesday, Thursday, Friday
         sugar: Monday, Thursday, Friday
   (B)   oatmeal: Monday, Tuesday, Thursday
         peanut butter: Tuesday, Wednesday, Thursday
         sugar: Monday, Wednesday, Thursday
   (C)   oatmeal: Tuesday, Wednesday, Thursday
         peanut butter: Wednesday, Thursday, Friday
         sugar: Tuesday, Thursday, Friday
   (D)   oatmeal: Monday, Tuesday, Thursday
         peanut butter: Monday, Wednesday, Thursday
         sugar: Monday, Thursday, Friday
   (E)   oatmeal: Monday, Thursday, Friday
         peanut butter: Tuesday, Wednesday, Thursday
         sugar: Monday, Thursday, Friday

14. How many of the days, Monday through Friday, are such that at most two batches of cookies could be made on that day?

   (A)   one
   (B)   two
   (C)   three
   (D)   four
   (E)   five

15. If the first batch of peanut butter cookies is made on Tuesday, then each of the following could be true EXCEPT:

   (A)   Two different kinds of cookie have their first batch made on Monday.
   (B)   Two different kinds of cookie have their first batch made on Tuesday.
   (C)   Two different kinds of cookie have their second batch made on Wednesday.
   (D)   Two different kinds of cookie have their second batch made on Thursday.
   (E)   Two different kinds of cookie have their third batch made on Friday.

16. If no batch of cookies is made on Wednesday, then which one of the following must be true?

   (A)   Exactly three batches of cookies are made on Tuesday.
   (B)   Exactly three batches of cookies are made on Friday.
   (C)   At least two batches of cookies are made on Monday.
   (D)   At least two batches of cookies are made on Thursday.
   (E)   Fewer batches of cookies are made on Monday than on Tuesday.

17. If the number of batches made on Friday is exactly one, then which one of the following could be true?

   (A)   The first batch of sugar cookies is made on Monday.
   (B)   The first batch of oatmeal cookies is made on Tuesday.
   (C)   The third batch of oatmeal cookies is made on Friday.
   (D)   The first batch of peanut butter cookies is made on Wednesday.
   (E)   The second batch of peanut butter cookies is made on Tuesday.

18. If one kind of cookie's first batch is made on the same day as another kind of cookie's third batch, then which one of the following could be false?

   (A)   At least one batch of cookies is made on each of the five days.
   (B)   At least two batches of cookies are made on Wednesday.
   (C)   Exactly one batch of cookies is made on Monday.
   (D)   Exactly two batches of cookies are made on Tuesday.
   (E)   Exactly one batch of cookies is made on Friday.[19]

---

[19] PrepTest 42, Sec. 1, Game 3, Qs 13–18

Explanations

STEPS 1 AND 2: **Overview and Sketch**

Your task is to lay out the weekly baking schedule for cookies made at a bakery. The framework, then, is familiar from the real world and any number of other Strict Sequencing games.

$$\underline{\text{M}} \quad \underline{\text{Tu}} \quad \underline{\text{W}} \quad \underline{\text{Th}} \quad \underline{\text{F}}$$

Figure 9.45

The first complicating factor you encounter in this game is in the setup's description of the entities. Instead of nine different kinds of cookies, you're asked to schedule three batches each of three kinds of cookies. You can start to take control of the task by writing the entities out like this:

$$O_1 \ O_2 \ O_3 \ P_1 \ P_2 \ P_3 \ S_1 \ S_2 \ S_3$$

$$\underline{\text{M}} \quad \underline{\text{Tu}} \quad \underline{\text{W}} \quad \underline{\text{Th}} \quad \underline{\text{F}}$$

Figure 9.46

Looking at the beginnings of your sketch reveals the second complicating factor. Like the Professor Hiring game you saw earlier in this chapter, you're going to have some spaces in your sequence with more than one entity. More importantly, there's nothing requiring you to schedule a batch every day. The bakery may have days off. Don't impose limitations where none exist.

STEP 3: **Rules**

Rule 1 tells you that you can't bake two batches of the same kind of cookie on the same day. Just note that next to your entity list.

$$O_1 \ O_2 \ O_3 \ P_1 \ P_2 \ P_3 \ S_1 \ S_2 \ S_3$$

Max.
1 per type per day

$$\underline{\text{M}} \quad \underline{\text{Tu}} \quad \underline{\text{W}} \quad \underline{\text{Th}} \quad \underline{\text{F}}$$

Figure 9.47

Rule 2 tells you to include at least one batch of cookies on Monday. If you hadn't caught the fact that there could be days without any batches scheduled, this rule should have put you on alert.

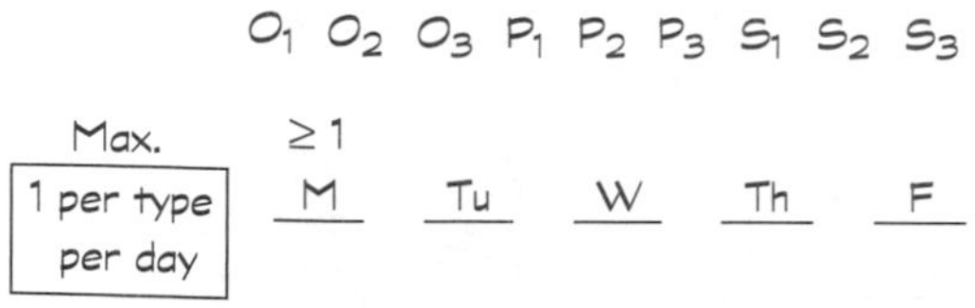

O_1 O_2 O_3 P_1 P_2 P_3 S_1 S_2 S_3

Max.	≥1				
1 per type per day	M	Tu	W	Th	F

Figure 9.48

Rule 3 creates a Block of Entities. O_2 and P_1 will be scheduled for the same day. I'll have you come back in Step 4 to think about how this rule interacts with Rule 1.

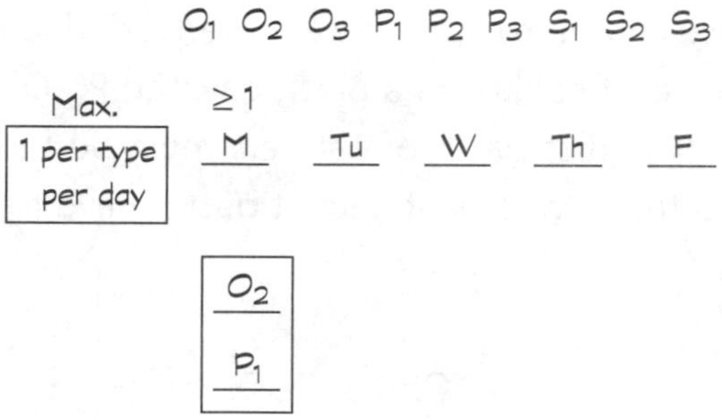

O_1 O_2 O_3 P_1 P_2 P_3 S_1 S_2 S_3

Max.	≥1				
1 per type per day	M	Tu	W	Th	F

O_2

P_1

Figure 9.49

Rule 4, thankfully, gives you an Established Entity. Put this restriction right in the framework.

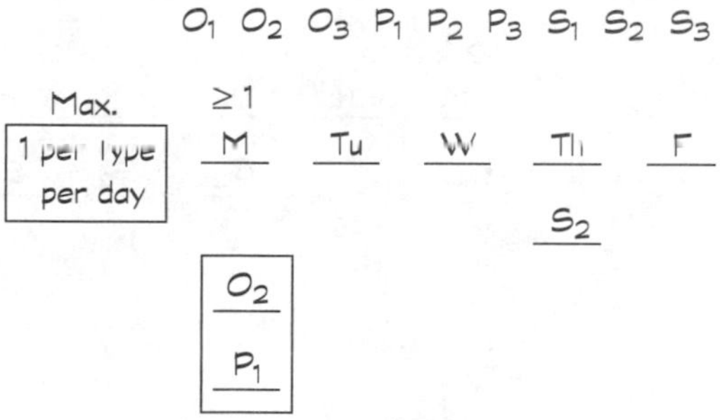

O_1 O_2 O_3 P_1 P_2 P_3 S_1 S_2 S_3

Max.	≥1				
1 per type per day	M	Tu	W	Th	F
				S_2	

O_2

P_1

Figure 9.50

At this point, it may seem as if you have six floaters, since only three of the batches have been cited in the rules. But that's not quite true. Because Rule 1 limits all batches of the same kind of cookie, you actually have some guidance here about all of the cookie batches you need to schedule. That will become even clearer in the Deductions step.

STEP 4: Deductions

Starting, as always with the most concrete restriction, you can add one more Established Entity into your sketch. Since S_2 is on Thursday, S_3 has to be on Friday.

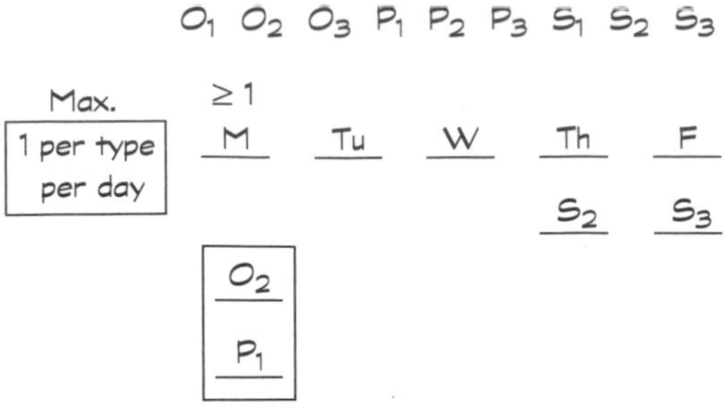

$$O_1 \quad O_2 \quad O_3 \quad P_1 \quad P_2 \quad P_3 \quad S_1 \quad S_2 \quad S_3$$

Max. 1 per type per day	≥ 1				
	M	Tu	W	Th	F
				S_2	S_3

$$\boxed{\begin{array}{c} O_2 \\ \hline P_1 \end{array}}$$

Figure 9.51

As I hinted, Rules 1 and 3 also combine to provide a powerful deduction. Since you cannot bake two batches of the same kind of cookie on a given day, the P_1–O_2 block can only be placed on Tuesday or Wednesday. The first batch of oatmeal must be baked before the second, of course, and the second and third batches of peanut butter have to follow the first. This leads to a Limited Options scenario:

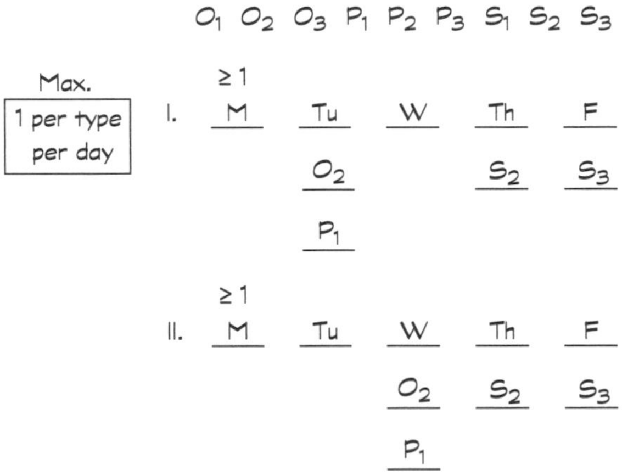

$$O_1 \quad O_2 \quad O_3 \quad P_1 \quad P_2 \quad P_3 \quad S_1 \quad S_2 \quad S_3$$

Max. 1 per type per day		≥ 1				
	I.	M	Tu	W	Th	F
			O_2		S_2	S_3
			P_1			

		≥ 1				
	II.	M	Tu	W	Th	F
				O_2	S_2	S_3
				P_1		

Figure 9.52

With a game this open and complex, you can be sure it's worth your time to explore the deductions thoroughly. In Option I, you know for sure that the bakery will make O_1 on Monday, while P_2 and P_3 will be baked sometime between Wednesday and Friday.

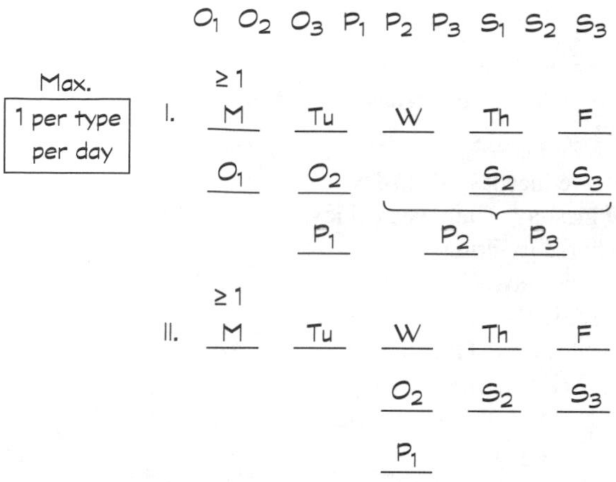

O_1 O_2 O_3 P_1 P_2 P_3 S_1 S_2 S_3

Max.
1 per type per day

I.
≥1

M	Tu	W	Th	F
O_1	O_2		S_2	S_3
	P_1	P_2	P_3	

II.
≥1

M	Tu	W	Th	F
	O_2	S_2	S_3	
	P_1			

Figure 9.53

Option II, on the other hand, locks down all three peanut butter batches. Since you know that the bakery makes at least one batch of cookies on Monday, you can be sure that S_1, O_1, or both occur that day. The bakery will make O_3 on either Thursday or Friday.

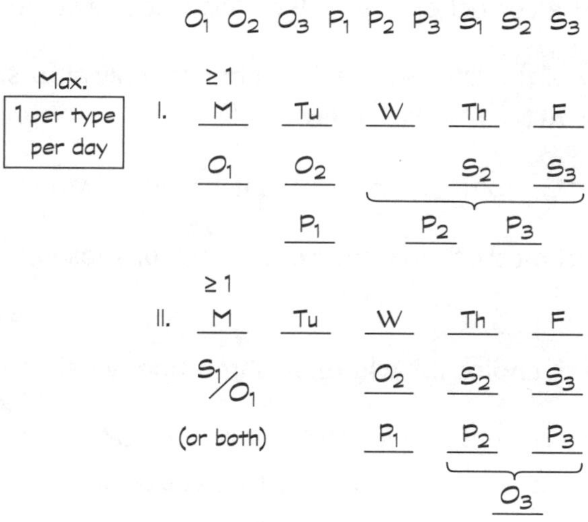

O_1 O_2 O_3 P_1 P_2 P_3 S_1 S_2 S_3

Max.
1 per type per day

I.
≥1

M	Tu	W	Th	F
O_1	O_2		S_2	S_3
	P_1	P_2	P_3	

II.
≥1

M	Tu	W	Th	F
S_1/O_1		O_2	S_2	S_3
(or both)		P_1	P_2	P_3

O_3

Figure 9.54

So it turns out that you have at least some information about all nine cookie batches that you need to schedule. In fact, with the Limited Options sketches in place and all of your deductions accurately reflected in them, the question set turns out not to be too bad after all.

STEP 5: Questions

The question set here contains an Acceptability question (that will be no problem for you at this point), a Minimum/Maximum-type question, and four "if" questions. Remember our discussion of "If" questions in Limited option games from chapter 5. The new "if" conditions will almost certainly put you into one option or the other. Use that to take on these questions more efficiently.

13. **(A)**

Which one of the following could be a complete and accurate list of the days on which the batches of each kind of cookie are made?

(A)   oatmeal: Monday, Wednesday, Thursday
       peanut butter: Wednesday, Thursday, Friday
       sugar: Monday, Thursday, Friday
(B)   oatmeal: Monday, Tuesday, Thursday
       peanut butter: Tuesday, Wednesday, Thursday
       sugar: Monday, Wednesday, Thursday
(C)   oatmeal: Tuesday, Wednesday, Thursday
       peanut butter: Wednesday, Thursday, Friday
       sugar: Tuesday, Thursday, Friday
(D)   oatmeal: Monday, Tuesday, Thursday
       peanut butter: Monday, Wednesday, Thursday
       sugar: Monday, Thursday, Friday
(E)   oatmeal: Monday, Thursday, Friday
       peanut butter: Tuesday, Wednesday, Thursday
       sugar: Monday, Thursday, Friday[20]

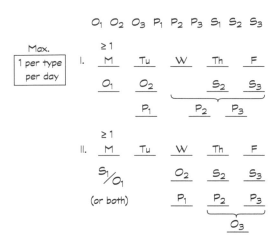

Figure 9.55

This is a routine Acceptability question. As always, use the rules to eliminate those answers that contain violations. The correct answer will be the last one standing.

Rule 1 isn't broken in any of the choices. Scanning horizontally across each line, you never see the same day mentioned twice for any kind of cookie.

Rule 2 gets rid of choice (C). None of the batches is baked on Monday in this answer.

Rule 3 knocks out both choice (D) and choice (E). Both of those choices have P_1 and O_2 on different days.

Finally, Rule 4 takes care of choice (B), where S_2 is improperly baked on Wednesday.

That leaves choice (A), the correct answer. Did you notice that choice (A) matches Option II of your Master Sketch? That's a good confirmation that you're on the right track with this tricky game.

---

[20] PrepTest 42, Sec. 1, Q 13

14. **(A)**

How many of the days, Monday through Friday, are such that at most two batches of cookies could be made on that day?

(A)   one
(B)   two
(C)   three
(D)   four
(E)   five[21]

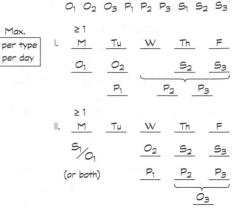

Figure 9.56

Make sure you understand what any question stem is calling for. Here, the correct answer is the number of days on which it's *impossible* to bake three batches of cookies. The answer choices, of course, range from one through five, since there are five days in the bakery schedule. Take a look at Option II. There, you can see that Thursday and Friday are days on which all three kinds of cookies can be made. Eliminate choices (D) and (E). In fact, eliminate choice (C) as well. If you have the bakery make S_1 on Wednesday, there's another day on which it can bake three batches. Now, the only question is whether Tuesday is a day that can have all three kinds of cookies. Option I shows that it is. You can have the bakery make S_1 on Tuesday in that option. Eliminate choice (B). Monday turns out to be the only day on which you must bake at most two batches of cookies, making choice (A) correct. The earliest you can bake P_1 is on Tuesday, although that's moot at this point, since the test makers did not include "zero" among the answer choices.

15. **(C)**

If the first batch of peanut butter cookies is made on Tuesday, then each of the following could be true EXCEPT:

(A)   Two different kinds of cookie have their first batch made on Monday.
(B)   Two different kinds of cookie have their first batch made on Tuesday.
(C)   Two different kinds of cookie have their second batch made on Wednesday.
(D)   Two different kinds of cookie have their second batch made on Thursday.
(E)   Two different kinds of cookie have their third batch made on Friday.[22]

I.

M	Tu	W	Th	F
O_1	O_2		S_2	S_3
	P_1		P_2	P_3

Figure 9.57

21 PrepTest 42, Sec. 1, Q 14

22 PrepTest 42, Sec. 1, Q 15

The "if" for this question lands you squarely in Option I. There's no need to redraw or add anything. Remember, though, to characterize the answer choices before you evaluate them. The four wrong answers here *could be true*. That means that the correct answer *must be false*.

There's no problem with choice (A). S_1 could be baked on Monday along with O_1. Eliminate it.

Choice (B) is acceptable as well. It just means that S_1 is baked on Tuesday. This choice could be true so it's wrong.

Choice (C), however, is impossible. In Option I, O_2 is on Tuesday and S_2 is on Thursday. Only P_2 could go on Wednesday. Choice (C) is the correct answer.

Choices (D) and (E) *could*, of course, *be true*. In Option I, both P_2 and S_2 could be baked on Thursday, and any of the third cookie batches could be baked on Friday.

16. **(D)**

If no batch of cookies is made on Wednesday, then which one of the following must be true?

(A)   Exactly three batches of cookies are made on Tuesday.
(B)   Exactly three batches of cookies are made on Friday.
(C)   At least two batches of cookies are made on Monday.
(D)   At least two batches of cookies are made on Thursday.
(E)   Fewer batches of cookies are made on Monday than on Tuesday.[23]

I.

M	Tu	W	Th	F
O_1	O_2		S_2	S_3
	P_1		P_2	P_3

Figure 9.58

This question stem's "if" condition puts you in Option I. (In Option II, remember, cookies have to be baked on Wednesday.) The correct answer here *must be true*. In Option I, the bakery has to make P_1 and O_2 on Tuesday, so choice (D) fits the bill. All four of the wrong answers offer statements that *could be false* in Option I.

17. **(A)**

If the number of batches made on Friday is exactly one, then which one of the following could be true?

(A)   The first batch of sugar cookies is made on Monday.
(B)   The first batch of oatmeal cookies is made on Tuesday.
(C)   The third batch of oatmeal cookies is made on Friday.
(D)   The first batch of peanut butter cookies is made on Wednesday.
(E)   The second batch of peanut butter cookies is made on Tuesday.[24]

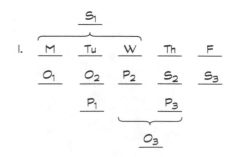

Figure 9.59

[23] PrepTest 42, Sec. 1, Q 16
[24] PrepTest 42, Sec. 1, Q 17

Here again, the question stem gives you an "if" that's only possible in Option I. Since the "if" allows only one batch of cookies on Friday, your mini-sketch (see above) should adapt Option I to reflect that P_2 and P_3 will be on Wednesday and Thursday, respectively, and that O_3 will be on either Wednesday or Thursday, although which one isn't important. That leaves only S_1 unaccounted for. The bakery could bake it on Monday, Tuesday, or Wednesday under these conditions.

The correct answer *could be true*. All four wrong answers *must be false*. As soon as you check choice (A), you see that it could be true. If you anticipated that S_1 would be involved in the correct answer, you are becoming an expert LSAT test taker. As the least restricted entity, it's the least likely to be included in a statement that must be false.

On test day, there would be no need for you to check the four remaining answer choices. The test maker will always include one demonstrably correct and four demonstrably incorrect answers. Go through choices (B) through (E) and confirm with the mini-sketch that they *must be false* if you want the practice. On test day, though, take the point and move on.

18. **(E)**

If one kind of cookie's first batch is made on the same day as another kind of cookie's third batch, then which one of the following could be false?

(A) At least one batch of cookies is made on each of the five days.
(B) At least two batches of cookies are made on Wednesday.
(C) Exactly one batch of cookies is made on Monday.
(D) Exactly two batches of cookies are made on Tuesday.
(E) Exactly one batch of cookies is made on Friday.[25]

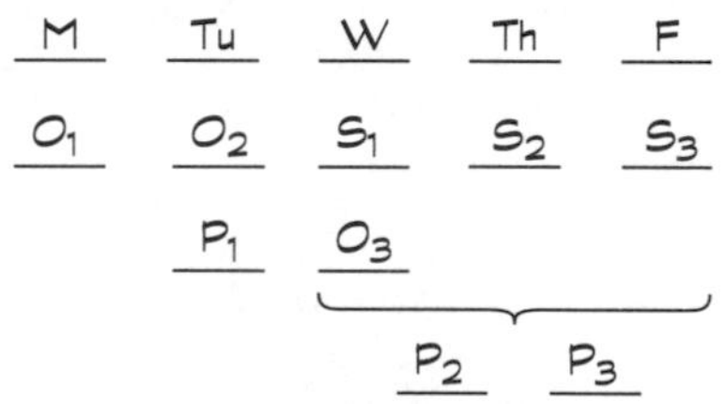

Figure 9.60

This "if" is tricky, but with a little thought, you'll see that it leads to a fantastically clear and conclusive deduction. There is only one day on which you bake one kind of cookie's first batch and another kind's third batch: Wednesday. That's the only day that can be followed *and* preceded by two other batches. Now, look at the Master Sketch and figure out how and where this "if" could be accommodated.

---

[25] PrepTest 42, Sec. 1, Q 18

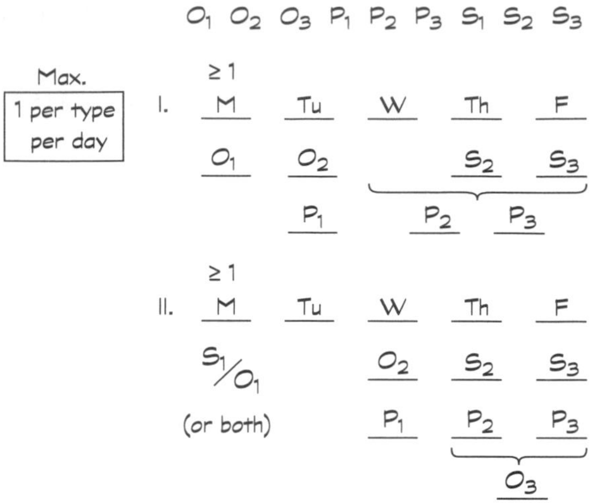

Figure 9.61

It has to happen in Option I, for sure. In Option II, all of the third batches are restricted to Thursday or Friday. But in Option I, S_1 and O_3 could be baked on Wednesday.

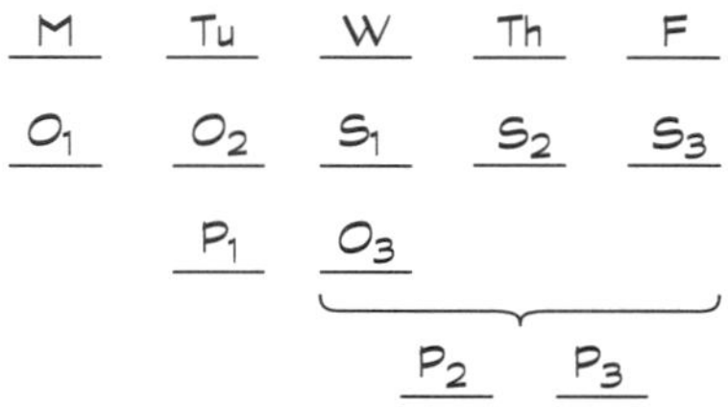

Figure 9.62

Now, evaluate the choices. The correct answer *could be false*, so all four wrong answers *must be true*. Remembering that P_2 and P_3 will be baked between Wednesday and Friday, choices (A) through (D) all *must be true*. Only choice (E) could be falsified, by having P_3 and S_3 both baked on Friday. Choice (E) is the correct answer, and you've conquered one of the most challenging Strict Sequencing games you're likely to encounter.

I wish I could say that you were unlikely to encounter a game this tough on test day, but that wouldn't be true. You will see one hard game and it might be a Strict Sequencing variant. What I can say, though, is that if you see such a game, it's going to share at least some of this game's elements—an unusual entity set, an uneven correspondence among entities and spaces, and broad or ambiguous rules. So you might ask, what do we do differently on these hardest examples? The answer, politely, is "Nothing." You used the Kaplan Method as you normally would, just with a little extra attention and little more patience. In most of the hardest games you'll encounter, the heavy lifting is done during Steps 1–4. By getting the Limited Options sketches and all of their deductions up front, you made the question set on this tough game no more difficult that it would be on any other.

Difficult Loose Sequencing

You've handled a tough Loose Sequencing game already, even in this chapter. The setup for the Bread Delivery game was as difficult as the one in the game featured next. But given the high number of these games in recent years (and the fact that the test makers have upped the ante in Loose Sequencing generally), it's worth your while to work through one more, questions and all. Without giving away too much, I'll remind you of the features common to difficult Loose Sequencing games. You'll see either conditional rules or rules that apply in one of two alternate ways, maybe both. Keep your eyes open for the opportunity to use Limited Options sketches to take control of the alternatives. Don't time yourself on this game. Be patient and thorough. It's important that you gain experience with how games like this one work. Speed and efficiency will come with your continued practice. If you find yourself struggling mightily with the questions, stop and compare your Master Sketch to the one developed in Steps 1–4 in the explanations. Once you're sure you've got the right starting point, return to the questions.

A competition is being held to select a design for Yancy College's new student union building. Each of six architects—Green, Jackson, Liu, Mertz, Peete, and Valdez—has submitted exactly one design. There are exactly six designs, and they are presented one at a time to the panel of judges, each design being presented exactly once, consistent with the following conditions:

Mertz's design is presented at some time before Liu's and after Peete's.

Green's design is presented either at some time before Jackson's or at some time after Liu's, but not both.

Valdez's design is presented either at some time before Green's or at some time after Peete's, but not both.

6. Which one of the following could be the order in which the designs are presented, from first to last?

(A) Jackson's, Peete's, Mertz's, Green's, Valdez's, Liu's
(B) Peete's, Jackson's, Liu's, Mertz's, Green's, Valdez's
(C) Peete's, Mertz's, Jackson's, Liu's, Green's, Valdez's
(D) Peete's, Mertz's, Valdez's, Green's, Liu's, Jackson's
(E) Valdez's, Liu's, Jackson's, Peete's, Mertz's, Green's

7. Mertz's design CANNOT be presented

(A) sixth
(B) fifth
(C) fourth
(D) third
(E) second

8. If Liu's design is presented sixth, then which one of the following must be true?

(A) Green's design is presented at some time before Jackson's.
(B) Jackson's design is presented at some time before Mertz's.
(C) Peete's design is presented at some time before Green's.
(D) Peete's design is presented at some time before Valdez's.
(E) Valdez's design is presented at some time before Green's.

9. If Jackson's design is presented at some time before Mertz's, then each of the following could be true EXCEPT:

(A) Jackson's design is presented second.
(B) Peete's design is presented third.
(C) Peete's design is presented fourth.
(D) Jackson's design is presented fifth.
(E) Liu's design is presented fifth.

10. Which one of the following designs CANNOT be the design presented first?

(A) Green's
(B) Jackson's
(C) Liu's
(D) Peete's
(E) Valdez's

11. Which one of the following could be an accurate partial list of the architects, each matched with his or her design's place in the order in which the designs are presented?

(A) first: Mertz; fourth: Liu; fifth: Green
(B) second: Green; third: Peete; fourth: Jackson
(C) second: Mertz; fifth: Green; sixth: Jackson
(D) fourth: Peete; fifth: Liu; sixth: Jackson
(E) fourth: Valdez; fifth: Green; sixth: Liu[26]

26 PrepTest 53, Sec. 2, Qs 6–11

Explanations

STEPS 1 AND 2: Overview and Sketch

There's nothing unusual about the task here. Six designs are presented, and you're asked to determine the order. They even come in one at a time, as you'd expect. At this point, you'll want to steal a glance at the rules to see whether you'll be using a strict or loose sketch. Since none of the rules mentions a specific space or gives you the specific distance between any two entities, you'll be making a Loose Sequencing "tree." There's no framework to draw, so just list the entities and move into the rules.

STEP 3: Rules

At this point, the complexity of this game becomes clear. You have three rules, each of which mentions three entities. Moreover, two of the rules present alternative possibilities. Jot down all three before you think about how to combine them.

Rule 1 is fairly straightforward, at least compared to the other two. It creates the following definite order:

Figure 9.63

Rule 2 gives you two possibilities. Either G comes before J and L, or G comes after J and L.

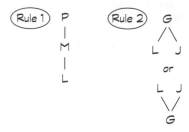

Figure 9.64

Rule 3 works the same way as Rule 2. Either V comes before G and P, or V comes after G and P.

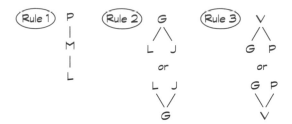

Figure 9.65

You can see that there are Duplications here: L appears in Rules 1 and 2, G appears in Rules 2 and 3, and P appears in Rules 1 and 3. But all those alternatives are making this game complicated.

STEP 4: Deductions

The alternate possibilities presented by Rules 2 and 3 suggest that you should make Limited Options sketches. But how do you decide which of the two alternatives to use as the basis for your dual sketches? The answer comes from recognizing that in order to use V in Rule 3, you need to know where P and G are. That will come from combining Rules 1 and 2 first. Copy the P-M-L chain from Rule 1, and attach one of the alternatives presented by Rule 2 to each.

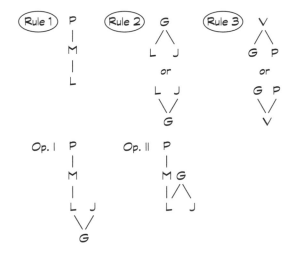

Figure 9.66

Now you can see that Rule 3 adds only one entity—V—to those you've already sketched. You might be tempted to create another set of dual sketches to show the possibilities for V, a sort of Option IA and IB, IIA and IIB format.

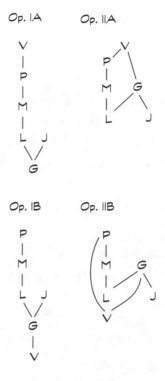

Figure 9.67

If you did that (and got everyone into the right orders), that's fine. But given the limited amount of space in the test booklet, I'd suggest something a little simpler. Just show that V can go in one of two places in either option, like so:

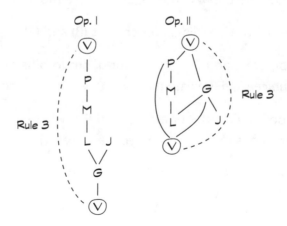

Figure 9.68

This is Loose Sequencing, so there are no floaters. And while there are still several ways that the presentations can be ordered, you've got about as clear a picture of basic options as possible. What you can know with confidence is that you have enough information to answer all of the questions.

step 5: Questions

If you're daunted by a tough game, one thing you can do to help yourself get a handle on the situation is to attack the clearest questions first. Here, that would be questions 6 (a standard Acceptability question), 7, and 10. The choices in those latter two are short, and you should be able to pick up the points quickly while gaining a little more familiarity with your complex sketch at the same time.

6. **(C)**

Which one of the following could be the order in which the designs are presented, from first to last?

(A) Jackson's, Peete's, Mertz's, Green's, Valdez's, Liu's
(B) Peete's, Jackson's, Liu's, Mertz's, Green's, Valdez's
(C) Peete's, Mertz's, Jackson's, Liu's, Green's, Valdez's
(D) Peete's, Mertz's, Valdez's, Green's, Liu's, Jackson's
(E) Valdez's, Liu's, Jackson's, Peete's, Mertz's, Green's[27]

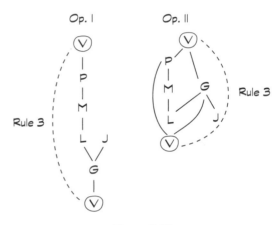

Figure 9.69

It's comforting to know that even the hardest games almost always give you the chance to get one point in such a routine way. As you would with any Acceptability question, use the rules one at a time and eliminate the answer choices that violate them.

Rule 1 created the P-M-L chain. That eliminates choices (B) and (E).

Rule 2 requires G to be before L and J or after L and J, but forbids him to be between them. He's between them in choice (A). Eliminate it.

Rule 3 requires V to be before G and P or after G and P. V will be between them in the one remaining wrong answer. That's choice (D), and you're all set. The correct answer is (C).

7. **(A)**

Mertz's design CANNOT be presented

(A) sixth
(B) fifth
(C) fourth
(D) third
(E) second[28]

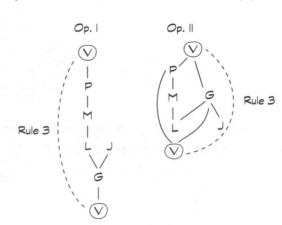

Figure 9.70

---

[27] PrepTest 53, Sec. 2, Q 6
[28] PrepTest 53, Sec. 2, Q 7

You can actually answer this question with nothing more than Rule 1. There are six designs presented in the game. M is always behind P and always ahead of L, so M cannot be first or sixth. That makes answer choice (A) impossible and thus correct.

Again, the test has given you an easy point within the context of a hard game. On test day, don't abandon an entire game; you're almost always able to get a least a couple of right answers to add to your score.

10. **(C)**

Which one of the following designs CANNOT be the design presented first?

(A) Green's
(B) Jackson's
(C) Liu's
(D) Peete's
(E) Valdez's[29]

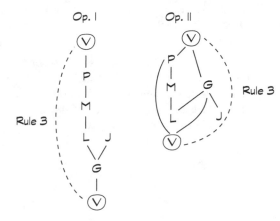

Figure 9.71

You can get the right answer to this question either by eliminating answers with entities who can be in first place (P, J, or V in Option I; P, G, or V in Option II) or by recognizing that Rule 1 makes it impossible for either M or L to ever be first. Either way, the correct answer—choice (C)—is unequivocal. Liu's design is never going to be the first presented.

That's now three points in your coffers in a matter of a few seconds each. The next two questions we'll cover—the "If" questions, numbers 8 and 9—will put your Limited Options sketches to the test.

8. **(A)**

If Liu's design is presented sixth, then which one of the following must be true?

(A) Green's design is presented at some time before Jackson's.
(B) Jackson's design is presented at some time before Mertz's.
(C) Peete's design is presented at some time before Green's.
(D) Peete's design is presented at some time before Valdez's.
(E) Valdez's design is presented at some time before Green's.[30]

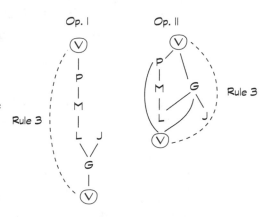

Figure 9.72

---

[29] PrepTest 53, Sec. 2, Q 10
[30] PrepTest 53, Sec. 2, Q 8

Whenever you approach an "If" question in a Limited Options scenario, ask, "Which option does this 'if' push me into?" Here, you can only consider Option II. That's because G has to follow L in Option I. Option II was created to account for the situations in which G is presented earlier than L and J. Thus, choice (A) *must be true*. If G comes before L, then it comes before J, too, according to Rule 2. All of the other answers could be either true or false in Option II.

9. **(D)**

If Jackson's design is presented at some time before Mertz's, then each of the following could be true EXCEPT:

(A) Jackson's design is presented second.
(B) Peete's design is presented third.
(C) Peete's design is presented fourth.
(D) Jackson's design is presented fifth.
(E) Liu's design is presented fifth.[31]

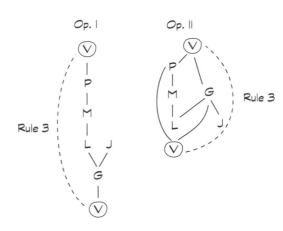

Figure 9.73

This question is alarming at first glance because it doesn't clearly put you into one of the two options. J could precede M in either case. But hold on for a moment. Do you remember what you learned about M's position in question 7? Right, it can never be sixth. So if J is to precede M, J's position cannot be fifth. That makes choice (D) correct in this "could be true EXCEPT" question. There's an irony to this question stem that leads to a strategic insight: Once you realize that either option is in play *and* notice that the four wrong answers all could be true (heck, lots of things could be true between the two options, right?), you should be telling yourself that the exact limitation described in the "if" must be the trigger to what makes the correct answer false. Students that aren't trained in the Kaplan Method are likely to use a time-consuming, confusing hunt-and-peck method and test all of the answer choices. Learning to appreciate the specific call of each question stem is one of the final pieces in true logic games mastery.

11. **(B)**

Which one of the following could be an accurate partial list of the architects, each matched with his or her design's place in the order in which the designs are presented?

(A) first: Mertz; fourth: Liu; fifth: Green
(B) second: Green; third: Peete; fourth: Jackson
(C) second: Mertz; fifth: Green; sixth: Jackson
(D) fourth: Peete; fifth: Liu; sixth: Jackson
(E) fourth: Valdez; fifth: Green; sixth: Liu[32]

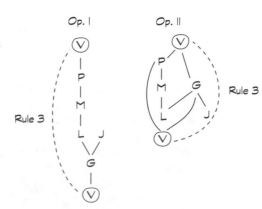

Figure 9.74

[31] PrepTest 53, Sec. 2, Q 9
[32] PrepTest 53, Sec. 2, Q 11

Although this is a Partial Acceptability question, it's probably the most difficult question in the set. That's true for a couple of reasons. First, Partial Acceptability questions are always tough in Loose Sequencing games, where you're used to assessing the entire pattern. Second, and specific to this question, the test makers have associated the entities with numbered spaces in the answer choices, something that the setup of this game doesn't easily lend itself to. Still, there's no better way to attack than to look for rule violators. Here's how you'd do it. Rule 1 eliminates choice (A): You know that M must follow P, so it can't be first. Rule 1 also takes care of choice (D): M has to follow P, and there's no room for it to do so here. Rule 2 states that G cannot be in between L and J, but G would have to be in between them in choices (C) and (E). Cross out those two, and you're left with only choice (B), the correct answer.

That game was complex, for sure, and somewhat time-consuming to set up. But like the Cookie Batches game, once you had a complete picture (or complete pictures, if you like), the question set was manageable. Probably the most important takeaway from this section on Difficult Sequencing is not to panic: The same approach you take on less complex games will get you through. In fact, it will have you outpacing your competition dramatically. Having learned the fundamentals first, you can confidently respond to quirky twists and variations.

In the final part of this chapter, I'll have you take a look at two extremely rare variations on Sequencing games. I don't expect that you'll see either of them on your test, but practicing them here will help you be ready for anything and give you another chance to see how the Kaplan Method and strategies unlock any task that the test makers can think up.

UNUSUAL SEQUENCING VARIATIONS

The games in this section are truly weird. These varieties have appeared only a few times over the past 20 years. Statistically, test takers have encountered such a game less than 2 percent of the time. So please don't give more than 2 percent of your practice or concern to them. Test takers who spend their time hunting down the strangest of games but who fail to master the fundamental logic games skills are at a great disadvantage. Those who master the Kaplan Method and its associated strategies are able to handle unusual, and unusually difficult, games by using what's familiar in them to create logical, useful sketches and recognizing the rules and deductions that provide the most restriction.

Circular Sequencing

Of the more than 260 games released by the LSAC at the time this book was written, just three fall under the category of Circular Sequencing. The first appeared in 1991, the second in 1998, and the third (the one you'll try here) in October of 2003. As the name implies, these games ask you to arrange entities in a circular pattern. In the example you're about to try, the scenario involves people eating around a circular picnic table. Getting a clear mental picture of your task is essential to making a useful framework for your sketch. Once you have that, it's pretty easy to anticipate what the rules and questions will be about. What are we always concerned about when choosing a seat? We want to know who's sitting next to us or across from us. The rules for these games, of course, work just the same way.

Give yourself eight and half minutes to set up the game and attempt the questions. If you find that you're struggling, check the explanations for Steps 1–4 of the Kaplan Method. Once you're sure you've got a useful sketch and have made the available deductions, go back and try the questions again. This game originally had seven questions associated with it. I'll only have you do five; that's more than enough to get a thorough understanding of how Circular Sequencing works.

Eight people—Fiona, George, Harriet, Ingrid, Karl, Manuel, Olivia, and Peter—are sitting, evenly spaced, around a circular picnic table. Any two of them are said to be sitting directly across from one another if and only if there are exactly three other people sitting between them, counting in either direction around the table. The following conditions apply:

Fiona sits directly across from George.

Harriet sits immediately next to neither Fiona nor Karl.

Ingrid sits immediately next to, and immediately clockwise from, Olivia.

18. Which one of the following could be the order in which four of the people are seated, with no one else seated between them, counting clockwise around the table?

    (A) George, Peter, Karl, Fiona
    (B) Harriet, Olivia, Ingrid, Karl
    (C) Ingrid, Fiona, Peter, Manuel
    (D) Olivia, Manuel, Karl, George
    (E) Peter, Harriet, Karl, Fiona

19. If Harriet and Olivia each sits immediately next to George, then which one of the following could be the two people each of whom sits immediately next to Peter?

    (A) Fiona and Karl
    (B) Fiona and Olivia
    (C) Harriet and Ingrid
    (D) Harriet and Karl
    (E) Karl and Manuel

21. If Manuel sits immediately next to Olivia, then which one of the following people must sit immediately next to Fiona?

    (A) Harriet
    (B) Ingrid
    (C) Karl
    (D) Manuel
    (E) Peter

22. What is the minimum possible number of people sitting between Ingrid and Manuel, counting clockwise from Ingrid around the table?

    (A) zero
    (B) one
    (C) two
    (D) three
    (E) four

23. If Karl sits directly across from Ingrid, then each of the following people could sit immediately next to Olivia EXCEPT:

    (A) Fiona
    (B) George
    (C) Harriet
    (D) Manuel
    (E) Peter[33]

[33] PrepTest 41, Sec. 2, Qs 18–19, 21–23

Explanations

STEPS 1 AND 2: Overview and Sketch

As I said in the introduction to this game, getting a clear mental picture of the task is essential. Fortunately, it's also pretty easy. The real-world situation described is familiar and simple. Probably the easiest way to picture it is to draw four lines, the end points of each representing the eight seats arrayed "evenly spaced" around the table.

Figure 9.75

The chairs aren't numbered or labeled with any other directional information (such as "north," "south," etc.), so you know that the restrictions will all involve who is or isn't next to or across from whom.

STEP 3: Rules

Rule 1 puts F and G at opposite ends of one of the lines.

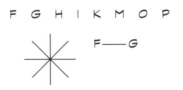

Figure 9.76

Rule 2 is the negative restriction you anticipated. H won't sit next to F or K. Make sure you show that F and K will not be adjacent to H on either side.

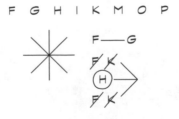

Figure 9.77

Rule 3 has the pair that wants to be together. I and O take consecutive seats, with I clockwise from O. Depict that in a way that allows you to see I's position relative to O no matter where around the circle you need to place them.

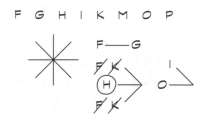

Figure 9.78

Make sure you recognize the familiar restrictions provided by Rules 1 and 3. Both create Blocks of Entities. Rule 1 could have been written in standard Sequencing language as "Exactly three seats will be between the seats in which F and G sit." Rule 3 could have been written "I sits in the seat immediately after the seat in which O sits" (provided that you substitute "after" for "clockwise," of course). Just as they would in a regular, linear Sequencing game, these rules will provide the basis for the greatest restrictions within the arrangement.

The floaters here are P and M. It's very important to make note of that in your Master Sketch.

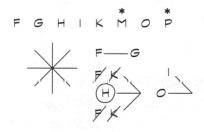

Figure 9.79

Those two will be able to sit anywhere, filling in any gaps around the table.

STEP 4: Deductions

There aren't really any deductions to add to this setup. That's less alarming when you note that the majority of questions contain "ifs" that are going to give you specific scenarios in which to test the rules. In the original appearance of this game, five of the seven questions had new "ifs." The only rules that share an entity are Rules 1 and 2. I suppose you could add the restriction on H and F to the F-G line, like so:

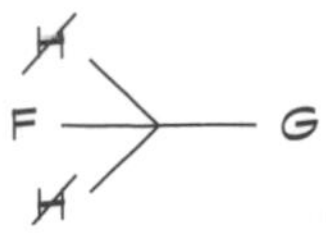

Figure 9.80

Even that's not much of a breakthrough, since the same information is visible in your depiction of Rule 2. At any rate, you've just learned a valuable lesson: Unusual games are just like normal ones in the sense that some have lots of deductions and some very few. With fewer deductions, you know to anticipate more "if" questions, and that's precisely what you get here.

STEP 5: Questions

This game had a Partial Acceptability question, a Minimum/Maximum type question, and as we noted already, five "If" questions, three of which I included for you to work on. You'll be drawing a lot of mini-sketches, no doubt.

18. **(C)**

Which one of the following could be the order in which four of the people are seated, with no one else seated between them, counting clockwise around the table?

(A)   George, Peter, Karl, Fiona
(B)   Harriet, Olivia, Ingrid, Karl
(C)   Ingrid, Fiona, Peter, Manuel
(D)   Olivia, Manuel, Karl, George
(E)   Peter, Harriet, Karl, Fiona[34]

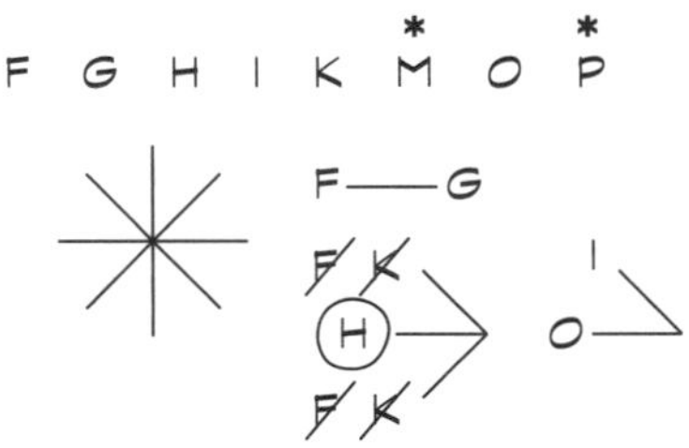

Figure 9.81

This is a Partial Acceptability question. Each answer shows four of the seats around the table in clockwise order. Use the rules to eliminate violators just as you would in any Partial Acceptability question. How do you check Rule 1 here? Since F and G must face one another, they will always have three seats between them on both sides.

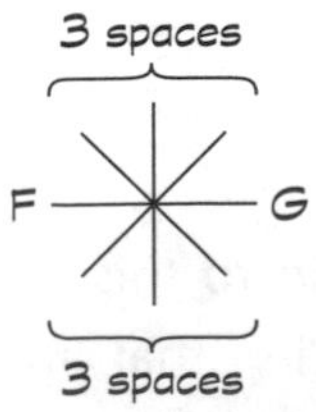

Figure 9.82

No matter how you slice it, any four consecutive seats you extract from the sequence will have one of F and G and will not have the other. That allows you to eliminate choice (A), where both F and G appear, and choice (B), where neither appears.

---

[34] PrepTest 41, Sec. 2, Q 18

Choice (E) violates Rule 2 by having H and K sit next to one another. And choice (D) violates Rule 3 by having M, instead of I, clockwise from O.

Choice (C) remains. It's the correct answer.

19. **(D)**

> If Harriet and Olivia each sits immediately next to George, then which one of the following could be the two people each of whom sits immediately next to Peter?
>
> (A) Fiona and Karl
> (B) Fiona and Olivia
> (C) Harriet and Ingrid
> (D) Harriet and Karl
> (E) Karl and Manuel[35]

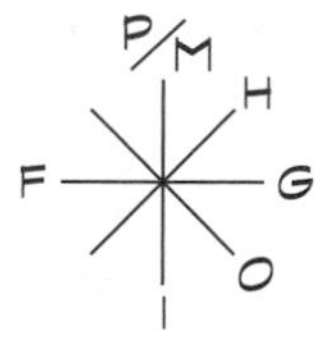

Figure 9.83

Here's the first of the "If" questions. Start your mini-sketch with the condition imposed by the question stem. For O to obey Rule 3, he'll have to sit clockwise from G. That puts H counter-clockwise from G.

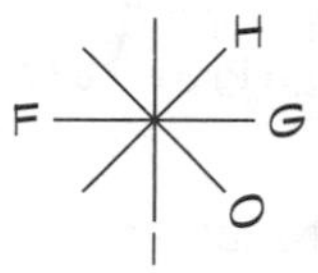

Figure 9.84

Of the remaining picnickers, only P and M (the floaters) can sit next to H.

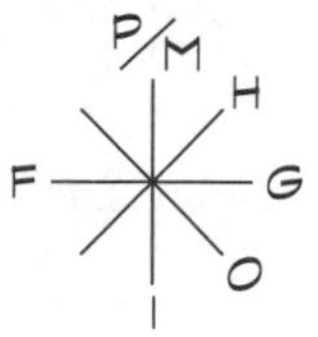

Figure 9.85

The question asks for two people who could sit next to P. Two of the answer choices include H, who you can see is one of P's possible neighbors. Choice (C) has H and I, but I would be across the table from P in this scenario. Eliminate that answer. Choice (D) has H and K. That would be possible, with K between F and P and M between I and F. Choice (D) is the correct answer here.

For the record, for choice (A) to work, K would have to sit next to H in violation of Rule 2. Choice (B) is impossible, since O is already between G and I. Choice (E) just cannot fit into the

---

35 PrepTest 41, Sec. 2, Q 19

spaces provided by this question's "if"; K and M could be on either side of F here, but not on either side of P.

21. **(C)**

If Manuel sits immediately next to Olivia, then which one of the following people must sit immediately next to Fiona?

(A) Harriet
(B) Ingrid
(C) Karl
(D) Manuel
(E) Peter[36]

Figure 9.86

Here's another "if" question calling for a new mini-sketch. In order for M to sit next to O, M needs to be counterclockwise from O so that I can sit clockwise from O in accordance with Rule 3.

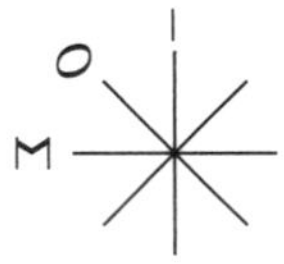

Figure 9.87

Now, you can add the F-G line. It doesn't matter which of those two sits next to M and which next to I.

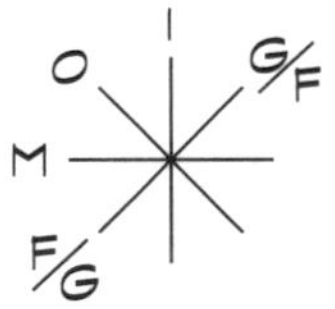

Figure 9.88

The remaining picnickers are H, K, and P. In order to keep K and H apart, P will have to sit directly across from O.

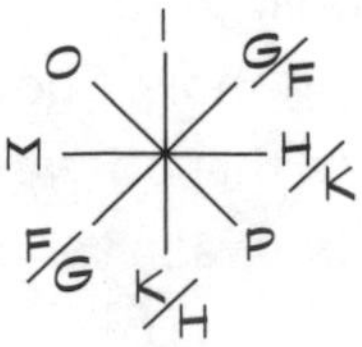

Figure 9.89

---

[36] PrepTest 41, Sec. 2, Q 21

Remember that H has to avoid being next to F, too, according to Rule 2. Therefore, K will have to take the seat next to F. That makes choice (C) the right answer.

While F *could* sit next to I (choice (B)) or M (choice (D)), the question stem asks for who F *must* sit next to. Regardless of which side of the table F sits on, K will be her neighbor there.

22. **(A)**

What is the minimum possible number of people sitting between Ingrid and Manuel, counting clockwise from Ingrid around the table?

(A) zero
(B) one
(C) two
(D) three
(E) four[37]

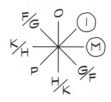

Figure 9.90

With a question like this one, make sure you understand the question stem. You need to see how close you can get I and M, with M to the clockwise side of I. The other way to make a simple, but fatal, error here is to miss the word "between." If M can be immediately next to I, there will be zero seats *between* them. Don't confuse that with M being *one* seat *away from* I; that's not what the question is asking.

If you're being very strategic here, you can answer this question in a few seconds. Remember the mini-sketch you made for question 19?

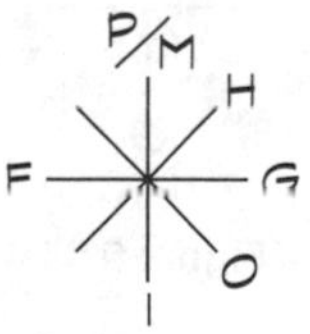

Figure 9.91

There, it was acceptable to place M between I and F. So M can sit immediately next to I, with zero seats *between* them. Choice (A) is the correct answer. No matter how bizarre the game, the Kaplan strategies work every time.

23. **(B)**

If Karl sits directly across from Ingrid, then each of the following people could sit immediately next to Olivia EXCEPT:

(A) Fiona
(B) George
(C) Harriet
(D) Manuel
(E) Peter

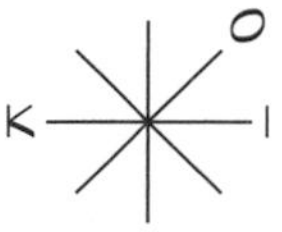

Figure 9.92

---

[37] PrepTest 41, Sec. 2, Q 22

Here's one more "If" question. Start your mini-sketch with the restriction in the stem.

Figure 9.93

Once you know I's position, Rule 3 dictates O's.

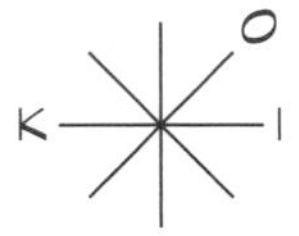

Figure 9.94

Now, think strategically about who could sit next to O on her counterclockwise side. The correct answer will be someone who *cannot* sit there. The floaters won't present a problem, so you can eliminate choices (D) and (E). Now, you can just test the three remaining choices. Placing F next to O presents no problems. G would be opposite F, and H could sit between I and G.

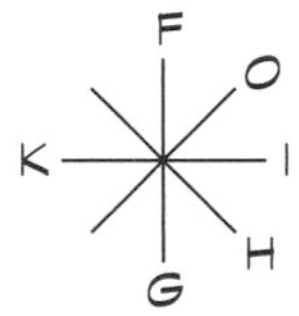

Figure 9.95

Eliminate choice (A).

When you try to put G next to O, you see the trouble. With F opposite G, there's nowhere for H that isn't next to either K or F, the two entities she's forbidden from sitting next to in Rule 2. G *cannot* sit next to O, and choice (B) is the correct answer.

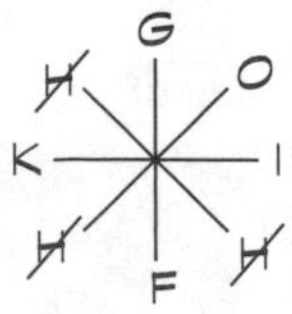

Figure 9.96

If you test choice (C), you'll of course find an acceptable arrangement. With H next to O on O's counterclockwise side, you can place G next to H, putting F across the table clockwise from I. The only remaining entities are the floaters—P and M—who can sit anywhere.

Chances are very slim that you'll encounter Circular Sequencing on your test. If you do see such a game, remember how much more prepared for it you are than someone who hasn't learned the Kaplan Method and the crucial skills and strategies that you have. Remember to base your sketch on the task described, which will allow you to anticipate the restrictions rewarded by the game. In a Circular scenario, that must involve who is or isn't next to someone else and how close or far apart they can be seated. Remember Circular Sequencing the next time you have to make seating arrangements for a wedding reception or social event. It might turn out to have real-life consequences.

There's just one more variation on Sequencing that the test makers have employed. It's almost as rare as Circular Sequencing, but its underlying task is actually closer to regular Strict Sequencing. Give it a look for the sake of completeness, but don't exaggerate its importance. Chances are, you won't see Circular Sequencing or Double Sequencing on your test.

Double Sequencing

Over the years, the LSAT has featured a couple of varieties of what I'll call Double Sequencing games. In one older example, two editors had to review the same six books, although they were restricted from reviewing the same book simultaneously. You'll see another later in this book, so I won't spoil the big "reveal" on that one. None of the four Double Sequencing games that have appeared on the LSAT are exactly identical, but they all ask you to sequence the entities twice or, in the game you're about to see, to schedule the entities once, but according to either of two criteria.

In the example that follows, you're asked to create a schedule for five pieces of music that will be performed at a concert. The "doubling" in this game derives from the fact that each of the pieces of music are performed on a specific pair of instruments. As you'll see, the rules restrict the acceptable sequences based on the instruments as well as the pieces being performed. I won't give too much away until you've had a chance to try the game on your own, but here's a hint: Pay attention to your main task—sequencing the pieces—and ask how knowing about the instruments helps you do that. The game ranks very hard based on test takers' responses, but a strategic test taker finds a lot of restrictions to guide her through the questions. Give yourself eight and half minutes and try to complete this game. If you get stuck, review the explanations for Steps 1–4 of the Kaplan Method. Then return to the question set.

Musicians perform each of exactly five pieces—Nexus, Onyx, Synchrony, Tailwind, and Virtual—once, and one at a time; the pieces are performed successively (though not necessarily in that order). Each piece is performed with exactly two instruments: Nexus with fiddle and lute, Onyx with harp and mandolin, Synchrony with guitar and harp, Tailwind with fiddle and guitar, and Virtual with lute and mandolin. The following conditions must apply:

> Each piece shares one instrument with the piece performed immediately before it or after it (or both).
> Either Nexus or Tailwind is performed second.

20. Which one of the following could be the order, from first to last, in which the pieces are performed?

    (A)   Nexus, Synchrony, Onyx, Virtual, Tailwind
    (B)   Synchrony, Tailwind, Onyx, Nexus, Virtual
    (C)   Tailwind, Nexus, Onyx, Virtual, Synchrony
    (D)   Tailwind, Nexus, Synchrony, Onyx, Virtual
    (E)   Virtual, Nexus, Synchrony, Onyx, Tailwind

21. Which one of the following instruments CANNOT be shared by the third and fourth pieces performed?

    (A)   fiddle
    (B)   guitar
    (C)   harp
    (D)   lute
    (E)   mandolin

22. If each piece (except the fifth) shares one instrument with the piece performed immediately after it, then which one of the following could be true?

    (A)   Virtual is performed first.
    (B)   Synchrony is performed second.
    (C)   Onyx is performed third.
    (D)   Nexus is performed fourth.
    (E)   Tailwind is performed fifth.

23. Each of the following could be the piece performed first EXCEPT:

    (A)   Nexus
    (B)   Onyx
    (C)   Synchrony
    (D)   Tailwind
    (E)   Virtual

24. If Synchrony is performed fifth, then which one of the following could be true?

    (A)   Nexus is performed third.
    (B)   Onyx is performed third.
    (C)   Tailwind is performed fourth.
    (D)   Virtual is performed first.
    (E)   Virtual is performed second.[38]

---

[38] PrepTest 38, Sec. 2, Qs 20–24

Explanations

STEPS 1 AND 2: Overview and Sketch

The opening paragraph that describes this game is quite long. That's a good sign that it will contain some helpful restrictions. The nature of your task is introduced at the beginning: Pieces of music "are performed successively." Up to that point, this is a very straightforward Sequencing task. You're creating the program for a performance.

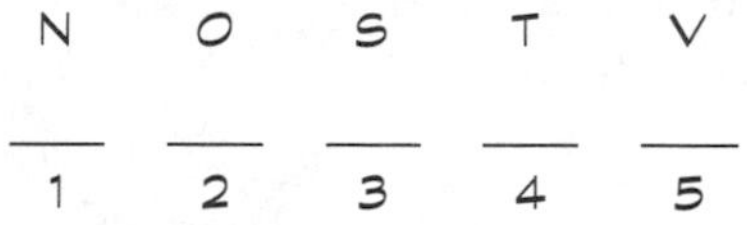

N   O   S   T   V

___ ___ ___ ___ ___
 1   2   3   4   5

Figure 9.97

The twist comes in when the paragraph starts describing the instruments that each piece is performed on. Although what restrictions the instruments provide isn't made clear until the rules, you can rest assured that you should record the instruments associated with each piece as you list the entities. We've all been at some kind of performance in which the featured artists are listed along with the pieces; in this case, it's the featured instruments that will be listed there.

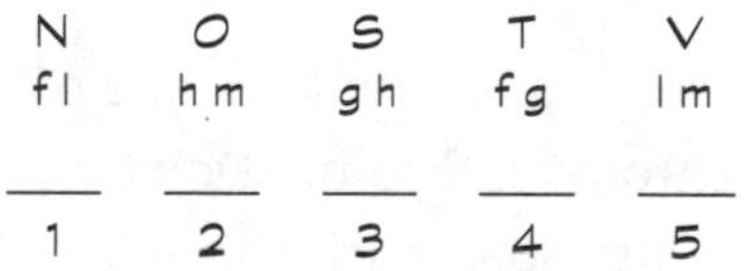

N   O   S   T   V
f l   h m   g h   f g   l m

___ ___ ___ ___ ___
 1   2   3   4   5

Figure 9.98

A glance at Rule 2 indicates that at least one specific space in the order is restricted, so a Strict Sequencing sketch is likely to be useful as you proceed.

STEP 3: Rules

There are only two rules, but each is very powerful.

Rule 1 tells you that each piece must share an instrument with the piece either before or after it in the schedule. There's no better way to diagram this rule than to note it in shorthand beside your sketch framework.

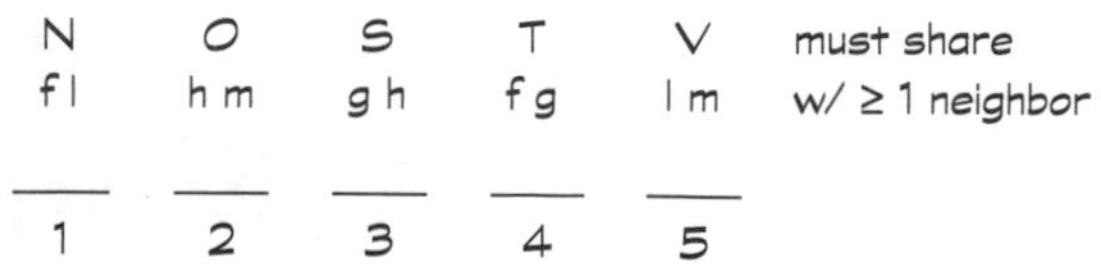

N   O   S   T   V   must share
f l   h m   g h   f g   l m   w/ ≥ 1 neighbor

___ ___ ___ ___ ___
 1   2   3   4   5

Figure 9.99

Did you take a moment to appreciate the impact of that rule on the game? Each piece is played on exactly two instruments. And each instrument is mentioned exactly two times. Thus, Synchrony, let's say, which is performed on guitar and harp, cannot be sandwiched in between Virtual and Nexus, neither of which feature guitar or harp. What's more, Synchrony couldn't be stuck at either end of the list if the only adjacent piece were Virtual or Nexus, either. In fact, the way the instruments are distributed, every piece has two other pieces with which it shares an instrument and two pieces with which it shares none. You can visualize that nicely by displaying the pieces in a ring so that each is joined to one with which it shares an instrument. It's a little reminiscent of a daisy chain:

N O S T V
fl hm gh fg lm
must share
w/ ≥ 1 neighbor
1 2 3 4 5
T S O V N
f g g h m h m l l f

Figure 9.100

This shows neatly that Nexus must be next to at least one of Tailwind or Virtual, Tailwind next to at least one of Virtual or Synchrony, and so on. Don't worry if you didn't come up with a fancy diagram, but take to heart just how much this rule actually gives you. Remember my hint? I told you to stay focused on your main job—sequencing the pieces—and to ask how the associated instruments would help you. From this one rule, you'll be able to eliminate literally dozens of unacceptable arrangements.

Rule 2 is much simpler, but no less important. It uses space 2 to create a Limited Options scenario.

N O S T V
fl hm gh fg lm
must share
w/ ≥ 1 neighbor
I.
fl
N
1 2 3 4 5
II.
T
1 2 3 4 5
fg
T S O V N
f g g h m h m l l f

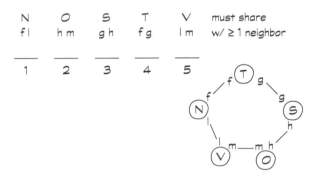

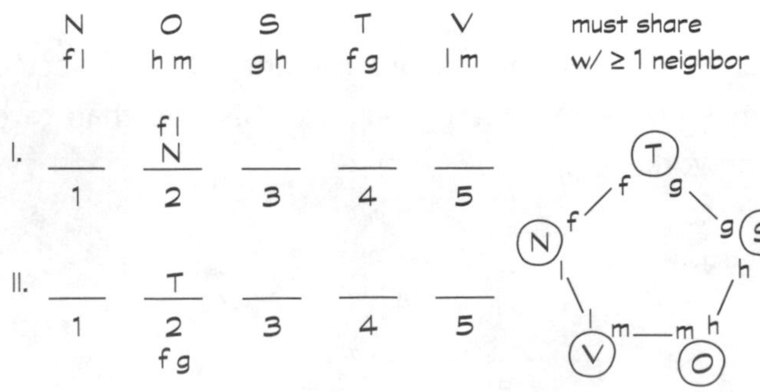

Figure 9.101

STEP 4: Deductions

There's really only one thing to add to your sketch under Step 4, but this one additional deduction will turn directly into points. Did you notice that there's a Duplication involved in the two rules? It comes from the fact that restricting space 2 to either Nexus or Tailwind also means restricting it to fiddle and lute (Nexus) or fiddle and guitar (Tailwind). Since the piece that is played first must share an instrument with the piece played second, you can see that in Option I, only Tailwind or Virtual could be the first piece, and in Option II, only Synchrony or Nexus.

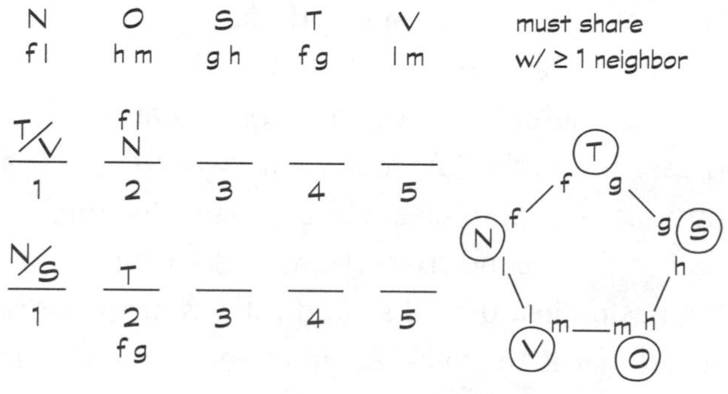

Figure 9.102

With that, you have everything you need to be able to answer the questions. The restrictions that come from Rule 1's requirement that every piece share an instrument with one of its neighbors will allow you to determine everything that can happen in either of the options.

STEP 5: Questions

One of the things that can cost test takers points and time is rushing to get to the questions. In this game, there are only five questions, and none of them are very long. When I teach students this game in class, I force them to spend four minutes on the setup, rules, and deductions to ensure that they get as complete a picture of their task and restrictions as possible. They often chafe a little at this. "What else are we supposed to do here?" But then they see the payoff. With a complete sketch and a thorough understanding of how the instruments limit the arrangement of pieces, they find that they can complete the question set easily in four minutes, sometimes far less. You can actually beat the timing average of eight and half minutes per game on a legendarily tough game like this one by being patient enough to extract all of the implications of the setup and rules before turning to the questions.

20. **(D)**

Which one of the following could be the order, from first to last, in which the pieces are performed?

(A) Nexus, Synchrony, Onyx, Virtual, Tailwind
(B) Synchrony, Tailwind, Onyx, Nexus, Virtual
(C) Tailwind, Nexus, Onyx, Virtual, Synchrony
(D) Tailwind, Nexus, Synchrony, Onyx, Virtual
(E) Virtual, Nexus, Synchrony, Onyx, Tailwind[39]

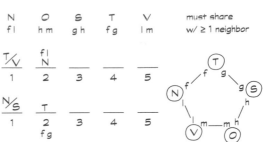

Figure 9.103

This is a run-of-the-mill Acceptability question in a decidedly *not* run-of-the-mill game. With only two rules, you know that at least one of them will eliminate multiple answer choices. Given that Rule 1 affects all of the entities, it's a good bet that it will do most of the heavy lifting. Since Rule 2 is so easy to check—just look for answer choices that have a piece other than N or T in the second spot—use it to clear out any clear violators first. Rule 2 knocks out only choice (A), which has S in the second space. Now, back to Rule 1. You'll need to find three choices in which an entity has no instrument shared with its neighbor(s). Even so, don't hunt blindly. Start with the easiest places to check, at either end of the program. In the remaining choices, the pieces in spaces 1 and 2 all share an instrument. Those you could check with just a glance at your Limited Options. The end of the program, however, reveals two violations. In choice (C), S shares nothing with V (glance at the ring of associated instruments if you need confirmation). In choice (E), T shares nothing with O. You're now left with choices (B) and (D). Look to the middle to make your final cut. In choice (B), O is sandwiched between T and N. Since neither of those pieces shares an instrument with O, choice (B) violates Rule 1, too. Only choice (D) is acceptable and, therefore, is the correct answer.

21. **(A)**

Which one of the following instruments CANNOT be shared by the third and fourth pieces performed?

(A) fiddle
(B) guitar
(C) harp
(D) lute
(E) mandolin[40]

Figure 9.104

39 PrepTest 38, Sec. 2, Q 20
40 PrepTest 38, Sec. 2, Q 21

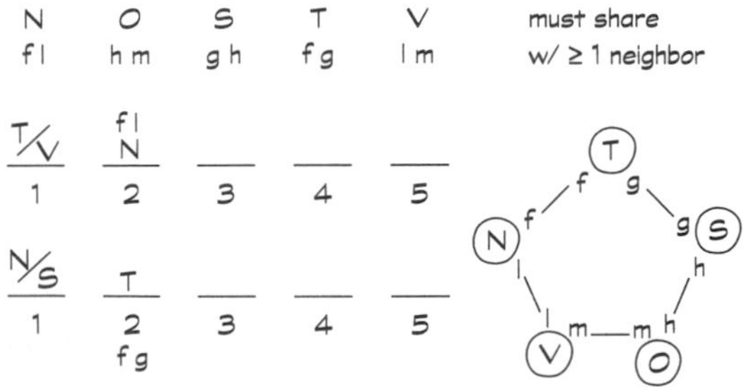

With your Limited Options sketch illustrating the instruments locked into space 2 with N or T, this is an easy point. Regardless of which option is in use, one of the two fiddles is dedicated to space 2. There's no way a fiddle could be shared between spaces 3 and 4. Choice (A) is correct, and you've got one more point in the bag.

22. **(A)**

If each piece (except the fifth) shares one instrument with the piece performed immediately after it, then which one of the following could be true?

(A) Virtual is performed first.
(B) Synchrony is performed second.
(C) Onyx is performed third.
(D) Nexus is performed fourth.
(E) Tailwind is performed fifth.[41]

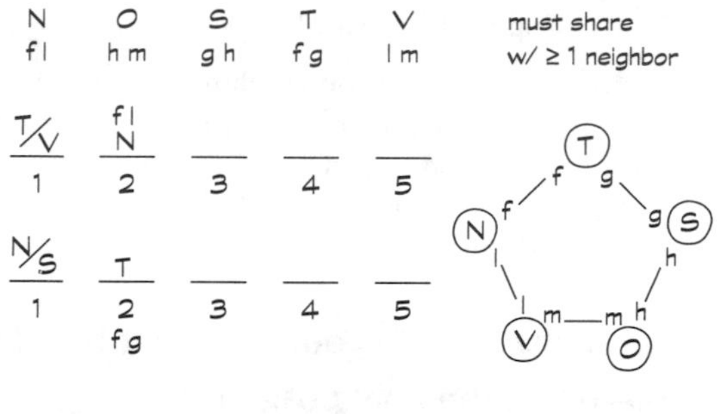

Figure 9.105

This is a rare "If" question that doesn't call for a mini-sketch. That's because instead of imposing a condition that places an entity within the arrangement, this "if" imposes an additional universal restriction on the game. In effect, the "if" here changes the original restriction that each entity share an instrument with at least one of its neighbors to require them to share an instrument specifically with the piece that follows. In other words, these arrangements simply proceed in order around the "daisy chain," as they must in order for every piece to share an instrument with the following piece. Looking at the Limited Options sketches, you see that there are four ways this can happen, one for each of the four possible first pieces. For Option I, the arrangements could go T-N-V-O-S or V-N-T-S-O. For Option II, they could be S-T-N-V-O or N-T-S-O-V. That observation is enough to prove that choice (A) is acceptable. The other four choices never occur within the four arrangements acceptable under this stem's "if."

23. **(B)**

Each of the following could be the piece performed first EXCEPT:

(A) Nexus
(B) Onyx
(C) Synchrony
(D) Tailwind
(E) Virtual[42]

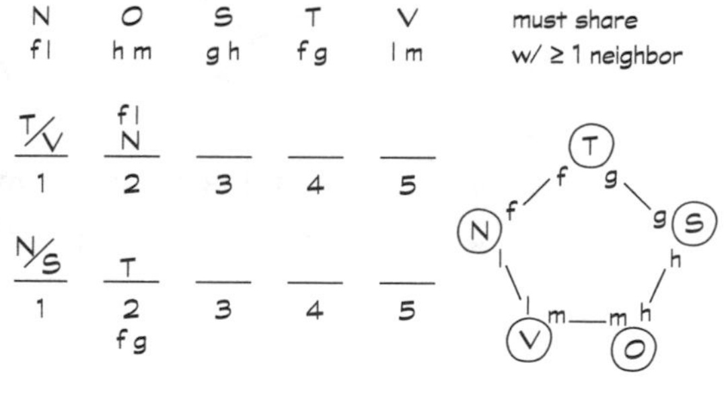

Figure 9.106

[41] PrepTest 38, Sec. 2, Q 22
[42] PrepTest 38, Sec. 2, Q 23

With the Limited Options diagrams, this question takes all of 10 seconds to answer. O is the one piece that cannot be first. That's choice (B).

24. **(D)**

If Synchrony is performed fifth, then which one of the following could be true?

(A) Nexus is performed third.
(B) Onyx is performed third.
(C) Tailwind is performed fourth.
(D) Virtual is performed first.
(E) Virtual is performed second.[43]

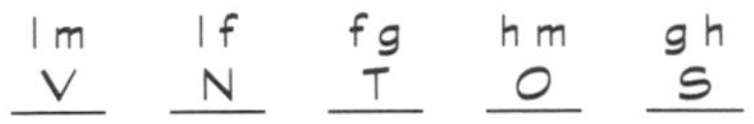

l m	l f	f g	h m	g h
V	N	T	O	S

Figure 9.107

Here, finally, is an "if" question that benefits from a mini-sketch. The "if" in the stem tells you to place S in the final position.

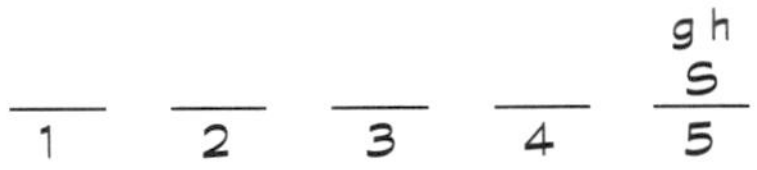

				g h
				S
1	2	3	4	5

Figure 9.108

S shares instruments with T and O, so you might as well make dual mini-sketches, one for each possibility.

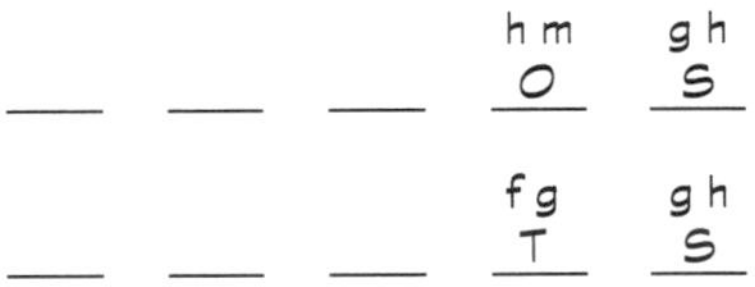

			h m	g h
			O	S

			f g	g h
			T	S

Figure 9.109

It doesn't take long to eliminate the second possibility from consideration. With T in space 4, N must take space 2. This puts you in Option I of the Master Sketch.

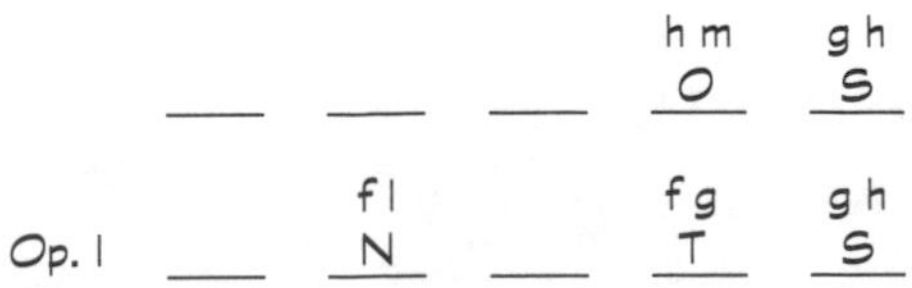

				h m	g h
				O	S
		f l		f g	g h
Op. I		N		T	S

Figure 9.110

Since T is in space 4, V must take space 1. That leaves O for space 3.

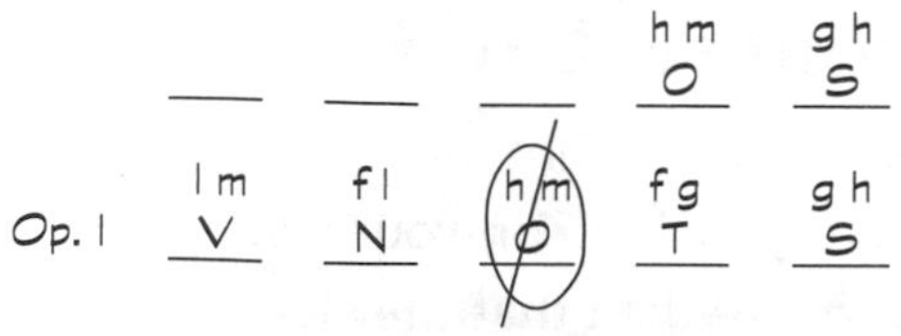

Figure 9.111

But O cannot take a position between N and T. It shares an instrument with neither. That alternative, with T in space 4, is impossible and you can eliminate choices (B) and (C).

While you're at it, eliminate choice (E), too. It violates Rule 2. V can never be second, "if" or no "if."

That leaves only choices (A) and (D) to consider. Test either one. If you find the acceptable choice, circle it and you're done. If you find the unacceptable one, cross it out and you're done.

Testing choice (A), you find that it doesn't work.

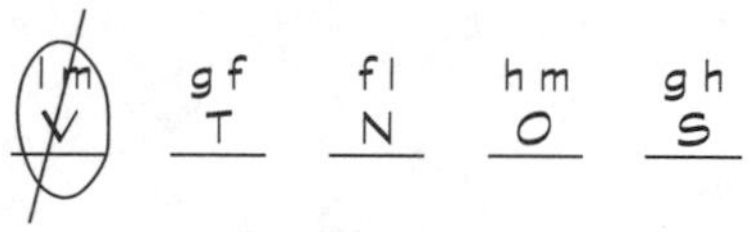

Figure 9.112

With N in space 3, T must take space 2. But that would require either S or N to take space 1, and here only V is left for space 1. Since choice (A) won't work, you know that choice (D) is correct. Test it if you need confirmation; you'll find that V can take the first position here when N takes the second position and T the third.

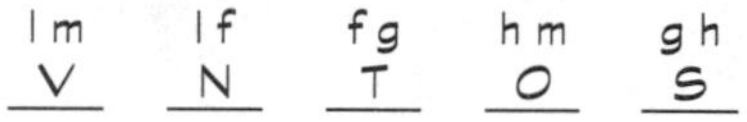

Figure 9.113

That is, indeed, a rare variation on Sequencing. You may never see one like it again. And yet, by starting from the familiar task—schedule these five pieces of music—you were able to turn the bizarre aspect of the game (the secondary attributes of the entities, the instruments) into a helpful set of restrictions. By adapting that game using the familiar Limited Options sketches, you were able to get a couple of the questions in a few seconds each. That's the underlying message of this chapter (of Part II, generally): Look for the familiar tasks, and leverage the familiar sketches and deductions. Then ask how the unfamiliar part of the game (if there is one) helps you determine the acceptable arrangements or eliminate the unacceptable ones.

YOU CAN HANDLE UNUSUAL GAMES

Don't let the unusual games in this part intimidate you. The chances are much greater that the Sequencing game or games you'll see on your test will be more like the Trail Signs game or the Water Treatment Plant game than that they'll be like one of the variations you've just seen. Keep in mind that you handled all of the games featured here—from the garden-variety examples to those with the strangest twists—using the Kaplan Method. In all of them, you see the importance of understanding your task, using the assistance of the rules, and having the patience to make all of the available deductions. Stick to those fundamental skills and you'll always have what you need to answer the questions. It comes back to the first statement in this book: Every question has an answer.

CHAPTER 10

DISTRIBUTION GAMES

Far less common than Sequencing, Distribution games are defined by tasks in which you will divide a set of entities into two or more groups. As you'll see clearly when we discuss real-life Distribution tasks, the salient question is always, "How many entities go into each group?" Sometimes the test makers will simply tell you; they might, for example, give you a game in which nine students are divided into three study groups of three students each. You'll appreciate it when that's the case, but it's more common for the test makers to leave the numbers initially ambiguous. When they do, use the rules and restrictions to determine as much as you can about the number of entities per group. At times, the numbers will reveal Limited Options scenarios such as, "Four employees serve on the charities committee and three on the travel committee, or vice versa." When you see that the numbers break down into only two possible arrangements in a Distribution game, make dual sketches and explore their implications.

REAL-LIFE DISTRIBUTION

You engage in Distribution tasks whenever you choose teams for a game, decide which piece of clothing goes in which closet, assign people to certain tasks or committees at work or school, or even when you deal out cards from a deck. The key thing to notice is that, in Distribution tasks, once you assign someone or something to a team or a place, you can't simultaneously assign it somewhere else; the grey suit can't hang in the hall closet and the bedroom closet at the same time; Joe can't play for the Blue team and for the Red team concurrently. Think of the entities in Distribution games as individual, physical beings or objects. You might move the green chair from the living room to the den, but it can't be in both places at once. This, by the way, is the main distinction between Distribution games and Matching games. In Matching tasks, you can use one set of entities multiple times. Serving coffee to Anne, for example, doesn't prevent you from serving it to Betty as well. I'll discuss the distinctions and overlap between these two tasks in the chapter on Matching games. For now, just keep the task of choosing teams as your model for Distribution.

Because real-world models for Distribution so often spring from activities like games and sports, your default assumption will often be that the teams or groups must be made up of equal numbers of players or entities. In most real-world games, each player gets the same number of cards or playing pieces to start. As I've said (and will again), check your assumptions at the door when you approach logic games. The test makers must be explicit about numbers restrictions in Distribution games. If they aren't, don't impose your own limitations.

While there are examples of Distribution tasks that follow an "equal groups" model, they're the exception. A better real-world model for most Distribution games is to picture something like a work assignment in which your boss tells you to assign eight employees to three different projects.

B C E J N O P R

$$\underline{log} \mid \text{mrkt} \mid \underline{r/e}$$

Figure 10.1

Your first question might be, "How many people do you want on each task?" But your boss responds, "You tell me. I want those projects finished ASAP. If the marketing initiative needs more bodies than the real estate plan, so be it." Like a Distribution setup on the test, your boss might impose some limits without giving you exact numbers: for example, "Just don't put more than four people on the real estate plan."

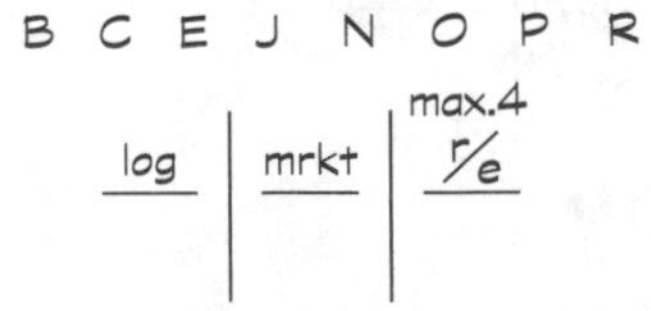

B C E J N O P R

$$\underline{log} \mid \text{mrkt} \mid \overset{\text{max.4}}{\underline{r/e}}$$

Figure 10.2

You might wish that your boss would be more definite, but you wouldn't let this response stop you from making the proposed assignments. Don't let the lack of numbers stop you from attacking a Distribution game, either.

What's definite in almost any real-world Distribution task is that there are certain people or items you'll want to keep together and certain ones you'll want to keep apart. In choosing basketball teams, you might say, "Tom and Dave are team captains," in order to keep the two tallest guys from being on the same team. Arranging your furniture, you might think, "The chair could go in the living room or the den, but either way, the ottoman has to go with it." Even your boss might tell you, "I don't care which project you put Peggy on, but don't assign Chuck to the same one," or, "Just make sure Evelyn and Nancy are working together; they're a good team."

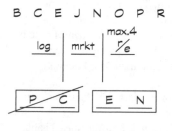

Figure 10.3

Thinking about how common such restrictions are in real life should take a lot of the sting out of formal logic rules in Distribution games. I doubt you'd wring your hands or get confused if your boss said, "Look, if you assign Evelyn to the marketing campaign, then put Rosa on the real estate planning team."

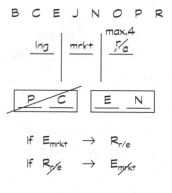

Figure 10.4

Don't let the test makers undermine your confidence when they use formal conditions, either.

STANDARD DISTRIBUTION

Up to this point in the book, you've seen a couple of Distribution games. Not surprisingly, they represent examples of the two standard Distribution subtypes: One had definite numbers for the assignments, and one had indefinite numbers. I'll refresh your memory of both and show you a couple of new examples for practice.

Distribution with Definite Numbers

Over the years, the LSAT has used Distribution games with definite numbers slightly less often than their more open-ended counterparts. In recent years, those with indefinite numbers have become the norm. Still, Distribution with definite numbers is the right place to start; these games provide the less complicated version of the task while using many of the same kinds of rules and restrictions to limit the placement of the entities. Here's an example that you worked with in Part I of the book:

On a field trip to the Museum of Natural History, each of six children—Juana, Kyle, Lucita, Salim, Thanh, and Veronica—is accompanied by one of three adults—Ms. Margoles, Mr. O'Connell, and Ms. Podorski. Each adult accompanies exactly two of the children, consistent with the following conditions:

If Ms. Margoles accompanies Juana, then Ms. Podorski accompanies Lucita.

If Kyle is not accompanied by Ms. Margoles, then Veronica is accompanied by Mr. O'Connell.

Either Ms. Margoles or Mr. O'Connell accompanies Thanh.

Juana is not accompanied by the same adult as Kyle; nor is Lucita accompanied by the same adult as Salim; nor is Thanh accompanied by the same adult as Veronica.[1]

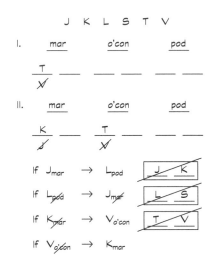

Figure 10.5

The key to the sketch is showing the number restrictions clearly. Each adult accompanies exactly two children. Even though you can't place many of the children into your initial Master Sketch, draw the individual slots beneath each chaperone. Do this whenever the test makers tell you how many entities are in each group.

The rules in this game are typical of Distribution games. The only one that's a little unusual is Rule 3, which creates the Limited Options based on the two possible placements for Thanh. The others you would expect to find in any game with a Distribution task. Rules 1 and 2 offer conditional formal logic restrictions, and Rule 4—which is really three rules in one—creates "impossible pairs," designating pairs of entities that cannot be assigned to the same adult as each other. Beyond noting that Veronica cannot share a chaperone with Thanh, there were no additional deductions here, so you can head in to the question set expecting to see "if" questions and questions that reward you for eliminating answers that violate the catalogue of rules. Try a couple of "if" questions from this game to practice applying Deduction game restrictions.

---

[1] PrepTest 52, Sec. 2, Game 2

9. If Ms. Margoles accompanies Lucita and Thanh, then which one of the following must be true?

    (A)   Juana is accompanied by the same adult as Veronica.
    (B)   Kyle is accompanied by the same adult as Salim.
    (C)   Juana is accompanied by Mr. O'Connell.
    (D)   Kyle is accompanied by Ms. Podorski.
    (E)   Salim is accompanied by Ms. Podorski.[2]

J   K   L̶   S̶   T̶   V̶

mar	o'con	pod

T   L   V   K̶/J   J̶/K   S

Figure 10.5A

The "if" condition tells you to use Option I, adding L under Margoles's heading. That leaves J, K, S, and V to be placed.

J   K   L̶   S   T̶   V

mar	o'con	pod

T   L   __   __   __   __

Figure 10.6

Since K isn't with Margoles in this question, Rule 2 requires V to go with O'Connell.

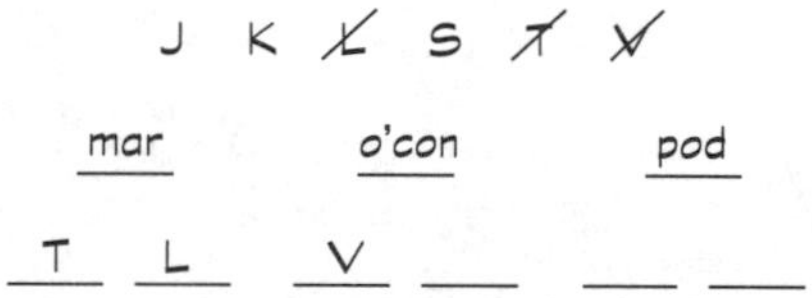

J   K   L̶   S   T̶   V̶

mar	o'con	pod

T   L   V   __   __   __

Figure 10.7

Rule 4 requires you to keep J and K separate, though there's no way to know which of those students will go with O'Connell and which with Podorski. Either way, it's clear that S must go with Podorski and your picture is complete.

J   K   L̶   S̶   T̶   V̶

mar	o'con	pod

T   L   V   K̶/J   J̶/K   S

Figure 10.8

The question stem calls for what must be true as a result of the new "if" condition. Unsurprisingly, choice (E) rewards you for deducing that S is chaperoned by Podorski. That's your correct answer. (It's also no surprise that all four wrong answers mention either J or K, the two entities whose placement *cannot* be completely determined here.)

That question is a good illustration of how the test makers write Distribution game rules so that they can be combined to lead to greater certainty. The next question works the same way, though its "if" will lead you to a different assignment of students to chaperones. Give it a try.

10. If Ms. Podorski accompanies Juana and Veronica, then Ms. Margoles could accompany which one of the following pairs of children?

    (A)   Kyle and Salim
    (B)   Kyle and Thanh
    (C)   Lucita and Salim
    (D)   Lucita and Thanh
    (E)   Salim and Thanh[3]

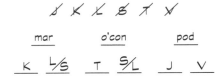

Figure 10.9

This time, you can begin your mini-sketch by assigning Podorski her charges based on the question stem.

Figure 10.10

You may think that leaves either option available, but consider the implications of Rule 2. Since V is not with O'Connell in this situation, the contrapositive of Rule 2 tells you that K must be assigned to Margoles.

Figure 10.11

---

[3] PrepTest 52, Sec. 2, Q 10

In Option I, that would mean that L and S are stuck together with O'Connell, but Rule 4 prevents you from placing L and S together. So you have to use Option II in order to accommodate this question's "if" condition and its resultant deductions.

Figure 10.12

Now, it doesn't matter which of L and S goes with Margoles or O'Connell. Either way, you're ready to answer the question.

Figure 10.13

The question asks for a pair of entities who *could* go with Margoles. You can see from your mini-sketch that the correct answer will say either "Kyle and Lucita" or "Kyle and Salim." Choice (A) has the second of those two possibilities and is correct. None of the other answers is a possible pair for Margoles here.

Distribution Practice

The next game is one that you haven't seen before. But like the Museum Chaperones game, it asks you to distribute entities in pairs. I'll let you try it out on your own and then go through the explanations with you. Here's one hint before you begin: The fact that the groups are days of the week gives some test takers the impression that this is a kind of Sequencing-Distribution Hybrid game. In fact, the days of the week work just like the three chaperones in the previous game. There are no rules or restrictions based on the ordering of the entities, nothing saying, for example, that K must come *earlier* or *later* in the week than P.

Give yourself eight and a half minutes for the game and its questions. If you feel stuck, review the explanations for Steps 1–4 of the Kaplan Method. Once you're sure you have a strong Master Sketch and understand the deductions, go back to the questions and complete your work.

During a certain week, an animal shelter places exactly six dogs—a greyhound, a husky, a keeshond, a Labrador retriever, a poodle, and a schnauzer—with new owners. Two are placed on Monday, two on Tuesday, and the remaining two on Wednesday, consistent with the following conditions:

The Labrador retriever is placed on the same day as the poodle.

The greyhound is not placed on the same day as the husky.

If the keeshond is placed on Monday, the greyhound is placed on Tuesday.

If the schnauzer is placed on Wednesday, the husky is placed on Tuesday.

7. Which one of the following could be a complete and accurate matching of dogs to the days on which they are placed?

   (A) Monday: greyhound, Labrador retriever
       Tuesday: husky, poodle
       Wednesday: keeshond, schnauzer
   (B) Monday: greyhound, keeshond
       Tuesday: Labrador retriever, poodle
       Wednesday: husky, schnauzer
   (C) Monday: keeshond, schnauzer
       Tuesday: greyhound, husky
       Wednesday: Labrador retriever, poodle
   (D) Monday: Labrador retriever, poodle
       Tuesday: greyhound, keeshond
       Wednesday: husky, schnauzer
   (E) Monday: Labrador retriever, poodle
       Tuesday: husky, keeshond
       Wednesday: greyhound, schnauzer

8. Which one of the following must be true?

   (A) The keeshond is not placed on the same day as the greyhound.
   (B) The keeshond is not placed on the same day as the schnauzer.
   (C) The schnauzer is not placed on the same day as the husky.
   (D) The greyhound is placed on the same day as the schnauzer.
   (E) The husky is placed on the same day as the keeshond.

9. If the poodle is placed on Tuesday, then which one of the following could be true?

   (A) The greyhound is placed on Monday.
   (B) The keeshond is placed on Monday.
   (C) The Labrador retriever is placed on Monday.
   (D) The husky is placed on Tuesday.
   (E) The schnauzer is placed on Wednesday.

10. If the greyhound is placed on the same day as the keeshond, then which one of the following must be true?

    (A) The husky is placed on Monday.
    (B) The Labrador retriever is placed on Monday.
    (C) The keeshond is placed on Tuesday.
    (D) The poodle is not placed on Wednesday.
    (E) The schnauzer is not placed on Wednesday.

11. If the husky is placed the day before the schnauzer, then which one of the following CANNOT be true?

    (A) The husky is placed on Monday.
    (B) The keeshond is placed on Monday.
    (C) The greyhound is placed on Tuesday.
    (D) The poodle is placed on Tuesday.
    (E) The poodle is placed on Wednesday.

12. If the greyhound is placed the day before the poodle, then which one of the following CANNOT be placed on Tuesday?

    (A) the husky
    (B) the keeshond
    (C) the Labrador retriever
    (D) the poodle
    (E) the schnauzer[4]

Answer Explanations follow on the next page.

Explanations

STEPS 1 and 2: Overview and Sketch

The similarities between this game and Museum Field Trip game are overwhelming. In both cases, six entities are grouped into three pairs and each pair assigned under a designated heading. It makes no difference at all that the headings were people in the prior game but days of the week in this one. If you called Margoles "Ms. Monday" or O'Connell "Mr. Tuesday," you'd wind up with exactly the same initial framework.

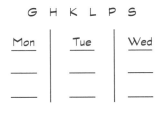

Figure 10.14

The more practice you do, the more these common patterns will show themselves and the greater your efficiency and confidence in setting up games will be.

STEP 3: Rules

The four rules from this game are about as typical a set of Distribution restrictions as you'll find. One establishes a pair of entities that must be together, one keeps a pair of entities apart, and two impose conditional restrictions on the distribution of pairs among the days of the week.

Rule 1 creates the established pairing.

Figure 10.15

Rule 2 designates the "impossible pair."

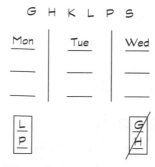

Figure 10.16

Rules 3 and 4 both involve formal logic. As you learned to do in Part I, translate each into "if then" notation and record its contrapositive as well.

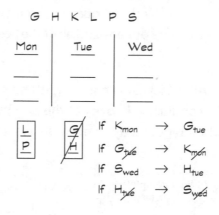

Figure 10.17

Those last two rules are the only ones that associate the entities—the dogs—with particular days of the week. Since they're conditional, you can anticipate a number of "if" questions here, each of which will designate the placement of certain dogs on certain days and reward you for being able to determine the implications of those designations.

STEP 4: Deductions

Each acceptable solution to this game's task will include three pairs. One of those pairs is established by Rule 1. Think about that in conjunction with Rule 2, and you'll realize that there are only two ways in which the remaining four dogs can be paired up. Since G and H must be kept apart, each will be paired with either K or S. There you have it.

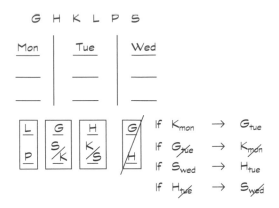

Figure 10.18

From here on out, everything in the game will focus on either those two possible pairings or on which days the various pairs are placed. "If" question stems will trigger the conditions in Rules 3 and 4, and you'll be able to figure out any and all of the acceptable arrangements easily.

STEP 5: Questions

Given that it's the formal logic rules that remain in play, it's no surprise to see that four of six questions here involve new "if" conditions. Knock out the Acceptability question and the one *must be true* example first, and then get ready to make several mini-sketches.

7. **(E)**

Which one of the following could be a complete and accurate matching of dogs to the days on which they are placed?

(A)   Monday: greyhound, Labrador retriever
        Tuesday: husky, poodle
        Wednesday: keeshond, schnauzer
(B)   Monday: greyhound, keeshond
        Tuesday: Labrador retriever, poodle
        Wednesday: husky, schnauzer
(C)   Monday: keeshond, schnauzer
        Tuesday: greyhound, husky
        Wednesday: Labrador retriever, poodle
(D)   Monday: Labrador retriever, poodle
        Tuesday: greyhound, keeshond
        Wednesday: husky, schnauzer
(E)   Monday: Labrador retriever, poodle
        Tuesday: husky, keeshond
        Wednesday: greyhound, schnauzer[5]

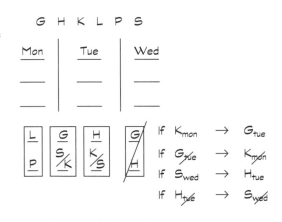

Figure 10.19

With four rules and four wrong answers, you should know what to anticipate from this Acceptability question: Look to knock out one violator with each rule. Rule 1 gets rid of choice (A); L and P aren't together there. Rule 2 gets rid of choice (C); G and H cannot be together. Rule

---

3 eliminates choice (B), which has K on Monday but doesn't have G on Tuesday. And Rule 4 knocks out choice (D), where S is on Wednesday but H isn't on Tuesday. That leaves the correct answer, choice (E).

8. **(B)**

Which one of the following must be true?

(A) The keeshond is not placed on the same day as the greyhound.
(B) The keeshond is not placed on the same day as the schnauzer.
(C) The schnauzer is not placed on the same day as the husky.
(D) The greyhound is placed on the same day as the schnauzer.
(E) The husky is placed on the same day as the keeshond.[6]

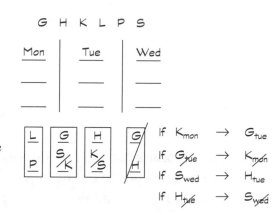

Figure 10.20

This question directly rewards the one big deduction you were able to make in Step 4 of the Kaplan Method. Just look at your diagram of the possible pairings, and you'll see that K and S must be placed on separate days. That's choice (B), the correct answer to this *must be true* question. You should even have been able to predict the four wrong answers here, one for each of the acceptable pairs: G is able to be placed on the same day as either K, choice (A), or S, choice (D); likewise, H can be placed on the same day as either K, choice (E), or as S, choice (C).

9. **(A)**

If the poodle is placed on Tuesday, then which one of the following could be true?

(A) The greyhound is placed on Monday.
(B) The keeshond is placed on Monday.
(C) The Labrador retriever is placed on Monday.
(D) The husky is placed on Tuesday.
(E) The schnauzer is placed on Wednesday.[7]

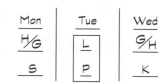

Figure 10.21

From here on out, it's all "If" questions. Begin your mini-sketch for this one with the information from the question stem.

[6] PrepTest 44, Sec. 3, Q 8
[7] PrepTest 44, Sec. 3, Q 9

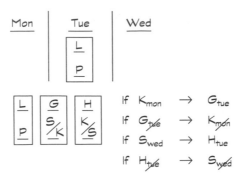

Figure 10.22

With P and, of course, L placed on Tuesday, Tuesday is full. That triggers the contrapositive of Rule 3. When G isn't placed on Tuesday, K can't be placed on Monday. Therefore, K (along with either G or H, to keep those two apart) is placed on Wednesday.

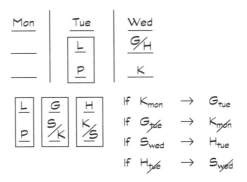

Figure 10.23

That means that S will go on Monday, along with either G or H.

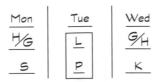

Figure 10.24

Since this is a *could be true* question, you should expect the correct answer to involve either G or H, the two dogs whose placement hasn't been established. Choice (A) is the right answer. G could be placed on Monday as the mini-sketch shows. The other four answers all *must be false*. Choice (D) mentions H but tries to place it on Tuesday, which is already occupied by L and P.

10. **(E)**

If the greyhound is placed on the same day as the keeshond, then which one of the following must be true?

(A)   The husky is placed on Monday.
(B)   The Labrador retriever is placed on Monday.
(C)   The keeshond is placed on Tuesday.
(D)   The poodle is not placed on Wednesday.
(E)   The schnauzer is not placed on Wednesday.[8]

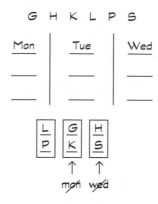

Figure 10.25

This time, the "if" establishes another pairing of dogs. If G and K are together, then so are H and S. Your three pairs are certain.

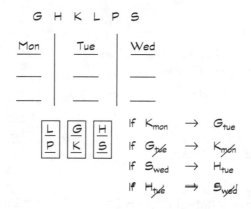

Figure 10.26

You can't know exactly the precise days on which any of the pairs are placed, but there are a couple of possibilities you can rule out. Rule 3 prevents the K-G pair from going on Monday, since placing K on Monday would mean placing G on Tuesday. Likewise, Rule 4 prevents the H-S pair from going on Wednesday, since placing S on Wednesday means placing H on Tuesday.

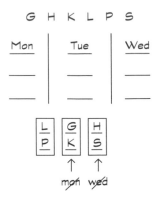

Figure 10.27

That's plenty of information to answer the question. The correct answer *must be true*. You know from the mini-sketch that S cannot be placed on Wednesday, and that's exactly what choice (E) says. All of the remaining choices could be true or false under the conditions established by this question stem.

11. **(D)**

If the husky is placed the day before the schnauzer, then which one of the following CANNOT be true?

(A)   The husky is placed on Monday.
(B)   The keeshond is placed on Monday.
(C)   The greyhound is placed on Tuesday.
(D)   The poodle is placed on Tuesday.
(E)   The poodle is placed on Wednesday.[9]

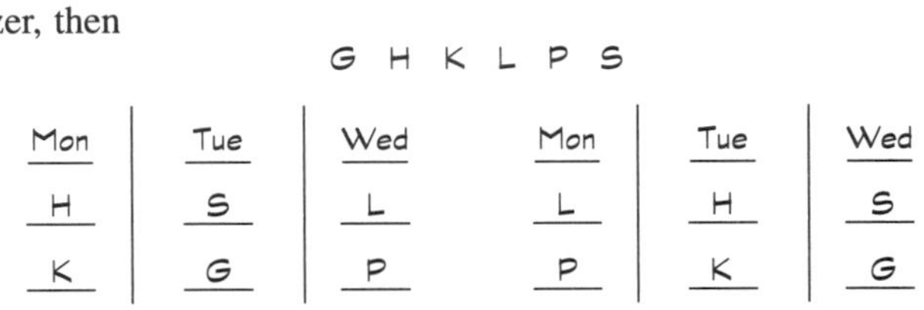

G H K L P S

Mon	Tue	Wed	Mon	Tue	Wed
H	S	L	L	H	S
K	G	P	P	K	G

Figure 10.28

There are two ways to accommodate this "if": H on Monday and S on Tuesday or H on Tuesday and S on Wednesday. Jot down both.

Figure 10.29

Since S isn't with H in either case, it has to be with G, and K has to be with H.

---

[9] PrepTest 44, Sec. 3, Q 11

G H K L P S

Mon	Tue	Wed	Mon	Tue	Wed
H	S	___	___	H	S
K	G	___	___	K	G

Figure 10.30

The remaining day—Wednesday in the first scenario, Monday in the second—belongs to the L-P pairing.

G H K L P S

Mon	Tue	Wed	Mon	Tue	Wed
H	S	L	L	H	S
K	G	P	P	K	G

Figure 10.31

That's a perfect picture of the two acceptable arrangements allowed by this question stem. Now, characterize the answer choices. The correct answer *must be false*. That fits choice (D), which cannot happen under either alternative. The other four choices are all possible in one of the two options acceptable here.

12. **(A)**

If the greyhound is placed the day before the poodle, then which one of the following CANNOT be placed on Tuesday?

(A) the husky
(B) the keeshond
(C) the Labrador retriever
(D) the poodle
(E) the schnauzer[10]

Mon	Tue	Wed	Mon	Tue	Wed
G	P	H	H	G	P
S/K	L	K/S	K/S	S/K	L

Figure 10.32

The "if" for this question works the same way as the one in question 11 did. G and P are either on Monday and Tuesday or on Tuesday and Wednesday, respectively.

Mon	Tue	Wed	Mon	Tue	Wed
G	P	___	___	G	P
___	___	___	___	___	___

Figure 10.33

[10] PrepTest 44, Sec. 3, Q 12

You know from the Master Sketch that either K or S accompanies G and that L always accompanies P.

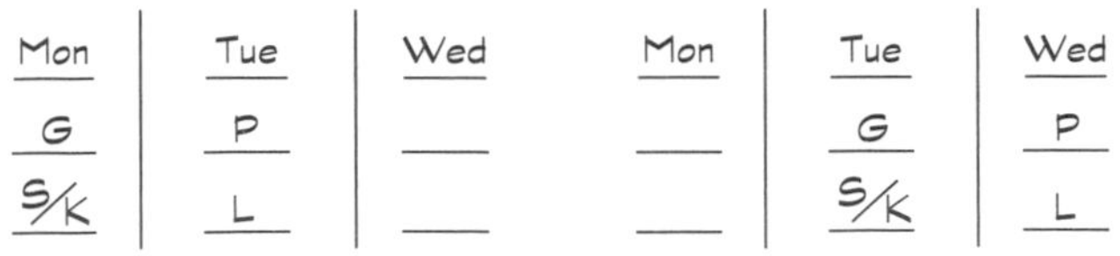

Mon	Tue	Wed	Mon	Tue	Wed
G	P	___	___	G	P
S̸/K	L	___	___	S̸/K	L

Figure 10.34

Now, H (along with either K or S) will take Monday or Wednesday, depending on which alternative you're considering.

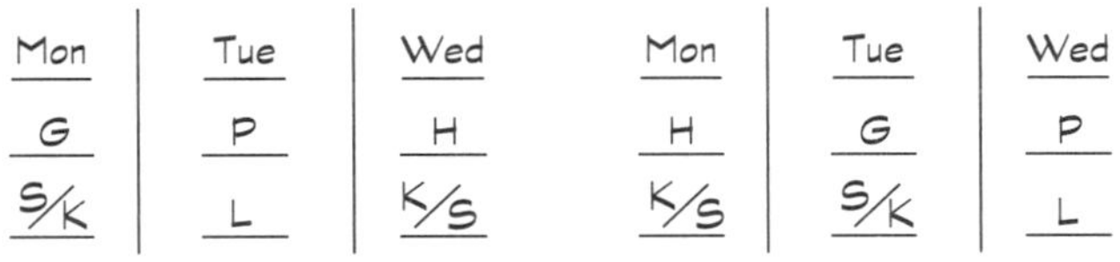

Mon	Tue	Wed	Mon	Tue	Wed
G	P	H	H	G	P
S̸/K	L	K/S	K/S	S̸/K	L

Figure 10.35

This time, the question asks for a dog that can *never* be placed on Tuesday. The only one ruled out is H, and that's the correct answer, choice (A). Every other dog can find its way to a Tuesday placement here. The four wrong answers *could be true*.

The two games you just saw began from almost exactly the same premise: Six entities will be distributed among three groups. The certainty with which the numbers were determined—two entities per group—allowed you to focus on two factors: the group to which an entity was assigned or the other entity it was paired with. Not every Distribution game with definite numbers will place pairs of entities—it could be trios of entities, or it could be two entities in two groups and three entities in another, or whatever. In any case, it is always helpful to have definite numbers in Distribution games. You can always take advantage of that clear restriction by drawing the slots that the entities will occupy into your Master Sketch. You'll know, too, to expect rules that affect the relationships between or among entities, as well as rules that require or forbid certain group assignments.

Now, turn your attention to the more common Distribution variation, in which the numbers aren't so definite at the outset. As you'll see, your Deductions step will be aimed at giving as much certainty as possible to numbers in each group.

Distribution with Ambiguous Numbers

Just as your boss left it up to you to determine how many employees should be assigned to each task in the "real-life" example near the beginning of this chapter, most Distribution games leave it up to you to determine how many entities can go in each group. But while the test makers don't tell you explicitly how many entities to assign per group, the rules always ensure that some restrictions within the numbers exist. Think about it like this: Any rule that tells you to keep two entities apart from one another is, at the same time, telling you that two of the groups get at least one entity each. To see this in action, look back at the Talent Agency game you learned to set up in Part I.

> Five performers—Traugott, West, Xavier, Young, and
> Zinser—are recruited by three talent agencies—Fame Agency,
> Premier Agency, and Star Agency. Each performer signs with
> exactly one of the agencies and each agency signs at least one
> of the performers. The performers' signing with the agencies
> is in accord with the following:
>> Xavier signs with Fame Agency.
>> Xavier and Young do not sign with the same agency as
>> each other.
>> Zinser signs with the same agency as Young.
>> If Traugott signs with Star Agency, West also signs with
>> Star Agency.[11]

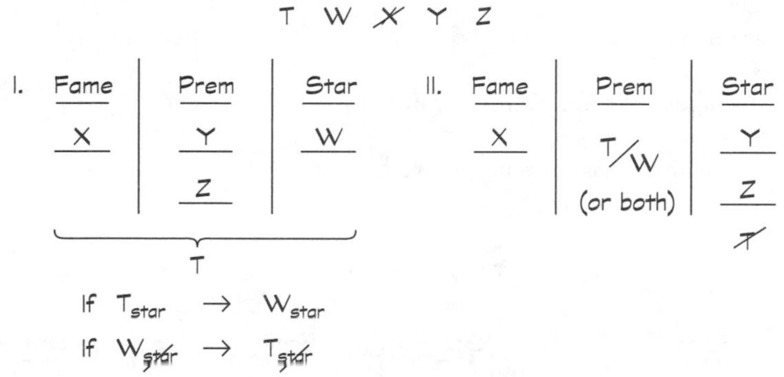

T W X̶ Y Z

I.	Fame	Prem	Star		II.	Fame	Prem	Star
	X	Y	W			X	T/W	Y
		Z					(or both)	Z
								T̶

(Option I) ‹—— T ——›

If T_{star} → W_{star}

If $W_{s̶t̶a̶r̶}$ → $T_{s̶t̶a̶r̶}$

Figure 10.36

Here, the first three rules allow you to create Limited Options sketches. X has to be placed with Fame, while Y must avoid X. That leaves only Premier or Star available for Y. Since Z accompanies Y, you have two options that account for three of the entities, for sure. Since the opening description of this game tells you that "each agency signs at least one of the performers," the number arrangements here are nearly set. In Option I, W has to sign with Star. To follow Rule 3, W will sign with Star if T does, and to ensure that Star represents at least one performer, W will have to sign there if T doesn't. Depending on where T is assigned in Option I, the number of performers per agency will be 2-2-1, 1-3-1, or 1-2-2 for Fame, Premier, and Star, respectively.

In Option II, placing T with Star is impossible (since Rule 3 would require W to be placed with Star as well, leaving Premier with no performers). So in this option, the possible number arrangements are 2-1-2, 1-2-2, or 1-1-3 for Fame, Premier, and Star, respectively, depending on where T and W wind up.

---

[11] PrepTest 53, Sec. 2, Game 1

The constant interplay between acceptable pairings of entities and the minimum and maximum number of entities per group is the feature that allows you to take full control of the acceptable and unacceptable arrangements within the game. The test directly rewards your understanding of that interplay, as these two problems illustrate. Take a minute to get familiar with the questions and then read the explanations that follow.

2. Which one of the following could be true?
    (A) West is the only performer who signs with Star Agency.
    (B) West, Young, and Zinser all sign with Premier Agency.
    (C) Xavier signs with the same agency as Zinser.
    (D) Zinser is the only performer who signs with Star Agency.
    (E) Three of the performers sign with Fame Agency.

3. Which one of the following must be true?
    (A) West and Zinser do not sign with the same agency as each other.
    (B) Fame Agency signs at most two of the performers.
    (C) Fame Agency signs the same number of the performers as Star Agency.
    (D) Traugott signs with the same agency as West.
    (E) West does not sign with Fame Agency.[12]

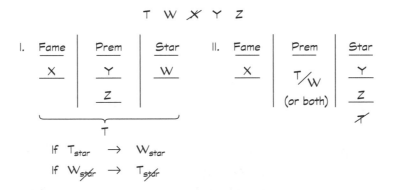

Figure 10.37

Choice (A) is the correct answer to question 2. W could be the one performer assigned to Star in Option I. Choice (B) is the correct answer to question 3. In either option, Fame cannot sign more than two of the performers. After all, in Option I, only T remains to be placed. In Option II, if Fame takes both T and W, no one is left to sign with Premier. Those questions illustrate just how central the issue of numbers is for all Distribution games. Whenever the test makers leave the numbers open, they'll design questions to reward you for determining any and all restrictions on the possible number of entities per group.

---

[12] PrepTest 53, Sec. 2, Qs 2–3

Distribution with Ambiguous Numbers Practice

The following game echoes the task of the Talent Agency game almost exactly. There are five entities (pieces of mail now, instead of performers) to distribute among three groups (housemates this time, instead of agencies). You can start with an identical framework. The rules are different, of course, because the test makers don't copy games exactly from one test to another. But one restriction (the most important one) remains the same: Each group (housemate, agency) is assigned at least one entity (piece of mail, performer). Use that as the starting point for your assessment of the acceptable number arrangements.

Give yourself eight and a half minutes to try this game (on the next page) and its question set. If you find that you're getting stuck, stop and review the explanations for Steps 1–4 of the Kaplan Method. Then return to the question set and see if you can finish it once you're clear on the deductions and Master Sketch.

There are exactly five pieces of mail in a mailbox: a flyer, a letter, a magazine, a postcard, and a survey. Each piece of mail is addressed to exactly one of three housemates: Georgette, Jana, or Rini. Each housemate has at least one of the pieces of mail addressed to her. The following conditions must apply:

> Neither the letter nor the magazine is addressed to Georgette.
>
> If the letter is addressed to Rini, then the postcard is addressed to Jana.
>
> The housemate to whom the flyer is addressed has at least one of the other pieces of mail addressed to her as well.

8. Which one of the following could be a complete and accurate matching of the pieces of mail to the housemates to whom they are addressed?

    (A) Georgette: the flyer, the survey
        Jana: the letter
        Rini: the magazine
    (B) Georgette: the flyer, the postcard
        Jana: the letter, the magazine
        Rini: the survey
    (C) Georgette: the magazine, the survey
        Jana: the flyer, the letter
        Rini: the postcard
    (D) Georgette: the survey
        Jana: the flyer, the magazine
        Rini: the letter, the postcard
    (E) Georgette: the survey
        Jana: the letter, the magazine, the postcard
        Rini: the flyer

9. Which one of the following is a complete and accurate list of the pieces of mail, any one of which could be the only piece of mail addressed to Jana?

    (A) the postcard
    (B) the letter, the postcard
    (C) the letter, the survey
    (D) the magazine, the survey
    (E) the letter, the magazine, the postcard

10. Which one of the following CANNOT be a complete and accurate list of the pieces of mail addressed to Jana?

    (A) the flyer, the letter, the magazine
    (B) the flyer, the letter, the postcard
    (C) the flyer, the letter, the survey
    (D) the flyer, the magazine, the postcard
    (E) the flyer, the magazine, the survey

11. Which one of the following CANNOT be a complete and accurate list of the pieces of mail addressed to Rini?

    (A) the magazine, the postcard
    (B) the letter, the survey
    (C) the letter, the magazine
    (D) the flyer, the magazine
    (E) the flyer, the letter

12. If the magazine and the survey are both addressed to the same housemate, then which one of the following could be true?

    (A) The survey is addressed to Georgette.
    (B) The postcard is addressed to Rini.
    (C) The magazine is addressed to Jana.
    (D) The letter is addressed to Rini.
    (E) The flyer is addressed to Jana.[13]

---

[13] PrepTest 49, Sec. 1, Qs 8–12

Answer Explanations follow on the next page.

Explanations

STEPS 1 and 2: Overview and Sketch

The situation described here is almost certainly something you've done in real life. You go to the mailbox to find five pieces of mail. You check who each one is addressed to and place them on that person's desk or dresser. As you start to draw a framework for this information, you'll see a picture that looks almost exactly like that described in the Talent Agency game.

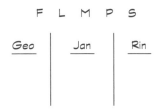

Figure 10.38

Beyond telling you that each piece of mail is addressed to one of the housemates and that each housemate gets at least one piece of mail, the setup gives you no guidance on the number limitations. So there's no way to add more than one slot under each housemate's name. You can anticipate learning more about the number possibilities from the rules and deductions, though.

STEP 3: Rules

Draw out each of the rules one at a time.

The first rule gives you two negative restrictions. You won't deliver L or M to Georgette.

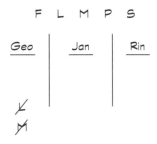

Figure 10.39

Rule 2 is conditional. Translate it into formal logic notation, and determine its contrapositive at the same time.

F L M P S
Geo
Jan
Rin
If Rin/L → Jan/P
If Jan/P̸ → Rin/L̸

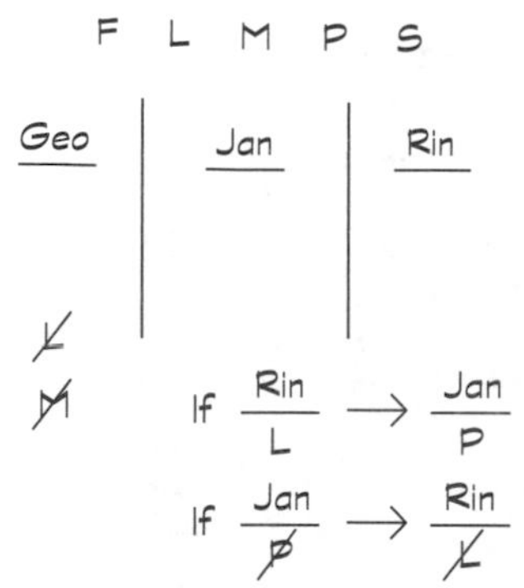

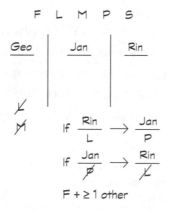

Figure 10.40

Rule 3 is verbose, but you can paraphrase it into a very simple restriction. F is delivered with at least one other piece of mail. No housemate will receive only F.

F L M P S
Geo
Jan
Rin
If Rin/L → Jan/P
If Jan/P̸ → Rin/L̸
F + ≥ 1 other

Figure 10.41

STEP 4: Deductions

Three of the five elements of the BLEND checklist are of little or no help to you here. The only block is created by Rule 3, and it tells you only that F is delivered as a block with at least one of the other pieces of mail; it doesn't tell you which one. There are no rules here that lead to a Limited Options scenario or that give you an Established Entity. So you won't have as complete-looking a Master Sketch as you did in the Talent Agency game. One area in which you can gain some traction is in the Number Restrictions. Because of Rule 3 and the limitation that requires each housemate to receive at least one piece of mail, you can be sure that the numbers will play out in one of two ways: Either two housemates will receive one piece of mail each and one will receive three, or one housemate will receive one piece of mail and the other two housemates will receive two pieces each. It's also worth noting that L is duplicated in Rules 1 and 2. L will be delivered to either Jana or Rini. And when Rini receives L, Jana has to get P.

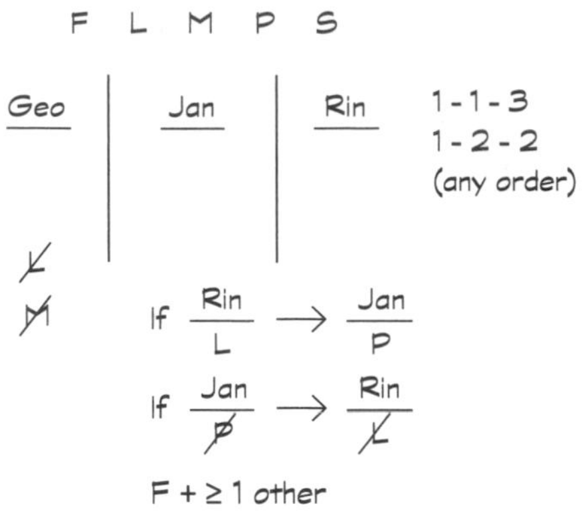

F   L   M   P   S

Geo ___ | Jan ___ | Rin ___   1-1-3
                                1-2-2
                                (any order)

L̸
M̸   If Rin/L → Jan/P

           If Jan/P̸ → Rin/L̸

F + ≥ 1 other

Figure 10.42

Make note of those two possible patterns within the numbers and move on to the questions.

STEP 5: Questions

The questions in this game are a little unusual. You might well have anticipated seeing three or four "if" stems in a game with this few deductions. Instead, the test makers give you three variations on the Complete and Accurate List question type. With a set of questions like this one, you'll be more efficient if you take on the Acceptability question and the "if" question first and then move on to the rarer Complete and Accurate List items.

8. **(B)**

Which one of the following could be a complete and accurate matching of the pieces of mail to the housemates to whom they are addressed?

(A) Georgette: the flyer, the survey
     Jana: the letter
     Rini: the magazine
(B) Georgette: the flyer, the postcard
     Jana: the letter, the magazine
     Rini: the survey
(C) Georgette: the magazine, the survey
     Jana: the flyer, the letter
     Rini: the postcard
(D) Georgette: the survey
     Jana: the flyer, the magazine
     Rini: the letter, the postcard
(E) Georgette: the survey
     Jana: the letter, the magazine, the postcard
     Rini: the flyer[14]

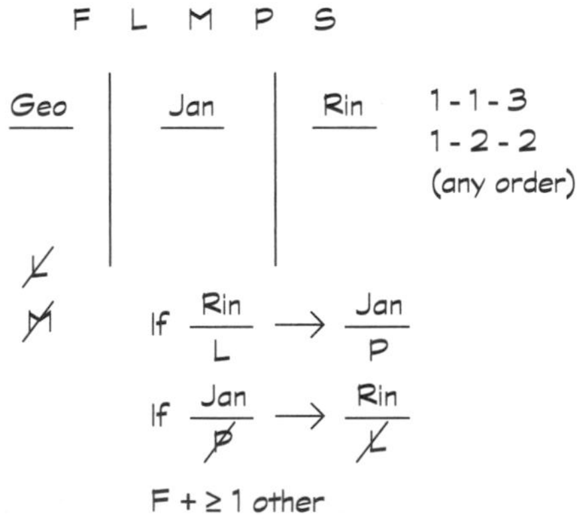

F   L   M   P   S

Geo ___ | Jan ___ | Rin ___   1-1-3
                                1-2-2
                                (any order)

L̸
M̸   If Rin/L → Jan/P

           If Jan/P̸ → Rin/L̸

F + ≥ 1 other

Figure 10.43

[14] PrepTest 49, Sec. 1, Q 8

In any Acceptability question, use the rules to eliminate answer choices that violate them. Here, Rule 1 knocks out choice (C), where Georgette receives M. Rule 2 eliminates choice (D), where Rini receives L but Jana doesn't get P. Rule 3 knocks out choice (E), where F is delivered alone. How can it be that you have gone through the rules but still have two choices left? Well, remember that the game's opening paragraph contains two more restrictions: Each housemate gets a piece of mail and all five pieces of mail need to be distributed. That helps you see that choice (A) is also impossible. It overlooks P and has only four pieces of mail delivered. Cross out choice (A), and you see that choice (B) is the correct answer here.

12. **(E)**

If the magazine and the survey are both addressed to the same housemate, then which one of the following could be true?

(A)   The survey is addressed to Georgette.
(B)   The postcard is addressed to Rini.
(C)   The magazine is addressed to Jana.
(D)   The letter is addressed to Rini.
(E)   The flyer is addressed to Jana.[15]

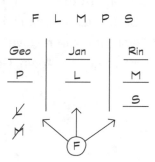

Figure 10.44

The "if" in this stem doesn't seem to assign any pieces of mail to a particular housemate, but don't be too hasty. Work through the deductions that follow from this "if," and you'll actually get quite a bit of certainty. Start by adding the "If" condition as a new rule.

Figure 10.45

Since Georgette is forbidden from receiving M, the newly formed M-S block must be delivered to either Jana or Rini.

---

[15] PrepTest 49, Sec. 1, Q 12

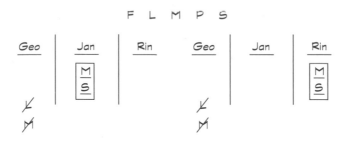

Figure 10.46

It only takes a moment to see that the first of these alternatives is impossible under the rules. F will have to be delivered along with L, P, or the M-S block. If you give P to Rini, there's nothing left that Georgette can receive. If you give L to Rini, on the other hand, P must go to Jana under the terms of Rule 2. Again, Georgette would be shut out.

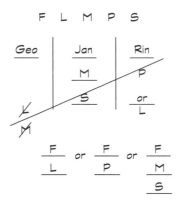

Figure 10.47

With only the second possibility in play, you can nearly complete the sketch. Georgette can't receive L, so she must get either F and P or just P as her mail.

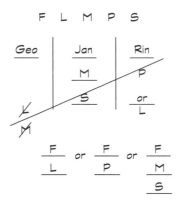

Figure 10.48

That leaves either F and L or just L as Jana's mail.

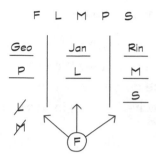

Figure 10.49

Now, characterize the answers and evaluate the choices. The correct answer here *could be true*. The four wrong answers *must be false*. Given that the right answer could be true, you should suspect that F is involved. After all, it's the only entity that isn't locked down. Indeed, choice (E), the only answer that includes F, is correct. Check the other four answers against the mini-sketch if you like; all four are impossible there.

Now, back up to the three Complete and Accurate List questions from this game.

9. **(B)**

Which one of the following is a complete and accurate list of the pieces of mail, any one of which could be the only piece of mail addressed to Jana?

(A) the postcard
(B) the letter, the postcard
(C) the letter, the survey
(D) the magazine, the survey
(E) the letter, the magazine, the postcard[16]

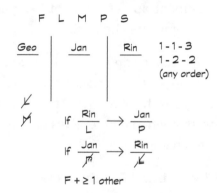

Figure 10.50

With any question of this kind, make sure you read the question stem carefully so that you know what will distinguish the one right answer from the four wrong ones. In question 9, the correct answer contains any and all pieces of mail that could be the *only* one Jana receives. You know from your mini-sketch for question 12 that it would be acceptable for her to receive only L.

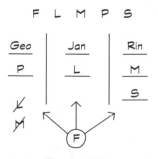

Figure 10.51

---

[16] PrepTest 49, Sec. 1, Q 9

That allows you to eliminate choices (A) and (D), both of which exclude L from the list.

Next, test P, which appears in both choice (B) and choice (E). If she can receive only P, you can eliminate choice (D). If she cannot receive only P, choice (D) is the correct answer. Giving only P to Jana leaves F, L, M, and S to be delivered. Georgette can't receive either L or M, so she'll have to get F and S. Rini would receive L and M in this situation.

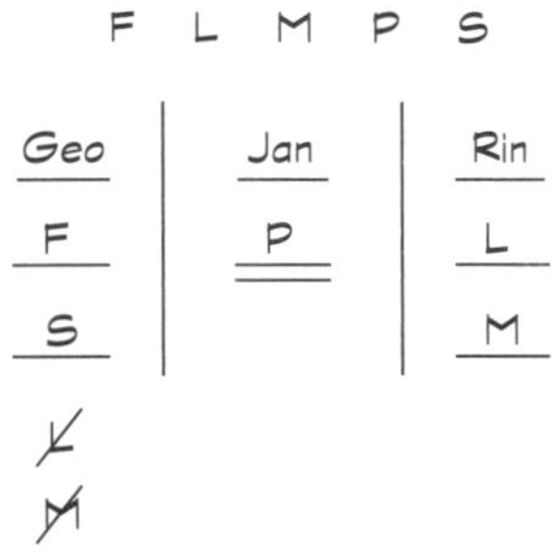

Figure 10.52

That arrangement abides by all of the rules, so P must be included in your complete and accurate list. Eliminate choice (D).

The only thing that distinguishes choices (B) and (E) is the presence of M in choice (E). It doesn't take long to see why M cannot be on the list. Try making M the only piece of mail Jana receives. In that case, you'd have to give L to Rini (L can never go to Georgette because of Rule 1). But Rule 2 says that when Rini receives L, Jana gets P. So M cannot be the *only* piece of mail Jana receives. Eliminate choice (E).

Choice (B), with L and P, is the correct answer. Only those two pieces of mail could be Jana's only deliveries.

10. **(E)**

Which one of the following CANNOT be a complete and accurate list of the pieces of mail addressed to Jana?

(A) the flyer, the letter, the magazine
(B) the flyer, the letter, the postcard
(C) the flyer, the letter, the survey
(D) the flyer, the magazine, the postcard
(E) the flyer, the magazine, the survey[17]

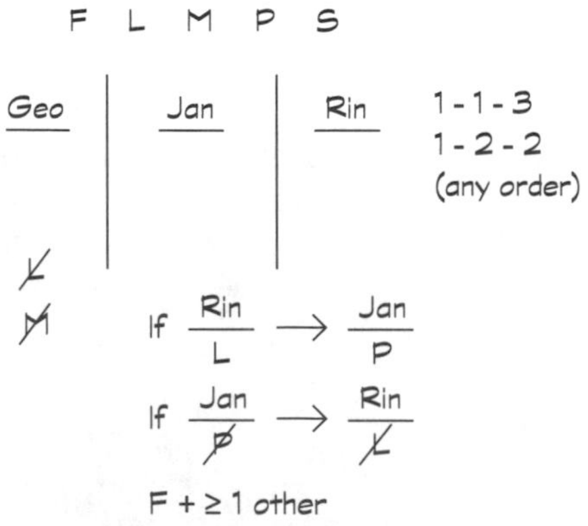

Figure 10.53

---

[17] PrepTest 49, Sec. 1, Q 10

For the untrained test taker (or for the test taker who isn't trained in the Kaplan Method and strategies), this question is a nightmare. The correct answer is the one that *cannot* be Jana's mail. Most test takers will have no choice but to start testing the answers. But you, realizing how important the numbers are, can be much more efficient. Each of these answer choices contains three entities, leaving only two to distribute. Take a moment to jot down which pieces of mail are left over next to each of the answer choices.

The answer that should now pop out to you is choice (E). With L and P left to distribute to Georgette and Rini, you've got a problem. Georgette can't get L, and when Rini gets L, Jana has to receive P (Rule 2), leaving Georgette with no mail. There's simply no way you can acceptably deliver F, M, and S to Jana, so choice (E) is the correct answer.

11. **(B)**

Which one of the following CANNOT be a complete and accurate list of the pieces of mail addressed to Rini?

(A) the magazine, the postcard
(B) the letter, the survey
(C) the letter, the magazine
(D) the flyer, the magazine
(E) the flyer, the letter[18]

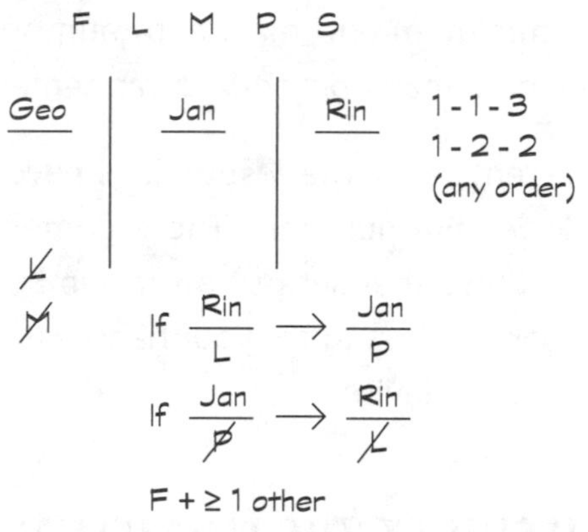

Figure 10.54

Here again, the correct choice is a list that cannot be acceptable. And again, the only option available to most test takers is a random, hunt-and-peck approach that will have them testing answers in the hope of finding the one that won't work out. You can be much more strategic. Consider who is mentioned in the question stem: Rini, who triggers Rule 2 when she receives L. Take a moment to think about the implications of L being delivered to Rini. In that case, Jana gets P.

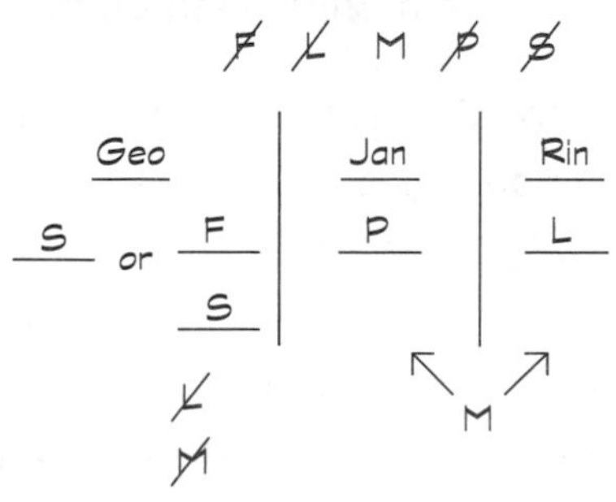

Figure 10.55

---

[18] PrepTest 49, Sec. 1, Q 11

That leaves F, M, and S to be delivered. Georgette needs to get mail, but she cannot be the recipient of M. That means she needs to get just S or F and S (since F cannot be delivered alone, according to Rule 3). Either way, Rini cannot get L and S at the same time. Choice (B) is the correct answer.

Comparing the Housemates' Mail game with the Talent Agencies game is a good exercise in seeing how the test makers can re-use a game format, and yet make one of the two games harder than the other. Housemates' Mail is harder, in part, because of its tough question set. But it also lacks some of the helpful rules (a definite Block of Entities, a key entity that leads to Limited Options) that gave the Talent Agencies game a clearer Master Sketch. What I hope is clear is that when the test makers do not define the number of entities per group, you should turn your attention to determining the number restrictions as best you can. Once you can see the minimum and maximum number of entities that a given group can take, you're able to eliminate many potential arrangements.

In recent years, the test makers have been much more likely to offer Distribution games that lack definite numbers. These games vary in difficulty, but for the most part, they're harder than those that set out a set number of entities per group. In the next section, I'll have you go back a ways to try your hand with one of the toughest Distribution games the test makers have ever devised.

DIFFICULT DISTRIBUTION

Unlike Sequencing games, the test makers don't seem to go out of their way to find many obscure twists on Distribution games. When they want to make them more challenging, they simply take one of the standard variations—with or without definite numbers—and make the game less concrete. In the one you're about to try, for example, you get no help from number restrictions in the setup text, and all five of the rules are conditional formal logic statements. Brace yourself for a challenge, but don't feel overwhelmed. You mastered the formal logic element back in chapter 3. Now, apply that expertise. See how the rules interact to give you more certainty, especially as regards the number restrictions.

Don't time yourself as you try this tough example. Approach it strategically and put each step of the Kaplan Method to work for you. Once you have a strong Master Sketch, you'll find that the questions are actually fairly straightforward. There's no trickery involved on the part of the test makers, just a challenging version of a standard game type. If you find yourself struggling with the questions, check through the explanations for Steps 1–4 of the Kaplan Method. Once you're sure you've got the ideal Master Sketch, return to the question set and get the points.

Each of exactly six doctors—Juarez, Kudrow, Longtree, Nance, Onawa, and Palermo—is at exactly one of two clinics: Souderton or Randsborough. The following conditions must be satisfied:

> Kudrow is at Randsborough if Juarez is at Souderton.
> Onawa is at Souderton if Juarez is at Randsborough.
> If Longtree is at Souderton, then both Nance and Palermo are at Randsborough.
> If Nance is at Randsborough, then so is Onawa.
> If Palermo is at Randsborough, then both Kudrow and Onawa are at Souderton.

19. Which one of the following could be a complete and accurate list of the doctors that are at Souderton?

    (A) Juarez, Kudrow, Onawa
    (B) Juarez, Nance, Onawa, Palermo
    (C) Kudrow, Longtree, Onawa
    (D) Nance, Onawa
    (E) Nance, Palermo

20. If Palermo is at Randsborough, then which one of the following must be true?

    (A) Juarez is at Randsborough.
    (B) Kudrow is at Randsborough.
    (C) Longtree is at Souderton.
    (D) Nance is at Randsborough.
    (E) Onawa is at Randsborough.

21. What is the minimum number of doctors that could be at Souderton?

    (A) zero
    (B) one
    (C) two
    (D) three
    (E) four

22. If Nance and Onawa are at different clinics, which one of the following must be true?

    (A) Juarez is at Souderton.
    (B) Kudrow is at Souderton.
    (C) Palermo is at Randsborough.
    (D) Four doctors are at Souderton.
    (E) Four doctors are at Randsborough.

23. Which one of the following CANNOT be a pair of the doctors at Randsborough?

    (A) Juarez and Kudrow
    (B) Juarez and Palermo
    (C) Kudrow and Onawa
    (D) Nance and Onawa
    (E) Nance and Palermo

24. If Kudrow is at Souderton, then which one of the following must be true?

    (A) Juarez is at Souderton.
    (B) Nance is at Souderton.
    (C) Onawa is at Randsborough.
    (D) Palermo is at Souderton.
    (E) Palermo is at Randsborough.[19]

---

[19] PrepTest 34, Sec. 4, Qs 19–24

Explanations

STEPS 1 AND 2: Overview and Sketch

You can't ask for a shorter setup or a clearer task from an LSAT logic game. There are two clinics and your job is to assign each of six doctors to one or the other. That task, no more complicated than separating whites and colors for the laundry or dividing friends into two teams for a board game, is easy to depict.

Figure 10.56

You'll just jot down each doctor under the headings for Souderton or Randsborough as you determine his or her placement. The one thing that's sorely missing, though, is any ability to determine how many of the doctors will be assigned to each clinic. From what you're given in the opening paragraph of this game, you could have 0 and 6, 1 and 5, 2 and 4, 3 and 3, 4 and 2, 5 and 1, or 6 and 0 of the doctors at Souderton and Randsborough, respectively. Steps 2 and 3 will have to reduce that daunting number of possibilities.

STEP 3: Rules

It doesn't take more than a glance to see that all of the rules here are conditional formal logic statements, although Rules 1 and 2 try to disguise this a little by placing the "if" clauses in the second half of the sentences.

You know what to do. Translate each of the rules and determine its contrapositive. Try as best you can to keep all of the "ifs" in a neat line so that you can see when the result of one rule triggers the "if" in another. Here's how you should depict the translations and contrapositives:

Rule 1:

$$\text{If } J_{sou} \rightarrow K_{ran}$$
$$\text{If } K_{sou} \rightarrow J_{ran}$$

Figure 10.57

Because there are only two possible placements for each doctor, and because all of the doctors will be placed, the negation of "K is at Randsborough" is, simply, "K is at Souderton." The negation of "J is at Souderton" is "J is at Randsborough." Keeping all of the formal logic in the affirmative makes it a lot easier to see the impact of each condition on the entities in the game. You'll notice that I will translate and contrapose the rules this way throughout the game.

Rule 2:

$$\text{If } J_{ran} \quad \rightarrow \quad O_{sou}$$
$$\text{If } O_{ran} \quad \rightarrow \quad J_{sou}$$

Figure 10.58

Rule 3:

$$\text{If } L_{sou} \quad \rightarrow \quad N_{ran} \text{ and } P_{ran}$$
$$\text{If } N_{sou} \text{ or } P_{sou} \quad \rightarrow \quad L_{ran}$$

Figure 10.59

Don't forget to change "and" to "or" when you contrapose clauses that contain more than one entity. Either N being placed at Souderton *or* P being placed there is sufficient to know that L must be placed at Randsborough. You don't need both of the triggers in the contrapositive to be true; just one is enough to trigger the result. The same is true of Rule 5, of course.

Rule 4:

$$\text{If } N_{ran} \quad \rightarrow \quad O_{ran}$$
$$\text{If } O_{sou} \quad \rightarrow \quad N_{sou}$$

Figure 10.60

Rule 5:

$$\text{If } P_{ran} \quad \rightarrow \quad K_{sou} \text{ and } O_{sou}$$
$$\text{If } K_{ran} \text{ or } O_{ran} \quad \rightarrow \quad P_{sou}$$

Figure 10.61

Most test takers, of course, cannot even get this far. But with your training, you can gain an even clearer picture of how this game will work out. Learning to front-load your work in Steps 1–4 of the Kaplan Method is probably the single most valuable lesson of this book when it comes to the most difficult games.

STEP 4: **Deductions**

Several of the rules in this game combine, and you could spend an inordinate amount of time working out all of the various possibilities. But the first two rules suggest an easy solution. The trigger for Rule 1 is "J is at Souderton," and the trigger for Rule 2 is "J is at Randsborough." That makes an easy starting point for Limited Options sketches. Try them out. You're sure to gain some important insights into the arrangements acceptable in this game.

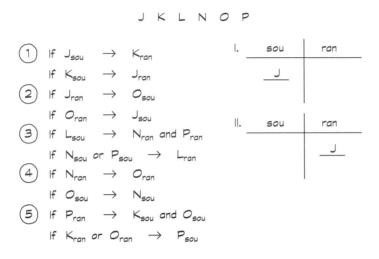

Figure 10.62

With J at Souderton, you know from Rule 1 that K is at Randsborough.

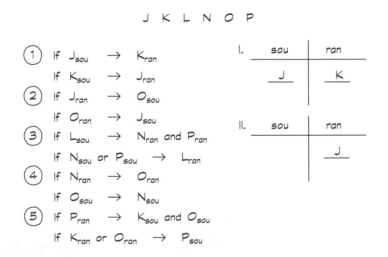

Figure 10.63

That, in turn, triggers the contrapositive of Rule 5. You can place P at Souderton, too. Notice how important it was to change that "and" into an "or" in the contrapositive of Rule 5.

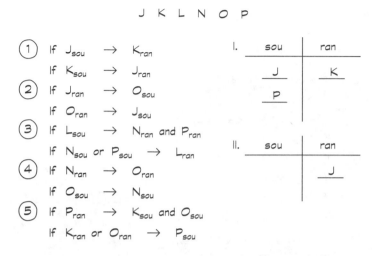

Figure 10.64

Placing P at Souderton means placing L at Randsborough. That's the contrapositive of Rule 3.

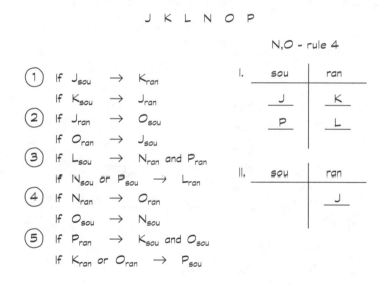

Figure 10.65

L's placement doesn't trigger any additional deductions. So Option I is complete, although it's worth noticing that the two entities that remain—N and O—restrict one another in Rule 4. Either they're together at one of the clinics, or N is at Souderton and O at Randsborough.

Go to work on Option II. With J at Randsborough, Rule 2 tells you to place O at Souderton.

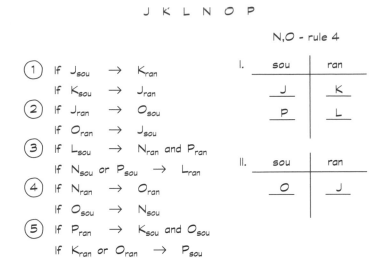

Figure 10.66

That requires N to be at Souderton as well, according to Rule 4.

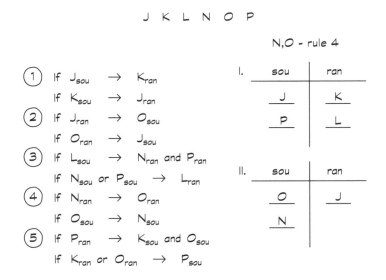

Figure 10.67

Placing N at Souderton triggers the contrapositive of Rule 3. L must take a place at Randsborough in this option.

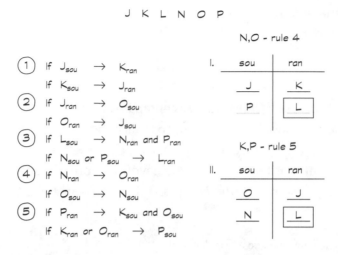

Figure 10.68

This is one of your breakthrough moments in this game. L, you now know, is always going to be placed at Randsborough because that must happen in both of your Limited Options. You've created an Established Entity in a game where you thought none existed.

You can't push Option II any farther, but here again, the two entities that remain—K and P—limit one another, this time in Rule 5: P is at Randsborough with K at Souderton, K is at Randsborough with P at Souderton, or P and K are together at Souderton.

When all is said and done (and deduced!), this game has only six acceptable arrangements. You could even list them out:

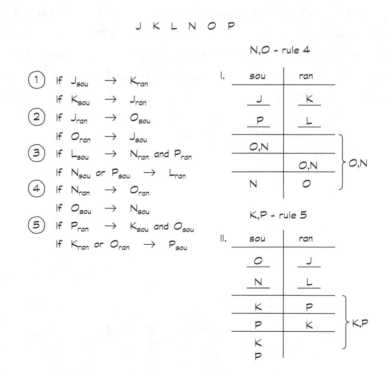

Figure 10.69

Whether you go to that extent or not, you'd do well to note that the possible number restrictions are down to 2 and 4, 3 and 3, or 4 and 2 of the doctors at Souderton and Randsborough, respectively.

STEP 5: Questions

This is a balanced question set: One Partial Acceptability, three "Ifs," one Minimum/Maximum, and one Must Be False question. There's no reason to take the questions out of order here. Given the Limited Options sketches you spent time making during Step 4, you should be prepared to tackle them all without hesitation. This is the payoff for your patience in Steps 1–4, and it's where you'll outshine your competition come test day on a game like this one.

19. **(B)**

Which one of the following could be a complete and accurate list of the doctors that are at Souderton?

(A) Juarez, Kudrow, Onawa
(B) Juarez, Nance, Onawa, Palermo
(C) Kudrow, Longtree, Onawa
(D) Nance, Onawa
(E) Nance, Palermo[20]

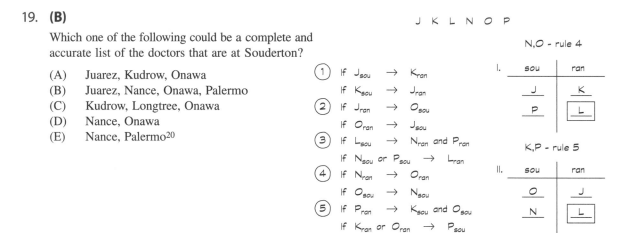

Figure 10.70

This is a Partial Acceptability question. In this case, use your Master Sketch to eliminate the violators. It's tough to apply the rules when only one side of the Distribution is visible in the answer choices, but in your sketch, you can zero in on Souderton and easily spot the unacceptable groupings there. First, L can never appear at Souderton, so cross out choice (C). Next, notice that when J is at Souderton (that's Option I, of course), P must be there, too. Eliminate choice (A), which has J but lacks P. The three remaining choices all contain N. You may notice that choice (B) is acceptable under Option I. Or you may eliminate choices (D) and (E) because neither N and O nor N and P can ever be the *only* entities at Souderton. Either way, choice (B) is the correct answer. Your Limited Options deductions will continue to pay dividends right down the line.

---

[20] PrepTest 34, Sec. 4, Q 19

20. **(A)**

If Palermo is at Randsborough, then which one of the following must be true?

(A) Juarez is at Randsborough.
(B) Kudrow is at Randsborough.
(C) Longtree is at Souderton.
(D) Nance is at Randsborough.
(E) Onawa is at Randsborough.[21]

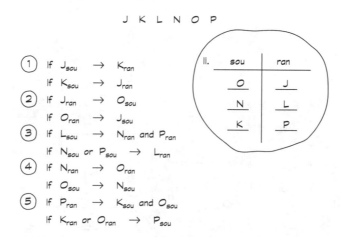

Figure 10.71

A quick check of the Master Sketch shows that P can only be assigned to Randsborough in Option II. When P is at Randsborough, Rule 5 requires that K be at Souderton. Now, you have the complete mini-sketch above. Choice (A), which is the very definition of Option II, *must be true*, making it the correct answer. All of the remaining choices *must be false* in this situation.

21. **(C)**

What is the minimum number of doctors that could be at Souderton?

(A) zero
(B) one
(C) two
(D) three
(E) four[22]

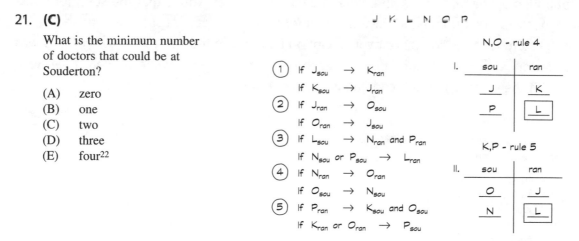

Figure 10.72

Here's a question you've known the answer to since you made your Limited Options sketches. The minimum number of doctors at either facility is two. Choice (C) is correct, and you're half-way home in this question set.

22. **(A)**

If Nance and Onawa are at different clinics, which one of the following must be true?

(A)   Juarez is at Souderton.
(B)   Kudrow is at Souderton.
(C)   Palermo is at Randsborough.
(D)   Four doctors are at Souderton.
(E)   Four doctors are at Randsborough.[23]

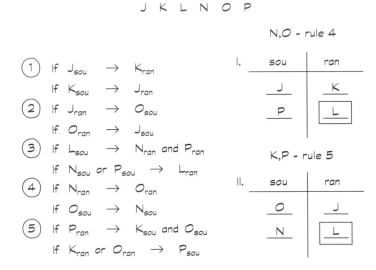

Figure 10.73

The "if" from this question stem can only happen in Option I. Choice (A), the very definition of Option I, *must be true* and is, therefore, the correct answer. Notice that the stem for question 20 put you in Option II and rewarded you for knowing that J must be at Randsborough, while the stem for question 22 put you in Option I and rewarded you for knowing that J was at Souderton. There's not much doubt that the test makers were aware of what they were doing with the complementary conditions in Rules 1 and 2.

23. **(E)**

Which one of the following CANNOT be a pair of the doctors at Randsborough?

(A)   Juarez and Kudrow
(B)   Juarez and Palermo
(C)   Kudrow and Onawa
(D)   Nance and Onawa
(E)   Nance and Palermo[24]

---

[23] PrepTest 34, Sec. 4, Q 22
[24] PrepTest 34, Sec. 4, Q 23

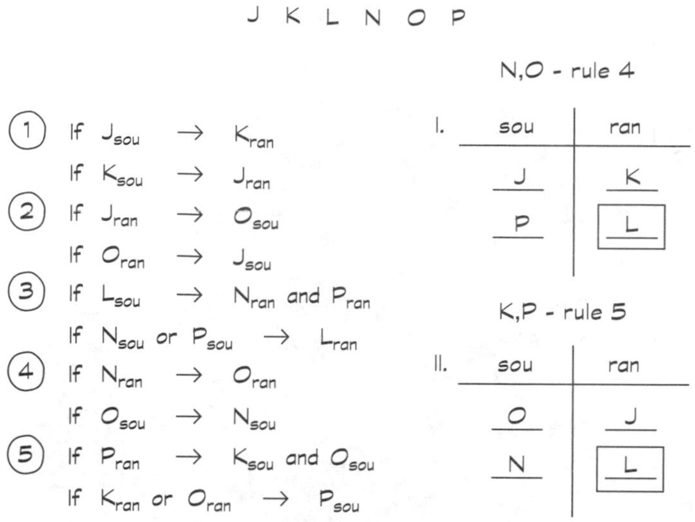

J K L N O P

N,O - rule 4

① If J$_{sou}$ → K$_{ran}$

If K$_{sou}$ → J$_{ran}$

② If J$_{ran}$ → O$_{sou}$

If O$_{ran}$ → J$_{sou}$

③ If L$_{sou}$ → N$_{ran}$ and P$_{ran}$

If N$_{sou}$ or P$_{sou}$ → L$_{ran}$

④ If N$_{ran}$ → O$_{ran}$

If O$_{sou}$ → N$_{sou}$

⑤ If P$_{ran}$ → K$_{sou}$ and O$_{sou}$

If K$_{ran}$ or O$_{ran}$ → P$_{sou}$

I.

sou	ran
J	K
P	L

K,P - rule 5

II.

sou	ran
O	J
N	L

Figure 10.74

With no new "if" condition, you know that this question can be answered from your Master Sketch (provided that you have an adequate one). The correct answer here *must be false*. So eliminate anything that could be true. Choices (A) and (B) are both possible in Option II. Choices (C) and (D) are both possible in Option I. N and P can never be together at Randsborough (a fact you could also derive by combining Rule 5 and the contrapositive of Rule 4). Thus, choice (E) is correct. In fact, if you check the Limited Options Master Sketch, you can see that either N or P is always assigned to Souderton. That's enough to make this correct answer apparent.

24. **(B)**

If Kudrow is at Souderton, then which one of the following must be true?

(A)   Juarez is at Souderton.
(B)   Nance is at Souderton.
(C)   Onawa is at Randsborough.
(D)   Palermo is at Souderton.
(E)   Palermo is at Randsborough.[25]

---

[25] PrepTest 34, Sec. 4, Q 24

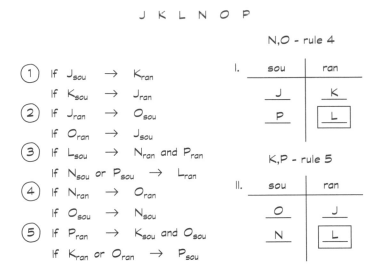

J K L N O P

N,O - rule 4

I.

sou	ran
J	K
P	L

① If J$_{sou}$ → K$_{ran}$
   If K$_{sou}$ → J$_{ran}$
② If J$_{ran}$ → O$_{sou}$
   If O$_{ran}$ → J$_{sou}$
③ If L$_{sou}$ → N$_{ran}$ and P$_{ran}$
   If N$_{sou}$ or P$_{sou}$ → L$_{ran}$
④ If N$_{ran}$ → O$_{ran}$
   If O$_{sou}$ → N$_{sou}$
⑤ If P$_{ran}$ → K$_{sou}$ and O$_{sou}$
   If K$_{ran}$ or O$_{ran}$ → P$_{sou}$

K,P - rule 5

II.

sou	ran
O	J
N	L

Figure 10.75

Here's one final "If" question. Its stem puts you into Option II, the only one that allows K to be at Souderton. The correct answer *must be true*. N must be at Souderton in Option II. Choice (B) is correct and you're done. For the record, choices (A) and (C) *must be false* in Option II, while choices (D) and (E) *could be* either true or false there.

That's a remarkable game. It's strained the brains of a lot of test takers. But it's also an example of a game in which the solution is hiding in plain sight. In fact, when you look at the set of rules now, you'll see that it's almost as if the test makers were trying to give you a clue.

> Kudrow is at Randsborough if Juarez is at Souderton.
> Onawa is at Souderton if Juarez is at Randsborough.
> If Longtree is at Souderton, then both Nance and Palermo
> are at Randsborough.
> If Nance is at Randsborough, then so is Onawa.
> If Palermo is at Randsborough, then both Kudrow and
> Onawa are at Souderton.[26]

Not only are those two rules written in a way that creates the Limited Options that unlock the game, but they're the only two in which the "if" clause is put at the end of the sentence. I don't want to encourage you to look for "secret messages" on the LSAT or to suggest that the test makers always leave obscure clues for you to discern. I do, however, want you to recognize that the information you need is always there, and it's always explicit.

As you've seen (and will continue to see throughout this section), the toughest examples of any game type always reward a little extra time in the Deductions step. Most test takers suffer through tough question sets because they haven't adequately interpreted and synthesized the rules and restrictions. All of the formal logic work you did on the Clinic Assignments game will help you again in the next chapter on Selection games.

---

[26] PrepTest 34, Sec. 4, Game 4

CHAPTER 11

SELECTION GAMES

Before you dive in to this chapter on Selection games, make sure you're fully familiar with formal logic, which is covered in chapter 3. Conditional statements are at the heart of every Selection game. That's because Selection tasks are all about choosing a smaller group out of a larger one. The situations described in these games' setups vary wildly, but you can always safely anticipate seeing rules that tell you, "If A is chosen, then B is not chosen," "If C is chosen, then D is chosen," or "If E is not chosen, then F is chosen," or some variation on those. It's a safe bet that you can combine some of the rules to make additional deductions, too. The most basic example would be a case in which the test makers include two rules such as, "If X is chosen, then Y is chosen" and "If Y is chosen, then Z is chosen." That means that choosing X entails choosing Y *and* Z. It also indicates that not choosing Z means not choosing Y *and* not choosing X. If it's not immediately apparent to you why that's the case, revisit chapter 3 of this book and shore up your formal logic skills.

REAL-LIFE SELECTION

You make selections all the time in your day-to-day life. You might be deciding which guests to invite to a wedding or a dinner. At work, you might need to choose which of six employees to send to a conference or meeting. Preparing to go to the conference, you might need to choose which of your clothes to pack for the trip. Often, the toughest part of real-life selection lies in figuring out what *not* to include. That's true on the LSAT as well. Always remember that coming up with a complete and accurate list of which ones are *not* chosen is just as valuable as the list of which ones *are*. In real life, these tasks involve wildly different numbers of choices, professional considerations, and even personal feelings. Fortunately, the LSAT always limits you to choosing from among a limited set of options, typically from among five to nine entities.

Thinking about a real-life selection task will reveal the variations that the test makers use when designing these games. Here's a typical case: Imagine that you and a roommate are going to throw a party; maybe you have friends coming over to watch a big football game. One of you asks, "What snacks should we have?" In real life, that question is open-ended. You could have as many or as few snacks as you like. As you try to make your decision, it's likely that your first question (much as it is in Distribution games) will be, "How many snacks will we serve?" You know enough about how LSAT logic games are constructed to anticipate that, for the most part, the test makers aren't going to answer that question directly. That's been true especially on more recent tests. All of the Selection games you've seen up to this point in the book put the burden on you to determine the minimum or maximum number of entities that could be chosen.

In the real-life version of the task, you could buy all of the snacks, make all of them at home, or decide on some combination of the two. You and your roommate might say, "We're too busy to make anything; let's just buy the snacks." Or you might decide, "Let's make two snacks and buy two others." It will always be important to note whether the test makers have designated subdivisions within the entities. They could, for example, say simply, "The roommates will choose from among eight snacks: almonds, cupcakes, garlic bread, licorice, meatballs, pretzels, tortilla chips, and wings." Or they could put the snacks into two categories, like so: "The roommates will choose from among four homemade snacks—cupcakes, garlic bread, meatballs, and wings—and four store-bought snacks—almonds, licorice, pretzels, and tortilla chips." When the test makers use one of the latter scenarios, look for restrictions based on the subcategories, with rules like "At least two homemade snacks and at least two store-bought snacks must be served," for example.

However the entity set is constructed, you can anticipate the types of rules that will be used. They're the same kinds of "rules" that guide your real-world decision. You might say, "If we serve pretzels, let's not have tortilla chips," or "If we have wings, then we have to have garlic bread." That leads to one of the friendliest features of Selection games: your sketch is basically no different than what you'd do in real life. "Okay, let's list out our potential snacks. We'll circle the ones we're going to serve and cross out the ones we're not."

Figure 11.1

You know that I'm a big fan of understanding logic games in a real-world context. Re-contextualizing a seemingly difficult LSAT task into a simple, real-life scenario will help you earn points confidently and quickly on test day.

STANDARD SELECTION GAMES

You've already seen a handful of the most representative logic games that appeared between PrepTest 33 and PrepTest 53. I'll reprint two of the games' setups and Master Sketches here to refresh your memory. If you can review these games and think, "Yeah, I've got it," then you're ready for the Selection game(s) you're most likely to see on test day.

An album contains photographs picturing seven friends: Raimundo, Selma, Ty, Umiko, Wendy, Yakira, Zack. The friends appear either alone or in groups with one another, in accordance with the following:

Wendy appears in every photograph that Selma appears in.
Selma appears in every photograph that Umiko appears in.
Raimundo appears in every photograph that Yakira does not appear in.
Neither Ty nor Raimundo appears in any photograph that Wendy appears in.[1]

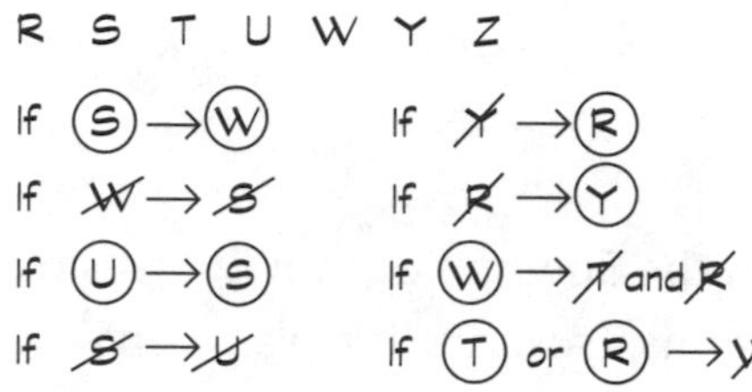

Figure 11.2

A summer program offers at least one of the following seven courses: geography, history, literature, mathematics, psychology, sociology, zoology. The following restrictions on the program must apply:

If mathematics is offered, then either literature or sociology (but not both) is offered.
If literature is offered, then geography is also offered but psychology is not.
If sociology is offered, then psychology is also offered but zoology is not.
If geography is offered, then both history and zoology are also offered.[2]

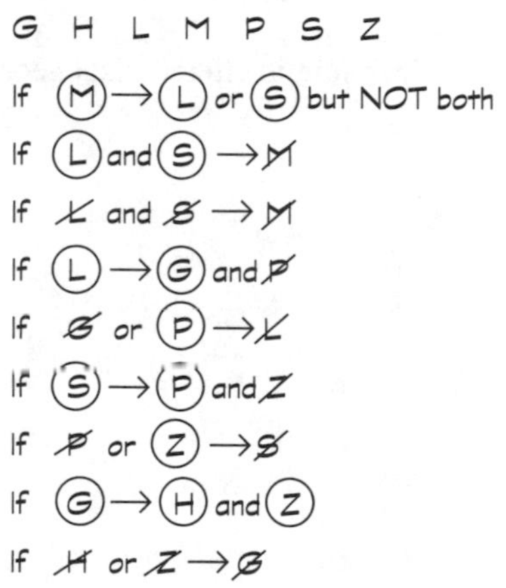

Figure 11.3

Those two games, especially the Summer School Courses game, are among the most difficult Selection games offered in the last decade. (The Dorm Room Appliances game from chapter 2 is one of the easier examples.) But notice that all of the Selection games you've seen have exactly the same task: Choose some of the entities and reject others. Each friend is either in the photograph or out of it; the courses are either offered or not offered during the summer. The games don't specify up front how many of the entities will be "in" or "out." They are anchored by formal logic, "if-then" rules. The big insight this reveals is that the test makers don't need to use weird twists or variations in order to make Selection games harder.

---

[1] PrepTest 45, Sec. 3, Game 3

[2] PrepTest 49, Sec. 1, Game 3

So what is it that makes these two games so much harder? One key consideration is simply the number of entities. It's inherently harder to choose from among seven items than it is to choose from among five. Notice, too, that in the Friends Photographs and Summer School Courses games, the test makers made the rules hard to translate. In Friends Photographs, they did this by making the sufficient and necessary terms harder to distinguish. The rule "Selma appears in every photograph that Umiko appears in" makes Umiko's inclusion sufficient to establish Selma's and Selma's inclusion necessary for Umiko's. It translates as follows, with the contrapositive included for good measure:

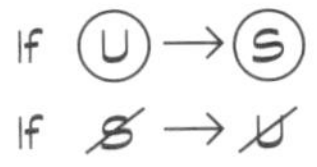

If $U \rightarrow S$
If $\cancel{S} \rightarrow \cancel{U}$

Figure 11.4

In the Summer School Courses game, there's no attempt to hide the sufficient and necessary terms. Each rule is a plain vanilla "if-then" statement. What they've done this time is include an additional term in the necessary clause and, in some cases, mix included and excluded entities into the same clause. Take this rule, for example:

If literature is offered, then geography is also offered but psychology is not.[3]

It translates:

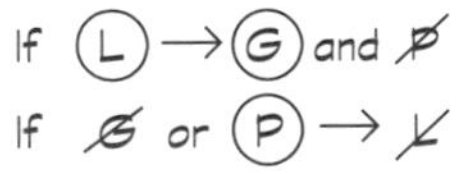

If $L \rightarrow G$ and $\cancel{P}$
If $\cancel{G}$ or $P \rightarrow \cancel{L}$

Figure 11.5

A mastery of formal logic rules, translations, and contrapositives is non-negotiable for the test taker who wants the points from a Selection game. While some test administrations have little or no formal logic in the Logic Games section, other (quite recent) tests have featured two Selection games, each packed with formal logic rules.

There's one more feature, also related to formal logic, common to all Selection games. In every case, some of the rules can be combined. In the Friends Photographs game, for example, there is a string of deductions triggered by the inclusion of Umiko.

---

[3] PrepTest 49, Sec. 1, Game 3

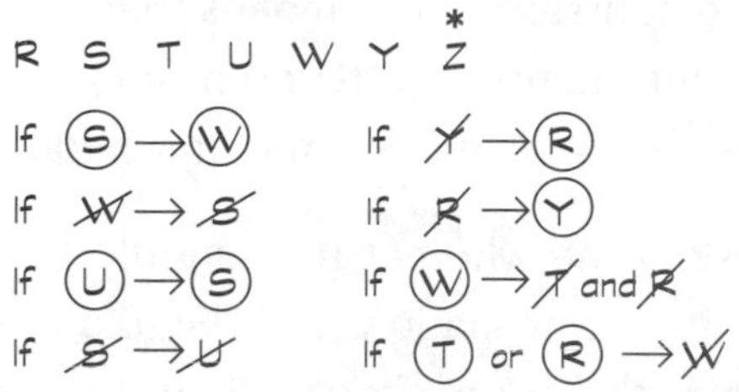

R S T U W Y Z*

If S→W   If X→R
If W→Z   If Z→Y
If U→S   If W→T and R
If Z→U   If T or R →W

Figure 11.6

Having Umiko in the picture requires having Selma (Rule 2). Selma's inclusion entails Wendy's inclusion (Rule 1). Once Wendy is in, Raimundo and Ty are out (Rule 4). And Raimundo's exclusion means that Yakira must be in the photo (Rule 3).

In the Dorm Room Appliances game, turning on the hairdryer means turning off the razor, the television, and the vacuum.

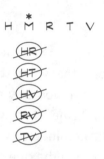

Figure 11.7

In the Summer School Course game, there are several strings of deductions triggered when one of the courses either is or is not offered. One example occurs when literature is offered.

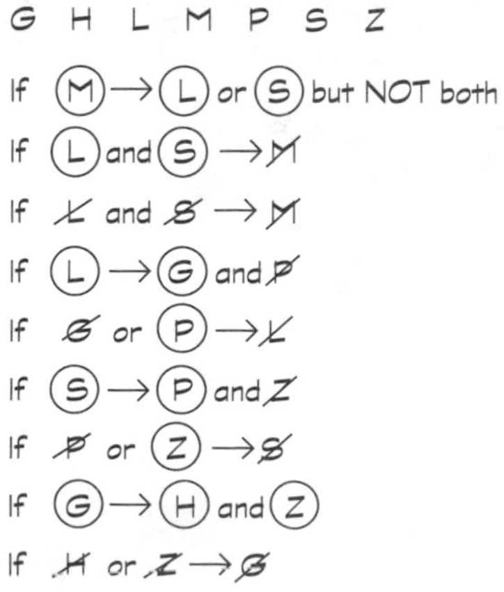

G H L M P S Z

If M→L or S but NOT both
If L and S →M
If L and S →M
If L→G and P
If S or P →L
If S→P and Z
If P or Z →S
If G→H and Z
If H or Z →S

Figure 11.8

Including literature among the courses offered means that geography must be offered, too (Rule 2). Including geography, in turn, means offering history and zoology (Rule 4). But including zoology means cutting sociology from the summer schedule (Rule 3, contrapositive).

Many of my students have asked me whether they should take the time to sketch out the implications of every possible rule combination, and I've told them not to. Adding all of those results to your scratch work runs the risk of simply filling the page with so much information that you can no longer see it clearly or use it effectively. Moreover, if you miss a combination, you could go into the questions thinking you've got every possible arrangement figured out when you don't. A better approach is to write out all of formal logic neatly in a line, as you see in the sample sketches. That way, you can scan all of the triggers quickly to see whether a given result triggers another statement. Combine all of the statements that you can. When you get to a result that doesn't trigger another statement, you have the information you need to answer the question at hand. Caution: You must be familiar and handy with formal logic to do this. Keep practicing what you learned in chapter 3 until forming contrapositives and combining statements is second nature.

Standard Selection Practice

There's one more standard Selection game that you saw in Part I. There, I had you do an exercise based on the game's rules in chapter 3 and you saw a couple of the questions in chapter 5, but you haven't had a chance to try the game all the way through. I'll reprint the game here, this time in its entirety. Take eight and half minutes to tackle this game and its question set. If you find that you're getting bogged down in the questions, stop and review the explanations for Steps 1–4 of the Kaplan Method. When you're sure you've got a complete and accurate picture of the game's rules and deductions, go back to the questions. Here's a hint: Pay special attention to rules that reduce the maximum number or increase the minimum number of entities that you can select.

A fruit stand carries at least one kind of the following kinds of fruit: figs, kiwis, oranges, pears, tangerines, and watermelons. The stand does not carry any other kind of fruit. The selection of fruits the stand carries is consistent with the following conditions:

If the stand carries kiwis, then it does not carry pears.
If the stand does not carry tangerines, then it carries kiwis.
If the stand carries oranges, then it carries both pears and watermelons.
If the stand carries watermelons, then it carries figs or tangerines or both.

1. Which one of the following could be a complete and accurate list of the kinds of fruit the stand carries?

    (A)   oranges, pears
    (B)   pears, tangerines
    (C)   oranges, pears, watermelons
    (D)   oranges, tangerines, watermelons
    (E)   kiwis, oranges, pears, watermelons

2. Which one of the following could be the only kind of fruit the stand carries?

    (A)   figs
    (B)   oranges
    (C)   pears
    (D)   tangerines
    (E)   watermelons

3. Which one of the following CANNOT be a complete and accurate list of the kinds of fruit the stand carries?

    (A)   kiwis, tangerines
    (B)   tangerines, watermelons
    (C)   figs, kiwis, watermelons
    (D)   oranges, pears, tangerines, watermelons
    (E)   figs, kiwis, oranges, pears, watermelons

4. If the stand carries no watermelons, then which one of the following must be true?

    (A)   The stand carries kiwis.
    (B)   The stand carries at least two kinds of fruit.
    (C)   The stand carries at most three kinds of fruit.
    (D)   The stand carries neither oranges nor pears.
    (E)   The stand carries neither oranges nor kiwis.

5. If the stand carries watermelons, then which one of the following must be false?

    (A)   The stand does not carry figs.
    (B)   The stand does not carry tangerines.
    (C)   The stand does not carry pears.
    (D)   The stand carries pears but not oranges.
    (E)   The stand carries pears but not tangerines.

6. If the condition that if the fruit stand does not carry tangerines then it does carry kiwis is suspended, and all other conditions remain in effect, then which one of the following CANNOT be a complete and accurate list of the kinds of fruit the stand carries?

    (A)   pears
    (B)   figs, pears
    (C)   oranges, pears, watermelons
    (D)   figs, pears, watermelons
    (E)   figs, oranges, pears, watermelons[4]

---

[4] PrepTest 36, Sec. 4, Qs 1–6

Explanations

STEPS 1 and 2: Overview and Sketch

Your task is pretty easy to picture. You have a warehouse with six kinds of fruits in it. Your job is to man the stand at which you sell the fruit, and it's your responsibility to pick which fruits will be displayed at any given time. You'll choose which fruits to display and which to leave in storage.

As a typical Selection task, this doesn't call for a special framework. Just list the entities in a line. Circle those that are included for display and cross out those that are rejected.

F   K   O   P   T   W

Figure 11.9

STEP 3: Rules

As usual in Selection games, all four of the rules are conditional formal logic statements. Take them one at a time. Translate and diagram the statements and their contrapositives as you go.

Rule 1 is a standard "if-then."

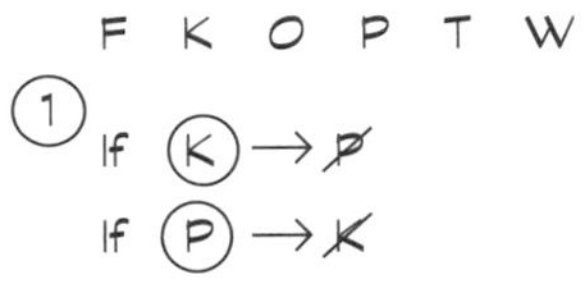

F   K   O   P   T   W

① If Ⓚ → P̶
If Ⓟ → K̶

Figure 11.10

Rule 1 reduces the maximum number of fruits that you can have on display at any given time. Either kiwis or pears must stay in the warehouse, since displaying either one would prevent you from displaying the other. It's fine if you display neither kiwis nor pears, but not if you display both.

Rule 2 is another standard "if-then," but this time the sufficient "trigger" is negative.

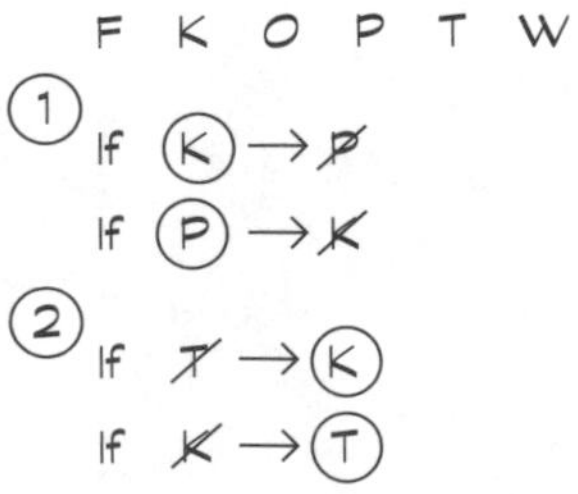

F   K   O   P   T   W

① If Ⓚ → P̶
If Ⓟ → K̶
② If T̶ → Ⓚ
If K̶ → Ⓣ

Figure 11.11

This rule increases the minimum number of fruits that you can have on display at any given time: Either tangerines or kiwis must be chosen. Note that nothing in this rule prevents you from having both, but you must at least have one or the other.

Rules 3 and 4 are formal logic statements that restrict three entities each. Rule 3 translates like this:

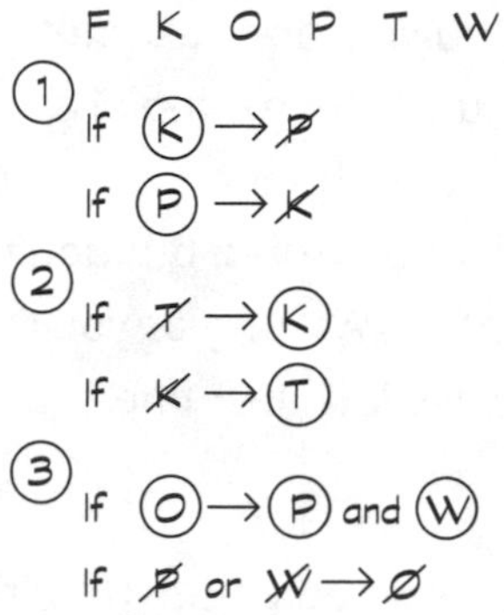

F   K   O   P   T   W

(1) If (K) → P̸

If (P) → K̸

(2) If T̸ → (K)

If K̸ → (T)

(3) If (O) → (P) and (W)

If P̸ or W̸ → Ø

Figure 11.12

Remember that when you negate "and," it becomes "or." Excluding either pears or watermelons forces you to exclude oranges.

Rule 4 looks weirder than it is.

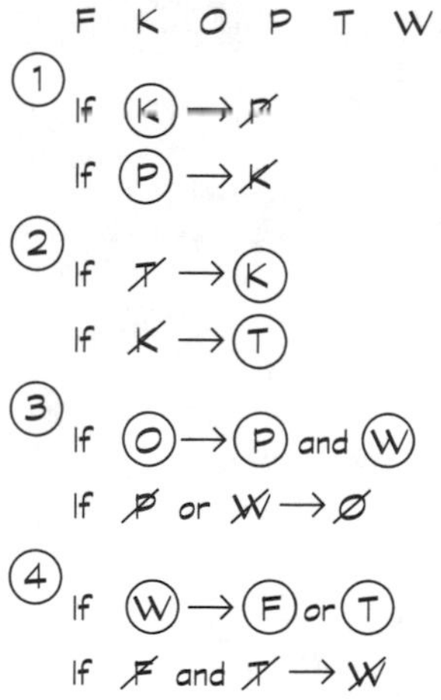

F   K   O   P   T   W

(1) If (K) → T̸

If (P) → K̸

(2) If T̸ → (K)

If K̸ → (T)

(3) If (O) → (P) and (W)

If P̸ or W̸ → Ø

(4) If (W) → (F) or (T)

If F̸ and T̸ → W̸

Figure 11.13

The "or both" at the end of the rule is actually redundant to the logic. If you display watermelons, you need to display at least one of figs or tangerines. If you display both figs and tangerines, you have, by definition, displayed at least one of them.

With a pure formal logic game like this (and this is like nearly all Selection games), keep your string of formal logic translations in a neat line. That will help you immensely when you need to see which of the rules combine.

STEP 4: Deductions

It's tempting to try to put all of the various combinations of formal logic together before moving on to the questions. But as I discussed above, this is usually more trouble than it's worth. For now, just scan the list of rules quickly and take note of which ones may potentially be combined. In the contrapositive of Rule 1, for example, choosing pears means excluding kiwis. That, in turn, triggers the contrapositive of Rule 2: Excluding kiwis means including tangerines. You could go on like this through all of the rules, but don't. The questions will signal which of the rules are at issue in a given situation. As long as you're able to see the implications of the rule(s) triggered, you'll handle the questions just fine.

STEP 5: Questions

This is a balanced question set for a balanced game. The first three questions can be answered without any new scratch work. The next three have new "ifs" (as you'll see, question 6 is actually a Rule-Changer) and will benefit from mini-sketches.

1. **(B)**

Which one of the following could be a complete and accurate list of the kinds of fruit the stand carries?

(A) oranges, pears
(B) pears, tangerines
(C) oranges, pears, watermelons
(D) oranges, tangerines, watermelons
(E) kiwis, oranges, pears, watermelons[5]

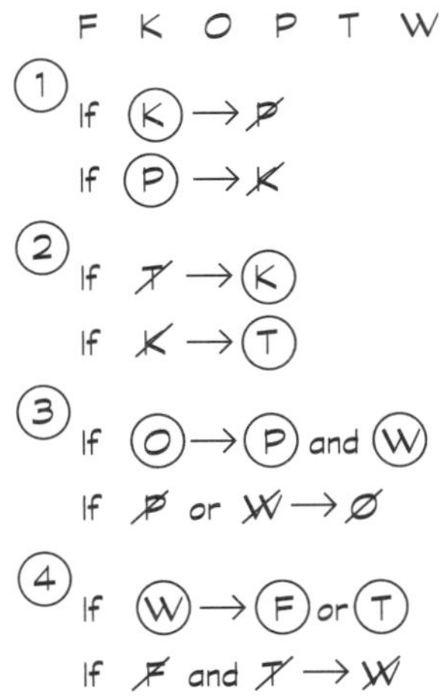

Figure 11.14

This is a standard Acceptability question. As you've done so often before, use the rules to eliminate answer choices that violate them. Rule 1 knocks out choice (E), where K and P are found together. Rule 2 eliminates choices (A) and (C), both of which lack both K and T. Rule 3 knocks out choice (D), which has O and W, but lacks P. That leaves choice (B), the correct answer.

---

[5] PrepTest 36, Sec. 4, Q 1

2. **(D)**

Which one of the following could be the only kind of fruit the stand carries?

(A) figs
(B) oranges
(C) pears
(D) tangerines
(E) watermelons[6]

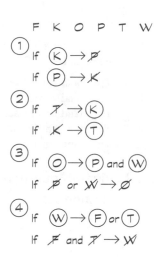

Figure 11.15

This is a funny little question that drives students crazy. That's because they dive in and try to test choices before they've taken time to think about the stem. What's the most important word there? It's "only." The correct answer is a fruit that could be on display without any other fruits being selected. This has to implicate Rule 2, which requires that, in every case, you must display either K or T. One of those two fruits must be the right answer. No matter what other fruit you put on display, you'd have to choose either K or T, too. So the right answer has either K or T. It turns out to be choice (D), with T. All four of the wrong answers have fruits that would have to be accompanied by either T or K and so cannot be the *only* fruit selected.

3. **(E)**

Which one of the following CANNOT be a complete and accurate list of the kinds of fruit the stand carries?

(A) kiwis, tangerines
(B) tangerines, watermelons
(C) figs, kiwis, watermelons
(D) oranges, pears, tangerines, watermelons
(E) figs, kiwis, oranges, pears, watermelons[7]

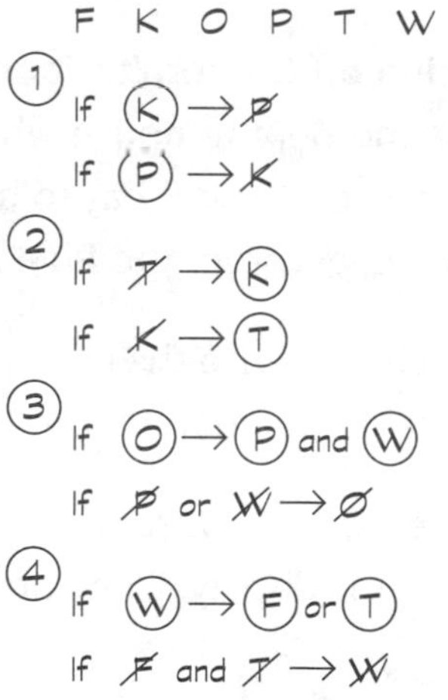

Figure 11.16

This is a *must be false* question. It functions like an anti-Acceptability question, where the one rule violator is the correct answer. Fortunately, you need only test Rule 1 in order to find the correct choice. Answer choice (E) includes both K and P. That means it cannot be an accurate list of the fruits on display, and it is therefore the correct answer.

---

[6] PrepTest 36, Sec. 4, Q 2
[7] PrepTest 36, Sec. 4, Q 3

4. **(C)**

If the stand carries no watermelons, then which one of the following must be true?

(A)   The stand carries kiwis.
(B)   The stand carries at least two kinds of fruit.
(C)   The stand carries at most three kinds of fruit.
(D)   The stand carries neither oranges nor pears.
(E)   The stand carries neither oranges nor kiwis.[8]

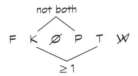

Figure 11.17

This is the first "If" question in the set. Copy your list of entities and cross off W in accordance with the question stem.

F   K   O   P   T   ~~W~~

Figure 11.18

Crossing off W means crossing off O according to the contrapositive of Rule 3.

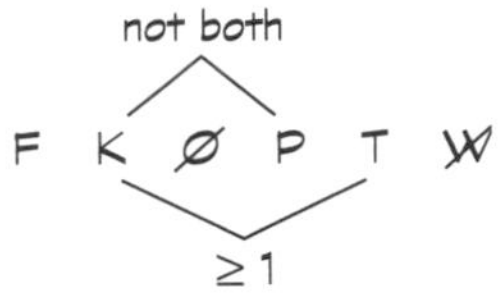

F   K   Ø   P   T   ~~W~~

Figure 11.19

Crossing off O doesn't trigger any of the other rules, so you're done with the mini-sketch. But take a moment to notice which of the fruits remain undetermined in your list: F, K, P, and T. At least one of K and P has to be excluded, according to Rule 1. At least one of K and T has to be included, according to Rule 2. F can stay or go; it's not restricted by anything here.

Now, characterize the choices. The correct answer *must be true*. The four wrong answers *could be false*. Evaluate them until you find the *must be true* choice.

Choice (A) *could be false*. You are required to have either K or T. So here, you might have T and leave K off display. Eliminate it.

Choice (B) *could be false*. You know from question 2 that K or T could be the only fruit displayed on a given day. Get rid of this answer, too.

Choice (C) *must be true*. At this point in the mini-sketch, four fruits remain possible for display. But two of them are K and P, which cannot be displayed together under Rule 1. So three fruits (either F, K, T or F, P, T) is the maximum that can go on display in this scenario. Choice (C) is correct.

---

[8] PrepTest 36, Sec. 4, Q 4

For the record, both of choices (D) and (E) could be false. The stand could display either P or K, respectively.

5. **(E)**

    If the stand carries watermelons, then which one of the following must be false?

    (A) The stand does not carry figs.
    (B) The stand does not carry tangerines.
    (C) The stand does not carry pears.
    (D) The stand carries pears but not oranges.
    (E) The stand carries pears but not tangerines.[9]

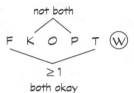

Figure 11.20

You saw this question in chapter 5, where I introduced the mini-sketch approach for "If" questions. Here's another "If," so start another mini-sketch. Copy the list of entities. This time, circle W, as the question stem instructs.

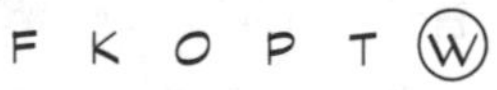

F K O P T Ⓦ

Figure 11.21

Circling W triggers Rule 4. Carrying watermelons means carrying figs, tangerines, or both. Those three possible results make this a little tricky to sketch, but something like this should suffice.

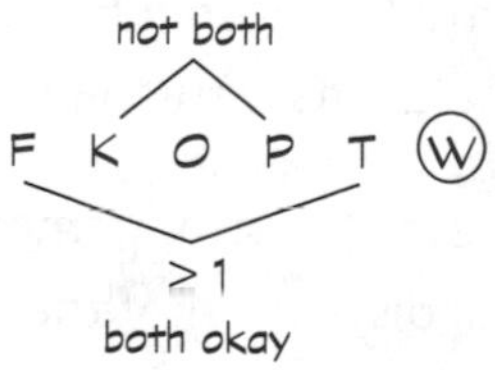

not both
F K O P T Ⓦ
≥ 1
both okay

Figure 11.22

Neither the inclusion of F nor that of T triggers any other results. (The *exclusion* of T is sufficient in Rule 2, but don't confuse that with its inclusion here.) You've exhausted the deductions, so evaluate the answer choices. The correct answer *must be false*. Each of the wrong answers *could be true*.

Choice (E) is the correct answer. Take a moment to see why choice (E) *must be false*. If you include P, Rule 1 says you must exclude K. But Rule 2 requires that you have either K or T in every case. You simply can't include P but exclude T. You don't even need the "if" from the question stem to know that this choice *must be false* in every instance.

Choices (A) through (D) all could be true. See chapter 5 for a fuller discussion if you are confused by any of them.

---

[9] PrepTest 36, Sec. 4, Q 5

6. **(C)**

If the condition that if the fruit stand does not carry
tangerines then it does carry kiwis is suspended, and all
other conditions remain in effect, then which one of the
following CANNOT be a complete and accurate list of
the kinds of fruit the stand carries?

(A) pears
(B) figs, pears
(C) oranges, pears, watermelons
(D) figs, pears, watermelons
(E) figs, oranges, pears, watermelons[10]

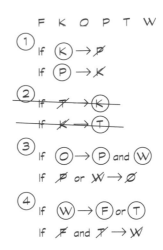

Figure 11.23

This question was also explained in chapter 5. It's a Rule-Changer, a rare question type, but
one you should know how to handle. Here, Rule 2 is suspended. The presence of Rule 2 in the
original Master Sketch told you that you had to have at least one of K or T. With that restriction
lifted, an arrangement with neither K nor T is fine, provided that it meets the game's other
requirements. You needn't do more than cross Rule 2 off the list and you're ready to evaluate
the answer choices.

Even without Rule 2, choice (C) cannot be an acceptable selection. It violates Rule 4, which is
still in effect under this question stem's terms. Including W requires including F or T, neither
of which is included in the answer choice. As a rule violator, choice (C) is the correct answer.

The wrong answers all represent acceptable arrangements under the altered circumstances
presented by the question stem. A full discussion of the wrong answers appears in chapter 5.

If you have a Selection game on your test, it's likely to remind you of the Fruit Stand game
or one of the others you've reviewed in this section. In recent years, the test makers haven't
often employed the twists and variations you'll see in the remainder of the chapter. However,
you might see something like the tasks that follow mixed into a Hybrid game. So practice the
games that follow to learn the basics of Selection involving definite numbers. Doing so will
give you additional formal logic practice, too.

SELECTION TWISTS

The main variation on Selection that you could see on test day involves telling you how many
entities to choose. Instead of saying, "There are seven people applying for jobs with your
firm; you'll hire some of them," these games say, "You will hire exactly four of the seven applicants." You should welcome such specificity with the numbers. It both makes your task clearer
and removes any possibility that you'll be tested on the minimum or maximum number of

---

[10] PrepTest 36, Sec. 4, Q 6

selections. Take a look at a couple of examples to see how the test makers construct games like this and how they try to make them more challenging.

Selection with Definite Numbers

Perhaps in order to compensate for the additional certainty that comes from giving you a definite number of entities to choose, the test makers almost always complicate the set of entities. I gave you an example of this above when I subdivided the snacks at your imaginary football party into subgroups: homemade and store-bought. This can seem confusing at first, but for the Kaplan-trained test taker, it's just one more way in which the test makers may restrict the acceptable solutions. Take a look at an example of a Selection game with definite numbers.

> A panel of five scientists will be formed. The panelists will be selected from among three botanists—F, G, and H—three chemists—K, L, and M—and three zoologists—P, Q, and R. Selection is governed by the following conditions:
>> The panel must include at least one scientist of each of the three types.
>> If more than one botanist is selected, then at most one zoologist is selected.
>> F and K cannot both be selected.
>> K and M cannot both be selected.
>> If M is selected, both P and R must be selected.[11]

Unlike any of the games in the first section of this chapter, this game tells you to choose exactly five of the nine scientists. It also subdivides the scientists into three categories: botanists, chemists, and zoologists. Look for ways in which those subdivisions can help you get a handle on the game's setup. In fact, the first two rules introduce further number restrictions based on the subgroups. Without those rules, you could make any of the following 12 arrangements.

Bot	Chem	Zoo
3	2	0
3	1	1
3	0	2
2	3	0
2	2	1
2	1	2
2	0	3
1	3	1
1	2	2
1	1	3
0	3	2
0	2	3

---

[11] PrepTest 42, Sec. 1, Game 1

Rule 1 tells you that you must have at least one of each category of scientist. That, by itself, knocks out half of the possible patterns.

Bot	Chem	Zoo
~~3~~	~~2~~	~~0~~
3	1	1
~~3~~	~~0~~	~~2~~
~~2~~	~~3~~	~~0~~
2	2	1
2	1	2
~~2~~	~~0~~	~~3~~
1	3	1
1	2	2
1	1	3
~~0~~	~~3~~	~~2~~
~~0~~	~~2~~	~~3~~

Rule 2 tells you that any time you have two or three botanists, you can have only one zoologist. That removes another possible arrangement within the selection.

Bot	Chem	Zoo
~~3~~	~~2~~	~~0~~
3	1	1
~~3~~	~~0~~	~~2~~
~~2~~	~~3~~	~~0~~
2	2	1
~~2~~	~~1~~	~~2~~
~~2~~	~~0~~	~~3~~
1	3	1
1	2	2
1	1	3
~~0~~	~~3~~	~~2~~
~~0~~	~~2~~	~~3~~

Rule 4 provides even more clarity. Since both K and M are chemists, you know that there's no way to select all three chemists. That knocks out one more arrangement, leaving you only four ways in which the numbers can work out in this game.

Bot	Chem	Zoo
~~3~~	~~2~~	~~0~~
3	**1**	**1**
~~3~~	~~0~~	~~2~~
~~2~~	~~3~~	~~0~~
2	**2**	**1**
~~2~~	~~1~~	~~2~~
~~2~~	~~0~~	~~3~~
~~1~~	~~3~~	~~1~~
1	**2**	**2**
1	**1**	**3**
~~0~~	~~3~~	~~2~~
~~0~~	~~2~~	~~3~~

Accounting for the possible number of entities that you can select from each subgroup makes your life much simpler when you need to identify acceptable and unacceptable arrangements in the questions.

Contrast that game with the following. Take a look and see why the subgroups are of less help than they were in the preceding example.

> For a behavioral study, a researcher will select exactly six individual animals from among three monkeys—F, G, and H—three pandas—K, L, and N—and three raccoons—T, V, and Z. The selection of animals for the study must meet the following conditions:
> F and H are not both selected.
> N and T are not both selected.
> If H is selected, K is also selected.
> If K is selected, N is also selected.[12]

Here again, you're asked to select a definite number: six out of nine, in this case. And just as they were in the Science Panel game, the nine entities are subdivided into three groups of three each. Did you notice, though, that there are no rules specifying the numbers that must be chosen for any of the subgroups? That's going to make this game a little more challenging. Rule 1 makes it impossible to have all three of the monkeys, but the numbers from each subcategory are otherwise up in the air.

---

[12] PrepTest 40, Sec. 2, Game 4

Selection with Definite Numbers Practice

Try this game out for practice. Give yourself eight and a half minutes to complete the setup, make the deductions, and try the questions. As always, if you find yourself struggling, consult the explanations for Steps 1–4 of the Kaplan Method. Then go back and try to finish the question set, knowing that you have all of the rules and deductions clearly represented on the page. I'll give you one hint: Remember that excluding three of the nine entities is the same as including six of them. You may make as much headway on some of the questions by noting what *cannot* be included as you will by figuring out what can.

For a behavioral study, a researcher will select exactly six individual animals from among three monkeys—F, G, and H—three pandas—K, L, and N—and three raccoons—T, V, and Z. The selection of animals for the study must meet the following conditions:

F and H are not both selected.
N and T are not both selected.
If H is selected, K is also selected.
If K is selected, N is also selected.

18. Which one of the following is an acceptable selection of animals for the study?

(A) F, G, K, N, T, V
(B) F, H, K, N, V, Z
(C) G, H, K, L, V, Z
(D) G, H, K, N, V, Z
(E) G, H, L, N, V, Z

19. If H and L are among the animals selected, which one of
the following could be true?

(A) F is selected.
(B) T is selected.
(C) Z is selected.
(D) Exactly one panda is selected.
(E) Exactly two pandas are selected.

20. Each of the following is a pair of animals that could be selected together EXCEPT:

(A) F and G
(B) H and K
(C) K and T
(D) L and N
(E) T and V

21. If all three of the raccoons are selected, which one of the following must be true?

(A) K is selected.
(B) L is selected.
(C) Exactly one monkey is selected.
(D) Exactly two pandas are selected.
(E) All three of the monkeys are selected.

22. If T is selected, which one of the following is a pair of animals that must be among the animals selected?

(A) F and G
(B) G and H
(C) K and L
(D) K and Z
(E) L and N

23. The selection of animals must include:

(A) at most two of each kind of animal
(B) at least one of each kind of animal
(C) at least two pandas
(D) exactly two monkeys
(E) exactly two raccoons[13]

---

[13] PrepTest 40, Sec. 2, Qs 18–23

Explanations

STEPS 1 AND 2: Overview and Sketch

Your task is straightforward. You have a list of nine animals, and you have to choose six of them. You don't need a special sketch. Just list the animals, noting their subcategories. You'll circle those that are selected for research and cross out those that aren't.

$$\underline{\text{Mon}} \qquad \underline{\text{Pan}} \qquad \underline{\text{Rac}}$$
$$\text{F G H} \qquad \text{K L N} \qquad \text{T V Z}$$

Figure 11.24

STEP 3: Rules

All four rules, in typical Selection game fashion, involve formal logic. Rules 1 and 2 create "impossible pairs." They're very easy to diagram.

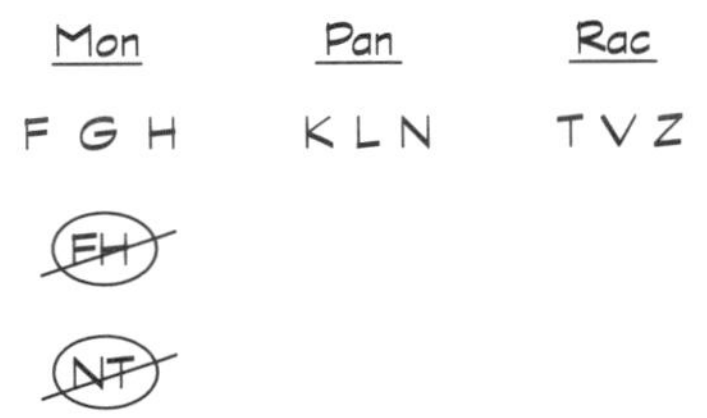

$$\underline{\text{Mon}} \qquad \underline{\text{Pan}} \qquad \underline{\text{Rac}}$$
$$\text{F G H} \qquad \text{K L N} \qquad \text{T V Z}$$

$\cancel{\text{FH}}$

$\cancel{\text{NT}}$

Figure 11.25

Rules 3 and 4 are straightforward "if-then" statements. Translate each and add its contrapositive.

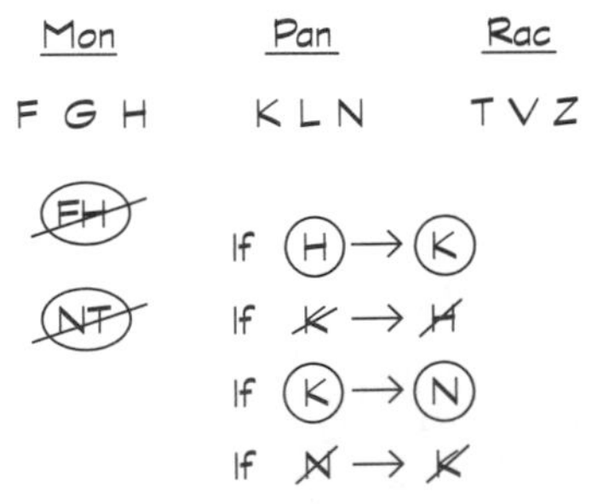

$$\underline{\text{Mon}} \qquad \underline{\text{Pan}} \qquad \underline{\text{Rac}}$$
$$\text{F G H} \qquad \text{K L N} \qquad \text{T V Z}$$

$\cancel{\text{FH}}$ If $\text{H} \rightarrow \text{K}$

$\cancel{\text{NT}}$ If $\cancel{\text{K}} \rightarrow \cancel{\text{H}}$

If $\text{K} \rightarrow \text{N}$

If $\cancel{\text{N}} \rightarrow \cancel{\text{K}}$

Figure 11.26

The contrapositives of those two rules tell you that when you reject either K or N, you'll have to reject additional animals as well. That could get dicey, given that you can only reject three of the nine animals.

It's worth noting, before you move on, that L, V, and Z are floaters. None of them are restricted by any of the rules.

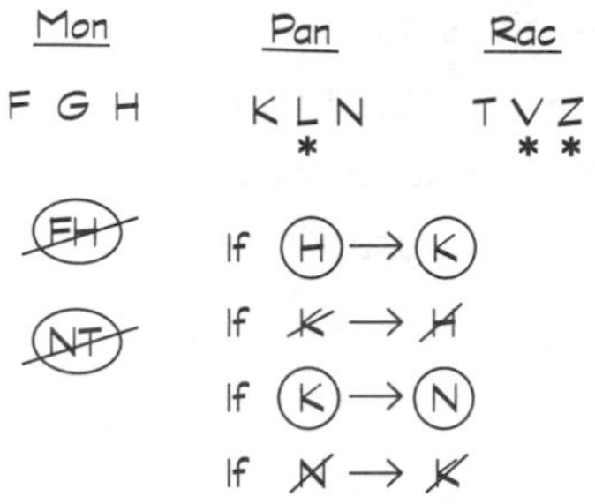

Figure 11.27

STEP 4: Deductions

There aren't many deductions to make in this game. Rules 3 and 4 share K and can thus be combined. If you choose H, you'll need to choose K and N. If you eliminate N, you'll have to eliminate K and H. But that much is clear at a glance.

The one place you get a little traction on the number restrictions is in Rule 1. Since F and H cannot both be selected, you'll have to choose either one or two of the monkeys. You may be thinking, "Wait, why can't I just have all six animals from the panda and raccoon subgroups and choose no monkeys at all?" The answer lies in Rule 2. Since N and T are an impossible pair, the sum of pandas and raccoons can never be more than five. You'll have to choose at least one animal from each subgroup in order to select six animals altogether.

You could, I suppose, try to figure out all of the possible selections from the monkey subgroup, where you could choose F-G, G-H, or just one of the monkeys F, G, or H. But that's five arrangements to work out, and there are only six questions. You're better off heading into the question set, aware of the restrictions as they are. The Acceptability question will help you gain some additional clarity, and there are three "If" questions that will be driven by mini-sketches anyway.

STEP 5: Questions

This is a balanced question set, featuring three questions with new "ifs" and three without. If you struggle with questions 20 or 23, complete the "If" questions first and use your work from them to help eliminate wrong answers in the Must/Could questions.

18. **(D)**

Which one of the following is an acceptable selection of animals for the study?

(A) F, G, K, N, T, V
(B) F, H, K, N, V, Z
(C) G, H, K, L, V, Z
(D) G, H, K, N, V, Z
(E) G, H, L, N, V, Z[14]

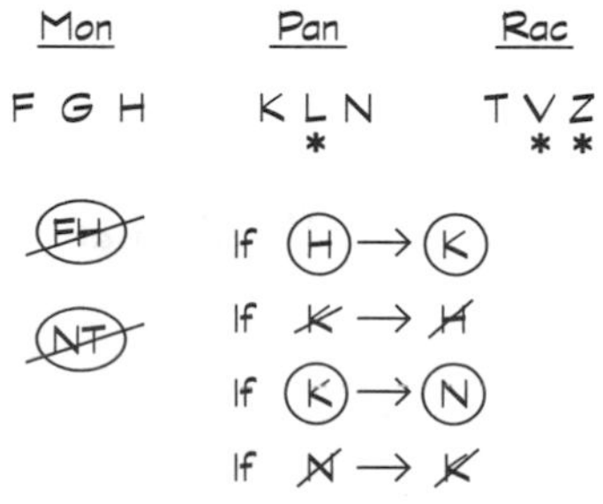

Figure 11.28

---

[14] PrepTest 40, Sec. 2, Q 18

Four rules, four wrong answers—this is as clear an Acceptability question as you could ask for. Choice (B) breaks Rule 1; you can't select both F and H. Choice (A) breaks Rule 2; you can't select both N and T. Choice (E) breaks Rule 3; when you choose H, you must choose K as well. Choice (C) breaks Rule 4; when you choose K, you must choose N as well. That leaves only choice (D), the correct answer.

19. **(C)**

If H and L are among the animals selected, which one of the following could be true?

(A)   F is selected.
(B)   T is selected.
(C)   Z is selected.
(D)   Exactly one panda is selected.
(E)   Exactly two pandas are selected.[15]

Figure 11.29

"If" questions are always welcome in Selection games; mini-sketches are easy to make by copying the entity list, and the "if" restriction will almost always set off a chain of deductions within the formal logic rules. Here, the question stem tells you to circle H and L in the list of animals.

Mon   Pan   Rac
F G Ⓗ   K Ⓛ N   T V Z

Figure 11.30

The inclusion of H triggers Rules 1 and 3. From Rule 1, you know to cross out F.

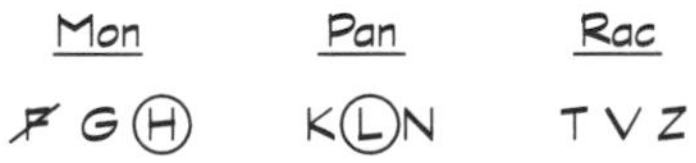

Mon   Pan   Rac
F̸ G Ⓗ   K Ⓛ N   T V Z

Figure 11.31

From Rule 3, you know to circle K.

Mon   Pan   Rac
F̸ G Ⓗ   Ⓚ Ⓛ N   T V Z

Figure 11.32

Including K sets off Rule 4 and then Rule 2. You need to circle N and cross out T.

---
[15] PrepTest 40, Sec. 2, Q 19

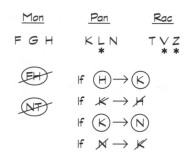

Mon Pan Rac

F̶ G H K L N T̶ V Z

Figure 11.33

Four of your selections—H, K, L, and N—are certain. The remaining two will come from among G, V, and Z. Assess the answer choices. The correct answer *could be true*; the four wrong answers all *must be false*.

Choice (C) is correct. Z is among the remaining possible selections. You can see that F and T have already been crossed off the list, making choices (A) and (B) incorrect. You can also see that you'll have to choose all three pandas, making choices (D) and (E) wrong answers, too.

20. **(C)**

Each of the following is a pair of animals that could be selected together EXCEPT:

(A) F and G
(B) H and K
(C) K and T
(D) L and N
(E) T and V[16]

Mon Pan Rac

F G H K L N T V Z
     *   * *

F̶H̶

N̶T̶

If H → K

If K̶ → H̶

If K → N

If N̶ → K̶

Figure 11.34

This question rewards you for being able to combine the rules. The correct answer is a pair of entities that cannot be selected together. The wrong answers all feature pairs that are acceptable together.

Choice (A) is incorrect. Nothing prevents F and G from being the two monkeys you select.

Choice (B) is also wrong. In fact, when H is selected, K must be.

Choice (C) is correct. Choosing K necessitates choosing N (Rule 4), and N and T are incompatible (Rule 2). Thus, K and T are incompatible as well.

Choices (D) and (E) both include floaters, N and V, respectively. Neither of those entities directly affects any other, so you know these choices are acceptable.

---

[16] PrepTest 40, Sec. 2, Q 20

21. **(B)**

   If all three of the raccoons are selected, which one of the
   following must be true?

   (A)   K is selected.
   (B)   L is selected.
   (C)   Exactly one monkey is selected.
   (D)   Exactly two pandas are selected.
   (E)   All three of the monkeys are selected.[17]

Mon	Pan	Rac
F G H̶	K̶ L K̶	Ⓣ Ⓥ Ⓩ

Figure 11.35

This question is one in which you'll derive the three animals that are *not* selected before you get to the six that are. Start your mini-sketch with the restriction from the stem. Circle all three raccoons—T, V, and Z.

Mon	Pan	Rac
F G H	K L N	Ⓣ Ⓥ Ⓩ

Figure 11.36

Of those three animals, only T entails additional restrictions. According to Rule 2, choosing T means rejecting N.

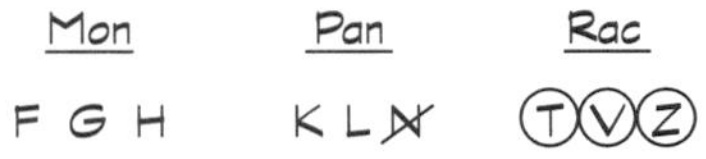

Mon	Pan	Rac
F G H	K L N̶	Ⓣ Ⓥ Ⓩ

Figure 11.37

Kicking N off your list means kicking K and H off, as well (Rules 3 and 4, contrapositives).

Mon	Pan	Rac
F G H̶	K̶ L N̶	Ⓣ Ⓥ Ⓩ

Figure 11.38

That's it. Once you've rejected three animals, the six that remain must be your final selection. F, G, and L must be selected along with the raccoons in this situation. That makes choice (B) the correct answer; it *must be true*. Your mini-sketch proves that all four wrong answers are false here.

---

[17] PrepTest 40, Sec. 2, Q 21

22. **(A)**

If T is selected, which one of the following is a pair of animals that must be among the animals selected?

(A)   F and G
(B)   G and H
(C)   K and L
(D)   K and Z
(E)   L and N[18]

Mon	Pan	Rac
F G H̸	K̸ L N̸	(T)(V)(Z)

Figure 11.39

The "if" to this question produces precisely the same mini-sketch as the one used for question 21. Since T's inclusion precipitates the exclusion of N (Rule 2), K (Rule 4), and H (Rule 3), exactly the same six animals chosen in question 21 must be selected again. Thus, choice (A), with F and G, represents a pair that must be chosen. Each of the four wrong answers includes at least one of the rejected entities—H, K, or L.

23. **(B)**

The selection of animals must include:

(A)   at most two of each kind of animal
(B)   at least one of each kind of animal
(C)   at least two pandas
(D)   exactly two monkeys
(E)   exactly two raccoons[19]

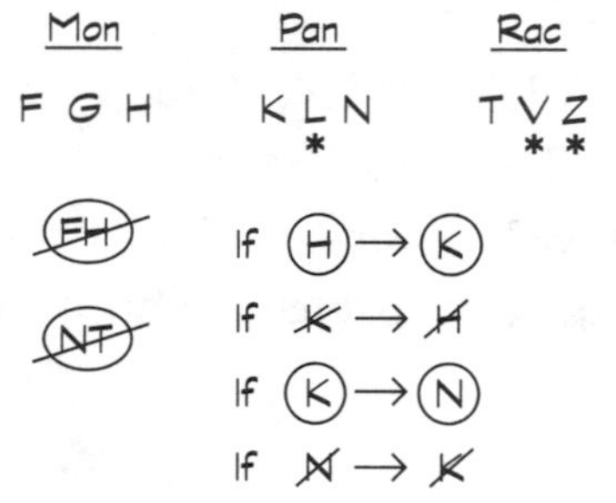

Mon	Pan	Rac
F G H	K L N	T V Z
	*	* *

(F̶H̶)   If (H) → (K)

(N̶F̶)   If K̸ → H̸

         If (K) → (N)

         If N̸ → K̸

Figure 11.40

You've known the answer to this question since you first added the rules to your sketch. Since Rule 1 allows you to take at most two of the monkeys and Rule 2 means that you can't have all six of the pandas and raccoons together, you must choose at least one animal from each of the subgroups. Choice (B) *must be true*, so it is correct.

When all is said and done, that game isn't so different from a standard Selection game. Moreover, the two big differences—the requirements that you select exactly six of the nine entities and at least one from each of the three subgroupings—played to your advantage. Although the test makers didn't include explicit limits on the number of animals from each subgroup, the questions wound up rewarding you for being able to see how many of the animals from a subgroup could or could not be chosen.

Selection with Entities Belonging to Multiple Subcategories

There's one more, very rare, twist on Selection that I want to make sure you have a chance to practice. The test makers haven't used anything exactly like this since PrepTest 35, originally administered in October of 2001. What makes the following game unique is that the entities

---

[18] PrepTest 40, Sec. 2, Q 22
[19] PrepTest 40, Sec. 2, Q 23

are subcategorized twice, with each entity belonging to one of two groups within each sub-category. Take a minute to read the game's setup text and you'll see what I mean.

> From among eight candidates, four astronauts will be selected for a space flight. Four of the candidates—F, J, K, and L—are experienced astronauts and four—M, N, P, and T—are inexperienced astronauts. F, M, P, and T are geologists whereas J, K, L, and N are radiobiologists. The astronauts must be selected according to the following conditions:[20]

The eight astronauts are each either experienced or inexperienced ("Ex" or "InEx"), and each does one of two jobs (G or R). Thus, each astronaut could receive one of four designations: "ExG," "InExG," "ExR," or "InExR." In the long run, all of this categorization will help you, since it provides additional restrictions along two dimensions. Initially, though, it puts the burden on you to categorize and mark the entities clearly and effectively.

Using what I've talked about so far, give this game a try. Take eight and a half minutes to tackle the game from top to bottom. If you find yourself struggling with the questions, stop and review Steps 1–4 of the Kaplan Method in the explanations. Once you're sure you have a strong Master Sketch, go back and complete the question set.

---

[20] PrepTest 35, Sec. 3, Game 1

From among eight candidates, four astronauts will be selected for a space flight. Four of the candidates—F, J, K, and L—are experienced astronauts and four—M, N, P, and T—are inexperienced astronauts. F, M, P, and T are geologists whereas J, K, L, and N are radiobiologists. The astronauts must be selected according to the following conditions:

   Exactly two experienced astronauts and two inexperienced astronauts are selected.
   Exactly two geologists and two radiobiologists are selected.
   Either P or L or both are selected.

1. Which one of the following is an acceptable selection of astronauts for the space flight?

   (A)   F, J, N, and T
   (B)   F, L, M, and P
   (C)   F, M, N, and P
   (D)   J, L, M, and T
   (E)   K, L, N, and T

2. If F and P are selected for the space flight, the other two astronauts selected must be:

   (A)   a radiobiologist who is an experienced astronaut and a radiobiologist who is an inexperienced astronaut
   (B)   a radiobiologist who is an experienced astronaut and a geologist who is an inexperienced astronaut
   (C)   a radiobiologist and a geologist, both of whom are experienced astronauts
   (D)   two radiobiologists, both of whom are experienced astronauts
   (E)   two radiobiologists, both of whom are inexperienced astronauts

3. If F and J are selected for the space flight, which one of the following must also be selected?

   (A)   K
   (B)   L
   (C)   M
   (D)   N
   (E)   T

4. If M and T are selected for the space flight, which one of the following could be, but need not be, selected for the flight?

   (A)   F
   (B)   J
   (C)   L
   (D)   N
   (E)   P

5. If N is selected for the space flight, which one of the following must also be selected?

   (A)   F
   (B)   J
   (C)   L
   (D)   M
   (E)   T[21]

Explanations

STEPS 1 AND 2: Overview and Sketch

In this game, Steps 1 and 2 are probably your biggest challenge; even so, the task isn't an unusual one in everyday life. Imagine you're staging a play that calls for a cast of four actors: one older woman, one older man, one young woman, and one young man. You might well have a list of actors who have auditioned, divided into groups for males and females and categorized by age group. Your task here is identical.

Start by listing the astronauts by experience level.

Exp				Inexp			
F	J	K	L	m	n	p	t

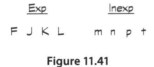

Figure 11.41

Now, under each one, list his or her job.

Exp				Inexp			
F	J	K	L	m	n	p	t
|	|	|	|	|	|	|	|
g	r	r	r	g	r	g	g

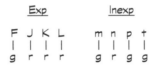

Figure 11.42

Right away, you notice something interesting. Only one of the experienced astronauts is a geologist, and only one of the inexperienced astronauts is a radiobiologist. Keep that in mind as you add the rules and deductions to this game. Astronauts F and N are sure to be central to at least some of the questions.

STEP 3: Rules

Rules 1 and 2 are similar, but focus on different subgroupings. Just make note of these two rules off to the side. They don't allow you to circle or cross out any entities yet.

Exp				Inexp			
F	J	K	L	m	n	p	t
|	|	|	|	|	|	|	|
g	r	r	r	g	r	g	g

2 Exp, 2 Inexp
2 g, 2 r

Figure 11.43

Rule 3 tells you that all acceptable selections in this game will follow one of three patterns. Probably the clearest way to depict this rule is by making a three-way Limited Options sketch.

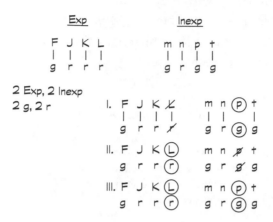

Figure 11.44

It's not always worth your while to make separate sketches when you have more than two options, but it is of paramount importance in this game that you maintain a clear picture of who's in and out, what their experience level is, and what job they do. So, the triple-sketch is probably worthwhile, especially with four "If" questions that are each likely to plop you into one of the options.

STEP 4: Deductions

Running through your BLEND checklist, there's simply nothing to add to your Master Sketch. Now you know why the test makers used so many "If" questions for this game.

STEP 5: Questions

As I had you note, the question set is dominated by "If" questions. You'll probably wind up making four mini-sketches here. Fortunately, with this being a Selection game, all that means is copying the list of entities and starting to circle them or cross them out.

1. **(D)**

    Which one of the following is an acceptable selection of astronauts for the space flight?

    (A)   F, J, N, and T
    (B)   F, L, M, and P
    (C)   F, M, N, and P
    (D)   J, L, M, and T
    (E)   K, L, N, and T[22]

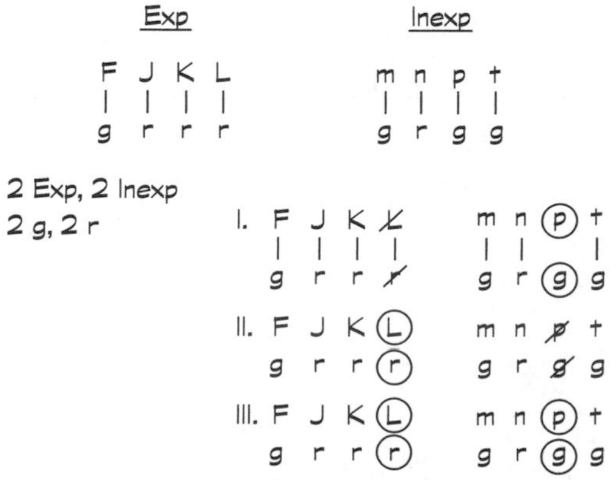

---

[22] PrepTest 35, Sec. 3, Q 1

Figure 11.45

No surprises here; the one "Non-If" question is a plain old Acceptability question. You know the drill. Use the rules to eliminate wrong answers. Rule 1 gets rid of choice (C), which has only one experienced astronaut along with three inexperienced ones. Rule 2 knocks out choice (B), which has too many geologists, and choice (E), which has too many radiobiologists. Rule 3 takes care of the final violator, choice (A), which has a list with neither L nor P. The last answer standing, choice (D), is acceptable and correct.

2. **(A)**

If F and P are selected for the space flight, the other two astronauts selected must be:

(A) a radiobiologist who is an experienced astronaut and a radiobiologist who is an inexperienced astronaut

(B) a radiobiologist who is an experienced astronaut and a geologist who is an inexperienced astronaut

(C) a radiobiologist and a geologist, both of whom are experienced astronauts

(D) two radiobiologists, both of whom are experienced astronauts

(E) two radiobiologists, both of whom are inexperienced astronauts[23]

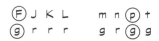

Figure 11.46

Start a mini-sketch with the condition from the question stem. Circle F and P (see figure above). The first thing to notice is that you now have both your geologists, including one experienced and one inexperienced. You'll need an "ExR" and an "InExR" to complete your selection. That's exactly what the correct answer, choice (A), says. All four wrong answers would produce the wrong mix of experience levels and jobs.

3. **(D)**

If F and J are selected for the space flight, which one of the following must also be selected?

(A) K
(B) L
(C) M
(D) N
(E) T[24]

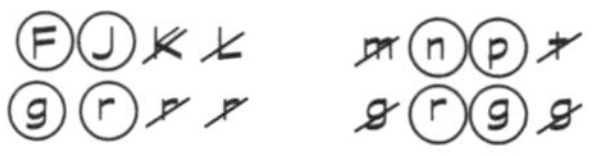

Figure 11.47

Use the "if" from the question stem to start your mini-sketch. Circle F and J in the list.

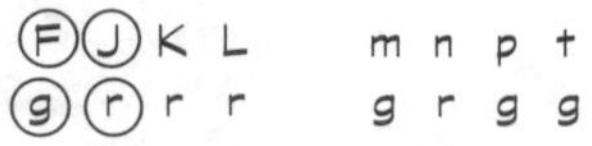

Figure 11.48

23 PrepTest 35, Sec. 3, Q 2
24 PrepTest 35, Sec. 3, Q 3

That tells you a lot. You have all of the experienced astronauts that you can take. Cross off K and L.

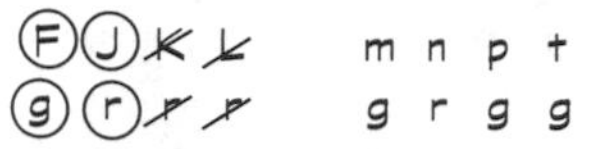

Figure 11.49

Once L is gone from the roster, you know from Rule 3 that you must include P.

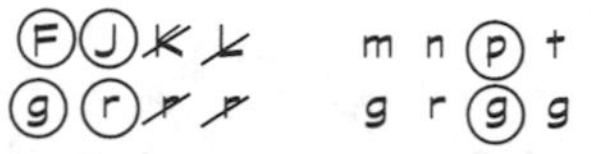

Figure 11.50

You need one more inexperienced astronaut who must also be a radiobiologist. The only acceptable entity is N.

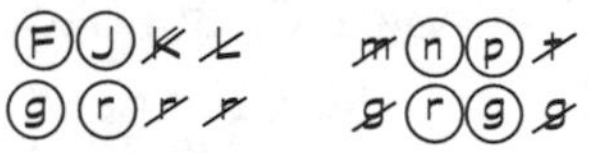

Figure 11.51

You now have the entire crew for your space flight. The correct answer to this question has an entity that must be included. That's choice (D), with N, your final deduction. Each of the wrong answers lists an astronaut who cannot go on the flight in this scenario.

4. **(B)**

If M and T are selected for the space flight, which one of the following could be, but need not be, selected for the flight?

(A)   F
(B)   J
(C)   L
(D)   N
(E)   P[25]

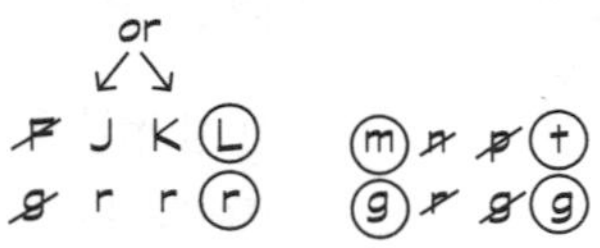

Figure 11.52

This question starts you off with two inexperienced astronauts. Create a mini-sketch and circle M and T, pursuant to the "if." Choosing M and T means you can't choose any more inexperienced astronauts or any more geologists, so N, P, and F are all out.

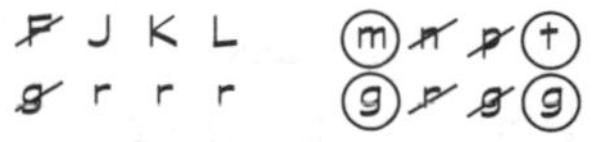

Figure 11.53

---

[25] PrepTest 35, Sec. 3, Q 4

With P no longer on your flight crew, Rule 3 requires that you have L; circle it.

Figure 11.54

Now you need one more crew member: an experienced radiobiologist. Your options are J and K.

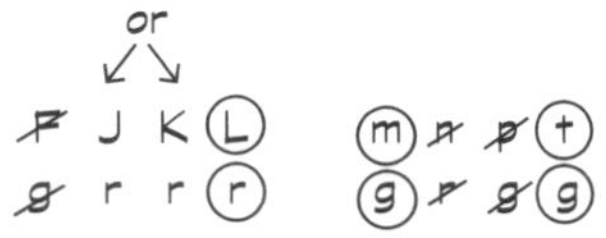

Figure 11.55

So what does the test maker ask you? Who could, but doesn't have to, be on the flight crew? You know that the correct answer will say either "J" or "K." Choice (B), which lists J, is the correct answer. A sloppy reader might fall for choice (C). But because L *must* go on the flight, choice (C) doesn't contain an astronaut who "could be, but need not be, selected for the flight." The other wrong answers simply list astronauts who cannot go on the flight in this case.

5. **(A)**

    If N is selected for the space flight, which one of the following must also be selected?

    (A) F
    (B) J
    (C) L
    (D) M
    (E) T[26]

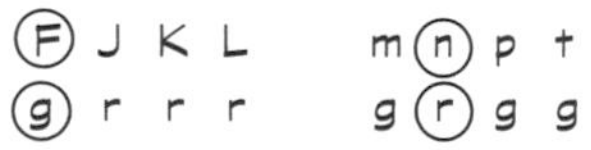

Figure 11.56

This is the hardest question from this game (and it's still not that hard, given the clear setup you have). Start your mini-sketch with the "if" condition—N is on the flight—and see what it reveals.

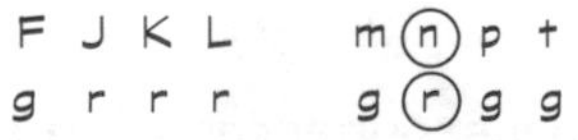

Figure 11.57

Do you remember why N is important? Because choosing N gives you the only inexperienced radiobiologist, the other inexperienced astronaut selected must be a geologist. That means that your two experienced astronauts need to be one geologist and one radiobiologist in order

---

for you to get the right mix of experience levels and jobs. The only experienced astronaut who is a geologist is F, so F must be on the flight.

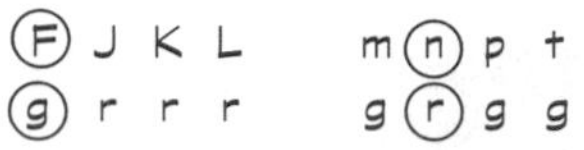

Figure 11.58

You can't determine for sure who the experienced radiobiologist or the inexperienced geologist is, but you don't need to. The question asks for an astronaut who *must* be selected. Choice (A), with F, is correct.

That game illustrates a unique twist on the Selection task, one that the test maker hasn't used much in the past and may not use again. But in a way, it's the exception that proves the rule. Ultimately, what makes this game manageable is what makes any game easier: the restrictions. By having two entities that each belong to two of four subgroups, the test makers severely restricted the possible choices in this game. Any time the test throws you an unusual variation or twist on a familiar action, look for what you know is true of how all games work. You'll wind up spotting the most important restrictions and letting the rest of the deductions work out from there.

DIFFICULT SELECTION

Believe it or not, you've already completed the most challenging examples of Selection representative of anything you're likely to see on test day. Unless there's a big reversal in the trend, the test makers seem unlikely to include Selection games with definite numbers. In the past decade, they've moved more and more to what I've called the "standard" Selection game type, with the numbers open-ended and questions that test your ability to determine minimums and maximums. Of the standard Selection games you've seen, Friends' Photographs, Summer School Courses, and Fruit Stand all rank about equal in difficulty and were all challenging for test takers. The main thing that makes those games tough is the inclusion of so much formal logic. But for you, conditional statements, translations, and contrapositives have been familiar since chapter 3. Provided that you continue your practice and keep your formal logic skills sharp, you've got little to worry about from this game type.

In the next chapter, we'll cover the last of the four common game tasks: Matching games. You've already managed a handful of these, so concentrate on their shared features and on what makes them recognizable. Once you know you're working with a Matching task, I don't expect you to have too much trouble recognizing the relevant restrictions.

CHAPTER 12

MATCHING GAMES

Matching games are the fourth and last of the standard game tasks that I'll cover. The games based on this task are distinguished by the fact that there are always two sets of entities. Your job is to assign the items or attributes in one set to the members of the other. You might, for example, have hikers who carry various types of equipment, or mannequins that receive different colors of clothing. Many test takers find the distinction between Matching and Distribution confusing. In fact, the two game types are very similar and use, at times, comparable sketches. The main difference is that, in Distribution, you may assign each entity only once. If you place Anna on the Blue Team, she can't play for the Red Team at the same time. Matching tasks, on the other hand, allow you to re-use the items or attributes on more than one of the other group's entities. Mannequins A and B can both wear blue shirts while mannequins B and C both have red pants. I'll point out this feature as I take you through the standard Matching examples below. In the end, it's less important that you give a game the "right" name than that you properly assess the task and restrictions.

REAL-LIFE MATCHING

Like all logic game tasks, Matching games correspond to real-life situations that you deal with regularly. Making decisions about what each of several guests will have for dinner provides a perfect illustration. Imagine you have five friends or family members coming over for a meal;

call them A, B, C, D, and E. You've prepared plenty of food for everyone. You have two kinds of soup: split pea and minestrone. You have three different entrées: ham, pasta, and roast beef. You've even made a dessert. In real life, absent any artificial rules, your guests could say, "Oh, I want to try both soups," or, "I'll have a little ham and a little of the pasta." Some of your guests will have dessert, and some might be too full. Your main concern—and this is what corresponds with the Matching task in a logic game—is that there's plenty for everyone. You can give B ham and still have some left to serve to D and E if they'd like to have it, too. Nothing (except running out) prevents you from serving everyone the roast beef, or anything else, for that matter.

Now, you can see how the LSAT imposes restrictions on this kind of game. The test makers can limit the number of entrées each guest has. (The simplest games would simply say, "Each guest will have exactly one kind of soup and exactly one entrée.") They could set restrictions among the guests, e.g., "C will not have any kind of food that A has," or, "B and D will have the same kind of soup." Likewise, they can impose restrictions based on the foods, e.g., "Any guest who has the split pea soup will have ham for an entrée," or, "No guest will have both the minestrone soup and the pasta." Number restrictions are just as important in Matching games as they are in Distribution or Selection games, but because the items to be matched can be re-used, the numbers will play out along two dimensions of the game. In our dinner example, you'll need to pay attention to how many kinds of food you serve to individual guests and how many servings of each kind of food you serve. It's always valuable in Matching to have a clear orientation (an *x*-axis and *y*-axis, if you will) for each part of your task.

	A	B	C	D	E
min					
s/p					
ham					
Pas					
r/b					
des					

Figure 12.1

Record the number restrictions along the appropriate rows and columns. That diagram isn't tough to understand, although this fictional menu is more complicated than any Matching game that has actually appeared on the LSAT over the last 10–12 years.

STANDARD MATCHING

In Part I, you saw a couple of games that exemplify the standard tasks you're likely to encounter if you should have a Matching game on your test. Review the following two setups to refresh your memory of what the test makers were asking you to do. Take special note of the fact that in each game, one set of entities is "stationary" (on the *x*-axis), and your job is to match one or more of the entities from the other set (on the *y*-axis) to members of the first group. There are more entities along the *x*-axis in the first game and more along the *y*-axis in the second, although the two games turn out to have exactly the same number of "cells" in their Master Sketches.

> In a repair facility there are exactly six technicians: Stacy, Urma, Wim, Xena, Yolanda, and Zane. Each technician repairs machines of at least one of the following three types—radios, televisions, and VCRs—and no other types. The following conditions apply:
>
> Xena and exactly three other technicians repair radios.
> Yolanda repairs both televisions and VCRs.
> Stacy does not repair any type of machine that Yolanda repairs.
> Zane repairs more types of machines than Yolanda repairs.
> Wim does not repair any type of machine that Stacy repairs.
> Urma repairs exactly two types of machines.[1]

	S	2 = U	W	X	Y	Z
4 = rad	✓	✓	X	✓	X	✓
tv	X				✓	✓
vcr	X				✓	✓

Figure 12.2

[1] PrepTest 48, Sec. 2, Game 3

Each of exactly six lunch trucks sells a different one of six kinds of food: falafel, hot dogs, ice cream, pitas, salad, or tacos. Each truck serves one or more of exactly three office buildings: X, Y, or Z. The following conditions apply:

The falafel truck, the hot dog truck, and exactly one other truck each serve Y.
The falafel truck serves exactly two of the office buildings.
The ice cream truck serves more of the office buildings than the salad truck.
The taco truck does not serve Y.
The falafel truck does not serve any office building that the pita truck serves.
The taco truck serves two office buildings that are also served by the ice cream truck.[2]

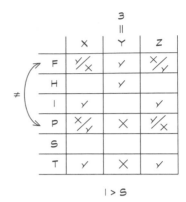

Figure 12.3

Test takers often ask, "How do I know which set of entities to put along the top and which to put along the side?" The answer is that it doesn't really matter. As long as the task is clear, you can orient the game in whichever way fits best in the space on the test booklet page. Most test takers simply acquire a habit of putting the "stationary" entities along one axis or the other (my personal tendency is to put them horizontally across the top of the sketch), but the orientation makes no difference in the logic or restrictions of the game.

As you reviewed those two games, did you notice what set them apart from a standard Distribution game? In the first game, several of the technicians repaired radios, several repaired TVs, and several repaired VCRs. In the second game, the trucks could serve multiple buildings. In both games, the number restrictions served to limit the number of matched items each "stationary" entity could receive *and* the number of times that the "movable" entities could be re-used.

In both games, the most important deductions came from those number restrictions (N in the BLEND checklist) and from the rules that had entities in common, the duplications (D in the BLEND checklist). This will almost always be the case in Matching games. In the Appliance Technician game, for example, Rule 2 affirmatively designated two matches that Yolanda would receive, while Rule 3 prevented Stacy from receiving any matches in common with Yolanda. That allowed you to figure out the exact matches that Stacy and Yolanda would receive and the ones they wouldn't. Rule 4 also duplicated Yolanda, relating her to Zane based on the number of matches each could receive. Again, the result was a precise deduction of exactly which appliances Zane would repair.

---

[2] PrepTest 43, Sec. 4, Game 4

Standard Matching Practice

Here's one more typical Matching game for you to try. It's different from those above in one significant way: As you conduct your Overview of the game, you'll see that each of the "stationary" entities (the nations) will export *exactly* two crops. Thus, you're likely to do better with a sketch that, beneath each nation, has two slots in which you can record the matches for that nation.

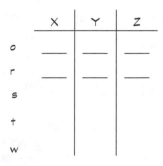

Figure 12.4

Use that as a template for your sketch and give the game a try. Take eight and a half minutes to cover the setup, rules, deductions, and questions. Then review the game with the explanations that follow. If you're struggling with the questions, stop and review Steps 1–4 in the explanations to make sure you have a complete Master Sketch. Then return to the question set and give it another try.

The Export Alliance consists of exactly three nations: Nation X, Nation Y, and Nation Z. Each nation in the Alliance exports exactly two of the following five crops: oranges, rice, soybeans, tea, and wheat. Each of these crops is exported by at least one of the nations in the Alliance. The following conditions hold:

> None of the nations exports both wheat and oranges.
> Nation X exports soybeans if, but only if, Nation Y does also.
> If Nation Y exports rice, then Nations X and Z both export tea.
> Nation Y does not export any crop that Nation Z exports.

18. Which one of the following could be an accurate list, for each of the nations, of the crops it exports?

    (A) Nation X: oranges, rice; Nation Y: oranges, tea; Nation Z: soybeans, wheat
    (B) Nation X: oranges, tea; Nation Y: oranges, rice; Nation Z: soybeans, wheat
    (C) Nation X: oranges, wheat; Nation Y: oranges, tea; Nation Z: rice, soybeans
    (D) Nation X: rice, wheat; Nation Y: oranges, tea; Nation Z: oranges, soybeans
    (E) Nation X: soybeans, rice; Nation Y: oranges, tea; Nation Z: soybeans, wheat

19. If Nation X exports soybeans and tea, then which one of the following could be true?

    (A) Nation Y exports oranges.
    (B) Nation Y exports rice.
    (C) Nation Y exports tea.
    (D) Nation Z exports soybeans.
    (E) Nation Z exports tea.

20. If Nation Z exports tea and wheat, then which one of the following must be true?

    (A) Nation X exports oranges.
    (B) Nation X exports tea.
    (C) Nation X exports wheat.
    (D) Nation Y exports rice.
    (E) Nation Y exports soybeans.

21. It CANNOT be the case that both Nation X and Nation Z export which one of the following crops?

    (A) oranges
    (B) rice
    (C) soybeans
    (D) tea
    (E) wheat

22. Which one of the following pairs CANNOT be the two crops that Nation Y exports?

    (A) oranges and rice
    (B) oranges and soybeans
    (C) rice and tea
    (D) rice and wheat
    (E) soybeans and wheat[3]

---

[3] PrepTest 45, Sec. 3, Game 4, Qs 18–22

Explanations

STEPS 1 AND 2: Overview and Sketch

It's understandable if this game reminded you of a Distribution game. The only thing that sets it apart is the fact that you'll have to use one of the crops twice. There are six spaces to fill in the Sketch, but only five different crops are exported.

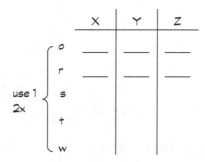

Figure 12.5

In fact, determining which of the crops is repeated is central to the Deduction step.

STEP 3: Rules

As expected, the rules cut across both dimensions of this game. Some restrict the crops that can be exported together, while others present restrictions among the nations.

Rule 1 provides that wheat and oranges cannot be exported by the same nation.

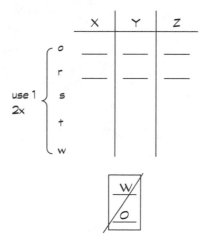

Figure 12.6

Rule 2 is a rare formal logic construction, the "if, and only if" statement. I actually showed you this rule back in chapter 3. As you'll recall, "if, and only if" (or as it is stated here, "if, *but* only if") makes the second term in the statement both necessary and sufficient for the first term. You can depict the rule like this:

$$\text{If } X_s \rightarrow Y_s \quad \text{If } Y_s \rightarrow X_s$$
$$\text{If } \cancel{Y_s} \rightarrow \cancel{X_s} \quad \text{If } \cancel{X_s} \rightarrow \cancel{Y_s}$$

Figure 12.7

Or like this:

$$X_s \leftrightarrow Y_s$$

Figure 12.7A

Either way, the important thing to take away from this rule is that either both Nations X and Y export soybeans, or neither does. That provides a Limited Options scenario that you can add to your Sketch.

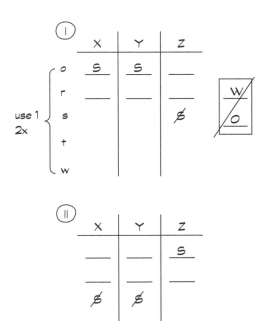

Figure 12.8

Rule 3 is another conditional formal logic statement, albeit of a more routine kind than Rule 2. Jot it down along with its contrapositive.

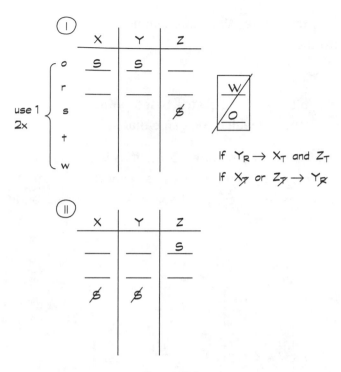

Figure 12.9

Rule 4 creates a restriction between two of the nations: Y and Z cannot have any exports in common.

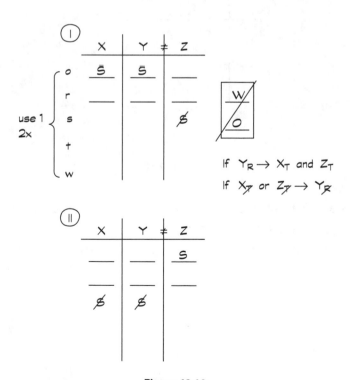

Figure 12.10

There are no floaters in this game. All of the nations and all of the crops have at least one restriction pertinent to them.

STEP 4: Deductions

If you didn't create a Limited Options sketch based on Rule 2, you'd need to do that now. Nothing creates more restriction within the game than that.

The next area to investigate is the number restrictions within the game. Since each nation exports exactly two crops, and since the opening paragraph of the game's setup tells you that all of the crops must be exported, you know that you'll use exactly one crop two times in any acceptable arrangement.

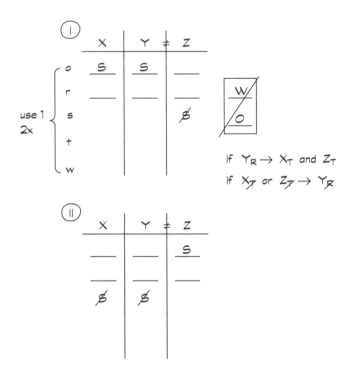

Figure 12.11

In Option I, where X and Y both export soybeans, the four other crops will be used only one time each. That implicates Rule 3. You can deduce that, in Option I, Nation Y cannot export rice. If it did, both Nation X and Nation Z would have to export tea. There wouldn't be any space left at that point to export both wheat and oranges. Add that deduction to the sketch for Option I.

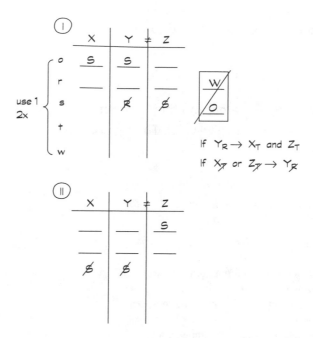

Figure 12.12

Nation Y can, but does not have to, export rice in Option II. You can note that Y may not export both rice and tea in Option II, however. Once Nation Y exports rice, both X and Z will export tea. Since you must use only one of the crops exactly two times and each of the others one time, you can safely conclude that Y won't be allowed to export both rice and tea.

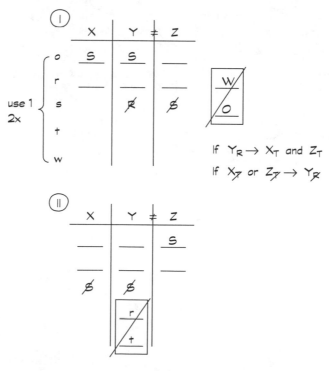

Figure 12.13

None of the remaining rules combine to lead to further deductions. So you're ready to tackle the questions.

STEP 5: **Questions**

There are five questions for this game, and they're arranged in the perfect order. The Acceptability question is first (as it nearly always is). Then you have two "If" questions. Finally, two Must Be False questions finish the set.

18. **(A)**

Which one of the following could be an accurate list, for each of the nations, of the crops it exports?

(A)   Nation X: oranges, rice; Nation Y: oranges, tea; Nation Z: soybeans, wheat

(B)   Nation X: oranges, tea; Nation Y: oranges, rice; Nation Z: soybeans, wheat

(C)   Nation X: oranges, wheat; Nation Y: oranges, tea; Nation Z: rice, soybeans

(D)   Nation X: rice, wheat; Nation Y: oranges, tea; Nation Z: oranges, soybeans

(E)   Nation X: soybeans, rice; Nation Y: oranges, tea; Nation Z: soybeans, wheat[4]

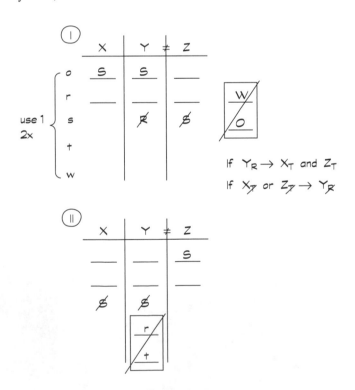

Figure 12.14

As always, attack this Acceptability question by using the rules to eliminate answer choices that break them.

Choice (C) breaks Rule 1 because it has Nation X exporting oranges *and* wheat.

Choice (E) breaks Rule 2; this answer has Nation X exporting soybeans, but not Nation Y.

Choice (B) breaks Rule 3; Nation Y is exporting rice, but Nation Z is not exporting tea.

Choice (D) breaks Rule 4; Nations Y and Z are both exporting oranges.

That leaves choice (A), the correct answer.

19. **(A)**

If Nation X exports soybeans and tea, then which one of the following could be true?

(A) Nation Y exports oranges.
(B) Nation Y exports rice.
(C) Nation Y exports tea.
(D) Nation Z exports soybeans.
(E) Nation Z exports tea.[5]

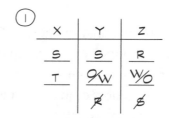

Figure 12.15

The "if" in this question stem places you in Option I (because Nation X is exporting soybeans) and adds some extra information as well. To start your mini-sketch, copy over Option I and add T under Nation X's column.

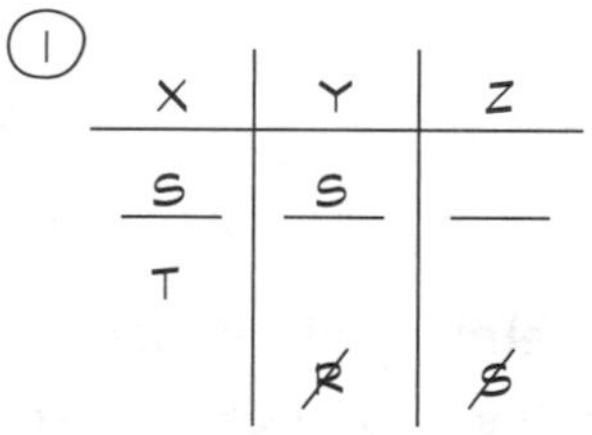

Figure 12.16

Now, consider the remaining crops—oranges, rice, and wheat—each of which must be exported. Oranges and wheat cannot be exported by the same country (Rule 1). So Nation Y will export one of them and Nation Z the other.

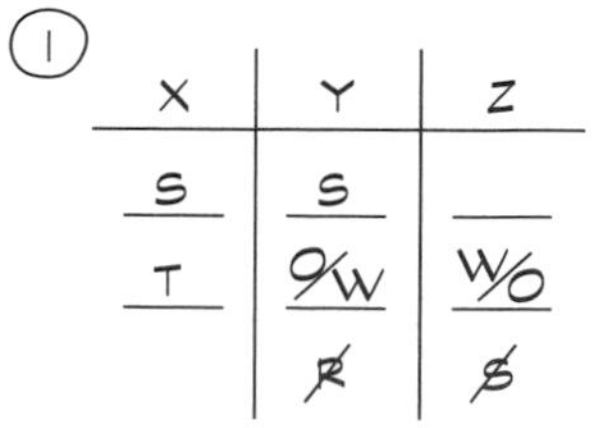

Figure 12.17

---

[5] PrepTest 45, Sec. 3, Q 19

That leaves only rice to be exported and only one open space within the framework. Nation Z must export rice.

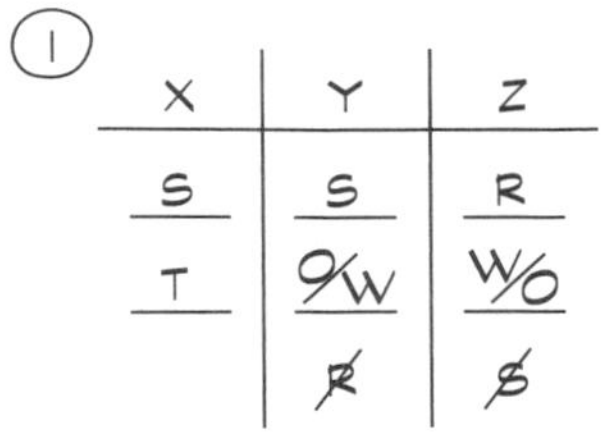

Figure 12.18

Now, characterize the answer choices. The correct answer *could be true* (you can already guess that it concerns oranges or wheat, the only two crops that aren't strictly determined), while the four wrong answers *must be false*. Choice (A) is the correct answer; Nation Y *could*, but does not have to, export oranges. A quick glance confirms that all four remaining answers are impossible in the mini-sketch for this question.

20. **(E)**

If Nation Z exports tea and wheat, then which one of the following must be true?

(A)   Nation X exports oranges.
(B)   Nation X exports tea.
(C)   Nation X exports wheat.
(D)   Nation Y exports rice.
(E)   Nation Y exports soybeans.[6]

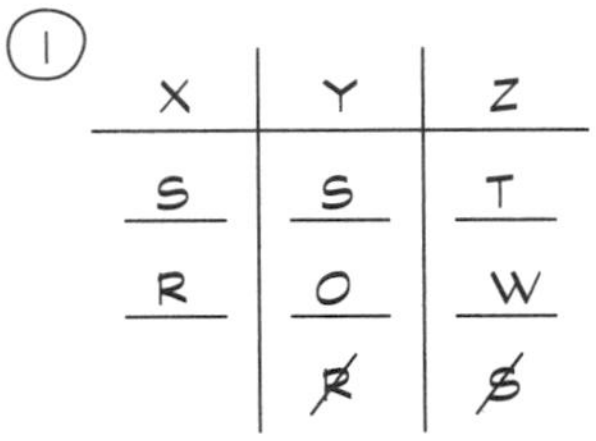

Figure 12.19

This question's "if" allows you to determine all six spaces within the framework. Since the "if" requires Nation Z to export tea and wheat, you know that you're in Option I (as Nation Z must export soybeans in Option II). Start a mini-sketch by using Option I and adding T and W in Nation Z's column.

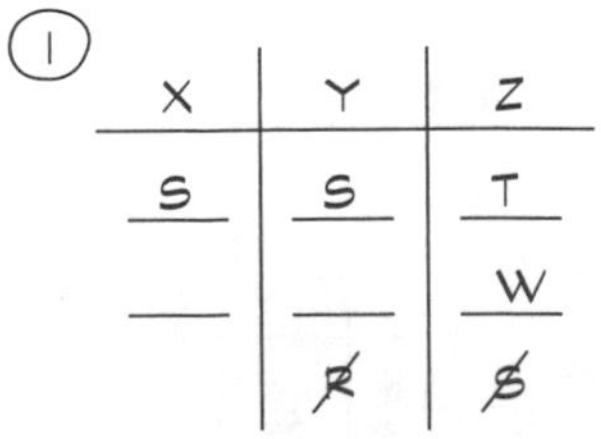

Figure 12.20

That leaves only rice and oranges to be placed. Nation Y cannot export rice in Option I. So Nation X will export rice and Nation Y, oranges.

---

[6] PrepTest 45, Sec. 3, Q 20

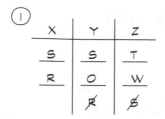

Figure 12.21

Naturally, with a completed sketch for this question, the stem calls for a *must be true* answer. That's choice (E); Nation Y will export soybeans here. As your mini-sketch illustrates, all four wrong answers are false under this question's conditions.

21. **(C)**

It CANNOT be the case that both Nation X and Nation Z export which one of the following crops?

(A)   oranges
(B)   rice
(C)   soybeans
(D)   tea
(E)   wheat[7]

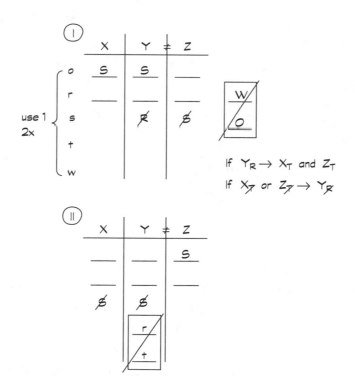

Figure 12.22

---

[7] PrepTest 45, Sec. 3, Q 21

This question goes straight to the heart of your Limited Options sketch. The crop that Nations X and Z cannot both export is soybeans, of course. Choice (C) gets it right. You've had it right since you analyzed Rule 2 in light of the overall number restrictions in this game.

22. **(C)**

Which one of the following pairs CANNOT be the two crops that Nation Y exports?

(A) oranges and rice
(B) oranges and soybeans
(C) rice and tea
(D) rice and wheat
(E) soybeans and wheat[8]

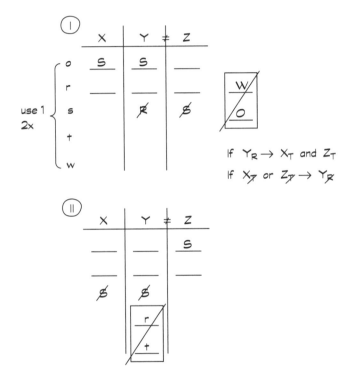

Figure 12.23

Like question 21, this question grants you a point simply for making deductions. Looking at your Master Sketch, you see two potential answers to this question. Nation Y may export neither soybeans and rice nor rice and tea. Choice (C) seizes on the second of those two forbidden pairs and is thus the correct answer. Recall how you deduced that Nation Y could not export both rice and tea: The overall number restrictions in the game provided that exactly one crop would be exported by two nations, and the other four crops by one nation each. When Nation Y exports rice, Rule 2 kicks in, and Nations X and Z export tea. So if you were to have Nation

---

[8] PrepTest 45, Sec. 3, Q. 22

Y export tea in this case, there would be three nations exporting tea and at least one crop would not be exported.

While the Sketch for this game looked a little different than those for the Appliance Technician and Lunch Trucks games, this game should still be considered a standard Matching task. There were "stationary" entities (the nations) and "movable" ones (the crops). The rules provided restrictions among both the "stationary" and the "movable" entities. Most importantly, one of the "movable" entities had to be re-used in order to complete the game. Be willing to modify your Sketch when doing so better fits a game's task and restrictions. Use that as your rule of thumb in the next section of this chapter, and the minor twists and variations that you encounter won't present more than a speed bump along your road to success with Matching games.

MATCHING TWISTS

Apart from Sequencing, Matching is probably the game type that has seen the greatest variety of minor departures from the norm over the years. Unlike Sequencing, where the variations themselves fall into categories (Loose Sequencing, Double Sequencing, Circular Sequencing, and the like), Matching variations tend to come along as one-time twists on the expected theme. This is probably because Matching isn't as common a task as Sequencing (which appears on nearly every LSAT). In this section, I'll show you three relatively recent Matching variants. What I want you to see is that, in each case, conducting a careful overview of the game allows you to create a useful, strategic sketch. Once that's in place, you can manage the game with no more difficulty (and sometimes considerably less) than in any of the standard Matching games you'll see in this book (or on your official test day).

The first Matching variant is a game that you saw in Part I of this book. Take a few moments to refresh your memory of the game and its restrictions. I'll give it a brief review below.

> A clown will select a costume consisting of two pieces and no others: a jacket and overalls. One piece of the costume will be entirely one color, and the other piece will be plaid. Selection is subject to the following restrictions:
>> If the jacket is plaid, then there must be exactly three colors in it.
>> If the overalls are plaid, then there must be exactly two colors in them.
>> The jacket and overalls must have exactly one color in common.
>> Green, red, and violet are the only colors that can be in the jacket.
>> Red, violet, and yellow are the only colors that can be in the overalls.[9]

---

[9] PrepTest 51, Sec. 4, Game 1

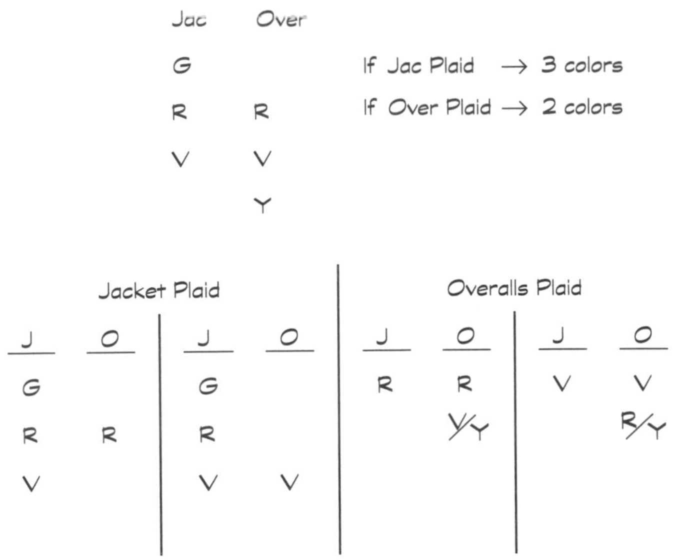

Figure 12.24

In this game, the "stationary" entities are the jacket and overalls. The "movable" entities are the colors. The test makers' use of "plain" and "plaid" at first appears to be a third consideration, but notice that it's actually just a clever way of introducing number restrictions. When the jacket is plaid, you match three colors to it; when the overalls are plaid, they get two matching colors. Once you use Rules 1 and 2 to set up dual Limited Options sketches, the further restrictions imposed by Rules 4 and 5 leave you only six ways in which this Matching puzzle can be solved. Test takers who spend the time to make a complete, thoughtful Master Sketch find the questions associated with this game to be a snap.

Matching with a Limited Pool of Entities

The next game is new to you, so take a few minutes to complete Steps 1–4 of the Kaplan Method and produce a Master Sketch reflecting all of the available deductions. As you set this one up, think about which of the "stationary" entities (the weeks) are the most restricted. Starting from the two most limited weeks, you can set off a string of deductions that leaves you with only a handful of acceptable arrangements. Take four minutes and see how much certainty you can derive.

A five-week adult education course consists of exactly five lectures with a different lecture given each week. No lecture is given more than once. Each lecture is delivered by a different speaker. The following conditions are true about the speakers and their lectures:

> Each speaker lectures on a philosopher in whom he or she specializes.
> No two speakers lecture on the same philosopher.
> The first week's speaker specializes in Kant, Locke, and Mill, and no other philosophers.
> The second week's speaker specializes in Kant, Locke, Mill, and Nietzsche, and no other philosophers.
> The third week's and fourth week's speakers each specialize in Mill and Nietzsche, and no other philosophers.
> The fifth week's speaker specializes in Nietzsche, Ockham, and Plato, and no other philosophers.[10]

By changing a couple of the rules, the test makers could easily turn this game into a Sequencing action. But notice why I don't categorize it that way. None of the rules here impose any restriction based on one entity being earlier or later than another. Nor do any of them require that any of the lectures be separated by a certain number of spaces. Thus, the five weeks of the philosophy program act as "stationary" entities. Your task is to match an acceptable lecture to each one.

Your overview should have noted that the primary restrictions pertain to the numbers. Each week sees one lecture, and the lectures are never repeated (an unusually tight limitation for a Matching action, but one that makes this game much easier in the long run).

```
1 per
wk.
          1    2    3    4    5
No
repeats
```

Figure 12.25

Four of the six rules fill in the possible matches for each week.

```
1 per    1    2    3    4    5
wk.
         K    K    M    M    N
No       L    L    N    N    O
repeats  M    M              P
         N    N
              N
```

Figure 12.26

---

[10] PrepTest 34, Sec. 4, Game 2

Remember that I told you to look for the two most restricted weeks. With this sketch, it's clear that they are weeks 3 and 4. What must happen during those two weeks? The M and N lectures, and only those lectures, must be delivered. There simply are no other alternatives. That means that you can cross M and N off of the list under any other weeks. That leaves:

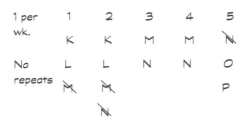

Figure 12.27

Weeks 1 and 2 will have lectures K-L or L-K; weeks 3 and 4 will have lectures M-N or N-M; week 5 will have either lecture O or lecture P. There are only eight acceptable arrangements for this game.

Take a look at how the test makers rewarded you for making those important deductions.

8. Which one of the following statements could be true?

   (A)   The first speaker lectures on Mill.
   (B)   The second speaker lectures on Mill.
   (C)   The second speaker lectures on Nietzsche.
   (D)   The fifth speaker lectures on Nietzsche.
   (E)   The fifth speaker lectures on Ockham.[11]

The first four answer choices all deal with lectures M or N. You know that those can only occur in weeks 3 and 4. Your Master Sketch reveals that choices (A)–(D) *must be false*. The correct *could be true* answer is choice (E); lecture O is possible in week 5.

The next one is a little bit harder. Use your Master Sketch to determine which answer would lock down the lecture schedule for all five weeks. Eliminate the choices that leave one or more of the weeks up in the air.

10. Which one of the following, if known, would allow one to determine the entire lecture schedule and identify for each week the philosopher who is lectured on that week?

   (A)   the weeks that Kant, Locke, and Mill are lectured on
   (B)   the weeks that Kant, Mill, and Nietzsche are lectured on
   (C)   the weeks that Kant, Mill, and Ockham are lectured on
   (D)   the weeks that Mill, Nietzsche, and Ockham are lectured on
   (E)   the weeks that Mill, Nietzsche, and Plato are lectured on[12]

---

[11] PrepTest 34, Sec. 4, Q 8
[12] PrepTest 34, Sec. 4, Q 10

In order to determine all five of the weeks' lectures, you'll need to know three things: the lecture for either week 1 or week 2, the lecture for either week 3 or week 4, and the lecture for week 5. Choice (C) is the one that provides all three. Thus, it's the correct answer. Notice that choices (A) and (B) both fail to clear up the lecture in week 5, while choices (D) and (E) both leave weeks 1 and 2 undetermined.

Matching with Spatial Restrictions

In the next game, you're asked to match one of three decorative light colors to each of 10 stores. If 10 stores sounds like a lot of entities for an LSAT logic game, it is. But pay attention to how those 10 "stationary" entities are arranged. With a strong overview, you can get a very clear picture of the task and lay out your sketch in a way that will allow you to anticipate most of the restrictions in this game. Take four minutes to go through Steps 1–4 of the Kaplan Method and produce your Master Sketch for this game.

There are exactly ten stores and no other buildings on Oak Street. On the north side of the street, from west to east, are stores 1, 3, 5, 7, and 9; on the south side of the street, also from west to east, are stores 2, 4, 6, 8, and 10. The stores on the north side are located directly across the street from those on the south side, facing each other in pairs, as follows: 1 and 2; 3 and 4; 5 and 6; 7 and 8; 9 and 10. Each store is decorated with lights in exactly one of the following colors: green, red, and yellow. The stores have been decorated with lights according to the following conditions:

　No store is decorated with lights of the same color as those of any store adjacent to it.

　No store is decorated with lights of the same color as those of the store directly across the street from it.

　Yellow lights decorate exactly one store on each side of the street.

　Red lights decorate store 4.

　Yellow lights decorate store 5.[13]

Did you use the description in the game setup to take control of this game's task? Although the opening paragraph is one of the longest you'll see, it conveys a very clear picture of the "stationary" entities' arrangement.

G, R, Y

| 1 | 3 | 5 | 7 | 9 |
| 2 | 4 | 6 | 8 | 10 |

Figure 12.28

Compare your sketch to that picture, and make sure you were rigorous in following the instructions laid out in the setup text.

---

[13] PrepTest 33, Sec. 4, Game 4

Once you saw how the shops were arranged, you should have anticipated the kinds of restrictions introduced in Rules 1 and 2. The game was so specific about which shops were next to or directly across from one another that the test makers must have had in mind that adjacent or facing shops would be subject to restrictions on their colors of lights.

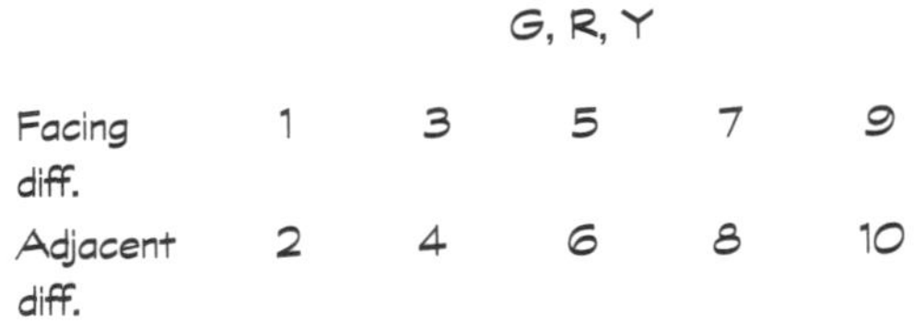

G, R, Y
Facing diff.
1 3 5 7 9
Adjacent diff.
2 4 6 8 10

Figure 12.29

Rule 3 further restricted the possible arrangements. In fact, the north side of the street will have one shop with yellow lights and four with either red or green.

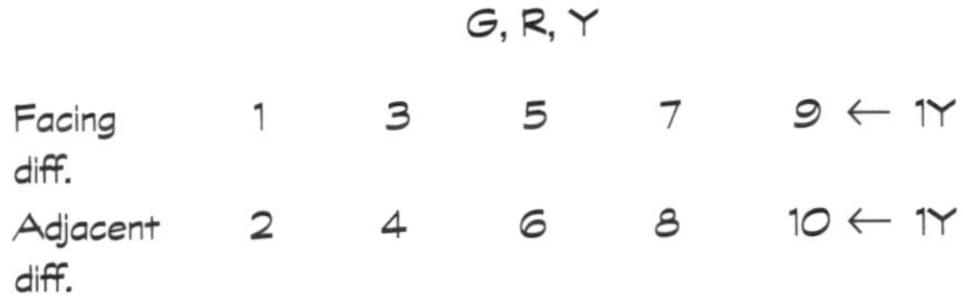

G, R, Y
Facing diff.
1 3 5 7 9 ← 1Y
Adjacent diff.
2 4 6 8 10 ← 1Y

Figure 12.30

Rules 4 and 5 imposed strict assignments for two of the stores.

G, R, Y
Y
Facing diff.
1 3 5 7 9 ← 1Y
Adjacent diff.
2 4 6 8 10 ← 1Y
R

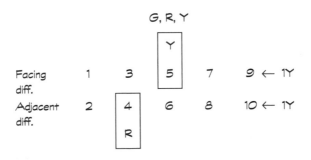

Figure 12.31

Did you use those last two rules to make further deductions about the shops adjacent to and across from stores 4 and 5? Since store 3 is next to a store with yellow lights and across from one with red, its lights must be green.

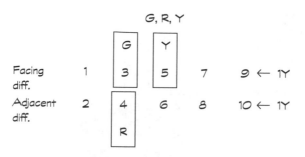

Figure 12.32

That, in turn, told you that store 1's lights must be red (remember, only one store per side of the street can have yellow lights according to Rule 3).

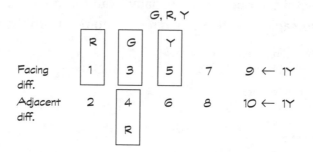

Figure 12.33

Like store 3, store 6 is also restricted from having yellow lights and from having red lights. Its lights must be green.

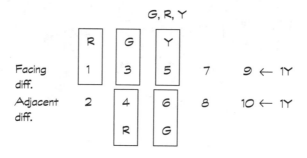

Figure 12.34

From what you have at this point, you can determine that stores 2, 8, 7, and 9 are limited to two options.

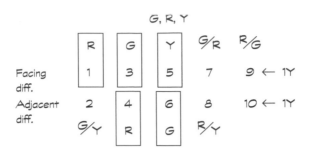

Figure 12.35

Only store 10 remains entirely unrestricted at the end of the Deductions step. Even it, of course, will be restricted by any further information about store 8 or store 9.

Take a look at a couple of the questions associated with this game, and you'll see how your use of Steps 1–4 of the Kaplan Method turn directly into points on the test.

20. If green lights decorate store 7, then each of the following statements could be false EXCEPT:

    (A)   Green lights decorate store 2.
    (B)   Green lights decorate store 10.
    (C)   Red lights decorate store 8.
    (D)   Red lights decorate store 9.
    (E)   Yellow lights decorate store 2.[14]

For this one, create a mini-sketch based on the new "if" condition introduced in the question stem.

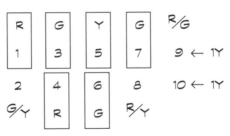

Figure 12.36

With store 7 assigned green lights, you know that store 9 must have red lights.

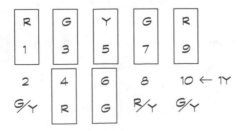

Figure 12.37

At this point, you cannot determine precisely which lights will decorate stores 2, 8, and 10. And that's the point. The four wrong answers in this question *could be false*, and all four of them—choices (A), (B), (C), and (E)—involve stores 2, 8, or 10. The correct answer *must be true* and goes directly to the deduction that follows from the question's new "if" clause. You determined that store 9 must have red lights, and that's exactly what the correct answer, choice (D), says.

21. Which one of the following statements must be true?

    (A)   Green lights decorate store 10.
    (B)   Red lights decorate store 1.
    (C)   Red lights decorate store 8.
    (D)   Yellow lights decorate store 8.
    (E)   Yellow lights decorate store 10.[15]

For this question, you needn't do more than characterize the correct answer—it *must be true*—and consult your Master Sketch. Store 1 must have red lights, just as the correct answer, choice (B), states. Notice that, here again, the wrong answers all involve stores whose color of lights can't be determined.

Those unusual Matching games are good examples of why, in the end, you shouldn't agonize over categorizing game types and subtypes and variations. In all three cases, you were able to manage the game by using the Overview step to assess the situation that the test makers described and what they were asking you to do with it. By attending to the task described in the setup, you were able to construct an effective sketch. You can see from those games that having a sketch that organizes the game's information in a clear, strategic way—a way that's *applicable to the game*—is more valuable than memorizing a limited number of set sketches and trying to make them accommodate every game action, regardless of how unusual or specific the test makers have designed it to be. Take what's familiar in a game and base your approach on that, but be open to what you need to do a little differently when the tasks described by the test makers don't fit the stereotype. The test makers always provide the information and restrictions needed to answer every question. Some test takers cut themselves off from the most helpful part of a game because it doesn't fit their preconceived notion of how a specific game type is "supposed to" work.

DIFFICULT MATCHING

The most difficult examples of Matching games are often built out of standard Matching game tasks. Rather than rely on unusual twists and turns to make these games harder, the test makers simply present the typical combination of "stationary" and "movable" entities, but provide fewer or less powerful restrictions.

---

[15] PrepTest 33, Sec. 4, Q 21

Difficult Matching Practice

Give the following game a try. Don't time yourself on this challenging example. Instead, go through it carefully, applying each step of the Kaplan Method appropriately. When you're finished, or if you find yourself struggling with the setup, check your work against the explanations. Here's a hint: Pay as much attention to which matches you *cannot* determine as you do to those you can.

For the school paper, five students—Jiang, Kramer, Lopez, Megregian, and O'Neill—each review one or more of exactly three plays: *Sunset*, *Tamerlane*, and *Undulation*, but do not review any other plays. The following conditions must apply:

Kramer and Lopez each review fewer of the plays than Megregian.

Neither Lopez nor Megregian reviews any play Jiang reviews.

Kramer and O'Neill both review *Tamerlane*.

Exactly two of the students review exactly the same play or plays as each other.

19. Which one of the following could be an accurate and complete list of the students who review only *Sunset*?

    (A) Lopez
    (B) O'Neill
    (C) Jiang, Lopez
    (D) Kramer, O'Neill
    (E) Lopez, Megregian

20. Which one of the following must be true?

    (A) Jiang reviews more of the plays than Lopez does.
    (B) Megregian reviews more of the plays than Jiang does.
    (C) Megregian reviews more of the plays than O'Neill does.
    (D) O'Neill reviews more of the plays than Jiang does.
    (E) O'Neill reviews more of the plays than Kramer does.

21. If exactly three of the students review *Undulation*, which one of the following could be true?

    (A) Megregian does not review *Undulation*.
    (B) O'Neill does not review *Undulation*.
    (C) Jiang reviews *Undulation*.
    (D) Lopez reviews *Tamerlane*.
    (E) O'Neill reviews *Sunset*.

22. Which one of the following could be an accurate and complete list of the students who review *Tamerlane*?

    (A) Jiang, Kramer
    (B) Kramer, O'Neill
    (C) Kramer, Lopez, O'Neill
    (D) Kramer, Megregian, O'Neill
    (E) Lopez, Megregian, O'Neill

23. If Jiang does not review *Tamerlane*, then which one of the following must be true?

    (A) Jiang reviews *Sunset*.
    (B) Lopez reviews *Undulation*.
    (C) Megregian reviews *Sunset*.
    (D) Megregian reviews *Tamerlane*.
    (E) O'Neill reviews *Undulation*.[16]

---

[16] PrepTest 42, Sec. 1, Game 4, Qs 19–23

Explanations

STEPS 1 AND 2: Overview and Sketch

The difficulty of this game is roughly equal to that of the first two games you reviewed in this chapter, the Appliance Technicians game and the one with the Lunch Trucks. So you've handled games of this caliber already. Here, the scenario described involves five student reporters who will each review one or more of three plays. The plays aren't going anywhere, so use them as your "stationary" entities.

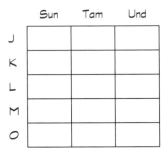

Figure 12.38

According to the opening paragraph of the game, each of the students reviews between one and three of the plays. The more clearly you understand the number restrictions in this game, the easier it will be.

STEP 3: Rules

The rules in this game impose limits either on the number of plays each student can review or on which students can review the same play(s) as one another.

Rule 1 tells you that K and L each review fewer plays than M. Just jot that down beneath the framework for the time being.

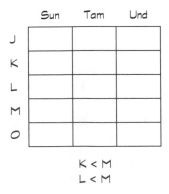

Figure 12.39

Rule 2 restricts L and M from reviewing any play that J reviews. You can depict that as formal logic or with a descriptive note.

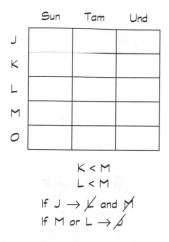

Figure 12.40

Rule 3 you can add into the framework. This concreteness is most welcome.

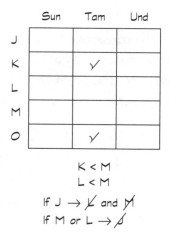

Figure 12.41

The last rule is worded in a tricky way. Make sure you capture its meaning with a quick paraphrase: Exactly two of the students (not three, not four) will review exactly the same roster of plays as one another. If a particular arrangement threatens to create three students with the same list of reviews, that arrangement is unacceptable.

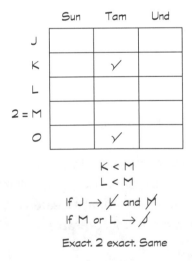

Figure 12.42

There are no floaters here. All of the students are restricted to some extent. But it's well worth noting that while O will definitely review *Tamerlane*, O has no restrictions with respect to any of the other students and thus may, or may not, review any of the other plays.

STEP 4: Deductions

You can learn a lot about this game by considering the number restrictions. Start with M, the most restricted entity in the game. M must review at least two plays (Rule 1), but can't review any play that J reviews (Rule 2). Thus, M cannot review all three plays. Add notation to your sketch signifying that M will review exactly two plays.

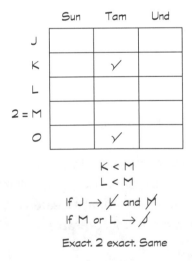

Figure 12.43

Since M reviews only two plays and reviews more plays than K or L (Rule 1), you can conclude that K and L review one play each.

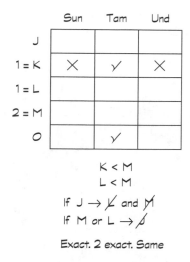

Figure 12.44

Notice that, thanks to Rule 3, K's row is now closed off. K reviews only *Tamerlane*.

Similarly, since M is reviewing two plays but cannot review any play that J reviews (Rule 2), you know that J reviews only one play as well.

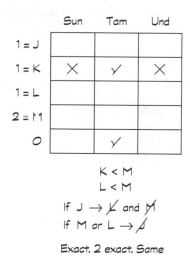

Figure 12.45

It's worth noting that J must review the one play M does not review, and M must review the two plays J does not. Between the two of them, they'll cover all three plays every time.

STEP 5: Questions

Expect the test makers to reward you for your deductions about the numbers. Expect, too, that they'll involve Rule 4—the one requiring exactly two students to review exactly the same play(s)—in at least one or two questions about acceptable arrangements.

19. **(A)**

Which one of the following could be an accurate and complete list of the students who review only *Sunset*?

(A) Lopez
(B) O'Neill
(C) Jiang, Lopez
(D) Kramer, O'Neill
(E) Lopez, Megregian[17]

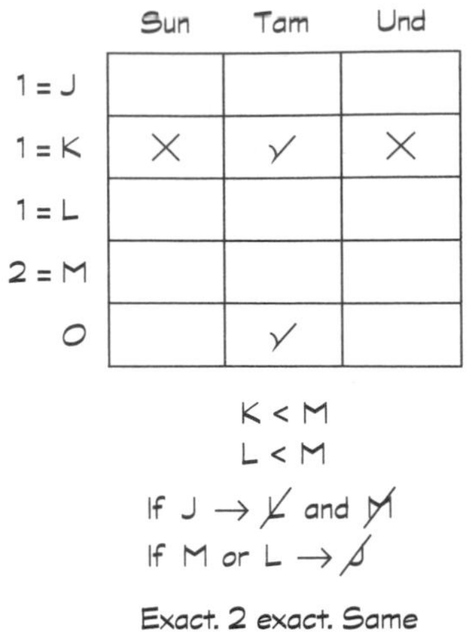

	Sun	Tam	Und
1 = J			
1 = K	✗	✓	✗
1 = L			
2 = M			
O		✓	

K < M
L < M
If J → ✗ and ✗
If M or L → ✗

Exact. 2 exact. Same

Figure 12.46

Make sure you read this question stem carefully. The correct answer is an acceptable list of those who review *only Sunset*. That allows you to get rid of choices (B) and (D) immediately. You know that K and O review *Tamerlane* (Rule 3). You can also eliminate choice (E), since M must review two plays. *Sunset* cannot be M's only review. That leaves choices (A) and (C). A check of the rules in your sketch reminds you that L and J may not review the same play(s) as one another. Eliminate choice (C). The correct answer is choice (A); L could be the only student who reviews only *Sunset*.

20. **(B)**

Which one of the following must be true?

(A) Jiang reviews more of the plays than Lopez does.
(B) Megregian reviews more of the plays than Jiang does.
(C) Megregian reviews more of the plays than O'Neill does.
(D) O'Neill reviews more of the plays than Jiang does.
(E) O'Neill reviews more of the plays than Kramer does.[18]

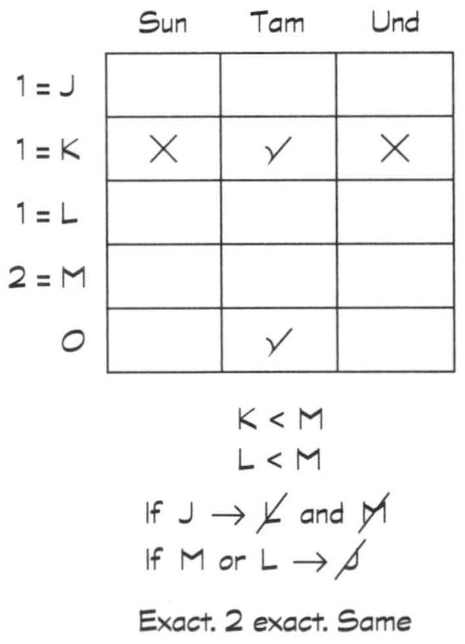

	Sun	Tam	Und
1 = J			
1 = K	✗	✓	✗
1 = L			
2 = M			
O		✓	

K < M
L < M
If J → ✗ and ✗
If M or L → ✗

Exact. 2 exact. Same

Figure 12.47

There's nothing fancy about this question. Characterize the answer choices and evaluate them based on your Master Sketch. The correct answer *must be true*. So each of the four wrong answers *could be false*.

---

[17] PrepTest 42, Sec. 1, Q 19
[18] PrepTest 42, Sec. 1, Q 20

Choice (A) is definitely false. J and L each review one play. Eliminate this choice.

Choice (B) must be true. You deduced that M reviews two plays and J one. This choice is correct and is the first point produced directly by your number-based deductions.

All three of the remaining choices—choices (C), (D), and (E)—include O, who you'll remember is the "almost floater" here. Since O can review one, two, or all three of the plays, there's no way to determine that O must review more or fewer plays than anyone else.

21. **(E)**

If exactly three of the students review *Undulation*, which one of the following could be true?

(A) Megregian does not review *Undulation*.
(B) O'Neill does not review *Undulation*.
(C) Jiang reviews *Undulation*.
(D) Lopez reviews *Tamerlane*.
(E) O'Neill reviews *Sunset*.[19]

	Sun	Tam	Und
1 = J			X
1 = K	X	✓	X
1 = L	X	X	✓
2 = M			✓
O		✓	✓

Figure 12.48

This is the first "If" question in the set. Create a mini-sketch by copying over your Master Sketch framework and adding the new condition.

	Sun	Tam	$\underset{\shortparallel}{3}$ Und
1 = J			
1 = K	X	✓	X
1 = L			
2 = M			
O		✓	

Figure 12.49

Consider how you could get three reviewers for *Undulation*. K is already out. Adding J would make it impossible to have L or M (Rule 2), leaving only two possible reviewers. Thus, you cannot have J review *Undulation*. The three student reviewers there will have to be L, M, and O.

---

[19] PrepTest 42, Sec. 1, Q 21

	Sun	Tam	Und
1 = J			X
1 = K	X	✓	X
1 = L	X	X	✓
2 = M			✓
O		✓	✓

Figure 12.50

Since L can review only one play, L's row is closed off.

At this point, you know that either J reviews *Sunset* and M reviews *Tamerlane*, or vice versa. But there's no way to determine which. You also have no way of knowing whether O reviews *Sunset*.

Since the question stem calls for a statement that *could be true*, one of the open possibilities just mentioned will be in the correct answer. The wrong answers, which *must be false*, will be ruled out in the mini-sketch.

Choices (A) through (D) all *must be false*. Check the mini-sketch and you'll see each of them contradicted there. The correct answer is choice (E). O could review *Sunset* under this question's conditions.

22. **(D)**

Which one of the following could be an accurate and complete list of the students who review *Tamerlane*?

(A) Jiang, Kramer
(B) Kramer, O'Neill
(C) Kramer, Lopez, O'Neill
(D) Kramer, Megregian, O'Neill
(E) Lopez, Megregian, O'Neill[20]

	Sun	Tam	Und
1 = J			
1 = K	X	✓	X
1 = L			
2 = M			
O		✓	

K < M
L < M
If J → K̸ and M̸
If M or L → J̸

Exact. 2 exact. Same

Figure 12.51

From Rule 3, you know that a list of students reviewing *Tamerlane* must include K and O. That allows you to eliminate choice (A), which lacks O, and choice (E), which lacks K. The three remaining choices all have K and O, but choices (B) and (C) lack both J and M. Remember that you deduced that between them, J and M would review all three plays. So one of J or M must be in a list of the students reviewing *Tamerlane*. Only choice (D) is acceptable and, therefore, the correct answer.

---

[20] PrepTest 42, Sec. 1, Q 22

23. **(D)**

If Jiang does not review *Tamerlane*, then which one of the following must be true?

(A)   Jiang reviews *Sunset*.
(B)   Lopez reviews *Undulation*.
(C)   Megregian reviews *Sunset*.
(D)   Megregian reviews *Tamerlane*.
(E)   O'Neill reviews *Undulation*.[21]

	Sun	Tam	Und
1 = J	✓	✗	✗
1 = K	✗	✓	✗
1 = L		✗	
2 = M	✗	✓	✓
O		✓	

Figure 12.52

Here's one more "If" question. Copy over the Master Sketch framework, and add in the new condition.

	Sun	Tam	Und
1 = J	✓	✗	✗
1 = K	✗	✓	✗
1 = L			
2 = M			
O		✓	

Figure 12.53

As soon as you know that J does not review *Tamerlane*, you can be certain that M does.

	Sun	Tam	Und
1 = J	✓	✗	✗
1 = K	✗	✓	✗
1 = L		✗	
2 = M	✗	✓	✓
O		✓	

Figure 12.54

That's as far as you need to go. The correct answer *must be true*. It's choice (D), which says that M reviews *Tamerlane*.

Congratulations. That was among the toughest Matching games to appear in the last ten years. Most test takers—those that haven't trained with the Kaplan Method, anyway—don't consider the impact that rules have on the number restrictions within the game. Because you've learned to look for the limitations that will allow you to reduce the number of acceptable arrangements

---

[21] PrepTest 42, Sec. 1, Q 23

down to a manageable handful, you're able to find the key deductions that the questions reward. The test makers may use unfamiliar patterns, odd scenarios, or obscure-sounding rules in their attempt to make some games harder. Your work with the Kaplan Method neutralizes all of those tactics.

In the next chapter, you'll see Matching tasks again, but they'll be mixed with Sequencing or Selection tasks. Hybrid games intimidate test takers who haven't trained in the fundamentals. For you, they're just one more way the test makers reward you for useful sketches, well-analyzed rules, and thorough deductions.

CHAPTER 13

HYBRID GAMES

Taken as a whole, Hybrid games are the second most common type of game on the LSAT, behind Sequencing games. While that statement is true, it's a bit misleading. Here's why. First, Hybrid games are created out of combinations of the four common logic games tasks. Test takers often handle Hybrids just fine without even realizing that they're dealing with Hybrids. In the midst of a Logic Games section, it's more important to clearly articulate your task than to define a game type. Being able to say, "I need to determine the order in which the seven trucks arrive and whether each one is green or red," is far more important than saying, "Aha, I have a Sequencing-Matching Hybrid here." Keep your focus in the overview on understanding what you're being asked for and designing a sketch that reflects the setup and restrictions. Second, the term Hybrid is a catch all phrase for games with multiple or multi-part tasks. So while Sequencing-Matching tasks are very common, Matching-Selection tasks have appeared all of two times in the past 20 years.

In this chapter, I'll have you review some of the Hybrid games you've already seen and solved in this book and introduce you to a couple of new examples of the most common Hybrid games. I'll finish up with a look at a couple of unusual Hybrid games to give you the flavor of just how diverse this category can be.

If you haven't done so already, review the portion of chapter 7 on handling complex games. There, I laid out two basic goals that you should try to accomplish any time you encounter a multi-part, multi-task game. First, determine the logical order of the tasks. If you have to schedule interviews for four out of six job candidates, you can't really schedule the interviews until you know who's being considered for the position. Thus, in a Selection-Sequencing Hybrid, the Selection task is logically prior to the Sequencing task. Second, always seek to integrate both tasks into your sketch. The Red and Green Trucks game is particularly illustrative. There, the rules sometimes created restrictions based purely on the Sequencing task ("Z arrives at some time before H"), purely on the Matching task ("No two consecutive arrivals are red"), or on a mixture of the two ("Exactly two of the trucks that arrive before Y are red"). You need a sketch that allows you to see how a restriction on one of the actions affects entities from the other action. In the examples that follow, pay attention to how the tasks are consistently integrated.

REAL-LIFE HYBRIDS

I suppose, if you think about it, almost everything we do in real life is a Hybrid task. I have a Kaplan colleague who likes to compare logic games to planning a wedding. You have to decide who you'll invite. That's Selection. You have to plan who'll sit together at dinner, like a huge Distribution game. You even have to decide the order in which the wedding party members will walk down the aisle, a kind of Matching-Sequencing task. As you plan that last task, you and your spouse-to-be will have some Rules that dictate who must walk earlier or later and others that determine who will walk with whom, exactly what the test makers would outline in a comparable logic game.

The one thing you can count on is that the tasks that are blended into an LSAT Hybrid game will, individually, be quite simple. The LSAT will never ask you to Sequence the six appliance technicians and assign each of them between one and three of the electronics categories to repair. They don't expect even the most expert test takers to be able to complete a game like that in eight and a half minutes. As you review and try the games below, take note of how the test makers limit the scope of one or both of the tasks. Usually, one of the two tasks is more complicated than the other. In both of the first two Sequencing-Matching games you'll review, the Sequencing task dominates your sketch. The Matching aspect of the game serves, as much as anything, simply to restrict some of the acceptable Sequencing arrangements. Take a look to see what I mean.

SEQUENCING-MATCHING HYBRIDS

In Part I, you saw several Sequencing-Matching Hybrid games. That's no surprise, given their prominence on recent tests. Between PrepTests 43 and 53, there were more Sequencing-Matching Hybrids than there were Selection or Distribution games. The most common pattern used by the test makers in these games is to ask you to sequence six or seven entities and to assign one of two conditions or attributes to each. The two examples that follow illustrate this "default" pattern that you first saw in Part I.

> Detectives investigating a citywide increase in burglaries questioned exactly seven suspects—S, T, V, W, X, Y, and Z—each on a different one of seven consecutive days. Each suspect was questioned exactly once. Any suspect who confessed did so while being questioned. The investigation conformed to the following:
>
> T was questioned on day three.
> The suspect questioned on day four did not confess.
> S was questioned after W was questioned.
> Both X and V were questioned after Z was questioned.
> No suspects confessed after W was questioned.
> Exactly two suspects confessed after T was questioned.[1]

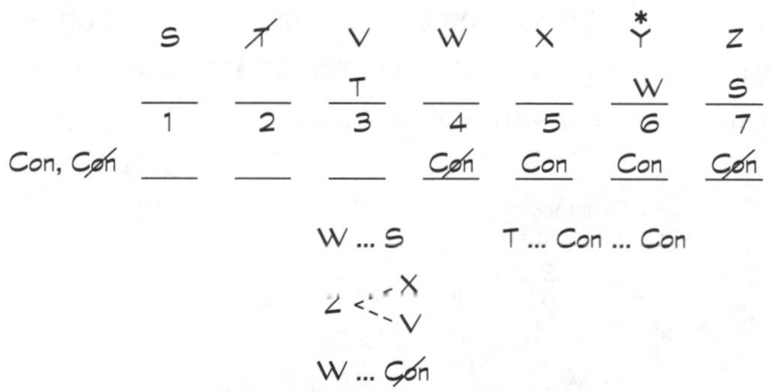

Figure 13.1

> A locally known guitarist's demo CD contains exactly seven different songs—S, T, V, W, X, Y, and Z. Each song occupies exactly one of the CD's seven tracks. Some of the songs are rock classics; the others are new compositions. The following conditions must hold:
>
> S occupies the fourth track of the CD.
> Both W and Y precede S on the CD.
> T precedes W on the CD.
> A rock classic occupies the sixth track of the CD.
> Each rock classic is immediately preceded on the CD by a
> new composition.
> Z is a rock classic.[2]

---

[1] PrepTest 53, Sec. 2, Game 3

[2] PrepTest 51, Sec. 4, Game 3

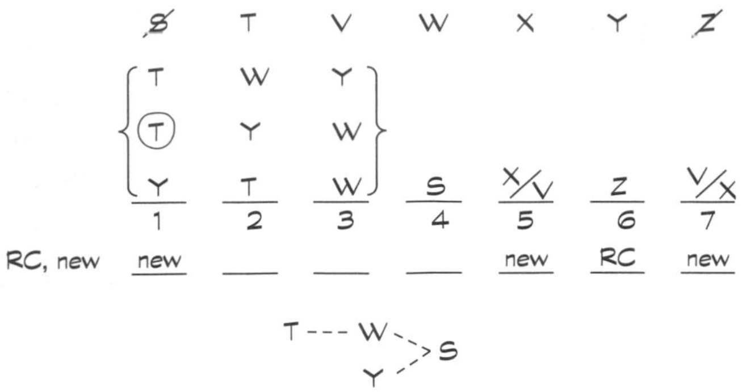

S̶   T   V   W   X   Y   Z̶

```
    ⎡ T    W    Y ⎤
    ⎢              ⎥
   {  (T)   Y    W  }
    ⎢              ⎥
    ⎣ Y    T    W ⎦     S    X/V    Z    V/X
      1    2    3         4    5     6    7
   RC, new   new   ___  ___   ___  new   RC   new
```

```
       T --- W ˜
                ˜˜> S
            Y ˜˜
```

Figure 13.2

I could just as easily have displayed the Thunderstorm game from chapter 1 or the Red and Green Trucks game from chapter 5 here. They're comprised of the same tasks and produce nearly identical sketches.

Notice that in both of the games, you were able to make some deductions along the "Sequencing line" where you arrange the suspects or songs, while you could make others along the "Matching line" where you assign the attributes (confess or not confess; new composition or rock classic). Indeed, learning that track 6 on the guitarist's CD is designated a rock classic allows you to deduce that song Z is the sixth track. Untrained test takers often try to deal with the two tasks in a Hybrid game in two different sketches.

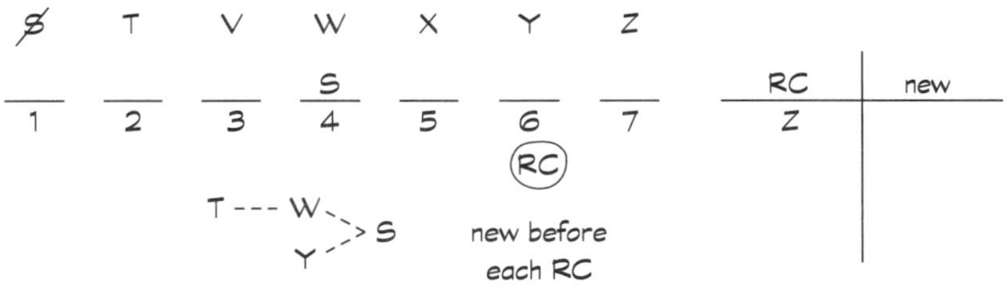

```
   S̶   T   V   W   X   Y   Z
                    S
   ___ ___ ___ ___ ___ ___ ___      RC  | new
    1   2   3   4   5   6   7        Z   |
                       (RC)             |
                                       |
       T --- W ˜                        |
                ˜˜> S     new before    |
            Y ˜˜          each RC        |
```

Figure 13.3

Trying to handle the tasks in that way risks missing important interactions between the two tasks. Integrated sketches, like those beside the games above, are always preferable.

The next game is another Sequencing-Matching Hybrid that you saw in Part I, and it's a game that illustrates the power of Limited Options sketches, a strategy I hope you now use without hesitation. Look at the game again, this time paying attention to the way in which the test makers blended Sequencing and Matching rules.

Exactly six people—Lulu, Nam, Ofelia, Pachai, Santiago, and Tyrone—are the only contestants in a chess tournament. The tournament consists of four games, played one after the other. Exactly two people play in each game, and each person plays in at least one game. The following conditions must apply:

Tyrone does not play in the first or third game.

Lulu plays in the last game.

Nam plays in only one game and it is not against Pachai.

Santiago plays in exactly two games, one just before and one just after the only game that Ofelia plays in.[3]

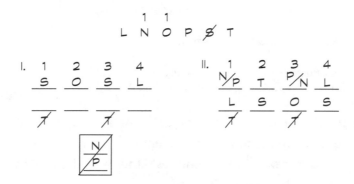

Figure 13.4

In this game, the test makers put a greater emphasis on the Matching aspect of the Hybrid by having you determine the possible "matchups" in the tournament as well as the order in which the games were played. Although three of the rules (Rules 1, 2, and 4) deal with the order in which participants appear, the final Master Sketch leaves open a number of questions about who faces whom in various games. As a result, the questions in this game rewarded you for determining the possible pairings of opponents.

You'll notice that in this game, two of the players play in two games each, while the other four play in only one game apiece. The test makers told you the number of games for three of the players (Nam, Ofelia, and Santiago), but left it up to you to determine the number of games for the other players. That added a little difficulty to the game, although you were able to clear up some of that uncertainty through your use of the Limited Options sketches.

In the next game, the test makers left the number restrictions even more wide open. While they limited the Sequencing task to just three entities—the eighth, ninth, and tenth centuries AD—they didn't specify that all three times had to be used. They pulled a similar stunt with the Matching task. Each site is found by one of the three archaeologists, but nothing requires all three archaeologists to have found sites. At this point in your practice, I'm not telling you anything new when I say, "Never assume restrictions that aren't explicit in the setup or rules." Many test takers have gone way off track with this game by assuming that all three times or

---

[3] PrepTest 45, Sec. 3, Game 2

all three archaeologists had to be used. Even if they eventually sorted out that not all of the entities had to be placed, they wasted a lot of time making unwarranted deductions.

A tour group plans to visit exactly five archaeological sites. Each site was discovered by exactly one of the following archaeologists—Ferrara, Gallagher, Oliphant—and each dates from the eighth, ninth, or tenth century (A.D.). The tour must satisfy the following conditions:

    The site visited second dates from the ninth century.
    Neither the site visited fourth nor the site visited fifth was discovered by Oliphant.
    Exactly one of the sites was discovered by Gallagher, and it dates from the tenth century.
    If a site dates from the eighth century, it was discovered by Oliphant.
    The site visited third dates from a more recent century than does either the site visited first or that visited fourth.[4]

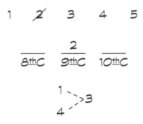

Figure 13.5

Notice one more interesting, and telling, feature of the Archaeological Sites game. While Rule 5 is, by definition, a Sequencing rule (it relates two entities chronologically, after all), the sketch is best integrated by assigning dates to the entities rather than the other way around. Imagine trying to set up the game with a sketch like this:

$$
\begin{array}{ccccc}
1 & \not{2} & 3 & 4 & 5 \\
\end{array}
$$

$$
\underset{\text{8thC}}{\rule{1cm}{0.4pt}} \quad \overset{2}{\underset{\text{9thC}}{\rule{1cm}{0.4pt}}} \quad \underset{\text{10thC}}{\rule{1cm}{0.4pt}}
$$

$$
\begin{array}{c}
1 \\
\;\;\diagdown\!\!>3 \\
4 \diagup
\end{array}
$$

Figure 13.6

You'd be hard-pressed to find a way to relate the sites to their discoverers without creating a separate, and thus confusing, second framework. Always let the sketch evolve naturally from a game's task. Test takers who memorize misleading "rules" (like, "Always write out the dates first and then put the entities underneath them") miss the opportunity to use the most helpful and strategic scratch work in their test booklets. Such test takers classify all Hybrids as "hard games" simply because they don't fit a familiar framework. In fact, Hybrid games have a range of difficulties. Make sure you're not allowing games to intimidate you for no good reason.

SEQUENCING-DISTRIBUTION HYBRIDS

The second most common Hybrid task is Sequencing-Distribution. The main distinction between this variation and Sequencing-Matching games is that, in Sequencing-Distribution games, each entity is used only once. These games call for the entities to be placed in an order, either chronological or hierarchical, and then grouped. Most often, some of the entities are paired with others in the groups while others take their positions alone in the sequence. The Concert Stages game provides an example that you worked with in Part I of the book.

> Three folk groups—Glenside, Hilltopper, Levon—and three rock groups—Peasant, Query, Tinhead—each perform on one of two stages, north or south. Each stage has three two-hour performances: north at 6, 8, and 10; south at 8, 10, and 12. Each group performs individually and exactly once, consistent with the following conditions:
>> Peasant performs at 6 or 12.
>> Glenside performs at some time before Hilltopper.
>> If any rock group performs at 10, no folk group does.
>> Levon and Tinhead perform on different stages.
>> Query performs immediately after a folk group, though
>> not necessarily on the same stage.[5]

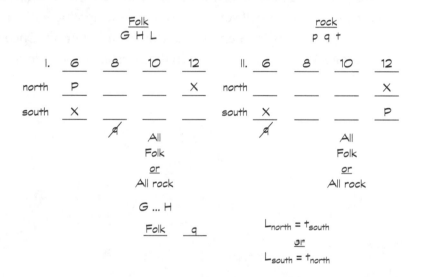

Figure 13.7

It's very important, in a game like this one, that you create a sketch that reflects the situation described in the setup. Offsetting the slots on the two stages so that you can see which groups are performing at the same time is essential.

Take note of which rules restrict which action within the Hybrid task. Rules 1, 2, and 5 refer exclusively to the Sequencing aspect of the game. Rule 4 limits only the Distribution of the two entities it names. Rule 3 refers explicitly to a time slot, but it affects both the order of the groups and their pairings.

The Concert Stages game is also a good reminder that all of the strategies you've learned thus far can be applied in Hybrid games. Rule 1 presents an "either/or" situation, calling for Limited

---

[5] PrepTest 48, Sec. 2, Game 4

Options sketches. While you can't fill in many of the slots initially, seeing that every acceptable arrangement must fit one of those two patterns proves very helpful as you attack the questions.

Sequencing-Distribution Hybrid Practice

Try one more Sequencing-Distribution game, one that you haven't seen before. Here, six paintings will be divided into two groups of three and then sequenced (early-, middle-, and late-period) within those groups. As you set up the game, take note of which rules and restrictions govern the Distribution task and which limit the Sequencing. Note, too, how the test makers can use rules from one of the tasks to affect the other. Here's a hint: If the first group already has a middle-period painting, it can't take another one.

Give yourself eight and a half minutes to try this game and all of its questions. Use the Kaplan Method to assess the game's task, create your sketch, add the rules, and make all of the available deductions. Then try the question set. If you find that you're struggling with one or more of the questions, check the explanations for Steps 1–4 of the Kaplan Method. Once you're sure you have a complete, accurate Master Sketch, return to the questions and give them another shot.

Questions 13–17

Exactly six of an artist's paintings, entitled *Quarterion, Redemption, Sipapu, Tesseract, Vale,* and *Zelkova,* are sold at auction. Three of the paintings are sold to a museum, and three are sold to a private collector. Two of the paintings are from the artist's first (earliest) period, two are from her second period, and two arc from her third (most recent) period. The private collector and the museum each buy one painting from each period. The following conditions hold:

> *Sipapu,* which is sold to the private collector, is from an earlier period than *Zelkova,* which is sold to the museum.
> *Quarterion* is not from an earlier period than *Tesseract.*
> *Vale* is from the artist's second period.

13. Which one of the following could be an accurate list of the paintings bought by the museum and the private collector, listed in order of the paintings' periods, from first to third?

    (A) museum: *Quarterion, Vale, Zelkova*
    private collector: *Redemption, Sipapu, Tesseract*
    (B) museum: *Redemption, Zelkova, Quarterion*
    private collector: *Sipapu, Vale, Tesseract*
    (C) museum: *Sipapu, Zelkova, Quarterion*
    private collector: *Tesseract, Vale, Redemption*
    (D) museum: *Tesseract, Quarterion, Zelkova*
    private collector: *Sipapu, Redemption, Vale*
    (E) museum: *Zelkova, Tesseract, Redemption*
    private collector: *Sipapu, Vale, Quarterion*

14. If *Sipapu* is from the artist's second period, which one of the following could be two of the three paintings bought by the private collector?

    (A) *Quarterion* and *Zelkova*
    (B) *Redemption* and *Tesseract*
    (C) *Redemption* and *Vale*
    (D) *Redemption* and *Zelkova*
    (E) *Tesseract* and *Zelkova*

15. Which one of the following is a complete and accurate list of the paintings, any one of which could be the painting from the artist's first period that is sold to the private collector?

    (A) *Quarterion, Redemption*
    (B) *Redemption, Sipapu*
    (C) *Quarterion, Sipapu, Tesseract*
    (D) *Quarterion, Redemption, Sipapu, Tesseract*
    (E) *Redemption, Sipapu, Tesseract, Zelkova*

16. If *Sipapu* is from the artist's second period, then which one of the following paintings could be from the period immediately preceding *Quarterion's* period and be sold to the same buyer as *Quarterion*?

    (A) *Redemption*
    (B) *Sipapu*
    (C) *Tesseract*
    (D) *Vale*
    (E) *Zelkova*

17. If *Zelkova* is sold to the same buyer as *Tesseract* and is from the period immediately preceding *Tesseract's* period, then which one of the following must be true?

    (A) *Quarterion* is sold to the museum.
    (B) *Quarterion* is from the artist's third period.
    (C) *Redemption* is sold to the private collector.
    (D) *Redemption* is from the artist's third period.
    (E) *Redemption* is sold to the same buyer as *Vale.*[6]

Explanations

STEPS 1 AND 2: Overview and Sketch

The opening paragraph of this game is lengthy, but it explains the game's premise in a way that allows you to draw a perfect sketch. You need to keep track of who (museum or private collector) bought each of the six paintings. At the same time, you need to record which of the artist's three periods each painting represents. The final limitation ("The private collector and the museum each buy one painting from each period") clarifies your sketch even more.

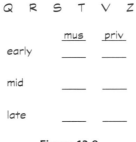

Figure 13.8

Now you can see that there will be a one-to-one matchup; in any acceptable arrangement, there will be one painting per slot.

STEP 3: Rules

The first rule affects both parts of the Hybrid action. You learn which buyers purchased S and Z, and you also learn their relative order.

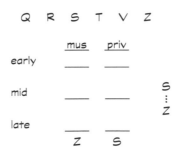

Figure 13.9

The second rule gives only a Sequencing relationship. Be careful: The rule says that Q cannot be earlier than T; that doesn't rule out their being from the same period.

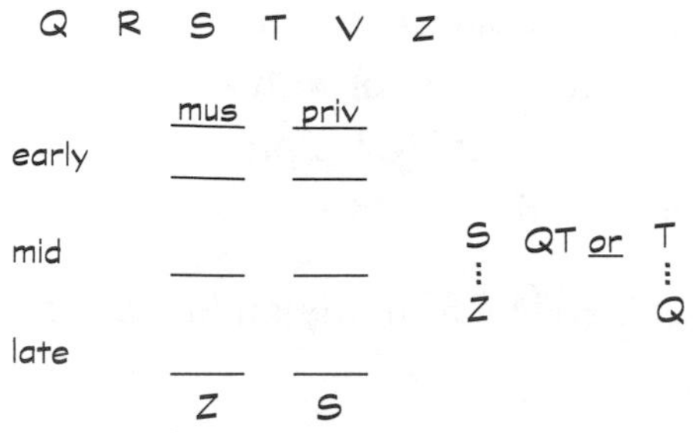

Q   R   S   T   V   Z

	mus	priv	
early	___	___	
mid	___	___	S⋮Z QT or T⋮Q
late	___	___	
	Z	S	

Figure 13.10

The final rule establishes V's period but not its buyer.

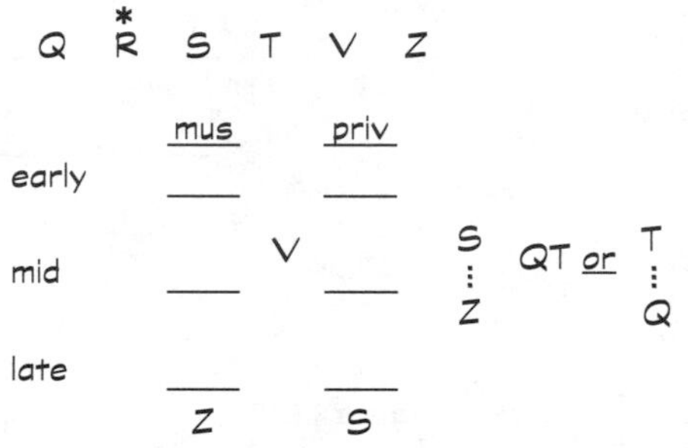

Q   R̊*   S   T   V   Z

	mus	priv	
early	___	___	
mid	___ V	___	S⋮Z QT or T⋮Q
late	___	___	
	Z	S	

Figure 13.11

Make sure you noted that R is a floater in this game, able to take either buyer and any of the three periods.

STEP 4: Deductions

The first rule in this game allows for a quasi-Limited Options approach. Since S must come from an earlier period than Z, you can set twin sketches like this:

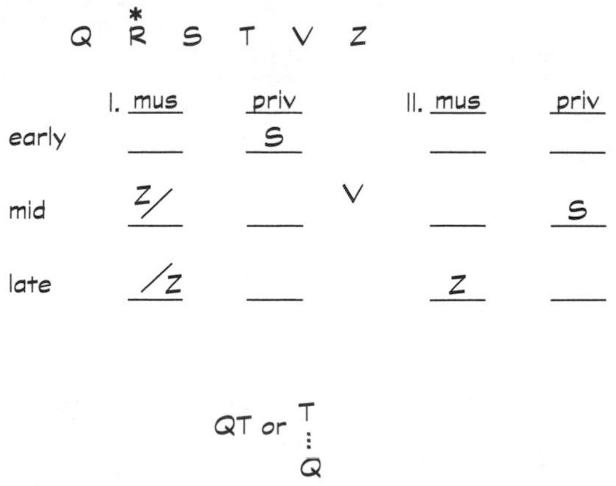

Q   R̊*   S   T   V   Z

	I. mus	priv		II. mus	priv
early	___	S		___	___
mid	Z̸	___	V	___	S
late	̸Z	___		Z	___

QT or   T⋮Q

Figure 13.12

In Option I, you can't lock Z into a specific space unless you want to draw a sort of Option I(a) with Z in the middle period and an Option I(b) with Z in the late period. That's fine, provided that it doesn't take you too long, but frankly, it's probably overkill. The previous sketches are more than sufficient to get the questions right.

In either option, you know that V will be from the middle period (Rule 2). That means that the museum purchased V in Option II.

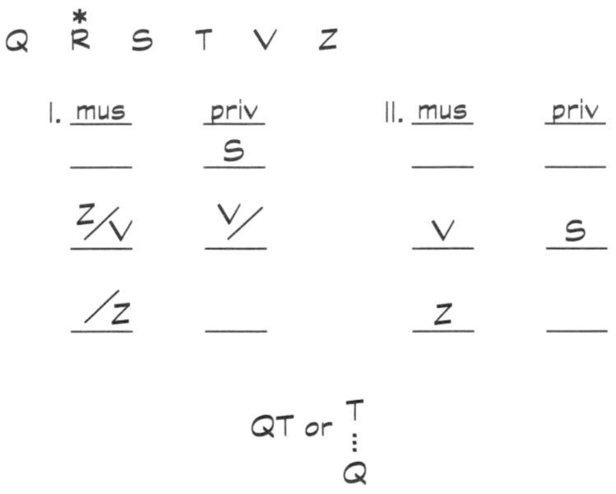

Figure 13.13

In Option I, you can't do more with Rule 2 than to note it to the side. In Option II, however, it's clear that T must be from the early period, while either Q or R is the private collector's purchase in the late period.

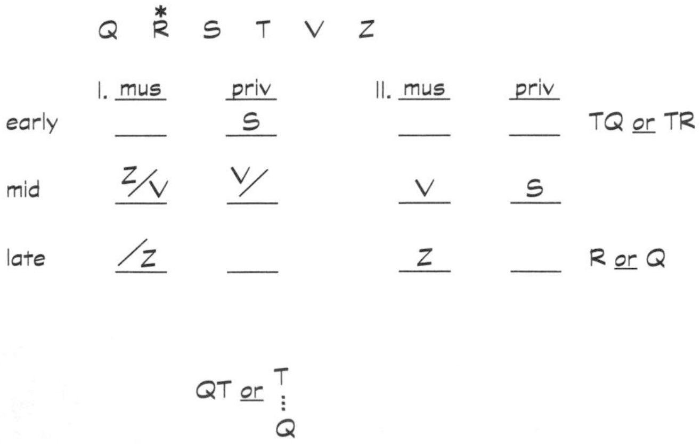

Figure 13.14

Like most Limited Options scenarios, one of the two arrangements leads to more certainty and one remains more open. Still, you have plenty to go on and the question set will add further clarity in its three "If" questions.

STEP 5: **Questions**

The questions from this game appear long and complex. Don't be thrown off, though. This is mostly just the effect of the entities' long, italicized names. In fact, the question set is pretty standard: One Acceptability question, one Complete and Accurate List question, and three "If" questions. Jump in and get the points.

13. **(B)**

Which one of the following could be an accurate list of the paintings bought by the museum and the private collector, listed in order of the paintings' periods, from first to third?

(A)   museum: *Quarterion, Vale, Zelkova*
    private collector: *Redemption, Sipapu, Tesseract*

(B)   museum: *Redemption, Zelkova, Quarterion*
    private collector: *Sipapu, Vale, Tesseract*

(C)   museum: *Sipapu, Zelkova, Quarterion*
    private collector: *Tesseract, Vale, Redemption*

(D)   museum: *Tesseract, Quarterion, Zelkova*
    private collector: *Sipapu, Redemption, Vale*

(E)   museum: *Zelkova, Tesseract, Redemption*
    private collector: *Sipapu, Vale, Quarterion*[7]

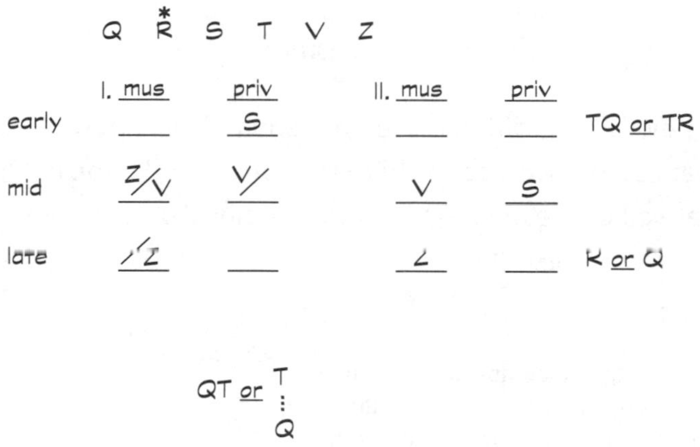

Figure 13.15

Approach this Acceptability question as you would any other. The fact that this is a Hybrid game is irrelevant to how you handle the questions.

Rule 1 knocks out choice (C), where S is sold to the museum, and choice (E), where Z is from the same period as S.

Rule 2 eliminates choice (D), where V is not found in the middle period.

Rule 3 gets rid of choice (A), where Q's period precedes T's.

That leaves only the correct answer, choice (B).

---

[7] PrepTest 43, Sec. 4, Q 13

14. **(B)**

If *Sipapu* is from the artist's second period, which one of the following could be two of the three paintings bought by the private collector?

(A)   *Quarterion* and *Zelkova*
(B)   *Redemption* and *Tesseract*
(C)   *Redemption* and *Vale*
(D)   *Redemption* and *Zelkova*
(E)   *Tesseract* and *Zelkova*[8]

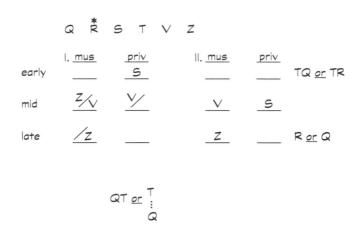

Figure 13.16

This question stem's new "if" condition places you squarely in Option II. The question asks for a pair of paintings that could have been sold to the private collector. In Option II, the museum buys V and Z. Eliminate all of the answers featuring either V or Z and you're left with only one choice, the correct answer, choice (B).

15. **(D)**

Which one of the following is a complete and accurate list of the paintings, any one of which could be the painting from the artist's first period that is sold to the private collector?

(A)   *Quarterion, Redemption*
(B)   *Redemption, Sipapu*
(C)   *Quarterion, Sipapu, Tesseract*
(D)   *Quarterion, Redemption, Sipapu, Tesseract*
(E)   *Redemption, Sipapu, Tesseract, Zelkova*[9]

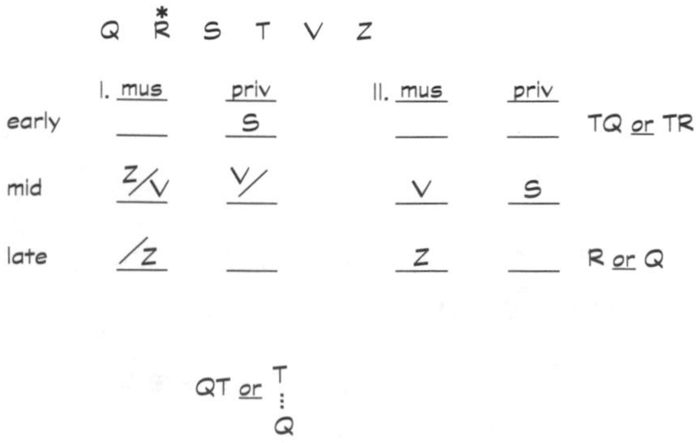

Figure 13.17

---

[8] PrepTest 43, Sec. 4, Q 14
[9] PrepTest 43, Sec. 4, Q 15

This question calls for any and all early-period paintings that could have been sold to the private collector. Glancing at the options, you can see that S is certainly a possibility. Eliminate choice (A), which lacks S in its list. At the same time, the options clearly reveal that Z cannot have been sold to the private collector. So cross out choice (E), which has Z in its list. The remaining possibilities from the list must come from Option II. There, the early-period paintings could be Q, R, or T. There's nothing restricting any of those paintings to the museum, so the correct answer must have those three paintings and painting S. That's choice (D), the correct answer.

16. **(B)**

If *Sipapu* is from the artist's second period, then which one of the following paintings could be from the period immediately preceding *Quarterion's* period and be sold to the same buyer as *Quarterion*?

(A) *Redemption*
(B) *Sipapu*
(C) *Tesseract*
(D) *Vale*
(E) *Zelkova*[10]

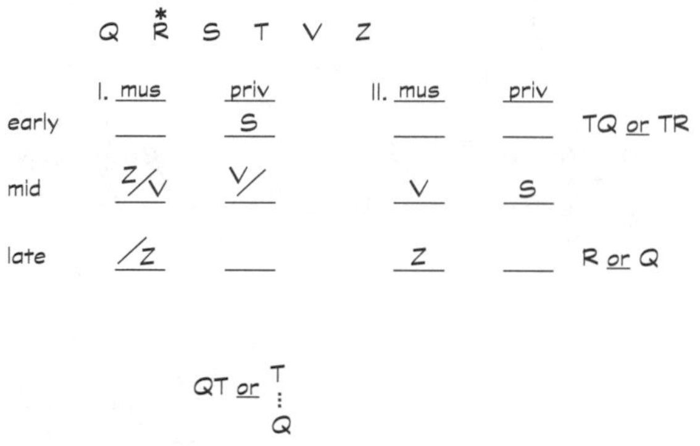

Figure 13.18

Did you notice that the "if" in this question is precisely the same as the one in question 14? So, here again, just consult Option II. The question asks for an entity that could immediately precede Q and be sold to the same collector. In Option II, the only way for Q to accommodate the question's "if" is to be the late-period painting sold to the private collector. That would be S from the immediately preceding period in the private collector's column. That's choice (B), the right answer to this question.

17. **(B)**

If *Zelkova* is sold to the same buyer as *Tesseract* and is from the period immediately preceding *Tesseract's* period, then which one of the following must be true?

(A) *Quarterion* is sold to the museum.
(B) *Quarterion* is from the artist's third period.
(C) *Redemption* is sold to the private collector.
(D) *Redemption* is from the artist's third period.
(E) *Redemption* is sold to the same buyer as *Vale*.[11]

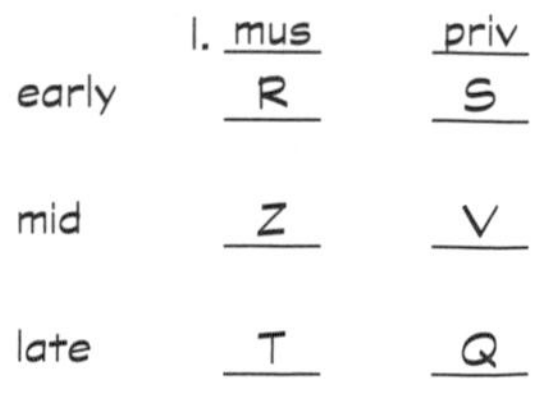

Figure 13.19

---

[10] PrepTest 43, Sec. 4, Q 16

[11] PrepTest 43, Sec. 4, Q 17

Here, at last, is an "if" question that will reward you for building a mini-sketch based on the "if" condition in the stem. The premise of the question, that Z comes from an earlier period than T, means you'll have to use Option I to begin your diagram. With Z immediately before T and both paintings sold to the same buyer, you have this:

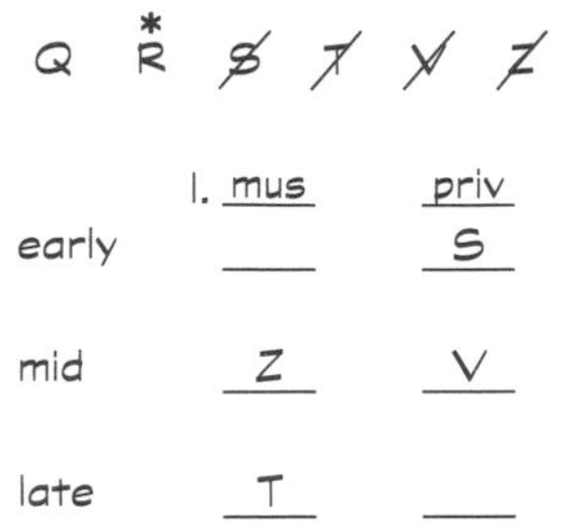

Figure 13.20

To accommodate Rule 2 in this mini-sketch, Q will have to be from the artist's late period and must be sold to the private collector.

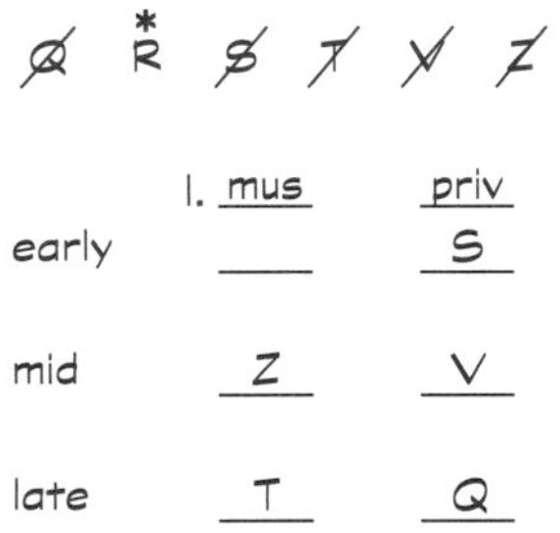

Figure 13.21

The only painting left to account for is the floater, R, which must be from the artist's early period and must be sold to the museum.

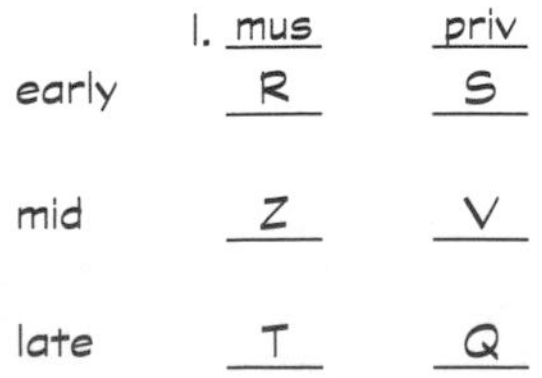

Figure 13.22

You have placed all six paintings precisely. The question calls for a *must be true* answer. Scan the choices and find the one answer that matches something in the mini-sketch. That's choice (B), and you're done with another game.

Sequencing-Distribution is much less common than Sequencing-Matching. When you encounter it, look for a way to design the sketch so that it reflects the grouping of the entities along one dimension and the order of the entities along the other. If you compare the sketch for the Concert Stages game with that for the Artist's Paintings game, you'll see that the Sequencing task ran horizontally in the first and vertically in the second. Either sketch could be rotated 90° without altering the basic information. The key is that both diagrams allow you to see how the Sequencing part of the Hybrid affects the Distribution, and vice versa. Don't sweat the small stuff. Get the fundamental tasks right and the game will fall into place.

SEQUENCING-SELECTION HYBRIDS

There's one more combination of tasks common enough to warrant its own section in this chapter, the Sequencing-Selection Hybrid. In these games, you'll always have more entities in the original list than you're allowed to place within the order required by the Sequencing action. The selection may be small (choose 5 of 6 entities) or, as in the game that follows, fairly large (choose 6 of 12 entities). Either way, the Selection part of the game is logically prior to the Sequencing element; you can't put the entities in order until you know who they are. Because of the Selection aspect present in the game, expect to see formal logic statements among the rules. Keep in mind that a condition sufficient to bring about a particular sequence of entities is, therefore, sufficient to bring about the selection of those entities. For example, in the following game, you find this rule: "A film in Italian is not shown unless a film in Norwegian is going to be shown the next day." Thus, showing an Italian film means selecting a Norwegian film *and* sequencing it for the next day after the Italian film, creating an I-N block, if you will.

Sequencing-Selection Hybrid Practice

Give this game a try. Take eight and a half minutes for the entire game and its question set. If you find yourself struggling with the questions, stop and review Steps 1–4 of the Kaplan Method in the explanations. Once you're satisfied that you have a complete Master Sketch, go back and finish the questions.

Questions 1–7

During an international film retrospective lasting six consecutive days—day 1 through day 6—exactly six different films will be shown, one each day. Twelve films will be available for presentation, two each in French, Greek, Hungarian, Italian, Norwegian, and Turkish. The presentation of the films must conform to the following conditions:

Neither day 2 nor day 4 is a day on which a film in Norwegian is shown.

A film in Italian is not shown unless a film in Norwegian is going to be shown the next day.

A film in Greek is not shown unless a film in Italian is going to be shown the next day.

1. Which one of the following is an acceptable order of films for the retrospective, listed by their language, from day 1 through day 6?

    (A) French, Greek, Italian, Turkish, Norwegian, Hungarian
    (B) French, Hungarian, Italian, Norwegian, French, Hungarian
    (C) Hungarian, French, Norwegian, Greek, Norwegian, Italian
    (D) Norwegian, Turkish, Hungarian, Italian, French, Turkish
    (E) Turkish, French, Norwegian, Hungarian, French, Turkish

2. If two films in Italian are going to be shown, one on day 2 and one on day 5, then the film shown on day 1 could be in any one of the following languages EXCEPT:

    (A) French
    (B) Greek
    (C) Hungarian
    (D) Norwegian
    (E) Turkish

3. If two films in Italian are shown during the retrospective, which one of the following must be false?

    (A) A film in French is shown on day 3.
    (B) A film in Greek is shown on day 1.
    (C) A film in Hungarian is shown on day 6.
    (D) A film in Norwegian is shown on day 5.
    (E) A film in Turkish is shown on day 4.

4. Which one of the following is a complete and accurate list of the days, any one of which is a day on which a film in Italian could be shown?

    (A) day 1, day 3, day 5
    (B) day 2, day 4, day 5
    (C) day 2, day 5, day 6
    (D) day 1, day 3
    (E) day 2, day 4

5. If two films in French are going to be shown, one on day 3 and one on day 5, which one of the following is a pair of films that could be shown on day 1 and day 6, respectively?

    (A) a film in French, a film in Turkish
    (B) a film in Greek, a film in Hungarian
    (C) a film in Italian, a film in Norwegian
    (D) a film in Norwegian, a film in Turkish
    (E) a film in Turkish, a film in Greek

6. If neither a film in French nor a film in Italian is shown during the retrospective, which one of the following must be true?

    (A) A film in Norwegian is shown on day 1.
    (B) A film in Norwegian is shown on day 5.
    (C) A film in Turkish is shown on day 4.
    (D) A film in Hungarian or else a film in Norwegian is shown on day 3.
    (E) A film in Hungarian or else a film in Turkish is shown on day 2.

7. If a film in Greek is going to be shown at some time after a film in Norwegian, then a film in Norwegian must be shown on

    (A) day 1
    (B) day 3
    (C) day 5
    (D) day 1 or else day 3
    (E) day 3 or else day 5[12]

Answer Explanations follow on the next page.

Explanations

STEPS 1 AND 2: Overview and Sketch

The first sentence of this game's setup is familiar. It implies a typical Sequencing game with six spaces. The second sentence is the one that may cause a moment of hesitation. Twelve entities? That seems inordinately high. It's a relief, then, to discover that the 12 films come from just six countries and they're evenly distributed, with 2 films from each. Did you reflect the entity list in a way that was easy to understand?

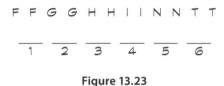

Figure 13.23

While it's clear from the game's description that you'll only be using half of the available films, nothing at the outset suggests that you need to take films from a minimum or maximum number of countries. You may be showing two films each from three countries, one film from each of the six different countries, or any other combination that gives you a total of six films for the festival.

STEP 3: Rules

There are only three rules, and none of them are very strict. You'll discover more about what can't happen than about what must.

Rule 1 tells you to rule out N for days 2 and 4.

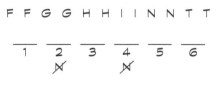

Figure 13.24

Rules 2 and 3 are conditional formal logic statements. Translate each into formal logic shorthand and formulate their contrapositives as well.

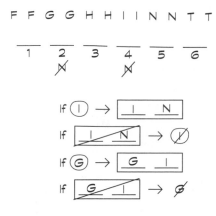

Figure 13.25

As I had you note earlier, both of these rules tell you something about the films that are chosen and about their order. You won't be able to show an Italian film without a Norwegian one being shown the next day, nor a Greek film without an Italian one immediately following. These rules will lead to big deductions when combined with the first rule.

STEP 4: **Deductions**

None of the rules give you anything positive that you can place into the sketch framework, but at least Rule 1 specifically ruled out a couple of film placements. Now, consider Rule 2 in light of what you know from Rule 1. Italian films cannot be shown on day 1 or day 3.

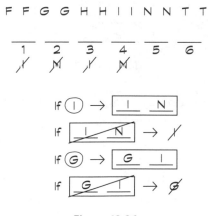

Figure 13.26

Did you notice that Italian films cannot be shown on day 6, either? Since that's the last day of the retrospective, there's no way an Italian film shown on day 6 could be followed by a Norwegian film the next day.

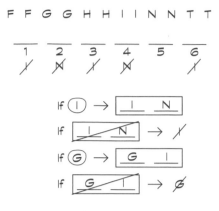

Figure 13.27

Make the comparable deductions stemming from Rule 3.

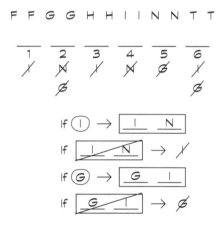

Figure 13.28

Since you can't show Italian films on days 3 and 6, you can't show Greek films on days 2 and 5. Nor can you show a Greek film on day 6, since there's no way it could be followed by an Italian film.

Now, realize there's every possibility that no Greek, Italian, or Norwegian films will be shown at all. Both French films, both Hungarian films, and both Turkish films act as floaters in this game. It's perfectly acceptable to schedule the retrospective with only those films. But it wouldn't make for a very fun logic game. Expect the test makers to reward your Deduction step with several questions that get at the intricate relationship among Greek, Italian, and Norwegian films.

STEP 5: Questions

Five of the seven questions associated with this game were "If"s. That shouldn't surprise you, given the dearth of affirmative deductions. Learning to trust that there's adequate information to answer every question—realizing that when you can't determine what must be true, the test makers will ask you for what *could be true*—is a key step in becoming a logic games expert. For your work here, I've selected five illustrative questions from the set.

1. **(E)**

   Which one of the following is an acceptable order of films for the retrospective, listed by their language, from day 1 through day 6?

   (A) French, Greek, Italian, Turkish, Norwegian, Hungarian

   (B) French, Hungarian, Italian, Norwegian, French, Hungarian

   (C) Hungarian, French, Norwegian, Greek, Norwegian, Italian

   (D) Norwegian, Turkish, Hungarian, Italian, French, Turkish

   (E) Turkish, French, Norwegian, Hungarian, French, Turkish[13]

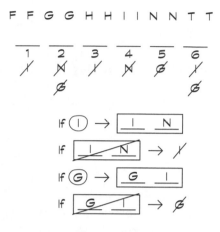

Figure 13.29

This is a straightforward Acceptability question. Each of the wrong answers will violate one of the rules. Testing each answer choice would cost you an inordinate amount of time. As always, use the rules to eliminate incorrect answer choices.

Rule 1 takes out choice (B), which has a Norwegian film on day 4.

Rule 2 gets rid of all the other wrong answers. Choice (A) is impossible because it has an Italian film (day 3) followed immediately by a Turkish film (day 4). Choice (C) violates the rule by scheduling an Italian film for day 6. Choice (C) breaks Rule 3 as well, by having a Greek film followed by a Norwegian one, but you needn't ever get that far. Choice (D) violates Rule 2 by having an Italian film (day 4) followed immediately by a French film (day 5).

The one answer choice that breaks none of the rules is correct; that's choice (E).

2. **(D)**

   If two films in Italian are going to be shown, one on day 2 and one on day 5, then the film shown on day 1 could be in any one of the following languages EXCEPT:

   (A) French
   (B) Greek
   (C) Hungarian
   (D) Norwegian
   (E) Turkish[14]

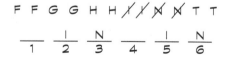

Figure 13.30

Use the "if" condition to start a mini-sketch for this question.

---

[13] PrepTest 49, Sec. 1, Q 1
[14] PrepTest 49, Sec. 1, Q 2

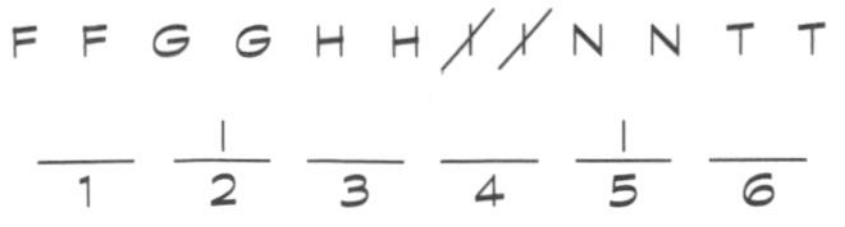

F F G G H H X X N N T T

$$\underset{1}{\quad} \underset{2}{|} \underset{3}{\quad} \underset{4}{\quad} \underset{5}{|} \underset{6}{\quad}$$

Figure 13.31

With Italian films on days 2 and 5, you know you must have Norwegian films on days 3 and 6.

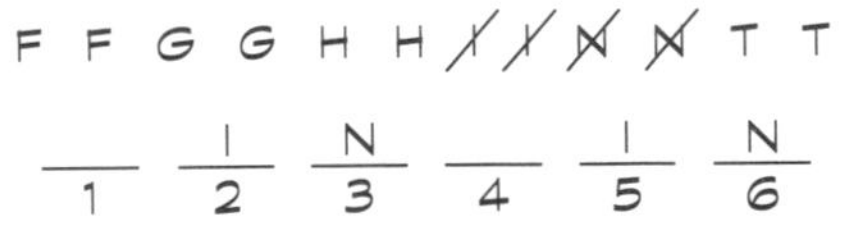

F F G G H H X X X X T T

$$\underset{1}{\quad} \underset{2}{|} \underset{3}{N} \underset{4}{\quad} \underset{5}{|} \underset{6}{N}$$

Figure 13.32

That uses up both Norwegian films in the roster, so the film on day 1 cannot be in Norwegian. That's choice (D). Test takers who forget the Selection element in this game or those who fail to list their entities in a way that reminds them that there are only two films in each language are stymied by this deceptively simple question.

3. **(A)**

    If two films in Italian are shown during the retrospective, which one of the following must be false?

    (A)   A film in French is shown on day 3.
    (B)   A film in Greek is shown on day 1.
    (C)   A film in Hungarian is shown on day 6.
    (D)   A film in Norwegian is shown on day 5.
    (E)   A film in Turkish is shown on day 4.[15]

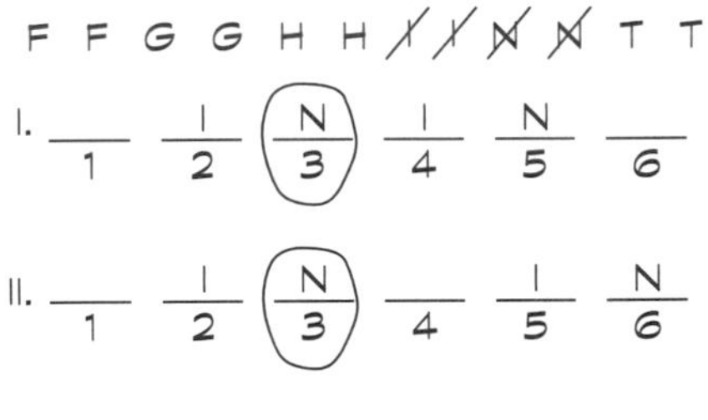

F F G G H H X X X X T T

I. $$\underset{1}{\quad} \underset{2}{|} \underset{3}{\boxed{N}} \underset{4}{|} \underset{5}{N} \underset{6}{\quad}$$

II. $$\underset{1}{\quad} \underset{2}{|} \underset{3}{\boxed{N}} \underset{4}{\quad} \underset{5}{|} \underset{6}{N}$$

Figure 13.33

Start a mini-sketch for this question based on the "if" condition in the stem. There are two ways to show two Italian films in the retrospective.

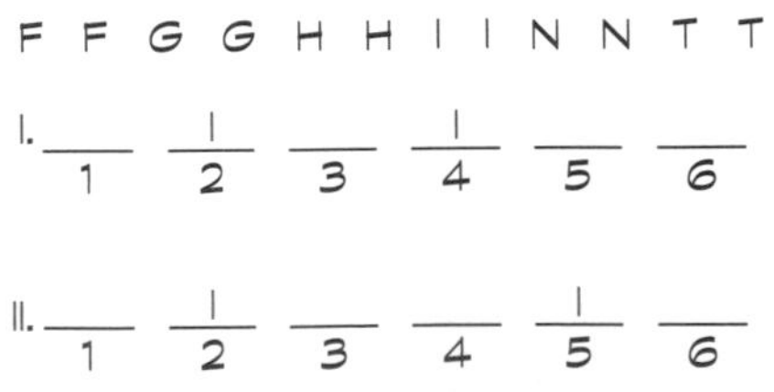

F F G G H H I I N N T T

I. $$\underset{1}{\quad} \underset{2}{|} \underset{3}{\quad} \underset{4}{|} \underset{5}{\quad} \underset{6}{\quad}$$

II. $$\underset{1}{\quad} \underset{2}{|} \underset{3}{\quad} \underset{4}{\quad} \underset{5}{|} \underset{6}{\quad}$$

Figure 13.34

In either case, Norwegian films must follow both Italian films. No matter what, an Italian film must be shown on day 2, so a Norwegian film must be shown on day 3.

---

[15] PrepTest 49, Sec. 1, Q 3

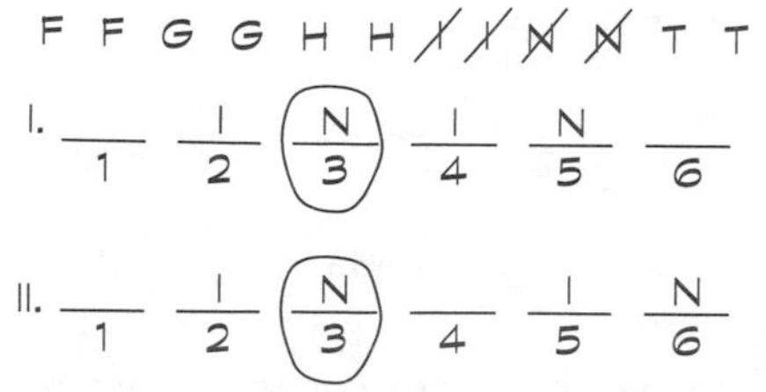

F F G G H H X X X X T T

I. ___ _|_ (N) _|_ N ___
     1   2   3   4   5   6

II. ___ _|_ (N) ___ _|_ N
      1   2   3   4   5   6

Figure 13.35

That means that choice (A) *must be false* and is the correct answer. All of the remaining choices could be true in one or both of the arrangements provided for in the mini-sketch.

4. **(B)**

Which one of the following is a complete and accurate list of the days, any one of which is a day on which a film in Italian could be shown?

(A) day 1, day 3, day 5
(B) day 2, day 4, day 5
(C) day 2, day 5, day 6
(D) day 1, day 3
(E) day 2, day 4[16]

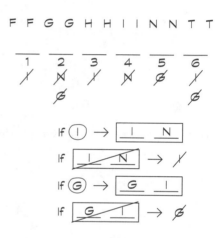

Figure 13.36

You can get the answer to this question from your Master Sketch or from the mini-sketch you just drew for question 3. Italian films may be shown on any of days 2, 4, and 5. That's choice (B).

5. **(D)**

If two films in French are going to be shown, one on day 3 and one on day 5, which one of the following is a pair of films that could be shown on day 1 and day 6, respectively?

(A) a film in French, a film in Turkish
(B) a film in Greek, a film in Hungarian
(C) a film in Italian, a film in Norwegian
(D) a film in Norwegian, a film in Turkish
(E) a film in Turkish, a film in Greek[17]

F̶ F̶ G G H H I I N N T T

___ ___ _F_ ___ _F_ ___
 1   2   3   4   5   6
 X   X   X   X
 ∅   ∅   ∅
           X

Figure 13.37

The "if" in this question allows you to place the two French films with certainty.

16 PrepTest 49, Sec. 1, Q 4
17 PrepTest 49, Sec. 1, Q 5

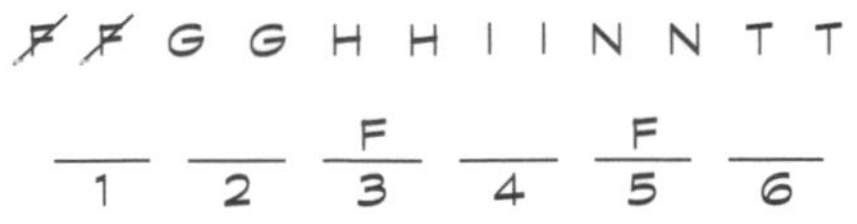

F̶ F̶ G G H H I I N N T T

$$\underline{}_1 \quad \underline{}_2 \quad \underline{F}_3 \quad \underline{}_4 \quad \underline{F}_5 \quad \underline{}_6$$

Figure 13.38

Since this precludes a film in Norwegian from being shown on day 3, you can add Italian to your list of films that cannot be shown on day 2.

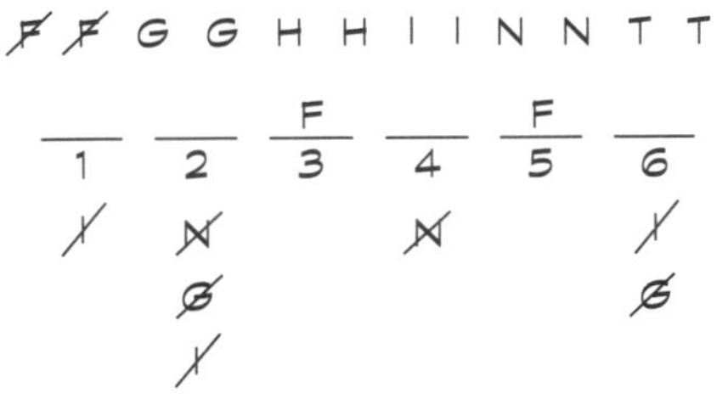

F̶ F̶ G G H H I I N N T T

$$\underline{}_1 \quad \underline{}_2 \quad \underline{F}_3 \quad \underline{}_4 \quad \underline{F}_5 \quad \underline{}_6$$

Figure 13.39

If no Italian film can be shown on day 2, no Greek film may be shown on day 1.

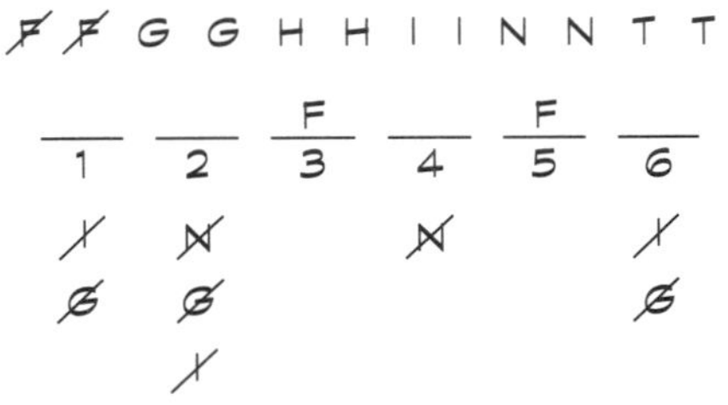

F̶ F̶ G G H H I I N N T T

$$\underline{}_1 \quad \underline{}_2 \quad \underline{F}_3 \quad \underline{}_4 \quad \underline{F}_5 \quad \underline{}_6$$

Figure 13.40

Now, characterize the answer choices. The correct answer is the one with acceptable films for days 1 and 6 under this question's "if" condition. Eliminate choices in which either day's film assignment is impossible in the mini-sketch.

Choice (A) is out; both French films are accounted for in days 3 and 5, so there can't be one shown on day 1. Choice (B) tries to show a Greek film on day 1. That won't work under these conditions, as you deduced while completing the mini-sketch. Get rid of choice (B), too. Choice (C) can't work; you can never show an Italian film on day 1 under any circumstances in this game. Choice (D) is fine. There are no restrictions on Norwegian films for day 1, and there are no restrictions at all for Turkish films. This answer's films are acceptable for days 1 and 6, and thus it's correct. Choice (E) goes wrong by trying to put a Greek film on day 6, something that's never acceptable in this game.

6. **(E)**
    If neither a film in French nor a film in Italian is shown during the retrospective, which one of the following must be true?

    (A) A film in Norwegian is shown on day 1.
    (B) A film in Norwegian is shown on day 5.
    (C) A film in Turkish is shown on day 4.
    (D) A film in Hungarian or else a film in Norwegian is shown on day 3.
    (E) A film in Hungarian or else a film in Turkish is shown on day 2.[18]

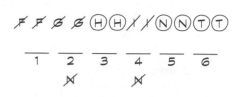

Figure 13.41

Question 6 strikes at the heart of the Selection component of this Hybrid game. Copy your Selection roster and cross off all the French and Italian films.

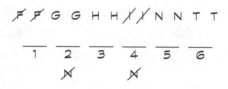

Figure 13.42

If you cannot show any Italian films, you cannot show any Greek films either. Strike the Greek films off the list, too.

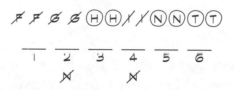

Figure 13.43

You can see the six films that will be shown in the retrospective. The only relevant restrictions involve the films in Norwegian. Rule 1 forbids them being shown on days 2 or 4.

The only answer that must be true here is choice (E); one of the two acceptable non-Norwegian films must be shown that day. All of the other choices could be false. The Norwegian films could be shown on days 3 and 6, so choices (A) and (B) need not be true. A film in Hungarian could be shown on day 4, so choice (C) doesn't have to be true. A Turkish film could be scheduled for day 3, so choice (D) need not be true, either.

---

[18] PrepTest 49, Sec. 1, Q 6

7. **(D)**

If a film in Greek is going to be shown at some time after a film in Norwegian, then a film in Norwegian must be shown on:

(A) day 1
(B) day 3
(C) day 5
(D) day 1 or else day 3
(E) day 3 or else day 5[19]

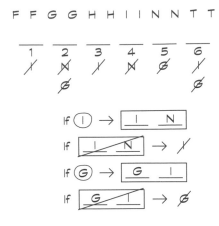

Figure 13.44

You can find the answer to this question by consulting your Master Sketch. Greek films may only be shown on days 1, 3, and 4. You can't have a Norwegian film on day 2. Thus, for a Greek film to follow one in Norwegian, the Norwegian film must be scheduled for day 1 or day 3. That's choice (D). There you have it. Yet another game falls to your strategic approach.

Sequencing-Selection Hybrids aren't common, and chances are fairly slim that you'll see one on test day. If you do, remember what you know about the two game types that combine to form this Hybrid task. Most test takers who go off track with a game like this one lose sight of one of the actions involved or simply lack the strategic approach to tackle a somewhat complex game.

OTHER HYBRIDS

Over the years, the test makers have combined any and all of the standard tasks to come up with what were, at the time, new Hybrid game types. Don't worry about trying to track them all down or come up with predetermined sketches. It's unlikely that you'll see anything exactly like any of them. Instead, concentrate your efforts on being rigorous and perceptive in the Overview step. When the test makers describe an apparently novel situation or combination of tasks, pay attention to what they're asking you to produce. That's just what you did with the Debate Teams game, a Hybrid in which you had to distribute six students into three two-person teams, match the resulting teams with three schools, and then sequence the schools into first, second, and third places. If you're dependent on knowing what a Sequencing-Distribution-Matching sketch is supposed to look like, you'll go nowhere with a game like that. But if you read the setup text strategically and think logically about how to organize the information, you'll come up with a serviceable framework in which you build a helpful Master Sketch.

---

[19] PrepTest 49, Sec. 1, Q 7

The three highest-placing teams in a high school debate tournament are the teams from Fairview, Gillom, and Hilltop high schools. Each team has exactly two members. The individuals on these three teams are Mei, Navarro, O'Rourke, Pavlovich, Sethna, and Tsudama. The following is the case:

Sethna is on the team from Gillom High.

Tsudama is on the second-place team.

Mei and Pavlovich are not on the same team.

Pavlovich's team places higher than Navarro's team.

The team from Gillom High places higher than the team from Hilltop High.[20]

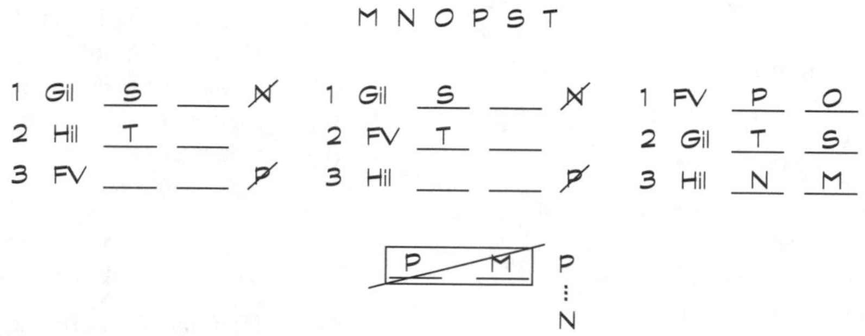

M N O P S T

1	Gil	S	___	~~N~~		1	Gil	S	___	~~N~~		1	FV	P	O
2	Hil	T	___			2	FV	T	___			2	Gil	T	S
3	FV	___	___	~~P~~		3	Hil	___	___	~~P~~		3	Hil	N	M

P — ~~M~~   P
        :
        N

Figure 13.45

By determining what the questions would ask you for, you were able to create a clear orientation for the order of the schools and for each school's team members. By the time you completed the deductions, you had a very small number of acceptable arrangements laid out for use in evaluating the questions. The key was "seeing" what you were being asked for and finding a simple, logical way to depict it. It's unlikely that particular sketch will ever be useful again, but the principles that led you to create it are helpful every time.

I'll have you try one more game in this chapter. Not to scare you, but it's almost legendary for being one of the toughest games ever to appear on a released LSAT test. I won't go into detail about the game until after you've had a chance to try it out. I will, however, give you one hint: Try your best to get a picture in your mind of the situation described, and then turn that into a simplified diagram in which you can record the given information. Do your best, too, to make your depiction of each rule look like the framework. That way, you'll be able to see how each rule potentially fits (or doesn't fit) into the framework under various conditions.

Don't time yourself on this game. And don't let it overwhelm you. As I said, it's a very hard game. Take it methodically and strategically, getting as much as you can from each step in the Kaplan Method. When you're done, I'll go through the game, break down the tasks that make up its Hybrid action, and show you a model sketch that will help you untangle its questions.

---

[20] PrepTest 53, Sec. 2, Game 4

Questions 14–18

Gutierrez, Hoffman, Imamura, Kelly, Lapas, and Moore ride a bus together. Each sits facing forward in a different one of the six seats on the left side of the bus. The seats are in consecutive rows that are numbered 1, 2, and 3 from front to back. Each row has exactly two seats: a window seat and an isle seat. The following conditions must apply:

Hoffman occupies the aisle seat immediately behind Gutierrez's aisle seat.
If Moore occupies an aisle seat, Hoffman sits in the same row as Lapas.
If Gutierrez sits in the same row as Kelly, Moore occupies the seat immediately and directly behind Imamura's seat.
If Kelly occupies a window seat, Moore sits in row 3.
If Kelly sits in row 3, Imamura sits in row 1.

14. Which one of the following could be true?

   (A)   Imamura sits in row 2, whereas Kelly sits in row 3.
   (B)   Gutierrez sits in the same row as Kelly, immediately and directly behind Moore.
   (C)   Gutierrez occupies a window seat in the same row as Lapas.
   (D)   Moore occupies an aisle seat in the same row as Lapas.
   (E)   Kelly and Moore both sit in row 3.

15. If Lapas and Kelly each occupy a window seat, then which one of the following could be true?

   (A)   Moore occupies the aisle seat in row 3.
   (B)   Imamura occupies the window seat in row 3.
   (C)   Gutierrez sits in the same row as Kelly.
   (D)   Gutierrez sits in the same row as Moore.
   (E)   Moore sits in the same row as Lapas.

16. If Moore sits in row 1, then which one of the following must be true?

   (A)   Hoffman sits in row 2.
   (B)   Imamura sits in row 2.
   (C)   Imamura sits in row 3.
   (D)   Kelly sits in row 1.
   (E)   Lapas sits in row 3.

17. If Kelly occupies the aisle seat in row 3, then each of the following must be true EXCEPT:

   (A)   Gutierrez sits in the same row as Imamura.
   (B)   Hoffman sits in the same row as Lapas.
   (C)   Lapas occupies a window seat.
   (D)   Moore occupies a window seat.
   (E)   Gutierrez sits in row 1.

18. If neither Gutierrez nor Imamura sits in row 1, then which one of the following could be true?

   (A)   Hoffman sits in row 2.
   (B)   Kelly sits in row 2.
   (C)   Moore sits in row 2.
   (D)   Imamura occupies an aisle seat.
   (E)   Moore occupies an aisle seat.[21]

---

[21] PrepTest 36, Sec. 4, Game 3, Qs 14–18

Answer Explanations follow on the next page.

Explanations

STEPS 1 AND 2: Overview and Sketch

To visualize this game, picture a typical bus. On each side of the aisle are two seats, one by the window and one by the aisle. This game deals with three such rows. It even tells you that the seats in question are on the left side of the bus. You should have no trouble turning that into a clear framework.

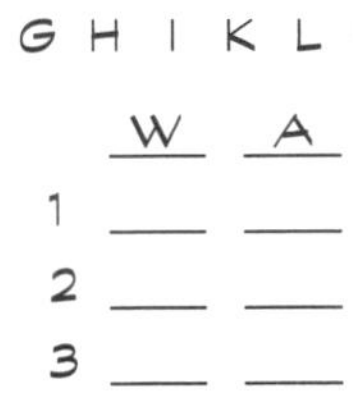

```
        G  H  I  K  L  M
            W     A
    1  ___  ___
    2  ___  ___
    3  ___  ___
```

Figure 13.46

The test makers go easy on you here in one respect. They provide six passengers and ask you to arrange them as you would expect to, one per seat.

So this game has a Sequencing element: The rows are numbered 1–3, and the rules restrict entities by placing them closer to the front or back relative to one another. There's also a Matching element: Some of the passengers may or may not sit with others. Finally, there's an aspect of Distribution: Certain rules are predicated on pairs of entities sitting in certain rows. When all is said and done, this game looks and feels an awful lot like the Debate Tournament, doesn't it?

STEP 3: Rules

There are five rules here, although four of them are conditional. It's the formal logic, more than anything, that makes this game tougher than the Debate Tournament game, despite their similar tasks.

Rule 1 creates a block of H and G and places the block in the aisle seats. With only three rows, this allows for a Limited Options approach to the game.

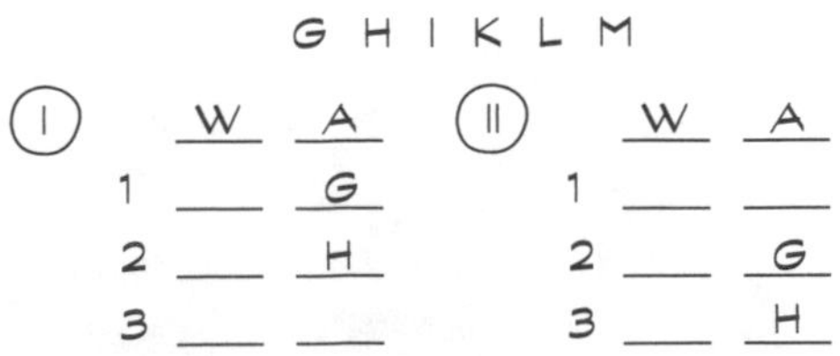

```
           G  H  I  K  L  M
   (I)    W    A        (II)    W    A
    1  ___  ___                1  ___  ___
    2  ___   G                 2  ___   G
    3  ___   H                 3  ___   H
```

Figure 13.47

You'll revisit those options several times as you work through the questions.

Rule 2 is triggered by M taking an aisle seat. When that happens, H and L occupy the same row. Thus, L will have to take the window seat, since Rule 1 already placed H and G in the aisle seats.

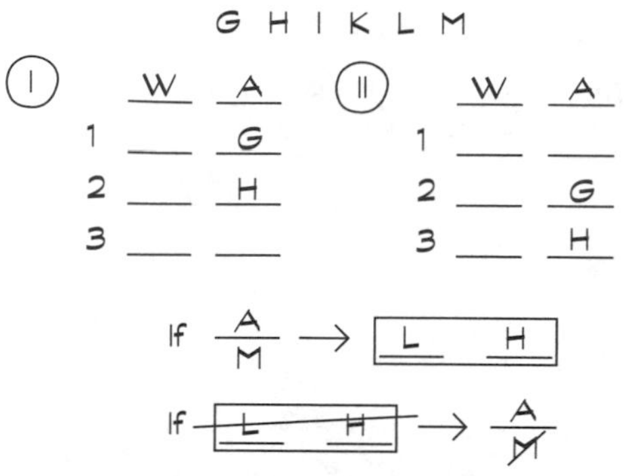

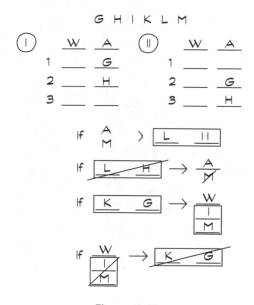

Figure 13.48

Rule 3 is triggered when K takes the window seat next to G. When that happens, I and M become a block, with M's seat directly behind I's. Did you notice that the I-M block can only take consecutive window seats? Remember, G and H will always be in two of the three aisle seats (Rule 1), so there's no room for another block of entities in the aisle column.

Figure 13.49

Rule 4 is relatively benign formal logic for this game. Translate it and diagram its contrapositive like so:

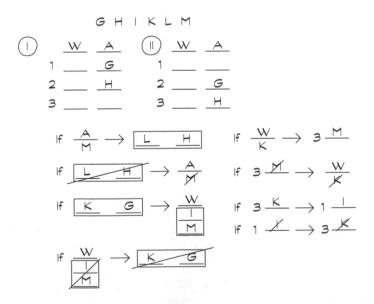

Figure 13.50

Rule 5 is another fairly straightforward formal logic rule. Here are the translation and contrapositive:

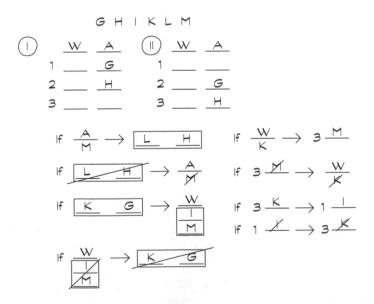

Figure 13.51

Nothing is more important to this game than getting the formal logic right. A close second is sketching each rule so that you can see clearly how it can or can't fit into the framework.

STEP 4: **Deductions**

Because Rules 2–5 are conditional, there's no way to make further affirmative deductions in this game. You'll have to wait until an "If" question triggers a sufficient statement in one of the rules or its contrapositive. That's all right. Four of the five questions here have new "if" conditions, so you can be sure you'll have a chance to work out the implications of the rules there.

STEP 5: **Questions**

As I just noted, four of the five questions here are "If" questions. Expect to use the options from Rule 1 along with whichever of the other rules might be put into play.

14. **(E)**

Which one of the following could be true?

(A) Imamura sits in row 2, whereas Kelly sits in row 3.
(B) Gutierrez sits in the same row as Kelly, immediately and directly behind Moore.
(C) Gutierrez occupies a window seat in the same row as Lapas.
(D) Moore occupies an aisle seat in the same row as Lapas.
(E) Kelly and Moore both sit in row 3.[22]

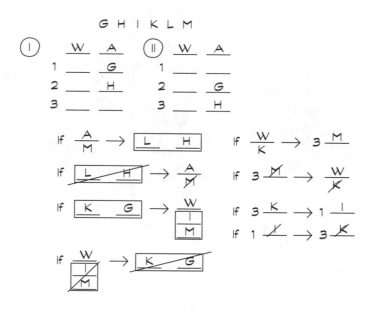

Figure 13.52

The correct answer to this question *could be true*. That means that each of the wrong answers *must be false*. Test the choices one at a time. Eliminate those that are impossible. The correct answer is the only one that will contain an acceptable statement.

---

[22] PrepTest 36, Sec. 4, Q 14

Choice (A) is impossible and can be eliminated. It directly violates Rule 5.

Choice (B) violates Rule 3. When G and K sit in the same row, M must sit behind I. There's not enough room in the aisle seats for I, M, G, and H. You can eliminate this one, too.

Choice (C) simply puts G in the wrong kind of seat. According to Rule 1, G is always on the aisle. Cross out choice (C).

Choice (D) violates Rule 2. When M sits in an aisle seat, L shares a row with H. Eliminate this choice and all that's left is the correct answer, choice (E).

15. **(A)**

If Lapas and Kelly each occupy a window seat, then which one of the following could be true?

(A) Moore occupies the aisle seat in row 3.
(B) Imamura occupies the window seat in row 3.
(C) Gutierrez sits in the same row as Kelly.
(D) Gutierrez sits in the same row as Moore.
(E) Moore sits in the same row as Lapas.[23]

Figure 13.53

Start a mini-sketch with the information from this question's "if" condition. There's no way to tell which of the options this triggers initially, so hold off on placing G and H for a moment.

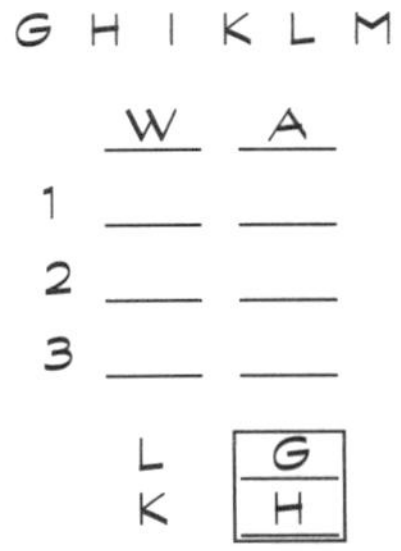

```
      G  H  I  K  L  M

          W    A
   1     ___  ___
   2     ___  ___
   3     ___  ___

          L  | G |
          K  | H |
```

Figure 13.54

By placing K in a window seat, the "if" here triggers Rule 4. You know that M sits in row 3, although not whether the seat will be window or aisle.

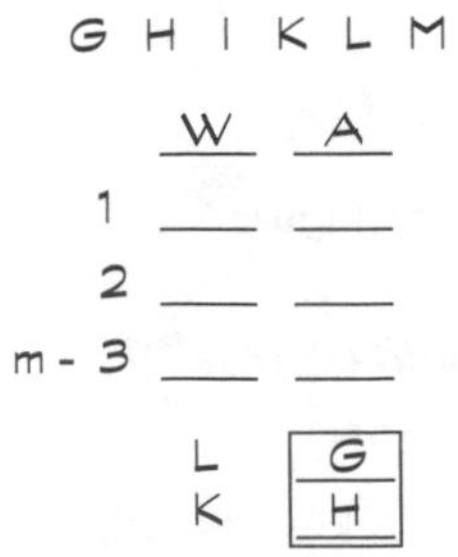

```
      G  H  I  K  L  M

          W    A
   1     ___  ___
   2     ___  ___
m-3     ___  ___

          L  | G |
          K  | H |
```

Figure 13.55

---

[23] PrepTest 36, Sec. 4, Q 15

Now, you can test the options. With Option I, try M in the aisle seat of row 3, behind H.

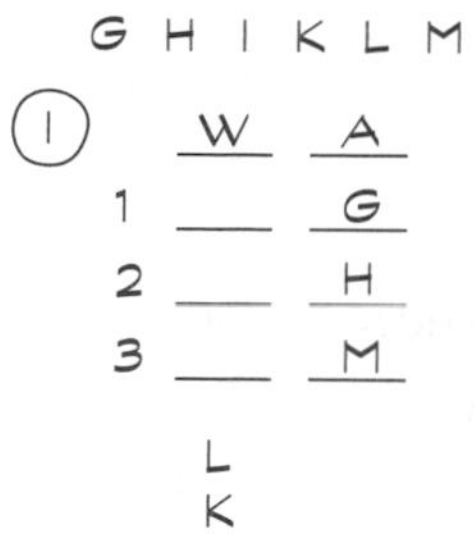

G H I K L M

I   W   A
1   ___ G
2   ___ H
3   ___ M
        L
        K

Figure 13.56

When M takes an aisle seat, Rule 2 is triggered. Place L in the window next to H in row 2.

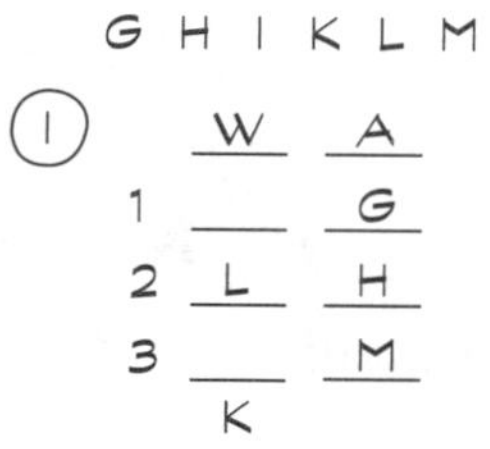

G H I K L M

I   W   A
1   ___ G
2   L   H
3   ___ M
        K

Figure 13.57

Now, you must place I and K. If you tried to put K in the window seat of row 1, you'd trigger Rule 3. But since there's no way for M to sit directly behind I in that case, you know K can't sit in the front row here. If you place K in row 3, however, everything's fine. Giving K a seat in row 3 triggers Rule 5. I can take the window seat in row 1 in this situation, so you've produced one acceptable option.

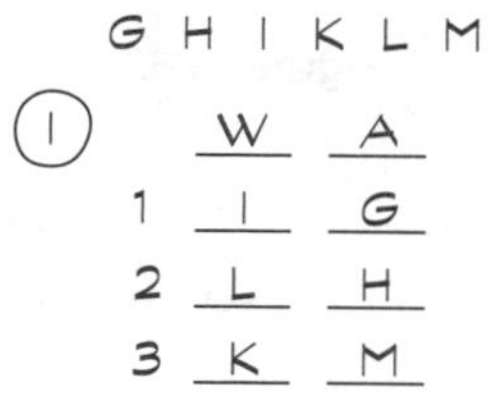

G H I K L M

I   W   A
1   I   G
2   L   H
3   K   M

Figure 13.58

That's actually enough to get you the right answer. This is a *could be true* question, and you've just shown that the statement in choice (A) is possible.

The remaining choices *must be false*, of course. Take a moment to consider why. The same sketch you just made rules out choice (B). Since M must take row 3 in this question, the only way for I to take the window seat in row 3 is for M to take the aisle. But you've just seen that when M takes the aisle, I winds up in row 1.

Choice (C) is impossible here because G and H are already occupying two of the aisle seats and this question's "if" has L and K occupying two of the window seats. Thus, one of I and M will be in a window seat and one in an aisle. Since Rule 3 says that I and M will both take window seats anytime G and K share a row, you know choice (C) is impossible here.

Choice (D) is out because this question requires M to take row 3, and G always takes either row 1 or row 2 as a result of Rule 1.

Choice (E) can't work under this question's conditions. Rule 2 makes clear that when M is in an aisle seat, L must sit in the same row as H. Since the question's "if" condition is that L is in a window seat, M's taking an aisle seat ensures that they won't be in the same row.

16. **(D)**

If Moore sits in row 1, then which one of the following must be true?

(A) Hoffman sits in row 2.
(B) Imamura sits in row 2.
(C) Imamura sits in row 3.
(D) Kelly sits in row 1.
(E) Lapas sits in row 3.[24]

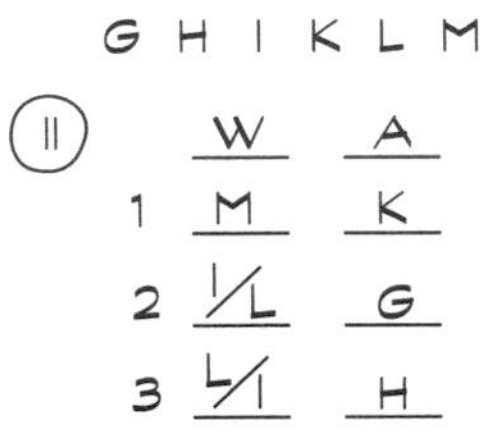

Figure 13.59

Start by sketching this question's "if" condition.

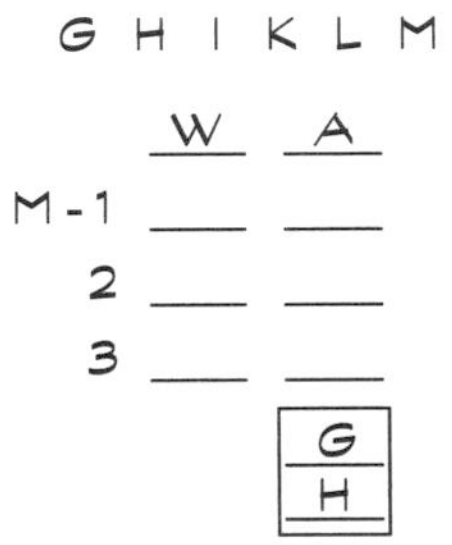

Figure 13.60

Placing M in row 1 triggers the contrapositive of Rule 4. If M is in row 1, then he certainly isn't in row 3. Whenever M is not in row 3, K takes an aisle seat.

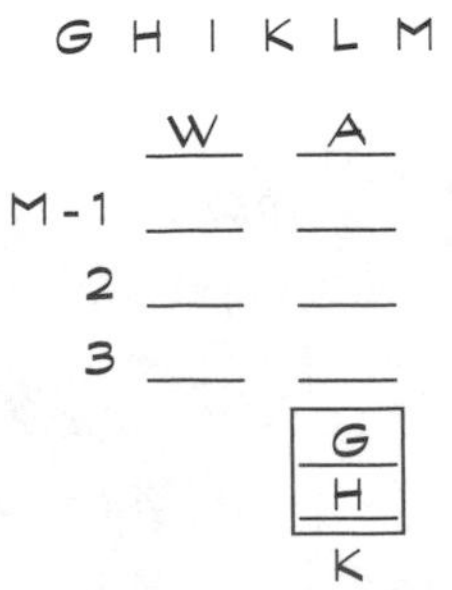

Figure 13.61

---

[24] PrepTest 36, Sec. 4, Q 16

There are now two possibilities for the aisle seats, corresponding to the two options in Rule 1: G-H-K or K-G-H in rows 1–3, respectively.

Figure 13.62

The first of those options is impossible. Placing K in row 3 triggers Rule 5, which requires that I take row 1. But there's no room in row 1 now. So only the second option is possible here.

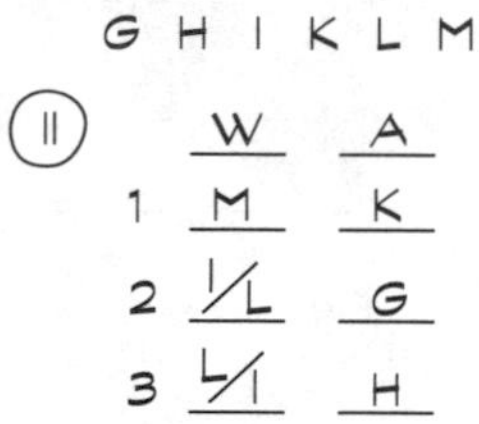

Figure 13.63

It doesn't matter which of the remaining seats I and L occupy; you've already got enough to answer this *must be true* question. Choice (D) says that K is in row 1, and that *must be true* under these conditions.

17. **(B)**

If Kelly occupies the aisle seat in row 3, then each of the following must be true EXCEPT:

(A) Gutierrez sits in the same row as Imamura.
(B) Hoffman sits in the same row as Lapas.
(C) Lapas occupies a window seat.
(D) Moore occupies a window seat.
(E) Gutierrez sits in row 1.[25]

Figure 13.64

In this question, the "if" is very specific. Start by copying the framework and placing K in the aisle seat of row 3. That only works in Option I, of course.

---

[25] PrepTest 36, Sec. 4, Q 17

Figure 13.65

Placing K in row 3 triggers Rule 5. I will take a seat in row 1. The only open seat there is by the window.

Figure 13.66

Nothing in this arrangement limits the acceptability of either remaining seat for L or M, so just list them as the alternatives for the window seats in rows 2 and 3.

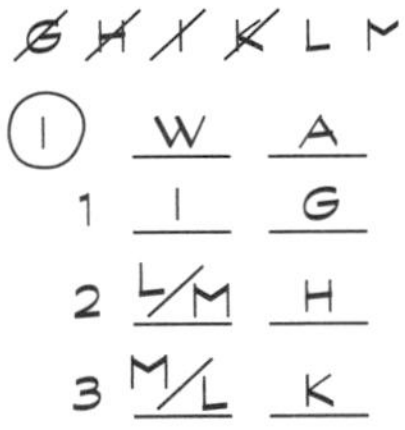

Figure 13.67

The question asks for the *could be false* answer. That's choice (B). Since L may sit in either row 2 or 3, it's possible that H doesn't sit next to L. The other four answers must be true, as your mini-sketch shows unequivocally.

18. **(C)**

If neither Gutierrez nor Imamura sits in row 1, then which one of the following could be true?

(A) Hoffman sits in row 2.
(B) Kelly sits in row 2.
(C) Moore sits in row 2.
(D) Imamura occupies an aisle seat.
(E) Moore occupies an aisle seat.[26]

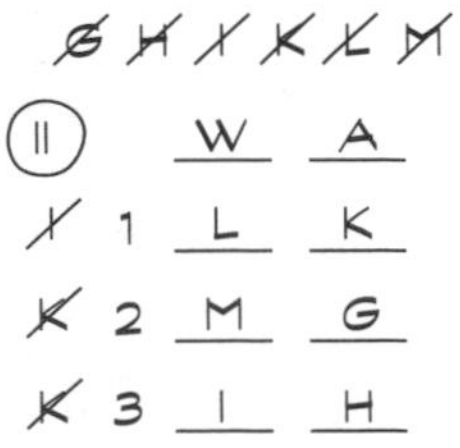

Figure 13.68

---

[26] PrepTest 36, Sec. 4, Q 18

The condition in the question stem is only possible in Option II. Start there, indicating that I cannot take a seat in row 1 either. That means that I will sit in a window seat.

Figure 13.69

Denying I a seat in row 1 triggers the contrapositive of Rule 5. K cannot take a seat in row 3 in this question.

Figure 13.70

K cannot sit in row 2 next to G, either. That would trigger Rule 3, and I and M would have to sit in consecutive window seats. That's impossible here. So you've narrowed K's seat down to row 1.

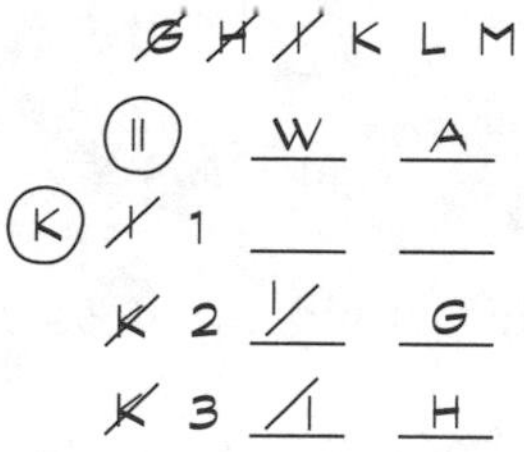

Figure 13.71

That's enough to eliminate three of the answer choices. The correct answer to this question *could be true*. Your mini-sketch already shows that choices (A), (B), and (D) must be false.

The two remaining choices both involve M. Test either one. If it produces an acceptable arrangement, it's the correct answer. If not, the other choice is correct.

Testing choice (C) produces an acceptable arrangement. If you place M in the window seat in row 2, you must place I in the window seat of row 3.

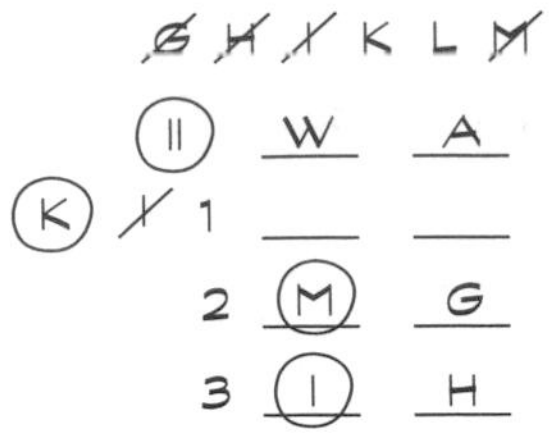

G H I K L M
(II) W   A
(K) 1 ___ ___
    2 (M) G
    3 (I) H

Figure 13.72

Since M isn't in row 3, you know from the contrapositive of Rule 4 that K will take the aisle seat in row 1.

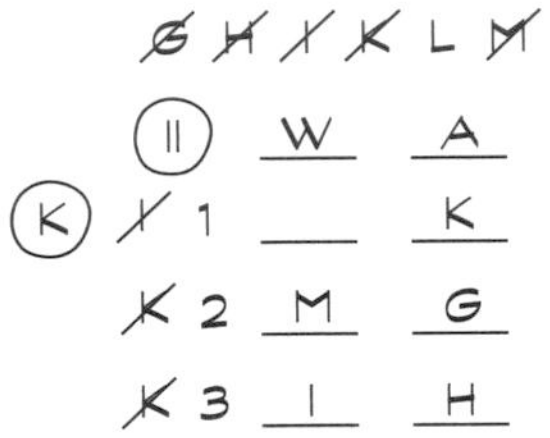

G H I K L M
(II) W   A
(K) 1 ___ K
    2 M   G
    3 I   H

Figure 13.73

That leaves the window seat in row 1 for L.

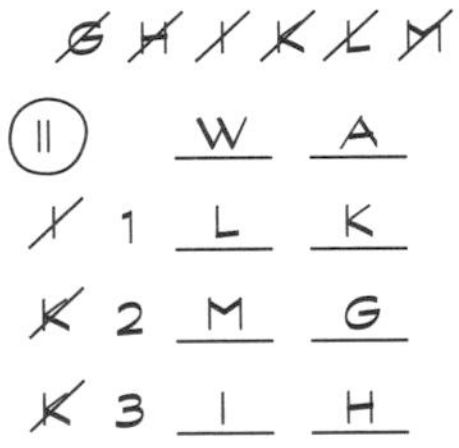

G H I K L M
(II) W   A
    1 L   K
    2 M   G
    3 I   H

Figure 13.74

There's no violation of the rules in this arrangement, so choice (C) is correct.

Were you to try choice (E), on the other hand, you'd be unable to complete the mini-sketch. The only aisle seat open for M is in row 1, which would put K in the adjacent window seat.

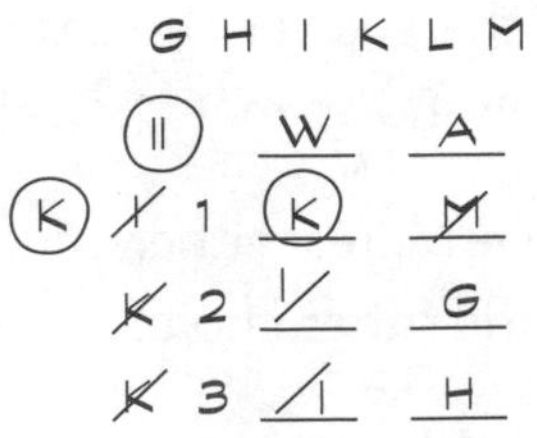

G H I K L M
(II) W   A
(K) 1 (K) M
    2 I   G
    3 I   H

Figure 13.75

But that contradicts Rule 4. When K takes a window seat, M has to be in row 3. Choice (E), therefore, must be false.

I know that I won't make any friends by introducing you to that game. The truth is, there have been few (if any) games more difficult than that in the past 20 years or so. All of those conditional rules make for quite a slog.

But step back for a minute and realize one thing: All of the questions did have one correct answer and four that were demonstrably incorrect. The test makers lived up to their end of the bargain by giving you all of the information you needed to distinguish the right answers from the wrong ones. If a game even close to this difficulty level appears on your test, it's going to be challenging for everyone taking the test. In fact, it will be much more challenging for those who haven't trained as effectively as you have. On every LSAT, you're scored against the other test takers for that administration. If you get two points out of a game like this and they only get one, you'll have the higher score.

Don't take the test personally. When it comes to the LSAT, the rain falls on everyone. By taking the time to assess the game's setup and task and turn that into a descriptive and useful sketch, at least you'll have the best umbrella in the room.

KEEP HYBRIDS IN A FAMILIAR CONTEXT

Hybrid games are important parts of your logic games practice. Taking all Hybrids as a group, they're second only to Sequencing games as the most common games to appear on the exam. But remember that Hybrids are always made up of familiar game tasks. Consider the tasks, combine them into a single, interrelated sketch, and pay attention to which of the rules affect which of the tasks, and you're right back on familiar ground.

CHAPTER 14

RECENT TRENDS

With all of the effort you're putting into your LSAT preparation, it's always important to stay on top of the latest trends and patterns appearing in the types of games and questions that the test makers are using. In this brief chapter, I'll outline the game types that have appeared on the exams released most recently at the time of this writing. While there's no guarantee that the test makers will use a particular assortment of games on your official test, the LSAT tends to change rather slowly, and patterns of game and question distribution are pretty similar from year to year.

The following chart shows the eight most recent exams released prior to this book's publication.

RECENT LSATs: LOGIC GAMES SECTIONS

PrepTest 61 (Oct '10)	**PrepTest 62 (Dec '10)**
Game 1—Distribution	Game 1 - Strict Sequencing
Game 2—Loose Sequencing	Game 2 - Matching
Game 3—Hybrid Selection/Sequencing	Game 3 - Hybrid Matching/Sequencing
Game 4—Strict Sequencing	Game 4 - Strict Sequencing
PrepTest 63 (June '11)	**PrepTest 64 (Oct '11)**
Game 1 - Distribution	Game 1 - Strict Sequencing
Game 2 - Strict Sequencing	Game 2 - Hybrid Distribution/Selection
Game 3 - Strict Sequencing	Game 3 - Matching
Game 4 - Strict Sequencing	Game 4 - Hybrid Distribution/Sequencing
PrepTest 65 (Dec' 11)	**PrepTest 66 (June '12)**
Game 1 - Loose Sequencing	Game 1 - Strict Sequencing
Game 2 - Strict Sequencing	Game 2 - Strict Sequencing
Game 3 - Selection	Game 3 - Distribution
Game 4 - Strict Sequencing	Game 4 - Hybrid Matching/Sequencing
PrepTest 67 (Oct '12)	**PrepTest 68 (Dec '12)**
Game 1 - Matching	Game 1 - Strict Sequencing
Game 2 - Strict Sequencing	Game 2 - Distribution
Game 3 - Strict Sequencing	Game 3 - Matching
Game 4 - Matching	Game 4 - Strict Sequencing

NOTE: The LSAC does not routinely release February exams to the public. Thus, the eight most recently released exams cover just over two years' worth of LSAT administrations.

Strict Sequencing Is Still the Favorite

The first takeaway from this chart is that Strict Sequencing, the old warhorse, remains by far the test makers' favorite game type. Nearly half of the games represented on these tests are single-task Strict Sequencing games. When you add in the Strict Sequencing tasks that are blended into Hybrid games, Strict Sequencing is involved in well over half of the test's most recent offerings.

It's also important to note that on PrepTest 63 three of the four games had Strict Sequencing tasks. There is no other game type that the test makers use in such a heavy concentration.

A handful of the recent Strict Sequencing games had twists like those you saw in chapter 9. In a couple of them, the setup described a situation—e.g., floors of a building or layers of a cake—in which you need to count from the bottom up. Another had a situation in which more than one of the entities could occupy the same position in the order; in this case, you were to rank six entities in four levels, so you knew that there would be some overlap. A couple of the games had a Double Sequencing feel to them. In one, for example, you had to schedule six entities over the course of three days, using one morning and one evening appointment each day.

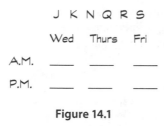

Figure 14.1

The rules played off the scenario, with some limiting certain entities to a time of day regardless of day and others limiting entities to certain days regardless of time. Still, this isn't true Double Sequencing. Each entity is assigned to only one position. Saying, "R takes an afternoon position," in this game is really no different than saying, "R is placed second, fourth, or sixth," in a run-of-the-mill Sequencing setup. Don't let seeming novelties throw you; look for the familiar core tasks of LSAT logic games that you've learned in this book, and you'll seldom run into anything unmanageable.

No New Game Types

The second takeaway from this chart should be that the test has introduced no new game types. The second and third most common games during this period were Matching and Distribution. If you've completed the work in this book up to this point, you've had ample practice with both of those game types. The recent games in both of these categories worked much like examples in this book, with the test makers adding little if anything in the way of twists or additions. Matching and Distribution reward careful analysis of Deductions such as Blocks, Limited Options, and especially Numbers. It's also worth noting that Matching was the only game type apart from Strict Sequencing to appear more than once on the same test.

The rarest find among these recent games is the Distribution-Selection Hybrid on PrepTest 64. While this game was made up of two common tasks, this particular blend has only been used a couple of times by the test makers. In this particular game, you were asked to choose three of five ambassadors and assign those three to three different countries. For test takers who can only perform if they've memorized standardized sketches, this game was intimidating. For those who were able to conduct a helpful overview and say, "The acceptable arrangements will have three ambassadors circled and two crossed out, and they'll use both the ambassadors and countries to limit which ones I can choose," this game, though an unusual Hybrid, was eminently manageable.

A New Question Type

For LSAT watchers, the biggest innovation in the past several years was the introduction of a new question type in June 2009. Really, the question type is a variation on the Rule-Changer. I'll refer to it as a Rule Substitution question. Here's what it looks like:

> Which one of the following, if substituted for the condition that Hibiscus must be hung somewhere before Katydid but cannot be the first photograph, would have the same effect in determining the arrangement of the photographs?[1]

> Which one of the following, if substituted for the restriction that if music is taken, then neither physics nor theater can be taken, would have the same effect in determining which courses the student can take?[2]

As you can see, these questions reward you for being able to assess the strength and effect of a particular rule. The standard Rule-Changer question got at this same ability by asking you to rethink the Master Sketch with one of the rules removed or altered. This newer variation poses the same puzzle by telling you, in effect, to remove a rule and then substitute the correct answer to wind up with exactly the same Master Sketch. When you think about it, this question type is really just asking you to paraphrase the original rule accurately. In fact, that's the strategy you should use as you approach these problems. Remove the rule from the Master Sketch and consider its effect. Then substitute the answer choices and choose the one that restores the Master Sketch to its original state. By rewarding your ability to paraphrase the rules, this question type is just one more way in which the test makers reward the core skill of Strategic Reading.

Indeed, remember that the test makers always reward the Core 4 LSAT Skills—Strategic Reading, Understanding Formal Logic, Analyzing Arguments, and Making Deductions—that you first encountered at the beginning of this book. With those key skills in mind, you're unlikely to encounter anything on test day (in any of the test's sections) that seems truly novel. If, at

---

[1] PrepTest 59, Sec. 1, Q 10
[2] PrepTest 58, Sec. 3, Q 23

first glance, you seem to be face-to-face with a game or question you haven't seen before, stop and get a handle on what you're being asked for. Then remember that the test makers always provide you with everything you need in order to determine the question's one correct answer. Approaching the LSAT from that perspective, all that you just learned about typical LSAT patterns is just icing on the cake.

PART III

FULL-SECTION PRACTICE

CHAPTER 15

TIMING AND SECTION MANAGEMENT IN A NUTSHELL

You're ready to put it all together. Timed, section-length practice is the final step in your preparation for LSAT logic games. You've been building up to this stage since the opening of chapter 1. Step-by-step, you've mastered the Kaplan Method, adopted the strategies associated with the various tasks and question types, and then learned to recognize the standard game types and variations that the test makers use. In Part II, you even did most of your practice on individual games under timed conditions. All of that was training and conditioning for taking the full Logic Games section—four games in 35 minutes—as you will on test day.

Here, in Part III, I'll introduce you to a handful of principles that will help you manage your time and maximize your score. Then you'll have the chance to take two complete Logic Games sections. Take them one at a time and review each of them thoroughly, studying the explanations for the game setups and all of the questions (even those you got right). Before you go any farther, though, I want to issue a strong CAUTION: **Don't take a timed section until you've completed Parts I and II of this book.** Taking a timed section without adequate preparation is likely to be a frustrating experience that won't contribute to your test day readiness. So if you're exploring this part of the book before you've completed the earlier chapters, go back and get yourself ready. If you have completed the earlier parts, please proceed.

EFFICIENCY VS. SPEED

"I could have gotten all of the questions right if I'd just had more time. How do I get faster?" I told you right at the beginning of the book that I've heard this question from my LSAT students hundreds of times, if not thousands. My response is always the same: You're much more likely to improve your score with improved efficiency than you are by blindly trying to speed up. Timing is a part of the test. The test makers are rewarding you for making smart, strategic decisions about how to spend your limited time. You'll face similar challenges in law school. There's simply too much to read and too much work to complete to take a plodding, bulldozer approach to the material. Just as you do on the LSAT, you'll learn to distinguish the relevant from the irrelevant and target the parts of the material that lead to points on your exams.

Ironically, one key to efficiency on the LSAT is patience. This is especially true in the Logic Games section. You've seen plenty of games in this book in which spending three or even four minutes creating a complete Master Sketch made it possible for you to answer all of the questions in a matter of a few seconds each. On the other hand, rushing the setup and making a mistake with one of the rules or missing a deduction can lead to disaster. Think about it like this: The test rewards only correct answers, so any time you spend producing a wrong answer is wasted time. Nobody will proudly proclaim, "Yeah, I missed all of the questions from that game, but I did it very fast." Even if you did the entire game in four minutes, you simply threw those four minutes away if they didn't produce correct answers.

OPTIMAL TIMING

Here's what you should be shooting for. With 35 minutes to complete four games, you need to average about eight minutes and 30 seconds per game. I'll talk about what to do with that leftover minute shortly. Within the eight and a half minutes you have for a given game don't hesitate to spend three to four minutes on Steps 1–4 of the Kaplan Method. (A few games may even reward you for spending longer. Think back to the Professors' Hiring game or the Music Program game in which each piece was performed on two instruments. Once you'd made all of the deductions in those games, the question sets wouldn't take you more than three minutes to complete.)

LSAT Logic Games Timing Guidelines	
Section—Four Games	35 minutes
Game—Setup and Questions	8 minutes 30 seconds
Setup (Kaplan Method Steps 1–4)	3–4 minutes
Questions (Kaplan Method Step 5)	4½ to 5½ minutes

Spending three to four minutes setting up the game leaves four and a half to five and a half minutes for the questions, which should be enough time, even if the set has several "If" questions.

Strategic Guessing

One important thing to remember is that, unlike the SAT, the LSAT has no wrong-answer penalty. You should enter an answer, even if it's a random guess, for every question. In fact, becoming a good strategic guesser can increase your score. If you come to a question that would take you two minutes to answer, ask yourself whether that time would be better spent setting up the next game, where you might be able to get five to seven more points.

Getting into an "ego battle" with the test is almost always detrimental. Our psychological tendency is to say, "I couldn't get it, so I had to give up and guess." I want you to change that message to yourself. From here on, say, "I made a smart decision to guess because battling it out with that one question wasn't in *my* best interest." Take the LSAT; don't let it take you.

It's tough to let go of a very difficult or time-consuming question once you have your teeth in it. But the best scorers do. They realize that the only glory on the LSAT comes from getting more points overall and that no one, not even the law school admissions officers, will ever see which questions you solved correctly and which you guessed on. Too many LSAT students try to be perfect and wind up costing themselves several points down the road. Learn not to over-invest in a single point.

SECTION MANAGEMENT: YOU'RE IN CONTROL
Section Triage: Ordering the Games

If you stick to an average of eight and a half minutes per game, you'll spend 34 minutes setting up games and answering questions. So what do you do with that one leftover minute in your section? The answer is that you spend it up front, deciding the order in which you want to tackle the games. The test makers do not necessarily arrange the games in the optimal order for you. Indeed, they often place the most time-consuming or difficult game second or third in the section. Nothing about the rules or structure of the LSAT obligates you to complete the games in order. You must work on only the announced *section* at any given time on test day, but you can move back and forth within that section in the way that's best for your performance.

So spend the first minute of the section (not more) assessing the difficulty of the four games. You'll want to tackle the easiest game first and leave the toughest game for last. In many aspects of life, it's good to get the hardest part out of the way and delay the easiest, most pleasurable part of your task. Not on the LSAT. This is an "eat dessert first" test. Taking on the easiest game first accomplishes three things: (1) It builds your confidence, (2) it offers the immediate reward of several points, and (3) it allows you to bank some additional time for the hardest game if you can complete the easiest one in less than eight and a half minutes.

Here's a chart showing student performance on a representative Logic Games section. Note that the bars indicate the percentage of students who gave *wrong* answers to each question.

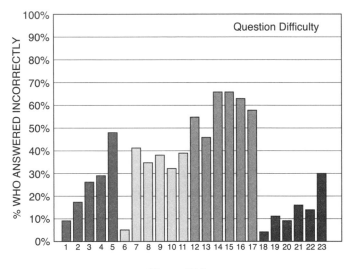

Figure 15.1

The hardest game on this exam was the third one. Many, maybe even most, of the students who took the section in order, just following the test maker's design, missed the opportunity for easier points in Game 4 or found themselves so rushed in the final game that they weren't able to take advantage of how much easier it was than Game 3.

How do you learn to identify the easiest and hardest games in just one minute? Kaplan calls this *triage*, after the procedure that doctors use to prioritize patients in emergency situations. The LSAT isn't as literally life-or-death, but you can still learn some good practices by following the doctors' example. When a big accident, for example, brings many patients into the hospital simultaneously, the doctor or triage nurse in charge assesses all of the patients and determines the order in which they'll be treated on the basis of several factors: how severely they're injured, how long it would take or how many staff members it would take to treat them, and the chances that they can be saved. The goal is to save as many of the patients as possible. To do that—and this is the real lesson for you as a test taker—the triage doctor may have to make the extremely difficult choice to postpone the treatment of the most severely injured patient. In order to help as many people as possible, the doctor says, "This person would require several hours and several doctors or nurses; we have to let his procedure wait." That's the kind of difficult but strategic decision you must make in order to get as many points on the test as possible.

In order for triage to work in the ER, doctors must be fast and confident in their assessments. They have guidelines that they follow in order to make their decisions quickly and accurately. You have one minute to assess your "patients," so you'll need the same thing. Fortunately, you're already familiar with the criteria you should use as you triage the section. Remember the four criteria you used to assess game difficulty in chapter 7?

WHAT MAKES LOGIC GAMES HARDER

Easier	Harder
Concrete	Ambiguous
Simple	Complex
Brief	Long
Familiar	Strange

Those are the same factors you should use to decide the order in which you'll handle the games. As you know from all of the work you've done up to this point, nothing is more salient to a game's difficulty than whether it's concrete or ambiguous. Simplicity and brevity can help make a game more manageable, but they won't compensate for rules and restrictions that are too open-ended. Familiarity is the wild card. If you simply don't know how to approach a certain game, you should put it off for later. The equivalent situation in the hospital would be a patient with an injury or condition that no one on duty knows how to treat. Of course, a well-run hospital will schedule its staff so that there's a wide range of expertise available at all times. Likewise, your practice should include all of the basic game types so that you're unlikely to run into a game you find utterly baffling.

In addition to the factors listed above, you may consider the number and types of questions associated with each game as you assess the section. If you find two games of equal difficulty, one of which has seven questions and the other only five, you should prioritize the former. Without a clear-cut case like that, though, you should base your priorities on the difficulty of the games' setups and rules.

Learning to triage effectively takes a little practice, something you can begin on the sections that follow. In order to be valuable, triage cannot take you several minutes to complete. Even if your assessment of the section is perfect, you can't afford more than about a minute to prioritize the games. (Imagine a doctor who correctly assessed each patient's prospects but ran out of time to treat them.) When you triage, be clear and decisive in your choices. In the end, I'd rather have you say, "If I had it to do over, I think I would have done Game 3 before Game 2," than to spend several minutes deciding between the two.

I'll review section triage in the explanations for each of the full-length sections that follow.

Question Triage: Ordering the Questions

Your ability to optimize your performance through strategic decision making doesn't end when you decide the order of the games. Within a given game, too, you can approach the questions in any order. Once you've completed Steps 1–4 and you have a strong, useful Master Sketch, take a moment to consider the questions. Are most of them "If" questions calling for new mini-sketches? Are they mostly Must/Could questions that you can answer from the deductions in your Master Sketch? Does the set have a balance of question types? You'll likely have an impression of what to expect from the questions based on the game type and how thoroughly you were able to fill in the framework in your Master Sketch. There's nothing wrong with taking the questions in the order presented and, most of the time, you probably will. But there are a handful of considerations that can help you better manage your time within a question set:

- Do Acceptability questions first. They're fast. Your approach—using the rules to eliminate the violators—is consistent. And the correct answer provides an acceptable arrangement you can use when evaluating answers to later questions.

- Your scratch work from "If" questions can help you answer Must/Could questions. For example, since the wrong answers to a *must be false* question all *could be true*, you can eliminate any choice that you've seen as acceptable in another question.

- Questions in which each answer choice is conditional are usually time-consuming. If a question's answer choices start with the word "if," consider skipping the question or guessing if time is tight. Remember that when the given conditions match the mini-sketches from any other question you've done, you can use your prior work to evaluate that answer.

- Always characterize the answer choices (e.g., the correct answer *could be true*, so the wrong answers *must be false*) before you evaluate them, regardless of the order in which you answer the questions. Answering the "wrong question" is always a waste of time and points.

The same caution that I issued with regard to section triage also applies when you assess the question set. Don't spend an inordinate amount of time (more than a few seconds, in this case) trying to come up with the perfect order. For the most part, take the questions in order, but be willing to skip a question as soon as you realize that it's not going anywhere. As you work through the rest of the questions for that game, you may get help with the question you skipped. If not, you can either guess strategically or come back to spend time with the question before you move on to the next game. What you *must* avoid is throwing off the timing for an entire game or section because you insist on getting the answer to a single question. The cost to you in time (and the emotional toll you pay for your frustration) simply isn't worth it.

That last statement, in many ways, summarizes the takeaway message of this chapter. The best test takers are those that get the most points. They don't let the perfect become the enemy of the good. Learn from them. They know that the test taker is in control of the section, and they'll take the games in whatever order is best for their overall performance. They're also willing to skip or guess on a question, when trying to complete it would be too time-consuming or is likely to end in frustration. The LSAT would be a different test if it reported to law schools which test takers had solved the toughest questions. It doesn't. It reports, quite simply, who answered *more* questions correctly. Use the test's design to your benefit. Learn to manage the section for maximum efficiency.

CHAPTER 16

FULL-LENGTH SECTION PRACTICE

In the following two chapters, you'll have the opportunity to take two full Logic Games sections, just as they appeared on the original exams. When you take them, make sure that you'll have 35 uninterrupted minutes in a quiet place. You'll want to time yourself strictly and follow the test instructions to the letter.

WHEN AND HOW TO USE SECTION PRACTICE

As I cautioned earlier, don't take a full-length section before you've completed the first two parts of this book. Section practice is about "putting it all together." Don't use section practice to learn game types or methods (although you'll certainly review your performance with the explanations that follow each section). Use section practice to improve your timing and performance with skills and strategies you've already mastered. Trying to practice timing before you've achieved a level of proficiency with the games will lead to mistakes and frustrations, and it will turn your review of the section into an exercise in learning the basics, when it should be an assessment of your efficiency in applying best practices to each game.

On your official test day, you will get credit only for the answers on your bubble sheet. No one will look in your test booklet to see what you've circled or indicated there.

Depending on how much time you have before your official exam, you may want to wait a few days between practice sections. Use what you learn from reviewing the first section to go back and refresh your understanding of the Kaplan Method, strategies, and game types as appropriate. One thing is for sure—if you take the sections back-to-back, you'll likely have almost exactly the same performance on the second that you did on the first.

HOW TO CALCULATE YOUR SCORE

With timed, section-length practice, your goal must be to get as many points as possible. Distinguish that from the goal of handling each game perfectly. Skip and guess as you need to in order to maximize your efficiency in the section and the overall number of correct answers you can produce.

Once you've completed the section, score your responses against the provided answer key. Mark each of the answers you got right or wrong, but review the entire game, Steps 1–5, using the explanations following the section. Test scores are calculated based on the overall number of correct answers you produced in all of the scored sections on a test, so there's no way to determine your overall LSAT score based on any single section. Here are a couple of score conversion tables from recently released LSATs. There are almost always 101 scored questions per LSAT, of which 22–24 come from the Logic Games section.

CONVERSION CHART		
For converting Raw Score to the 120–180 LSAT Scaled Score LSAT Prep Test 47		
REPORTED SCORE	LOWEST RAW SCORE	HIGHEST RAW SCORE
180	99	100
179	98	98
178	97	97
177	96	96
176	--*	--*
175	95	95
174	94	94
173	93	93
172	92	92
171	91	91
170	90	90
169	89	89
168	88	88
167	87	87
166	85	86
165	84	84
164	83	83
163	81	82
162	80	80
161	78	79
160	77	77
159	75	76
158	73	74
157	72	72
156	70	71
155	68	69
154	66	67
153	65	65
152	63	64
151	61	63
150	59	60
149	57	58
148	55	56
147	54	54
146	52	53
145	50	51
144	48	49
143	46	47
142	45	45
141	43	44
140	41	42
139	40	40
138	38	39
137	36	37
136	35	35
135	33	34
134	32	32
133	30	31
132	29	29
131	27	28
130	26	26
129	25	25
128	24	24
127	22	23
126	21	21
125	20	20
124	19	19
123	18	18
122	17	17
121	16	16
120	0	15

*There is no raw score that will produce this scaled score for the test.

CONVERSION CHART		
For converting Raw Score to the 120–180 LSAT Scaled Score LSAT Prep Test 50		
REPORTED SCORE	LOWEST RAW SCORE	HIGHEST RAW SCORE
180	98	100
179	97	97
178	--*	--*
177	96	96
176	95	95
175	94	94
174	--*	--*
173	93	93
172	92	92
171	91	91
170	90	90
169	89	89
168	88	88
167	86	87
166	85	85
165	84	84
164	83	83
163	81	82
162	80	80
161	78	79
160	77	77
159	75	76
158	73	74
157	72	72
156	70	71
155	68	69
154	66	67
153	64	65
152	63	63
151	61	62
150	59	60
149	57	58
148	55	56
147	53	54
146	52	52
145	50	51
144	48	49
143	46	47
142	45	45
141	43	44
140	41	42
139	40	40
138	38	39
137	36	37
136	35	35
135	33	34
134	32	32
133	30	31
132	29	29
131	27	28
130	26	26
129	25	25
128	23	24
127	22	22
126	21	21
125	20	20
124	18	19
123	17	17
122	16	16
121	15	15
120	0	14

*There is no raw score that will produce this scaled score for the test.

Figure 16.1

```
┌──────────────────────────────────────────────────────┐
│                   SCORING WORKSHEET                    │
│                                                        │
│  1.  Enter the number of questions you answered        │
│      correctly in each section                         │
│                                                        │
│                             NUMBER                     │
│                             CORRECT                    │
│                                                        │
│      SECTION I . . . . . . . . . .  _____             │
│                                                        │
│      SECTION II . . . . . . . . .   _____             │
│                                                        │
│      SECTION III. . . . . . . . .   _____             │
│                                                        │
│      SECTION IV . . . . . . . . .   _____             │
│                                                        │
│                                                        │
│  2.  Enter the sum here:   _____   THIS IS YOUR       │
│                                     RAW SCORE.         │
│                                                        │
└──────────────────────────────────────────────────────┘
```

Figure 16.2

By estimating the number of correct responses you'd generate from the remaining sections of the test, you can gain an idea of the impact your logic games performance will have on your score. To improve your performance on the other sections of the test, study this book's companion volumes, *LSAT Reading Comprehension: Strategies and Tactics* and *LSAT Logical Reasoning: Strategies and Tactics*.

Remember that there is no "guessing penalty," so fill in an answer for every question, just as you would on test day. If you're able to eliminate two or three of the wrong answers, guess from among the remaining choices. When you review the section, you can look to see how you would be able to answer the question quickly and effectively, but don't let that deter you from guessing and skipping when it's in your interest to do so.

Good luck on the sections. Do your best.

CHAPTER 17

FULL-LENGTH SECTION I[1]

Time—35 minutes

22 Questions

Directions: Each group of questions in this section is based on a set of conditions. In answering some of the questions, it may be useful to draw a rough diagram. Choose the response that most accurately and completely answers each question and blacken the corresponding space on your answer sheet.

---

[1] PrepTest 47, Sec. 4

Questions 1–5

Exactly seven products—P, Q, R, S, T, W, and X—are each to be advertised exactly once in a section of a catalog. The order in which they will be displayed is governed by the following conditions:

Q must be displayed in some position before W.
R must be displayed immediately before X.
T cannot be displayed immediately before or immediately after W.
S must be displayed either first or seventh.
Either Q or T must be displayed fourth.

1. Which one of the following CANNOT be the product that is displayed first?

    (A)   P
    (B)   Q
    (C)   R
    (D)   T
    (E)   X

2. If X is displayed immediately before Q, then which one of the following could be true?

    (A)   T is displayed first.
    (B)   R is displayed fifth.
    (C)   Q is displayed last.
    (D)   Q is displayed second.
    (E)   P is displayed second.

3. If P is displayed second, then which one of the following could be displayed third?

    (A)   R
    (B)   S
    (C)   T
    (D)   W
    (E)   X

4. Which one of the following could be true?

    (A)   Q is displayed fifth.
    (B)   Q is displayed seventh.
    (C)   R is displayed third.
    (D)   W is displayed third.
    (E)   X is displayed fifth.

5. If R is displayed sixth, then which one of the following must be displayed fifth?

    (A)   P
    (B)   Q
    (C)   T
    (D)   W
    (E)   X

<u>Questions 6–11</u>

A lighting control panel has exactly seven switches, numbered from 1 to 7. Each switch is either in the on position or in the off position. The circuit load of the panel is the total number of its switches that are on. The control panel must be configured in accordance with the following conditions:

If switch 1 is on, then switch 3 and switch 5 are off.
If switch 4 is on, then switch 2 and switch 5 are off.
The switch whose number corresponds to the circuit load of the panel is itself on.

6. Which one of the following could be a complete and accurate list of the switches that are on?

(A)   switch 2, switch 3, switch 4, switch 7
(B)   switch 3, switch 6, switch 7
(C)   switch 2, switch 5, switch 6
(D)   switch 1, switch 3, switch 4
(E)   switch 1, switch 5

7. If switch 1 and switch 3 are both off, then which one of the following could be two switches that are both on?

(A)   switch 2 and switch 7
(B)   switch 4 and switch 6
(C)   switch 4 and switch 7
(D)   switch 5 and switch 6
(E)   switch 6 and switch 7

8. If exactly two of the switches are on, then which one of the following switches must be off?

(A)   switch 3
(B)   switch 4
(C)   switch 5
(D)   switch 6
(E)   switch 7

9. If switch 6 and switch 7 are both off, then what is the maximum circuit load of the panel?

(A)   one
(B)   two
(C)   three
(D)   four
(E)   five

10. If switch 5 and switch 6 are both on, then which one of the following switches must be on?

(A)   switch 1
(B)   switch 2
(C)   switch 3
(D)   switch 4
(E)   switch 7

11. What is the maximum circuit load of the panel?

(A)   three
(B)   four
(C)   five
(D)   six
(E)   seven

Questions 12–17

In Crescentville there are exactly five record stores, whose names are abbreviated S, T, V, X, and Z. Each of the five stores carries at least one of four distinct types of music: folk, jazz, opera, and rock. None of the stores carries any other type of music. The following conditions must hold:

Exactly two of the five stores carry jazz.

T carries rock and opera but no other type of music.

S carries more types of music than T carries.

X carries more types of music than any other store in Crescentville carries.

Jazz is among the types of music S carries.

V does not carry any type of music that Z carries.

12. Which one of the following could be true?

   (A)   S carries folk and rock but neither jazz nor opera.
   (B)   T carries jazz but neither opera nor rock.
   (C)   V carries folk, rock, and opera, but not jazz.
   (D)   X carries folk, rock, and jazz, but not opera.
   (E)   Z carries folk and opera but neither rock nor jazz.

13. Which one of the following could be true?

   (A)   S, V, and Z all carry folk.
   (B)   S, X, and Z all carry jazz.
   (C)   Of the five stores, only S and V carry jazz.
   (D)   Of the five stores, only T and X carry rock.
   (E)   Of the five stores, only S, T, and V carry opera.

14. If exactly one of the stores carries folk, then which one of the following could be true?

   (A)   S and V carry exactly two types of music in common.
   (B)   T and S carry exactly two types of music in common.
   (C)   T and V carry exactly two types of music in common.
   (D)   V and X carry exactly two types of music in common.
   (E)   X and Z carry exactly two types of music in common.

15. Which one of the following must be true?

   (A)   T carries exactly the same number of types of music as V carries.
   (B)   V carries exactly the same number of types of music as Z carries.
   (C)   S carries at least one more type of music than Z carries.
   (D)   Z carries at least one more type of music than T carries.
   (E)   X carries exactly two more types of music than S carries.

16. If V is one of exactly three stores that carry rock, then which one of the following must be true?

   (A)   S and Z carry no types of music in common.
   (B)   S and V carry at least one type of music in common.
   (C)   S and Z carry at least one type of music in common.
   (D)   T and Z carry at least one type of music in common.
   (E)   T and V carry at least two types of music in common.

17. If S and V both carry folk, then which one of the following could be true?

   (A)   S and T carry no types of music in common.
   (B)   S and Z carry no types of music in common.
   (C)   T and Z carry no types of music in common.
   (D)   S and Z carry two types of music in common.
   (E)   T and V carry two types of music in common.

<u>Questions 18–22</u>

Maggie's Deli is open exactly five days every week:
Monday through Friday. Its staff, each of whom works on
at least one day each week, consists of exactly six people—
Janice, Kevin, Nan, Ophelia, Paul, and Seymour. Exactly
three of them—Janice, Nan, and Paul—are supervisors.
The deli's staffing is consistent with the following:

Each day's staff consists of exactly two people, at least
one of whom is a supervisor.

Tuesday's and Wednesday's staffs both include
Ophelia.

Of the days Nan works each week, at least two are
consecutive.

Seymour does not work on any day before the first
day Paul works that week.

Any day on which Kevin works is the first day during
the week that some other staff member works.

18. Which one of the following could be an accurate
staffing schedule?

(A)   Monday: Janice, Kevin
      Tuesday: Nan, Ophelia
      Wednesday: Nan, Paul
      Thursday: Kevin, Paul
      Friday: Janice, Seymour
(B)   Monday: Paul, Seymour
      Tuesday: Ophelia, Paul
      Wednesday: Nan, Ophelia
      Thursday: Kevin, Nan
      Friday: Janice, Seymour
(C)   Monday: Janice, Kevin
      Tuesday: Nan, Ophelia
      Wednesday: Nan, Ophelia
      Thursday: Kevin, Paul
      Friday: Paul, Seymour
(D)   Monday: Janice, Kevin
      Tuesday: Janice, Ophelia
      Wednesday: Nan, Ophelia
      Thursday: Nan, Seymour
      Friday: Kevin, Paul
(E)   Monday: Paul, Seymour
      Tuesday: Ophelia, Paul
      Wednesday: Nan, Ophelia
      Thursday: Janice, Kevin
      Friday: Nan, Paul

19. If Kevin and Paul work Thursday, who must work
Friday?

(A)   Janice
(B)   Kevin
(C)   Nan
(D)   Paul
(E)   Seymour

20. Each of the following could be true EXCEPT:

(A)   Janice works Monday and Tuesday.
(B)   Kevin and Paul work Friday.
(C)   Seymour works Monday and Friday.
(D)   Janice and Kevin work Thursday.
(E)   Paul works Monday and Friday.

21. Which one of the following CANNOT be the pair of
staff that works Monday?

(A)   Janice and Seymour
(B)   Kevin and Paul
(C)   Paul and Seymour
(D)   Nan and Ophelia
(E)   Janice and Nan

22. Which one of the following could be true?

(A)   Nan works Wednesday and Friday only.
(B)   Seymour works Monday and Paul works
      Tuesday.
(C)   Kevin works Monday, Wednesday, and Friday.
(D)   Nan works Wednesday with Ophelia and
      Thursday with Kevin.
(E)   Ophelia and Kevin work Tuesday.

ANSWER KEY

1.	E	9.	C	17.	B
2.	A	10.	C	18.	C
3.	C	11.	C	19.	E
4.	A	12.	E	20.	B
5.	D	13.	D	21.	A
6.	B	14.	B	22.	B
7.	A	15.	C		
8.	B	16.	C		

TRIAGE REVIEW

This is a Logic Games section that can be taken in order. The easiest game for most students is the first, which is a standard Strict Sequencing game. Although it doesn't have a great many deductions up front, it has five rules that limit the possible arrangements down to a manageable number.

The second and third games are the two that you might have taken in either order. They are basically equal in difficulty for the majority of test takers. The second is a standard Selection game with one unusual feature—a special term that's defined in the game's setup and which you must understand in order to use one of the rules. The third game is a fairly complex Matching game, but one on which you can do most of the work up front. It has six rules that, if combined, solve more than half the game before you ever tackle a question. Your decision about which of those two games to do first should be guided, frankly, by personal preference. If you are comfortable with formal logic and you like Selection, take on game two first. If you've tended to do well with the Matching games you've seen thus far, prioritize game three.

The final game was the hardest for most students and not just because it came last. It's a Strict Sequencing game, but one in which you have to re-use some of the entities. Moreover, you have to schedule two entities on each of five days, so there's a Double Sequencing feel to the task. With only five questions, it's an easy one to leave for last. But given that it has an Acceptability question and three short "Non-If" questions, it's definitely in your interest to try to leave adequate time to get to this game. You're likely to add at least a few more right answers to your score.

EXPLANATIONS

Game 1—Product Advertisements

Questions 1–5

> Exactly seven products—P, Q, R, S, T, W, and X—are each
> to be advertised exactly once in a section of a catalog. The
> order in which they will be displayed is governed by the
> following conditions:
>> Q must be displayed in some position before W.
>> R must be displayed immediately before X.
>> T cannot be displayed immediately before or
>> immediately after W.
>> S must be displayed either first or seventh.
>> Either Q or T must be displayed fourth.[2]

STEPS 1 AND 2: Overview and Sketch

There's nothing out of the ordinary in this standard Sequencing game. You have seven products to arrange in order, one at a time. A quick glance at the rules shows that they mention definite spaces in the order, and one gives the precise number of spaces between two of the entities. These rules call for a Strict Sequencing framework.

P Q R S T W X

___ ___ ___ ___ ___ ___ ___
 1   2   3   4   5   6   7

Figure 17.1

STEP 3: Rules

There are five rules here, but only a couple that can be built directly into the framework.

Rule 1 gives the relative order of (but not the distance between) Q and W.

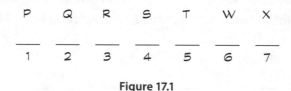

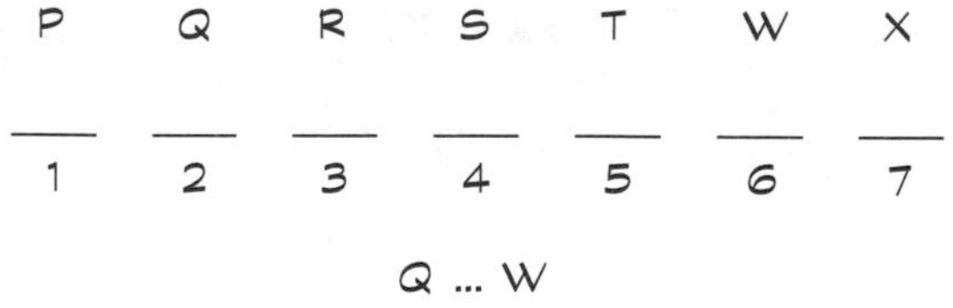

P Q R S T W X

___ ___ ___ ___ ___ ___ ___
 1   2   3   4   5   6   7

Q ... W

Figure 17.2

Rule 2 creates a block of entities.

---

[2] PrepTest 47, Sec. 4, Game 1

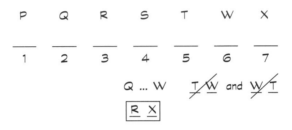

Figure 17.3

Rule 3 restricts two entities from being next to each other, regardless of their order.

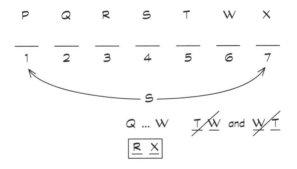

Figure 17.4

Rule 4 gives S only two options. Given that S's position doesn't affect any of the other entities, however, you need not make two separate sketches. Depicting Rule 4 like this works just fine:

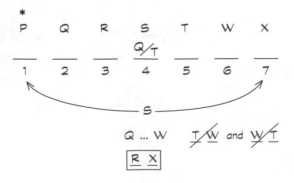

Figure 17.5

Rule 5 gives you two options for a specific space within the order.

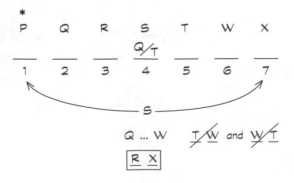

Figure 17.6

Note, too, that P is marked as the floater. That's the one product not mentioned in any of the rules.

STEP 4: Deductions

The only firm deduction available here is relatively minor. You know that R cannot take space 3, since X cannot take space 4. Likewise, you know that X can't take space 5, since R cannot take space 4.

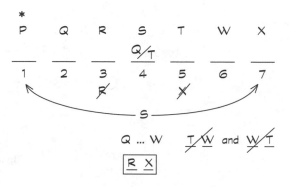

Figure 17.7

There are no additional deductions to be made in this game. The rules that share entities—W appears in Rules 1 and 3, T in Rules 3 and 5, and Q in Rules 1 and 5—are suggestive, but not strong enough to allow you to add any specifics into the framework. Rather than spend time speculating ("What if T is in space 4?" or, "What if Q is there?"), move into the questions. The three "If" questions will definitely give you the additional specificity you need to build mini-sketches.

STEP 5: Questions

This is a fairly standard question set, with three "If" questions and two Must/Could questions. If you struggle with either of the Must/Could questions, work through the "If" questions first to see if their mini-sketches help you evaluate the Must/Could answer choices.

1. **(E)**

   Which one of the following CANNOT be the product that is displayed first?
   (A) P
   (B) Q
   (C) R
   (D) T
   (E) X[3]

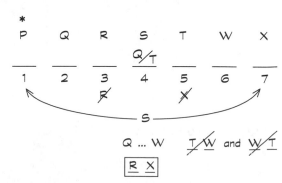

Figure 17.8

_____

[3] PrepTest 47, Sec. 4, Q 1

Looking through the rules, only two entities are prevented from being first: W (Rule 1) and X (Rule 2). One of those two entities must be in the correct answer. It turns out to be X, in choice (E).

2. **(A)**

If X is displayed immediately before Q, then which one of the following could be true?
(A)   T is displayed first.
(B)   R is displayed fifth.
(C)   Q is displayed last.
(D)   Q is displayed second.
(E)   P is displayed second.[4]

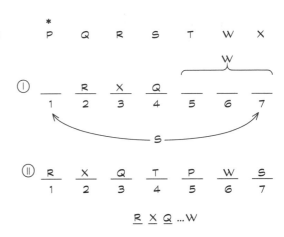

Figure 17.9

The "if" condition in the question stem calls for a mini-sketch. Start your mini-sketch with the "if" from the stem.

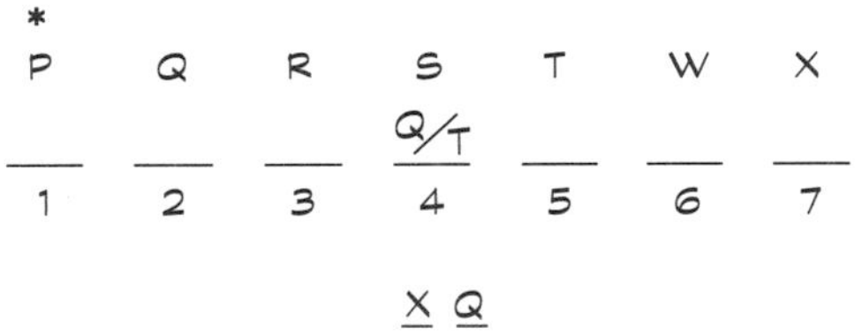

Figure 17.10

Rule 2 places R immediately before X in every case.

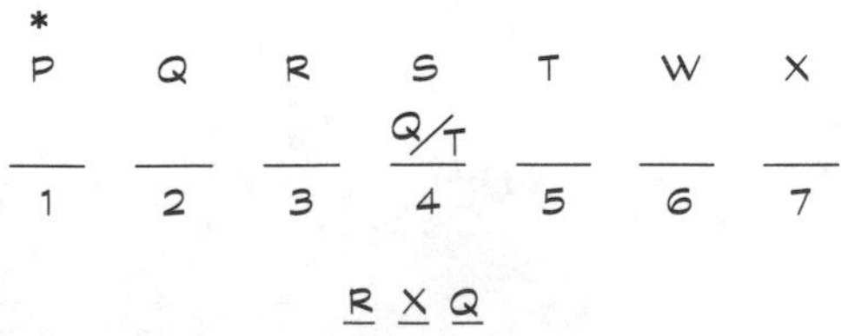

Figure 17.11

Rule 1 tells you that W must follow Q.

---

[4] PrepTest 47, Sec. 4, Q 2

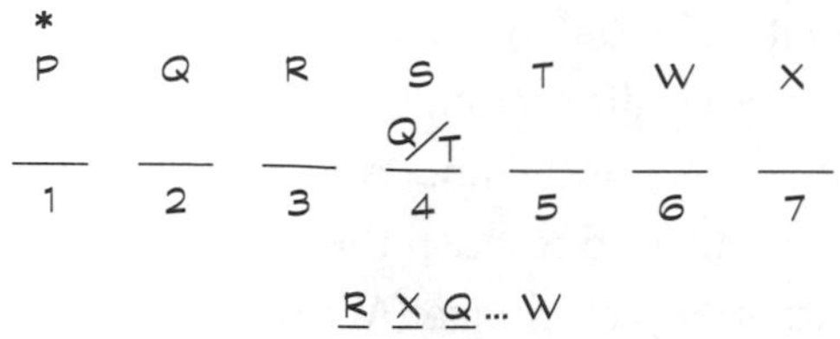

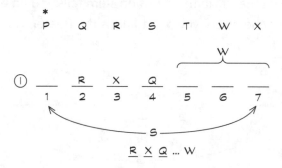

Figure 17.12

That's enough to eliminate three of the wrong answers. The correct answer *could be true*, so each of the four wrong answers *must be false*. Choice (B) is impossible since R is followed by three entities. Choices (C) and (D) are impossible since Q is followed by W and preceded by two entities. Now, you need to check whether T can be first (choice (A)) or whether P can be second (choice (E)).

Consider where the list you've created can fit in light of Rule 5. When Q is in space 4, R and X take spaces 2 and 3, respectively, and W takes a space between 5 and 7.

Figure 17.13

When T takes space 4, R-X-Q must take spaces 1–3, and W must take space 6 in order to avoid being adjacent to T and thus violating Rule 3. S will have to take space 7 in this scenario, since space 1 is occupied by R. That leaves space 5 for the floater, P.

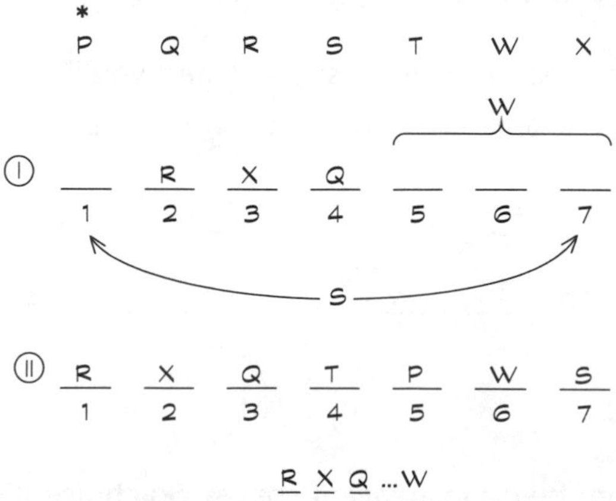

Figure 17.14

Either way, there's no possibility of P being in space 2. Choice (E) is impossible and, therefore, choice (A) is correct. If you need confirmation, test T in the first option (where Q takes space 4). In that case, S would take space 7 and P and W would takes spaces 5 and 6 in either order. No problem. You may not have needed to push the mini-sketch to this level of completeness. Once you were able to confidently pick choice (A) or eliminate choice (D), you were done.

3. **(C)**

    If P is displayed second, then which one of the following could be displayed third?

    (A) R
    (B) S
    (C) T
    (D) W
    (E) X[5]

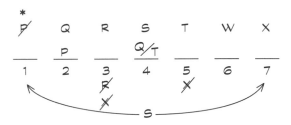

Figure 17.15

Adding the one entity from the "if" in the question stem tells you an enormous amount about the sketch. That's because the entity you're adding is the floater, P.

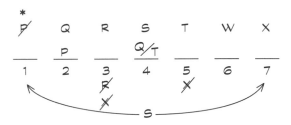

Figure 17.16

The question calls for an entity that can take space 3. S can never take space 3 (Rule 4), so you can get rid of choice (B). R can never take space 3, since X must follow immediately after it (Rule 2), so eliminate choice (A). And with P in space 2, you know that X cannot take space 3 either, since X must follow immediately after R (Rule 2). Eliminate choice (E), too.

Now, all you need to do is check T or W for space 3, and you'll have the answer. If you try W in space 3, Q would have to take space 1 to comply with Rule 1. That would put T in space 4.

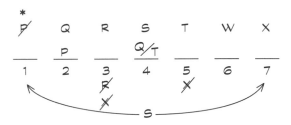

Figure 17.17

Rule 3 forbids T and W from being in adjacent spaces. So choice (D) is incorrect.

That means choice (C) must be acceptable, and indeed, placing T in space 3 works out fine. S would take space 1 in this situation, and W and the R-X block would bring up the rear (their precise order is irrelevant).

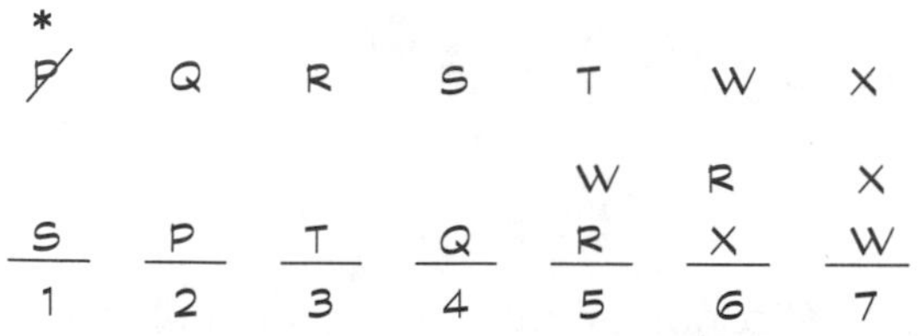

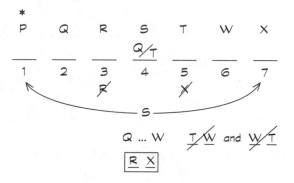

Figure 17.18

4. **(A)**

    Which one of the following could be true?
    (A)   Q is displayed fifth.
    (B)   Q is displayed seventh.
    (C)   R is displayed third.
    (D)   W is displayed third.
    (E)   X is displayed fifth.[6]

Figure 17.19

The correct answer to this short question *could be true*. That means that each of the wrong answers *must be false*. The quickest route to the right answer is to eliminate each of the impossible choices.

Choice (B) won't work because of Rule 1; if Q was in the final position, there'd be no room for W in the sequence.

Choice (C) is out because of Rule 2; X is unable to take space 4.

Choice (D) cannot happen. You discovered why this is true as you tested choice (D) in question 3. If W takes space 3, Q must take space 1 or space 2 and leave space 4 for T. If W and T are contiguous, Rule 3 is violated.

Choice (E) breaks Rule 2. X can never take space 5 since R can never take space 4.

Voilà. Choice (A) is correct. It's the only answer with an acceptable placement.

---

[6] PrepTest 47, Sec. 4, Q 4

5. **(D)**

If R is displayed sixth, then which one of the following must be displayed fifth?
(A) P
(B) Q
(C) T
(D) W
(E) X[7]

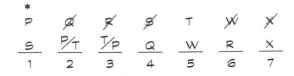

Figure 17.20

Push the implications of the "if" condition from this stem until space 5's occupant is clear. Start with R in space 6.

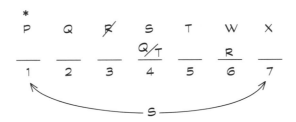

Figure 17.21

R must, of course, be followed by X (Rule 2).

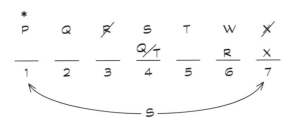

Figure 17.22

With X in the final spot, S needs to take space 1.

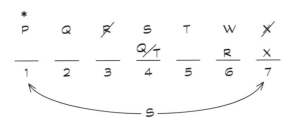

Figure 17.23

At this point, you can see that W may not take space 2 (there's no room for Q to be in front of W). Nor can W take space 3 (that would put Q in space 2 and T in space 4, and Rule 3 would be violated). So W will have to take space 5.

---

[7] PrepTest 47, Sec. 4, Q 5

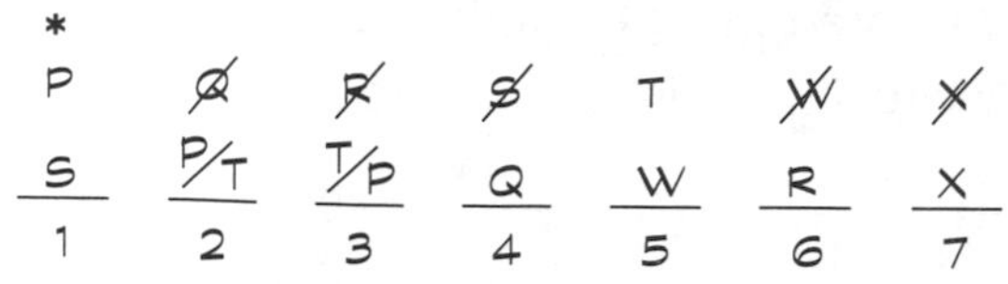

Figure 17.24

That makes choice (D) the correct answer.

This game was a standard Strict Sequencing game. The lack of strong deductions up front meant that you had to be patient in making mini-sketches and applying the rules to eliminate wrong answers. Provided that you did those things, this game likely proved manageable.

Game 2—Light Switches

<u>Questions 6–11</u>

A lighting control panel has exactly seven switches, numbered from 1 to 7. Each switch is either in the on position or in the off position. The circuit load of the panel is the total number of its switches that are on. The control panel must be configured in accordance with the following conditions:

If switch 1 is on, then switch 3 and switch 5 are off.
If switch 4 is on, then switch 2 and switch 5 are off.
The switch whose number corresponds to the circuit load of the panel is itself on.[8]

STEPS 1 AND 2: Overview and Sketch

Picture the task that's being described, and the game type will be revealed. You have a panel of seven numbered switches.

Figure 17.25

Each switch is either *on* or *off*.

Figure 17.26

You've seen this pattern many times. This is a standard Selection game. There's no need for any other sketch or framework; a roster of the entities that you can circle or strike through is perfect.

The one oddity here is the specially defined term "circuit load." When the test offers a made-up term like this, it will always give you a definition. For this game, "circuit load" means the

---

[8] PrepTest 47, Sec. 4, Game 2

total number of switches that are turned on. If three switches are on, the circuit load is three. If four switches are on, the circuit load is four. Just follow the definition and you'll be fine.

STEP 3: Rules

The first two rules, as you should expect with Selection, are conditional formal logic statements. Translate each and jot down its contrapositive, too. Remember to change "and" to "or" as you form the contrapositive.

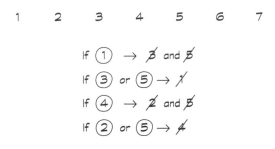

Figure 17.27

The third rule requires you to read carefully. The rule tells you that the switch with the number corresponding to the circuit load must be on. So if three switches are on, switch 3 must be on. If four switches are on, switch 4 must be on. Just note that rule in a shorthand paraphrase you'll be sure to understand.

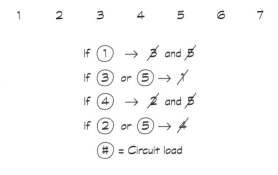

Figure 17.28

STEP 4: Deductions

There's just one big deduction to make, and it comes from the number restrictions. With any standard Selection game, it's valuable to consider the minimum and maximum numbers. In this game, the minimum number of switches that must be on is zero. No rule or restriction requires that you turn on any switch. The maximum is a little trickier. That's because of Rule 3, which states that the maximum number of switches that can be on must include the switch with that number. By combining Rules 1 and 2, you can see that it's impossible to have more than five switches on; turning on switch 1, switch 4, or switch 5 requires you to turn two other switches off. So the relevant question is: Can you have a maximum number (a circuit load, if you will) of five switches on? To abide by Rule 3, switch 5 has to be one of the five switches turned on. Turning on switch 5 entails turning off switches 1 and 4.

Figure 17.29

But once those two are off, nothing prevents the remaining five from being on simultaneously. Your maximum circuit load (the maximum number of switches that can be on) is five.

STEP 5: Questions

The question set is perfectly suited to a standard Selection game. It has one Acceptability question, four "If" questions, and (lo and behold) a Minimum/Maximum question, one that you've already figured out. Start off with the two quickest points—questions 6 and 11—and then work your way through the "Ifs," using mini-sketches to make your work concrete.

6. **(B)**

Which one of the following could be a complete and accurate list of the switches that are on?

(A) switch 2, switch 3, switch 4, switch 7
(B) switch 3, switch 6, switch 7
(C) switch 2, switch 5, switch 6
(D) switch 1, switch 3, switch 4
(E) switch 1, switch 5[9]

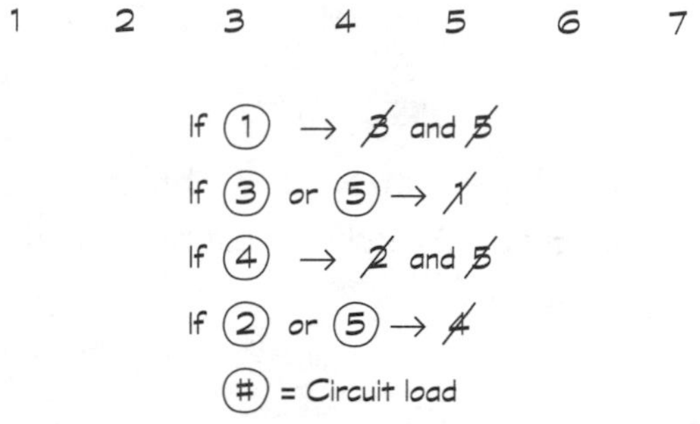

1   2   3   4   5   6   7

If ① → 3̶ and 5̶

If ③ or ⑤ → 1̶

If ④ → 2̶ and 5̶

If ② or ⑤ → 4̶

(#) = Circuit load

Figure 17.30

The correct answer here is an acceptable selection of switches that are turned on. Use the rules to eliminate the unacceptable choices. Rule 1 eliminates choice (D) and choice (E); if switch 1 is on, switches 3 and 5 must both be off. Rule 2 gets rid of choice (A); switches 2 and 4 cannot be on simultaneously. Rule 3 knocks out choice (C); the circuit load here is three, yet switch 3 is off. (Notice that Rule 3 would eliminate choice (E) as well; there, the circuit load is two, but switch 2 is not on.) The correct answer is choice (B), the only answer that doesn't break any of the rules.

7. **(A)**

If switch 1 and switch 3 are both off, then which one of the following could be two switches that are both on?

(A) switch 2 and switch 7
(B) switch 4 and switch 6
(C) switch 4 and switch 7
(D) switch 5 and switch 6
(E) switch 6 and switch 7[10]

Figure 17.31

---

[9] PrepTest 47, Sec. 4, Q 6
[10] PrepTest 47, Sec. 4, Q 7

For each of the "If" questions in this game, create mini-sketches based on the conditions laid out in the question stems. Here, begin by listing the switches and crossing out switches 1 and 3.

1 2 3 4 5 6 7

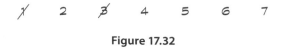

Figure 17.32

That leaves five switches. The most important are switches 2 and 4, which are in conflict due to Rule 2. Thinking about the implications of that rule, you soon realize that switch 4 must be off. Turning it on would mean turning off switches 2 and 5. That would leave you with three switches, but without switches 1, 2, and 3. So you'd have no way of turning on the switch with the number matching the circuit load.

1 2 3 4 5 6 7

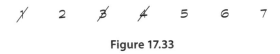

Figure 17.33

Now, you have four switches, but switches 1, 3, and 4 are off, so the maximum circuit load possible is two. Switch 2 must be turned on along with one other switch.

1 2 3 4 5 6 7
1 of these

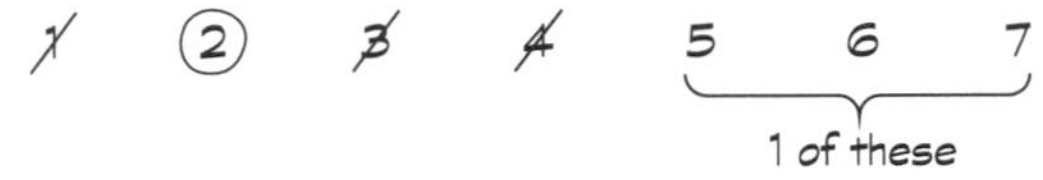

Figure 17.34

The only answer that matches this arrangement is choice (A), the correct answer.

8. **(B)**

If exactly two of the switches are on, then which one of the following switches must be off?

(A) switch 3
(B) switch 4
(C) switch 5
(D) switch 6
(E) switch 7[11]

(2 on/5 off)
1 2 3 4 5 6 7

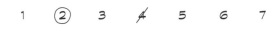

Figure 17.35

The "if" in this stem tells you more than you might realize at first. If exactly two switches are on, the circuit load is two. According to Rule 3, then, switch 2 must be turned on in this situation.

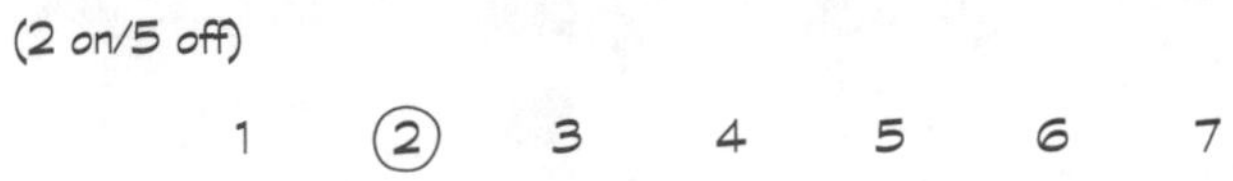
(2 on/5 off)
1 2 3 4 5 6 7

Figure 17.36

---

[11] PrepTest 47, Sec. 4, Q 8

Turning on switch 2 triggers Rule 2. Switch 4 must be turned off.

(2 on/5 off)

1   ②   3   ⚡   5   6   7

Figure 17.37

That makes choice (B) the correct answer. Switch 4 must be off.

9. **(C)**

If switch 6 and switch 7 are both off, then what is the
maximum circuit load of the panel?

(A)   one
(B)   two
(C)   three
(D)   four
(E)   five[12]

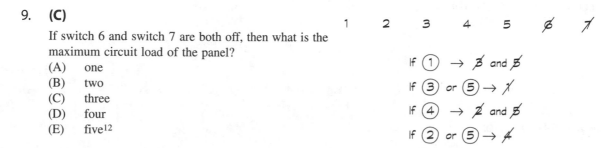

1   2   3   4   5   ⚡   ⚡

If ① → ⚡ and ⚡
If ③ or ⑤ → ⚡
If ④ → ⚡ and ⚡
If ② or ⑤ → ⚡

Figure 17.37A

Once you cross off switches 6 and 7 in accordance with the "if" in the question stem, you
can deduce the answer to this question. Rules 1 and 2 make it impossible to have more than
three of the remaining switches turned on. You can achieve a circuit load of three by having
switches 2, 3, and 5 turned on. Choice (C) is correct.

10. **(C)**

If switch 5 and switch 6 are both on, then which one
of the following switches must be on?

(A)   switch 1
(B)   switch 2
(C)   switch 3
(D)   switch 4
(E)   switch 7[13]

Cir. load   ⚡   ⚡   ③   ⚡   ⑤   ⑥   ⚡
   3
Cir. load   ⚡   ②   ③   ⚡   ⑤   ⑥   ⑦
   5

Figure 17.38

Start your mini-sketch by circling switches 5 and 6 as instructed by the question stem.

1   2   3   4   ⑤   ⑥   7

Figure 17.39

---

[12] PrepTest 47, Sec. 4, Q 9
[13] PrepTest 47, Sec. 4, Q 10

Turning on switch 5 requires you to turn off switches 1 and 4 (see Rules 1 and 2).

$$\cancel{1} \quad 2 \quad 3 \quad \cancel{4} \quad ⑤ \quad ⑥ \quad 7$$

Figure 17.40

The remaining switches are all compatible under the rules, provided that the switch with the circuit load number is on (Rule 3). To follow that requirement, you have two possibilities. The circuit load might be three:

$$\text{Cir. load } \cancel{1} \quad \cancel{2} \quad ③ \quad \cancel{4} \quad ⑤ \quad ⑥ \quad \cancel{7}$$
$$3$$

Figure 17.41

Or it might be five:

$$\text{Cir. load } \cancel{1} \quad \cancel{2} \quad ③ \quad \cancel{4} \quad ⑤ \quad ⑥ \quad \cancel{7}$$
$$3$$
$$\text{Cir. load } \cancel{1} \quad ② \quad ③ \quad \cancel{4} \quad ⑤ \quad ⑥ \quad ⑦$$
$$5$$

Figure 17.42

In either case, switch 3 *must be* turned *on*, making choice (C) the correct answer. The switches in choices (A) and (D) *must be off* in this scenario, while those in choices (B) and (E) *could* but don't *have to be on*.

11. **(C)**

What is the maximum circuit load of the panel?
(A) three
(B) four
(C) five
(D) six
(E) seven[14]

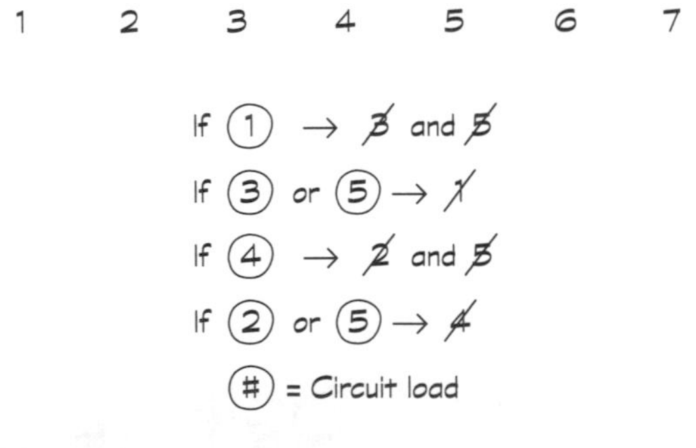

$$1 \quad 2 \quad 3 \quad 4 \quad 5 \quad 6 \quad 7$$

If ① → $\cancel{3}$ and $\cancel{5}$
If ③ or ⑤ → $\cancel{1}$
If ④ → $\cancel{2}$ and $\cancel{5}$
If ② or ⑤ → $\cancel{4}$
(#) = Circuit load

Figure 17.43

You've known the answer to this question since Step 4. The maximum number of switches that can be on (that's the definition of "circuit load") is five: switches 2, 3, 5, 6, and 7. Rule 3 requires that you turn on the switch with the number corresponding to the circuit load. Since the circuit load is five and switch 5 is on, you're fine here. Choice (C) is the correct answer.

The one aspect of that game that most students complain about is the unusual definition of "circuit load." Instead of calmly remembering that the test makers will always define an unusual

---

[14] PrepTest 47, Sec. 4, Q 11

term, they panic and say, "I don't know what that means." But those specially defined terms always result in important restrictions within the game. (Remember the professors who "shared a specialty" in the Professors' Hiring game from chapter 7?) Make sure you understand how the test makers are defining the special term, and make note of it next to or beneath your sketch. Do that, and you'll be at an enormous advantage over other test takers who aren't patient enough to take full advantage of the game setup and restrictions.

Game 3—Crescentville's Record Stores
Questions 12–17

In Crescentville there are exactly five record stores, whose names are abbreviated S, T, V, X, and Z. Each of the five stores carries at least one of four distinct types of music: folk, jazz, opera, and rock. None of the stores carries any other type of music. The following conditions must hold:

Exactly two of the five stores carry jazz.
T carries rock and opera but no other type of music.
S carries more types of music than T carries.
X carries more types of music than any other store in Crescentville carries.
Jazz is among the types of music S carries.
V does not carry any type of music that Z carries.[15]

STEPS 1 AND 2: Overview and Sketch

While record stores aren't as common as they were a few years ago, you can still picture this task pretty easily. You arrive in a new town and you want to see where you can shop for different kinds of music. According to the game's setup, there are five record stores to check and four types of music you're interested in. Since you're a fastidious LSAT test taker, you can keep track of your findings in a brief chart.

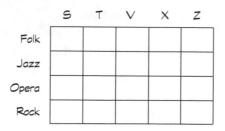

	S	T	V	X	Z
Folk					
Jazz					
Opera					
Rock					

Figure 17.44

When you find out that a certain record store carries a type of music, put a check mark in the corresponding box. When you find out it doesn't, record that with an X. Once you see this framework, you know you're working with a Matching game. In fact, this game should remind you a lot of the Appliance Repair Shop game with radios, TVs, and VCRs.

---

[15] PrepTest 47, Sec. 4, Game 3

STEPS 3 AND 4: **Rules and Deductions**

There are six rules. Provided that you are patient and record them one by one, you'll wind up with a lot of restriction here. This game provides an example of a fairly rare phenomenon; it's a game in which you can actually make the deductions as you're listing the rules. That's because the rules are listed in a logical order, such that each new rule builds off of something you've already put into the sketch framework. It doesn't happen often, so don't expect to see it on test day. But if you encounter a game built like this, take advantage of the opportunity to take the two steps together.

Rule 1 establishes the number of stores that carry jazz records.

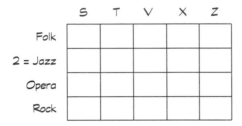

Figure 17.45

Rule 2 establishes T's column precisely.

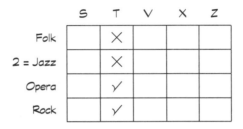

Figure 17.46

Rule 3 allows you to determine that store S carries either three or four types of music.

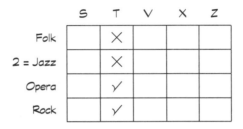

Figure 17.47

Rule 4 gives even more clarity to the numbers. Since store X carries the most types of music, you can now determine that store S carries exactly three types and that store X carries all four types.

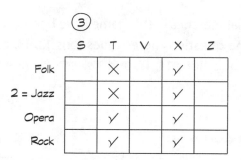

Figure 17.48

Rule 5 tells you to check the jazz box in store S's column. Notice that you now know exactly which stores carry jazz—S and X. You can close off the jazz row.

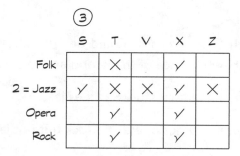

Figure 17.49

Finally, Rule 6 is one that you'll just have to list under the framework. You'll use it when the questions give you additional information about store V or store Z.

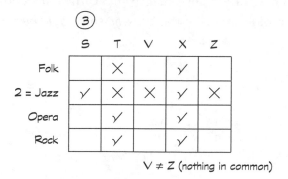

Figure 17.50

That's your Master Sketch. Eleven of the 20 boxes are determined. Some restrictions apply to each of those that remain open: Store S will carry a total of three types of music, and stores

V and Z have to avoid having any overlap. You should be amply prepared to breeze through this question set.

STEP 5: Questions

Just over half of the potential matches in this game have been established or ruled out. It's no surprise then that half of the questions here—questions 12, 13, and 15—reward you for your Master Sketch, while half—questions 14, 15, and 17—are "If" questions that will add information for those open boxes.

12. **(E)**

Which one of the following could be true?
(A) S carries folk and rock but neither jazz nor opera.
(B) T carries jazz but neither opera nor rock.
(C) V carries folk, rock, and opera, but not jazz.
(D) X carries folk, rock, and jazz, but not opera.
(E) Z carries folk and opera but neither rock nor jazz.[16]

③

	S	T	V	X	Z
Folk		✗		✓	
2 = Jazz	✓	✗	✗	✓	✗
Opera		✓		✓	
Rock		✓		✓	

V ≠ Z (nothing in common)

Figure 17.51

Just use your Master Sketch to answer this Could Be True question. The correct answer is acceptable within the sketch, while each of the wrong answers *must be false*.

Choice (A) must be false. You know that store S carries jazz.

Choice (B) must be false. Store T carries opera and rock but not jazz.

Choice (C) must be false. V cannot carry all three of folk, rock, and opera. That would leave nothing for store Z to carry and would thus violate Rule 6.

Choice (D) must be false. Store X carries all four types of music.

That leaves choice (E) as the correct answer. If store Z carries folk and opera, store V can carry rock. There's no violation of Rule 6 with this answer, so it *could be true*.

13. **(D)**

Which one of the following could be true?
(A) S, V, and Z all carry folk.
(B) S, X, and Z all carry jazz.
(C) Of the five stores, only S and V carry jazz.
(D) Of the five stores, only T and X carry rock.
(E) Of the five stores, only S, T, and V carry opera.[17]

③

	S	T	V	X	Z
Folk		✗		✓	
2 = Jazz	✓	✗	✗	✓	✗
Opera		✓		✓	
Rock		✓		✓	

V ≠ Z (nothing in common)

Figure 17.52

---

[16] PrepTest 47, Sec. 4, Q 12
[17] PrepTest 47, Sec. 4, Q 13

This question works exactly like question 12 did. Use your Master Sketch to eliminate the four *must be false* answers.

Choice (A) must be false. Rule 6 prevents V and Z from having any types of music in common.

Choice (B) must be false. Rule 1 allows for exactly two stores to carry jazz music.

Choice (C) must be false. You know from your Master Sketch that stores S and X are the ones that carry jazz.

Choice (D), however, *could be true*. Stores T and X definitely carry rock according to your Master Sketch. There's no rule that requires stores S, V, or Z to carry rock. Store S could carry folk, jazz, and opera as its three types of music. Of stores V and Z, one could carry opera and the other folk. This is the correct answer.

You already know that choice (E) is definitely false and therefore wrong. Store X always carries opera.

14. **(B)**

> If exactly one of the stores carries folk, then which one of the following could be true?
> (A)   S and V carry exactly two types of music in common.
> (B)   T and S carry exactly two types of music in common.
> (C)   T and V carry exactly two types of music in common.
> (D)   V and X carry exactly two types of music in common.
> (E)   X and Z carry exactly two types of music in common.[18]

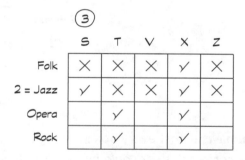

Figure 17.53

This question benefits from a mini-sketch. Some students avoid making mini-sketches in Matching games (or other games with somewhat complex frameworks) for fear that it will take them too long to copy the Master Sketch. With a little practice, though, it should take you only 10–15 seconds to copy your Master Sketch. The time you save (and the wrong answers you avoid) by doing so is well worth this small time investment. Trying to alter your Master Sketch and then erase when another new "if" is introduced is no faster and will, in short order, lead you to a messy sketch and confusion over what was in the original sketch and what you added for a particular question. Watch how well it works. Start your mini-sketch by copying over your Master Sketch and crossing out all boxes in the "folk" row except for Xs.

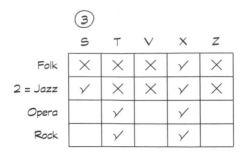

Figure 17.54

Now, you can see that store S will carry jazz, opera, and rock as its requisite three types of music. Moreover, between stores V and Z, one will carry rock and the other opera, although which carries which doesn't matter.

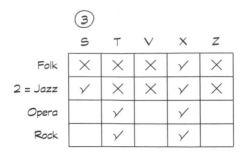

Figure 17.55

You have almost every box in the framework filled in. Evaluating the choices should be a snap. The correct answer *could be true*. The four wrong answers, therefore, *must be false*.

Choice (A) must be false under these conditions. After all, store V will carry only one type of music.

Choice (B) is the correct answer. It must, in fact, be true. In this case, stores S and T will both carry opera and rock.

Choices (C), (D), and (E) must all be false. Each answer includes either store V or store Z, which you know will carry only one type of music each under the conditions of this question.

15. **(C)**

Which one of the following must be true?
(A)   T carries exactly the same number of types of music as V carries.
(B)   V carries exactly the same number of types of music as Z carries.
(C)   S carries at least one more type of music than Z carries.
(D)   Z carries at least one more type of music than T carries.
(E)   X carries exactly two more types of music than S carries.[19]

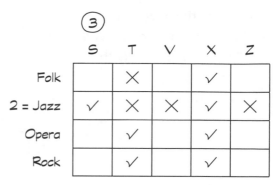

Figure 17.55

To answer this question, simply refer to your Master Sketch. The correct answer *must be true*, so you can eliminate any choice that *could be false*.

Choice (A) could be false. Store T always carries two types of music, but store V may carry only one.

Choice (B) could be false as well. Stores V and Z might carry one type of music each, but nothing prevents one of them from carrying two types as long as it doesn't duplicate the type of music that the other carries.

Choice (C), on the other hand, must be true. It's the correct answer. Store S will always carry three types of music. Store Z can carry, at most, two types of music. If it carried three types, it would share a type of music carried by store V in violation of Rule 6.

You know that choices (D) and (E) are wrong answers. In fact, both *must be false*. For review, make sure you can articulate why that's the case. Choice (D) is false because store T carries two types of music, and store Z can carry either one or two types. Choice (E) is false because store X carries exactly *one* more type of music than store S carries.

16. **(C)**

If V is one of exactly three stores that carry rock, then which one of the following must be true?
(A)   S and Z carry no types of music in common.
(B)   S and V carry at least one type of music in common.
(C)   S and Z carry at least one type of music in common.
(D)   T and Z carry at least one type of music in common.
(E)   T and V carry at least two types of music in common.[20]

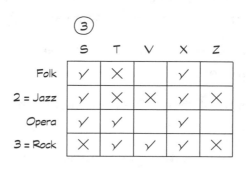

Figure 17.56

---

[19] PrepTest 47, Sec. 4, Q 15
[20] PrepTest 47, Sec. 4, Q 16

Here again, the new "if" in the question stem calls for a mini-sketch. Quickly copy over the Master Sketch information and add a check mark in the rock box under store V's column. Because the "if" says that exactly three stores carry rock, you can close off the rock row at this point.

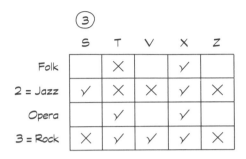

Figure 17.57

With store S unable to carry rock, its three types of music must be folk, jazz, and opera.

③

	S	T	V	X	Z
Folk	✓	✗		✓	
2 = Jazz	✓	✗	✗	✓	✗
Opera	✓	✓		✓	
3 = Rock	✗	✓	✓	✓	✗

Figure 17.58

The only boxes left undetermined are those for folk and opera in store V's and store Z's columns. You know that store Z will have to carry at least one of those types of music and, of course, that stores V and Z can have no types of music in common (Rule 6).

Take the time to characterize the answers before you evaluate the choices. The correct answer *must be true*. That means that each of the wrong answers *could be false*.

Eliminate choice (A). Store S carries two types of music—folk and opera—that store Z might carry, too.

Get rid of choice (B) as well. Store V may carry only rock and have no types of music in common with store S.

Choice (C) is the correct answer. It *must be true* that store S, which carries folk, jazz, and opera in this case, shares at least one type of music with store Z, which will have to carry folk, opera, or both.

In the scenario created by this question's "if" condition, choice (D) could be false. Store T carries rock and opera and no other types of music; store Z might carry only folk music here.

The same is true of choice (E). In this situation, store V may or may not carry opera. There's no way to know for sure.

17. **(B)**

If S and V both carry folk, then which one of the following could be true?
(A) S and T carry no types of music in common.
(B) S and Z carry no types of music in common.
(C) T and Z carry no types of music in common.
(D) S and Z carry two types of music in common.
(E) T and V carry two types of music in common.[21]

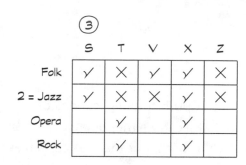

Figure 17.59

The "if" in this question stem isn't as restrictive as some you've seen in this game. Still, basing a mini-sketch on it will allow you to make all of the available deductions and ensure you have the information you need to answer the question. Start by copying the Master Sketch information and adding to it that stores S and V carry folk.

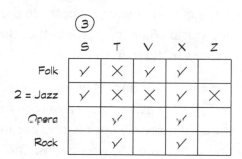

Figure 17.60

Knowing that store V carries a type of music tells you that store Z won't carry it. Indicate that store Z cannot carry folk in this case.

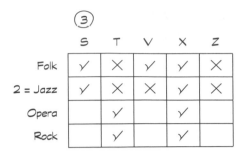

Figure 17.61

You can't push the implications of the "if" any further than that. At this point, you know that store S will carry either opera or rock but not both. As for stores V and Z, each will carry opera or rock or both, but that's as certain as it gets here.

So characterize the answer choices and dive in. The correct answer *could be true*. That means that all four wrong answers *must be false*. It should be relatively easy to spot the impossible answer choices and eliminate them.

Choice (A) must be false. Store T always carries opera and rock, and store S will have to carry one of those here.

Choice (B) *could be true*. This is the correct answer. It's possible that store S will carry rock and store Z will carry opera, or vice versa. While it's possible that they carry a type of music in common, they aren't required to by anything in this scenario.

At this point, you know that choices (C), (D), and (E) must be false. For the purposes of review, make sure you see why. Choice (C) is out because store Z will carry either opera or rock or both, giving it some overlap with store T. Choice (D) goes wrong because, no matter what, store S can carry only one of opera and rock, store Z's two options. Choice (E) is false because store V, which carries folk under the "if" of this question, can carry only one of opera and rock. It has to leave the other for store Z. Thus, stores T and V can have, at most, one type of music in common.

This is a game that puts a high premium on your initial sketch and deductions. That's often true of Matching tasks. The payoff comes when you use your thorough Master Sketch to make short work of the questions.

Game 4—Maggie's Deli Schedule

Questions 18–22

> Maggie's Deli is open exactly five days every week:
> Monday through Friday. Its staff, each of whom works on
> at least one day each week, consists of exactly six people—
> Janice, Kevin, Nan, Ophelia, Paul, and Seymour. Exactly
> three of them—Janice, Nan, and Paul—are supervisors.
> The deli's staffing is consistent with the following:
>
> > Each day's staff consists of exactly two people, at least
> > one of whom is a supervisor.
> >
> > Tuesday's and Wednesday's staffs both include
> > Ophelia.
> >
> > Of the days Nan works each week, at least two are
> > consecutive.
> >
> > Seymour does not work on any day before the first
> > day Paul works that week.
> >
> > Any day on which Kevin works is the first day during
> > the week that some other staff member works.[22]

STEPS 1 AND 2: Overview and Sketch

It's very important that you're patient with the Overview step in this game. You've probably worked at a job that had a weekly schedule for who's on duty each day. It may even have designated a "shift leader" or manager on duty, as this game does. At Maggie's Deli, the fictional business in this game, every member of the staff works on at least one day of the week. Rule 1 tells you that exactly two people work each day, Monday through Friday, and that at least one is a supervisor (but notice that doesn't preclude two supervisors working together). Form a mental picture of the weekly schedule as it might be posted on the office door, and translate it into a framework for the game:

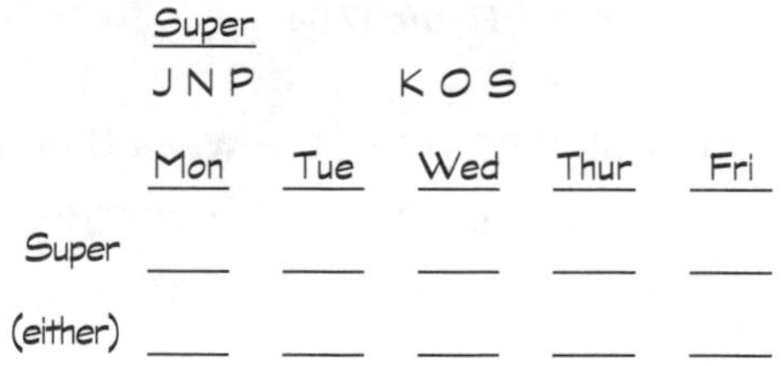

Figure 17.62

Make sure your initial sketch clearly distinguishes the supervisors, and include a note that reminds you that each day needs at least one supervisor but may have two.

STEP 3: Rules

The game has five long rules. They'll provide helpful restrictions but only if you take the time to make sure you know what each says (and what it doesn't) and find a clear way to add it into or underneath the sketch framework.

---

22 PrepTest 47, Sec. 4, Game 4

The first rule you've already worked into the overall framework. It's more of a global limitation than a specific rule.

Rule 2 allows you to place O on two days. O is not a supervisor, so make sure to enter her on the bottom row in your sketch.

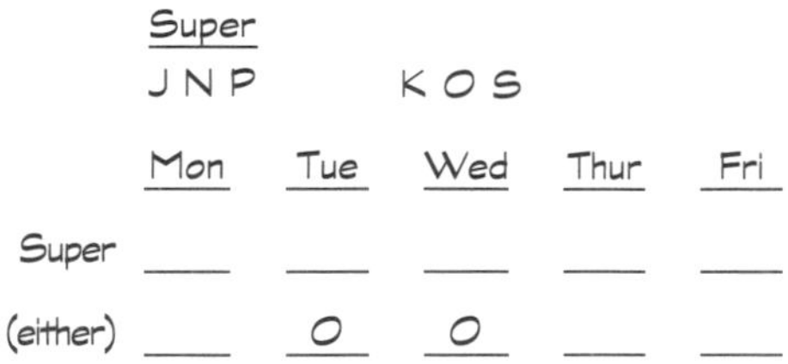

Figure 17.63

Make sure you didn't over-interpret the rule. It doesn't tell you that Tuesday and Wednesday are necessarily O's only days.

Rule 3 tells you that you'll need to have two days in a row with N scheduled. Again, note that she may or may not work more than that.

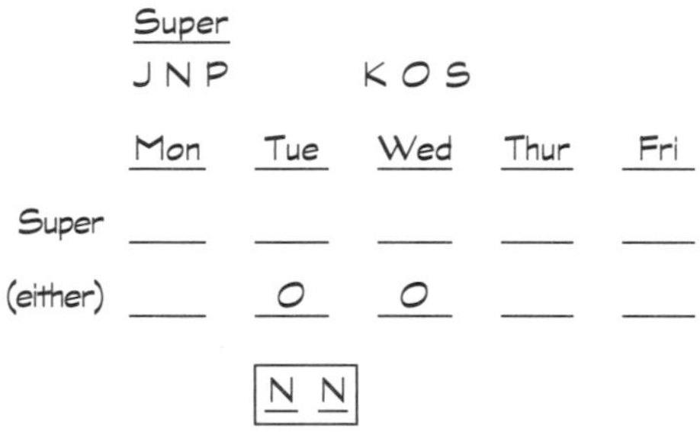

Figure 17.64

Rule 4 restricts S from being scheduled *earlier* in the week than P. Make sure you appreciate that S and P may have the same first day in the week, however.

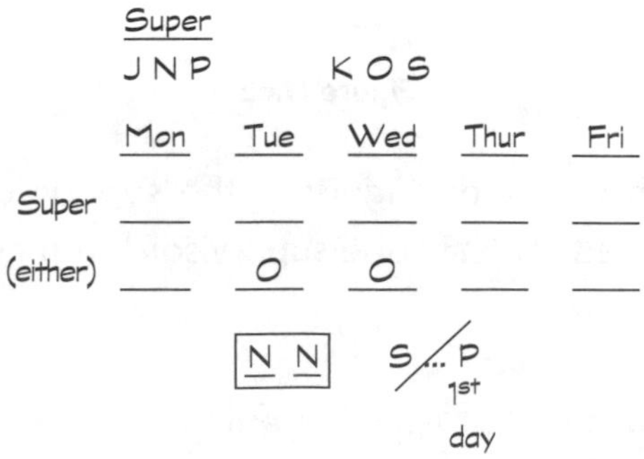

Figure 17.65

Rule 5 sounds a little bizarre, but it actually provides a very clear restriction. Any time K works, it's the shift's other worker's first day that week.

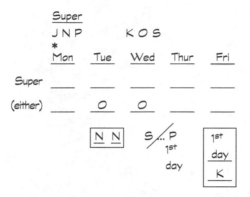

Figure 17.66

As you depict that rule, keep in mind that K is not a supervisor. Show him always on the bottom row in the framework. Note, too, that J is the floater, with no rules or restrictions limiting her placement.

STEP 4: Deductions

There aren't any solid deductions that you can add to your Sketch for this game. It is not a good use of your time, especially on the final game in the set, to start speculating about all the possibilities. Go quickly through the BLEND list of potential deductions. When you discover there aren't any, trust that the rules as they are will give you everything you need to determine the right and wrong answers.

STEP 5: Questions

With the exception of the Acceptability question, where the answers must display the entire five-day schedule, the questions here are short. There is only one "If" question, so you can tell that you'll be asked to assess the acceptability or unacceptability of arrangements based on the original rules and the small amount of information you've been able to put in your Master Sketch.

18. **(C)**

Which one of the following could be an accurate staffing schedule?

(A) Monday: Janice, Kevin
Tuesday: Nan, Ophelia
Wednesday: Nan, Paul
Thursday: Kevin, Paul
Friday: Janice, Seymour

(B) Monday: Paul, Seymour
Tuesday: Ophelia, Paul
Wednesday: Nan, Ophelia
Thursday: Kevin, Nan
Friday: Janice, Seymour

(C) Monday: Janice, Kevin
Tuesday: Nan, Ophelia
Wednesday: Nan, Ophelia
Thursday: Kevin, Paul
Friday: Paul, Seymour

(D) Monday: Janice, Kevin
Tuesday: Janice, Ophelia
Wednesday: Nan, Ophelia
Thursday: Nan, Seymour
Friday: Kevin, Paul

(E) Monday: Paul, Seymour
Tuesday: Ophelia, Paul
Wednesday: Nan, Ophelia
Thursday: Janice, Kevin
Friday: Nan, Paul[23]

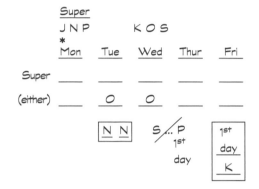

Figure 17.67

There's a lot of information to look through, but each answer choice is organized in the same way, so be methodical. One thing that the test makers did not do for you is to distinguish the supervisors from the other employees. It will be helpful that you've distinguished the supervisors in your Master Sketch.

Rule 1 says that each day must have at least one supervisor. If you find a day without J, N, or P, eliminate the entire answer choice. Scanning the answers, you never find this rule violated. Move on to the next one.

Rule 2 requires O on Tuesday and Wednesday. That rule is broken in choice (A). One down.

Rule 3 says that, during the week, you need to have N on consecutive days at some point. Be careful, N may work on other days, too. The rule simply requires that, at least once, she works back-to-back days. Choice (E) violates that rule. Eliminate it.

Rule 4 says that you may not find S scheduled prior to P's first day during the week. Again, be careful. S can be scheduled *on* P's first day, just not before it. That rule knocks out choice (D), where P's first day is Friday, but you find S scheduled on Thursday.

Finally, Rule 5 tells you that any day on which K is scheduled is the other employee's first day of work for the week. In other words, if K is working alongside someone who has previously worked during the week, you can cross out that answer choice. The answer that violates this rule is choice (B). Thursday in choice (B) is both N's second day and a day on which K is scheduled.

That leaves only the correct answer, choice (C), the one answer that's violation-free.

19. **(E)**

If Kevin and Paul work Thursday, who must work Friday?

(A) Janice
(B) Kevin
(C) Nan
(D) Paul
(E) Seymour[24]

	Mon	Tue	Wed	Thur	Fri
Super	___	___	___	P	___
(either)	___	O	O	K	S

Figure 17.68

This question rewards you for understanding Rules 4 and 5. The relationship of the "if" in the question stem to those rules is made absolutely clear once you start your mini-sketch. Copy the framework, and put P and K in the Thursday column.

	Mon	Tue	Wed	Thur	Fri
Super	___	___	___	P	___
(either)	___	O	O	K	___

Figure 17.69

You know from Rule 5 that Thursday must be P's first day for the week. That, in turn, triggers Rule 4. S cannot work prior to P's first day. Since S cannot work with P on Thursday in this question, he must work on Friday.

	Mon	Tue	Wed	Thur	Fri
Super	___	___	___	P	___
(either)	___	O	O	K	S

Figure 17.70

That matches the correct answer, choice (E).

---

[24] PrepTest 47, Sec. 4, Q 19

20. **(B)**

Each of the following could be true EXCEPT:
(A)   Janice works Monday and Tuesday.
(B)   Kevin and Paul work Friday.
(C)   Seymour works Monday and Friday.
(D)   Janice and Kevin work Thursday.
(E)   Paul works Monday and Friday.[25]

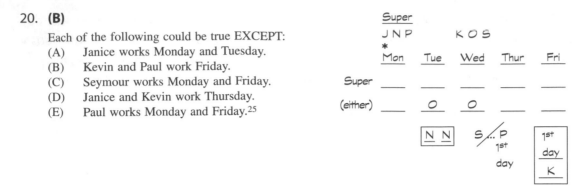

Figure 17.71

For this question, characterize the answer choices and then evaluate each against the rules and the Master Sketch. The correct answer here *must be false*. Each of the wrong answers *could be true*.

Choice (A) *could be true*. In fact, J is the floater, with no restrictions at all in the setup or rules.

Choice (B) *must be false*, so it's the correct answer. If K and P work together on Friday, there's no room in the schedule for S. This answer works just like the "if" from question 19, except that K and P are moved one day later in the week. But just like the preceding question, you're rewarded for understanding how Rules 4 and 5 work together.

You can check the remaining choices if you like, but you know that each will produce an acceptable result. On test day, you should stop once you find choice (B), the *must be false* answer.

21. **(A)**

Which one of the following CANNOT be the pair of staff that works Monday?
(A)   Janice and Seymour
(B)   Kevin and Paul
(C)   Paul and Seymour
(D)   Nan and Ophelia
(E)   Janice and Nan[26]

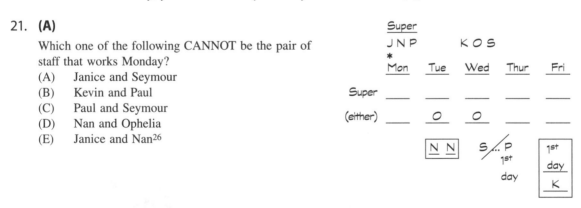

Figure 17.72

The last two questions had you looking at the end of the week. This one puts the focus on the beginning of the week. The correct answer is an unacceptable pair of employees for Monday. As soon as you see choice (A), you're done. Rule 4 tells you that S may not work prior to P's first day. Since choice (A) schedules S on Monday with someone other than P, this answer is unacceptable.

---

[25] PrepTest 47, Sec. 4, Q 20
[26] PrepTest 47, Sec. 4, Q 21

The pairs in the remaining choices are all fine for Monday assignments. You'll notice that choice (C) also schedules S, but this time, the other employee is P, so there's no violation of Rule 4.

22. **(B)**

Which one of the following could be true?
(A) Nan works Wednesday and Friday only.
(B) Seymour works Monday and Paul works Tuesday.
(C) Kevin works Monday, Wednesday, and Friday.
(D) Nan works Wednesday with Ophelia and Thursday with Kevin.
(E) Ophelia and Kevin work Tuesday.[27]

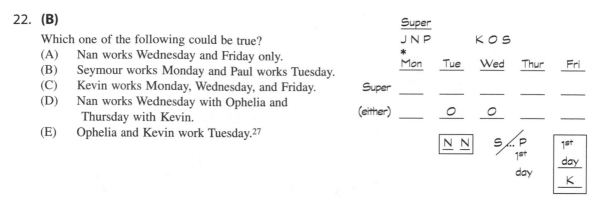

Figure 17.73

The stem for this final question is simple, but as you'll see, the correct answer has a trick up its sleeve. The correct answer here *could be true*. That means the four wrong answers *must be false*.

Choice (A) must be false. Rule 3 requires that N be scheduled on consecutive days at some point in the week, but here, her two days are non consecutive.

Choice (B) could be true. This is the correct answer. Rule 4 requires that if S works on Monday, then so does P. That rule doesn't forbid P from working on other days, too. Most test takers who miss this answer do so because they *misread* this answer. It does not say that Tuesday is P's first or only day.

For the record:

Choice (C) must be false. Any day on which K works must be the other employee's first day of the week (Rule 5). Wednesday is, at least, O's second day. Also, if K and O are the employees scheduled for a given day, there's no room for a supervisor on that day.

Choice (D) must be false. This answer, too, violates Rule 5 by having Kevin work alongside N on her second day.

Choice (E) must be false. Neither K nor O is a supervisor, and Rule 1 requires that a supervisor be scheduled each day.

[27] PrepTest 47, Sec. 4, Q 22

CHAPTER 18

FULL-LENGTH SECTION II[1]

Time—35 minutes
22 Questions

Directions: Each group of questions in this section is based on a set of conditions. In answering some of the questions, it may be useful to draw a rough diagram. Choose the response that most accurately and completely answers each question and blacken the corresponding space on your answer sheet.

---

[1] PrepTest 50, Sec. 3

Questions 1–5

At each of six consecutive stops—1, 2, 3, 4, 5, and 6—that a traveler must make in that order as part of a trip, she can choose one from among exactly four airlines—L, M, N, and O—on which to continue. Her choices must conform to the following constraints:

Whichever airline she chooses at a stop, she chooses one of the other airlines at the next stop.

She chooses the same airline at stop 1 as she does at stop 6.

She chooses the same airline at stop 2 as she does at stop 4.

Whenever she chooses either L or M at a stop, she does not choose N at the next stop.

At stop 5, she chooses N or O.

1. Which one of the following could be an accurate list of the airlines the traveler chooses at each stop, in order from 1 through 6?

   (A) L, M, M, L, O, L
   (B) M, L, O, M, O, M
   (C) M, N, O, N, O, M
   (D) M, O, N, O, N, M
   (E) O, M, L, M, O, N

2. If the traveler chooses N at stop 5, which one of the following could be an accurate list of the airlines she chooses at stops 1, 2, and 3, respectively?

   (A) L, M, N
   (B) L, O, N
   (C) M, L, N
   (D) M, L, O
   (E) N, O, N

3. If the only airlines the traveler chooses for the trip are M, N, and O, and she chooses O at stop 5, then the airlines she chooses at stops 1, 2, and 3, must be, respectively,

   (A) M, O, and N
   (B) M, N, and O
   (C) N, M, and O
   (D) N, O, and M
   (E) O, M, and N

4. Which one of the following CANNOT be an accurate list of the airlines the traveler chooses at stops 1 and 2, respectively?

   (A) L, M
   (B) L, O
   (C) M, L
   (D) M, O
   (E) O, N

5. If the traveler chooses O at stop 2, which one of the following could be an accurate list of the airlines she chooses at stops 5 and 6, respectively?

   (A) M, N
   (B) N, L
   (C) N, O
   (D) O, L
   (E) O, N

Questions 6–11

The members of a five-person committee will be selected from among three parents—F, G, and H—three students—K, L, and M—and four teachers—U, W, X, and Z. The selection of committee members will meet the following conditions:

The committee must include exactly one student.
F and H cannot both be selected.
M and Z cannot both be selected.
U and W cannot both be selected.
F cannot be selected unless Z is also selected.
W cannot be selected unless H is also selected.

6. Which one of the following is an acceptable selection of committee members?

   (A) F, G, K, L, Z
   (B) F, G, K, U, X
   (C) G, K, W, X, Z
   (D) H, K, U, W, X
   (E) H, L, W, X, Z

7. If W and Z are selected, which one of the following is a pair of people who could also be selected?

   (A) U and X
   (B) K and L
   (C) G and M
   (D) G and K
   (E) F and G

8. Which one of the following is a pair of people who CANNOT both be selected?

   (A) F and G
   (B) F and M
   (C) G and K
   (D) H and L
   (E) M and U

9. If W is selected, then any one of the following could also be selected EXCEPT:

   (A) F
   (B) G
   (C) L
   (D) M
   (E) Z

10. If the committee is to include exactly one parent, which one of the following is a person who must also be selected?

    (A) K
    (B) L
    (C) M
    (D) U
    (E) X

11. If M is selected, then the committee must also include both

    (A) F and G
    (B) G and H
    (C) H and K
    (D) K and U
    (E) U and X

Questions 12–17

Within a five-year period from 1991 to 1995, each of three friends—Ramon, Sue, and Taylor—graduated. In that period, each bought his or her first car. The graduations and car purchases must be consistent with the following:

Ramon graduated in some year before the year in which Taylor graduated.

Taylor graduated in some year before the year in which he bought his first car.

Sue bought her first car in some year before the year in which she graduated.

Ramon and Sue graduated in the same year as each other.

At least one of the friends graduated in 1993.

12. Which one of the following could be an accurate matching of each friend and the year in which she or he graduated?

    (A)   Ramon: 1991; Sue: 1991; Taylor: 1993
    (B)   Ramon: 1992; Sue: 1992; Taylor: 1993
    (C)   Ramon: 1992; Sue: 1993; Taylor: 1994
    (D)   Ramon: 1993; Sue: 1993; Taylor: 1992
    (E)   Ramon: 1993; Sue: 1993; Taylor: 1995

13. Which one of the following could have taken place in 1995?

    (A)   Ramon graduated.
    (B)   Ramon bought his first car.
    (C)   Sue graduated.
    (D)   Sue bought her first car.
    (E)   Taylor graduated.

14. Which one of the following must be false?

    (A)   Two of the friends each bought his or her first car in 1991.
    (B)   Two of the friends each bought his or her first car in 1992.
    (C)   Two of the friends each bought his or her first car in 1993.
    (D)   Two of the friends each bought his or her first car in 1994.
    (E)   Two of the friends each bought his or her first car in 1995.

15. Which one of the following must be true?

    (A)   None of the three friends graduated in 1991.
    (B)   None of the three friends graduated in 1992.
    (C)   None of the three friends bought his or her first car in 1993.
    (D)   None of the three friends graduated in 1994.
    (E)   None of the three friends bought his or her first car in 1995.

16. If Taylor graduated in the same year that Ramon bought his first car, then each of the following could be true EXCEPT:

    (A)   Sue bought her first car in 1991.
    (B)   Ramon graduated in 1992.
    (C)   Taylor graduated in 1993.
    (D)   Taylor bought his first car in 1994.
    (E)   Ramon bought his first car in 1995.

17. If Sue graduated in 1993, then which one of the following must be true?

    (A)   Sue bought her first car in 1991.
    (B)   Ramon bought his first car in 1992.
    (C)   Ramon bought his first car in 1993.
    (D)   Taylor bought his first car in 1994.
    (E)   Taylor bought his first car in 1995.

Questions 18–22

A child eating alphabet soup notices that the only letters left in her bowl are one each of these six letters: T, U, W, X, Y, and Z. She plays a game with the remaining letters, eating them in the next three spoonfuls in accord with certain rules. Each of the six letters must be in exactly one of the next three spoonfuls, and each of the spoonfuls must have at least one and at most three of the letters. In addition, she obeys the following restrictions:

The U is in a later spoonful than the T.
The U is not in a later spoonful than the X.
The Y is in a later spoonful than the W.
The U is in the same spoonful as either the Y or the Z, but not both.

18. Which one of the following could be an accurate list of the spoonfuls and the letters in each of them?

    (A) first: Y
         second: T, W
         third: U, X, Z
    (B) first: T, W
         second: U, X, Y
         third: Z
    (C) first: T
         second: U, Z
         third: W, X, Y
    (D) first: T, U, Z
         second: W
         third: X, Y
    (E) first: W
         second: T, X, Z
         third: U, Y

19. If the Y is the only letter in one of the spoonfuls, then which one of the following could be true?

    (A) The Y is in the first spoonful.
    (B) The Z is in the first spoonful.
    (C) The T is in the second spoonful.
    (D) The X is in the second spoonful.
    (E) The W is in the third spoonful.

20. If the Z is in the first spoonful, then which one of the following must be true?

    (A) The T is in the second spoonful.
    (B) The U is in the third spoonful.
    (C) The W is in the first spoonful.
    (D) The W is in the second spoonful.
    (E) The X is in the third spoonful.

21. Which one of the following is a complete list of letters, any one of which could be the only letter in the first spoonful?

    (A) T
    (B) T, W
    (C) T, X
    (D) T, W, Z
    (E) T, X, W, Z

22. If the T is in the second spoonful, then which one of the following could be true?

    (A) Exactly two letters are in the first spoonful.
    (B) Exactly three letters are in the first spoonful.
    (C) Exactly three letters are in the second spoonful.
    (D) Exactly one letter is in the third spoonful.
    (E) Exactly two letters are in the third spoonful.

ANSWER KEY

1.	D	9.	A	17.	E
2.	B	10.	E	18.	B
3.	C	11.	B	19.	D
4.	E	12.	B	20.	E
5.	B	13.	B	21.	D
6.	E	14.	C	22.	A
7.	D	15.	A		
8.	B	16.	E		

TRIAGE REVIEW

This section mixes in some variations on the standard game types. Remember not to assume that twists necessarily make games harder. Concreteness (above all), along with simplicity and brevity, is what indicates the easier games.

Game 1 is a Strict Sequencing game, but you have only four entities to fill six spaces. You know you'll re-use at least one of the entities as you schedule the traveler's flights. Still, with five rules and a fairly balanced question set, you should be able to make some headway on the acceptable arrangements in the Rules and Deductions steps.

Game 2 is a Selection game with definite numbers. You're tasked with choosing five committee members from among nine people who are divided into three subcategories. While Selection with definite numbers and subgroups is less common than a simple "choose some of the entities" Selection task, the restrictions involved here indicate a game that won't be inordinately challenging.

Game 3 is Double Sequencing. You must decide the order in which certain people graduated and the order in which they got their first cars. This game isn't likely to be the easiest in the set, but with five rules, it won't be unmanageable either.

Game 4 is a Hybrid of Distribution and Sequencing. The setup looks long and complicated, so you'll need to make sure that you understand and sketch the task appropriately. Look for help from the number restrictions. There are only a handful of ways to split six entities up into three groups.

You will likely be best served taking the two Sequencing games—Game 1 and Game 3—first. Then you could take Game 2 and finish up with Game 4. If you know that Selection is your weakest area, you may reasonably decide to take Game 4 before Game 2. Otherwise, 1-3-2-4 is probably your optimal order.

EXPLANATIONS
Game 1—Flights and Airlines
Questions 1–5

At each of six consecutive stops—1, 2, 3, 4, 5, and 6—that a traveler must make in that order as part of a trip, she can choose one from among exactly four airlines—L, M, N, and O—on which to continue. Her choices must conform to the following constraints:

>Whichever airline she chooses at a stop, she chooses one of the other airlines at the next stop.
>She chooses the same airline at stop 1 as she does at stop 6.
>She chooses the same airline at stop 2 as she does at stop 4.
>Whenever she chooses either L or M at a stop, she does not choose N at the next stop.
>At stop 5, she chooses N or O.[2]

STEPS 1 AND 2: Overview and Sketch

It's not hard to picture your task. Just imagine yourself planning out a business trip with six destinations. For each, you have to decide which airline to fly to the next stop. There is nothing special about the departure points; they're just called stops 1–6. Several of the rules mention specific stops, so a standard Strict Sequencing framework is called for.

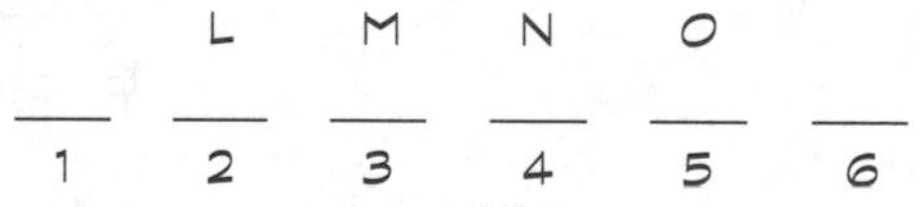

$$\begin{array}{cccccc}
\text{L} & \text{M} & \text{N} & \text{O} & & \\
\underline{} & \underline{} & \underline{} & \underline{} & \underline{} & \underline{} \\
1 & 2 & 3 & 4 & 5 & 6
\end{array}$$

Figure 18.1

The twist comes from the fact that there are only four airlines to choose from. So one or more of the entities (the airlines) will appear more than once in the list of flights. It is essential that you notice that there is no requirement that all four airlines be used. Remember never to impose restrictions that aren't explicit in the game's setup and rules.

STEP 3: Rules

Rule 1 is simple but important: You can't use the same airline at consecutive stops.

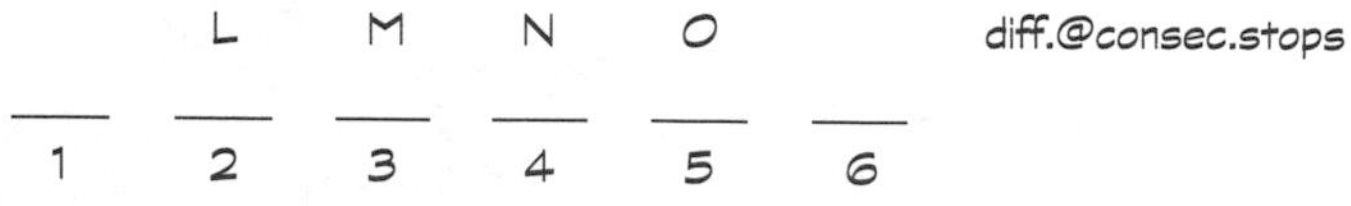

$$\begin{array}{ccccccc}
\text{L} & \text{M} & \text{N} & \text{O} & & & \text{diff.@consec.stops} \\
\underline{} & \underline{} & \underline{} & \underline{} & \underline{} & \underline{} & \\
1 & 2 & 3 & 4 & 5 & 6 &
\end{array}$$

Figure 18.2

Rule 2 tells you to use the same airline at stops 1 and 6.

---

[2] PrepTest 50, Sec. 3, Game 1

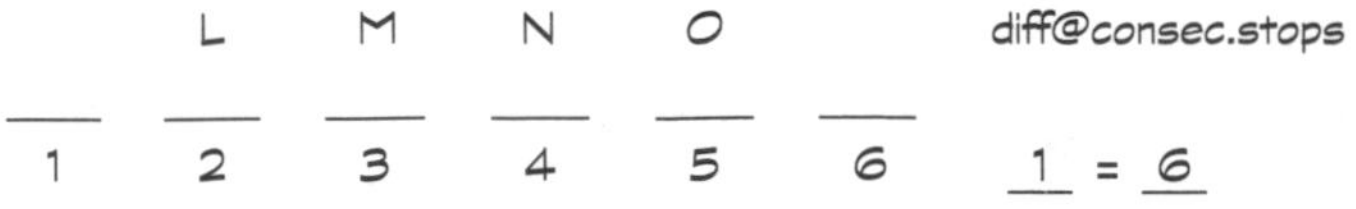

Figure 18.3

Rule 3 offers the same restriction as Rule 2, this time for stops 2 and 4.

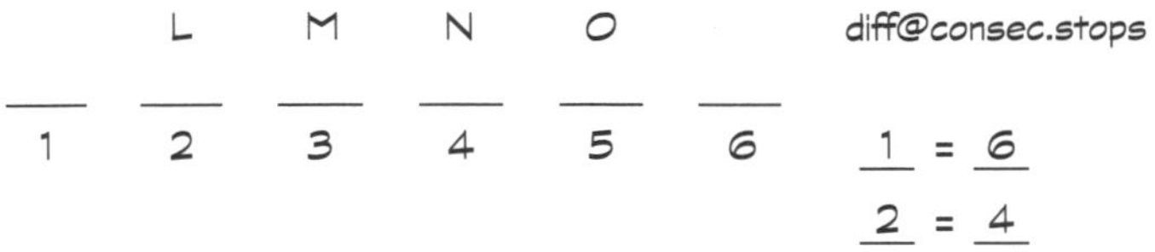

Figure 18.4

Rule 4 creates two "anti-blocks." Airline N can't be at the next stop after either airline L or airline M is used.

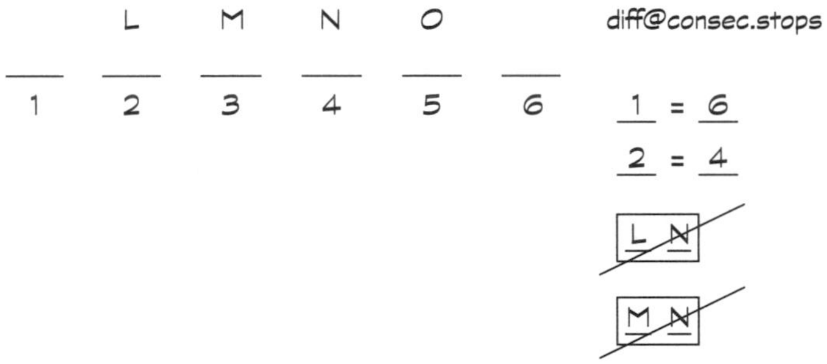

Figure 18.5

Rule 5 creates a Limited Options scenario based on the airline used for stop 5.

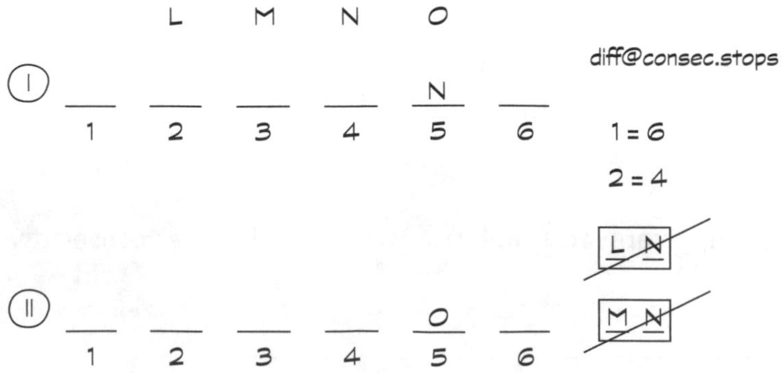

Figure 18.6

There are no floaters in the game. So move on to deductions. It's pretty clear that the Limited Options will provide the starting point for additional exploration of this game's restrictions.

STEP 4: Deductions

Start with Option I, where N is the airline at stop 5. Rule 4 makes it clear that neither L nor M can be the airline at stop 4, while Rule 1 excludes the possibility of having N at consecutive stops, so you must use O there.

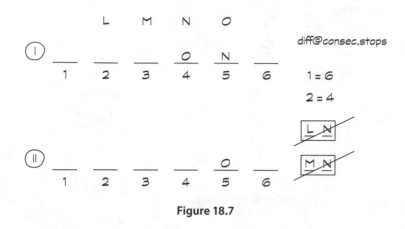

Figure 18.7

Placing O in stop 4 triggers Rule 3. O must be the airline at stop 2 as well.

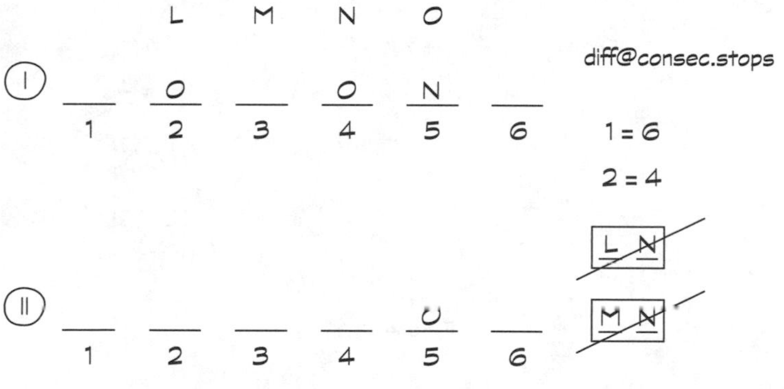

Figure 18.8

Don't forget the implications of Rule 1 for this option. Since N is at stop 5, it cannot be used again at stop 6. Likewise, since O is at stop 2, it can't be used again at stops 1 or 3.

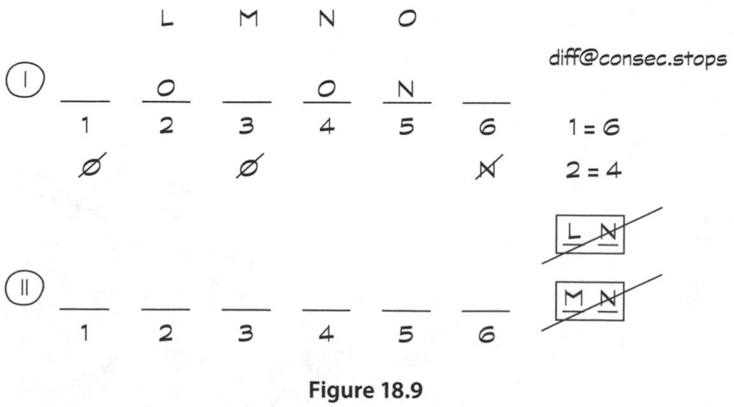

Figure 18.9

Since Rule 2 requires the same airline for stops 1 and 6, you now know that those two stops will use either airline L or airline M.

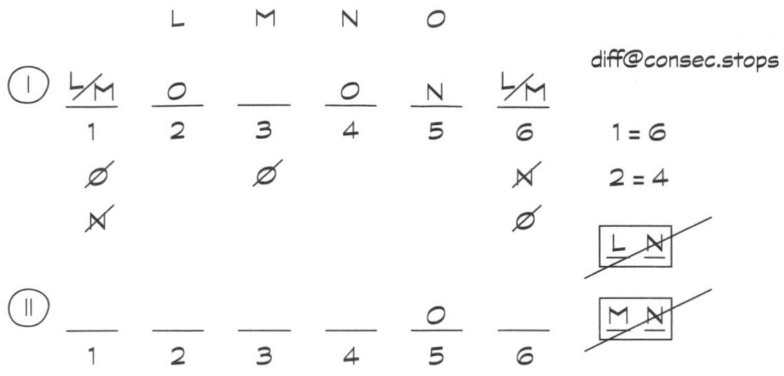

Figure 18.10

Only stop 3 has more than two possibilities in this option.

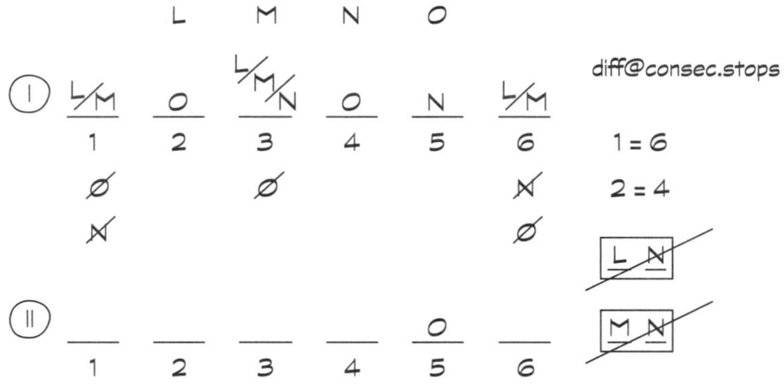

Figure 18.11

In Option II, you can't make nearly as much headway. With O used at stop 5, you know it will not be used at either stop 4 or stop 6.

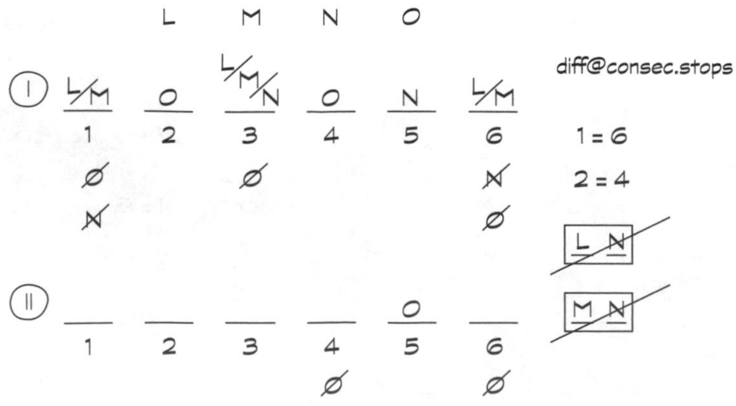

Figure 18.12

By extension, Rules 2 and 3 mean that O cannot be the airline for stops 1 or 2 either.

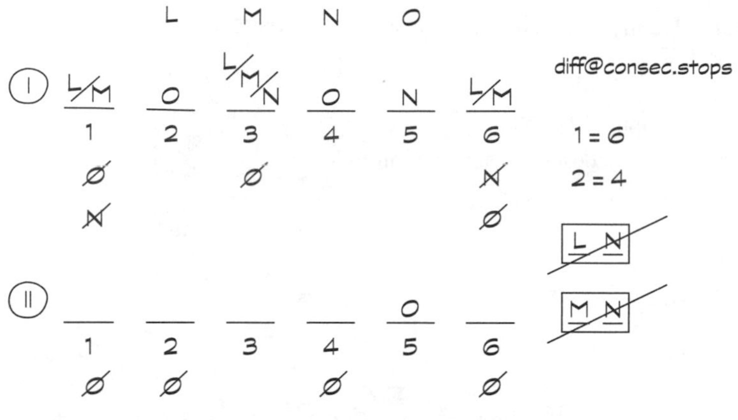

Figure 18.13

Since airline O is the only one that can be used at a stop immediately preceding a stop of N's, you can conclude that airline N will not be used at stops 2 or 3. And of course, if N isn't the airline at stop 2, it cannot be the airline for stop 4 (Rule 3).

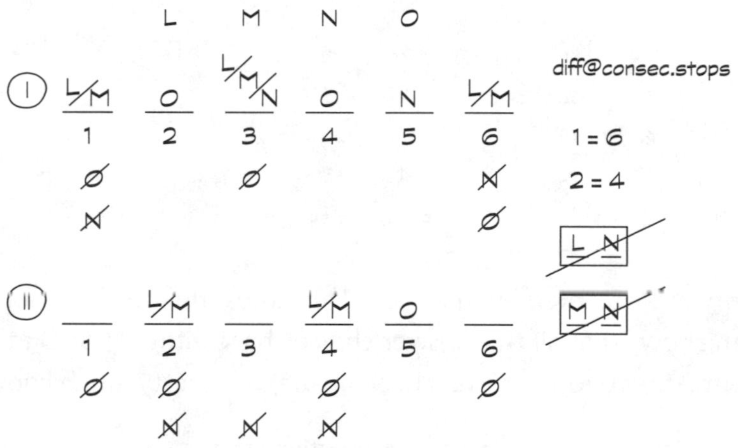

Figure 18.14

That last deduction brings home the value of always asking about both the positive and the negative implications of any restriction found in a logic game. Once you're aware that one arrangement cannot happen, ask, "Well, then, what can?" Once you find an affirmative requirement, ask, "And what does that rule out?"

Even with fewer affirmative deductions in Option II, you have a lot of certainty in this game. This Master Sketch should make the questions a snap.

STEP 5: Questions

There are three "If" questions in this set, but each of them should put you into one or the other of the options, dramatically reducing the amount of resketching you'll need.

1. **(D)**

    Which one of the following could be an accurate list of the airlines the traveler chooses at each stop, in order from 1 through 6?

    (A)   L, M, M, L, O, L
    (B)   M, L, O, M, O, M
    (C)   M, N, O, N, O, M
    (D)   M, O, N, O, N, M
    (E)   O, M, L, M, O, N[3]

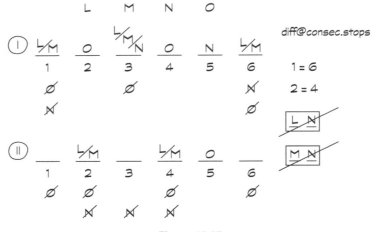

Figure 18.15

This is a straightforward Acceptability question. The easiest rule to check for violations is Rule 5. But a quick scan shows that all five answer choices have either N or O at stop 5. With four rules left to check and four wrong answers to eliminate, you pretty much know what to expect.

Rule 1 eliminates choice (A); M appears at consecutive stops.

Rule 2 eliminates choice (E); O flies from stop 1, but N from stop 6.

Rule 3 gets rid of choice (B); L flies from stop 2 and M from stop 4.

Rule 4 knocks out the final violator, choice (C); airline M immediately precedes airline N at stops 1 and 2, respectively.

That leaves only the correct answer, choice (D).

---

[3] PrepTest 50, Sec. 3, Q 1

2. **(B)**

If the traveler chooses N at stop 5, which one of the following could be an accurate list of the airlines she chooses at stops 1, 2, and 3, respectively?

(A)   L, M, N
(B)   L, O, N
(C)   M, L, N
(D)   M, L, O
(E)   N, O, N[4]

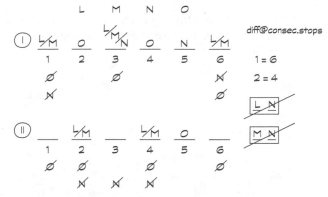

Figure 18.16

This question's new "if" condition simply tells you, "Consult Option I." Do so, and choose the one answer that would be acceptable for stops 1–3 there. Glancing at your Master Sketch, you see that airline O must fly from stop 2 in Option I. That allows you to strike through choices (A), (C), and (D). Since either airline L or airline M must fly from stop 1 in Option I, you can eliminate choice (E), too. The correct answer is choice (B), just that fast.

3. **(C)**

If the only airlines the traveler chooses for the trip are M, N, and O, and she chooses O at stop 5, then the airlines she chooses at stops 1, 2, and 3, must be, respectively,

(A)   M, O, and N
(B)   M, N, and O
(C)   N, M, and O
(D)   N, O, and M
(E)   O, M, and N[5]

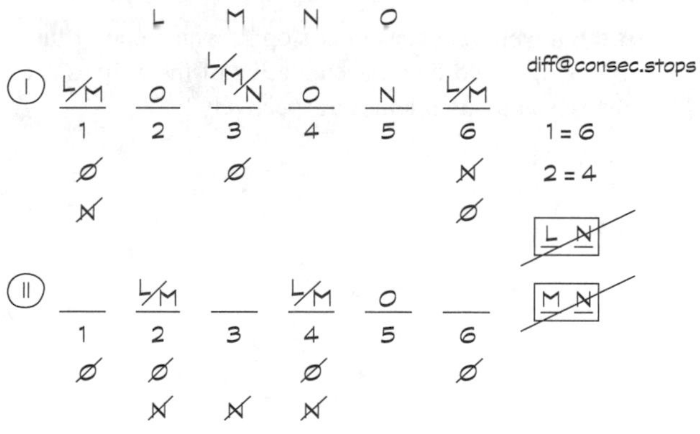

Figure 18.17

There are two parts to the "if" in this question. Take the second clause of the stem—"she chooses O at stop 5"—first. That puts you in Option II. Now, consider the first clause in light of Option II. If you use only airlines M, N, and O in this option, the first two airlines you use

4 PrepTest 50, Sec. 3, Q 2
5 PrepTest 50, Sec. 3, Q 3

must be N and M, respectively. The only choice that begins "N, M" is choice (C). That's the right answer and you can move on.

4. **(E)**

    Which one of the following CANNOT be an accurate list of the airlines the traveler chooses at stops 1 and 2, respectively?

    (A)   L, M
    (B)   L, O
    (C)   M, L
    (D)   M, O
    (E)   O, N[6]

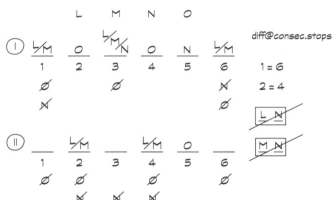

Figure 18.18

This question does not have an "if" clause. You need to consider both options here. The correct answer is the one with an unacceptable pair of airlines for stops 1 and 2. Stop 2 is the easier one to check. It can have only airline O in Option I and only airlines L or M in Option II. In other words, airline N can never be used at stop 2. That, by itself, is enough to show that choice (E) is impossible and, therefore, the correct answer.

5. **(B)**

    If the traveler chooses O at stop 2, which one of the following could be an accurate list of the airlines she chooses at stops 5 and 6, respectively?

    (A)   M, N
    (B)   N, L
    (C)   N, O
    (D)   O, L
    (E)   O, N[7]

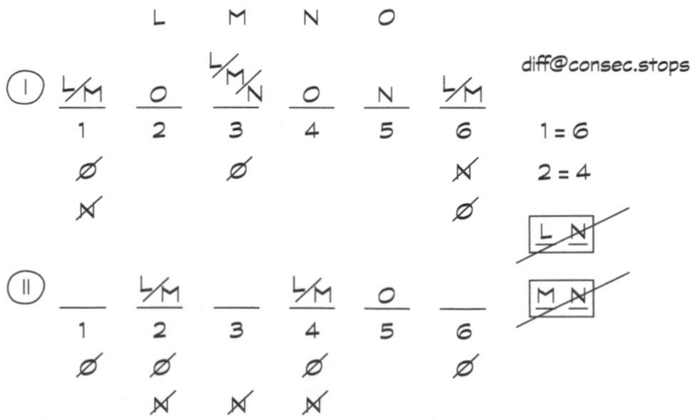

Figure 18.19

---

[6] PrepTest 50, Sec. 3, Q 4

[7] PrepTest 50, Sec. 3, Q 5

Once again, the "if" condition makes it clear which option you may use. Choosing airline O at stop 2 is tantamount to saying, "Use Option I." Now that you know which option to employ, consider the rest of the question stem. It calls for airlines acceptable at stops 5 and 6, respectively. In Option I, airline N must be used at stop 5. Eliminate choices (A), (D), and (E). Airlines L and M are the only acceptable choices for stop 6 in Option I. Choice (C) is thus unacceptable, but choice (B) works just fine. It's the correct answer.

That game looked a little unusual at first with just four entities for six spaces. Once you made your way through the rules, however, the possibility of Limited Options sketches emerged and the result was an extremely helpful set of deductions. If you were patient enough to create a complete Master Sketch, you may even have been able to complete the question set quickly enough to bank some time for the tougher games later in the section.

Game 2—Student-Parent-Teacher Committee

Questions 6–11

> The members of a five-person committee will be selected
> from among three parents—F, G, and H—three
> students—K, L, and M—and four teachers—U, W,
> X, and Z. The selection of committee members will meet
> the following conditions:
>> The committee must include exactly one student.
>> F and H cannot both be selected.
>> M and Z cannot both be selected.
>> U and W cannot both be selected.
>> F cannot be selected unless Z is also selected.
>> W cannot be selected unless H is also selected.[8]

STEPS 1 AND 2: Overview and Sketch

Here, your task is to select the members of a 5-person committee from among 10 people. The people are designated as parents, students, or teachers. So you can anticipate that the game will impose restrictions on how many of the committee's members can come from one or more of the subgroups. Make sure your roster of entities reflects the subgroups.

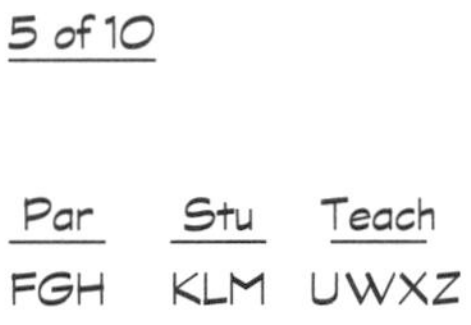

5 of 10

Par	Stu	Teach
FGH	KLM	UWXZ

Figure 18.20

You'll circle the chosen entities and strike through the rejected ones, just as you would in any Selection game. It's a good idea to write "5 of 10" near the roster so that you remember the specific number restriction in this game.

STEP 3: Rules

With the entities divided into subgroups, you can anticipate that one or more of the rules will limit the number of entities you can select from each subgroup. Indeed, that's exactly what Rule 1 tells you.

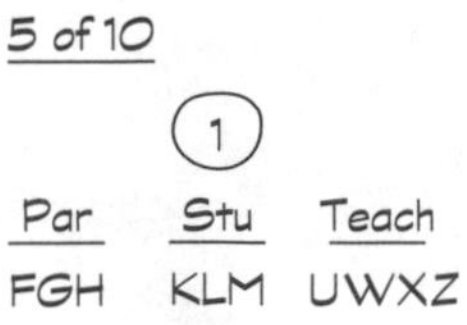

5 of 10

①

Par	Stu	Teach
FGH	KLM	UWXZ

Figure 18.21

---

[8] PrepTest 50, Sec. 3, Game 2

That rule will prove to be the most important in the Deductions step, but get the other restrictions down first. Then circle back and consider them in light of the number restrictions.

Rules 2, 3, and 4 each create "impossible pairs."

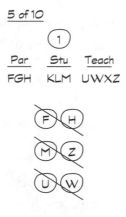

Figure 18.22

The last two rules are routine formal logic statements. Translate them and diagram the contrapositives as you learned to do in chapter 3.

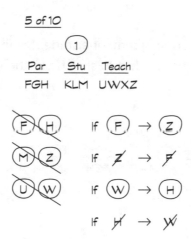

Figure 18.23

With your sketch at this point, you would be able to work your way through all of the questions, albeit somewhat slowly. With a little attention to the number restrictions, you'll be able to breeze through this question set.

STEP 4: **Deductions**

Rule 1 provides a clear limit; just one student must serve on the committee. That leaves four committee members to account for.

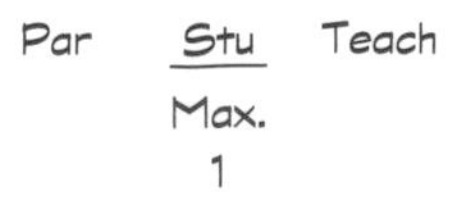

Par   Stu   Teach
      Max.
       1

Figure 18.24

Rule 2 limits you to using just one or two parents on the committee. Since F and H cannot serve together, there is no way you can use all three parents.

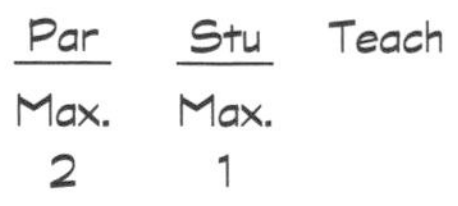

Par   Stu   Teach
Max.   Max.
 2   1

Figure 18.25

Rule 4 has a comparable effect on the teacher subgroup. Since U and W cannot serve together, you can have at most three teachers on the committee.

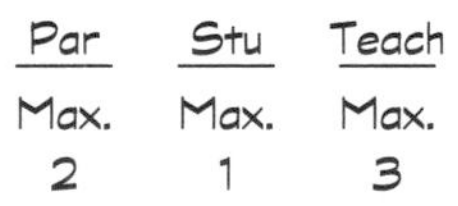

Par   Stu   Teach
Max.   Max.   Max.
 2   1   3

Figure 18.25A

Thus, you have only two options: one parent, one student, and three teachers; or two parents, one student, and two teachers. It's worth it to sketch out the implications of each option.

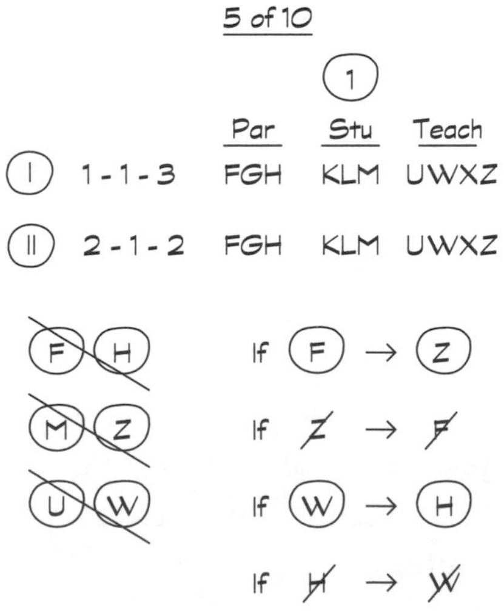

5 of 10

(1)

Par   Stu   Teach
I   1-1-3   FGH   KLM   UWXZ
II   2-1-2   FGH   KLM   UWXZ

F̶X̶H̶   If F → Z
M̶X̶Z̶   If Z̶ → F̶
U̶X̶W̶   If W → H
               If H̶ → W̶

Figure 18.26

In Option I, the teachers will have to be X, Z, and one of U or W.

5 of 10
Par Stu Teach
I 1-1-3 FGH KLM UWXZ
II 2-1-2 FGH KLM UWXZ
F H
M Z
U W
If F → Z
If Z → F
If W → H
If H → W

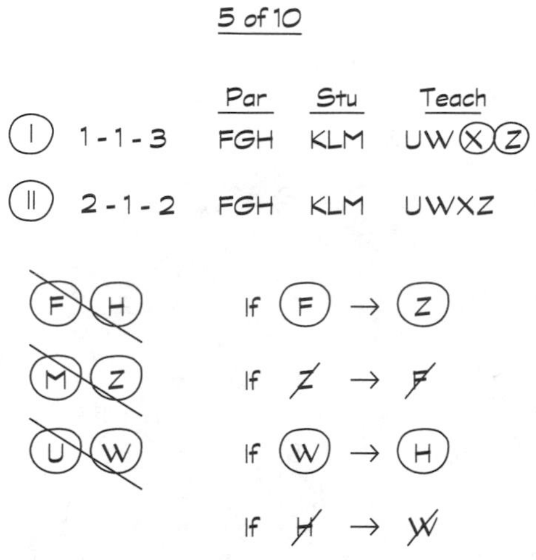

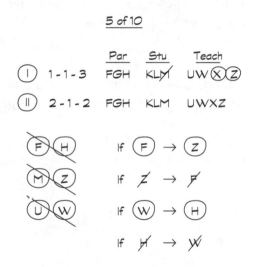

Figure 18.27

Because Z is included among the teachers on the committee, M cannot be the student (Rule 3).

5 of 10
Par Stu Teach
I 1-1-3 FGH KLM UWXZ
II 2-1-2 FGH KLM UWXZ
F H
M Z
U W
If F → Z
If Z → F
If W → H
If H → W

Figure 18.28

Any one of the three parents can serve on the committee in Option I, though if the parent is not H, the third teacher will have to be U, not W (Rule 6).

In Option II, you can't make as many additions to the sketch. Using Rule 2, you know that the parents will be G and either F or H.

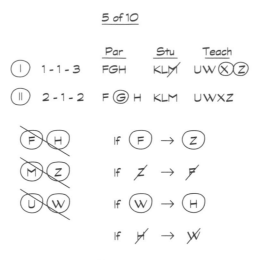

Figure 18.29

The remaining selections in Option II will depend on the "impossible pairs" restricted by Rules 3 and 4 and on the formal logic in Rules 5 and 6. That's too speculative to pursue without some additional information. Move on to the questions.

STEP 5: Questions

This question set contains a standard Acceptability question, a Must Be False question, and four "If" questions, some of which may guide you to one or the other of the two options.

6. **(E)**

Which one of the following is an acceptable selection of committee members?

(A) F, G, K, L, Z
(B) F, G, K, U, X
(C) G, K, W, X, Z
(D) H, K, U, W, X
(E) H, L, W, X, Z[9]

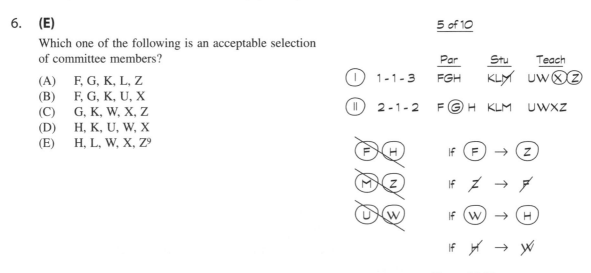

Figure 18.30

This is a typical Acceptability question. Test the rules one at a time, and cross off any answer that breaks a rule.

Rule 1 eliminates choice (A), which includes two students, K and L.

[9] PrepTest 50, Sec. 3, Q 6

Rule 2 isn't broken in any of the choices.

Nor is Rule 3 violated anywhere.

Rule 4, though, eliminates choice (D), which has both U and W.

Rule 5 eliminates choice (B), where F is included without Z.

Finally, Rule 6 takes out choice (C); there, W is included without H.

That leaves the correct answer, choice (E).

7. **(D)**

If W and Z are selected, which one of the
following is a pair of people who could also be
selected?

(A)   U and X
(B)   K and L
(C)   G and M
(D)   G and K
(E)   F and G[10]

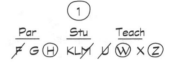

Figure 18.31

The "if" from this question's stem doesn't automatically limit you to one of the options, so build a mini-sketch to see the implications of the new condition. Start with the entity list and circle W and Z.

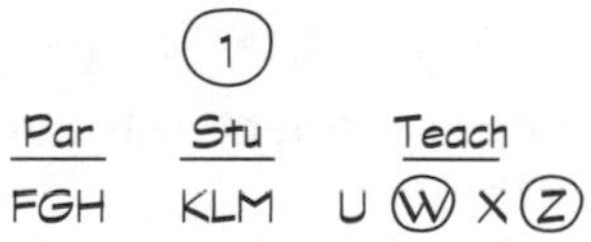

$$\textcircled{1}$$

Par	Stu	Teach
FGH	KLM	U $\textcircled{W}$ X $\textcircled{Z}$

Figure 18.32

Including Z triggers Rule 3. Cross M off the list.

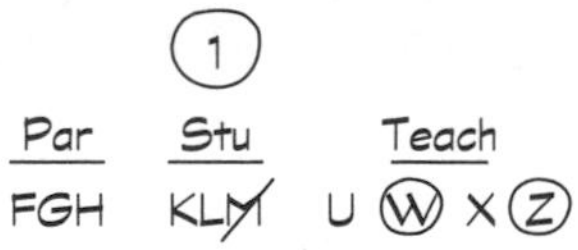

$$\textcircled{1}$$

Par	Stu	Teach
FGH	KL̶M̶	U $\textcircled{W}$ X $\textcircled{Z}$

Figure 18.33

Including W triggers Rule 4. Get rid of U.

---

[10] PrepTest 50, Sec. 3, Q 7

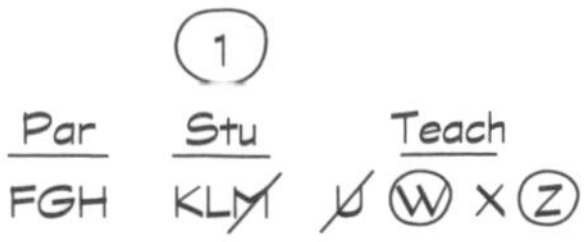

Figure 18.34

W's inclusion also triggers the formal logic in Rule 6. You must select H in this question.

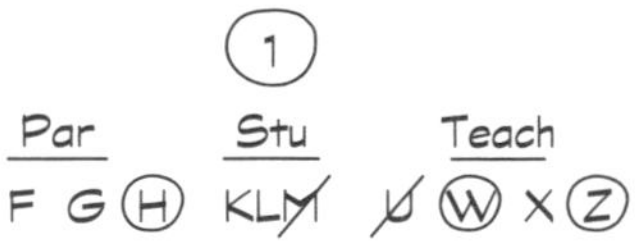

Figure 18.35

H is incompatible with F according to Rule 1. So strike F off the list here.

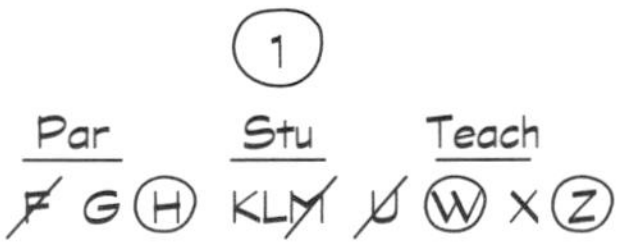

Figure 18.36

It's still impossible to tell which option you're in, but you can't push the deductions any further. Go ahead and characterize the answer choices. The correct answer is a pair of entities that can both be selected. That means each wrong answer will include at least one entity that cannot be selected or will be a pair that cannot be selected together.

Get rid of any answer that includes an entity you've already crossed off the list. That eliminates choice (A), which includes U, choice (C), which includes M, and choice (E), which includes F.

Which of the remaining choices is impossible? That's choice (B), which has two students. You know from Rule 1 that only one student will serve on the committee. Cross out choice (B), leaving only the correct answer, choice (D). G and K can both serve on the committee under the conditions given in this question stem.

8. **(B)**

Which one of the following is a pair of people who CANNOT both be selected?

(A) F and G
(B) F and M
(C) G and K
(D) H and L
(E) M and U[11]

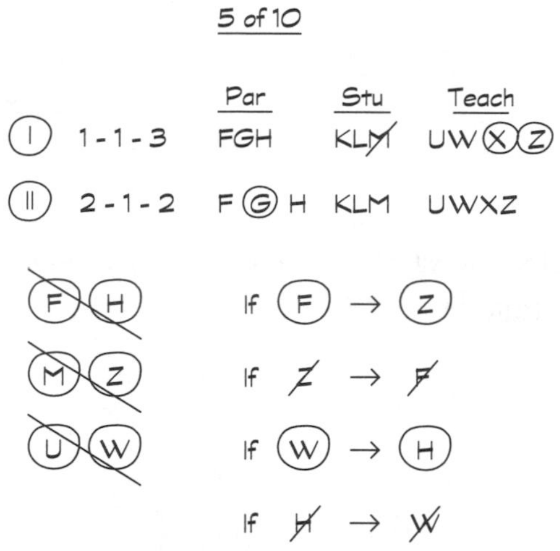

Figure 18.37

If you find yourself struggling with this question or tempted to just start writing out mini-sketches in an attempt to test each answer, slow down and take a more strategic approach. The correct answer is an "impossible pair"—two entities who cannot serve together on the committee. That means each of the four wrong answers contains an acceptable pair. You can eliminate any answer choices that contain pairs you've already seen in acceptable arrangements. Thus, you can get rid of choice (D). After all, H and L both appear in the correct answer to question 6; that choice is, by definition, an acceptable arrangement. You can also get rid of choice (C); G and K were acceptable as a pair in the correct answer to question 7.

From here, you can either wait until you finish the remaining "If" questions to see if they help you eliminate other acceptable pairs or you can test the remaining answer choices. Either way, you'll find that the correct answer—with the "impossible pair"—is choice (B). When F is selected, Z must be as well (Rule 5); and Z cannot serve with M (Rule 3). Thus, F and M cannot serve together on the committee.

9. **(A)**

If W is selected, then any one of the following could also be selected EXCEPT:

(A) F
(B) G
(C) L
(D) M
(E) Z[12]

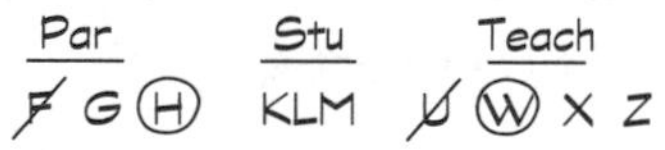

Figure 18.38

Selecting W does not, by itself, place you in either of the Limited Options. So copy out the list of entities and circle W.

---

[11] PrepTest 50, Sec. 3, Q 8
[12] PrepTest 50, Sec. 3, Q 9

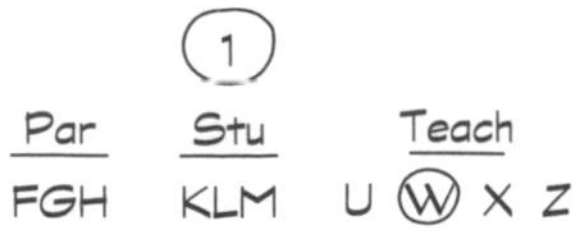

$$\text{①}$$

Par	Stu	Teach
FGH	KLM	U Ⓦ X Z

Figure 18.39

Selecting W has two direct consequences: You must eliminate U (Rule 4), and you must include H (Rule 6).

Par	Stu	Teach
F G Ⓗ	KLM	~~U~~ Ⓦ X Z

Figure 18.40

Selecting H triggers Rule 2. You must reject F in this case.

Par	Stu	Teach
~~F~~ G Ⓗ	KLM	~~U~~ Ⓦ X Z

Figure 18.41

That's as far as you can push the deductions, but it's (of course) enough to answer the question easily. The correct answer is an entity that cannot be selected under these conditions. That's F, choice (A).

10. **(E)**

If the committee is to include exactly one parent, which one of the following is a person who must also be selected?

(A) K
(B) L
(C) M
(D) U
(E) X[13]

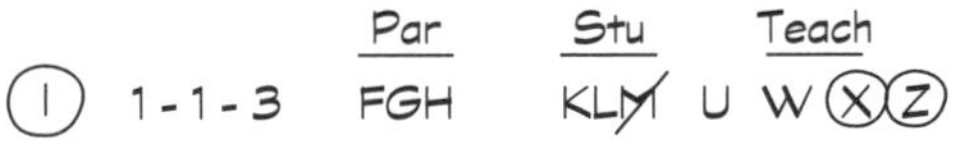

$$\text{①}\quad 1\text{-}1\text{-}3$$

Par	Stu	Teach
FGH	KL~~M~~	U W ⓍⓏ

Figure 18.42

The "if" for this question steers you straight to Option I. Checking that option, you see that both X and Z must be selected for the committee. X is in choice (E), making it the correct answer.

11. **(B)**

If M is selected, then the committee must also include both:

(A) F and G
(B) G and H
(C) H and K
(D) K and U
(E) U and X[14]

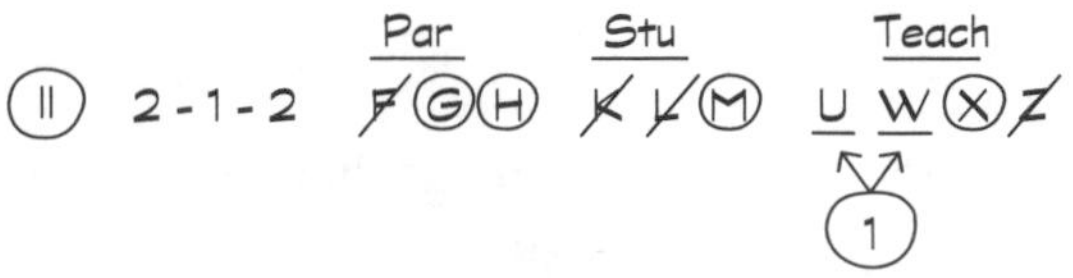

$$\text{②}\quad 2\text{-}1\text{-}2$$

Par	Stu	Teach
~~F~~ⒼⒽ	~~K~~ ~~L~~Ⓜ	U W Ⓧ~~Z~~

$$\text{①}$$

Figure 18.43

---

[13] PrepTest 50, Sec. 3, Q 10
[14] PrepTest 50, Sec. 3, Q 11

This question's "if" restricts you to Option II. That's because M cannot be used in Option I. Create a mini-sketch based on Option II with M as the student on the committee.

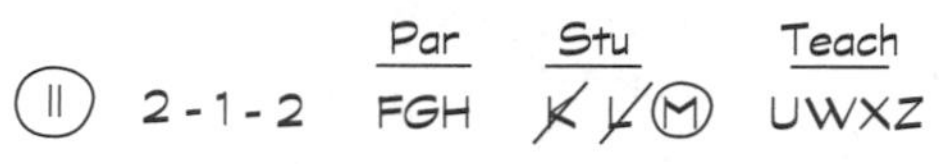

$$\text{II} \quad 2\text{-}1\text{-}2 \quad \overset{\text{Par}}{\underline{\text{FGH}}} \quad \overset{\text{Stu}}{\cancel{K}\,\cancel{L}\,\boxed{M}} \quad \overset{\text{Teach}}{\underline{\text{UWXZ}}}$$

Figure 18.44

Selecting M means rejecting Z (Rule 3). Thus, the teachers on the committee must be X and one of U and W (you cannot select both U and W because of Rule 4, remember).

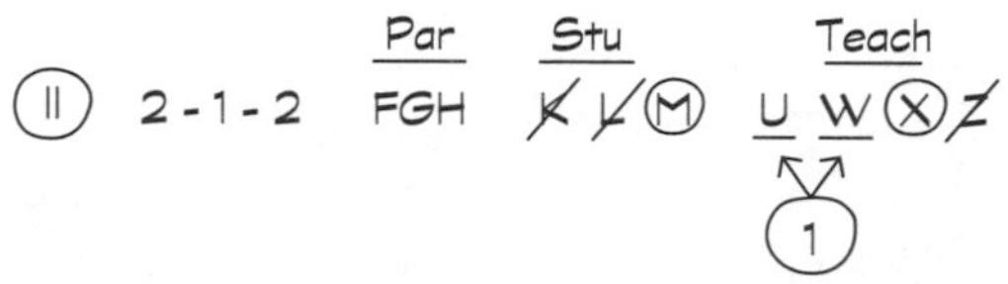

$$\text{II} \quad 2\text{-}1\text{-}2 \quad \overset{\text{Par}}{\text{FGH}} \quad \overset{\text{Stu}}{\cancel{K}\,\cancel{L}\,\boxed{M}} \quad \overset{\text{Teach}}{\underline{U}\,\text{W}\,\cancel{X}\,\cancel{Z}}$$

Figure 18.45

Finally, without Z on the committee, you aren't permitted to select F (Rule 5).

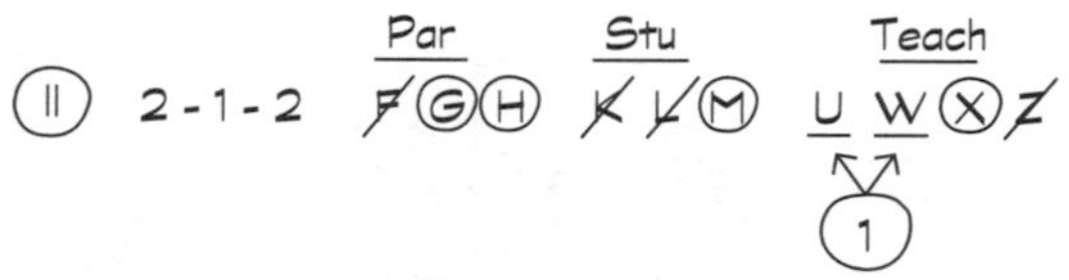

$$\text{II} \quad 2\text{-}1\text{-}2 \quad \overset{\text{Par}}{\cancel{F}\,\boxed{G}\boxed{H}} \quad \overset{\text{Stu}}{\cancel{K}\,\cancel{L}\,\boxed{M}} \quad \overset{\text{Teach}}{\underline{U}\,\text{W}\,\cancel{X}\,\cancel{Z}}$$

Figure 18.46

Thus, the parents for this arrangement must be G and H. Those are the entities listed in choice (B). Since the question stem calls for a pair of entities that *must be selected*, choice (B) is the correct answer.

Choices (A), (C), and (D) all include entities that cannot be selected in this situation (F and K), while choice (E) includes U, which doesn't have to be selected here.

Game 3—Graduation and First Car

<u>Questions 12–17</u>

> Within a five-year period from 1991 to 1995, each of three friends—Ramon, Sue, and Taylor—graduated. In that period, each bought his or her first car. The graduations and car purchases must be consistent with the following:
>
> > Ramon graduated in some year before the year in which Taylor graduated.
> > Taylor graduated in some year before the year in which he bought his first car.
> > Sue bought her first car in some year before the year in which she graduated.
> > Ramon and Sue graduated in the same year as each other.
> > At least one of the friends graduated in 1993.[15]

STEPS 1 AND 2: Overview and Sketch

This game sounds like a conversation you may have had with people you met in college, although it's pretty unlikely that you would have made a chart to keep track of everyone. You will here, although it will just be a standard Strict Sequencing line with five slots for the five years covered by the game's setup.

$$\underline{\quad} \quad \underline{\quad} \quad \underline{\quad} \quad \underline{\quad} \quad \underline{\quad}$$
$$91 \qquad 92 \qquad 93 \qquad 94 \qquad 95$$

Figure 18.47

Some test takers try to make this game much more complicated than it needs to be by making one line for graduations and one for cars. In fact, you should just treat each friend's graduation and car as two separate entities. Use "G" and "C" after the letter representing the friend to distinguish his or her graduation from his or her getting a car.

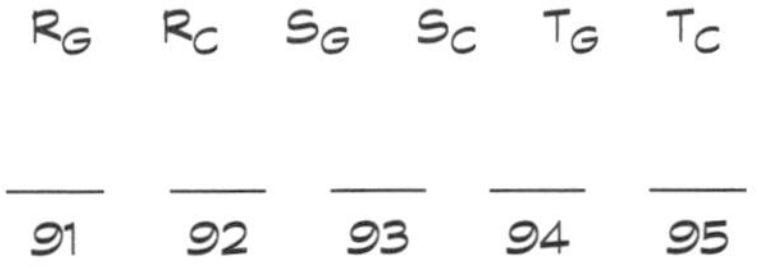

$$R_G \quad R_C \quad S_G \quad S_C \quad T_G \quad T_C$$

$$\underline{\quad} \quad \underline{\quad} \quad \underline{\quad} \quad \underline{\quad} \quad \underline{\quad}$$
$$91 \qquad 92 \qquad 93 \qquad 94 \qquad 95$$

Figure 18.48

Now, you have six events to fit into five years, so you know that at least one year saw two of the events occur. That's all right, there's no restriction saying that one event has to happen each year. There may even be years in which three or four of these events or none of these events happened. The rules will give you more clarity on that.

---

[15] PrepTest 50, Sec. 3, Game 3

STEP **3: Rules**

The first rule relates Ramon's graduation (R_G) to Taylor's graduation (T_G). You can't place that into the framework yet.

$$R_G \quad R_C \quad S_G \quad S_C \quad T_G \quad T_C$$

$$\underline{} \quad \underline{} \quad \underline{} \quad \underline{} \quad \underline{}$$
$$91 \qquad 92 \qquad 93 \qquad 94 \qquad 95$$

$$R_G \ldots T_G$$

Figure 18.49

The second rule can simply be appended to the first. Taylor's first car (T_C) followed his graduation (T_G).

$$R_G \quad R_C \quad S_G \quad S_C \quad T_G \quad T_C$$

$$\underline{} \quad \underline{} \quad \underline{} \quad \underline{} \quad \underline{}$$
$$91 \qquad 92 \qquad 93 \qquad 94 \qquad 95$$

$$R_G \ldots T_G \ldots T_C$$

Figure 18.50

The third rule gives the order of S's two events.

$$R_G \quad R_C \quad S_G \quad S_C \quad T_G \quad T_C$$

$$\underline{} \quad \underline{} \quad \underline{} \quad \underline{} \quad \underline{}$$
$$91 \qquad 92 \qquad 93 \qquad 94 \qquad 95$$

$$R_G \ldots T_G \ldots T_C$$
$$S_C \ldots S_G$$

Figure 18.51

The fourth rule tells you that Ramon and Sue graduated the same year ($R_G = S_G$).

$$R_G \quad R_C \quad S_G \quad S_C \quad T_G \quad T_C$$

$$\underline{} \quad \underline{} \quad \underline{} \quad \underline{} \quad \underline{}$$
$$91 \qquad 92 \qquad 93 \qquad 94 \qquad 95$$

$$R_G \ldots T_G \ldots T_C \quad \boxed{\begin{array}{c} R_G \\ \hline S_G \end{array}}$$
$$S_C \ldots S_G$$

Figure 18.52

Did you note that Rule 4 allows you to join the S_C-S_G block to the R_G-T_G-T_C string you already diagrammed? If so, that's great. If not, you would have gotten it as you considered the duplications (the rules sharing the same entity) under Step 4.

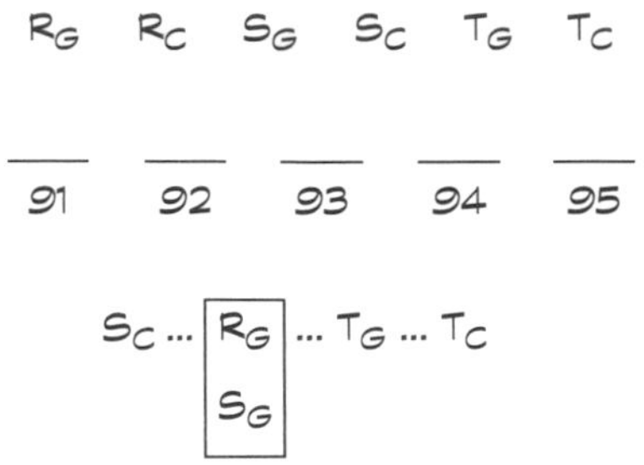

Figure 18.53

The final rule tells you that at least one of the graduations happened in '93. Just make a note of this rule beneath the framework.

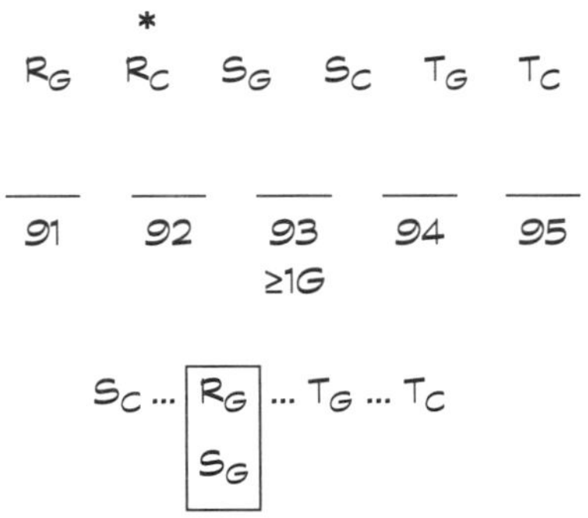

Figure 18.54

It's about to become very important. Notice, too, the asterisk above RC, reminding you that it is the floater.

STEP 4: Deductions

As I pointed out when discussing Rule 4, the first four rules all connect to form a string of relationships among five of the six entities.

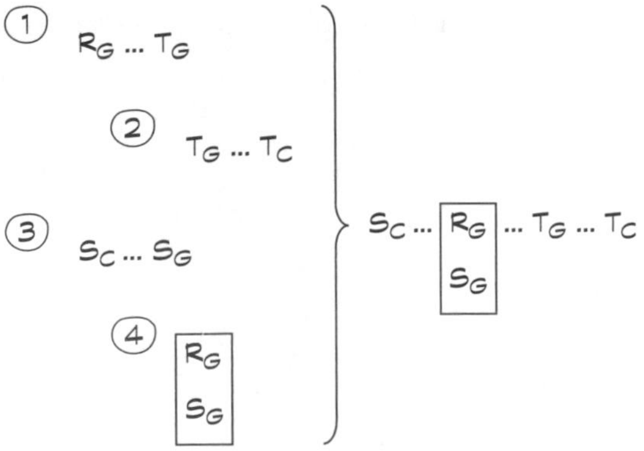

Figure 18.55

Consider how that string can fit into the framework in light of Rule 5, which says that at least one graduation took place in 1993. You quickly see that either '93 was the year of Sue's and Ramon's graduations, or it was the year of Taylor's. That allows you to set up dual Limited Options sketches.

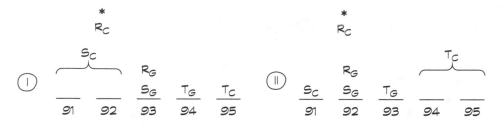

Figure 18.56

When Sue and Ramon are the '93 grads, Taylor's graduation must take place in '94 and the purchase of his first car in '95. In Option I, Sue gets her car in either '91 or '92. When Taylor is the '93 grad, Sue's car gets pushed back to '91, and Sue's and Ramon's graduation occurs in '92. Taylor gets his car after his graduation, so in Option II, he'll get it in either '94 or '95. Remember that the one unknown in either option is when Ramon got his car.

STEP 5: Questions

Since so much of this game could be determined in the Deduction step, it's not surprising to see only two "If" questions. Keep the fact that R_C is a floater in mind when you're asked what *could be true*.

12. **(B)**

Which one of the following could be an accurate matching of each friend and the year in which she or he graduated?

(A)   Ramon: 1991; Sue: 1991; Taylor: 1993
(B)   Ramon: 1992; Sue: 1992; Taylor: 1993
(C)   Ramon: 1992; Sue: 1993; Taylor: 1994
(D)   Ramon: 1993; Sue: 1993; Taylor: 1992
(E)   Ramon: 1993; Sue: 1993; Taylor: 1995[16]

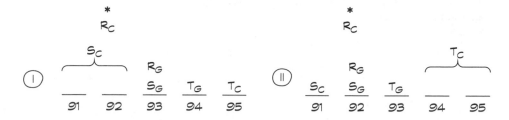

Figure 18.57

---

[16] PrepTest 50, Sec. 3, Q 12

This is a Partial Acceptability question, asking only for the possible graduation dates. With the Master Sketch you have, you can see that there are only two possible solutions: either R_G/S_G in '92 and T_G in '93, or else R_G/S_G in '93 and T_G in '94. Choice (B) matches the first of those two arrangements and is the correct answer.

13. **(B)**

Which one of the following could have taken place in 1995?

(A) Ramon graduated.
(B) Ramon bought his first car.
(C) Sue graduated.
(D) Sue bought her first car.
(E) Taylor graduated.[17]

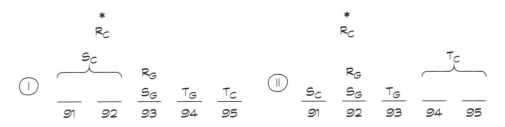

Figure 18.58

Checking the Master Sketch, you can tell that only two events could have taken place in '95, T_C or R_C (the floater, as you recall, which can go anywhere). The only choice that matches one of these possibilities is (B), so it's the correct answer.

14. **(C)**

Which one of the following must be false?

(A) Two of the friends each bought his or her first car in 1991.
(B) Two of the friends each bought his or her first car in 1992.
(C) Two of the friends each bought his or her first car in 1993.
(D) Two of the friends each bought his or her first car in 1994.
(E) Two of the friends each bought his or her first car in 1995.[18]

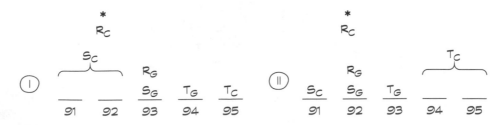

Figure 18.59

[17] PrepTest 50, Sec. 3, Q 13
[18] PrepTest 50, Sec. 3, Q 14

Here is yet another question that can be answered straight from the Master Sketch. The correct answer *must be false*, meaning that the four wrong answers *could be true*. If you find a choice acceptable in either option, eliminate that answer.

Choice (A) is acceptable in either option; Sue and Ramon could both have gotten their cars in '91. Cross out this answer.

Choice (B) is acceptable in Option I; there, Sue and Ramon could both have gotten their cars in '92. Get rid of choice (B), too.

Choice (C) is impossible, and thus, the right answer. Only Ramon could have gotten his car in '93.

For the record, choices (D) and (E) are both possible in Option II, where the two friends to have gotten their cars would be Taylor and Ramon.

15. **(A)**

Which one of the following must be true?

(A)   None of the three friends graduated in 1991.
(B)   None of the three friends graduated in 1992.
(C)   None of the three friends bought his or her first car in 1993.
(D)   None of the three friends graduated in 1994.
(E)   None of the three friends bought his or her first car in 1995.[19]

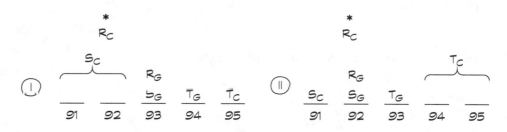

Figure 18.60

One last "Non-If" question: this one asks for what *must be true*. That means that each of the wrong answers *could be false* in one or both of the options. You don't have to look far to find the right answer. Choice (A) *must be true*; all three graduations take place in '93 and '94 (Option I) or '92 and '93 (Option II). Each of the wrong answers, choices (B)–(E), could be false in at least one of the two options.

[19] PrepTest 50, Sec. 3, Q 15

16. **(E)**

If Taylor graduated in the same year that Ramon bought his first car, then each of the following could be true EXCEPT:

(A)   Sue bought her first car in 1991.
(B)   Ramon graduated in 1992.
(C)   Taylor graduated in 1993.
(D)   Taylor bought his first car in 1994.
(E)   Ramon bought his first car in 1995.[20]

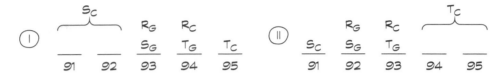

Figure 18.61

The "if" condition described in this question stem could happen in either of the two options. In Option I, R_C would occur in '94. In Option II, R_C would happen in '93. If it's helpful, you can add that to a quick mini-sketch like the one you see above.

Make sure you characterize the answer choices on an "EXCEPT" question like this one. The correct answer *must be false*. Since R_C can happen only in '93 or '94, choice (E) cannot be true and is, therefore, the correct choice. You'll notice that all of the remaining choices are possible in one or both of the options.

17. **(E)**

If Sue graduated in 1993, then which one of the following must be true?

(A)   Sue bought her first car in 1991.
(B)   Ramon bought his first car in 1992.
(C)   Ramon bought his first car in 1993.
(D)   Taylor bought his first car in 1994.
(E)   Taylor bought his first car in 1995.[21]

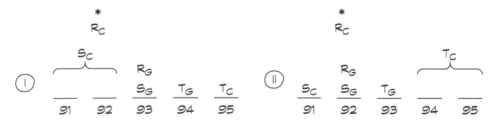

Figure 18.62

This question's "if" puts you squarely in Option I. Simply consult that option and determine which answer *must be true*. It's unclear in Option I whether Sue got her car in '91 or '92, so choice (A) could be false. Eliminate it. Ramon could have gotten his first car in any one of the

---

[20] PrepTest 50, Sec. 3, Q 16
[21] PrepTest 50, Sec. 3, Q 17

five years in either option; R_C is this game's floater. That allows you to eliminate choices (B) and (C). Taylor gets his car in '95 in Option I. That makes choice (D) false and wrong. But the same fact means that choice (E) *must be true*.

This game stands as one more example illustrating that somewhat oddball variations on game types needn't make games more difficult. By sticking to the fundamental and strategic approach guaranteed by the Kaplan Method, you were able to make a Master Sketch with which you could just mow down the question set. In the end, the complexity involved in sequencing each entity in two distinct ways was neutralized by treating them as six distinct events.

Game 4—Alphabet Soup Game
Questions 18–22

A child eating alphabet soup notices that the only letters left in her bowl are one each of these six letters: T, U, W, X, Y, and Z. She plays a game with the remaining letters, eating them in the next three spoonfuls in accord with certain rules. Each of the six letters must be in exactly one of the next three spoonfuls, and each of the spoonfuls must have at least one and at most three of the letters. In addition, she obeys the following restrictions:

The U is in a later spoonful than the T.
The U is not in a later spoonful than the X.
The Y is in a later spoonful than the W.
The U is in the same spoonful as either the Y or the Z, but not both.[22]

STEPS 1 AND 2: **Overview and Sketch**

Admittedly, this is one of the odder situations described in an LSAT logic game. But haven't we all done something like this, trying to get only the red cereal in our spoon or eating the monkeys before the lions from our animal crackers? Whether or not you can imagine playing this game yourself, it's not hard to picture this situation. The child will take three more spoonfuls of soup. Each spoonful will have between one and three pasta letters in it. This is a Distribution-Sequencing task.

Figure 18.63

You can anticipate at least some rules about which letters can or cannot be together in a spoonful and others about the relative order of the letters, which ones she eats in earlier or later bites.

---

[22] PrepTest 50, Sec. 3, Game 4

STEP 3: **Rules**

None of the rules is concrete. None says, "T Is in spoonful 1," or, "T and Z are in the same spoonful." So at least initially, there's nothing to draw inside the framework. Record each of the rules beside or beneath the framework and assess their relationships in step 4.

Rule 1 gives you the relative order of T and U.

Figure 18.64

Read Rule 2 carefully. U can be in an earlier spoonful than X or in the same spoonful as X, just *not* in a later one.

Figure 18.65

Rule 3 tells you that Y follows W.

Figure 18.66

The final rule tells you that U has at least one partner, either Y or Z. The "but not both" language at the end is important. Without it, U could share a spoonful with Y and Z. But in this game, that possibility is ruled out. Make note of that.

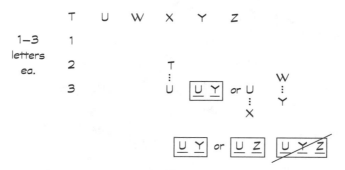

Figure 18.67

You can tell that U, which appears in three of the five rules, will be the lynchpin of what can happen in any acceptable arrangement.

STEP 4: Deductions

The biggest drawback to this game is the impossibility of any concrete deductions. Don't waste your time chasing down every speculative arrangement. Start with the most restricted (and restrictive) entity and see what you can learn, but once you're just stabbing at possibilities, draw the line and move on to the questions.

As you noted above, U is most restricted entity in the set. According to Rule 4, U must share a spoonful with either Y or Z, but not both.

Figure 18.68

In either case, T must be an earlier spoonful than U.

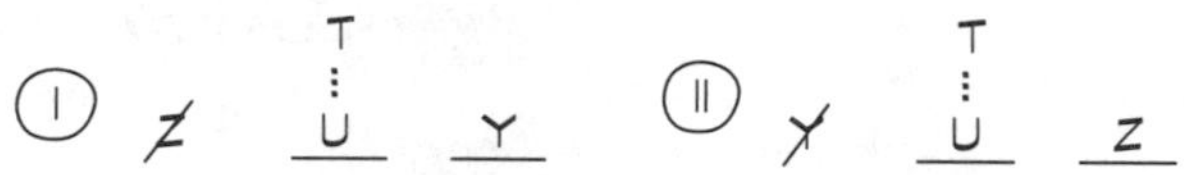

Figure 18.69

U's other rule is Rule 2. X may share U's spoonful or come later. Note that like this:

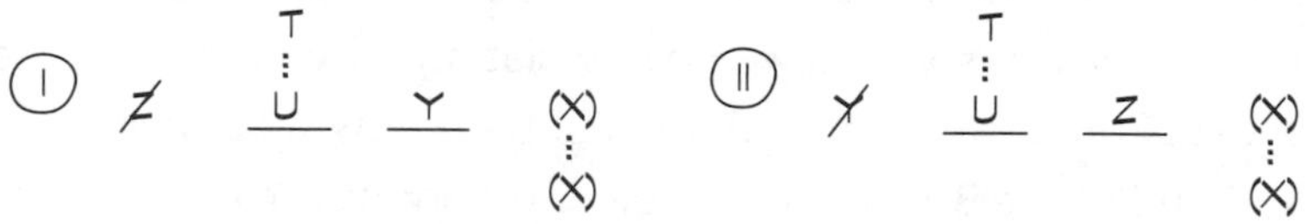

Figure 18.70

In the first option, you can add Rule 3, which requires that W be in an earlier spoonful than Y. In Option II, you'll just have to note that relationship off to the side.

Figure 18.71

W could partner with U and Z in the second option, but only if X and Y are found in the third spoonful.

There's nothing more that you can add with certainty. Trust that the test makers have given you everything you'll need to answer the questions, and move on.

STEP 5: **Questions**

Of the five questions in this set, three have new "if"s—not surprising, given the number of possible arrangements that remain open. Question 21 is a Complete and Accurate List question. You may be able to use what you've learned from the "If" questions to help you answer it.

18. **(B)**

Which one of the following could be an accurate list of the spoonfuls and the letters in each of them?

(A) first: Y
second: T, W
third: U, X, Z

(B) first: T, W
second: U, X, Y
third: Z

(C) first: T
second: U, Z
third: W, X, Y

(D) first: T, U, Z
second: W
third: X, Y

(E) first: W
second: T, X, Z
third: U, Y[23]

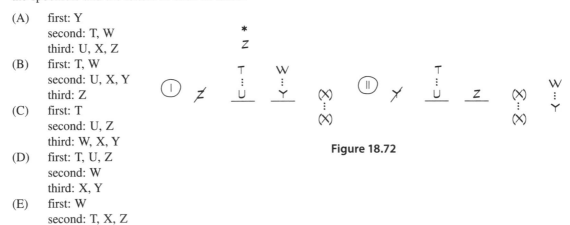

Figure 18.72

The concreteness (or lack thereof) in a game doesn't change your approach to Acceptability questions. Just use the rules to spot and remove violating answer choices. Here, Rule 1 takes out choice (D); U must be in a *later* spoonful than T. Rule 2 gets rid of choice (E); U must *not* be in a later spoonful than X. Rule 3 eliminates choices (A) and (C); Y must be in a *later* spoonful than W. That leaves only the correct answer, choice (B).

---

19. **(D)**

If the Y is the only letter in one of the spoonfuls, then which one of the following could be true?

(A) The Y is in the first spoonful.
(B) The Z is in the first spoonful.
(C) The T is in the second spoonful.
(D) The X is in the second spoonful.
(E) The W is in the third spoonful.[24]

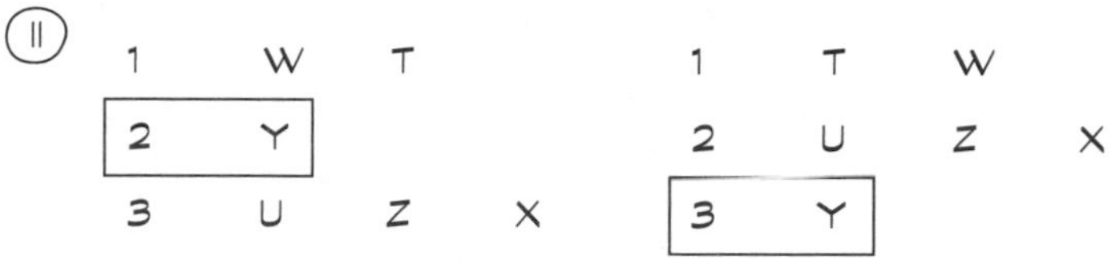

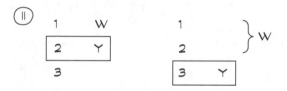

Figure 18.73

If Y is alone in one of the spoonfuls, then Option II is the only option in play. Since Y must follow W (Rule 3), Y can only be in spoonful 2 or spoonful 3, with W in an earlier spoonful.

Figure 18.74

Since the question stem requires Y to be alone, you know Z must accompany U (Rule 4). U, of course, must always follow T (Rule 1).

Figure 18.75

Think for a moment about where T and U-Z can go in each option.

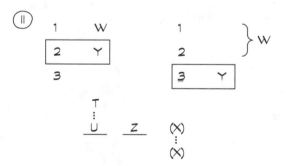

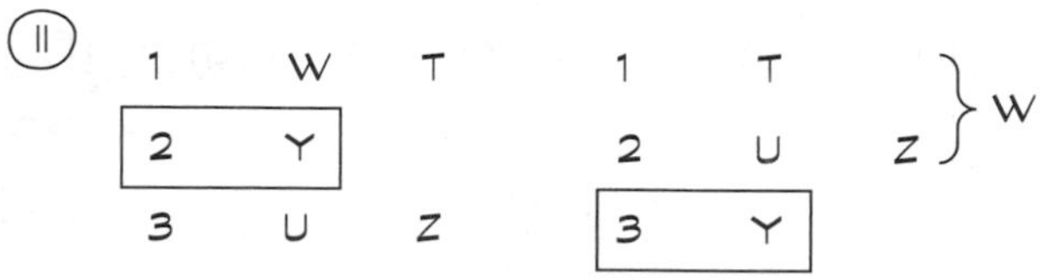

Figure 18.76

---

24 PrepTest 50, Sec. 3, Q 19

Now, add X to each side of the mini-sketch, pursuant to Rule 2. Remember that Y must stay alone according to this question's stem.

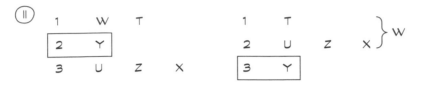

Figure 18.77

This makes it clear that W must be in the first spoonful in either possible arrangement, since the maximum number of letters that can appear in a spoonful is three.

Figure 18.78

With this mini-sketch, you can evaluate the choices in a few seconds. Only choice (D) could be true (in the second arrangement), so it's the right answer.

20. **(E)**

   If the Z is in the first spoonful, then which one of the following must be true?

   (A)   The T is in the second spoonful.
   (B)   The U is in the third spoonful.
   (C)   The W is in the first spoonful.
   (D)   The W is in the second spoonful.
   (E)   The X is in the third spoonful.[25]

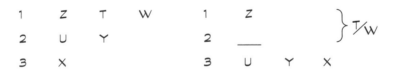

Figure 18.79

The "if" in this stem produces another two-option mini-sketch. Start by placing Z in the first spoonful.

1   Z

2

3

Figure 18.80

[25] PrepTest 50, Sec. 3, Q 20

Since U cannot be in the first spoonful (U must follow T because of Rule 1), you know that Y will share U's spoonful (Rule 4). They'll be either in spoonful 2 or spoonful 3.

Figure 18.81

In the first option, W must take spoonful 1 in order to appear earlier than Y (Rule 3). That leaves only X to appear in spoonful 3.

Figure 18.82

In the second option, X must take spoonful 3 in order not to break Rule 2. At least one of T and W must be in the second spoonful, although it's fine if both are.

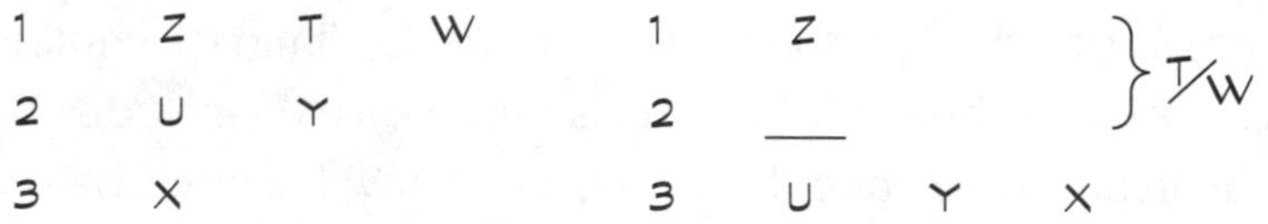

Figure 18.83

Now, characterize the answer choices. The correct answer *must be true*. That means that the four wrong answers *could be false*. Only choice (E) *must be true* in either option. The other four choices include entities that can move into either of two possible spoonfuls under this question's conditions.

21. **(D)**

   Which one of the following is a complete list of letters,
   any one of which could be the only letter in the first
   spoonful?

   (A)   T
   (B)   T, W
   (C)   T, X
   (D)   T, W, Z
   (E)   T, X, W, Z[26]

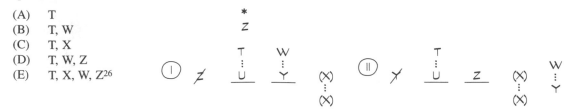

Figure 18.84

The answer to question 20 helps you answer this question in a matter of seconds. You saw in
the preceding question that Z could be alone in spoonful 1.

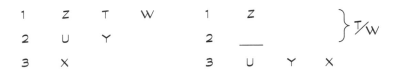

Figure 18.85

Since the correct answer to this question must include Z, eliminate choices (A), (B), and (C).
The only difference between choices (D) and (E) is that choice (E) includes X. Since Rule 2 tells
you that X cannot be in an earlier spoonful than U, you know X cannot be in spoonful 1 alone.
Eliminate choice (E) and you're left with the correct answer, choice (D). There's another point
for you, and it took you all of 10 seconds to get it.

22. **(A)**

   If the T is in the second spoonful, then which one of the
   following could be true?

   (A)   Exactly two letters are in the first spoonful.
   (B)   Exactly three letters are in the first spoonful.
   (C)   Exactly three letters are in the second spoonful.
   (D)   Exactly one letter is in the third spoonful.
   (E)   Exactly two letters are in the third spoonful.[27]

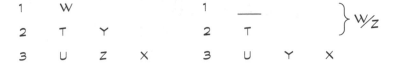

Figure 18.86

---

[26] PrepTest 50, Sec. 3, Q 21
[27] PrepTest 50, Sec. 3, Q 22

Here's another "If" question and, again, a mini-sketch will reveal the limitations that result from the new condition. Start with T in spoonful 2.

```
1
2    T
3
```

Figure 18.87

Placing T triggers Rule 1. U will have to take spoonful 3.

```
1
2    T
3    U
```

Figure 18.88

Because of Rule 2, X must also be in spoonful 3 in this case. And because of Rule 4, either Y or Z will be there, too.

```
1
2    T
3    U    Y/Z    X
```

Figure 18.89

That leaves either W and Z or W and Y still to be determined. When Z takes spoonful 3, every letter's spoonful can be established.

```
1    W              1
2    T    Y         2    T
3    U    Z    X    3    U    Y    X
```

Figure 18.90

When Y is in the third spoonful, however, W and Z can be in spoonful 1 or 2, alone or together, as long as at least one of them is in spoonful 1.

```
1    W              1    ___
2    T    Y         2    T          } W/Z
3    U    Z    X    3    U    Y    X
```

Figure 18.91

The question stem calls for the answer that *could be true*. The four wrong answers in this question *must be false*. Choice (A) could be true; W and Z could be together in spoonful 1. That's the correct answer, and you're done with this game. Note that choices (B)–(E) all contain impossible placements under the terms of this question.

This game stands as a great example of a game in which you may be tempted to spend far too long on the Deductions step. You could spend minutes figuring out all of the possible permutations, but it wouldn't be a good investment of your time. Since the most restricted entity in the game—letter U—didn't lead to any concrete deductions, you know you can (and should) move on to the questions. The test maker always gives you the information you need to answer every question. Sometimes you're allowed to figure out almost all of the possible arrangements up front; other times, you have to wait until the questions give you more guidance. Learning to assess when it's time to move from Step 4 to Step 5 is one of the final stages in complete logic games mastery.

PART IV

THE TEST DAY EXPERIENCE

CHAPTER 19

GET READY FOR TEST DAY

Congratulations. Your work with the Kaplan Method and strategies gives you the knowledge and practice you need for LSAT success. Now, it's time for you to schedule a test date, register for the exam (if you haven't done so already), and put yourself in the right frame of mind to take the next step on the road to law school.

The details of registering for the test are covered in "An Introduction to the LSAT" at the beginning of the book. Follow the steps and recommendations mentioned there to ensure that you have a spot at the next test administration or on the test date that's best for you. In the remainder of this chapter, I'll cover what you need to do to have yourself mentally and emotionally ready for the rigors and rewards of test day.

YOU ARE PREPARED

First, remember (and remind yourself) that you are prepared. By learning the lessons and doing the work from this book, you can know, with confidence, that there is nothing else you need to *know* about LSAT logic games. The Kaplan Method, the specific strategies, and the analysis of the games that I've presented in this book are the result not only of my own 15-year tenure as an LSAT instructor; they're the summation of five decades of Kaplan expertise and research. Hundreds of great LSAT minds—including those of perfect scorers, legal scholars, and psycho-metricians—have contributed to the development, testing, and refinement of Kaplan's LSAT pedagogy. If we know it, you now know it. So strike from your mind any concern that there's one more secret to uncover or a mysterious LSAT Rosetta Stone to search for. You have the most complete, proven system for LSAT Logic Games success available. If you've already studied and practiced from this book's companion volumes—*Kaplan LSAT Reading Comprehension: Strategies and Tactics* and *Kaplan LSAT Logical Reasoning: Strategies and Tactics*—you can say the same thing about the entire exam.

Now, saying that you *know* everything you need to about the Logic Games section doesn't mean you're ready to *do* everything you need to do to achieve your goal score. You need to continue to practice and review. Indeed, I'll cover that in the next section of this chapter. But first, I want to make sure you're translating your comprehensive knowledge of logic games into confidence on test day. From now until the day you sit for your official administration of the LSAT, you need to exhibit the confidence your preparation has earned you.

There are some very practical steps you can take to reinforce your test day confidence. Once you're registered for the test, visit your test site. You may even want to take a logic game to practice in the very room where you'll be sitting for the real test. At a minimum, know where you're going to be, how you'll get there, and where you'll park or where public transportation will drop you off. You want no surprises on the morning of your official LSAT.

The day before your test, relax. There's no way to cram for a skills-based exam. While your competition is scrambling and fretting, go to the gym, watch your favorite movie, or have a nice dinner. Gather what you need for the next day, and keep yourself one step ahead of everything you need to do. It sounds a little corny, but acting confident will actually make you feel more confident. Get to bed relatively early, have a good night's sleep, and wake ready to have the best day of your (test-taking) life.

The following is a list of what you'll need to have with you on test day:

LSAT SURVIVAL KIT

You MUST have the following:

- Admissions ticket
- Photo ID
- Passport-style photos
- Several sharpened #2 pencils
- 1-gallon transparent zip-top bag

You SHOULD also have:

- Pencil sharpener
- Eraser
- Analog wristwatch
- Aspirin
- Snack and drink for the break

You CANNOT have:

- Cell phone
- MP3 player
- Computer or electronic reader
- Electronic or digital timers
- Weapons
- Papers other than your admission ticket

That list conforms to the rules for the test site as they stand at the time of this writing. You should check www.lsac.org periodically before your test date to make sure there haven't been any changes or amendments to the Law School Administration Council's (LSAC) policies.

Of course, the "MUSTs" are non-negotiable. You need those to be allowed entry to the testing room. Some of the "SHOULDs," on the other hand, you may not need at all. But if you begin to feel a little headache coming on, or if you find your stomach grumbling midway through Section 3 of the test, you'll be awfully glad you took along those "just in case" items. As for the "CANNOTs," do yourself a favor and avoid any conflict with the proctors or test administrators. Just leave your phone or electronics in the car or at home.

One other very practical thing you can do is to dress in layers. The LSAT is usually administered during the weekend and almost always in a large, institutional building. It's really tough to predict whether the room will be too hot or too cold or whether it will fluctuate throughout the day. Take the Goldilocks approach and make sure the temperature is always "just right" for you by wearing or taking the kind of sweater or light jacket that's easy (and quiet) to slip on or off.

The stress levels of test takers around you will be high. But if you demonstrate nothing but preparation and confidence on the morning of the test, you'll feel calmer, more clear-headed, and ready for the real challenges of the test itself.

CHAMPIONS PRACTICE. VIRTUOSOS PRACTICE. YOU PRACTICE.

To put my earlier point about practice into formal logic terms, knowledge of the test is necessary, but not sufficient, for test day success. Mistaking this relationship is something that leads a lot of test takers off track. They haven't achieved the score they want, so they say, "There must be something I don't know yet," or, "What am I missing?" The fact is that many of these test takers know all about the test, but they haven't practiced taking the test. Ask almost any great performer, musician, public speaker, or athlete and they'll tell you that the key to their success is practice. A great violinist may study a composer's compositional theory, historical context, or even personal life in order to better understand a piece before performing it. But all of that will mean little if the performer hasn't practiced. The audience would be pretty disappointed if the violinist showed up to give a lecture about the composer instead of playing a concert. It's the same with the LSAT. Your audience, law school admissions officers, won't care what you know about the exam, just how well you perform on it.

So how can you best practice? First, lay out a study and practice schedule for yourself that runs from now until test day—one that's ambitious but practical. Fill in as much as you can about which sections or question types you'll be practicing each day or week. If you're working on different parts of the test, vary the sections you're practicing and the materials you're using.

If you haven't completed and reviewed the full-section practice in this book, make sure you do so. Leave time for review of your work. Remember that you're not just checking to see whether you produced the correct answer, you're asking whether you did so as efficiently and effectively as you could have. That means that you should always be reviewing the questions you got right as well as those you got wrong. Look for what features in a game or question you're likely to see again on test day. You won't see the games from this book on your test, but every game on your test will have similarities—in the setup, the entities, the rules and deductions, and the questions—to those you've practiced here.

If you're looking for additional practice, consider the following additional resources:

OTHER KAPLAN LSAT RESOURCES

Logic Games On Demand
Logical Reasoning On Demand
Reading Comprehension On Demand
Comprehensive, section-specific courses for in-depth instruction and targeted practice.

LSAT Advantage—On Site, Anywhere or On Demand
Our most popular option—complete, targeted, and focused prep designed for busy students.

LSAT Extreme—On Site or Anywhere
Maximum in-class instruction plus tutoring for students who want extra time, review, and more practice.

LSAT One on One—On Site or Anywhere
An expert tutor designs a one-on-one, custom program around your individual needs, goals, and schedule.

LSAT Summer Intensive
Six weeks of total LSAT immersion in a residential academic program at Boston University

Check out *www.kaplanlsat.com* for courses and free events live, online, and in your area.

All of those additional resources will provide the outstanding instruction, coaching, and practice you expect from Kaplan test prep. Consider which ones work best for your schedule, learning style, and admissions timeline. Kaplan is committed to helping you achieve your educational and career goals.

THE PSYCHOLOGICAL DIMENSIONS OF TEST DAY

There's no doubt that taking your official LSAT is one of the most important steps (maybe *the* most important) you'll take on the road to law school. That's a lot of pressure. It's natural to have a little excitement and some extra adrenaline for such a big event. Those are actually healthy things to feel, provided that you channel your emotions into energy and concentration, rather than anxiety and confusion. I'd be pretty disappointed if, after weeks or months of practice and preparation, one of my students said, "Eh, I don't really care what happens on the test." Of course you care. That's why you're reading this book and working so hard. So embrace the big day.

I've already talked about how you can begin to foster an attitude of confidence and act in ways that support and sustain it. Here are a couple of practical steps you can take to carry your confidence right into the testing room.

Know What to Expect

It is easy to lay out the order of events on test day. Here's a chart that shows you what will happen from the time you arrive at the test site.

Event	What Happens	Time
Check-In	Show admissions ticket, ID, and passport-style photos, get room and seat assignment	10–30 minutes
Rules and Procedures	Test booklets distributed, proctor reads the rules, test takers fill out grid information	30 minutes
LSAT Administration		
Section 1	Logic Games, Logical Reasoning, or Reading Comprehension Section	35 minutes
Section 2	Logic Games, Logical Reasoning, or Reading Comprehension Section	35 minutes
Section 3	Logic Games, Logical Reasoning, or Reading Comprehension Section	35 minutes

Break	Test booklets and grids collected, test takers have break, return to seats, booklets and grids redistributed	12–20 minutes (10 minute break with additional time for administrative tasks)
Section 4	Logic Games, Logical Reasoning, or Reading Comprehension Section	35 minutes
Section 5	Logic Games, Logical Reasoning, or Reading Comprehension Section	35 minutes
Prepare for Writing Sample	Test booklets and grids collected, test takers given a chance to cancel scores, Writing Sample booklets distributed	5–10 minutes
Writing Sample	Test takers produce Writing Samples	35 minutes

You can see that even if everything goes as smoothly as possible, you're in for around five hours from start to finish. This is another reason that it's so important to be rested, comfortable, and nourished. Students who are too groggy to be at their best in Section 1 or too exhausted and hungry to keep up their performance in Section 5 will have trouble competing with someone like you, who's prepared for the entire testing day, from start to finish.

One thing that star performers do—I don't care if you're thinking of singers, actors, athletes, or even great trial lawyers—is to warm up before they "go on." You can do the same on the morning of your test by reviewing a Logic Game, Logical Reasoning question, or Reading Comprehension passage that you've done before. As you revisit the game or question, go over the steps in the Kaplan Method that allowed you to be successful with the item before. This will get your brain warmed up just as a quarterback would loosen his arm or a singer would warm up her vocal cords. Don't try new material, and certainly don't try a full section. Just start reading and thinking—calmly and confidently—in the LSAT way. You'll be miles ahead of the unprepared test taker who looks shell-shocked for most of Section 1.

In order to maintain a high level of performance, it's important to stay hydrated and nourished. Mental work makes most people hungry. So drink water at the break and have a small, healthy snack. Don't, however, eat a sleep-inducing turkey sandwich or gobble sugar that will have you crashing out during Section 5.

Knowing what to expect also helps you manage your mental preparation for test day in other small, but important, ways. A lot of test takers don't know that the proctors will ask whether anyone in the room wants to cancel his or her score right after Section 5 is completed and the test booklets are collected. If you're not expecting that question, it can throw you into a moment of self-doubt. It's human nature to underestimate your performance on the test. You will remember the handful of questions that gave you trouble while ignoring the dozens of questions you answered routinely with no problem. I've personally known students who canceled their scores when they shouldn't have. The LSAC allows you a number of days after the test to cancel your score, so don't worry about it during the exam. Complete the Writing Sample to the best of your ability. You can always consider things that might have caused you to underperform—illness, a personal crisis—after you've completed the test.

You Will Panic, but Don't Panic

Over the course of four to five hours of rigorous, detailed, strictly timed test taking, you're going to reach a point at which you lose focus, feel overwhelmed, or just downright panic for a moment. It's normal. So first thing, don't feed the panic by blaming yourself or saying, "Oh, I knew this would happen." There's nothing wrong with you for having those feelings. In fact, panic is a physical response to high-pressure situations. It's related to the autonomic nervous system, the "flight or fight" response we've adapted to survive danger. Your heart beats faster; blood leaves your brain to go to your extremities; your breathing gets rapid and shallow. That's all very important when the danger you face is a predator or enemy. It's just not very helpful when you're facing a standardized test.

If—when—you face a point of doubt, confusion, or panic on test day, take a moment. Collect yourself physically first. Take a deep breath; sit up in a straight, comfortable posture; put both feet flat on the floor and lower your shoulders; even close your eyes for a second while you breathe. Then open your eyes and remind yourself that whatever you're looking at, it's just an LSAT question. The fact is that you've seen one like it and done one like it before. You know that's the case because of your preparation. Get your concentration back by reciting the Kaplan Method as you work through the problem. You know that will provide a strategic, purposeful approach every time.

Worry Only about What's in Your Control

When I have students in LSAT prep courses, they often ask a lot of questions about what to do if things go wrong on test day. "What if the proctor doesn't give us a verbal five-minute warning?" "What if someone is being noisy right behind me?" "What if the school marching band is rehearsing in the courtyard under the window?" All of those and a few weirder, more distracting things have happened to test takers. But my students' concern about such occurrences before test day is misplaced. They should be taking care of the things that are within their control—learning the Kaplan Method, practicing logic game setups and deductions—not worrying about the things that aren't. The vast majority of LSAT administrations go off without more than a minor hitch. Your job is to be ready to have a peak performance on a routine test day.

When the unexpected happens, stay calm. If there is something that you notice before the test begins—a window is open, letting in cold air or street noise; the lights in the back of the room aren't turned on, making it dark where you're sitting—just let the proctor know (politely) and ask if it can be remedied. If something happens during a section—another test taker is unconsciously tapping his pencil; the proctor forgets the five-minute announcement—keep working. Raise your hand and get a proctor's attention. When they come to your seat, quickly and quietly explain the situation. Most of the time, they'll take action to remedy the situation. But don't let those things throw you off your game. If something truly bizarre happens that seriously impedes your performance—a fire alarm goes off, a wrecking crew starts to jackhammer the building—follow the proctor's instructions, keep a record of what happened, and follow up with the LSAC by telephone or in writing after the test concludes. You are welcome to contact 1-800-KAPTEST and ask for advice from one of our LSAT experts, too. A word to the wise: The LSAC will not add points to a score as a remedy for a distracting test administration, but they have found other ways to accommodate test takers who, through no fault of their own, have been unable to complete the test or who encountered unmanageable distractions.

GET READY FOR TEST DAY

This chapter really boils down to one message: Prepare yourself for the perfect test day. Display confidence and preparation in all that you do. Get ready for consistent, focused performance from start to finish. When that's the attitude you take into the test, you're more likely to outperform your competition and have your best day regardless of what else does or doesn't happen.

CHAPTER 20

SECRETS OF THE LSAT

The "secrets" of the LSAT aren't really secrets at all. They're well-known facts that many test takers fail to take full advantage of. The best test takers use the structure and format of the test to their advantage. Just as a great football or basketball coach adjusts the team's strategy when time is running out on the clock, or just as a great conductor rearranges an orchestra to take advantage of the acoustics in a new venue, you can learn to adjust your approach to the test you're taking. We might well laud the insightful coach or conductor by saying, "Wow, he really knows the 'secrets' of this game (or stadium or theater)." But in fact, he's simply taking account of all the circumstances and making the right strategic decisions for that time and place. Consider a handful of facts that make the LSAT a unique testing experience, and see how you can use them to your advantage.

EVERY QUESTION IS WORTH THE SAME AMOUNT TO YOUR SCORE

Many tests you've taken (even some standardized tests) rewarded you more for certain questions or sections than for others. In school, it's common for a professor to say, "The essay counts for half of your score," or to make a section of harder questions worth five points each while easier ones are worth less. With such exams, you may simply be unable to get a top score without performing well on a given question or topic. It makes sense, then, to target the areas the professor will reward most highly.

As you well know, that's not the case on the LSAT. Every question—easy or hard, short or long, common or rare—is worth exactly the same amount as every other question. That means that you should seek out the questions, games, and passages that are the easiest for you to handle. Far too many test takers get their teeth into a tough question and won't let go. That hurts them in two ways. First, they spend too much time—sometimes three or four minutes—on such a question, sacrificing their chances with other, easier questions. Second, since questions like these are tough or confusing, they're less likely to produce a right answer no matter how much time you spend. Learn to skip questions when it's in your interest to do so. Mark questions that you skip by circling the entire question in your test booklet. That way, those questions will be easy to spot if you have time left after you complete the other questions in the section. If you've eliminated one or two obviously incorrect answer choices, strike them through completely so that you don't spend time rethinking them when you come back to the question.

When schools receive your score report, the only thing they see is your score. They don't know—and they don't care—whether you've answered the easiest or the toughest questions on the LSAT. They only care that you answered more questions correctly than the other applicants. Becoming a good manager of the test sections is invaluable. You'll do that, in part, by triaging the games or passages and choosing to put off the toughest for last. Even more often, you'll manage the section by skipping and guessing strategically. Don't slug it out with a tough question for minutes and then grudgingly move on. Boldly seek out questions on which you can exert your strengths, and be clearheaded and decisive in your decisions to move past questions you know are targeted at your weaknesses. Take the test; don't let it take you.

ONE RIGHT, FOUR ROTTEN

I'm sure you've had the experience, on a multiple-choice test in school, of having a teacher tell you, "More than one answer may be correct, but pick the best answer for each question." Given that you're a future law student, I wouldn't be surprised to learn that you may even have debated with your instructor, making a case for why a certain answer should receive credit. As a result, you're used to comparing answer choices to one another. On the LSAT, however, that's a recipe for wasted time and effort. The test makers design the correct answer to be unequivocally correct; it will respond to the call of the question stem precisely. Likewise, the four wrong answers are demonstrably wrong, not just "less good."

For the well-trained test taker—for you, that is—this leads to an important, practical adjustment in strategy. Throughout the test, you should seek to predict the correct answer before assessing the answer choices. In Logical Reasoning, you will, on most questions, be able to anticipate the content of the correct answer, sometimes almost word for word. In Reading Comprehension and Logic Games, you should spend the time up front to have a clear passage road map or game sketch. At a minimum, you must characterize the correct and incorrect answers (if the correct answer *must be true*, for example, each of the wrong answers *could be false*). Then seek out the one answer that matches your prediction or characterization.

The bottom line is that, on the LSAT, you are always comparing the answers against what you know must be correct, not against one another. When locating the correct choice is difficult or time-consuming, you can always turn the tables on the test maker and eliminate the wrong ones.

In Logic Games, Acceptability questions provide the perfect example. Testing answer choices to find the passable arrangement can take minutes, but using the rules to eliminate the choices that violate them takes only a few seconds. Because you know that there will always be one correct choice and that you can always identify the characteristics that make wrong answers wrong, you can always take the most direct route to the LSAT point.

THERE'S NO WRONG-ANSWER PENALTY

This point is easy to understand, but sometimes hard to remember when you're working quickly through an LSAT section. The LSAT is scored only by counting the number of correct responses you bubble in. Unlike some standardized tests—the SAT is the most notorious example—you're not penalized for marking incorrect responses. Simply put, there's nothing to lose, so mark a response, even if it's a blind guess, for every answer.

Of course, strategic guessing is better than just taking a wild stab at the correct answer. Even if a question gives you a lot of trouble, see if you can eliminate one or more answer choices as clearly wrong. When you can, take your guess from the remaining choices. Removing even one clearly incorrect choice improves your chances of hitting on the right one from 20 percent to 25 percent; getting rid of two wrong answers, of course, gives you a one-in-three chance of guessing correctly. Provided that you do it quickly (not taking time away from questions you can handle with little trouble), strategic guessing can improve your score.

Students ask another question related to this point about the answer choices. They want to know if a particular answer choice—(A), (B), (C), (D), or (E)—shows up more often than others, or whether it's better, when guessing, to pick a particular choice for all guesses. The answer to both questions is no. Over the course of a full LSAT, all five answer choices show up just about equally. There's no pattern associated with particular question types. You're no more likely to see any particular answer early or late in a section. Thus, when you're blind guessing, you have a one-in-five chance of hitting the correct answer whatever you choose. And there's no benefit from guessing choice (C) or choice (D) over and over. It's far more valuable to spend your limited time trying to eliminate one or more wrong answers than it is to fret over any illusory patterns within the choices.

THE LSAT IS A MARATHON . . . MADE UP OF SPRINTS

At this point in your academic career, you've had long tests and you've had tests that put time pressure on you. But chances are, you've never encountered as intense a combination of the two as you will on the LSAT. In the last chapter, I already talked about the importance of stamina. Including the administrative tasks at the beginning, the breaks, and the collection and distribution of your testing materials, you're in for around a five-hour test day. It's important to remember that, over the course of that marathon, the first and fifth sections are just as valuable as those in the middle. Unsurprisingly, Kaplan's research has shown that, for the untrained test taker, those sections are likely to produce the poorest performance. You can counteract the inherent difficulties in the schedule by doing a little warm-up so that you're ready to hit the ground running at the start of Section 1, and by staying relaxed and having a healthy snack at the break so that you're still going strong at the end of Section 5. Just taking these simple steps could add several points to your score.

At the same time that you're striving to maintain focus and sustain your performance, you're trying to manage a very fast 35 minutes in each section. I've talked already about how you can triage a section to maximize your opportunity to attack the easiest games, passages, and questions. Combine that with confident, strategic guessing and you'll be outperforming many test takers who succumb to the "ego battle" with tough or time-consuming questions. But there's one more thing that you have to add to your repertoire of test day tactics: You have to learn to not look back. Over the years, I've talked to many students who could tell me how they thought they performed on each of the test's sections. To be honest with you, I find that a little disappointing. Sure, you may remember that the game with the Cowboys and Horses or the passage on Nanotechnology was really challenging, but it's a waste of time and mental capacity to try and assess your performance as you're taking the test. Once you've answered a question, leave it behind. Give your full concentration to what you're working on. This is even more important when it comes to sections. Once time is called, you may no longer work on the section, not even to bubble in the answers to questions you completed in your test booklet. If a proctor sees you continuing to work on a section for which the time has expired, he or she can issue you a misconduct slip, and the violation will be reported to all of the schools to which you apply. More importantly, you're harming your work on the current section.

There's no rearview mirror on the LSAT. Work diligently, mark the correct answers, and move on to the next question. Keep this in mind: Even if you could accurately assess your performance as you worked (you can't, but imagine it for a moment), it wouldn't change anything. You'd still need to get the remaining questions right. So learn this lesson—and the other "secrets" of the LSAT—now. Be like those seemingly brilliant coaches and performers. By knowing how the LSAT test day works, you can gain an edge over test takers who treat this just as they have every other exam in their academic careers.

CHAPTER 21

LSAT STRATEGIES AND TACTICS

At last, I'll bring you full circle back to the premise at the start of this book. The LSAT may be unlike any other test you've studied or prepared for, but it need not be mysterious or overwhelming. The underlying principle that has informed this book is that **every question has an answer**. The twist is that you're not expected to know the answers. How could you? This is a test that rewards what you can do, not what you've learned. In that sense, you can't *study* for the test. And you certainly can't cram for it. What you can do, indeed what you've been doing throughout this book, is to *practice* for the test. Instead of thinking of the LSAT as a test, think of it as your law school audition or tryout. A play's director or a team's coach doesn't ask you what you know; she wants to see what you can do. And just as the director or coach will give you everything you need to demonstrate your skill, the test makers always give you everything you need to produce the correct answers on the LSAT.

THE LSAT REWARDS THE CORE 4 SKILLS

Law schools don't expect incoming students to know the law. Indeed, much as the LSAT does, your professors may try to use your outside knowledge and assumptions against you. What the schools are looking for is incoming students who have the skills they'll need to succeed through the coming three years of rigorous legal training. That, at least in part, is what they're looking for your LSAT score to indicate. That's why the LSAT is a skills-based, rather than a knowledge-based, exam. Back near the beginning of this book, you learned the central skills rewarded on the test.

THE CORE 4 LSAT SKILLS

1. Strategic Reading
2. Analyzing Arguments
3. Understanding Formal Logic
4. Making Deductions

USE WHAT YOU'VE LEARNED THROUGHOUT THE TEST

One nice thing to realize is that much of the work you've done here, preparing for the Logic Games section specifically, will translate to exceptional performance throughout the test. Your understanding of the sufficient-necessary relationship highlighted by formal logic rules will be rewarded by several questions in each of the Logical Reasoning sections. Your discipline in setting up a complete Master Sketch mirrors the process of mapping passages in the Reading Comprehension section. To be successful on the LSAT, you must make deductions and draw valid inferences from related rules and statements dozens of times in every scored section.

So let me leave you with this: The LSAT is designed to reward the skills that will make you a successful law student. You know that you have those skills. You are, after all, seeking this path with passion and focus. The work you've done in this book is all about honing your skills and preparing you for a successful test day. Take the insights you've gathered about LSAT logic games and apply them throughout the exam. Take what you've learned about yourself as a test taker, and use it not only for a stronger, more confident performance on test day, but also throughout your law school endeavor, during your bar exam, and into your legal career. Best of luck to you. Now, go out and accomplish great things.

Kaplan's Most Sought After LSAT Instructors Break-It-Down

KAPLAN
LSAT
LOGIC GAMES

Second Edition
STRATEGIES & TACTICS

- 100% official LSAT PrepTest® questions with explanations for every answer
- 2 full-length logic games practice sections
- Proven strategies to build your skills and increase your score
- Comprehensive review of every question type for the logic games section

By Glen Stohr, JD

HIGHER SCORE GUARANTEED*

KAPLAN
LSAT
LOGICAL REASONING

Second Edition
STRATEGIES & TACTICS

- 100% official LSAT PrepTest® questions with explanations for every answer
- 2 full-length logical reasoning practice sections
- Proven strategies to build your skills and increase your score
- Comprehensive review of every question type for the logical reasoning section

By Deborah Katz, JD, PhD

HIGHER SCORE GUARANTEED*

KAPLAN
LSAT
READING COMPREHENSION

Second Edition
STRATEGIES & TACTICS

- 100% official LSAT PrepTest® questions with explanations for every answer
- 2 full-length reading comprehension practice sections
- Proven strategies to build your skills and increase your score
- Comprehensive review of every question type for the reading comprehension section

By Scott Emerson

HIGHER SCORE GUARANTEED*

All NEW 2nd Editions!

KAPLAN
PUBLISHING

NOTES

NOTES

NOTES